The Vernacular Architecture of Brittany

The Vernacular Architecture of Brittany

An essay in
historical geography

GWYN I. MEIRION-JONES

BSc, MPhil, PhD, FSA

City of London Polytechnic

JOHN DONALD PUBLISHERS LTD

EDINBURGH

ISBN 0 85976 060 X

Exclusive distribution in the United States
of America and Canada by Humanities Press Inc.,
Atlantic Highlands, NJ 07716, USA.

Phototypesetting by H.M. Repros, Glasgow.
Printed in Great Britain by Bell & Bain Ltd., Glasgow.

PREFACE

THIS study of the traditional vernacular buildings of Brittany, begun in 1970, was designed as a long-term survey, it being intended from the outset that results would be published from time to time in the form of papers in scientific journals. The completion of the first stage of the work in 1977 was marked by the submission of a PhD thesis to the University of London.[1] The present book is a slightly abridged, but updated, version of that thesis, incorporating new work resulting from four periods of intensive fieldwork during the years 1977–79.

An opportunity has been taken to discard the twenty-one maps of the sample areas on which the original survey was based and any reader requiring these is referred to the thesis. Detailed descriptions of the buildings, interleaved with the drawings in the original work, have also been removed, the necessary information being incorporated in the text. Because certain material has recently been published in article form, it has also been possible to shorten a few of the original chapters.

Distribution maps have been improved as a result of recent work, both by revision and addition. In some cases the distributions shown are much fuller than those on the 1977 maps. Additional data derive both from field-mapping and from the *dossiers* of the *Commission d'Inventaire de Bretagne*. The field-mapping expeditions of 1977–79 chiefly concentrated on the accurate location of the two features described as the 'bed-outshot' and the 'table-outshot'. At the same time, notable additions were also made to the maps of circular farm buildings, first-floor halls and carpentry features. During the summer of 1979 it was possible to examine the available records of the Commission d'Inventaire for those *communes* and *cantons* for which either a *pré-inventaire* or an *inventaire* had been made. The terms of reference of the French *Commissions d'Inventaire* charge them with making an inventory of the *'richesses artistiques de la France'*. Emphasis is consequently upon those works considered to be of artistic merit, and the staff of the *Commissions d'Inventaire* are all art historians. Inventories are consequently mostly concerned with greater buildings, although increasing attention is now being paid to the lesser traditional buildings, particularly where they display obvious craftsmanship. Interpretation of the large number of photographs of vernacular buildings in the *Inventaire* made possible the addition of a total of over five hundred examples to the distribution maps, chiefly of carpentry features, but also of first-floor halls, lateral chimney-stacks, circular buildings, and timber-frame buildings in the countryside. As a result of these additions the distribution maps carry considerably more authority, and although there have been no changes in the overall patterns of distribution, conclusions which depend on the maps can be drawn more firmly. It should be noted, however, that the *Commission d'Inventaire de Bretagne* is responsible for only four of the *départements* of the historic Duchy. The fifth, Loire-Atlantique, comes under the aegis of the *pays de la Loire* commission and it has not yet been possible to add data for this *département*. In order to cope with these additions, it has mostly been necessary to abandon the original method of mapping each example with a symbol. The congestion and cartographic distortion which would result from the continued use of symbols is not acceptable and the more generalized quadrat mapping, based on a uniform five-kilometre grid, has been substituted. In the present series of maps the density of the population of any given feature within the relevant quadrat is indicated in a few cases only. For the majority, it is felt that the census is still at too early a stage for quadrat mapping on a grid density basis to be meaningful.

The work is based on the maps of the *Institut Géographique National* at scales of 1:250,000, 1:50,000 and 1:25,000. The UTM or 'military' Grid is the one used for references and quadrat mapping (Fig. 2). Whilst the Lambert co-ordinates are in many ways preferable, only the UTM Grid is printed in full on maps and is consequently the only one capable of being read rapidly in the field in what are often adverse weather conditions. Several general maps of Brittany are reproduced in the text including geology, relief and place-name maps and an outline grid-map which, when used in conjunction with the others, should enable the reader to locate approximately any of the buildings described or referred to in the text. Grid references are given in a way exactly comparable to those of the British National Grid. Orthography of place-names is generally that of the *Institut Géographique National*, but, unfortunately, place-names are few, even on the 1:25,000 maps, and where farms and hamlets are unnamed, either the 'official' version, or that locally used, has been adopted. Sadly, the result is far from scholarly, for Breton place-names are all too often highly Gallicized, and a strange orthography, part Breton, part French, is common. For the location of many of the towns, principal rivers, ranges of hills and *pays*, the reader is referred to Figures 7 and 8.

The architectural drawings were all prepared by the author and each bears the date of survey. Penny Tommis drew the maps and Mavis Teed prepared the plans of the sites at Kerlano and Pen-er-Malo which are based on the original published work of Patrick André and Roger Bertrand. The photographs were taken by the author.

Financial assistance has been gratefully received from the City of London Polytechnic, the Centre National de la Recherche Scientifique, Paris, the Colt Fund of the Society for Medieval Archaeology, the Dudley Stamp Memorial Fund, the University of London, which made grants from both its Central Research Fund and the Banister Fletcher Fund, and from the British Academy.

The author owes a considerable debt of gratitude to his wife, not least for tolerating his long absences abroad, and to French acquaintances, almost too many to name, who have given both of their time and local knowledge. Thanks are particularly due to Professor Pierre Flatrès who from the outset showed considerable interest in the work and willingly shared his great knowledge of his native land; to Professor André Mussat, Vice-President, and Madame Françoise Hamon, Secrétaire, both of the *Commission d'Inventaire de Bretagne*, and their invariably most friendly and helpful staff, who have always provided an hospitable welcome and permitted access to both records and library; to René Sanquer, *Directeur des Antiquités Historiques de Bretagne*, under whose overall guidance the work of the medieval archaeologists of Brittany is now developing; to the unfailingly helpful staff of the five *archives départementales* and particularly to Monsieur Jacques Charpy whose *guide* to the *Archives du Finistère*,[2] a model of its kind, enables a newcomer quickly to find his way; and to the ever-hospitable Breton farmers who have received him at all times and seasons and allowed free access to their buildings. Dr. E. M. Yates, of King's College in the University of London, has given guidance and encouragement, not only during the course of this work, but throughout a long association begun in July 1961, when he first introduced the writer to geographical fieldwork in the Weald of south-east England.

CONTENTS

ONE

INTRODUCTION

Brittany has long been regarded with fascination. One of the many peninsulas that constitute the 'Atlantic ends of Europe', it has, through nearly all the phases of its history, been a crossroads of much-frequented maritime routes (Fig. 1). During the Neolithic it was a centre of intense political, social and religious activity as the large number of surviving Megalithic monuments testify. At the dawn of the Christian period the existing Gallo-Roman population was reinforced by large-scale immigration from south-west Britain, the 'Welsh' escaping from the pressures of the Saxons in the east and the Irish to the west, and probably organized by the Romans to fill a population vacuum. The resulting stock formed the Breton population which, over the centuries, moulded a landscape of tiny hedged fields, the *bocage*, and dispersed settlement that reached its maximum development in the late-nineteenth and early-twentieth centuries. This landscape is both characteristic of Celtic Europe as a whole and yet distinctive. Large towns are relatively few and the predominantly agricultural population dwelt almost entirely in hamlets and isolated farms. Notwithstanding wide regional variations, the pattern of rural settlement has been a generally dense one until recent times when, with rapid rural depopulation and the consolidation of farm holdings, there has been considerable change. Brittany became a land of survival of ancient customs and traditions.

The region was chosen for a long-term survey of domestic buildings because it is the one Celtic country, save Galicia, of which British scholars know little, one where old customs and traditions have survived, and where the house-types and building techniques may help to explain the development of the house in western Europe generally.

Vernacular architecture is the study of traditional domestic buildings, those which, given historical perspective, are seen to have been widely accepted and understood in a region at a particular time. It follows that they are, or were, present in large numbers and are a social as well as an architectural phenomenon. They are 'of traditional form, are built in traditional ways with traditional materials, and use traditional ornament'.[3] Whilst a vernacular building has much in common with its neighbours, it must be distinguished from the great buildings which may also exist, perhaps in some numbers, in the same region. Some workers have used the term 'polite architecture' for 'those buildings — cathedrals and palaces, town halls and parish churches — which have been designed by professional designers, whether acting under the title of architect or not, according to rules accepted nationally or internationally'.[4] Vernacular buildings, in contrast, farmhouses and cottages, barns and other farm buildings, are the work of craftsmen, carpenters and masons, working according to long-standing tradition. They tend to be conservative in design and make use of local materials. The work of these craftsmen, often aided by the unskilled labour of the prospective owner, must be distinguished at the lower end from 'primitive' building or that which wholly results from the work of the non-specialist. Such a term would describe the many simple constructions found in Breton farmyards, the work of the farmers who use them. They too are built according to well-established rules, but have not required the employment of specialist tradesmen in their construction. The distinction between 'polite' and 'vernacular' architecture is not necessarily a sharp one and the boundary is often arbitrary. Influences can be demonstrated to have descended the social scale, as the lower social orders sought to imitate and adopt the styles and fashions of their superiors. The larger country houses fall into the polite category but there are many dwellings which may loosely be described as belonging to the 'manor-house' class, and which display characteristics of both polite and vernacular architecture. In general, this work will only be concerned with the houses of the social classes directly engaged in agriculture. This includes those of the 'gentry' who played an active part in the working of their land and whose homes, by their plans, demonstrate this attachment to the land. As soon as plan becomes more elaborate, with the number of rooms

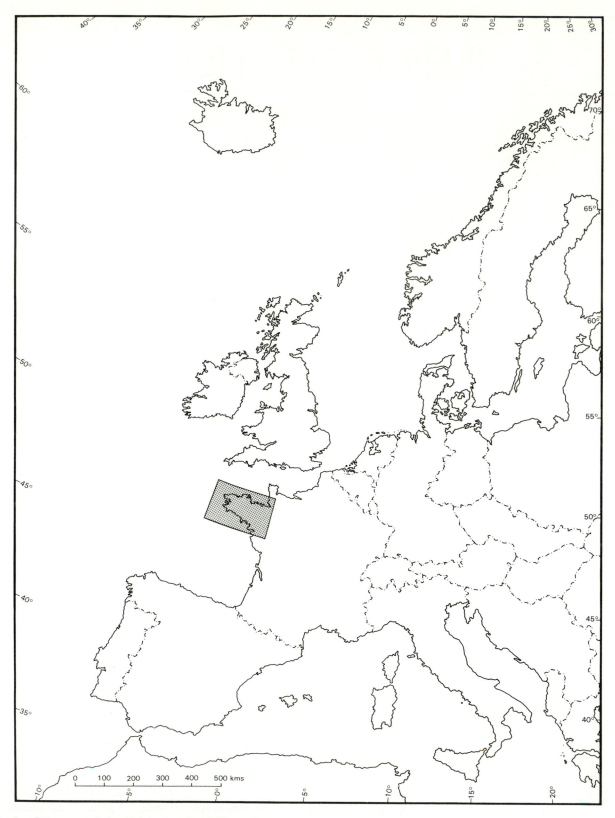

Fig. 1. Brittany and the 'Atlantic ends of Europe'.

suggesting a pattern of life divorced from the land, the houses are held to be polite rather than vernacular and are the concern of this study only in so far as they might have been the source and inspiration for architectural detail at the vernacular level. The study is also principally concerned with the dwelling-house, and is in no sense a study of *l'habitat rural* as understood by French geographers. Many smaller domestic, and a few non-domestic, buildings are included in the survey where it is felt that their inclusion assists explanation of construction and evolution. The study of farm buildings separated from the house, and the evolution of farmyard plan, topics that require separate treatment, are dealt with only briefly in this work.

Whereas in the British Isles, the coming of the railways, *c.* 1840, is often taken as an upper terminal date for the study of vernacular buildings, in France, old ways lingered and this is especially true of Brittany where 'primitive' houses existed in large numbers until World War I, and a few relics survived into the 1940s. This study is thus concerned in general with traditional buildings from earliest times to *c.* 1920, it being understood that in certain places, traditional methods continued later in use, and also that new techniques and materials, often of industrial provenance, were diffused following the arrival of the railway during the nineteenth century, partly as a result of improvements in agriculture.

Although it was in the countries of north-west Europe that research in the subject developed, the study of vernacular architecture in France is still at a relatively early stage. For the best examples of regional and systematic studies illustrating methods and techniques for the study of vernacular building it is necessary to turn to the British Isles, Scandinavia and Germany. Scholars like Campbell,[5] Erixon,[6] Peate[7] and Evans,[8] exponents of the 'folk-life' approach, saw the peasant house, not just as an example of vernacular architecture, but as a structure adapted to family needs which had evolved over the centuries in response to changing economic, social, agricultural and industrial conditions. They studied not only the fabric of the building, its materials, construction and plan, as well as the archaeological and architectural evidence of change, but also the folk-ways of those who inhabited it, their customs, superstitions, habits of work and play, their music, literature and oral traditions. The former line of enquiry led to the classification of houses based on building materials, structure and plan, and the establishment of an evolutionary sequence and chronology, whilst the second permitted a much fuller understanding and interpretation of vernacular buildings. Studies of building construction and techniques in the British Isles by Addy[9] and Innocent[10] have become

classics, but the first regional study on any scale was *The Welsh house*[11] followed soon afterwards by *Monmouthshire houses*[12] then by a series of enquiries into the lesser domestic buildings of England.[13] More recently, Mercer[14] and Smith[15] have produced major works on England and Wales respectively.

Architects long neglected the study of the lesser buildings, having been chiefly concerned with those of the upper social classes. An exception is a notable series of regional and systematic studies produced in the School of Architecture of the University of Manchester under Cordingley.[16] The architect is conscious of detail and ornament which help to elucidate changes in fashion, the spread of new ideas and styles, and which cast light generally on the process of cultural diffusion.

Archaeologists, perhaps partly motivated by the thought that such studies would assist in the interpretation of excavated dwellings, have also turned to an examination of vernacular architecture. The dwelling is treated as an artefact, a product of human art and workmanship. The archaeologist shows how it has developed and changed, and examines evidence of earlier form and modifications to the construction. At its best this approach is exemplified in the work of Fox and Raglan,[17] a now classic study, whose aim was to discover how each style developed, its time range, and to define gaps in the evolutionary record by a detailed study of building techniques and house plans. The work has served as a methodological textbook for many a worker since, but few would now agree that such an enquiry can be carried out solely by archaeological methods.

Buildings are historical documents in their own right. Dwellings must be placed in their historical context, and the influence of historical changes may be related to changes in house-type. Inventories listing furniture room by room, the number and type of farm implements, and the disposition of buildings around the farmyard, provide valuable data to enable the dwelling to be related to the argrarian economy. Barley[18] and Hoskins[19] have shown just how essential is the need to undertake parallel archive work. Wills, marriage contracts and probate inventories may enable the worker to identify the people who lived in a house and define their social status and work. Such documents often list rooms, their number and disposition, furniture and household goods, providing information on the wealth of the occupant as reflected in his material possessions, occasionally allowing the identification of the house referred to and permitting the reconstruction of the physical organization of the interior. Information is forthcoming about conditions for areas and periods poorly represented by surviving houses. In those areas rich in surviving buildings, documents help further to illuminate the problems.

Study of the cultural landscape and its evolution has long been the historical geographer's concern. Field systems and settlement patterns have been examined in detail, although with one or two notable exceptions these enquiries have stopped short of the dwelling house itself. Yet the house is a prominent element whose colour, texture and form play a significant part in giving a landscape its particular character and further assists the process of areal differentiation and the understanding of spatial organization which are the concern of every geographer. Evidence afforded by the house and its ancillary buildings, agricultural or industrial, may provide insights into present and past economic conditions which, along with evidence of settlement pattern and field systems, helps to elucidate earlier geographies. Establishment of an evolutionary sequence and a chronology of house-types leads to an ability to estimate the age of buildings. Since cartographic and documentary coverage vary widely both in time and space and may be very lean before *c.* 1800, it may be possible, by dating buildings, to show that a site was inhabited perhaps two to three centuries before this can be shown by documentary evidence. Furthermore, the survival of an old house is sufficient to establish continuity of settlement since the time of its earliest datable element. It follows that a village with many surviving medieval buildings was obviously a village in medieval times, whatever changes may have occurred since.

The student of folk life, the archaeologist, the architect, the economic and social historian and the geographer may each contribute to the study of the peasant house and in so doing demonstrate the value of a multi-disciplinary approach.

The present study was conceived as a primary survey of the whole of Brittany, comprising the five *départements* of the historic Duchy. Its aim is essentially exploratory and attempts to bring to light new material, to outline the principal *traits* of Breton vernacular architecture and to extend existing knowledge of certain west European house-plans and constructional techniques, making possible new definitions and hypotheses. It is concerned with construction, distribution and evolution. Construction includes assembly of building materials and particularly the carpentry of roof structure. By distribution is meant not only the relationship of one house to another, whether dwellings are isolated, loosely grouped in hamlets, arranged in rows or terraces or nucleated in villages, but also the distribution of various house-types and their features over the whole of the Breton peninsula. Evolution is that of house-plan and the development of room-functions, and of constructional techniques, particularly carpentry. It is argued that the consideration of construction, distribution and evolution eventually permits an attempt at regional characterization, and finally that the domestic buildings of Brittany can be related to those of western Europe generally.

Rural life in Brittany, as in much of western Europe, is changing rapidly. Growth of full-time education, changing social consciousness, improvement in living conditions and the revolutionizing of private transport have made the countryman more independent and mobile. Many local markets have disappeared and since 1945 there has been a large-scale abandonment of traditional forms of agricultural labour, increased mechanization of farm work and an agricultural revolution of considerable scale and effect. These changes in the social order, agrarian structure and rural economy have been dramatic in themselves, but their effect is catastrophic as vast amounts of unrecorded data, material and oral, have been destroyed. Massive rural depopulation together with the restructuring of agriculture has resulted in the abandonment of farm-houses and the conversion and destruction of others. In areas like the Monts d'Arrée where once a hamlet may have consisted of ten or a dozen small farms all actively worked, now only one or two may remain. Houses and cottages have either been handed down to a younger generation for use as holiday homes or they have been purchased by outsiders with the result that whole hamlets come to life for only a few weeks in the summer. The time is thus ripe for a study of Breton vernacular architecture, for there are many crumbling and ruinous buildings which can often be studied more readily and profitably than houses which are inhabited. Houses that have become second homes are, however, mostly closed and shuttered. Restoration by town dwellers is often disastrous and the original plan and form may be changed beyond recognition and the materials obscured by cement rendering.

Improvement grants for farmers are also responsible for the destruction and transformation of many peasant dwellings. Roofs of traditional materials have been renewed, stone and clay walls given a cement rendering, old windows and door frames torn out and replaced with standard suburban-type substitutes. In the face of the cataclysmic changes that have taken place in the French countryside during the last fifteen years, the student of vernacular architecture is faced with an urgent task. Very little work has so far been accomplished and each year sees the destruction of still more valuable evidence and the need for both regional and systematic studies is great.

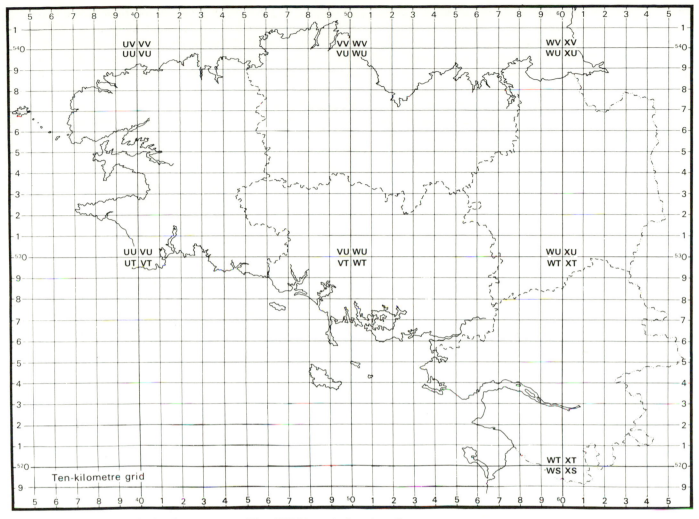

Fig. 2. Brittany: Grid reference map (The U.T.M. or 'military' grid).

The study falls into two distinct parts. An extensive survey comprised the superficial examination of the buildings within each of twenty-one quadrats, 2.50 kilometres square, a nested sample ensuring randomness coupled with a relatively even distribution across the Duchy and an absence of periodicity so important in a region displaying a marked geological grain. A subjective assessment entered into the choice of buildings and not every house in each quadrat was recorded. Many were post-1920 and not vernacular. Others had once been of the traditional type, but now so heavily altered as to render them of doubtful value as evidence. It soon became evident that the vast majority of Breton houses are simple structures, some little more than rectilinear stone shells that may readily be converted to new use, any evidence of earlier functions being obliterated. In some quadrats, notably those near the coast, only a handful of buildings were thought worthy of consideration, in others over a hundred were recorded. In this way a total of 1055 buildings was recorded and photographed. Some were selected for more detailed investigation, but evidence in certain quadrats proved so meagre that given the acute problem of time, no further enquiry was made. At some future stage these might repay more careful and detailed examination. In a few quadrats, the architecture was of the greatest interest and numerous buildings were measured. It was clear, however, that the selection of random quadrats, valuable though they were, failed to pick up many regional variations which could not be ignored. Such regions were subsequently selected for closer study. Examination within the quadrats also showed the existence of certain types of building and roof structure, further examples of which had to be sought over the former Duchy at large if their presence and distribution was to be explained. A particular problem is that relatively few buildings of the 'manor-house' category fall within the quadrats. This is not surprising, for although there are large numbers of these houses, they are proportionately few. Being large, they are also difficult and laborious to measure and record. This work can then only indicate the existence of some of these and hope to point the way to further research. The superficial data was recorded using a modified Brunskill[20] system but as this work progressed, greater emphasis was laid on plan and construction and it was felt that a detailed study of architectural features was not only unnecessary at this stage, but to a certain extent irrelevant.

The results from the areas subjected to superficial survey are presented in maps of plan-type and number of storeys (Figs. 79, 101, 102). Data from the quadrats also appear, combined with data gathered additionally from the region at large, in several other maps, notably those of first-floor halls (Fig. 205) and the distribution of various carpentry features (Figs. 60 to 69).

The more detailed studies of individual buildings are presented in the form either of full drawings, or of plans only. Some buildings were measured because they were thought or known to be in imminent danger of demolition or severe alteration, and this element of 'rescue archaeology' is felt to be an important one. Together with the photographic record of some six thousand slides, for the years 1970–76, the field notes and measured drawings form an archive and scientific record that remains to be re-interpreted long after hypotheses have been rendered obsolete by new discoveries. Much data was recorded just in time before it was destroyed for ever, and a record now exists of many buildings which no longer survive. The selection of buildings was partly the result of chance discovery and partly the result of the deliberate choice in areas found to be rich in vernacular building, but not represented by the twenty-one sample quadrats. The discovery of such areas came about partly from local recommendation, but chiefly as a consequence of making 'transects' across the country from one random quadrat to another. These transects were not systematically chosen, but over the period of six years of fieldwork, very good coverage of Brittany was possible by varying routes taken. Fields and field-patterns have also been observed and an attempt made, where appropriate, to relate buildings, not only to each other, but also to the landscape of which they are a part.

Archive work was carried out parallel to the later stages of fieldwork and use is made of the material so gathered where relevant in the text. The richest sources of data are the *minutes notariales* in which are located probate inventories, wills and marriage contracts, together with a miscellany of documents including many farm leases. The latter often describe the buildings of the farmyard in great detail. Probate inventories are extensively used to elucidate the arrangements of the interiors and the number and functions of the rooms. Other important documentary material includes the reports of the *Comités d'Hygiène* from the mid-nineteenth century, a considerable quantity of miscellaneous material, the *Fonds Stany Gauthier*,[21] articles in local publications, photographs, prints and drawings.

Existing published work relevant to the study of vernacular architecture of France in general has been outlined elsewhere[22] and a bibliography listing these and all other known writings has recently been compiled.[23] It is against this body of work that the buildings of Brittany must be assessed. Only a handful of articles on the vernacular architecture of Brittany are of a standard that would currently be accepted by British workers. There is, nevertheless, a considerable body of literature, often dealing very superficially with the house, which provides useful preliminary information on a region, or gives a clue to the existence of a house-type. Sometimes the approach is an ethnological one, with details of interiors and folk-life. That most prolific writer, J.-S. Gauthier, travelled widely and much of his work provides useful leads. A series of publications by the Vicomte Frotier de la Messelière, on the Côtes-du-Nord, is profusely illustrated with line drawings of buildings mostly of the 'manor-house' category, some of which can be interpreted, others giving clues for further investigation. Among studies in regional geography, Vallaux,[24] Fournier,[25] M. Gautier,[26] Guilcher[27] and Le Lannou[28] give very good accounts of the rural house. Several authors, Bernard,[29] Colin[30] and Keravel,[31] base regional accounts largely on probate inventories, whilst others like Buffet[32] include chapters on the house in works dealing generally with the culture of a region, sometimes with an ethnological approach. Other writers, claiming no particular specialization, give fascinating glimpses of houses and ways now lost,[33] and numerous authors provide fragments of relevant information. An excellent early study of the houses of the Monts d'Arrée is that by Giese,[34] and more recently there is evidence of renewed interest in the subject.[35] Recent work in medieval archaeology has brought to light valuable house-plans in Morbihan which may be related to simple structures surviving in the twentieth century.[36]

This survey, believed to be the first serious study of a major French region, attempts to combine techniques from several disciplines in an interdisciplinary approach. It is hoped, nevertheless, that the result bears the unmistakable stamp of the historical geographer.

TWO

THE PHYSICAL LANDSCAPE OF BRITTANY

Les ajoncs éclatants, parure du granit,
Dorent l'âpre sommet que le couchant allume;
Au loin, brillante encor par sa barre d'écume,
La mer sans fin commence où la terre finit.

J.-M. de Hérédia, *Les Trophées*,
Paris (1895), 142.

From the line of fortified towns along the eastern Marches, marking the historic frontier with France, westwards to the windswept peninsulas where the resistant rocks of Finistère are pounded by the waters of the Atlantic, stretches a country whose vigorous personality makes it one of the most distinctive of natural regions (Figs. 3, 4, 5, and 6). Extending from latitudes forty-seven to forty-nine degrees north, and longitudes one to five degrees west, the Armorican peninsula is one of the many 'Atlantic ends of Europe'. Brittany is some three hundred kilometres in extent from east to west and about two hundred kilometres from north to south at its maximum. Its total area of 35,313 sq. kilometres is rather less than twice the size of Wales.

The two broad traditional regional subdivisions, the coastlands and the interior, *Armor*, the land of the sea, and *Arcoët*, the land of the wood, are today blurred. The forested heart of the country, the great central Forêt de Broceliande of the Arthurian legend, for long a hindrance both to settlement and communication, is now reduced to a few remnants of which the forests of Loudéac, Quénécan and Paimpont are examples. It is a land of relatively subdued relief to which peoples from south-western Britain emigrated during the Early Christian period. Subsequent human activity has produced a landscape both characteristic of Celtic Europe as a whole and yet distinctive. Much of the country, until the recent agrarian changes, was characterized by a multitude of tiny hedged fields, the Breton *bocage*, interrupted by *landes*, rough grazing of heath, gorse and broom, which,

before the enclosures of the nineteenth century, appeared as 'waste' occupying over half the country.[37] Large towns are relatively few and the predominantly agricultural population dwells almost entirely in hamlets and isolated farms. Notwithstanding wide regional variations, the pattern of rural settlement has been a generally dense one until recent times when, with rapid rural depopulation and the consolidation of land holdings, there has been considerable change. Maximum population for the province as a whole in 1911 was 3,271,712, or 92.4 per sq. kilometre, falling by 1946 to 3,001,884 or 85 per sq. kilometre, about ten persons per sq. kilometre more than the average for France.[38] Relatively isolated from mainland France for much of historical time, Brittany became a land of survival for ancient customs and traditions.

The most striking features of the Breton landscape are the subdued land-forms. At its most vigorous, the landscape is characterized by a relatively low amplitude of relief, ridges occur in narrow bands and summits are usually flat, occasionally broken by an outcrop of granite or by a band of slate or schist. Amplitude is only 100 metres in the Blavet valley upstream of the Lac de Guerlédan, 75 metres on the Vilaine at Pont-Réan and 60 metres on the Trieux near its confluence with the Leff (Figs. 5 and 8).

The Armorican *massif* is a region of folded structures. Essentially east–west in direction, basic structures are chiefly Hercynian but incorporate some Caledonian folds. Although trend-lines are complex, a central synclinal furrow is discernible from the west coast through the basins of Châteaulin and Rennes, whilst south of the Landes du Mené the downfold is marked by a narrow band of Carboniferous rocks. To the north and south of this synclinorium, upfolds run west-south-west to east-north-east in Léon, and north-west in Cornouaille. This folding has left a clear grain on the landscape. Large numbers of faults demarcate horst-like uplands and

Fig. 3.   Pointe du Raz, Cap Sizun, Finistère. 'The windswept peninsulas where the resistant rocks of Finistère are pounded by the waters of the Atlantic.'

distinct basins, and explain the rapid succession of long narrow exposures of different rocks (Figs. 5 and 6). Erosion platforms dominate much of the landscape and support the greater part of the human settlement (Fig. 9). Three principal levels have been recognized in Basse-Bretagne: the Léon platform, or Breton peneplain (90–110 metres), the Sainte-Marie-du-Menez-Hom platform (180–200 metres) and the Monts d'Arrée platform (280–300 metres).[39] Resistant granites and granulites have been exposed. Crystalline schists form extensive plateaux over much of central Armorica and small patches of Tertiary rocks are preserved in depressions and basins: Oligocene and Miocene limestones and clays west and south-west of Rennes, and several scattered Pliocene outcrops east of Redon (Fig. 6).

Topography reflects the structure faithfully; the schistose depression of the Rennes basin and the long corridor from the Baie des Trépassés to south-east Brittany have been excavated and large blocks of granite

exposed. The Montagnes Noires and Monts d'Arrée (Figs. 6, 9 and 10), major breaks in the Breton peneplain, constitute the residual relief of hard rocks. Anticlinal folds appear as high ground in the narrow ridges of quartzite enclosed by thin outcrops of schist and sandstone in the Montagnes Noires, and north of Redon where clusters of narrow ridges are separated by long depressions. An east–west axis lying nearer to the north than the south coast marks roughly the line of the irregular watershed, the south-flowing streams being twice as long as the north-flowing ones (Figs. 5 and 8). The greatest altitude is in the north, the Monts d'Arrée (Roc'h Trévézel 344 metres, Toussaine 384 metres and the Montagne Saint-Michel 391 metres) owing their prominence to the Tertiary tilting of the Breton peneplain as well as to the relative resistance of their rocks (Figs. 9 and 10). In the east, the Landes du Mené are formed of relatively soft schists. A north–south axis separates the area of Tertiary depression in the east from the more vigorous relief of western Brittany. Other contrasts

Fig. 4.   Pointe de Penhir, Crozon, Finistère. 'The Rade de Brest . . . and the Baie de Douarnenez penetrate deeply on either side of the Crozon peninsula.'

prevail. Basse-Bretagne is higher in the north whilst Haute-Bretagne continues the plains of the Paris basin. Granite ridges and massifs are higher in the west and lower in the east (Figs. 5 and 6).

The coastal lowlands are only truly plateaux in the north-west. Trégorrois falls uniformly from 130 to 80 metres towards the sea and both here and in Léon the surfaces are deeply gashed with valleys. To the east of the Baie de Saint-Brieuc, the lowlands widen, becoming more diversified, and between Lamballe and the Couesnon the relief is composed of a series of low hills and basins in which both the north-west–south-east Armorican trend, and the south-west–north-east trend are evident (Figs. 5 and 6). Tectonic influences with numerous fault scarps are strongly evident here and lithology further complicates the detail. Between Dol-de-Bretagne and Pontorson the granite ellipse of Saint-Broladre rises above depressions in Pre-Cambrian schist (Figs. 6 and 11).

In the south, the littoral plateaux are narrower and soon give way northwards to long ridges. From the Blavet to the Vilaine, the *pays vannetais* is bounded to the north by the granulitic spine of the Landes de Lanvaux (Fig. 12). The belt of country from the Loire to the Crozon peninsula extends in a wide arc. East of the Vilaine, the plateau is broken into asymmetrical blocks whose steepest slopes generally face the areas of deposition along the coast: the great peat fen of the Grande Brière (Fig. 13), the *marais salants* between Guérande and Le Croisic (Fig. 14) and the cultivated *marais breton* on the borders of the Vendée. The breaks which mark out this pattern take the north-west–south-east Armorican trend and determine some abrupt monoclines like the *sillon de Bretagne* always under 100 metres altitude and only 50 metres overlooking the *pays brièron*.

The central node of miscellaneous plateaux, known generally as the Plateau de Rohan, covers the interior regions of Côtes-du-Nord and north Morbihan and lacks the clear-cut structure and topography of Finistère and

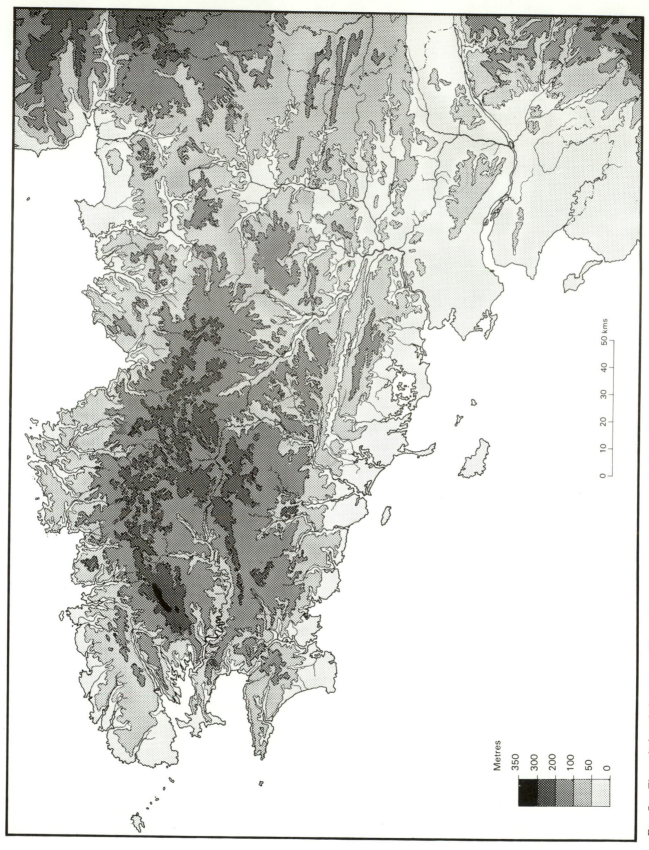

Metres
350
300
200
100
50
0

Fig. 5.   The relief and drainage of Brittany.

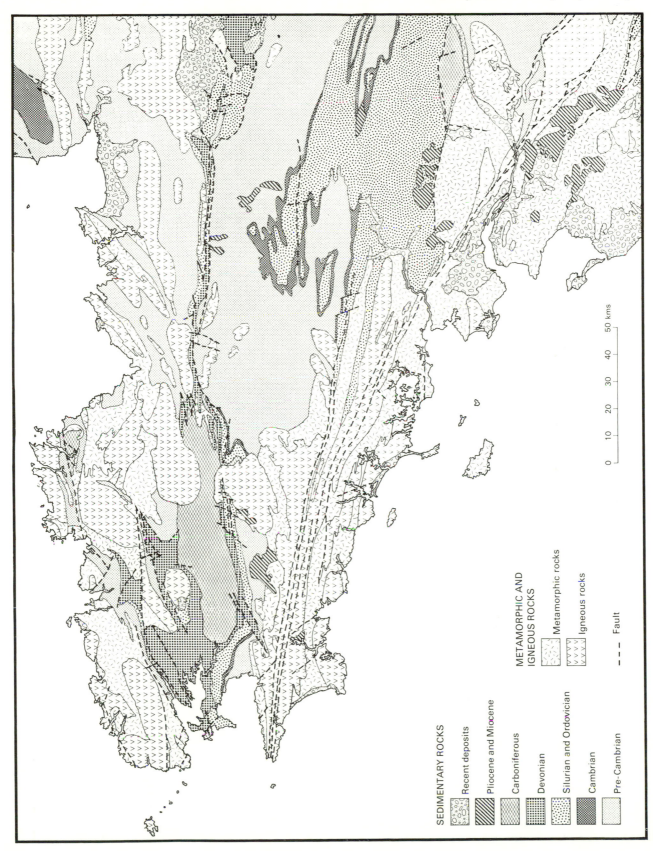

SEDIMENTARY ROCKS

Recent deposits

Pliocene and Miocene

Carboniferous

Devonian

Silurian and Ordovician

Cambrian

Pre-Cambrian

METAMORPHIC AND
IGNEOUS ROCKS

Metamorphic rocks

Igneous rocks

– – – Fault

Fig. 6. The geology of Brittany.

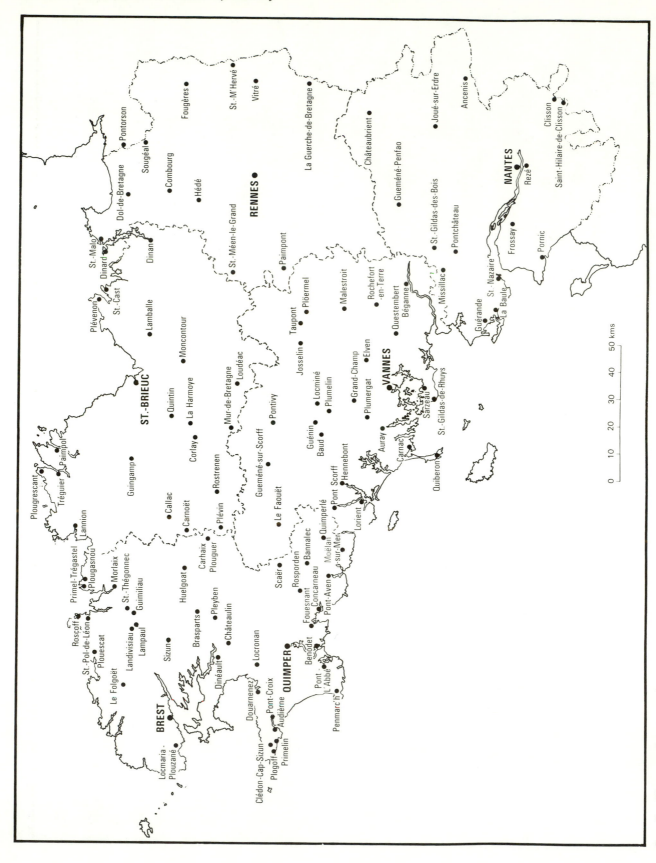

Fig. 7. Places and *pays* — I.

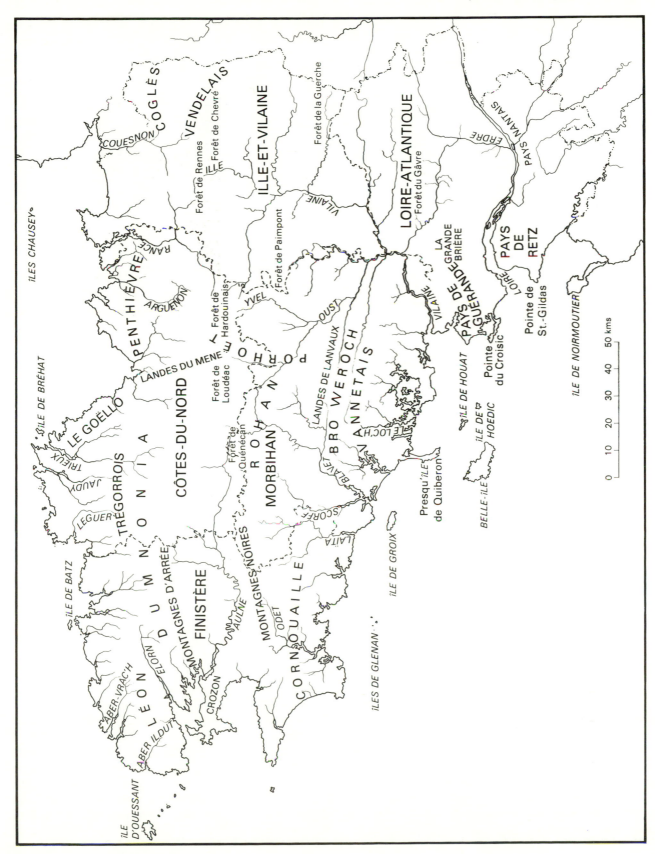

Fig. 8. Places and *pays* — II.

Fig. 9.   Monts d'Arrée, Finistère. View north-west from the Roc'h Trévézel (384 metres). Erosion platforms 'dominate much of the landscape and support the greater part of the human settlement'.

Ille-et-Vilaine. It is a confused mass of sandstone hills, granitic ridges and schistose basins, cut with deep valleys, sometimes gorge-like. Towards the north-east this relatively high region is terminated by the Landes du Mené (340 metres), and to the north-west by the granite mass of Quintin–Duault. To the south its limits are more confused and robust. The Landes de Lanvaux are only a poor barrier between the hills and basins of the areas around Pontivy and Josselin, and the littoral region of the *pays vannetais*. The Châteaulin basin, cut in Carboniferous schists, has moderately vigorous relief and is framed by the Monts d'Arrée and the Montagnes Noires, the Aulne cutting between the steep sides to escape westwards. In contrast, the Rennes basin, cut in Pre-Cambrian schists, is very old; Tertiary deposits of great thickness occupy the southern part, and the Vilaine and Ille flow in broad shallow valleys.

The coastline has a total length of about 3500 kilometres including the many rocky islands. Marine transgression during late Quaternary times inundated the margins of the plateaux and drowned the lower parts of the river valleys. The Rade de Brest, with the Elorn and Aulne, and the Baie de Douarnenez, penetrate deeply on either side of the Crozon peninsula (Figs. 4 and 5). Along the north-west coast of Léon, *les abers*, Aber-Vrac'h, Aber-Ildut and Aber-Benoît bite deeply into the plateau (Fig. 15). In the south, the valleys of the transverse rivers, the Odet, Ellé, Blavet and Vilaine, have all been submerged. Along the north coast many short streams flow from the Monts d'Arrée and the Landes du Mené, cutting deep winding valleys, drowned to form the estuaries of the Penzé and Morlaix rivers, the Jaudy, Trieux and Rance (Fig. 5). Several shallow inundated areas are laid bare at low tide to reveal wide expanses of mud-flats: the Golfe du Morbihan, the Baie du Mont-Saint-Michel, the Baie de la Frêneye and the Anse d'Yffiniac. The rise in sea-level also resulted in the formation of many islands to be numbered in hundreds along the north coast (Fig. 16), some little more than granite stumps.

Fig. 10. Saint-Rivoal, Finistère. View north-east from Saint-Michel-de-Brasparts towards the Monts d'Arrée which owe 'their prominence to the Tertiary tilting of the Breton peneplain as well as to the relative resistance of their rocks'.

Bold cliffs are formed of resistant granitic rocks as at Saint-Cast, hard Devonian feldspathic sandstones form Cap Fréhel (Fig. 17), and diorite Fort la Latte and Cap d'Erquy. The headlands of Penmarc'h and Quiberon are of granite, whilst sandstones, quartzites and schists of Devonian, Silurian and Ordovician age form the Crozon peninsula (Fig. 4). Granitic rocks dominate (Fig. 6). In the less resistant slates and shales, deep inlets, *baies* and *anses* have been eroded. Elsewhere, sedimentary deposits of shingle, sand and gravel with the backing of dunes, marsh and accompanying sedimentation have resulted in a wide flat coastline like that of the Marais de Dol, first dyked in 1324 (Fig. 18).

Settlement and agriculture owe much to the Breton climate. The mild West European climate is relatively uniform over the whole province although differences in position, relief and aspect result in climatic variations between the west and the east, north and south, the coastal plateaux and the uplands of the interior. The west is remarkably temperate whilst continental influences are just detectable in the east. Relief has a considerable effect on precipitation. The many islands are noted for their low rainfall, but inland, totals increase with altitude, notably in the Monts d'Arrée. In the drier east, with warmer summers and lower rainfall, the cultivation of cereals is successful. The south-east, with higher summer temperatures, has witnessed the survival of viticulture, once extensive in Haute-Bretagne, on a commercial scale. The mildness of the winters permits the growth of exotic species, magnolia, mimosa, agave and palms, almong the coast. Abundant and evenly distributed rainfall favours the establishment of forests, once more extensive in interior Brittany.

The great variety of soils derive from the complex tangle of old rocks, the Quaternary *limon* and the alluvial deposits of the valleys and coastal lowlands. Sandstones and quartzites decompose to give a sandy soil, generally very permeable. Rainfall rapidly drains away and sandstone ridges develop a dry *lande* which man has sometimes attempted in vain to plant with coniferous

Fig. 11.   Tertre de la Claie, La Boussac, Ille-et-Vilaine. '. . . between Lamballe and the Couesnon the relief is composed of a series of low hills and basins.' This view, looking south-east from the granite ellipse of Saint-Broladre, shows a depression in Pre-Cambrian schist in the country east of Dol-de-Bretagne.

trees. The Breton sandstone, the *grès armoricain* of the lower Silurian and Ordovician, and some of the quartzites, often have no effective vegetal cover. Granites, granulites and gneisses provide soils of greater variety. Quartz grains help to render a soil strongly permeable and support a *lande* richer in gorse, broom and heath than that found on the sandstone ridges, with occasional woodland on the decomposed granites of the Monts d'Arrée. On slopes, fine quartz sands provide permeable soils, less fertile but easy to work, often extending across the upper slopes of valleys, favouring the location of numerous hamlets. On the lower slopes and in the valley bottoms accumulations of clay give rise to heavier land more difficult to cultivate. Schists give soils of great variety.

Heavy soils are characteristic of the schist basins, especially those floored with Brioverian schist. Whilst light soils cover the sandstone ridges, the granite plateaux are more varied and generally possess a catena.

Generalization is difficult and it is not uncommon to find a wide range of soils within the lands of a single village. This variety is only one of the factors of polyculture and the resistance to a modern agricultural economy. The Breton peasant grows a little of everything to make best use of a wide variety of soils. Some soils are rich in potash, but poor in lime and phosphorus. Whilst acidity enables certain plants to flourish, gorse, bracken, the potato and sarrazin, lime-loving plants such as barley, lucerne and sainfoin respond poorly. Until the twentieth century, lime was obtained from shelly beach deposits, *trez*, and transported up to about twenty-five kilometres inland. From 1864 it was imported from Mayenne, firstly by the Nantes–Brest canal and then, after 1890, by rail, resulting in considerable change. Natural chemical deficiencies, only relatively recently corrected, help additionally to explain the relative backwardness of agriculture. Traditionally, fertility was restored by long periods of fallow and by using large areas of *lande* for

Fig. 12. Plumelec, Morbihan. A view towards the granulitic spine of the Landes de Lanvaux, looking south-west across the valley of the Claie, eroded in Ordovician sandstone.

grazing. Cereals were cultivated in small patches and rye, particularly, was rotated from field to field. *Landes* and forest were essential to provide adequate grazing for animals, resulting over many centuries in considerable modification to the vegetation.[40]

Whether the forest cover of the interior was ever as continuous and impenetrable as some historians allege would seem to be doubtful.[41] Legend and history have left much tradition surrounding the Forêt de Broceliande. In the western peninsulas it seems likely that woodland never made much headway, except in some sheltered valleys. *Lande* is the climax type, as on Cap Fréhel (Fig. 17), the Pointe du Raz and the Crozon peninsula where the *grès armoricain* supports dwarf gorse (*Ulex gallii*) and heath (Figs. 19 and 20).[42] The greatest surviving relic of woodland is the Forêt de Paimpont (Fig. 21) and the place-name Bresselien, a hundred kilometres west of this, has been used to suggest that the Forêt de Broceliande once extended that far. Other place-name evidence suggests that the central forest was far from continuous by the sixth century. Several hundred Gallo-Roman *fundi* have been identified within its bounds.[43]

The use of the place-names (Br.) Penhouet and (Br.) Lescouat suggests limits of the woodland at the time of the Breton settlement, a forest already cut up into large clearings, a *pagus trans sylvam* or *porhoet*.[44] The term 'forest' has probably been given too literal a meaning by some historians. More likely it was a stretch of wild country with wood and *lande* mixed. Long and vigorous human interference has reduced the total area of woodland to under five per cent of the land area of which planted and sub-spontaneous conifers are now an important element. Among the most striking aspects of the historical landscape are the *landes* as Arthur Young observed.[45] The old agrarian system was hostile to forest and favourable to *lande*, which complemented the small enclosed fields. Gorse, well cared for and often planted and cultivated in rows, gave forage for animals and made excellent fuel for bread ovens. Broom was often used for thatching whilst bracken made excellent litter. The last century has seen a great transformation, with much enclosure, so that Brittany is no longer a country of immense *landes* (Figs. 22 and 23).

Fig. 13.   Mayun, Loire-Atlantique. The Grande Brière.

Fig. 14.   Guérande, Loire-Atlantique. View northwards across the *marais salant* to the town of Guérande on its granite ridge.

Fig. 15.   Aber Wrac'h, Plouguerneau, Finistère. 'Along the north-west coast of Léon, *les abers* . . . bite deeply into the plateau.

Fig. 16.   Castel Meur, Plougrescant, Côtes-du-Nord. 'The rise in sea-level also resulted in the formation of many islands to be numbered in hundreds along the north coast, some little more than granite stumps . . .'

Fig. 17.   Plévénon, Côtes-du-Nord. View of Fort la Latte from Cap Fréhel. 'Hard Devonian feldspathic sandstones form Cap Fréhel . . . and diorite, Fort la Latte.'

Fig. 18.   Dol-de-Bretagne, Ille-et-Vilaine. The marais de Dol, first dyked in 1324, seen from Mont Dol.

THREE

THE CULTURAL LANDSCAPE

During prehistoric times, and particularly the Neolithic and Bronze Ages, Armorica was the centre of the great Megalithic culture, the remains of which are so distinctive a part of the modern Breton landscape. The *alignements* of Carnac and around the Baie de Quiberon alone total nearly three thousand stones. Other megalithic survivals include the great passage grave of the Gavr'Inis in the Golfe du Morbihan, 'one of the most remarkable tombs in western Europe'.[46] Though the purpose and origin of many of these monuments is unknown, they betray a region of wealth, with a well-developed social and political system and a religious, commercial and intellectual centre of great influence in western Europe.[47] During the Neolithic period settled agriculture appeared, beginning the profound changes which led to the eventual creation of the pattern of isolated farms, hamlets and *bocage*. Indeed, Megalithic directions may have had an influence on subsequent field patterns.[48] The sea gave Brittany a privileged position, and by the western seaways were diffused goods, ideas and people.[49] '*Sortie de son isolement primitif, la péninsule a brillament rayonné au loin et pris une parte prépondérante au*

Fig. 19.   Crozon-Morgat, Finistère. The *village-rangée* associated with highly fragmented former openfield and *landes*.

Fig. 20.   Kerdreux, Crozon-Morgat, Finistère. The *village-rangée* may contain several parallel *rangées*. Adjacent *landes* vegetation is quick to colonize former openfield.

Fig. 21.   Lèzillac, Taupont, Morbihan. 'true openfield . . . associated with *rangées.*' The forêt de Paimpont lies on the horizon.

Fig. 22.   Kerdalibot, Plumergat, Morbihan. *Landes* and small fields.

progrès de la civilisation européenne.[50] The Bronze Age left a wealth of field monuments and, like the Neolithic period, depended greatly on the western sea-routes for its contacts. In general, it was less brilliant, and before it merges into the Gallo-Roman period, the sea-routes had waned in importance. The prehistory and protohistory of Brittany have recently been summarized in two volumes.[51]

From the time of the earliest written records, Brittany has been a Celtic country whose inhabitants spoke a language related to the Gaulish branch of the Brythonic group of Celtic languages. The introduction of the Celtic language into Armorica probably took place during the Iron Age, and the arrival of the Belgae strengthened the first Celtic elements in the population. The latter were undoubtedly Gauls who established city-states, tribal territories whose boundaries were of subsequent cultural significance (Fig. 24). The first towns, and possibly many small settlements, originated in this period. Only the Redones have a name that is definitely Celtic[52] and it is probable that these tribes were pre-Celtic peoples later Celticized. Their territories broadly correspond to the five *départements* of post-1789 Brittany, themselves based on the feudal divisions of the historic Duchy. Roman conquest brought roads and milestones, the former radiating from the chief towns, Vannes, Nantes, Carhaix-Plouguer, a network suggesting a substantial population. The troubles which beset the Roman Empire from the third century A.D. onwards led to the building of walls around Rennes, Vannes and Nantes. In an attempt to protect western Gaul, the tribal capitals of Armorica were transferred from the interior to the coasts, and the population and defences concentrated on the Gaulish border, leaving the west of the peninsula largely unprotected,[53] and greatly facilitating the immigration of the Celtic population from Great Britain. The Saxons had failed to effect a permanent settlement or to dislodge the earliest Breton immigrants, and Chadwick[54] suggests that the Roman authority prevailed, the west being deliberately relegated to immigrant Britons by the Romans.

With the arrival of the Britons probably from the third century A.D. onwards, Armorica, an outpost of the Roman Empire, gradually became Brittany, 'a country with its back to Gaul, and with its contacts, its culture, and its relations and political sympathies, its Church and its population closely united with that of the British Isles'.[55] The new population entered the peninsula by the sea-routes, occupying large areas of the interior, especially the west. The cause of the exodus from Britain

Fig. 23.   Saint-Jean-Baptiste-des-Landes. Joué-sur-Erdre, Loire-Atlantique. Large square fields formed by the enclosure of former *landes* in the late-nineteenth century.

is not clear but it seems likely that the pressure of Saxon colonization in eastern Britain was not the sole cause and that earlier Irish pressures from the west, both piracy and permanent settlement, were probably greater factors. It seems more than likely that the migration was encouraged, and possibly actively organized, by the Romans to fill a population vacuum. The earliest settlers, and eventually the majority, appear to have come from Devon and Cornwall, but with many Welsh leaders.

By the middle of the sixth century, Armorica had become Brittany and the Breton language was spoken over the western part of the peninsula. The number of colonists, in relation to the number of surviving Gauls, is the subject of controversy, as is the extent to which Gallo-Roman speech survived to influence the subsequent Breton language.[56] It now seems likely, however, that the Gallic tongue was alive in Armorica at the beginning of the Dark Ages, and that it was a vigorous language when the Bretons began to arrive, chiefly on the northern coast. The immigrants found a population low in numbers, but very close to them in language, history and

religion. From this period onwards, the history of settlement is closely tied up with the movement and influence of the Celtic saints. As leaders of the immigrant Britons, their influence was substantial; in their legacy of place-names, an extraordinarily high proportion of which contain the elements *plou-*, *tref-*, *lann-* and *loc-*, it was profound. The strength of ecclesiastical influence is demonstrated by the number, pattern and density of such place-names, suggesting peaceful, rather than military, conquest.[57] Some of the Breton saints were *peregrini* seeking solitude on fringing islands, but most came as leaders of the migration.[58] Almost all are represented in tradition as educated members of the princely families of Wales. This close relationship suggests an organized political immigration with the saints exercising, in addition to spiritual leadership, a diplomatic and legal role, and playing an active part in the acquisition of land. Links with Wales and Cornwall continued for centuries. By the mid-sixth century three great political divisions are recognized: Dumnonia covering all the north, Cornouaille stretching south from the Monts d'Arrée and east

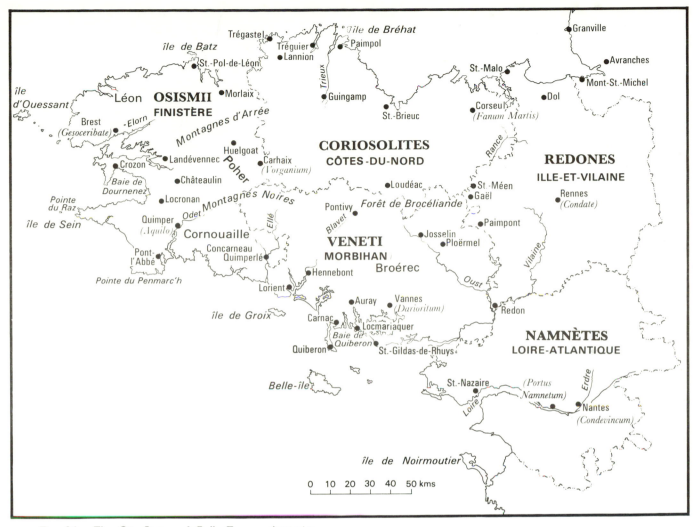

Fig. 24. The City-States of Gallo-Roman Armorica.

to the Ellé river, and Bro Weroc'h, the remainder of the south (Fig. 8). Whilst the Bretons were settling in Armorica, the Frankish kings were establishing themselves in Gaul, and had reached the boundaries of Brittany before the end of the fifth century. Continual military skirmishes occurred throughout the Middle Ages and led to the building of castles and the creation of Marcher lordships which were to contribute significantly to the landscape of the Border regions.

It is assumed that at those places bearing the names of Welsh and Cornish saints, churches and settlements were founded either by the saints themselves or by their disciples. St. Illtud, from mid-Glamorgan, was one, as was a disciple of his, St. Sampson, founder of the great monastic church of Dol, and later first bishop of that see. The spheres of influence of these church leaders form well-defined cultural areas (Fig. 25). Thus St. Sampson's sphere of influence is chiefly confined to eastern Brittany

where settlements named after him are evenly distributed from the north coast down to the Loire, with a further small concentration in Tréguier (Dumnonia) and an isolated settlement in western Léon. A close relative, St. Méen, is responsible for the monastic foundations at Gaël and Saint-Méen-le-Grand, both in the Forêt de Broceliande.[59]

St. Gildas and his followers penetrated Brittany from the north, as did St. Maudez. In both cases, the distributions are striking and the cultural enclaves founded by these and other saints formed the core of the medieval sees of Dol, Saint-Malo, Saint-Brieuc, Tréguier and Saint-Pol-de-Léon (Fig. 26).[60]

The group of saints which includes SS. Petroc, Brioc, Carantoc and Nonna is associated with the outer sea-routes. St. Guenolé settled in western Finistère and founded the great abbey of Landévennec. The evidence for the settlements of the Celtic saints in Brittany shows the importance of the western sea-routes in transmitting populations and ideas across the Atlantic peninsulas of Europe. These settlements and associated territorial organization were of great importance to the subsequent development of the landscape.

The colonization is verified by history and by linguistic and place-name evidence. Archaeological evidence of the advent of the Bretons has been lacking, and is only now beginning to yield information of prime importance.[61] Anthropology shows that the immigrants were no different from the rest of the inhabitants of the Atlantic world, and brought with them the same physical characteristics, a mixture of mesocephalic and brachycephalic peoples, with a predominance of the latter in Haute-Bretagne, and the former in Basse-Bretagne, notably in the coastal areas, for they give way to brachycephalic types in the interior.[62]

A characteristic feature of Brittany is the body of place-names, many of the elements of which are shared with other Celtic languages, but unique in combination and totality. The line of maximum extent of the Breton language, reached during the ninth century, passes from the mouth of the Couesnon, to the west of Rennes, and south to the Loire, by-passing Nantes to the west (Fig. 27, line 1). The maximum area of Breton speech is thus considerably less than the extent of the medieval Duchy. The zone shrank during the Middle Ages, so that by 1650 only Finistère, western Côtes-du-Nord and western Morbihan as far as Vannes were Breton-speaking. A further recession had occurred by the end of the nineteenth century (Fig. 27, lines 2 and 3). That Breton failed to establish itself in the east, and subsequently withdrew westwards, is probably due to the fact that Breton immigrants were there in a minority insufficient to establish the language, rather than to any subsequent Norman or other colonization.[63] An exception is the *pays de Guérande* which has remained an island of Breton culture just north of the Loire (Figs. 8 and 27). Gautier considers that there may have been a medieval 'Breton invasion' into the *pays gallo* where, in the regions around Ploërmel, Plélan-le-Grand and Ploubalay, there is evidence of Breton place-names, the *domaine congéable* (see below), and a dispersion of population more appropriate to *Bretagne bretonnante*.[64] This dichotomy of Breton and non-Breton Brittany, Basse-Bretagne and Haute-Bretagne, or *Bretagne bretonnante* and *pays gallo,* is strengthened by contrasts in place-names. In the east, the element -*ac*, designating former Gallo-Roman *fundi*,[65] survives in some numbers in the area from which Breton has retreated. Some examples have been retained in their original form as in Mériadec, Missillac, Callac and Herbignac, others have evolved to '-*é*' or '-*y*',

as in Marcigné, Aubigné, Erquy and Bubry (Fig. 28).[66]

The occurrence of the place-name elements *plou-*, *tré-*, *loc-*, *lann-* and their association with personal names of the Celtic saints has already been noted. *Plou-*, a parish (Welsh *plwyf*; Cornish *plu-*), highly concentrated in the west, is an index of the religious settlement of the sixth and seventh centuries, and compounded in names given by the Breton settlers and their immediate descendants. *Tré-* (Welsh *tref*; Cornish *tre*) for the most part is compounded either with the name of a saint or with a topographic element and is of ecclesiastical origin, implying dependence upon a parish church. Not all these names are old, or of the same religious origin, but many date from the sixth and seventh centuries. *Lan-* (Welsh *llan*; Cornish *lan*), designating a church, monastery, or consecrated land, is generally compounded with the name of a Celtic saint. *Loc-* (Welsh *llog*), originally a cell, or place (Latin *locus*), implies a religious origin,[67] probably later than the other three elements and not earlier than the eleventh century (Fig. 27).[68] It seems likely that the religious leaders, having established their monasteries and churches, sought to organize territorially, for religious purposes, the scattered settlement pattern of hamlets and isolated farms, some time after, perhaps in some cases a long time after, the immigration. The limits of the parish or *plou-* were imposed by the needs of the clergy and not by any grouping of agricultural holdings generally. They were the areas of land that a priest could visit and administer and from which the furthermost inhabitants could find their way to church, and had little to do with economic life.[69] Physical barriers, ridges and watercourses, valleys deeply entrenched into the plateaux, forests and *landes*, were often limiting factors.

The modern administrative units, the *communes*, are usually based on, and formerly coincided with, the ancient parishes. The parishes of 1789, however, were the consequence of an evolution during which some were combined and others sub-divided so that a *tref* sometimes became a parish. Before 1789, the average area of *communes* in the interior was *c.* 60 sq. kilometres; now it is *c.* 23 sq. kilometres in Finistère, 22 in Morbihan and 33 in Loire-Atlantique.[70] Thébaut has shown how there was an overall tendency towards the splitting up of *communes* with consequent reduction in size, and the land-use factor seems to have played a major role in determining the original dimensions.[71] The big early parishes have remained large. Those containing the element *plou-*, *tré-*, or *lan-* are amongst the most common, with a high concentration in western Brittany (Fig. 27).[72] The *tré* or *tref*, originally a hamlet, often came in time to be served by a chapel, and perhaps subsequently became a parish in its own right as

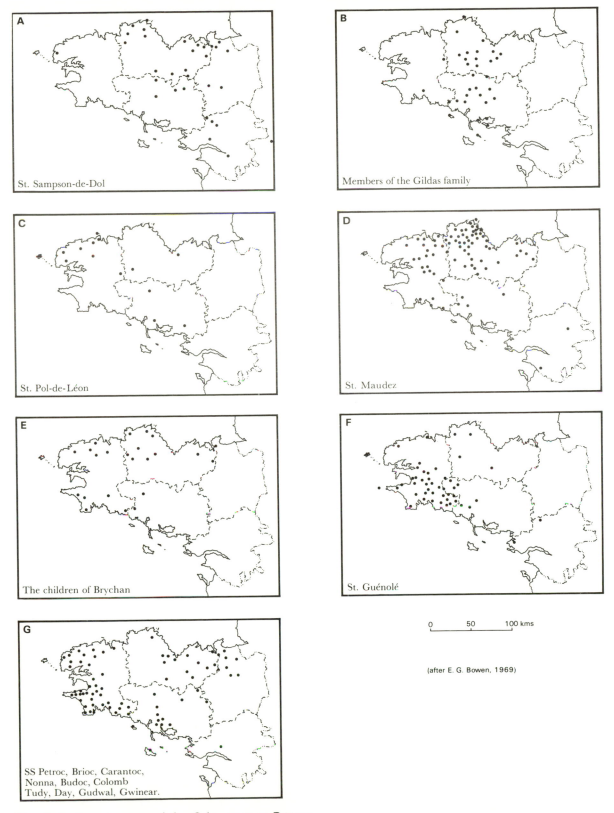

Fig. 25. Dedications to some of the Celtic saints in Brittany.

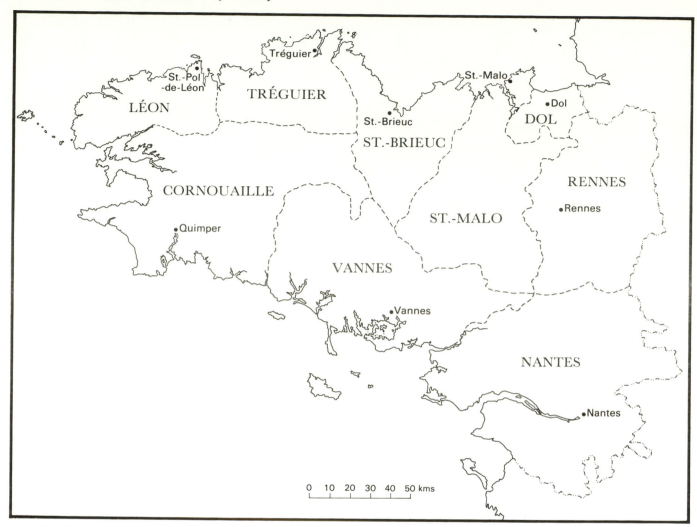

Fig. 26.   The Breton dioceses in the Middle Ages.

settlement increased and population grew. While some of these secondary parishes are of early date, others post-date the Revolution. Organizational structure grew but slowly, the Gallo-Roman *civitas* disappearing and a new administrative structure gradually appearing in the Middle Ages along with diocesan organization (Fig. 26). Most parishes seem to have been completed by the twelfth century, a church being built in a central location and a *bourg* developing around it. The latter performs a service function for the *commune*, with shops, cafés, craftsmen, a smithy, and, to-day, a garage. Often it comes to life only on Sundays and market days. Some *bourgs* are scarcely bigger than many of the neighbouring hamlets and sometimes smaller. The early routes were those from the church to the hamlets and farms. Towns were slow to establish themselves. Nantes, Rennes and Vannes were centres of Gallo-Roman city-states, Carhaix was the node

of a remarkable system of Roman roads, but in general, Breton town development had to await the feudal period. Towns began to grow during the eleventh and twelfth centuries around the *seigneurial* castle, as at Josselin, Vitré, Combourg and Machecoul.[73] Some towns, Quimperlé, Redon and Saint-Méen, grew up around an abbey. Many feudal towns like Bécherel and Moncontour have scarcely grown since the Middle Ages. Others in more favoured locations — Fougères, Lannion, Brest, Quimper — have become important centres of population. Some, located at the lowest crossing point of a river as at Pont-Croix, Pont-l'Abbé or Hennebont, were the scene of maritime and commercial activity from the fourteenth century onwards. Whether the Norman harassment had something to do with the depopulation of the coast or not, at a time when feudal towns were beginning to grow, during the eleventh and twelfth

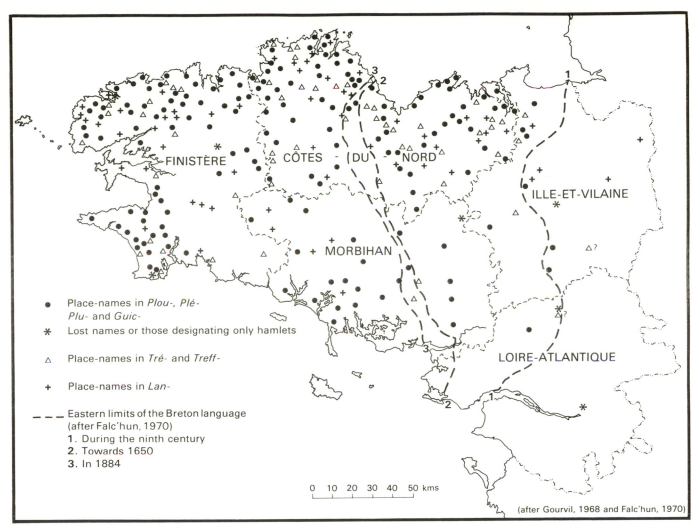

Fig. 27. Brittany: distribution of place-name elements in *Plou-*, *Guic-* *Tré-* and *Lan-*.

Legend on map:

● Place-names in *Plou-*, *Plé-* *Plu-* and *Guic-*

* Lost names or those designating only hamlets

△ Place-names in *Tré-* and *Treff-*

+ Place-names in *Lan-*

– – – Eastern limits of the Breton language (after Falc'hun, 1970)
1. During the ninth century
2. Towards 1650
3. In 1884

0 10 20 30 40 50 kms

(after Gourvil, 1968 and Falc'hun, 1970)

centuries, small ports with the prefix *loc-* were established, as at Loctudy and Locquirec, as the hamlets of fishermen.[74] The great ports, Brest, Nantes and Saint-Malo, developed later, from the thirteenth century onwards, as coastal Brittany began to play its part in mercantile activity. During the period from the thirteenth to fifteenth centuries, towns flourished and began to free themselves of the old parishes, illustrating the dichotomy between the old rural settlement with its origins in the Breton immigration, and the new outward-looking towns and ports that sought to trade far and wide.[75]

The map of Brittany displays a classic pattern of rural dispersion with an overwhelming number of hamlets and isolated farms. In the *pays gallo* the original unit of settlement may have been the Gallo-Roman *fundus* bearing the suffix *-ac* (Fig. 28). From these nuclei

settlement dispersed, during the eleventh to the thirteenth centuries, into the surrounding waste. These additional hamlets and farms appear to have been individual colonizations bearing place-names compounded of a personal name followed by *-ière* or *-ais* (La Havardière, La Renaudière, La Bernardais).[76] Names in *-ière* and *-erie* date from the eleventh century, those in *-ais* and *-aie* from the twelfth century, with maximum extension during the thirteenth century. This extension of settlement is to be explained by the quieter political conditions following the Norman invasions, the need, with increasing population, to colonize the *landes* and clear the woodland, and by the fact that in the west of France, serfdom disappeared early, partly as a result of the relatively small social and economic differences between the nobility and others. Here lie the beginnings of the small peasant proprietor.[77] These place-name

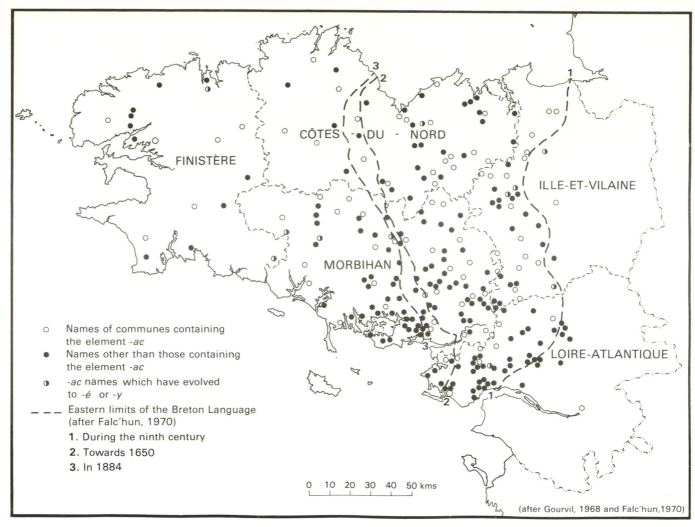

Fig. 28.   Brittany: distribution of place-name elements in *-ac*.

elements are widely distributed in western France and extend in Brittany up to the line of Breton speech in 1650 (Fig. 28). There is a zone of mixing where hybrid forms appear and where names in the Breton *ker* (see below) are the equivalent of names in *-ière* and *-ais*.[78]

The next major period of settlement was the nineteenth century, when the use of artificial fertilizers aided the conquest of the *landes* and led to the creation of new farms with characteristic names: Belle-vue, Le Point-du-Jour, Beau Soleil, Saint-Jean-Baptiste-des-Landes (Fig. 23). Thus in eastern Brittany the pattern appears to have been one of dispersal from the Gallo-Roman *fundus*, a centrifugal movement of colonists and assarters, still evident in the circular clearings visible in the field patterns.[79]

In the west, evolution took a different course, although early forms of settlement remain obscure. The eleventh

to the thirteenth centuries saw active secondary colonization. After the Norman devastations many new settlements appeared, some with the prefix *ker-* (Welsh, *caer*; Cornish, *car*), originally an enclosure and later a fortified settlement. The 18,000 *ker* names are one of the most characteristic features of *Bretagne bretonnante* (Fig. 29). Generally, *ker* implies a unique colony rather than a group, although many settlements later developed into hamlets and villages, and it sometimes occurs in the name of a *bourg* or town.[80] The element appears relatively late, there being few recorded examples before the eleventh century.[81] It is usually combined with a personal name, Kerjean, Kermenguy, Kergonan, or a descriptive element, Kerloc'h (lake house), Kervrug (heath house), Kernevez (new house), Kergoz (old house), Kervihan (small house), Ker an dour (house by the water). Subsequent history shows the same tendency

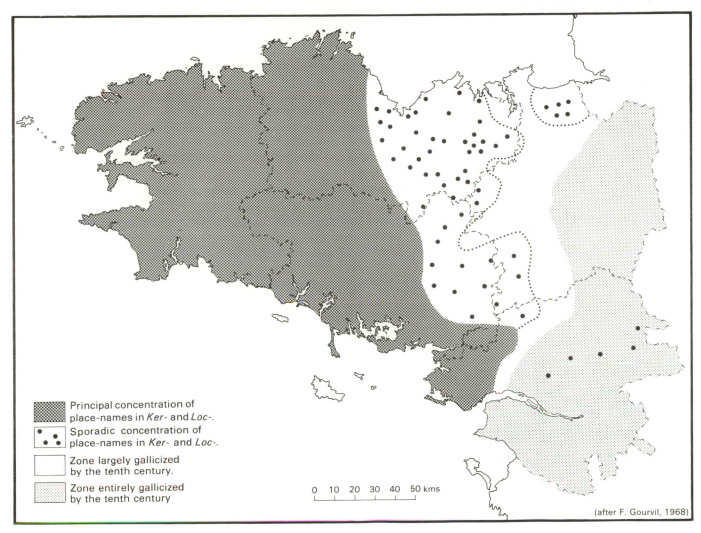

Fig. 29. Brittany: distribution of place-name elements in *Ker-* and *Loc-*.

to dispersion. At the start of the nineteenth century, the *landes* were still extensive and an integral part of the agricultural system. After 1850, with the coming of the railways and the use of lime, a new era of colonization dawned and farms were established in the former *landes* surrounded by new rectilinear fields (Fig. 23). Place-names betray such farms: Kerhuel (high farm), Keravel (windy farm). Sometimes the element *ty-*, a house, is used instead of *ker-*. These last stages of rural colonization have the same characteristics as those that preceded them and represent '*les prolongements d'un processus très ancien et très uniforme d'installation rurale marqué du même signe de l'individualisme*'.[82]

The initial settlement has been modified, not only by further colonization, but also by subdivision and fragmentation of land. Additional houses were built next to the original settlement site and not 'in the fields', so

that the hamlets grew from single farmsteads. The *domaine congéable* (see below), the need by larger farms to hire and house additional labour, and the operation of partible inheritance laws may help to explain the dense hamlet groupings of the interior. By different processes of evolution the patterns of settlement in eastern and western Brittany, notwithstanding strong regional variations, come to much the same. One contrast is between *Armor* and *Arcoët*. By the sea, where fragmentation of holdings is often extreme, hamlets tend to be smaller and isolated farms greater in number, perhaps a reflection of better quality land and more favourable conditions.

The Breton hamlet varies greatly both in the space it occupies and in the number of its constituent dwellings. While some contain only two farms bearing a common name, others may consist of twenty, thirty or even forty

Fig. 30.   Saint-Igneuc, Jugon, Côtes-du-Nord. *Landes,* small fields and hamlets of the *bocage.*

or more independent dwellings, each having an agricultural function (Figs. 30 and 31). The spatial relationship of the constituent dwellings is also subject to variation. Some hamlets are *extraordinarily amorphous,* in others distinct patterns occur. Meynier has drawn attention to the small, low, single-storeyed houses, often of only one cell, with adjacent byres and other farm buildings.[83] These dwellings are arranged in rows (*rangées, barres, rues*) of three to eleven houses (Figs. 31 and 32). In the *pays Nord-Bigouden, villages* are located close to the great *landes,* their houses grouped gable against gable in a long *rangée.*[84] In the Pollues the houses open into a yard divided into parcels, whilst behind the dwellings and in front of the yard are the *courtils,* sometimes entirely enclosed, sometimes with sub-divisions marked by *bornes.* This systematic subdivision of the *village-rangée* is repeated in the subdivision of the openfield or *trest* and is interpreted as the work not of individuals, but of a group (Fig. 32). Villages with strip-divided openfields are located in the *haut-pays* amid *landes* and *bocage* and would appear to have been founded by groups in the midst of deserted territory.[85] In

south Finistère *villages* of twenty to thirty hearths, or *feux,* are common in upland regions. Along the littoral, in the Bassin de Châteaulin, and in south Cornouaille, hamlets of five to ten, or ten to twenty, *feux* predominate. Fundamental hamlet plans are repre-sented: the *village-rangée,* a long line of four, five or six farms, and the hamlet of independent farms. The former, pronounced in the Crozon peninsula (Figs. 19 and 20), may contain several parallel *rangées.* Elsewhere, one or more *rangées* may be mixed with independent dwellings. In the second category, buildings are dispersed around yards and no plan may readily be discernible. A characteristic *trait* of many hamlets is the *placître* or green. Often outside the hamlet and triangular in form, it appears to represent the last shred of an old *lande.* Many hamlet groups are nebulous. In the Monts d'Arrée they bear a common name, but along the littoral, small villages with different names are found crowded around a common green. The isolated farms, many bearing a 'ker-' name, are widely distributed in Finistère, except in Crozon.[86] A further element in the settlement, especially in Finistère, is the *penty,* in its strict sense a house at the

Fig. 31.   Linsard, Taupont, Morbihan. In some areas dwellings are grouped in *rangées* which appear to be related to adjacent openfield.

end of a piece of ground. Forming part of a larger farm, it was traditionally allocated to the principal farm servant, the *grand valet,* but is now usually the home of an agricultural worker or *journalier,* and is accompanied by one or two fields. The numbers of *penty* greatly multiplied after the early-nineteenth century, with the growth of population, and were most numerous at the period of population maximum between 1900 and 1910. Their names usually begin with *ty-, loch-* or *menez-,* and never with *ker-.*[87]

Around the Golfe du Morbihan, the *rangée* is again widespread and most of the hamlets in the Presqu'île de Rhuys, around Locmariaquer, Arradon and Baden, are formed of one or two rows of adjacent long-houses, usually south-facing. Many dwellings are in ruins, and where formerly a hamlet may have contained seven or eight *exploitations,* there are now only one or two. Behind each house is a *courtil* or *liors* surrounded by a *talus* or a stone wall. The settlements were traditionally characterized by the *rangée,* the strip-divided openfield, and the survival of communal cultivation practices.[88] In

the heart of the *pays gallo,* south of Rennes, the existence of openfield is related to characteristic hamlet forms which seem older than the isolated farms and *métairies* that lie scattered between the hamlets. Rows of farms are known as *rangées* or *rangs,* the long-houses standing in lines of up to a dozen, although the system is in decay and many former dwellings have been converted to farm use. The relationship between the *rangées* and openfield appears indisputable. Each *commune* contains several agglomerations of this kind separated by areas of dispersed habit and *bocage.* In Messac, each *rangée* corresponds to one or more domaines.[89] The *rangée* is evident in a well-developed form in eastern Ille-et-Vilaine, north Morbihan (Fig. 31) and in Loire-Atlantique. *Rangées* of two or three farms are common all over Brittany, whilst in some areas the highly dispersed pattern appears to predominate (Figs. 33 and 34). In many areas there are gradations between the group of one or two farms and the serried ranks of *rangées* (Fig. 35).

One characteristic of the hamlet is the almost complete

Fig. 32 Penhors, Pouldreuzic, Finistère. Short *rangées* grouped into a large hamlet on the edge of openfield.

Fig. 33. Lilia, Plouguerneau, Finistère. In some areas the highly dispersed pattern of settlement predominates.

Fig. 34. Toul-al-lan, Île d'Ouessant, Finistère. The tiny fields, high stone walls and scattered farms of Ouessant.

absence of services, save perhaps for a chapel. The service function is provided by the *bourg*, the *chef-lieu* of the *commune*. Essentially a non-agricultural nucleated settlement developed around the parish church, it comes to life on Sundays and market days, but for the rest of the week gives the impression of being lifeless. Occasionally the centre of the parish may have been moved to a new site close to a modern road, leaving the former *bourg*, often called *Vieux Bourg*, to survive as an agricultural hamlet, the old parish church becoming a dependent chapel as at Taupont, Morbihan. In a few rare cases the church may be isolated. An agricultural community may form part of the *bourg*, or exist adjacent to it, but functionally it rests apart. Some *bourgs* are minute. Treffiagat consists only of church and *presbytère*, others have only a few houses. This seems to have been general until the nineteenth century. The large *bourgs* with their two-storey houses are very much a product of the second half of the nineteenth and the twentieth centuries, representing growth of the small nuclei. Roads radiate to outlying farms and hamlets on the parish boundary and often go no further. A *placître*, a triangular space, usually

lies on the periphery and is often lined with farms.[90] Other modern essentials of a bourg are its *mairie*, post-office, a school, shops, cafés, agricultural tradesmen and a weekly market on the *place*.

The most general impression of the Breton countryside until recent agrarian reforms and *remembrement* was of a patchwork of small, narrow fields enclosed by stone walls or earthen banks with or without stone revetments planted with pollarded oaks and shrubs (Figs. 9-12; 18; 23; 30; 33-42). The dense network of lanes, many sunken, the *chemins creux*, may be prehistoric in origin with directions related to the sub-divisions of the fields[91] or the result of the need to demarcate and enclose fields in medieval and later times, or both.[92] Earthen banks, *talus*, serve as land boundaries, provide firewood from the pollarded trees, and act as wind-breaks. On the western peninsulas, stone walls alone serve to bound the fields (Fig. 34) and in some areas field boundaries are formed from slabs of schist. Granite slabs are used in the area around Névez and Trégunc. On the more recently enclosed *landes* banks are often much lower and less well-built, and in some areas posts and wire are common

Fig. 35.   Saint-Jean, Campénéac, Morbihan. A hamlet consisting of two farms and a chapel.

(Fig. 23). Characteristically, Breton fields are small, often minute (Figs. 34; 37-40), many of them long, narrow and strip-like, displaying an aratal curve, perhaps betraying the former existence of common openfield.

Post-war studies show the Breton *bocage* to be far from irregular, comprising cohesive groups of fields.[93] Meynier identifies four principal agrarian landscapes:

regular geometrical enclosures, bounded by generally bare *talus,* but with some hedges and occasional trees, mostly date from the enclosure of the *landes* in the late-eighteenth and nineteenth centuries;

the much more frequent roughly regular enclosures which display approximate orientation over long distances. (The *talus* is nearly always planted with trees and shrubs, but dating is difficult. This type appears to have reached its maximum extent at the end of the nineteenth century, since when fields have steadily been enlarged and *talus* destroyed);

ribbon-like enclosures, long, narrow and some-times incurved and bounded by trees casting shadows over the whole parcel (Fig. 38);

openfield with *bornes* to mark the boundaries and common names for whole parcels of parallel strips. (Groups of curved parcels are frequent and enclosure of the whole is generally by a *talus* (Figs. 19, 20, 39, 40, 41).[94]

Frequently observed are the elliptical and circular groups of fields, nearly always linked to a hamlet.[95] A few bear Gallo-Roman or Gaulish names, but many have Breton names in *ker-* often compounded with *coat* or *coët,* and sometimes *penhoët,* suggesting assarting. In the *pays gallo, -ais* names suggest clearances of the thirteenth century. Meynier argues that prehistoric routeways served as a 'base' for colonization and that even as late as the nineteenth century clearances were aligned on them, showing the strength, and length, of tradition.[96] The size of the fields indicates clearance by small groups who subdivided the land, cultivating some as common openfield or *méjou.*

Other field groups are rectilinear with curvature that may be aratal. Field orientation in three major directions, north–south, north–north-east and north–north-west, is almost tyrannic, and maintains an indifference to

Fig. 36.   Caradeuc, Plouasne, Côtes-du-Nord. View north across the *bocage* of Côtes-du-Nord from the terrace of the Château de Caradeuc.

Fig. 37.   Trébouic, Dingé, Ille-et-Vilaine. Narrow fields with earthen banks often planted with pollarded oaks and shrubs.

Fig. 38.   Le Courtil, Paimpont, Ille-et-Vilaine. 'Ribbon-like enclosures, long, narrow . . . bounded by trees casting shadows over the whole parcel.'

accidents of relief, even when rivers, gorges and the coast intervene. Centuriation is known to have occurred over only a part of Brittany but the correspondence of agrarian orientation with the direction of Megalithic alignments has been demonstrated.[97]

Much discussion has centred on the origin of the *bocage,* the enclosed field and the *talus.* Guilcher draws attention to the great variety of enclosure banks (Fr. *fossé,* Br. *kleuz, -iou*), and ditches (Fr. *douve,* Br. *foz*), planted with gorse, trees, and sometimes quick-set hedges (Br. *garz*).[98] Near the sea, dry-stone walls are common and in certain areas orthostat walls are found. In Basse-Bretagne, the *fossé* was already present in the ninth century and Guilcher regards this as a sign of appropriation.[99] In Haute-Bretagne, enclosure and openfield lay side by side, very similar to the present, but with more *landes.* The density of *bocage* cannot accurately be estimated. Meynier regards *bocage* as having gradually replaced the openfield,[100] Flatrès thinks it partly resulted from a movement of population inland following Norse piracy,[101] whilst Souillet sees in the *bocage* a form of individual colonization during the

eleventh to thirteenth centuries.[102] Chaumeil takes a different view, regarding *clôture* as initially a means of keeping cattle out when cultivation formed a small part in a largely pastoral economy.[103] Lefeuvre shows how the peasantry had need of commons to pasture their cattle and to provide fertilizer owing their right to concessions by, or to the tolerance of, the *seigneur.*[104] The rights of the *seigneur* seem to have been strongly marked in Brittany and many enclosed their commons, giving the peasantry a proportion, half or two-thirds, according to their status, not, however, without causing considerable hostility.

Openfield, sub-divided into strips and formerly cultivated in common, has been identified all over Brittany. It appears to have been in existence by the ninth century.[105] The *pays gallo* was an area of big estates, with openfield, the *pays breton* an area where property was held by individuals. Transactions were individual ones, partible inheritance is demonstrable, and groups of two or three co-inheritors or neighbours occurred. Territorial divisions seem to be less rigid than in the east. *Talus,* uncultivated *landes* and *domaines* are all present, and

Fig. 39.   Tal-ar-Groas, Crozon, Finistère. 'Groups of curved parcels are frequent and enclosure of the whole is generally by a *talus.*'

indications are that the habitat was already dispersed in small cells of several hearths and isolated farms.[106] The unit of holding was the *ran,* or *tigran,* with both enclosures and openfield.[107] The Breton rural structures thus differed from those of the *pays gallo.* As a result of the subsequent evolution of the latter, differences became small and contrasts seem largely to disappear.[108] This interpretation is supported by evidence for the persistence of *Gaulois* in the east.[109]

Meynier has outlined three types of openfield: true openfield often associated with *rangées* (Fig. 21) and, rarely, a 'green' village; elongated openfield in the middle of the *bocage,* with an axial road or interfluve, fields which may belong to a period of expansion; small groups of fields, often near hamlets, whose frequency leaves no doubt that they were important.[110]

A multitude of collective local names have been used to describe openfield. In the *pays bretonnant,* they include *trest* and *méjou,* in the *pays gallo, champagne, landelle, plaine, domaines* and *gaigneries.*[111]

The origin of the *méjou* is obscure. On the best soils it may be early, but when associated with centrally placed

hamlets, it probably results from the clearance of the *landes.* As with the *bocage,* extreme variations of age appear to characterize it.[112] The small openfield, associated with from three to seven dwellings and obligatory collective practices, was known in the Saint-Brieuc region in the thirteenth century, and openfield seems to have been more extensive near the sea and rarer in the interior.[113] In the Loire-Atlantique, *méjou* coincides with the pattern of Breton place-names, perhaps suggesting a tenth- or eleventh-century origin.[114] Other regional descriptions are provided.[115]

Micro-openfield is associated with *rangées,* and there is a constant link: no *hameau-rangée* unless there is *méjou* in proximity.[116] The extent of the *méjou* has been greatly reduced since the eighteenth century, accompanied by enclosure and sometimes *remembrement,* and always with depopulation of the *hameaux-rangées.* Decay of openfield was fully under way before the nineteenth-century rise in population, although some new *méjou* was created during that century in Finistère and Côtes-du-Nord.[117]

In the *pays* Nord-Bigouden each farm had a few

Fig. 40.   Penantre, Plougasnou, Finistère. 'Openfield . . . and common names for whole parcels of strips.'

enclosures or *park* beyond the openfield. Not all hamlets were *rangées,* some being loosely grouped around a chapel in the midst of the *trests,* with a multitude of transitional types. Other settlements were isolated amid the *bocage.* The most infertile soils carried openfield and at certain periods there must have been a colonization of poorer land by groups. Documentary evidence, of eleventh-century date, suggest hamlets and strip fields isolated amid the *landes.*[118] Ancient fields and openfield dependent on small villages, individual lands around the farms and pioneer lands on the borders of the waste have been identified all over south Finistère. The littoral regions seem to have been densely populated for a long time, for the parishes are ancient and there are many Megalithic monuments. Interior plateaux were once sparsely populated and were used, by the colonization of the *landes,* to reduce population pressure on the coast. Nearly all the *landes* have been enclosed during the last hundred years as the geometrical network of recent *talus* shows. Consistent *traits* in south Finistère are the co-existence of isolated farms and hamlets, of openfield and enclosures, and, above all, the survival of minute parcels of land.[119]

In the south-east, Charaud has outlined the existence of openfield in the Loire country, mostly on the plateaux to the north of the river where *villages,* grouped into *fréries* to which the commons belong, are built around the *pâtis* and *gast* on which stand the communal well and bake-oven.[120] Two great areas of marsh, the Grande Brière and the Marais de Donges, illustrate quite different, but highly individual, landscapes with some openfield and communal organization, and a memory of compulsory rotation of crops.[121]

Openfield, group habitat and collective practices, which survived in parts until the mid-twentieth century, appear to be related. There is oral evidence for the survival of compulsory rotation up to 1914 over a great part of southern Brittany, and much later on the Presqu'île de Rhuys and some of the islands. During the nineteenth century *vaine pâture,* the right to graze the common fields after harvest and during fallow, was widespread. Eighteenth-century documents deplore the continued use of practices of feudal origin. On Rhuys the openfield is highly fragmented and strips very narrow, with great problems of access. Compulsory rotation is biennial, with grazing after harvest and all the year round

Fig. 41.   La Jarrie, Frossay, Loire-Atlantique. Former openfield south of the Loire.

on fallow.[122] *Vaine pâture* existed on the whole of the peninsulas of Rhuys and Locmariaquer on stubble and on the fallow of which the farmer was proprietor. Agreement was needed to sow and harvest on the same day and fallow was one year in two. With population densities approaching three hundred per sq. kilometre in the early-nineteenth century, enclosure was impossible.[123]

Considerable regional variations occurred. In some areas the proprietor considered a hamlet and its fields to be a single tenancy, leaving the occupants to pay rent as a group, and presumably to organize themselves as they chose. In the Monts d'Arrée, there are memories of collective clearances, of *écobuage* in common. Some *communes* are divided into sections, *souarties*, for self-help. There is eighteenth- and nineteenth-century evidence of biennial compulsory rotation, free pasture after harvest, and collective herding on the meadows.[124] In the Josselin-Ploërmel region, rotation was by agreement, and not compulsory, some on openfield created in the nineteenth and twentieth centuries.[125] At

the end of the nineteenth century, compulsory rotation was the rule south of Rennes, followed by free pasture over all the common field after harvest[126] By the mid-twentieth century fallow had been shortened to one year, but had formerly been two, three, four and up to ten years or more. Harvesting was by hand, with the sickle, until well into the twentieth century, and the *landes*, dwarf gorse and heath, were cut for litter.[127] In Crozon, sheep were pastured from Michaelmas to Candlemas, but by World War II beasts were tied to a stake to prevent straying.[128]

Flatrès outlines the common rights and stresses the sharp distinction from time immemorial between enclosed cultivated land and the unenclosed parcels.[129] *Landes* were the property not of *communes* or individuals, but of the adjacent hamlets, a situation challenged by the *seigneurs* under the *Ancien Régime* but overturned at the Revolution. The inhabitant of a *cabane*, without land, had rights to the common on the same basis as the largest landowner. By the end of the nineteenth century the greater part of the *landes* had

Fig. 42.   Louargat, Côtes-du-Nord. View northwards from Menez Bré across the *bocage* of Côtes-du-Nord.

been enclosed, but much still remains. Rights included pasture for cattle, prohibited about 1900, turbary, for fuel and fertilizer, the cutting of *landes* for litter and feed, and *écobuage*. Turbary and *écobuage* have ceased, but cutting of the *landes* continues. Such products were for the exclusive use of the commoner and their sale was forbidden. The enclosure of the waste for a limited period was permitted. The land so enclosed, a form of openfield, was sown with oats or rye for a period of two or three years, after which the fields had to be broken down and the land returned to common. Strictly, during this period, the commoner had to give up his right of common grazing, but the rule seems rarely to have been strictly applied. There is documentary evidence of men establishing themselves on the *landes* and clearing with the tolerance of their co-proprietors. There was other common land, *leucar,* the verges of the roads, the *placître* or village green, and common meadow. Fifteenth-century documents give the impression that each tenant enjoyed exclusively his house, his *courtil* and a part of the yard or *aire*. Each parcel of land in *méjou* or *trest* was, in theory, for the exclusive profit of one tenant,

although restrained by common practice. Other restraints included the obligation to plant the same crop in all parcels of a *méjou* and the difficulties over access. Signs are that common pasture has now all but disappeared, but traces of common grazing will no doubt survive until all is enclosed. By the mid-twentieth century free grazing was in decay and cattle had to be staked to prevent straying.[130]

It would thus appear that the strip-divided openfield, whose date of origin is unknown, corresponds in general to a population of small farmers who, at various periods, and sometimes right up to the present day, have practised a partially collective rural economy.[131]

Poor soils, the great extent of the *landes,* small, often minute and widely scattered land holdings, a dispersed pattern of settlement and relative isolation have characterized Breton agriculture. Until the 1950s and the rapid change that followed the creation of the European Economic Community, farms over forty hectares were rare in the interior. The practice of partible inheritance among male heirs resulted in sub-division and fragmentation, and the chief force controlling farm size has been the capacity of a family to cultivate an area of land without assistance. A notable characteristic was the absence of hired labour on a regular basis. During the 1930s in Bulat-Pestivien, only seven per cent of the agricultural population fell into this category.[132] Assistance was provided by the *journalier,* who held a *penty,* or by another family lending a helping hand. This characteristic *intraide,* far from being an indication of weakness, actually served to strengthen the system. The use of female and child labour was an essential feature. A farmer starting with ten hectares might lease a further five hectares as soon as his eldest son could work, increasing gradually to a peak of twenty to twenty-five hectares before progressive diminution set in as his children set up on their own.[133] Such variations were made possible only by the great elasticity of ownership and tenure.

Statistics of farm size before the great post-War changes took effect provide a useful indication of the position not long after the last of the truly vernacular houses had been built. In Finistère, large farms over twenty-five hectares constituted five per cent of the total, occupying twenty per cent of the land area; medium-sized farms, ten to twenty-five hectares, formed twenty-five per cent of the total occupying fifty-one per cent of the area; small farms, under ten hectares, constituted seventy per cent of the total, occupying twenty-nine per cent of the area. In Côtes-du-Nord, there were 121,270 farms of which 62,528 were under ten hectares, 16,674 were between ten and twenty hectares, and 4,571 were between twenty and fifty hectares. Only 235 farms exceeded fifty hectares. In Morbihan, of 57,215 farms in 1929, 35,362 were under ten hectares, 15,216 between ten and twenty hectares, 6,300 between twenty and fifty hectares and only 337 over fifty hectares. These figures illustrate the change from the turn of the century when population was nearing its maximum. In 1892, 24,298 farms were under one hectare, 20,475 between one and five hectares, 13,348 between five and ten hectares, 9,716 between ten and twenty hectares, 5,029 between twenty and fifty hectares, and 322 over fifty hectares. In Ille-et-Vilaine, 47,912 farms were under ten hectares, occupying 29.25 per cent of the land area; 12,790 between ten and twenty hectares, or 31.20 per cent of the area; 6,883 over twenty hectares, or 39.55 per cent of the area. In Loire-Atlantique, 55,700 farms were under ten hectares, 12,200 between ten and twenty hectares, 6,575 between twenty and fifty hectares and 181 over fifty hectares.[134] Holdings are often very small near the coast, where the growing of early vegetables or market gardening was practised, where tenants had additional employment as *journaliers,* masons, fishermen or had retired from the national or merchant marine to a small farm in their home parish.

The average farm was frequently split up into fifteen or twenty pieces, and fifty or more was not unknown. In general, the smaller farms were the most fragmented. Farmers frequently bought a field two or three kilometres from their home to enlarge a holding. Partible inheritance seems to have been the chief factor in this fragmentation, but the enclosure of the *landes* further increased the tendency.[135] Fragmentation was extreme on the islands. In mid nineteenth-century Ouessant, 1,562 hectares were divided into 35,245 parcels, averaging four *ares* per parcel (Fig. 34). Subdivision was greater on Bréhat and Batz, and worst on the Île de Sein where the tiny walled fields were of only ten to thirty square metres each. In general the smallest holdings lay on the islands and along the coastlands of *Armor* from Saint-Brieuc to Brest and from Brest to Vannes. Absence of forests and extensive *landes* and marsh, the presence of a maritime population able to supplement its living from the sea and the pressure of population on land, were all contributory factors. In the interior, on the northern peneplains, the smallest farms occurred in Goëllo, Trégorrois, the *pays de Morlaix* and Léon, extending south to the Monts d'Arrée. In *Arcoët,* in the mountains and on the southern peneplains, they did not dominate, but they were conspicuous near Quimper, in the Montagnes Noires between Briec and Laz, in the *pays de Rohan* and, above all, in the *pays vannetais.*[136]

The initial dispersion of settlement which has been strongly maintained is a pre-eminent characteristic little altered by subsequent history. Feudalism and the division of land into *seigneuries* rested relatively lightly on the Breton peasant. '*La féodalité a dû ici ménager les travailleurs, et permettre ainsi que se perpétuât une démocratie rurale née des établissements pionniers du VIe siècle*'.[137] Of several modes of tenure, the most curious was the *domaine congéable* which existed throughout Basse-Bretagne until 1789 and of which fragments survived to the mid-twentieth century. In origin the system seems to have derived from the granting by the *seigneur* of fallow or waste land to a *domanier* who cleared and cultivated it and became proprietor of the buildings and crops but who was required to pay a small rent for the land. The *seigneur* retained the right to dismiss the *domanier* but on doing so had to pay to him the value of the *édifices* and *superfices.* The system seemed to discourage improvement in agriculture and buildings and was seen as an example of feudal oppression. Other forms of tenure existed in a land essentially '*une région de ferme démocratie terrienne*'.[138]

Its greatest concentration lay in the *pays de Rohan,* Bro Weroc'h and Cornouaille.[139]

The *domaine congéable* had all but disappeared and *métayage* was rare by 1950, comprising under one per cent of holdings in Basse-Bretagne. At the end of the nineteenth century, in the north and east, *métayage* seems to have been a system with positive advantages if the proprietor with capital to invest was matched by a hard-working tenant.[140] At the turn of the century, Vallaux was able to write that *métayage* was not numerous in Basse-Bretagne except around Saint-Brieuc.[141] Most of the 11,141 *métairies* in 1892 lay on the eastern edges of Côtes-du-Nord and Morbihan.

By the late 1930s, tenant-farming and owner-occupancy had become the most favoured forms of holding. In Finistère sixty-two per cent of agriculturalists were owner-occupiers, thirty-seven per cent tenants and one per cent *métayers.* In Côtes-du-Nord the figures were forty-six per cent owner-occupiers, fifty-three per cent tenants and one per cent (a total of 496 persons) *métayers;* in Morbihan, sixty-one per cent owner-occupiers, thirty-eight per cent tenants and one per cent *métayers;* in Ille-et-Vilaine, forty-two per cent owner-occupiers and fifty-eight per cent tenants.[142]

The tendency of owner occupation is for the land to be grouped as closely as possible about the farm. Regroupment has taken place from time to time either by purchase or by renting. Many farms are neatly situated in the centre of their fields, but in others parcels are small and widely scattered, the dwellings and buildings often being a kilometre or more from the nearest field. Most farms have some land close by and some widely scattered.

At Bulat-Pestivien, 6,514 pieces of land appear on the *cadastre,* the average area being 0.5 hectare, and nearly ninety per cent of the fields were under 1.0 hectare in area. The mixture of ownership and tenancy was striking. A farmer often let some of his own land, and not always that furthest from his farm, simultaneously renting land from a neighbour.[143]

Whatever the form of tenure, Breton farms have been traditionally small, sometimes extremely small, with holdings often widely scattered. Nor do there seem to have been great discrepancies in the amount of land held by the majority of families in a given region. The size, form and function of the agricultural holdings may find expression in the houses and buildings of the families who worked them.

FOUR

BUILDING MATERIALS

The choice of building materials and the spatial and temporal variations of their occurrence and use depend on a number of factors which include geology, relief and its altitude, amplitude and denudational history, the extent and nature of the soil cover, the possession of extraction techniques, the level of building technology and the generally prevailing economic conditions. Concern with building materials has been uppermost in many studies of rural buildings in France, and materials and their treatment are usually of paramount interest to owners of second homes in the countryside. Several authors treat this subject sensitively with reference to Breton houses.[144]

The complex structural history of the Armorican peninsula — the essentially east–west Hercynian trends, complex in detail, broad in outline but with considerable regional variations — has been described in Chapter 2. Brittany is largely a land of hard old rocks, and the combination of an east–west grain, faulting and folding often results in tightly packed ribbon-like patterns in which different rocks give way rapidly one to the other in a north–south direction, but which may extend tens of, and occasionally a hundred, kilometres, or more, in an east–west direction.

Granite is the stone traditionally associated with Breton architecture, but in reality there is a great diversity of building material. Large quantities of granites are certainly used, both fine- and coarse-grained varieties, and walling of grey and rose-coloured stones is well known. But schists and mica-schists in colours varying from red and purple to grey and black are common and blocks of massive sandstone of diverse colours and subtle nuances are also widely used. It was not for any great love of stone that it was used for building, rather because it was the best available material, the alternatives being wood and cob. The latter, known in French variously as *terre, torchis* or *pisé,* is derived from the clay subsoil and puddled before use. Stone was rarely sought from afar, except for building at the highest social levels. Indeed, the correlation between the solid geology and the walling

material of the lesser domestic buildings shows an almost tyrannical relationship, the material usually changing within a few hundred metres or so of any lithological change. In every parish there were formerly small quarries wherever stone of adequate quality lay close to the surface. Often there were several, sometimes one to each hamlet, and on many farms it is not necessary to look further than the shallow depressions in nearby fields, or on an adjacent *lande,* to learn where building stone came from. The poorer buildings were constructed with door and window dressings of the same material and with lintels of wood where stone of sufficient size and mechanical strength was not available. For many of the better-built peasant houses, dressed stone for door and window dressings, lintels and sometimes quoins, was sought further afield.

The overwhelming impression gained by the traveller in Brittany is of the apparent preponderance of igneous rocks, but whilst igneous material is certainly present in considerable quantities, there are also large amounts of sedimentary and metamorphic rocks. The long east–west bands of igneous rocks are conspicuous in the south, the trend-lines being less uniform and more broken in the north, taking a generally north-east–south-west orientation (Figs. 5 and 6). From the Pointe du Raz a whole belt of individual bands of igneous rock stretches across south Finistère and southern Morbihan where it fans out, finding physical expression in the Landes de Lanvaux and their eastward extensions, and in the Sillon de Bretagne which closes the estuarine lowlands of the Loire at the northern end. These igneous rocks intersect the Loire at Nantes and continue south-eastwards to form the upland areas around Clisson. The principal igneous belts of southern Brittany are formed of riebeckite and muscovite granites. To the north of these lies the gneissic belt of the Landes de Lanvaux, and in the west, a belt of mica-schist. Eastwards, the Landes de Lanvaux give way to a complex assemblage of mica-schists and Silurian and Ordovician sedimentary rocks. In an arcuate belt around the north and east of Nantes are mica-schists, gneiss, and intrusions of amphibolite. The southern littoral is underlain by migmatite which occurs in a belt several kilometres wide from the Baie d'Audièrne through to the Loire, and is interrupted by intrusions of riebeckite and muscovite granite, gneiss, crystalline schist and anatectic granite. A notable intrusion of biotite granite, between Concarneau and Pont-Aven, gives rise to a material from which are derived the long flat slabs of granite used for the orthostat walling of many buildings in that district. Throughout this southerly belt, the granite, gneiss and crystalline schists are used for walling material but their texture and colour vary locally. Approximately from the valley of the Scorff eastwards to the Loire, the weathered stone takes on a light to medium-brown hue which, coupled with the high proportion of thatched roofs in that district, gives the farms and hamlets a honey-coloured aspect. West of the Scorff, in southern Finistère, the granite is colder and greyer to the eye.

Along the northern edges of this southern belt of igneous rocks occur further igneous intrusions, mostly of riebeckite and muscovite granites, but also of granites and biotite granites. These extend northwards to mingle with the strongly east–west orientated Devonian and Silurian sandstones and schists of the Montagnes Noires, the ridges of which overlook the lowlands of the Châteaulin basin to the north.

The northern part of the peninsula is less regular, but the Hercynian trend is nevertheless unmistakable. Whereas in the south the igneous belts follow closely one upon the other, in the north there are often wide areas of Pre-Cambrian (Brioverian) schists between the igneous outcrops. Large intrusions of granites and biotite granites occur in western Léon, north of Brest, around Plouescat, north of Belle-Isle-en-Terre, around Quintin, Moncontour and near Dol-de-Bretagne. Large granite intrusions appear again near Fougères. All provide excellent building stone. Other igneous intrusions in the north are the extensive amphibolites around the Baie de Saint-Brieuc and western Côtes-du-Nord, and a small patch in north-west Léon. There is a belt of migmatite along the north-west fringe of Léon and a large intrusion of gabbro occurs just north of Morlaix. Muscovite and biotite granite also occur in some quantity near Guingamp, Belle-Isle-en-Terre and around Dinan and Saint-Malo. Intermixed with these granitic intrusions are large areas of mica-schist and stretches of Pre-Cambrian (Brioverian) schists. Extending from Belle-Isle-en-Terre eastwards to the Baie du Mont-Saint-Michel is an area in which north–south aligned igneous dykes of diabase, dolerite and porphyrite have been intruded.

The igneous complexes of the north and south are separated by the central depressions of Rennes and

Châteaulin. That of Châteaulin is a true basin sharply upturned along the northern front of the Montagnes Noires to the south, and the southern edge of the Monts d'Arrée to the north. Apart from the granitic inlier of Huelgoat, the Montagnes Noires and the Monts d'Arrée, composed for the most part of Devonian sandstones and schists, may be considered along with the Châteaulin basin, floored in its central part by the Carboniferous rocks. Silurian and Ordovician sandstone and schists form the backbone of the Montagnes Noires and, along with the Devonian, the greater part of the Crozon peninsula to the west. From Châteaulin in the west to Rostrenen in the east, the basin is floored by Dinantian schists around the margins of which are long, narrow and discontinuous igneous intrusions. To the south, Devonian schists and quartzites rise along the frontal edges of the Montagnes Noires. To the north, the Ordovician *grès armoricain,* extensive on, and around, the Monts d'Arrée, extends in tongues westwards, into and around the Rade de Brest. A large variety of building stone is thus available in these central western areas, from the finest of slates and schists for walling and roofing, in the Montagnes Noires, to coarse blocks of Ordovician *grès armoricain,* the common Breton sandstone.

In the east, the basin is closed by the granite masses of Quintin, Moncontour and that between Rostrenen, Plouay and Pontivy. East of Pontivy, the solid geology is Pre-Cambrian with occasional granite intrusions, except for the patches of Pliocene deposits and the large deposits of Ordovician and Cambrian material between Rennes and Ancenis. In the dissected country to the west of the Rennes Basin, especially around Loudéac and Pontivy, the bedrock is never far below the surface, but for ten or twenty kilometres around Rennes, it lies beneath a thick covering of later deposits. Stone is not abundant here and *torchis* has been widely used as a walling material. In certain areas, notably around the margins of the basin, a mixture of *torchis* and stone is used with stone footings rising to a height sometimes of a metre or more before giving way to *torchis* above. Where there is sufficient stone the whole of a building may be fronted with it. The other area notable for *torchis* is the Grande Brière. Here, where stone outcrops on the islands or around the margins it is used, but otherwise walling is of *torchis.* The transition here from stone availability to non-availability is sharply reflected in the houses and shows that building material in the main was not carried more than a few hundred metres, and often much less, for the homes of the majority of the population. Only the upper social classes could afford to bring stone from further afield and then it was usually for dressings only, the walling being of whatever material was commonly available. Even the multi-cell gentry houses are built largely of *torchis* in the region around Rennes. Close to the Loire, the *tuffeau* of Anjou, an almost white soft Cretaceous limestone, was occasionally used for dressings. There was considerable trade in this material, but, to carry it so far, even for use at the upper levels of rural society, is remarkable when the greater part of the population was content to look for building stone little further than its own backyard.

Walling was thus usually the material of the immediate neighbourhood, but for dressings it was occasionally necessary to look further afield. In some areas, lithological change conveniently provides two contrasting materials, as near Antrain, where schist and granite occur in close juxtaposition so that dressings of the highest quality are available for use with a common walling material.

Lime mortar was virtually unknown in the countryside until the twentieth century, and stone was bonded in a simple clay mortar made in exactly the same way as the *torchis*. Other building materials are timber for beams, roof structure, door and window frames, doors and shutters, very important before the days of glass, and the roof covering. The method of utilization of these will be discussed in the next chapter and it is sufficient here to note the type of material and its provenance. Timber is widely available except in the western peninsulas and on certain islands, and most farms had some fields enclosed by high banks bearing trees (see Chapter 3). In addition, wood was available on the waste ground and in the greater forests. Timber of sufficient scantling must often have been expensive and difficult to come by, for beams are often of poor quality. Generally, ceiling beams of 0.20–0.25 metres square and about 6.00 metres long are required and these usually, but not always, serve also as tie-beams for the roof trusses. Oak was the most favoured wood but chestnut is often found. The principal rafters also need to be cut from timber of similar dimensions and it is thus not surprising that many, if not most, roof timbers bear evidence of second-hand use: sound timber was used again when a new building replaced an old one. Common rafters and purlins are sometimes of sawn timber, but often they are simple rough poles from one of the many chestnut coppices which abound in Brittany, tied together with straw rope.

Roof covering south of the Loire is universally of 'Roman' tiles. North of that river, the traditional material is thatch. Reed thatch is still commonly used where it is available, as in the Grande Brière, the valley of the Vilaine and around Châteaulin, where reeds are taken from the flood-plain of the Aulne, and one or two other small areas. Over the greater part of the country, however, thatch was of rye straw, the hardest and most durable of straws, and since rye was a staple item of food, there was little difficulty in obtaining the straw, although as it was cut before fully ripe, the seed crop was inevitably lost. Red-tile covering is not unknown, especially along the north coast, and tiles here seem to have originated at Bridgwater in Somerset, from which port bricks and tiles were widely exported during the eighteenth and nineteenth centuries. French tiles of twentieth-century date are occasionally to be found, widely distributed. From about the middle of the nineteenth century, thatch gradually came to be replaced by slate, not least as a result of pressure from insurance companies, and slate roofing gained ground rapidly. It had probably been used for hundreds of years on buildings of the wealthy, but during the period 1850–1914 the countryside saw a change from a state in which the vast majority of peasant buildings were thatched, to one in which, except for a few areas such as south Morbihan, the greater number were roofed in slate. Many small local quarries formerly existed, notably in the interior on the schists and slates, and a ready supply was obviously an important factor in the early diffusion of the material. The absence of slate along the granitic lowlands south of the Landes de Lanvaux is certainly a factor in the continued presence there of large numbers of thatched houses. With the coming of the railway, however, in the later-nineteenth and early-twentieth century, the superior slate of Anjou became readily available and much of the present slate roofing of Brittany comes from Angers. Cleft oak shingles may have been commonly used before slate. A ruined house at La Villette, Villamée, Ille-et-Vilaine, is entirely roofed with it, an outbuilding at Le Beuchet, Saint-M'Hervé, has its gable covered with oak shingles, and a restored turret and chapel in the castle of Châteaubriant is roofed with the material, suggesting that it is a traditional material for major medieval buildings.

FIVE

CONSTRUCTION — I

The construction of the house was traditionally accompanied by superstitious and religious practices. Careful preparations were made to choose a site that would not subsequently prove to be unlucky. In parts of Morbihan, two chickens were buried in their plumage in the midst of the proposed building area and if, after several days, they were found still to be intact, this was considered to be a sign that the spirits had refused the offering, thereby showing their displeasure in the choice of site. The blood of a cock was sprinkled on the foundations of a house, in Finistère, before the walls were constructed. During the construction of a house, in Morbihan, *c.* 1850, a cock was killed and the living area of the house sprinkled with its blood, the corpse then being thrown outside. It was never eaten, for that was believed to bring bad luck, nor was it buried, but left to decay in the open yard. A similar usage is reported near Quimper, performed to assure the solidarity of the house and the luck of the occupants.

In Basse-Bretagne, masons believed that if the foundation were not so sprinkled with blood, the first person to enter the house would die within the year, for when the sill was put in place, (Br.) *Ankou*, the personification of death, would come and seat himself there in wait for the first occupant. Only the sacrifice of an animal, or the blood of a cock, would appease him. An egg would also suffice, providing it had been taken from a brood.[145] This is perhaps the origin of burying an egg under the hearthstone of a new-built house.[146] To enter a new-built house for the first time was to court disaster unless preceded by a domestic animal, a dog, hen or a cat.[147]

The laying of the first stone was an occasion for ceremony. In Morbihan, coins were laid beneath it and a prayer offered for the protection of the house. Sometimes a stone bearing an engraved cross was placed in the wall, and the date of construction marked on a lintel or other place.[148] The first peg to be placed in the roof timbers was driven home by the owner, who, when the roofing was complete, provided a celebration meal.

Building tradesmen, masons and carpenters, usually received nourishment in part-payment of their work. The thatcher, or coverer, was also fed during the course of his work. In Morbihan, if the food was good, he planted seeds of flowers in the clay capping of the ridge. If it had been poor, then weeds were sown instead. Similar practices are described in association with construction in Haute-Bretagne.[149] At Pont-Croix in 1884, the laying of the first stone was the occasion for a party of the family and neighbours. When the construction was finished, a *bouquet* was placed on the ridge, the house blessed by the priest and a big meal given to the family and friends.[150]

The blessings of a house by the priest was also universal, and linked with this is the custom of placing a cross on the wall of the house. This is occasionally cut into the lintel or wall as at Kervaly (Fig. 183) or, as is still commonly the case in Loire-Atlantique, painted in white on the wall, usually alongside the doorway. The latter practice is widespread in the east,[151] Bachelot de la Pylaie observed it in Finistère,[152] and Pelras in Cap-Sizun.[153] It was not confined to Brittany, though, and sometimes extends to other Christian symbols such as the sacred monogram or the elements of the Mass.[154] A chalice bearing the letters IHS is common. Blessing by the priest often took the form of the sprinkling of the interior of the house with holy water. The soil so dampened was then dug up and placed in a small bag, to be kept as a talisman against illness. The hole so formed grew larger with time and sweeping, and with the practice of throwing waste into the centre of the room.[155]

It seems probable that the earliest buildings were simple tent-like structures resting on the ground, like Bouleguy 2 (Chapter 8, Fig. 160). Walls were introduced to provide greater headroom, maximizing the utilization of the living space. They were a protective curtain defining the house and in certain forms of construction served also as a support for the roof timbers. The earliest walls were low, rising perhaps to a little more than a metre or so, except near the doorway, and never to more than the height of a man. A pigsty at Kerguestoc (Fig. 112) provides one example of a circular building with such walls whilst the excavated houses at Kerlano and Pen-er-Malo (Figs. 70 and 71) show the remains of low walls in medieval oval buildings (Chapter 8). Low walling has survived into the twentieth century as at Bouleguy 3 (Fig. 161). Several houses were recorded in the same *commune*, Plumelin.[156] Of these, two long-houses at Talforest have walls rising only to *c.* 1.60 metres, one of which, a platform-house, cut into the natural slope of the ground, has a rear wall rising only 1.00 metres to the eaves on the outside. At Kerspec in the same *commune*, a single-cell house is cut back into the ground so that the rear and end walls are formed entirely by an earthen bank.[157] Only the front elevation is wholly of built walling. It is not clear from the drawings whether the walls formed against the earth banks have an interior stone revetment, but this seems probable. The free-standing walls, 0.65 to 0.90 metres thick at the base, tapering to *c.* 0.60 metres, are formed of a course matrix of stone rubble and clay as at Pon Digeu in the same *commune* (Fig. 166). Such walling, though essentially of stone, is rather crude, and courses are badly formed. At Pon Digeu, the door and window openings have insufficient mechanical strength and require a wooden frame, but there is no evidence of such framing in the houses referred to above. It is, however, common in *torchis* houses (see below). Corners are often imperfectly squared, and round corners survive in some regions (see Chapter 8).

Two other houses from the same area of Morbihan illustrate the survival of this 'primitive' walling into the twentieth century. At Botcol, a small long-house has some of the characteristics of the houses in Plumelin, the rubble walling is poorly coursed, has a high clay content, and contains timber posts to give it added strength (Fig. 72). In a similar house nearby the walls barely rise to the level of the doorway lintel (Fig. 167).[158] Other forms of primitive walling survive, including the use of timber, and these will be considered below.

Walling of earth and clay, known in England as 'cob', is commonly referred to in north-west France as *terre*, *pisé* or *torchis*. An essential distinction is between *torchis* and *pisé*, the latter term being frequently confined to a clay mixture without vegetable content. The raw material is the partly weathered clay found below the topsoil, at a variable depth, but *c.* 0.60 metres. If the clay does not contain a proportion of fine gravel or grit, this must be added. *Torchis* is prepared in the hole from which the clay is dug and is worked for a length of time, varying with the district, which is presumably a function of the texture of the clay. As little as an hour or so may be sufficient, more usually several hours are necessary, and

it may be left some days. The clay must be thoroughly soaked in water, and can be worked with a spade, but puddling by trampling is better, as in Normandy where the masons tread it barefoot.[159] In the Grande Brière, the *torchis* was mixed until the 1940s by men who trod it barefoot, linking arms as they did so, dancing and singing. When well-mixed, straw cut to a length of 0.15 to 0.20 metres was added and the dance repeated. The mixing completed, it was lifted with a fork and placed on the stone footings to a height of 0.60 to 0.80 metres, and left to dry for two or three days before the process began again for the next 'lift'. When complete, the walls were pared with the edge of a fork.[160] In Ille-et-Vilaine, the preparation seems to have been similar, chopped straw, hay or heath added, and sometimes also *balle d'avoine*, *des cosses de fève*, or *de la filasse*. The resulting mixture is known as *menu massé* in the *pays de Combourg*, *baouche* or *bauge* at Plouasne and Paimpont, *mardra* at Plélan-le-Petit and *madraille* at Quintenic.[161] In some

Fig. 43. Marland, Saint-André-les-Eaux, Loire-Atlantique. A wall of *torchis*, showing the texture.

Fig. 44.   Les Hauts Talus, Montgermont, Ille-et-Vilaine. The *pisé* rendering has largely fallen away exposing the *torchis* walls.

areas, heath plants or other vegetable matter are used in place of straw. Gravel helps to stabilize the material, straw to bind, and cow-dung is frequently added further to assist adhesion. If the whole wall is to be constructed of *torchis*, it is applied in 'lifts' or layers of from 0.60 to 0.80 metres at a time. Wall thickness, 0.65 metres on average, varies from *c.* 0.55 to *c.* 0.80 metres (Figs. 168, 174 and 191). Foundations are laid either directly on the ground, or in a shallow trench never more than 0.50 metres deep. For most buildings, footings of stone are laid first, rising to 0.20 or 0.30 metres, but in poorer dwellings, earth walls rest directly on the ground. Two principal techniques are used. A relatively liquid mixture may be run into the mould formed by pegged wooden shutters and left to dry before the shutters are removed and the process repeated at a higher level. Alternatively, the mixture may be allowed partly to dry before building starts. The stiff mixture is then lifted by fork and placed along the line of walls to the required height. These are then trimmed along their inner and outer faces with the blade of a spade. Drying time for each 'lift' appears to vary with the district. One week has been quoted at Paimpont, whilst a

month seems more common. Buffet gives a six-month wait between each lift in the Coglais,[162] but generally a whole house could be constructed in this time. The drying period no doubt varied according to regional practice as well as to local variations in the material. The texture of the resulting wall can be seen at Marland (Fig. 43). Such a wall will set very hard, and provided that it is protected from the rain may last hundreds of years, but it disintegrates rapidly if the rain is allowed to penetrate. Finished walls were consequently rendered in *pisé* for protection, but this rendering has mostly fallen away from surviving houses and has not been replaced, so that wall faces show considerable signs of weathering (Fig. 44). At Les Hauts Talus traces of the rendering can be seen on the façade. Colour varies, according to district, from an almost whitish grey to a deep ochre. A variation on the above methods is to mix the clay without vegetable matter. The walls are then built with blocks of earth, laying straw, heath or gorse between each course, and the use of small blocks of *torchis* in the form of unbaked bricks is also recorded.[163] Narrow horizontal courses of *torchis,* separated by layers of straw, were recorded at

Koh-Coët, Guénin[164] and a recently abandoned *loge* at Koh-Coët also has walls of this type (Fig. 168). In the Marais de Dol these are laid in a herring-bone pattern, but horizontally laid courses are reported near Loudéac.[165] The extraction of the clay in quantities necessary to build a house often leaves a deep hole which subsequently fills with water and serves as a farm pond (Fig. 44).

Torchis and *pisé* are also used in the construction of timber-frame walls, as a roof covering and for the flooring of lofts. The *terre battue* floors are essentially of the same material as *pisé*. The latter is a 'mortar' universally used in the building of stone walls before the advent of lime mortar. Almost without exception, the traditional stone walls were laid with it before *c.* 1920 (Fig. 45). Before the nineteenth century, rubble stone walls were rendered with *pisé*, and traces of this remain on many buildings as at Koh-Coët (Fig. 167). It is difficult to assess the former distribution of houses with walls of *torchis*. Today they are confined to Haute-Bretagne within which the Rennes basin is the best-known region, the zone of *torchis* extending in an ellipse from a point east of Rennes, westwards to Loudéac (Fig. 46). Recent fieldwork suggests, however, that houses and farm buildings of *torchis* were once much more widespread and accord closely with the occurrence of superficial deposits of *loess*, or *limon*. Detailed mapping is currently in progress and has produced examples, in some numbers, between Saint-Brieuc and Lamballe. Clay farm buildings occur also between Saint-Brieuc, Guingamp and Paimpol and widely in the north and east of Ille-et-Vilaine. In places their distribution reaches the north coast and extends eastwards almost as far as Fougères and Vitré. The greatest concentration of *torchis* houses lies between Rennes and Merdrignac, but towards the edges of the zone is a transitional area in which houses wholly of *torchis* are intermingled with those wholly of stone. Stone 'footings' frequently rise to a height of *c.* 1.00 metre, with *torchis* above (Fig. 190). Sometimes stone is carried to first-floor level in the front elevation, but not at the rear and sides, and occasionally the whole façade may be of stone. It is on the edges of the region that the proportion of stone in the walls is noticeably higher. Availability of stone and the wealth and social aspirations of the owner were important factors. In some areas, as around Paimpont, stone may be used in greater or lesser quantities in the houses, but byres and outbuildings frequently display quantities of *torchis*, perhaps with stone used around door and loft openings, but not the window opening (Fig. 91). Another area in which clay buildings survive in some numbers is the Grande Brière where they are found alongside stone buildings. In outlying areas concentrations of *torchis*, as from

Fig. 45. Kerdren, La Harmoye, Côtes-du-Nord. Traditional walling of stone rubble bonded with a mortar of *pisé*.

Lamballe towards Val-Saint-André, and in the Marais de Dol and south of Saint-Broladre, have now been shown by fieldwork to be part of the larger distribution. Nevertheless, the density of surviving examples varies considerably and the mixture of stone and *torchis* houses on the fringes suggests that the 'clay' areas were formerly more extensive and that their boundaries have receded with time. The fact that *torchis* is used for farm buildings in areas where stone is universal for houses confirms this, the superior material being reserved for houses, as does the fact that surviving examples of poor housing contain clay, when better quality housing is of stone. Buffet records the survival in the *arrondissements* of Fougères and Vitré of *subites*, essentially timber-frame structures, but dependent upon large quantities of *torchis*.[166] At Run Moan, Loc-Envel, *torchis* is used as an infilling for a post-and-plank house.[167] Two English travellers suggest that clay building was formerly more extensive during the

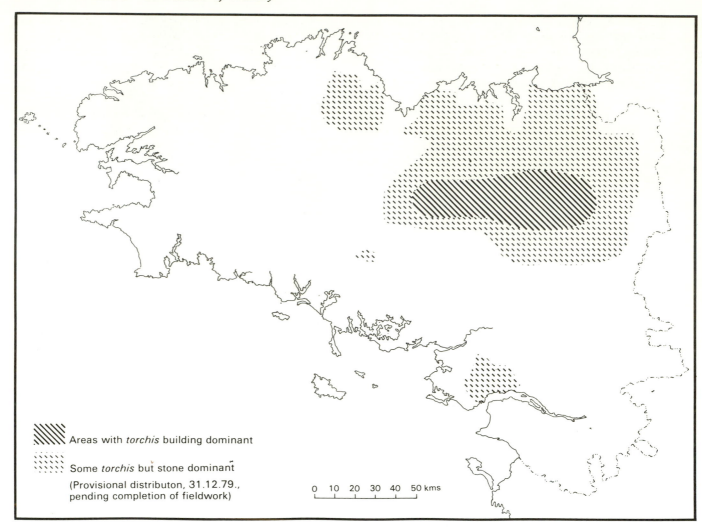

Fig. 46.   Distribution of building in 'cob' or *torchis*.

In the legend of the map:

Areas with *torchis* building dominant

Some *torchis* but stone dominant
(Provisional distributon, 31.12.79.,
pending completion of fieldwork)

0   10   20   30   40   50 kms

nineteenth century. Stothard observes that the 'Bretons dwell in huts, generally built of mud; men, pigs, and children live all together without distinction, in these cabins of accumulated filth and misery. . . .' and that 'The Breton houses (excepting in the towns) are generally built of mud, without order or convenience'.[168] Later in the century, Blackburn, commenting on Stothard's description, added that the 'mud houses are before us, and the description holds good to-day'.[169] It is possible, however, that the traveller mistook stone houses rendered with *pisé*, formerly a common practice, for houses whose walls were wholly of earth. It seems that clay building, once more extensive, survived at the lower levels of society well into the nineteenth century, and has now receded to a few areas where it has found expression in a relatively permanent form (Fig. 46).

Stone walls, whether of rubble, dressed stone or a mixture of the two, are traditionally erected with a 'mortar' of *pisé*. Inner and outer faces are separated by a rubble-and-*pisé* infill, the smaller stones being reserved for this core. The wall depends for its strength on the effectiveness of the *pisé* bond as well as on the laying of the stone, for the technique of placing through-stones seems little used, and walling is consequently often weak (Fig. 45). It is evident that in a large number of houses the outer face of a wall has fallen away and has had to be re-built, for with such a high clay content a wall quickly 'runs' if rainwater gets into it. By far the largest proportion of Breton buildings have walls entirely of rubble but cut stone is frequently used for door and window dressings, and for quoins. This dressed stone may be purchased several kilometres away at one of the many small quarries. In Côtes-du-Nord, for example, quarries at Perros-Guirec, Gouedic and Regrit supplied granite, Pléhérel and Erquy *grès rose*, Île Grande *granit bleu* and Pyric granulite, all of good quality for cutting. Limestone of excellent quality, seen in the houses around Bécherel, came from Le Quiou in the valley of the Rance, and a limestone was also available at Cartravers in La Harmoye. In Loire-Atlantique, around Guérande, building is often of very high quality. Granite rubble for much of the walling comes from Guérande, and dressings from granite quarries at Clis and Queniquen. The quality of much of the work in this area is attributed to the former activity and example of the monks of Landévennec. Only in a few limited areas was stone of good quality sufficiently abundant for walls wholly of ashlar to be built.

A wide variety of rubble walling is evident in the twenty-one sample areas (Fig. 79). Much of it is random uncoursed or poorly coursed, especially when the rubble is of small granite blocks. The *granit rose* at Castel and Plougasnou (Figs. 80 and 82) provides a good example. Roughly coursed rubble is also evident at Locmaria, Carnoët, Dinéault, Saint-M'Hervé and Frossay (Figs. 81, 83, 88, 92 and 99). Well-laid courses are seen at Plévenon, Pont-Scorff, Grand-Champ, Béganne, Joué-sur-Erdre and Saint-Hilaire-de-Clisson (Figs. 85, 94, 95, 96, 97, 100). Good examples of fine coursing in granite rubble may be seen near Guérande, the courses being carried round the corners with roughly squared quoins of the same material (Fig. 98). Polychrome effects are sometimes possible as near Paimpont where purple and light-brown stone combine to give a striking appearance further enhanced by the presence of areas of *torchis* (Fig. 91). Some areas, usually those with sandstone or schist, display remarkably fine coursing as at La Harmoye, Sougéal and Taupont (Figs. 84, 86 and 90). In Sougéal, the use of 'staggered' quoins is remarkable and has not been observed elsewhere. At La Harmoye, a strong contrast is obtained by the juxtaposition of a dark-coloured schist and fine light-grey granite dressings, ashlar for door and window dressings, roughly squared blocks for the quoins. Wood is used for lintels and larger rubble blocks to frame the openings at Taupont. Large granite blocks contrast sharply with the rubble walls at Plévin, where the windows are probably later insertions (Fig. 89). Dressed stone at Moëlan-sur-Mer is used only for the lintels, the jambs being of rubble like the remainder of the walling (Fig. 93). One of the most striking areas for walling is Sougéal where the Silurian schist lies close to the granite outcrop. The latter, light in colour, is used for dressings, providing a strong contrast to the dark brown schist.

Several areas stand out in contrast because of the large amount of ashlar walling: the regions around Saint-Malo, Fougères, and the area of fine limestone houses north of Bécherel and the grey granite of Cap-Sizun. Ashlar

façades are found in other areas too, used for the houses of the wealthy, but not in the same numbers. The cost of transport, as well as that of the stone itself, was an important factor in the diffusion of dressed stone. In Cap-Sizun, chimney-stacks, cornices, quoins, and door and window dressings are almost universally of dressed stone, but not always the façades. Ashlar is often used for the front elevation, but nearly always gives way to rubble at the rear end in the gables. When rubble is used for the front elevation, it is frequently rendered (Fig. 87).

Walling formed entirely of orthostats, large flat vertical slabs of stone with their lower ends embedded in the ground, has been recorded in six locations, but only in south Finistère, in the region between Concarneau and Pont-Aven, do large numbers of buildings incorporating this type of walling survive. Here, an intrusion of calco-alkaline biotite-granite is sufficiently fissile to yield large slabs. A rapid extensive survey produced forty farms and hamlets containing at least one orthostat-walled building (Fig. 47), all but two examples confined to the granite outcrop, and intensive survey would undoubtedly lead to further discoveries. Several transects were made across the northern boundary of the granite and these confirmed that the orthostats are confined to that outcrop. The arcuate distribution is partly to be explained by the need for additional fieldwork, and partly by the heavily wooded nature of the country and the existence of a large estate in the northern part of the area where building density is low. Numbers and distribution are sufficient to demonstrate a well-established tradition in this form of construction.

Specific examples are illustrated by Figs. 48, 49 and 50. The orthostats are normally cut to a length of c. 2.50 metres and stand with the lower 0.50 metres embedded in the ground, leaving a full 2.00 metres of free-standing wall. In the more regular examples, the orthostats are c. 0.40 metres wide and 0.25 to 0.30 metres thick. Fifteen orthostats are needed for the lateral wall at Tréberouan 1, and even for a house of modest length like Saint-Philibert 1, the total in the rear wall is twenty-six. In many houses, front, rear and gable walls are built with orthostats, only the chimney gable being of coursed walling, necessary in order to accommodate the heavy granite chimney-piece and flue, which could never be supported on the thin short orthostats. Tréubert 1 and Saint-Philibert 1 have front and rear walls of orthostats with gables of coursed stone. At Tréberouan 1, the front wall and the lower gable are of orthostats, the rear wall and the upper gable being of coursed rubble.

The limited height of the orthostats has resulted in the preservation of the hipped roof, elsewhere but rarely found now, and the houses are all of one storey as it is

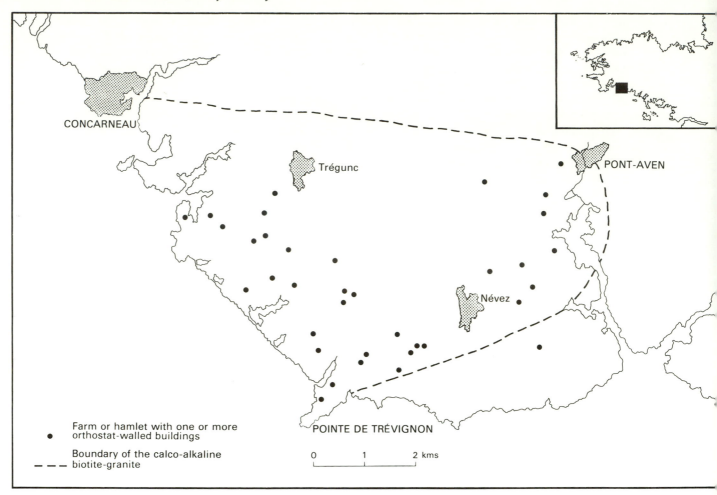

Fig. 47. Orthostat-walled buildings in south Finistère

technically impossible to build on top of such thin and relatively unstable walling. Tie-beams, with exposed ends, generally rest on a wall-plate laid along the top of the orthostat wall, spaces between the beams being filled either with carefully cut stone, or with rubble (Fig. 48). Figs 48, 49 and 50 show finely-cut orthostats with flat surfaces and straight edges so that they fit closely, any gaps being filled with *pisé*. Interior surfaces bear no trace of plaster, and finish is usually confined to painting with whitewash. Some houses, however, are constructed with more irregularly cut stones, and here a greater infill of *pisé* is necessary. A few buildings have walls of orthostats separated by short stretches of coursed walling. Both the latter technique, and that of continuous orthostat walling, are of high antiquity and examples of both may be found in many of the Megalithic chambered tombs of Brittany.[170] Obviously, where stone with straight sides cannot be obtained, there is a need for rubble infill, and this form of walling is probably typologically earlier, although it does not follow that examples are themselves earlier in date

than the technically superior examples illustrated. Chronology in this area is difficult to establish, for the few dated houses belong to the nineteenth century. Saint-Philibert 1 is of 1857. Many of the most carefully cut orthostats have drill marks showing that dynamite was used in quarrying. The area is also characterized by the extensive use of smaller orthostats as field boundaries, some of which are undoubtedly of great antiquity, and it is these that probably provide the continuous link with the past. A small walled enclosure close to a bake-oven at Kermeun illustrates this technique (Fig. 133). Some of the surviving orthostat houses may be of seventeenth- or eighteenth-century date, for Cambry in the 1790s was able to write of the '*grandes pierres de taille plates, longues de sept à huit pieds, comme à Trégunc*',[171] but it would seem that there was a renaissance of this type of construction in the nineteenth century following the acquisition of a technically more advanced quarrying skill and the use of explosives.

All the houses observed are either single-cell

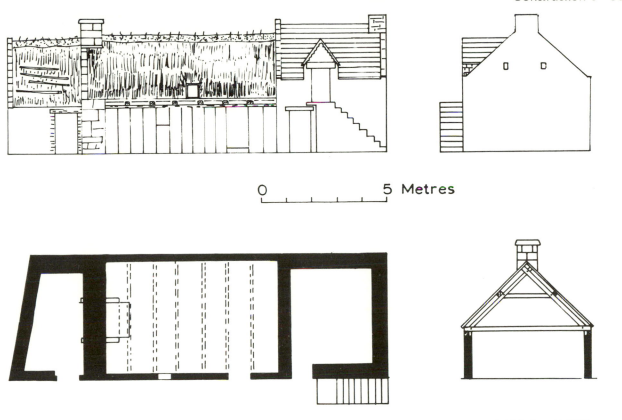

0   5 Metres

G.I.M.-J.   5. 7. 71.

Fig. 48.   Tréubert 1, 2, Trégunc, Finistère

structures, pure long-houses, single-cell houses whose lower ends may once have served as byres, or long-house first derivatives, with a separate door into the byre. An excellent example of the latter type, and also a good example of the regional style, is Goëlan-Trégonal, Trégunc (Fig. 51). Here the grey granite orthostats, used for three walls, have their *pisé* infill picked out in white paint. At the lower end the reed-thatched roof is hipped, whilst at the upper end the plain dressed-granite chimney rises from the roughly-dressed granite gable wall. Doorways provide entry to the hall, lighted by a single window, and to the byre, with its own smaller window for ventilation. A large number of farm buildings in this area, especially byres and stables, are also built of orthostats.

Orthostat walling has been recorded in four other widely separated areas. In two examples, orthostats of slate are set in a wooden frame. At Les Portes 5 and 6 in La Harmoye, slabs of slate rest on a heavy wooden sill and form a dividing wall between the two houses. At Kergiquel, Neuillac, Morbihan, large slabs of schist are used as infill in a timber-frame farm building. In two other locations, orthostats of schist are used to form the external walling of some numbers of houses. At Laniscat,

Côtes-du-Nord, and in a belt towards Rostrenan, orthostat-walled houses are rigidly confined to a long narrow outcrop of schist. Schist orthostats are also present in houses near Nozay, Loire-Atlantique. A whole straggling series of houses, squatters' cabins built on the roadside waste, with orthostat walls, was recorded at Pont-Rot, Plounévez-Quintin.[172] Measured drawings were made of only three houses, but all have walls of schist, embedded in the ground like those in the Névez–Trégunc area. The orthostats were wider and shorter than in Finistère, varying from 0.60 to 0.80 metres wide with a height from ground to eaves of 1.70 metres, so that the houses stand lower than those in south Finistère. All four walls are of orthostat construction and the fully hipped roof structure rests on heavy wall-plates. A light chimney-hood, of wooden planking nailed to a frame, stands over the hearth placed against the end wall. These houses have now all been demolished. The use of orthostat walling is thus attested in six widely separated parts of Brittany and it is possible that it represents the survival of a technique whose origin lies in the Megalithic period.

Breton towns, from Quimper and Saint-Renan in the

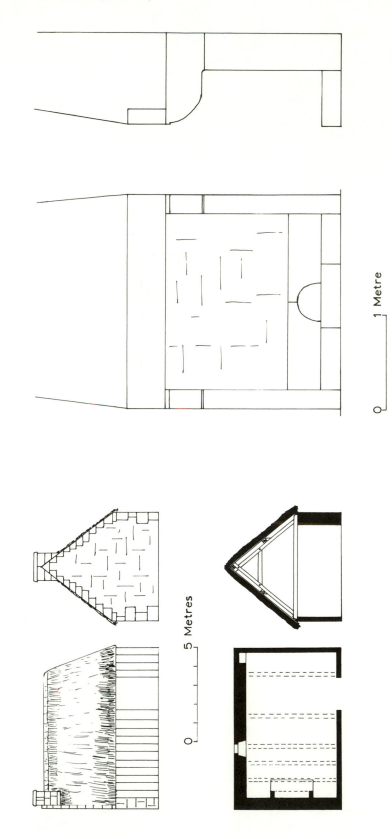

G.I. M.-J.   **5 . 7 . 71.**

1 Metre

5 Metres

Fig. 49.   Tréberouan 1, Trégunc, Finistère

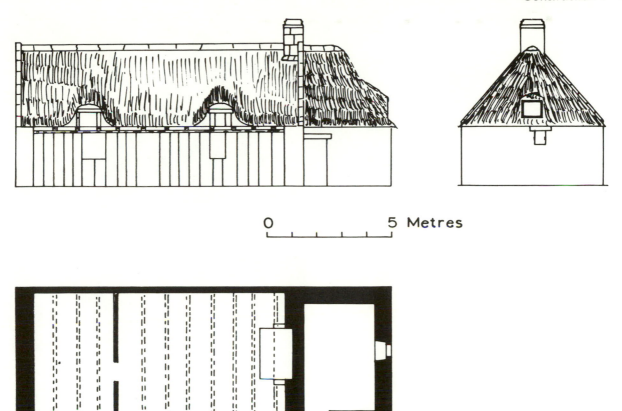

G.I.M.-J. 15.9.70.

Fig. 50.   Saint-Philibert 1, Trégunc, Finistère

west to Vitré, Fougères and Châteaubriant in the east, display a wealth of building that demonstrates a strong urban tradition of wall construction wholly or in part of timber-frame. In contrast, evidence of timber-framing in the countryside is often either absent or meagre, and this apparent dichotomy between town and country raises the question of whether there was ever a tradition of timber-building in the countryside generally. It has been suggested above that a high proportion of rural housing may have been of *torchis* and this possibility is further considered in Chapter 8. Nevertheless, the surviving peasant houses over the greater part of the province are substantial stone-built structures and in south Finistère, at least, there seems to be a possibility of the continuity of building in stone from prehistoric times.

Against the considerable legacy of stone building, evidence for timber-frame construction is much less. The farm-building at Kergiquel, Neuillac, Morbihan, with orthostats set in a timber-frame, may not be of any great age. The framing is light and rests on a low stone plinth into which the posts are sunk, passing through an interrupted sill-beam. This feature, also observed in Normandy, suggests typologically early framing, only

one stage removed from an interrupted sill with earth-fast posts. Two other widely separated buildings provide fragmentary evidence. A house at Botcol (Fig. 72) contains three timber posts embedded in the stone and *pisé* wall, suggesting a lack of confidence in the strength of the wall such as might be expected with a new technique. The building, unlikely to be of any age, is probably no earlier than the mid-nineteenth century. A similar technique is seen in a farm building recorded at Le Pélo, Saint-Lyphard, Loire-Atlantique where timber posts are embedded in the corners of a *torchis* building, on the outside, to give added support to the end trusses.

Examples of the primitive use of timber were recorded by the E.A.R. In Finistère, buildings wholly or partly of timber-frame are recorded at Celerou, Scaër, where rough posts embedded in stone walls support a hipped roof-structure, and more remarkably, at Miné Tréouzal in the same *commune*, where the *penty* consists of a hipped roof structure resting on posts embedded in stone walls. The corner- and lateral-posts are exposed inside the building and only the posts in the middle of the gables are visible also from outside. At the same farm, the byre, built against the farmhouse, has timber posts embedded in the

Fig. 51.   Goëlan-Trégonal, Trégunc, Finistère
A long-house, first derivative, and a good example of the regional style. Grey-granite orthostats are used for three walls, their *pisé* infill picked out in white paint. The reed-thatched roof is hipped at one end.

walls in such a way that they are exposed on the inside of the building but not on the outside. In none of these examples are the posts earthfast, but the buildings are, nevertheless, extremely rudimentary.[173] A similar case occurs at Guiscriff where the builder appears to have had little faith in the stone walls and to have erected a series of posts within the lateral walls, visible inside the building, but not outside, with corner posts also on the inside and a post centrally placed in each of the gables.[174] An example of a very simple timber house is provided at Run Moan, Loc-Envel. The upper gable, containing the chimney-piece and flue, is of stone, but the other three walls of this single-storey structure are formed of earthfast posts spaced *c.* 1.00 metre apart and to which weather-boarding is nailed both inside and out. In the spaces formed between the posts and the weather-boarding, an infill of *torchis* has been placed, and on the rear, or western, wall a covering of broom is fastened to the boards as an additional protection against the weather.[175] These examples are all extraordinarily rudimentary and

must represent either evidence for timber-framing at its earliest stages of development or in its final stages of degeneration. It is remarkable that they should have survived into the mid-twentieth century. In contrast, examples of relatively advanced structures are to be seen in eastern Brittany.

At Saint-M'Hervé, Ille-et-Vilaine, there is some evidence of timber-frame farm buildings. An aisled barn at Le Mesnil, with an attached wheelhouse, has the aisle trusses embedded in stone walls which perform only a limited load-bearing function. Nearby, at L'Orrier, a rectilinear barn has an orthodox king-post roof-truss and stone walls, but the ends of the tie-beams are supported on posts embedded in the walls and not visible from the outside. Other examples exist in the district, as well as a large number of barns and cow-sheds whose roof structures are supported on free-standing timber posts as at Le Beuchet, Lanjuères and the several examples at La Boucherie. These free-standing buildings generally have timber posts resting on the ground, either directly, or on

Fig. 52.   Fresnay Normandie, Melesse, Ille-et-Vilaine
'A series of buildings to the north of Rennes combines stone walls with a jettied timber-frame front to the second storey, the "three-quarter" style, reminiscent of much urban architecture of the sixteenth and seventeenth centuries.'

stone pads, and are occasionally open but in some instances are walled with either vertically or horizontally laid timber cladding. The posts embedded in the walls may again indicate a lack of confidence in a new stone technique, leading to retention of the posts of the old timber tradition, or may be indicative of the replacement of an original timber wall with a stone curtain. Whilst the joints of the primitive buildings appear to be rudimentary, in eastern Brittany the framing is the product of skilled carpentry. Examples of this primitive construction can be found all over Brittany, and further examples will be described in Chapter 8. Numerous examples of field-shelters occur along the eastern Marches, particularly in eastern Ille-et-Vilaine, one, south of Vitré, observed with a row of central posts. Between Vitré and Avranches and between Vitré and Joué-sur-Erdre they are very common and have wattle and *pisé* infill. Indeed, there is much timber framing in farm buildings around Fougères and such structures may be seen from that area westwards as

far as Rennes. There are even small timber-framed houses near Fougères. In addition, timber-framed gables on buildings otherwise wholly of stone are occasionally to be found.

In the Rennes basin, particularly in the *torchis* area, large numbers of buildings, wholly or partly of timber-frame, survive. At Billé, a timber-frame gable has a full king-post truss with bracing and close-studding, and a framed outbuilding stands on a stone plinth. Le Mesnil in Melesse is a single-cell building of timber-frame, the posts rising from a sill placed on a stone plinth. The building is close-studded with bracing of herring-bone and a scissors pattern between the posts. A second example, at Melesse, is of a house with only the front wall of timber-frame, rising out of a continuous sill.[176] In this area infill is of either wattle and *pisé* or lath and *pisé*. These buildings are in complete contrast to the primitive structures outlined above, are properly framed and represent a fully developed tradition. Furthermore, unlike the farm building at Kergiquel, the posts are tenoned into a continuous sill and do not appear to have been lifted straight out of the ground, as do the timber-frame buildings with interrupted sills, resting on stone plinths. This latter category, represented in considerable numbers in Normandy, represents typologically a transition between buildings with earth-fast posts and those with continuous sills.

Many further examples have been observed. Some of the timber-framed buildings are entirely coated on the outer surface with *pisé* and from a distance may be mistaken for *torchis* structures. Close-studding is a universal characteristic, often with multiple bracing of herring-bone or scissors patterns. All the buildings observed are associated with either the full king-post, or the upper king-post, truss. A series of buildings to the north of Rennes combines stone walls with a jettied timber-frame front to the second storey, the 'three-quarter' style, reminiscent of much urban architecture of the sixteenth and seventeenth centuries. Fresnay Normandie in Melesse is a good example (Fig. 52), showing patterns of bracing. These buildings are substantial structures and obviously the homes of well-to-do farmers, and it is possible that this style was diffused from the towns, particularly from Rennes, by *bourgeois* buying land and seeking to invest in agriculture and become *petits seigneurs*. These 'three-quarter' houses apart, confined to an area close to Rennes, the timber-frame buildings of Ille-et-Vilaine have much in common with those of Normandy, where both continuous and interrupted sills have been observed, where the king-post truss is widespread, and where similar forms of bracing may be seen.

A recent examination of photographs in the *dossiers* prepared by the Commission d'Inventaire de Bretagne in connection with both its *pré-inventaires* and *inventaires*, shows that timber-frame construction exists widely in Ille-et-Vilaine at most levels of society including the highest. The Château de la Robinais in Bain-de-Bretagne has a large quantity of timber-frame in walls of coursed rubble and one of the finest timber-frame structures is La Grand'Cour in Betton; the Manoir des Grandes Cours de Coësmes of 1675 in Cesson-Sevigné is a timber-frame first-floor hall, and the fine gatehouse at the Manoir du Plessis-Beaucé, in La Chapelle-des-Fougeretz, with its superb full king-post roof, is also entirely of timber, once completely rendered in *pisé*. There are many more examples in the Rennes basin. In Morbihan, the Château of La Gaudinais, Ploërmel, has much timber-frame, with schist nogging, in the upper part of its walls. A number of timber-frame outbuildings are recorded in Pontivy.

Likewise in Côtes-du-Nord, the Manoir de Goas-Froment in Plouëzec has fine timber-frame corner turrets, there is a timber-frame gatehouse at La Tisonnais in Saint-Maden, and a timber outbuilding at Maritaine in Saint-Aaron. Even in Finistère, evidence for big-scale timber-frame construction is not wanting. The former convent of Notre-Dame-des-Anges at Landéda, on the extreme north-west coast, has a timber-frame galleried structure as well as a timber-frame gatehouse.[177]

There thus seems once to have been a widespread timber-frame tradition in Brittany. The fragmentary evidence of the primitive examples suggests that this tradition in the countryside remained technically low and the poor primitive framing appears to be a late survival of a very early tradition. More advanced timber-frame techniques were diffused into eastern Brittany in the Middle Ages, partly to be replaced, during and after the sixteenth century, by the advent of stone building, particularly stone houses, timber-frame continuing to be used for farm buildings. It may be that these styles in eastern Brittany represent a diffusion from metropolitan France, which would likewise have got into the Breton towns of the Middle Ages, and not directly related to the poor timber-frame structures in rural western Brittany. The improved carpentry techniques spread to the towns in the west and may not have been greatly diffused into the countryside, except in buildings of the upper social classes, but in view of what has been said of the low level of much of Breton housing, this is perhaps not surprising. It is significant that much of the surviving timber frame is in farm buildings, exactly what might be expected if surplus wealth had to be utilized to renew the house in stone, leaving the other buildings to be rebuilt later, as resources permitted.

During the survey, very few houses were observed with original flooring other than of *terre battue*. After World War I, the replacement of earth floors with concrete began on a small scale, and then mostly near the coast, but it was not until after 1945 that this change gathered pace. A survey of housing conditions in 1939 recorded *terre battue* as dominant in Côtes-du-Nord, tiles being too costly. It was universal in Finistère, as also in Morbihan for the hall, although where a second room existed this was sometimes paved. Little *terre battue* flooring was recorded in Loire-Atlantique except in the Grande Brière, although observation during the present investigation suggests that there was in fact a great deal of *terre battue* in Loire-Atlantique.[178] A high proportion of the older houses in south Morbihan still had earth floors in the 1970s. Only in a few areas has stone paving been observed, and that where schist or slate is near at hand, as at Châteaulin (Fig. 176), and Saint-Jean-Trolimon (Fig. 210). At Kerrio (Fig. 211) the kitchen was paved, but not the hall, although the latter was provided with a finer chimney-piece. Presumably, wear on the floor of the kitchen, where the domestics lived, was a factor and perhaps the earth floor of the hall was felt to be warmer and more comfortable for the *seigneur*. Certainly, until recently, the greater part of the peasantry knew of nothing but the beaten-earth floor. This is confirmed in the writings of earlier travellers. Cambry wrote of the floor that *'jamais il n'est carrelé, ni boisé, ni pavé, la terre inégale en sert'*, but although it could be very uneven, shallow holes developing with time, these were unlikely ever to be deep enough for the unwary to fall into them and break a leg, as he suggests.[179] In Bas-Léon, at the end of the nineteenth century, there was no floor covering save *'un pisé argileux carroyé et battu sur place'*.[180] Stothard[181] observed 'no flooring but the substantial earth. When it rains, the kennel from the street runs over through the door, and makes a soft mud carpeting', and Blackburn saw 'the old farm houses . . . and mud floors'.[182]

In the vast majority of rural houses of Haute-Bretagne during the nineteenth century the *place*, i.e. the ground floor, was formed of earth. To prepare it, stones were carefully removed, and it was then dampened and perhaps mixed with a little lime or some *balle d'avoine*. This was necessary, for it had to take not only the wear and tear of everyday life, but also the rainwater that came in by the door and the *eaux ménagères* commonly thrown into the centre of the room. The 'beating' to form the *terre battue* resulted from holding *fouleries de place*. Friends and neighbours were invited to the new house to dance *'au son du violon'* during which the host *'fait circuler des pots de cidre, et chacun danse de son mieux pour niveler et durcir le sol'*. Notwithstanding attempts by the clergy to suppress dancing, this remained throughout the length and breadth of Brittany the means by which a new floor was made.[183] There is oral evidence from Saint-Rivoal that the practice continued well within living memory in the Monts d'Arrée and it was also the method used to harden the outside threshing floor following the communal labour of laying the clay.[184] There is no doubt that the unevenness was a source of inconvenience. Hélias describes how as a child he fell often enough *'à cause de ces maduits trous justement'*. The advantage of such a surface was that it was *'facile à entretenir, comme elle est commode à vivre! Nul besoin de nettoyer les sabots avant d'entrer. La boue que nous apportons sous nos semelles ne salit rien du tout. Ou elle s'amalgame au reste ou elle est balayée dehors, une fois sèche, à l'aide*

d'une branche de genêt. On jette sur le sol, sans aucune gêne, les os et les débris pour le chien . . .'. Known in the *pays bigouden* as *l'argile à crapaud*, the *terre battue* was laid in the manner described and levelled and hardened under the dancing sabots of the owner, his family and friends.[185]

In the Côtes-du-Nord, except along the littoral, the majority of houses had floors of *terre battue* as late as 1950, which were widely believed to be warmer and more comfortable than concrete. Repairs were carried out each year, and they were renewed, at least partially, every few years — occasions for more dancing. When houses were more than usually prone to damp, however, *'le sol en terre battue forme au milieu, auprès des lits, des cavités remplies d'eau, au point qu'on en prend dans ses sabots'*.[186] Dampness is a recurring complaint of the Comités d'Hygiène, as is the fact that floor-levels were lower than the ground outside, allowing rainwater to seep in, but in view of the compacting effect of the making of the floor, this is hardly to be wondered at.

Buffet describes the *fouleries de place* as one of the *'fêtes les plus joyeuses que se rattachaient à la construction de la maison'*. They took place every five or six years in Haute-Bretagne, as the floor needed renewing. The old floor was removed with a pick and the *place* or *piace* renewed with clay well sieved of stones and mixed with *gâpas,* hayseeds, dried grass, chopped straw and *balle d'avoine* before the young people danced on it.[187]

Flooring for the upper storeys was also required. Frequently this is of wooden boards nailed to the beams. In a large number of houses in south Morbihan, Finistère, Côtes-du-Nord and parts of Loire-Atlantique, notably the Brière, a flooring of *terre battue* is common. All the houses at Kervaly have it (Figs. 178–184) and it has been observed in the above areas. From inspection, the method of laying the clay floor seems to be everywhere the same except for a few details. In the Brière, the loft flooring is called *doubli* or *doublyi* and consists of batons of wood and clay, the batons called *grenouilles* or *baguettes* in the dialect of Loire-Atlantique. A *baton* some 0.55 to 0.65 metres in length is selected and a mixture of clay and hay wound around it. The resulting *baguettes* are then laid from beam to beam at intervals of 0.08 to 0.10 metres. As each *baton* is 0.08 to 0.10 metres in diameter, they touch to form a continuous platform. When dry, a surface layer of *pisé* is applied to the upper surface to form a smooth floor. The *torchis* for this *terrasse* is very similar to that used for the walls, but the straw, or hay, is cut longer. Flooring thus reaches a thickness of 0.10 to 0.12 metres. Loft flooring was not

Fig. 53.   Niou, Île d'Ouessant, Finistère
A roof of *torchis* plastered over a covering of turfs previously laid over the rafters.

always so substantial, however, and Souvestre observed that although the *'terre battue servait de plancher'*, the loft floor was formed only by *'quelques fascines de noisetiers encore couvertes de leurs feuilles sèches, et soutenues sur ses perches transversales'*.[188]

Thatch was used almost universally as a roof covering for houses before the advent of slate, the raw material being available naturally and as an agricultural by-product. Providing it was carefully laid an kept in repair, good-quality thatch could last twenty or thirty years. Its use was frequently observed by travellers. Cambry records *'une multitude de chaumières abattues, abandonnées . . .'* near Carhaix, Bachelot de la Pylaie found the houses at Kerveden du Fret *'couvertes en paille'* and Souvestre, also writing of Finistère, found the houses generally *'couvertes en chaume ou en genêt'*.[189] Transition to slate covering began during the nineteenth century as in Bas-Léon where, at the end of the century, slate was replacing the once universal rye-straw thatch.[190] Although large numbers of thatched houses remain, their occurrence is localized, they are present in small numbers

in many of the sample areas (Fig. 79; Quadrats 2, 7, 9, 11, 14, 15), and in others they survive in large numbers (Fig. 79; Quadrats 16, 17). In south Morbihan, notably the *pays vannetais*, and adjacent parts of Loire-Atlantique including the Grande Brière, thatch roofs are common. Elsewhere they form a minority, but frequently when houses were re-roofed in slate, thatch was retained for farm buildings where it survives. Mostly, however, it is not being repaired, and much thatch will soon give way to slate or other covering.

Several types of thatch were once common, but by far the most widespread was that of rye-straw, harder and more durable than oat-, wheat- or barley-straw. All the thatched houses around Grand-Champ and Plumergat are roofed with it (Figs. 55, 95, 178–184, 187, 188). Rye is still grown in small quantities. In September 1977 the thatch of a *lokenn* (see Chapter 8) near Pontivy had been repaired using rye-straw threshed with a flail. The best straw was cut in June before the heads were fully formed, but this entailed the loss of a crop. It was common to use the straw left after threshing. Close to

Fig. 54. Kerdreux, Île d'Ouessant, Finistère
Thatch of *roseau* weighted down on ridge, eaves and gables with bands of *torchis*.

river valleys and marshland, reeds were used as in Béganne (Quadrat 17), the Grande Brière (Fig. 56), Dinéault (Quadrat 9) and on the Île d'Ouessant. It was probably once used also near other estuarine areas.

As the surviving examples of thatching are representative of the lower ends of the social scale, there is no evidence that elaborate decorative techniques were ever used. All the thatched roofs observed are uniformly simple. The common rafters are laid over purlins, either close-spaced and tied with straw rope (Fig. 55), or more widely spaced so that the numerous spars and rafters form squares of *c.* 0.10-1.15 metres (Fig. 56). Whichever framework is used, the thatch is laid directly on it in small bundles and tied with straw, twine or wire. Mostly it is not stitched along the eaves, or the gables, but a few examples of outbuildings have been observed in which the gables are pegged and stitched to prevent the wind lifting them. Occasionally spars were pegged lengthways across the thatch to prevent it lifting (Fig. 160). The ridge was finished either with *torchis* or with *torchis* covered with turfs pegged into the ridge. Turfs or

mottes are green sods cut off the fields and placed along the ridge, usually overlapping (Figs. 48, 49, 72). These ridging techniques are still used on new thatch. No underthatch of any kind has been observed, but the possibility of its once being used must not be discounted.

In two widely separated areas, the use of clay-and-thatch has been recorded. There is oral evidence for the former use of a mixture of clay and thatch in Taupont (Quadrat 11), but no details are available. This may have taken the form of alternate layers of clay and thatch as in Scotland[191] or it may have taken one of the forms used on the Île d'Ouessant where several buildings at Niou have a complete covering of clay. Here, *torchis* is plastered over a covering of turfs previously laid over the rafters (Fig. 53). A second method is to thatch with reeds and lay bands of *torchis* along the ridge, in broad strips along the eaves lines, the gable ends, and in one or two horizontal bands over the line of the side-purlins. After exposure to the weather, the *torchis* washes into the thatch and sometimes gives the impression of having been mixed with the straw (Fig. 54). The object of this practice is not

Fig. 55.   Kerdalibot, Plumergat, Morbihan
'The common rafters are laid over the purlins either close-spaced and tied with straw rope or more widely spaced so that the numerous spars and rafters form squares of *c.* 10-15 cms . . . the thatch is tied directly . . . with straw, twine or wire.'

only to waterproof the weak points, ridge and gables, but also to give added weight to the thatch, so necessary in a very windy climate. Evidence at Taupont and Ouessant indicates that the use of clay may once have been much more common, and recent archaeological evidence from Jersey suggests that it may have been used there during the medieval period.[192]

Clay-and-thatch roof covering is known in Ouessant as *gleds,* a word which may derive from *terre glaise.* The same term is widely used on the mainland to signify a thatch roof without clay content, but the possibility that it may be a survival from the days when clay was used must not be overlooked, particularly as it occurs frequently in documents. Examples of houses and outbuildings in Ouessant, each *'couverte de gleds'* are given in 1830, 1832, 1835, 1842.[193] A distinction between *gleds* and thatch is drawn at Keralaouen in 1832, where there was *'une maison couverte en pailles'* and *'deux étables couvertes de gleds'.*[194] That the use of clay was not confined to houses is shown by an entry for a farm at

Trouguennour, Cléden-Cap-Sizun in 1747 where there was a *'soue a porsseau en forme ronde couvert de terre'*,[195] but whether this circular pigsty had a thatch or turf roof, or a corbelled stone vault, under the clay, is unclear. Certainly bake-ovens were once given a weather-proofing of clay, a practice observed across the whole length of the country, as remains testify, but because annual repairs were necessary, slate roofs later came to be built over the ovens in some areas (Figs. 136-138; 143-146). Not all the eighteenth- and nineteenth-century documents speak of *gleds* and there are many references also to *chaume.* The house, pigsty, stable and byres of Lantrennou in Plougasnou were roofed with slate in 1774, but the *maison à four* with *gleds,* as was the new barn.[196] At Kerziguet Bian in the same parish in 1774, the house, pigsty and bake-house were covered with *gleds,* but other buildings with slate, and *gleds* is mentioned in Brasparts in 1764.[197] Buildings covered with *gleds* are recorded at Tréverrec in Châteaulin in 1789 but the byre was thatched with

Fig. 56. Bréca, Saint-Lyphard, Loire-Atlantique

roseau.[198] In Dinéault there are repeated references between 1750 and 1800 to houses and buildings *couverte de gleds* or *couverte de genêts. Genêt,* the common broom, was also widely used for thatching farm buildings until after World War II. Although it is now rare, the circular pigsty at Coat ar C'herno (VU 536691) is still covered with *genêt,* and a few other decaying examples have recently been recorded. At Perherel, Plougasnou, in 1776 the house and subsidiary buildings were thatched with it,[199] as were houses in Commana in 1801.[200] *Gleds* and *genêts* are repeatedly quoted in Plougasnou during the eighteenth and early-nineteenth century, and several houses thatched with *genêts* are referred to in Plougonver, Côtes-du-Nord in 1768.[201] The use of the term *gleds* thus remains ambiguous, but there is a strong possibility that its widespread survival indicates a former practice of roofing with clay or clay-and-thatch. Other plants were also used for thatching and even gorse is not unknown, for Du Fail writes of a house covered '*de Paille et Ioncz entremelez*' in the mid-sixteenth century.[202] Several varieties of reed or *roseau* were used in the

regions of Redon and Châteauneuf, some with very long life.[203] Even after World War II. the poor houses of Côtes-du-Nord were often covered with *genêts* or even with heath. Along the eastern Marchlands there seems to be a tradition of covering roofs with shingles. Around Fougères, cleft shingles, *essengles,* of chestnut, were used to protect *torchis* walls from the weather but these 'wooden slates' were also used for roofing. Oak is used on the chapel roof of the castle at Châteaubriant, and cleft shingle roofs have been seen on barns at Le Beuchet in Saint-M'Hervé (Fig. 79; Quadrat 13) and elsewhere.

It appears that slate began to be used in the towns, along the coast and on the islands in the eighteenth century,[204] but was little known in the countryside before the nineteenth century except for the larger houses in areas with a local supply, as at Plougasnou where Kermorfezan was already slate-covered in 1780, and Traon ar Run in 1775.[205] It was probably used for the greater rural buildings by the end of the Middle Ages, but not until the nineteenth century did it gain widespread favour for the vast majority of humbler buildings. Small

Fig. 57.   La Ville Bonne 12, Taupont, Morbihan
An upper king-post truss. The king-post supports a ridge-purlin to which it is braced both ways. The lateral purlins, overlapping at the trusses, are supported on cleats. The slates are nailed to laths laid across the common rafters.

quarries were once widespread among the schists and the quartzitic *grès*, notably the Silurian schists of the Montagnes Noires, along the Nantes–Brest canal, and north of Plévin within the Carboniferous basin of Châteaulin. Maël-Carhaix had important quarries and those of La Roche-Derrien long provided the large chunky slates for the region of Lannion, Tréguier, Paimpol and Pontrieux. Poorer quality stone was obtained at Callac, Locarn and Collinée.[206] Buffet comments on the thick local slates at Saint-Cast, Broons, Mauron (Côtes-du-Nord), Ploërmel, Plumelec and Rochefort (Morbihan), Saint-Péran, Saint-Gilles and Coësmes (Ille-et-Vilaine), and old slate roofs can be seen in the towns of Rennes, Ploërmel, Redon and Vitré.[207] The technique of cutting slate seems to have become more widely practised from about 1811.[208] By the mid-nineteenth century in Finistère, all the houses at Lanvaux were slate-covered, whilst at Brasparts there were numerous town houses *remontant aux XIVe et XVe siècles, qui se présentaient avec leurs pignons pointus,* *avec leurs étages en saillie par encorbellements successifs, et avec un manteau d'ardoises sur toute leur façade'.*[209]

The mid-nineteenth century seems to have been a turning point after which slate made great headway, well illustrated by the census of 1856 for Côtes-du-Nord. Of a total of 144,327 houses, 81,028 were thatched, 63,299 roofed in slate. In Callac in 1856, 413 houses were thatched and 208 covered in slate. By 1861, the figures were 223 and 385 respectively. In Carnoët in 1856, 430 were thatched, but by 1861 the number was 412. In La Harmoye, 279 were thatched in 1856, 266 in 1861. By the end of World War I, thatch had been completely replaced by slate in many areas, but elsewhere the change was still in progress, for *'de plus en plus, l'ardoise se substitue au chaume'*[210] and, a little later in Finistère, *'le chaume a presque disparu de nos jours et la grande majorité est recouverte en ardoise d'Angers qui sont employées de préférence à celles dites de Quimper, considérées comme trop lourdes'.*[211] Some areas were

Fig. 58.   La Touquellerie, Frossay, Loire-Atlantique
A 'Roman' tile roof and a chimney-stack of the thin red bricks typical of the area south of the Loire.

slow to change, though, and Lestang was able to write of the Vannetais that whilst thatch was usual in the countryside, slate was common in the towns.[212] In Bas-Léon, where roofing was once universally of thatch, *'depuis quelques années le logis du fermier, l'étable et la grange ont été couvertes en ardoise'*. Although the change reduced the risk of fire, it appears not to have been appreciated by all the inhabitants *'que le chaume arbritait mieux que l'ardoise contre les variations de la température extérieure'*.[213]

In central Brittany at the end of World War II, thatch was still common except close to the quarries at Mur, Caurel, Ploërmel and Mauron and in the valley of the Arz, where small, thick heavy slates are still to be seen on houses. Factors which encouraged conversion to slate during the latter part of the nineteenth century included the encouragement of its *conseils généraux*, the danger of fire, higher insurance premiums and the use of harvesting machines cutting close to the soil and damaging the straw. The nineteenth century also saw the

introduction of slate from Angers, light in weight and higher in quality. The Nantes–Brest canal made possible cheap transport into the heart of Brittany and the railways further assisted the process during the last quarter of the nineteenth century.[214] By World War II, the change from thatch to slate was still being encouraged by the *département* in Côtes-du-Nord with financial assistance to owners. Today, thatch survives on farm buildings rather than on houses, in the south rather than in the north, and in granite areas rather than on schist.

Red tiles are occasionally seen in all five *départements*, and in some areas, notably around Coglais, Combourg and Tinténiac, they are quite common, and were produced in the tilery at Québriac until 1858.[215] Tiles became popular around Lannion and in areas served by the railways before the advent of slate, and were produced locally at Saint-Ilan (Saint-Brieuc) and Saint-Méen.[216] Tiles and bricks were also formerly imported into the Lannionais and Trégorrois from Bridgwater in Somerset (Figs. 80, 81).[217] South of the

Loire, and in the area characterized by the low-pitch short king-post roof (Figs. 62 and 63) the half-round tile is found on almost every building (Figs. 58, 99, 100, 147, 148). Known locally as *tiges de bottes, tuiles creuses* or *tuiles romaines,* these tiles appear to be of considerable antiquity and southern origin.[218]

The great majority of houses are gable-ended, with the chimney-stack incorporated into one of the gables. Hipped roofs are rare at the lower levels of society and appear to survive only as a relic of 'primitive' building (see Chapter 8), except in the east where the fully-hipped Renaissance house is quite common at the level of the *manoir,* notably in the Rennes basin (Fig. 44). This roof-form appears in the seventeenth and eighteenth centuries, an intrusion from metropolitan France. Only rarely does it occur in the west. Roof pitch is generally of the order of forty-five to fifty degrees, but in the thatched-roof areas of Morbihan it occasionally reaches fifty-five degrees. South of the Loire, the red-tile roofs average twenty to twenty-five degrees, and on some houses roof-pitch may be as little as seventeen to eighteen degrees.

SIX

CONSTRUCTION — II

Roof structure is the most important single aspect of the construction of a building. The need for shelter implies, first and foremost, the existence of a roof. A house, or other building, may be so simple as to consist only of a roof structure resting directly on the ground, but a house cannot be said to exist unless it has a roof. Walls increase space and volume within the house and act as a curtain separating inside from outside. In most buildings they also support the roof. It is to the construction of the roof, to span ever-increasing areas, that the ingenuity of carpenters and stonemasons has been directed over the centuries. In recent years there has been considerable debate, amongst British scholars in particular, in an attempt to explain the origin and development of various types of roof-carpentry, and notwithstanding the considerable progress in this field of learning, there remain many gaps in our knowledge. The paucity of serious studies on the carpentry of France has been one great handicap. Only during the last few years has the existence, in a number of French regions, of features long known in other parts of Europe, been attested.

A provisional study of the roof-carpentry of Brittany has recently been published.[219] Following an examination of the records of the Commission d'Inventaire de Bretagne during the summer of 1979, it has been possible to make many additions to the maps of carpentry types. The continued use of the dot map would now lead to such congestion that it has been abandoned in favour of quadrat mapping. The maps that follow are all therefore revised and up-dated versions of those previously published. No attempt has been made, however, at density-mapping. Although in many of the quadrats there may be a dozen or more examples of the feature illustrated, selection has been much too uneven to merit density-mapping, and vast numbers of buildings are as yet unrecorded. The maps therefore indicate only that features have been observed in certain places.

Stone-vaulted buildings are well-known in certain areas. Although no discovery has yet been made of the use of the tunnel- or barrel-vault in houses or ancillary buildings, it does occur in a few structures with special functions, of essentially vernacular character. At the Pointe de Primel, Plougasnou, Finistère (VU 398967), a *guérite* (coastguard look-out) is probably of late seventeenth-century date, and tunnel-vaulted beneath its slate roofing (Fig. 59). Walling is entirely of *granit rose*, rubble being used for the greater part but with some roughly dressed blocks for the quoins and the door and window dressings. Externally the building measures 7.20 metres by 6.10 metres and internally 5.75 metres by 3.85 metres. There is a small lean-to outshot which further extends the length of the building by 1.75 metres and it is 2.30 metres wide. Internally the outshot measures 1.25 metres wide by 1.60 metres long. The length extends partly into the gable wall of the main building. The gable walls are 0.70 metres thick and the lateral walls 1.10 metres thick. Walling is laid with a mortar of *pisé* and the barrel-vaulted roof is covered with large, coarse slates. The small outshot is roofed firstly with flat slabs of granite, then the slope built up with granite rubble and finally finished with similar slates. A fine but plain chimney-piece is sited at the upper end, there being two breastsummers to support the chimney-hood of roughly coursed granite rubble. There is no longer a chimney-stack and the back of the hearth is provided with a hole, presumed to be for ventilation purposes. The floor is of *terre battue*. Door and window dressings are finely cut but plain. Only the doorway to the outshot has an offset cut provided to receive the wooden door which presumably opened outwards. Light is provided by a single window and ventilation at the lower end by a slit. The building was intended to serve as a look-out at a prominent point on the coast, hence its solid construction and stone-vaulted roof. It is interesting in that the plan is that of the simple long-house, and although the furniture and arrangements of the interior are not known, it is probable that some sort of living accommodation was provided at the upper end whilst horses or other animals might have been given temporary accommodation in the lower end.

Built by order of the State as one of a series of *guérites*

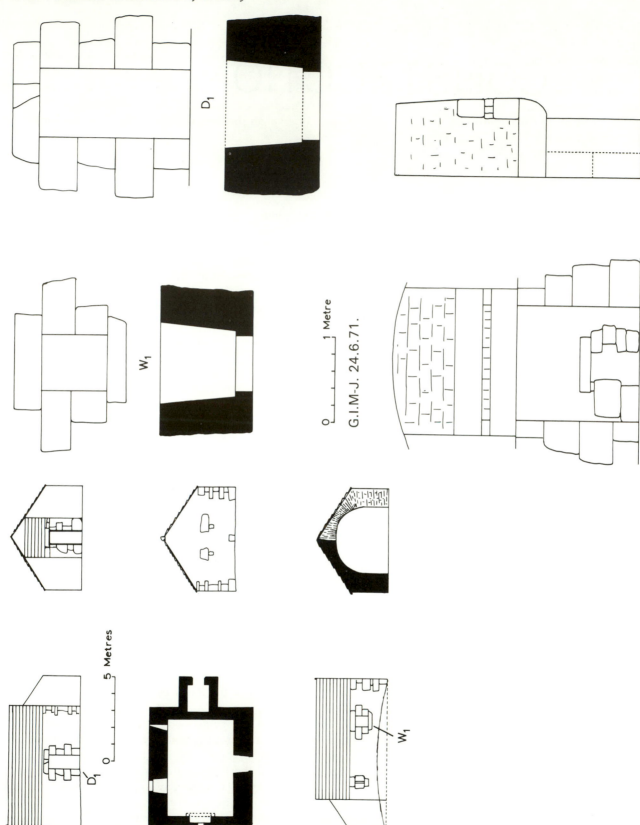

D_1

W_1

0   1 Metre

G.I.M-J. 24.6.71.

D_1

0   5 Metres

W_1

Fig. 59. A coastguard lookout, or *guérite*, on the Pointe de Primel, Plougasnou, Finistère

at intervals along the coast, defensive needs alone are insufficient to explain its construction, for the window and door openings would make it vulnerable. Need to withstand surprise attack by small bands of men, or even cannonade, may have been a factor in the design of such a substantial structure. The desire to make it durable as well as completely weatherproof in such a windy and exposed situation is a more likely explanation. Two other *guérites*, rectilinear in plan, recorded at Le Verger (WU 825946) and the Pointe du Meinga (WU 784944) on the north coast are essentially similar in construction. That at the Pointe du Meinga has a look-out tower of square plan and corbelled vault built against the western gable. A former *guérite*, now a house, at Le Valade (WU 835959) may be tunnel-vaulted. Yet another stands on the Cotentin coast just north of Avranches, and many lie at intervals, particularly along the north coast and on certain islands.

The tunnel-vault is of some antiquity and appears to have been a common feature of both Iron Age and medieval *souterrains*. Distribution is essentially coastal, and medieval examples occur with great frequency in western Léon and Cap-Sizun. Isolated examples have been recorded elsewhere in Finistère, as at Kerberez in Locmaria-Plouzané. It is often difficult to distinguish between *souterrains* of medieval and Iron Age date. They generally take the form of a rectilinear room cut into the rock. Drystone work lines the walls from which rises the vault. After construction, the roof was covered with earth levelled with the ground outside to camouflage the existence of the structure. Access is either by a hole cut into the vault or by a lateral doorway approached by a vertical shaft. A date between the fourteenth and sixteenth centuries is given for some medieval examples, pre-dating the *guérites* by no more than two hundred years.[220] Continuity of building tradition is thus likely. A tunnel-vaulted building, St. Hervé's hermitage, ascribed to the Early Christian period, at Lanrivoaré in north Finistère, measures 3.50 by 2.50 metres, the floor sunk 0.40 metres below ground level. The tunnel-vault rises to 2.50 metres above the floor, and the wall incorporates some orthostats and is provided with two keeping-places. A hearth-stone stands in a corner, with a hole for keeping cinders alive during the night.[221]

The circular stone vault, a barrel-vault in the round, whether constructed of stone or brick, is universally used for bake-ovens, whilst circular corbelled dove-cots are frequent. Only two corbelled stone farm buildings have been discovered, both in the same yard at the Manoir de Quéhéon in Ploërmel (Fig. 117). The only rectilinear structure known to have corbelled vault is the tower of

the *guérite* at Le Verger, above. Fuller details of circular stone-vaulted buildings are given in Chapter 7.

The termination of a corbelled vault with a large flat slab is not uncommon, is frequently met with in well covers as at La Croix-Havard (Fig. 120), and is also encountered occasionally in larger buildings like the small *guérite* on the eastern side of the Anse du Verger (WU 833947). Here, the first few courses of the roof are corbelled and the arch then bridged with large closely-fitting flat slabs. The triangular-section roof is built up with stone rubble and finished with a slate covering. This form of structure, of considerable antiquity, is known from the Megalithic period[222] and is used to roof some of the medieval *souterrains*.[223]

A consideration of carpentry must begin with the aisled hall, a few examples of which have been recorded in the countryside, two within a short distance of each other at Mesnil and La Brosse in Saint-M'Hervé (Fig. 79; Quadrat 13). Both are barns, that at La Brosse having only one aisle. At Mesnil, the structure is enclosed by stone walls, the end trusses being visible in the gables and the stone-work playing only a partial load-bearing function. A full king-post rises from the tie-beam which rests on square-set arcade-plates in the orthodox manner. The aisle-plates are carried on horizontal timbers braced downwards to the aisle posts, the latter, in turn, being braced upwards to the tie-beam. There is a building with one aisle at the Manoir de la Ronce in Billé (XU 303495), and La Rivière in Châtillon-sur-Seiche (WU 992212) appears to be an aisled hall. Further examination is required here, but if it is correct this will be the first aisled hall found in Brittany used as a dwelling.[224] Market halls are the only class of aisled buildings, except, of course, for the churches, known to survive at Plouescat, Clisson, Questembert and Le Faouët. The former market hall at Guipry was aisled,[225] as was that at Guémené-sur-Scorff, and it is virtually certain that the now demolished market halls of many other towns such as Morlaix, Quimper, Auray, Rennes and Nantes were timber aisled structures. Only that at Questembert, firmly dated to 1675, has been subjected to serious study;[226] for that at Le Faouët, a date at the end of the fifteenth century or the beginning of the sixteenth century has been suggested.[227] The aisled market hall at Brasparts, described by Bachelot de la Pylaie,[228] and of which a plan survives,[229] was demolished in 1878. It is probable that most of these halls belong to the period from the fifteenth to the seventeenth centuries.

The aisled hall is certainly part of the vernacular tradition elsewhere in France where it survives widely in market halls, churches and barns. In the Basque country and other parts of south-west France, as well as the

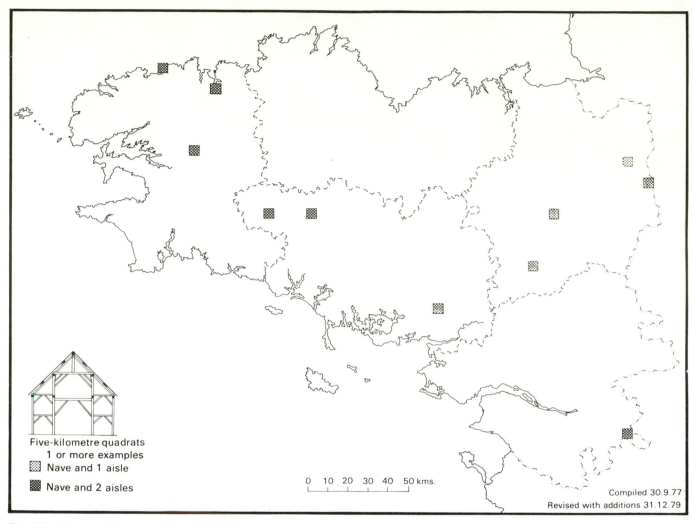

Fig. 60.   The distribution of the aisled-hall truss

Alpine regions, it is used for houses.[230] The distribution in Brittany (Fig. 60) shows the widely separated market halls combined with the few known rural examples in the east. The almost total absence of the aisled hall at the vernacular level in the Breton countryside suggests that either it was never known there, and that it was introduced into the towns from metropolitan France during the late-medieval or early-modern period, which might explain the rural survival in the east, or that it was once part of the timber-frame tradition in the countryside, already postulated, but that all trace of it has disappeared. In view of the general poverty of Breton rural architecture, the former seems the more likely. The Breton examples all have full king-post trusses, often heavily braced to other members. A second tie-beam is sometimes used and secondary ties are also known in the aisles. Multiple straight bracing is common. The better

quality timber roofs at 'manorial' or comparable social levels frequently have a longitudinal member between the king-posts placed at some distance below the ridge, but braced upwards to it either with single or multiple straight braces or with scissors braces. This is the (Fr.) *sous-faîtage*, generally best translated as 'under-ridge purlin'. Where, as in some cases, more than one such member exists, these may be distinguished as 'first' and 'second' under-ridge purlins.

Rafter roofs, that is, roofs formed of close-set pairs of rafters, each pair linked by a collar and sometimes additionally, or alternatively, by a tie-beam, have been observed in western Brittany. These roofs are characterized by the absence of a ridge-purlin and lateral purlins, and may be described as 'single' roofs in that the whole weight of the roof covering rests directly on the rafters. All other Breton roofs are 'double' roofs, having a

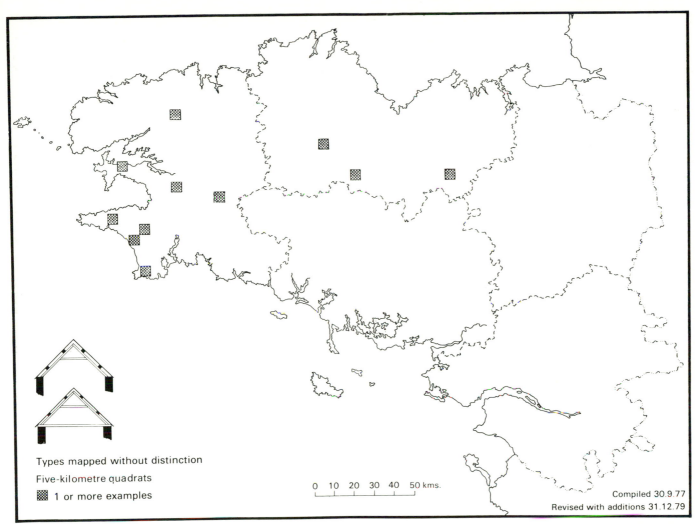

Types mapped without distinction

Five-kilometre quadrats

1 or more examples

0 10 20 30 40 50 kms.

Compiled 30.9.77
Revised with additions 31.12.79

Fig. 61.   The distribution of rafter roofs

second set of rafters, the common rafters, riding over the purlins and supporting the roof covering. Only ten rafter roofs have been recorded, eight in Finistère, where they are widely distributed, and two in Côtes-du-Nord (Fig. 61). In each case the houses have stone gables at both ends providing added longitudinal support to the roof. One example at Plomeur is dated 1818, the trusses being placed at 1.00 metre intervals, and examples at Lanvéoc, of 1856, and at Pouldreuzic, of 1870, have similar closely spaced rafters.[231] In all these, the trusses are held in place by horizontal boards nailed to them to which the slates are fastened. Not a single example in Finistère belongs to a house other than of a convincingly nineteenth-century date. In Côtes-du-Nord, at Saint-Gilles-Vieux-Marché, a house of 1768 has a rafter roof but it seems likely that the roof timbers date, not from the original building, but from a period of re-roofing in the

nineteenth century. This explanation would be consistent with what is known of the extensive conversion from thatch to slate from the mid-nineteenth century onwards.

The rafter roof is known to have been used on the larger buildings of medieval France and it survives in some of the aisled-hall houses of the Basses-Pyrénées.[232] It is possible that the Breton examples cited represent a survival of this early form of construction in the remote west. If this is so, examples might be expected in the large number of obviously early and more 'primitive' houses and outbuildings. However, all the older houses and outbuildings observed, which retain an 'original' thatch roof, have without exception principal rafter roofs with purlins and especially a ridge purlin. The rafter roofs, on the other hand, are uniquely associated with the boarded and slated roofs of nineteenth-century date. It therefore seems likely that they represent an 'industrial' innovation

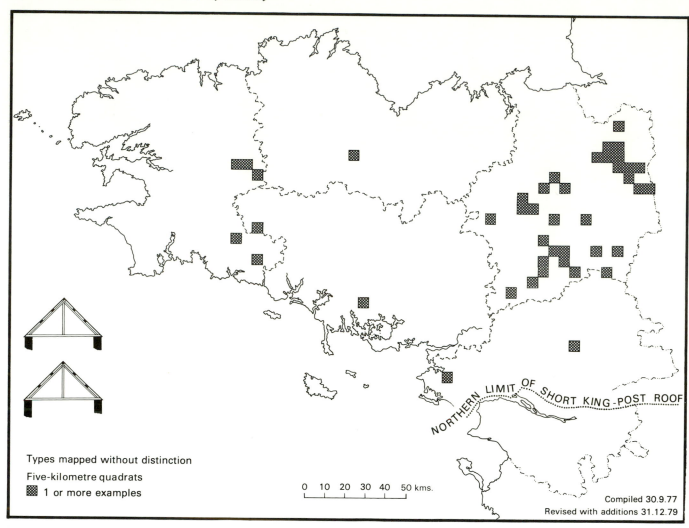

Fig. 62.   The distribution of the full king-post truss

designed to economize in the use of timber by using boarding both for lateral roof support as well as a surface on to which the slates may be nailed. These roofs predate the arrival of the railways, and diffusion of the technique from a centre or centres in the west must be a possibility, the idea perhaps originating in a builder's pattern book. The distribution in the far west remains puzzling, and if this explanation is correct, future examples in central and even eastern Brittany should eventually be forthcoming.

The king-post and upper king-post trusses appear to be almost universal in ecclesiastical buildings in Brittany, and examples have also been recorded in domestic buildings (Figs. 62 and 63). They appear to be by far the most common form of truss in northern and western France generally, and the full king-post in a shortened form occurs in the low-pitch 'Mediterranean'-type Roman-tiled

roofs of the south.[233] The latter reach as far north as the Loire in south-east Brittany.[234] Examples of the king-post, upper king-post and short king-post trusses are illustrated in Figs. 163, 195, 201, 202, 204 and 209. The examples mapped are derived both from fieldwork and from photographs in the collection of the Commission d'Inventaire de Bretagne.

Fieldwork, both by the writer and the Commission d'Inventaire, has inevitably been confined to limited areas, the greater part of the country remains to be worked, and to this extent the distributions shown are merely an index of accomplished fieldwork. The patterns illustrated by the maps of carpentry forms (Figs. 60–67) are to be interpreted generally for what they show, rather than for what they do not show. Nevertheless, with caution, some generalizations and comments may be made. Both subjective assessment of unrecorded field

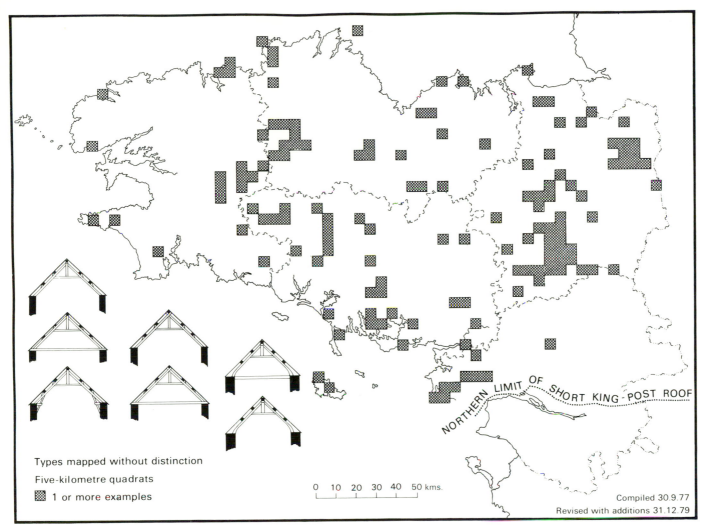

Fig. 63.   The distribution of the upper king-post truss

observations and the recorded data indicate that the full king-post occurs in great numbers in eastern Brittany, but only rarely at the domestic level in the west. Eventually a dense pattern may emerge along the whole of eastern Ille-et-Vilaine and possibly in Loire-Atlantique as well. Numbers appear to thin out somewhat to the west of Rennes. The king-posts are often finely moulded and sometimes magnificently tapered. Westwards, away from the Marches, they become plainer parallel-sided pieces of timber, without ornament and lacking elegance, save perhaps for an occasional flat-splay chamfer.

At the domestic level, probably because it allows unimpeded access to the loft space universally used for storage, the upper king-post is much more common. All the variants of the upper king-post including those combined with the upper cruck, and two of the upper king-strut are shown on Fig. 63. Clusters again show

those places subjected to intensive fieldwork, and although dense patterns will probably eventually emerge over a large areas, it seems that, as with the king-post, the distribution is denser in the east, thinning out markedly to the west. This interpretation is supported by subjective assessment in the field. In the east, the upper king-post occurs frequently in houses representative of a relatively low social status, as at Les Landes de l'Etriac 1 (Fig. 174), where it is braced longitudinally by an under-ridge purlin, a feature only to be expected at the higher social levels in the west. It also occurs, along with the full king-post, in houses of 'manorial' status like La Salle in Plurien (Fig. 217). The full king-post is oocasionally found in the far west in the greater houses. A superb example is to be found in the Manoir de Kerligonan in Kergloff, Finistère.[235] In general the upper king-post truss is common in the east where it may be said to represent

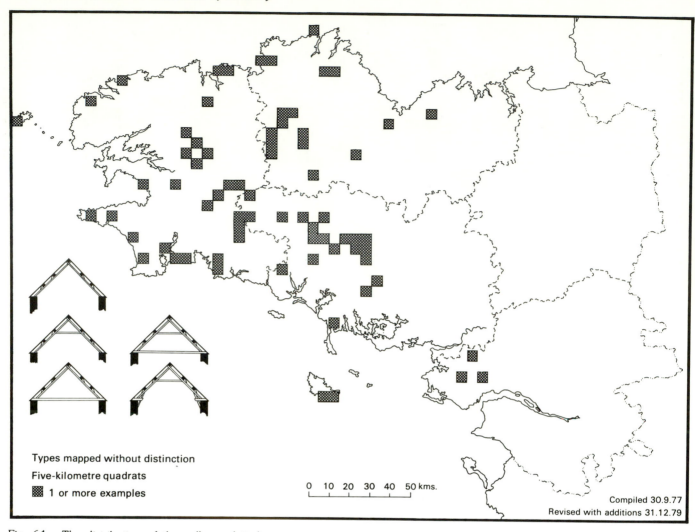

Fig. 64.   The distribution of the collar and tie-beam truss

the norm at the middle level of rural society, but gives way to other types westwards. In the far west, although the numbers decrease to the point of being almost non-existent at the lower levels of society, they remain almost universal in houses of those of upper-rural social status. The gradation is such that it is felt the task of mapping according to 'social status' is, at least for the present, too difficult. The *manoirs* of the west are frequently very small compared with those of the east.

Only a few examples of the full cruck are known (Fig. 65), the finest being in the now demolished house at Talforest in Plumelin.[236] Here, three trusses of the collar and tie-beam type supported the roof in the classic manner. The house, with its low walls of *torchis*, was of a relatively primitive type but illustrates well the full development of the cruck at a low social level. Another, but poorer, example has recently been recorded in the

neighbouring *commune* of Guénin, at Koh-Coët (WU 062055) (Fig. 167). A further example is the cruck barn at Penhap in Marzan (Fig. 226). Here there is a collar but no tie-beam, the blades rising from the walls to intersect at the apex and carry the ridge. In size and form these blades closely resemble those widely found in use as upper-crucks.

Examples of the use of full crucks, as distinct from inverted V-trusses, are occasionally found in a *lokennou*. In one such building, near Callac, now used as a garage, the owner had built the shelter using curved blades obtained by splitting hedgerow trees to obtain like pairs, in the manner practised in the district for generations. There are no walls, the feet of the rafters rest on the ground, and there is a collar but no tie-beam. Another recently discovered example lies at Hôtel Neuf, Guillac, Morbihan. The barn at La Ville Gauthier at Saint-

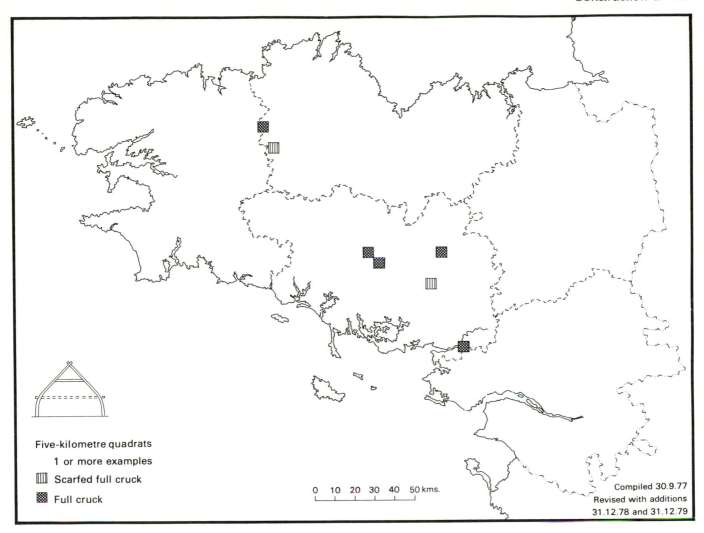

Fig. 65.   The distribution of the full cruck-truss

Guyomard, Morbihan (WT 359937), a primitive structure, is supported by scarfed crucks, also with collar, but no tie-beam. Other examples of crude scarfing are known, as at Goaz Henry (VU 604587) and Koh Coët (WU 058053) but it must be admitted that these are no more than rafters pegged into vertical posts. Technically, however, they are crucks. Of these examples, the only ones displaying any degree of refinement in finish are those at Talforest and Penhap. In each case, the ridge-purlin is carried in the V-notch formed by the intersecting principal rafters. Notwithstanding low numbers, the distribution shows that the type is known across the length of Brittany from the mouth of the Vilaine to the foothills of the Monts d'Arrée.

The upper-cruck truss appears with and without collar and tie-beam in five variants, two of these with upper king-post. There are also examples of truncated upper-crucks, sometimes known as base upper-crucks (Figs. 66 and 67). Clusters in the distributions again highlight areas of intensive fieldwork, notably at La Harmoye (Quadrat 13), Béganne (Quadrat 17), Grand-Champ (Quadrat 16) and the adjacent *commune* of Plumergat, Guérande (Quadrat 19), and the adjacent regions of the Grande Brière and the *pays blanc*. The distribution suggests that the variant without a collar is rare, whilst that with collar and tie-beam is common and fairly evenly distributed in central and eastern Brittany, with only two examples in the north and west. The upper-cruck and collar truss on present evidence seems localized in south Morbihan, whilst the upper king-post types are fairly evenly distributed in the centre and east. To these distributions must be added the evidence of two surveys, one which suggests that there are many more upper-crucks in the older houses of the *pays blanc*[237] and the other that they

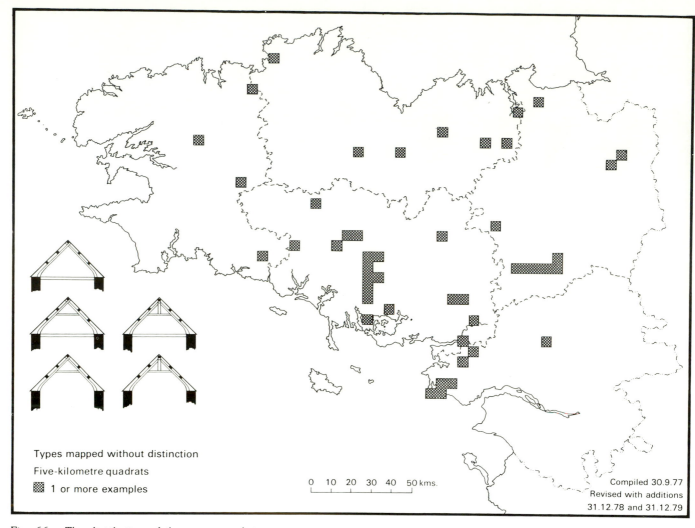

Fig. 66.   The distribution of the upper-cruck truss

exist in some numbers in the older houses in the southern part of Ille-et-Vilaine.[238] As precise locations for these regions are not available, examples cannot be added to the maps, but the evidence is believed to be reliable. Recent fieldwork suggests that the upper cruck is also likely to be found in the older houses of northern Ille-et-Vilaine, and the same may yet prove to be true of Côtes-du-Nord, for the few examples so far encountered are of good quality. Evidence thus suggests that the upper-cruck is common in central Brittany and certainly in the western part of Ille-et-Vilaine and Loire-Atlantique. Only two examples have so far been discovered in Finistère and it is possible that it is little known there.

Truncated upper-crucks are few in number (Fig. 67). At Le Verger in Gestel (Quadrat 15), in a mill dated 1656, there were originally four such trusses, the blades recessed in slots in the stone walls. A second example,

somewhat different, is that at the Moulin d'Haroult in Saint-M'Hervé (XU 428390). Two examples of the truncated upper-cruck are recorded in Ille-et-Vilaine by the Commission d'Inventaire, one in the *bourg* of Pléchâtel, the other at La Gandouflais in Poligné.[239] Unlike the other examples illustrated in Fig. 68, these have a curved principal rising from the tie-beam to be morticed into the straight principal which extends from the ridge down to the wall-head where it is tenoned into the spur. This is identical in principle to the roof truss of the *greniers-à-sel* at Honfleur[240] with its curved principals. Both upper-crucks and truncated upper-crucks occur elsewhere in France.

In addition to the structurally unsound couple truss, of which one example is known near Scaër, there are four variants of the collar and tie-beam type of truss, one with a sling-braced stub tie-beam (Fig. 64). With the exception

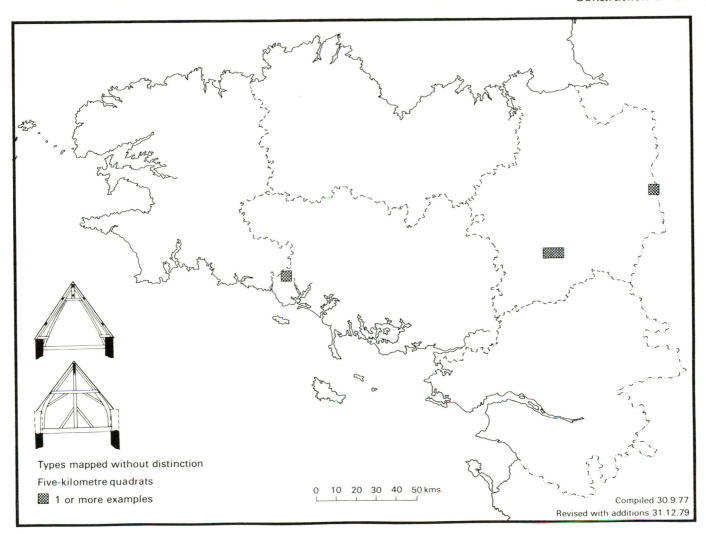

Types mapped without distinction

Five-kilometre quadrats

1 or more examples

0 10 20 30 40 50 kms.

Compiled 30.9.77
Revised with additions 31.12.79

Fig. 67.   The distribution of the truncated upper-cruck truss

of the collar and tie-beam truss, which occurs in some numbers in the Grand Brière, the distribution of all these variants is almost entirely confined to western Brittany. It is difficult to believe that, even allowing for the uneven nature of the fieldwork, examples would not have been found in the east had the type been known there. The sling-braced truss occurs only in the south, but the other forms show a wide and fairly even distribution across the west.

Any interpretation of the evolution of carpentry must partly rest on assumptions concerning the nature of the diffusion process. Opinion is divided between those who argue for evolution from a single origin and those who accept the possibility of independent invention and multiple origins. It is argued here that the whole of western Europe is sufficiently small a geographical entity to permit of single origins for carpentry forms, providing

other factors allow. Carpentry, unlike portable forms of material culture which may be traded, requires the movement of people for its dissemination, either of craftsmen on some scale, or the migration of a people.[241] Only two periods of history would seem to fulfil these conditions for Brittany: the Iron Age with the first influx of Celtic peoples, and the Breton invasions of the Early Christian period. The movement of skilled carpenters independently of these folk movements may be associated with the periods of church and castle building in the later Middle Ages, or with the extensive building of houses and churches following the Renaissance. Whilst most of those craftsmen might have been Breton or French, there were strong links between Brittany and England during the medieval period, and the possibility of movement of craftsmen across the Channel should not be discounted.

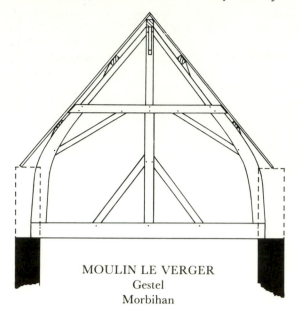

MOULIN LE VERGER
Gestel
Morbihan

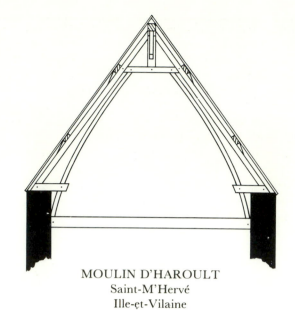

MOULIN D'HAROULT
Saint-M'Hervé
Ille-et-Vilaine

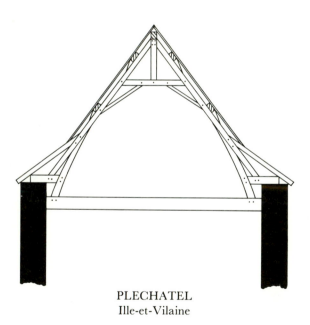

PLECHATEL
Ille-et-Vilaine

LA GANDOUFLAIS
Poligné
Ille-et-Vilaine

Fig. 68.   The truncated upper-cruck truss

One of the principal characteristics of Brittany is the survival, in remote areas, of ancient ways and customs into recent times. Roof structures, generally accepted to be typologically early, have also survived. A field building with a row of central posts was observed in eastern Ille-et-Vilaine in the 1970s, and in 1946 two houses at Plumelin, one at Kerspec, the other at Talforest, had their ridge-beams supported by vertical posts. Both houses had fully hipped roofs. At Kerspec, the centre of the ridge

was supported by a *stridsuler*-type truss, the feet of the two posts placed immediately on either side of the open hearth, and the ends of the ridge were supported by vertical posts. At Talforest, a sloping post, aided by a prop, supported the roof in the centre.[242] Here is indisputable evidence for the survival of the central post into the mid-twentieth century, in domestic buildings at the lowest social levels.

At what stage the aisled hall and the king-post first

began to supersede the hall with a central row of posts at the upper social levels in France is impossible to say, but the late survivals in Brittany suggest that the disappearance of the central roof supports may have been a gradual one occupying a period in excess of two thousand years. The orthodox view is that both the aisled hall and the king-post roof developed through the need to clear the earliest halls of the row of central posts supporting the roof which so impeded movement within them.[243] It is interesting to note that the distribution of king-post roofs in Great Britain is now predominantly northern and, amongst vernacular buildings, almost wholly northern. The earliest surviving roofs in the north, however, are without king-posts and the type is now known in greater numbers in southern England. It appears that *c.* 1400 the king-post was widely known in England.[244] It thus seems probable that the British king-post region once formed part of a greater region incorporating most of France, where the king-post remains dominant. The problem is further clouded because, given the present stage of medieval archaeology in France, there is little knowledge of the type of building in which the majority of Bretons lived up to the end of the Middle Ages. It is probable, however, that the primitive structures described in Chapter 8 represent the norm, and that relatively permanent housing dates only from the sixteenth century. Remarkably few medieval domestic buildings survive, even at the upper levels of rural society, most of the larger rural houses being of late-medieval or Renaissance date or later. The problem is further aggravated by the absence of serious study of French carpentry, except for one notable example.[245] Dates can only occasionally be ascribed with certainty to carpentry, and then rarely before the sixteenth century. In the absence of archaeological evidence, it is not known whether the aisled hall existed in medieval Brittany at the domestic level, but the distribution of surviving examples (Fig. 60) strongly suggests that it did not but was introduced to the towns at a late-medieval or early-modern date, being diffused into the countryside of the Breton Marches about the same time. Rafter roofs (Fig. 61) are best regarded as a late and localized introduction until more evidence concerning their date is available.

The king-post, cruck, and collar and tie-beam trusses must be considered in more detail. The number of variants within these types is remarkably few and carpentry is relatively simple compared, for example, with the complex derivatives found in the British Isles. The two apex forms illustrated (Figs. 61–66) are universal and there is no trace of any of the strange apex forms found in Britain. It should be noted, however, that recent studies in Limousin have produced apex forms

strikingly similar to those described for England and quite unlike Breton ones.[246] It has already been demonstrated that the essential contrasts of distribution lie between the king-post and cruck trusses on one hand, and the collar and tie-beam forms on the other. The former are more common in the east, whilst the latter are mostly confined to the west but with survivals also in the culturally retarded areas of south Morbihan and the *pays de Guérande.* The heavy concentration of cruck forms in the south may be directly related to the intensity of fieldwork, but the possibility that it is of wider significance must not be discounted.

Some of the simplest structures surviving in Brittany are the *lokennou,* on farmyard buildings (see Chapter 8), with inverted 'v' collar-trusses carrying ridge and lateral purlins, the feet of the principal rafters resting directly on the ground. The lifting of this type of structure on to low walls results in a conventional collar-truss and, if the walls are high enough to give adequate headroom, a tie-beam may be added. This may be the origin of the trusses shown on Fig. 64, they may be typologically the oldest surviving form of roof truss, and their survival in the west and the more conservative areas of the south may be explained by the fact that here is an area of cultural survival into which later forms have made little headway. Whether or not there has been continuity of building in stone, as has been suggested in southern Finistère, is essentially irrelevant to the survival of this type of roof, for the argument rests solely on the raising of a simple inverted 'v' truss, first on to low walls, whether of earth, timber or stone, and then on to walls of full height. In the larger halls associated with the leaders of society, the ridge beam could be supported by a row of central posts, although as the examples at Plumelin have shown, this technique was also favoured for small houses of lowly status. At some stage, and probably at the higher social levels, the full king-post truss came into being, as a result of lifting the central post on to a tie-beam. Such a truss is effective for a building in which no great use is made of the roof space, but as soon as the latter comes to be used for the storage of hay or grain, the posts are an obstruction. If the post is again lifted on to the collar, the upper king-post truss results. In the majority of Breton farms the lofts are so used for storage and it is not surprising that the upper king-post truss is far commoner than the full king-post version. The distribution of these two variants (Figs. 62 and 63) suggests that they originated in the east, that diffusion has taken a westerly direction and that the type was accepted in the west almost exclusively at the middle and upper levels of society, whilst in eastern Brittany they are found at lower social levels. The origin of the king-post appears to be east of the language divide and probably outside Brittany.[247] The short king-post roof so strongly associated with the Mediterranean area is also of considerable antiquity and was diffused northwards to the Loire, probably in Roman times (Figs. 62 and 63). There is no reason to believe that the carpentry forms so far described do not belong at the latest to the Roman period.

The cruck truss poses more problems and has already been the subject of much controversy in the British Isles.[248] The number of full cruck-trusses (Fig. 65) is too few to be more than an indication of its existence in Brittany and of a probable former wide distribution. Many of the larger numbers of upper-crucks (Fig. 66) are concentrated in areas of intensive fieldwork, and new discoveries may considerably alter the picture. Applying Childe's principle[249] to the upper-cruck distribution, it would appear that the upper-cruck, collar and tie-beam truss is the oldest type being most accurately reproduced in the greatest number of distinct regions followed by the form with the upper king-post added. Variants without a tie-beam, localized in southern Morbihan, would be later in the typology. The survival of large numbers of these structures in south Morbihan may be indicative of their origin in Brittany. The reconstruction of former carpentry from post-hole evidence in excavated buildings is notoriously difficult, and the buildings at Pen-er-Malo, in Guidel, Morbihan, are no exception in this respect. Whilst there is little evidence to assist in the reconstruction of Building A, there remains the possibility that the inclined post-holes of Building B once housed the feet of crucks (see Chapter 8).[250] Even if this archaeological evidence be set aside, a prehistoric origin may still be argued, however, on the grounds of wide distribution. If the cruck form existed among the Armorican population, the clusters in Morbihan could be attributed to the survival there, only to be re-diffused over the whole Province after the Breton invasions, which may themselves have brought knowledge of the cruck. If a medieval or later date is sought, then a more probable explanation is that the cruck came via the Loire valley during the Renaissance by way of the southern coastline to be diffused throughout the Province from south Morbihan where it took root.

Forms of cruck construction are widely distributed in northern and western France and in other parts of Europe.[251] The most common form so far recorded in north-west France is the upper-cruck. In view of the wide distribution in France, a prehistoric origin is preferred. Variants of the upper-cruck show various degrees of curvature at the elbow to the point at which the blade is almost perfectly straight, and the truss becomes indistinguishable from the collar and tie-beam truss.

These forms belong to the same family whose typological development is suggested in Fig. 69. The immediate antecedent of the cruck is the inverted 'v' truss which could have evolved directly to the collar and tie-beam truss. As low walls developed, evolution to the full-cruck was also possible. Early walls, whether of *torchis,* stone or timber, may have been too weak to bear the weight of the roof. The full-cruck is therefore appropriate as it transmits the weight directly to the ground. In addition, the development of the full-cruck may have been related to the postulated timber-frame tradition in the countryside. As walls increased in height, suitable long timbers may have become harder to obtain, and as walling techniques improved they developed a greater load-bearing capacity. The answer to both increased headroom and the desire to achieve maximum storage space in the loft is the upper-cruck in association with a house of one-and-a-half storeys. Its survival in Brittany is almost certainly owed to the tradition of living entirely on the ground floor, leaving the loft for storage. Earlier development of a full second storey would have been followed by the demise of the upper-cruck.

The combination of the upper-cruck and the upper king-post associated with better quality housing must be seen either as a hybrid preferred in some areas, or to the fact that the two are closely related, the juxtaposition perpetuating their evolution as a solution to the clearing of a row of central posts from the early halls. The carpentry distribution should be compared with the cultural distributions. The striking dichotomy lies between Haute-Bretagne and Basse-Bretagne. The close relationship between collar and tie-beam roofs with Breton-speaking areas, and their medieval dioceses, on the one hand, and the relationship of king-post roofs at the lower levels of society, with the Pays Gallo, is extraordinary, and requires more than a change in language to explain it.

The concentration of collar and tie-beam trusses in the west may indicate that crucks never made much headway in an area where more ancient forms persisted, or that they developed directly from the inverted 'v' truss, and that they are an older type. Alternatively, they may represent the last stages of the cruck cycle, crucks having died out because they had lost their purpose or through an insufficiency of suitable timber, or both. Continuity of building in stone, in Finistère, from prehistoric times, may have resulted in walls sufficiently strong so that crucks were never needed. If the cruck is particularly associated with the timber-frame tradition, this may well be the case.

The former existence of the open hearth in Brittany is shown by archaeological evidence, by the observation of travellers and by a few examples that survived World War

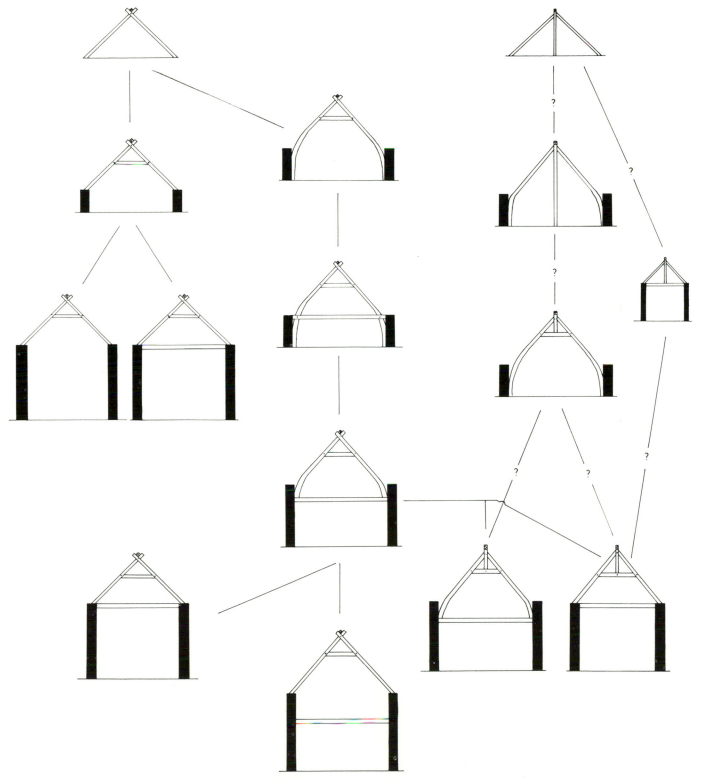

Fig. 69.   Cruck construction: a proposed typology

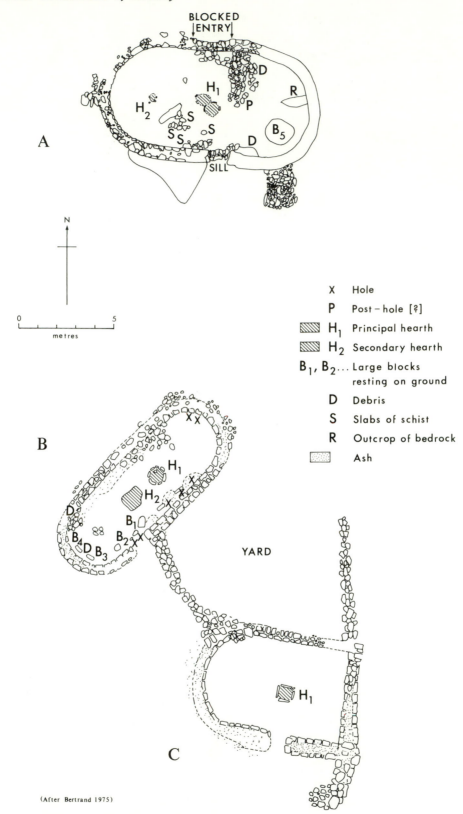

Fig. 70. Buildings excavated at a medieval site: Pen-er-Malo, Guidel, Morbihan

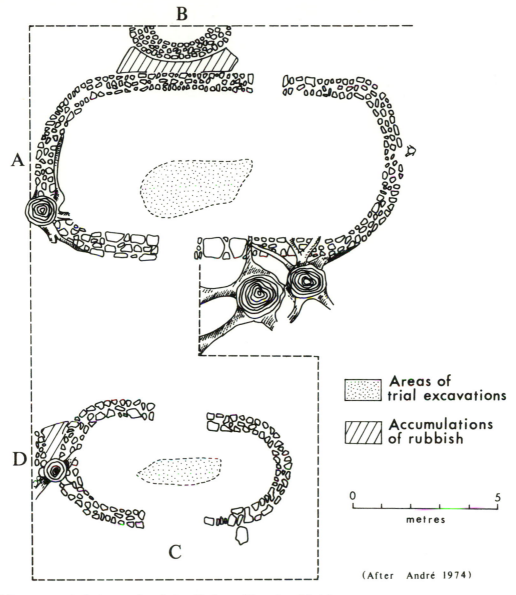

Fig. 71. Buildings excavated at a medieval site: Kerlano, Plumelec, Morbihan

II. Only recently has medieval archaeology made progress in France, but already two sites in Brittany have been excavated to reveal oval buildings. At Pen-er-Malo, Guidel, Morbihan, three structures were uncovered, two with remnants of more than one hearth (Fig. 70). In all cases the hearths were centrally placed, roughly circular, with a diameter of 0.72–0.75 metres. In building A, of long-house form, Hearths H_1 and H_2 are delimited by vertically set stones, four for hearth 1, two for hearth 2. The western hearth, H_2, is simpler and bounded by five blocks of granite. This building is securely dated by two coins of Conan III to the mid-twelfth century. Buildings B and C also have central hearths, that of B, 0.80 metres in

diameter, with a pyramidal stone placed in the centre, perhaps intended to support the *marmite* or cooking pot. The irregular depth of cinders seems to indicate that the hearth was not used all over, but that the fire lay off-centre, proportional to the heat needed. There is similarity of form between this hearth and that of building A. In the case of building C, the rectilinear hearth is bounded by four fine slabs of mica-schist embedded in the earth.

The second excavation, at Kerlano, Plumelec, Morbihan, unfortunately brought no evidence of the existence of hearths, but buildings A and C here are both oval in plan, have opposing doorways and are of long-

In figure: B, A, D, C, Areas of trial excavations, Accumulations of rubbish, 0 ... 5 metres, (After André 1974)

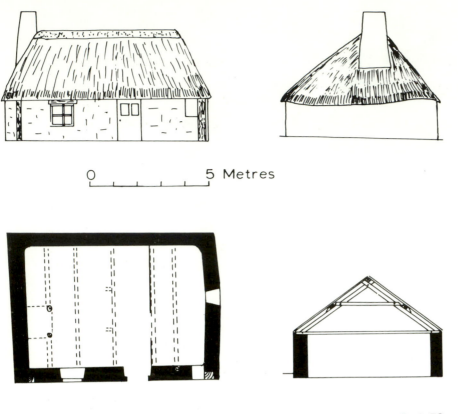

0   5 Metres

Not to
scale

G.I.M.-J.   16.10.76.

Fig. 72.   Botcol, Guénin, Morbihan

house form (Fig. 71). A link between these medieval structures and the modern period is provided by a sub-rectilinear structure at Bouleguy 2, Plumelin, Morbihan (Fig. 160). This farmyard building, or (Br.) *lokenn*, is of a type formerly very common all over Brittany, scarcely a farm being without one and used for the storage of implements, crops and animals. The example at Bouleguy, although built and still in use as a pigsty, is significant, not just as a survival of an archaic type, but because the tenant himself lived in a similar building as a child, and tells how there were formerly a hundred or so in the parish. These dwellings apparently differed from the pigsty only in that the whole structure was laid upon a low bank of earth to give better headroom and wall-space within. Heat was provided by a fire or an open hearth set in the middle of the floor, opposite the door, smoke escaping through a hole in the roof immediately above. There was no chimney or louvre, and smoke was 'guided' up to the hole by a tripod of chestnut poles upon which was suspended the cooking pot. The floor was of *terre battue* and furniture of the simplest kind. This structure at Bouleguy fits precisely the oval plans of Kerlano and Pen-er-Malo and it appears that this type of

house was current from the medieval period until World War I in the more conservative areas.[252]

Guilcher records the presence of the *huttes des sabotiers* in Plouvien, a type adapted to nomadism, '*une hutte de chaume et de fougère, sans cheminée (la fumée passe à travers le toit)*'.[253] Although no further details are given, the implication is that the type was formerly common, a view echoed by Le Braz who found the *sabotiers'* home warm, rather like a byre, with a fire burning in the middle of the room on a circular hearth of primitive masonry, rough stones and wetted clay, smoke escaping through a hole in the roof. Light from the fire also served to illuminate the windowless cabin.[254] Souvestre records the circular huts of forest workers in the Forêt du Gâvre, Loire-Atlantique, with what appear to be wattle chimneys raised over open hearths, one at least of which was centrally placed.[255] In the 1860s, a group of five or six roughly circular huts were recorded in Brandivy and Grand-Champ, Morbihan, each with a hole in the roof to allow smoke to escape. The hearths consisted of flat slabs of granite.[256] Vallaux also observes them (see Chapter 8).[257]

Dwellings with an open hearth are not peculiar to

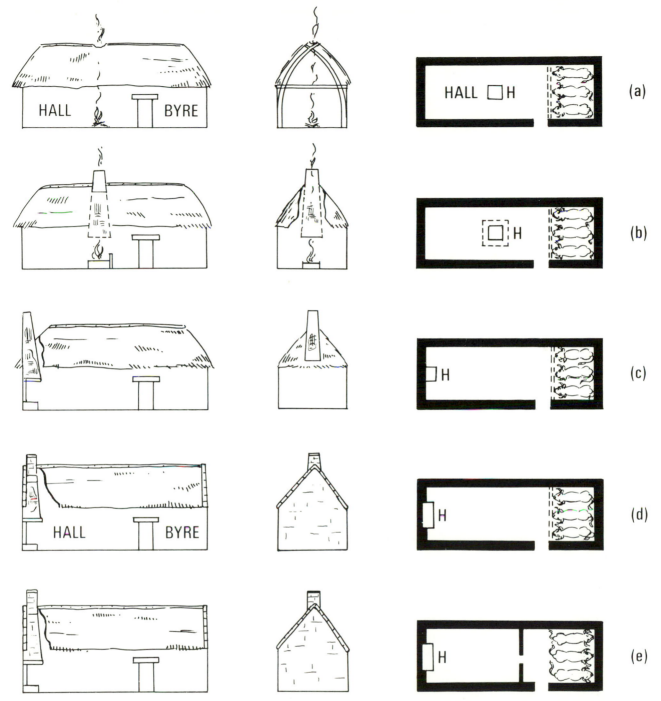

Fig. 73. The evolution of the hearth

temporary habitations, as is shown by examples recorded at the end of World War II.[258] These mark the transition stages from the true open hearth to the enclosed hearth. By chance, all three were recorded in the commune of Plumelin in which the Bouleguy example was found and which clearly lay in a conservative area. At Kerspec stood a stone-walled, high-roofed dwelling, partially cut into the slope. A solitary doorway led into a single-cell dwelling with central hearth. The roof was supported on two vertical posts placed at the ends of the ridge, the centre of which was supported on an inverted 'v' truss, the feet resting on either side of the hearth. The latter was

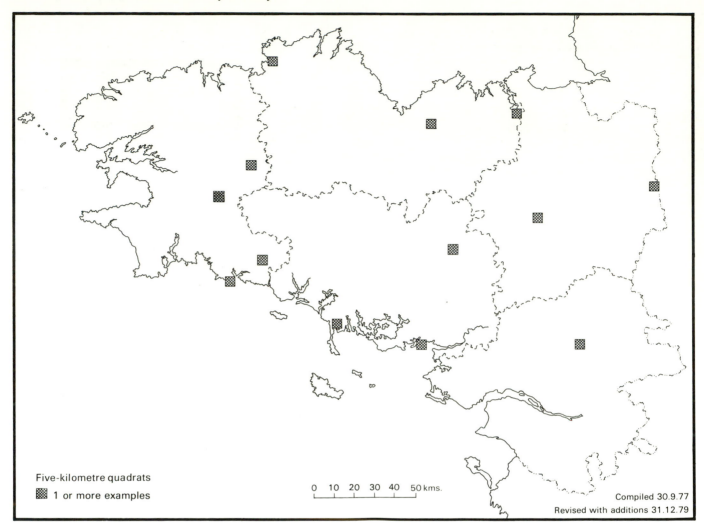

Fig. 74.   The distribution of the lateral chimney-stack

raised on a platform above the earthen floor and had a low stone wall as a fire-back. On either side of the hearth was a wooden bench. There was no window and no means of illumination other than the open door and the light of the fire, nor was there a hole in the roof for the smoke to escape; the interior must have been very smoky. The first of two houses in the nearby hamlet of Talforest was also a stone-and-clay structure partially set into the earth bank. In this long-house, a centrally placed hearth close to the only roof truss, slightly off-centre, was raised above the floor on a stone platform above which rose a hood and chimney of wattle and clay. Here is the hearth in its central position with the possible later addition of a flue. In the third example, the hearth has migrated to the gable end, is again built on a low stone platform and has a similar wattle and clay chimney cover.

The hearth is raised and a three-legged pot is shown standing on it. These examples, which are fully illustrated elsewhere, have no loft, the hall being open to the roof even when a chimney hood exists.[259] Here is further evidence for the former existence of the open hall.

Guilcher notes that at Plouvien, Finistère, the traditional house is a low building without a loft: '*Il y a seulement parfois une sorte de plafond de planches sur la pièce unique; plus souvent, ce plafond n'existe que près de la cheminée.*'[260] This half-loft is an intermediate stage between a fully open hall and one with a *grenier* or other rooms above. A further example at Botcol, recently examined, also shows the hearth located against the gable wall of a hipped roof house (Fig. 72). The hearth-back is not recessed into the gable wall, the hearth stone simply built against it and a chimney of wickerwork and clay, rectangular in cross-section, supported on a wooded breastsummer and corbels. This must surely represent a transitional stage between the hearth independent of the wall structure, and a hearth fully integrated with the wall. A further intermediate stage is illustrated by the curved hearth-backs, examples of which may be seen in the excavation at Le Coudray[261] and the *guérite* at Le Verger near Cancale. The full evolutionary sequence is thus represented from the simple open centrally placed hearth in a circular building with a hole in the roof, to an oval building with low walls and simple stone hearths, over which chimney hoods were built, sometimes at a later date, to rectangular buildings with stone walls and hipped roofs with contemporary wattle and daub chimneys. The final stage occurs when hipped roofs have given way to gable types and the wattle-and-clay of the chimney hoods has been replaced by stone. A more detailed outline of this sequence has been published elsewhere and is summarized in Fig. 73.[262]

Dating these buildings, and their hearths, is very difficult. One of the excavated buildings is firmly dated to the twelfth century. Some of the examples cited are of nineteenth- and twentieth-century date. It is thus clear that the open hearth survived in Brittany until the twentieth century, the last example disappearing in the late 1940s. The open hall [263] certainly went out of fashion earlier on the Continent than in the British Isles, perhaps a hundred years earlier in France generally, but in Brittany old ways die hard. It is difficult to say when the chimney first came to replace the open hearth in buildings of the social level of the well-to-do peasantry and the minor gentry, still less at the lower social levels. Medieval houses with stone-built chimneys are known. In the greater houses and castles, chimneys were known at a very early date, well before the end of the Middle Ages. As the earliest surviving dated peasant houses belong to the end of the sixteenth century, and as these have fully developed stone chimneys, it is probable, but not yet proven, that the introduction of the chimney-stack began not later than the latter part of the sixteenth century. It seems that the new fashion was slow to make progress and that the poorer people, including the forest workers, continued to live in buildings with open hearths for a very long time afterwards, in the more remote and conservative areas, and in increasingly small numbers as time went by. The transition seems to have lasted for a period of at least four to five hundred years.

The hearth having remained open and centrally placed, probably for several thousand years, has come to the gable end, a place it has now occupied almost without exception, for only a few lateral hearths have so far been encountered (Fig. 74). In the vast majority of Breton houses, one- and two-roomed structures, the hearth lies at the gable end. Never does it abut the cross-passage, which is rarely defined in stone in the peasant house.

The other architectural change which was to follow the migration of the hearth to the gable wall is the building of a full gable in stone, or cob, and the complete disappearance of the hipped roof, except for one locality where, for special reasons, it has remained. Mériadec-en-Plumergat has hearths in the gables and is formed of two separate dwellings with no internal communication, a long-house and a single-cell dwelling. The chimney-piece is typical (Fig. 185). The hood is of stone rubble plastered with earth and rests on a wood frame corbelled out, wood corbels over stone. There are no keeping places in the chimney-back, but one lies immediately to the right. A date, 1689, and a phallic symbol appear on the door lintel. At Kervaly 1, 2 (Fig. 178) the chimney-piece is identical in construction to that of Mériadec. The fire is set on a raised stone platform, the hood of stone rubble is supported on a wood frame and corbelled out. Invariably the ends of the wood or stone corbels project outside and are an infallible guide as to whether a hearth exists. The three chimney-stacks are misleading, as one is false. A superstitious practice of providing a chimney for the cattle is reported from both Finistère and Morbihan and may be related to the fact that with the abandonment of the central hearth, and the building of a partition separating hall and byre, the practice of building a stack had something to do with the need to provide a 'hearth' for the cattle. That the resulting effect was to give some symmetry to the building may have helped to sustain it. This hearth is provided with keeping-places. Vieux Coët Sal is a gentry long-house of extraordinary quality (Fig. 189). The stone chimney-piece is identical in construction to the wooden ones, but of a superior construction appropriate to the status of its former occupants. Other examples at Kervaly 12, 13, 14 (Fig. 184) and Kervaly 7, 8 (Fig. 181) illustrate the same principles of construction. The wooden chimney-corbels protrude on the outside of the gable.

Chimney-pieces vary in size, shape and quality, in the number of keeping-places and in materials, but the principle of construction is the same throughout Brittany, as Figs. 75, 76, 228, 232–235 and 237 show. Some chimney-pieces are wholly built of stone whilst others have hoods of stone rubble resting on wooden frames supported on either wood or stone corbels. Keeping-places vary in number and position and are often completely absent. In some areas a ledge at the back of the hearth replaces them (Fig. 76). A hole for cinders is sometimes provided (Figs. 49, 75, 76). Where stone of sufficient length or mechanical strength cannot be

Fig. 75. Le Pré Rondel, Taupont, Morbihan
Some chimney-pieces are wholly of stone, others have hoods of stone rubble resting on wooden frames supported on either wood or stone corbels. Note the three keeping-places in the chimney-back.

obtained, a wooden breastsummer is used even in houses of the highest quality (Fig. 217). In poor houses, the quality of the wood may be very low indeed (Fig. 75). In some areas, notably the Rennes basin and south of the Loire, thin bricks are found in the construction of the fire-back, and also in the chimney. Keeping-places are usually built into the walls as well as into the hearth-backs (Fig. 235) and used for storing salt and other items.

Except for a handful of primitive survivals in limited areas, all the vernacular houses have firehoods and chimney-stacks of stone, usually rubble, laid with a mortar of *pisé* and supported on a frame of either wood or stone. Exceptionally, in the finer houses, the hood will be of ashlar, perhaps with a shield-of-arms on the breastsummer as at Kerrio (Fig. 211). Ashlar is used more frequently for that part of the stack visible outside (Figs. 49 and 50), and is sometimes given a moulded stone capping. In a few nineteenth-century houses in Ille-et-Vilaine and Côtes-du-Nord, stacks of red brick have been observed, notably in areas of *torchis* walling (Figs. 136–138, 140) but in Loire-Atlantique they have a longer history, particularly south of the Loire where the characteristic thin bricks are used decoratively (Fig. 58). At Kerat, Larmor-Baden, Morbihan, and La Salle, Plurien (Fig. 217), both probably of late-medieval date, the rubble-stone stacks are of circular cross-section above the roof line, and similar chimney-stacks of circular cross-section occur in the Saint-Malo region.

Several wattle and *torchis* hoods and chimney-stacks have been found, at Botcol, in Guénin (Fig. 72), and others once existed here and in other parts of Morbihan.[264] A recent discovery, not shown on Fig. 77, is a *loge* built of *torchis* at La Broussette, Maxent, Ille-et-Vilaine. An example with wooden planks nailed to the frame was recorded at Plounévez-Quintin[265] and it is probable that many *torchis* chimney-hoods still exist in the Grande Brière. On the Île Fédrun, lumps of *torchis* were hung on spars laid horizontally across the wooden

Fig. 76. Folhaie 8, Guérande, Loire-Atlantique
In this massive granite chimney-piece, a ledge serves as a keeping-place and the hole at the base is where ashes are kept 'live' during the night.

frame.[266] In all these examples, the inner and outer surfaces are given a rendering of *pisé* and many of the stone-rubble examples are similarly finished. The distribution of the wood-frame chimneys shows them to be confined to the culturally conservative areas of Morbihan and the Grande Brière (Fig. 77).

The impression conveyed by writers and travellers, that window openings were traditionally small and few, and sometimes totally absent, is supported by recent field observation. Cambry describes the solitary window as letting in only a ray of light,[267] and Bachelot de la Pylaie, also writing of Finistère, observed '*La petite fenêtre qui éclaire la table à manger et le foyer en même temps n'a point de vitres, et ne se trouve fermée, la nuit, qu'au moyen d'un simple volet; de sorte que les courants d'air qui entrent en jour par la porte qu'on laisse toujours ouverte pour éclairer le fond de l'appartement, ainsi que par cette fenêtre, rendent l'intérieur de la maison aussi froid que le dehors; il en résulte qu'il n'y a d'autre*

différence entre le feu d'un bivac et celui des maisons de nos paysans, que parce qu'on est ici à l'abri de la pluie . . .'.[268] At Kerveden du Fret, the picture is one of even less comfort where '*les maisons chétives . . . n'ont que des espèces de trous non vitrés pour fenêtres. C'est encore ici la continuation des XIVe et XVe siècles . . . .*'.[269] Souvestre found that houses in Finistère were '*d'une seule pièce*' with '*une très-étroite croisée fermée par un volet de bois au milieu duquel apparaissant deux petits carreaux semblables à deux yeux, donne, concourremment avec la porte qui est toujours ouverte, tout ce que l'on trouve de jour et d'air à l'intérieur*'.[270] Le Bail regarded '*l'exiguïté des ouvertures*' to be one of the chief features of the traditional farmhouses of Basse-Bretagne.[271] Sée is undoubtedly correct in his view that during the two centuries before the Revolution dwellings had but one room lighted only '*par de petites fenêtres, sans vitres*'.[272] Dupuy, writing of eighteenth-century Basse-Bretagne, thought that '*les chaumières n'ont pas*

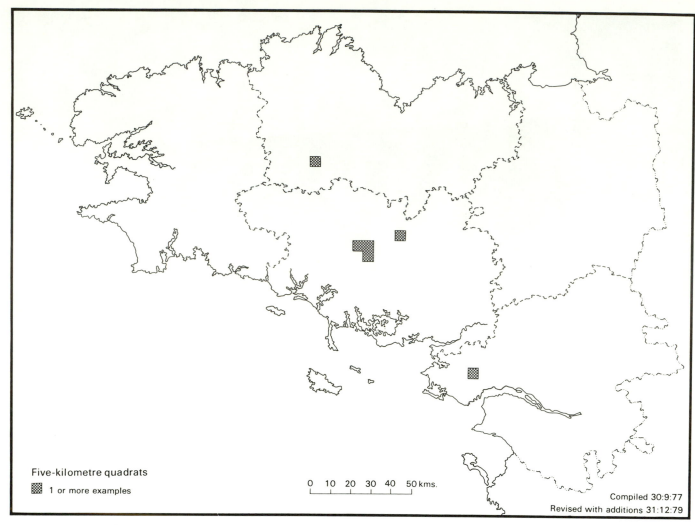

Fig. 77.   The distribution of wood-framed chimney-stacks

de fenêtres; elles n'ont d'autre ouverture que la porte,[273] but, as a generalization, this is too sweeping, for archaeological evidence shows that a large number of houses did have windows from the sixteenth century onwards. Nevertheless many were certainly without them and occasionally one may still find a windowless cottage in the countryside, abandoned in its original state. Even as late as 1946, an inhabited dwelling at Kerspec, Plumelin, had no windows,[274] and numerous houses in the Grande Brière lacked them, on the Île de Fédrun, the Île de Pandille and in Mayun.[275]

It thus appears that whilst some houses formerly had no windows, the majority possessed only one small, often very small, opening lighting a single-cell dwelling (Figs. 178–184, 82, 87, 90, 92–95). Until a relatively late date, window openings were unglazed, and in some areas these survive (Figs. 194, 195). It seems certain

from the evidence at Laz and Saint-Rivoal and other field evidence that houses with unglazed windows continued to be inhabited until well into the twentieth century. Whilst the smallest of the openings appear to have been closed by a simple shutter, others, as at Saint-Rivoal, had plain wood mullions and transoms and were closed by two or four shutters (Fig. 195). Many of the larger houses formerly had iron *grilles* over the windows, and some of these remain, usually at the higher social level (Fig. 52). Field evidence has so far failed to produce a single example of a glazed window-frame convincingly earlier than the nineteenth century, and, furthermore, many houses, now glazed on the ground floor, have the original shutters at first-floor level or in the loft. This evidence strongly suggests that, although precise dates are not yet available, the glazing of windows began to be fashionable in rural areas during the nineteenth century,

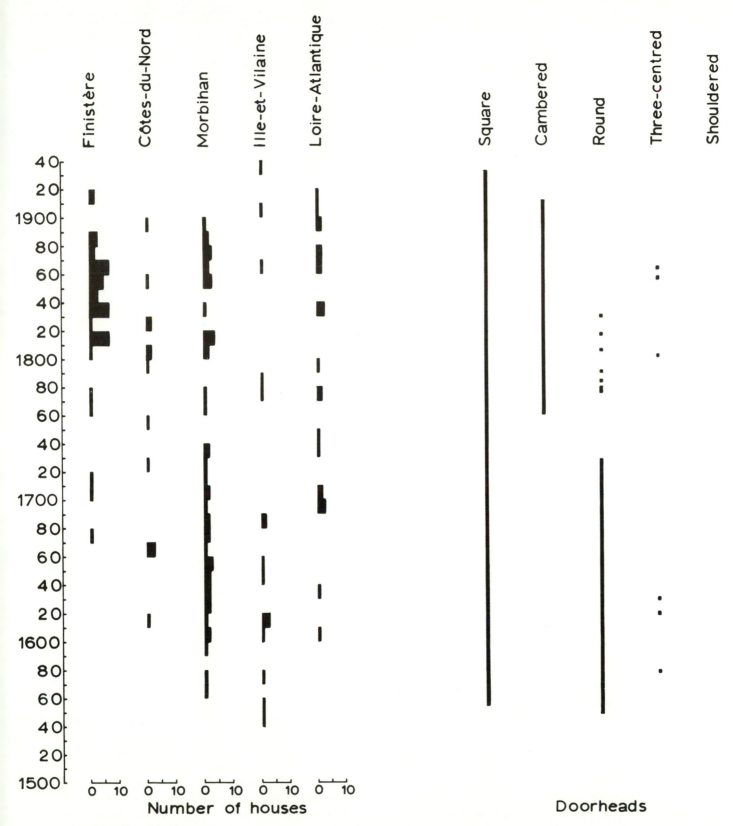

Fig. 78. Dated houses

and that unglazed houses survived into the twentieth century. As in other matters, the west was almost certainly later in adopting glass windows than the east. The need to enlarge windows was repeatedly urged by the Comités d'Hygiène during the mid-nineteenth century. At Rostrenen in 1852 the houses were said to lack air, having only one small window rarely opened. The door was always open during the day, being a means of lighting and airing the house. At Saint-Nicholas-du-Pélem, windows were only 0.40–0.50 metres wide. At Loudéac, shortage of air was especially commented upon, such as there was '*introduit par une seule porte et par une énorme cheminée, grâce à laquelle les habitants ne sont pas asphixiés pendant la nuit*'. It is also clear that not all houses had glazed windows, and among improvements commonly called for by the Comités is the need to glaze windows and enlarge openings to provide more air.[276]

Only rarely does a room have more than one window. In Cap-Sizun (Quadrat 8) all the houses have a small opening to light the working area round the hearth (Fig. 87), but this is a regional characteristic in Cornouaille, and a function of interior arrangement (see Chapter 15). Generally over the whole Province the single-cell house has only one window, always on the south side, even when the doorway is in the northern wall. During the later-nineteenth and twentieth centuries, many of the traditional small windows were enlarged (Figs. 83, 88, 89), but large numbers of houses retain their original stone or wood framing. Stonework is frequently moulded, the flat-splay chamfer being the most common, but other and more elaborate mouldings are found (Figs. 177, 217). The majority of houses had only one doorway, although sometimes there was a second at the back. Doorways can be more elaborately treated, and as houses often bear a date, a rough chronological sequence is possible. Few doors of any age appear to survive and many were no doubt renewed. The older ones, usually harr-hung, are of planks pegged to battens, and a small opening, closed by a wooden shutter, is often found. In the simplest dwellings and those of woodland dwellers, the 'rush' door was known, an example surviving at Bouleguy (Fig. 160).

No attempt is made here to examine in depth the art-historical aspects of the Breton house. Mouldings and details have been recorded but these are yet insufficient in number for general conclusions to be possible. Tentative conclusions may be drawn, however, from the temporal variations of dated houses and of doorhead design. Not every house was necessarily built at the time indicated by an inscribed date, for the date may indicate an alteration, addition or modernization, the date of marriage, of the

taking of possession or some other event. Nevertheless, a careful subjective assessment suggests that some 142 houses taken from all over Brittany were probably built at the time shown by their date-stones, the error in making this assumption probably being very small. A clear pattern of buildings emerges from these dates, plotted by *département* (Fig. 78). Finistère has a large number of early and mid nineteenth-century houses, particularly in Cornouaille, and whilst many earlier buildings undoubtedly exist in Finistère, the overall impression is of a considerable rebuilding during the nineteenth century. Many of these dated houses were recorded in Cap-Sizun where the great majority of buildings are of late eighteenth- or nineteenth-century date. Here the houses are not necessarily newly built, and some can be shown archaeologically to be rebuilds of earlier long-houses. Cap-Sizun thus appears to have enjoyed a period of great prosperity in the nineteenth century. Even allowing for the weighting of the sample towards Cornouaille, the absence of earlier dated houses in Finistère tends to confirm the impression of travellers that it was a very poor *département* during early modern times. The dated houses of Côtes-du-Nord, Loire-Atlantique and Ille-et-Vilaine are more widely scattered in time. There is substantial evidence of building in the sixteenth and seventeenth centuries in Ille-et-Vilaine. The seventeenth, eighteenth and nineteenth centuries are all represented in Côtes-du-Nord, but as in all the *départements*, although building took place during the eighteenth century, it was a somewhat quieter period than either the preceding or subsequent centuries. There seems to have been considerable building activity, from the mid-sixteenth century to about 1730, in Morbihan, and then a lull until it recommenced about 1790 and lasted through the nineteenth century. The resurgence of building activity during the nineteenth century, most noticeable in Finistère, Morbihan and Loire-Atlantique, is in part a response to increasing prosperity and improved agriculture, but also to growing population and the large-scale colonization of the waste (see Chapter 3 and Fig. 23).

Doorheads classified by date also fall into periods (Fig. 78). The square-headed doorway appears at all periods. The earliest example, of 1554, is Beau Normandie 2, Paimpont (Quadrat 12, Fig. 219) with a wood lintel, and many of this type occur in areas where ashlar is not readily available. This category hides, however, the variations in the eighteenth- and nineteenth-century square-headed stone doorways whose form, both with and without chamfers, varies subtly. The cambered doorheads, usually formed with an undercut stone lintel, are confined to the period from 1760 to 1910. Of the

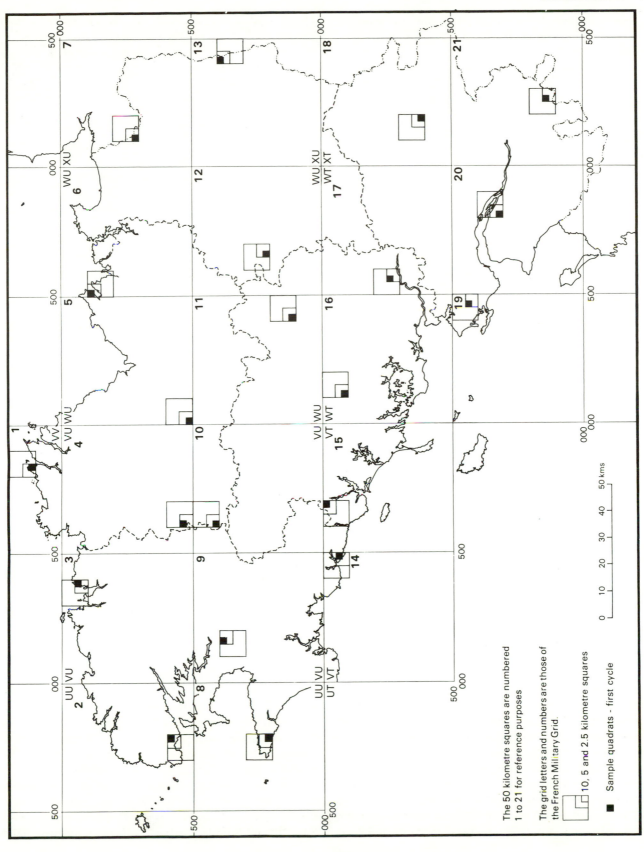

The 50 kilometre squares are numbered
1 to 21 for reference purposes

The grid letters and numbers are those of
the French Military Grid.

☐ 10, 5 and 2.5 kilometre squares

■ Sample quadrats - first cycle

Fig. 79. Sample quadrats: survey of lesser domestic buildings of Brittany, 1970-76.

Fig. 80.   Castel 6, Plougrescant, Côtes-du-Nord
A two-cell single-storey house built of *granit de Perros-Guirec.* Note the red-tile roofs, common along the north coast.

remaining three types, the three-centred doorway has a remarkably wide distribution from 1578 to 1863. The examples of 1578, 1619 and 1629 are probably genuine enough, but the possibility exists that those of 1801, 1856 and 1863 are later dates added to earlier buildings. Alternatively, they may represent the survival or revival of a type, in conservative areas. Only one shouldered doorhead, of 1694, was found. The round-headed arch, so common that it is popularly, but wrongly, regarded as 'typical', is a Renaissance feature and its span can safely be drawn from 1548 to 1738. The late eighteenth- and early nineteenth-century examples may, like the three-centred arch, be a survival or a revival, or they may be re-dated houses. Two of this group of seven are found in each of Côtes-du-Nord and Finistère. It would thus appear that this type entered Brittany through Morbihan, always a conservative area, where it survives in greatest numbers, to be diffused westwards and northwards. If this is correct, then this Renaissance feature probably entered Brittany from metropolitan France via the Loire valley. In a recent article, Mussat confirms these *traits* and gives a perceptive summary from an art-historian's point of view.[277]

The above conclusions accord to some degree with views expressed in the latest volume of the *Inventaire topographique.* In the cantons of Le Faouët and Gourin in west Morbihan, round and three-centred arches co-existed during the sixteenth and seventeenth centuries whilst the gothic arch disappeared from the houses of the upper social classes at the start of the seventeenth century, but remained a further half century on peasant houses. The round arch replaced the gothic arch at the start of the seventeenth century. In peasant houses, the three-centred arch continued to the end of the eighteenth century. The square-headed arch became fashionable from the beginning of the eighteenth century.[278]

The twenty-one sample squares illustrate a considerable variety of building construction, colour, texture and miscellaneous detail. Buildings in Quadrat 1 (Figs. 79 and 80), where there seems to have been much

Fig. 81. Locmaria 2, Locmaria-Plouzané, Finistère
A symmetrical two-cell, two-storey house.

rebuilding, are generally undistinguished with little obviously earlier than the nineteenth century, although some of the larger farms may be of eighteenth-century date. There are many small single-storey fishermen's cottages with outbuildings for storage, and the small farms are also usually of one storey, with byre attached. It is the larger houses that rise to two storeys. Walling, of the *granit de Perros-Guirec,* varies in colour from pink to black, and whilst red-tile roofs are common, most roofing is of slate. Many houses have stone or wood cornices and a small square window to light the working space by the hearth, as in Cap Sizun. Of the twenty-nine houses recorded, twenty-two are of one storey, the remainder of two storeys, forty-five per cent of one cell, fifty-two per cent of two cells, and only one long-house (Figs. 101 and 102).

A considerable nineteenth-century rebuilding is also evident in Quadrat 2 (Figs. 79 and 81), where many of the two-cell dwellings are probably rebuilt long-houses. As in Cap Sizun, the upper rooms appear to have been in use as bedrooms, rather than for storage, at least since the end of the nineteenth century. Although red tile is quite common, roof covering is mostly of slate. Walling is of micaschist and granite, the latter being used for dressings. Of the eighteen houses recorded, sixteen are of two storeys, and two of one storey, eighty-nine per cent are two-cell dwellings, the remainder of one cell (Figs. 101 and 102).

A rich and interesting variety of houses is evident in Quadrat 3. Walling is everywhere of *granit rose* and all the roofs are of slate, some of a chunky local variety. Whilst thirty-nine of the forty-eight houses recorded are of one storey, seven are of two storeys and two of one-and-a-half storeys. Single-cell dwellings form twenty-nine per cent of the total, two-cell dwellings forty per cent, and twenty-one per cent are long-houses (Figs. 101 and 102). Trovern 1, 2 (Fig. 82) are excellent examples of the tiny one-cell single-storey houses of the district of early eighteenth-century date.

Quadrat 4 lies on Carboniferous deposits and walling is

Fig. 82.   Trovern 1, 2, Plougasnou, Finistère
'. . . excellent examples of the tiny one-cell single-storey houses of the district of early eighteenth-century date'.

entirely of schist with little ashlar in evidence. Of the fifty-seven houses, fifty are of one storey, one of one-and-a-half storeys and six of two storeys. Single-cell dwellings form twenty-eight per cent of the total, two-cell dwellings fifty-one per cent and twenty-eight per cent are proven long-houses (Figs. 101 and 102). Most of the two-cell houses are probably converted long-houses, as at Quinquis Simon (Fig. 83) where only the upper cell is heated and the large window openings are recent enlargements.

Of the forty-one houses recorded in Quadrat 5, twenty-four are of one storey, fourteen of one-and-a-half storeys and only three of two storeys. Single-cell dwellings constitute thirty-nine per cent of the sample, two-cell dwellings twenty-nine per cent, and thirty-two per cent are long-houses (Figs. 101 and 102). Most of the walling material is schist with dressings of sandstone. Clevry 7 is a good example of the one-cell, single-storey dwelling, typical of the area (Fig. 84). The schist walling is well-laid, the quoins are roughly squared, and the

doorway and window dressings severe. This area also has many 'modern' two-cell houses with unheated second cells, probably converted long-houses.

In Quadrat 6, thirty-one of the thirty-three houses recorded are of one-and-a-half storeys, and one each of two, and two-and-a-half storeys. One-cell dwellings constitute eighteen per cent of the total, two-cell dwellings thirty-six per cent, and forty-five per cent are long-houses, mostly of the derived type with separate entrances to the byre (Figs. 101 and 102). Walling is mostly of schist with sandstone dressings and roofing of slate. Characteristic features are the very wide chimney stacks and the hipped dormers with undercut wood lintels (Fig. 85).

The juxtaposition of granite and Brioverian schist provides the building materials in Quadrat 7, the dark schist walls contrasting sharply with the lighter-coloured dressings. Notable are the double-arched polylithic door-ways characteristic of the Saint-Malo region, and the curiously 'staggered' quoins. Of the seventy-one houses

Fig. 83. Quinquis Simon, 2, Carnoët, Côtes-du-Nord
A single-storey two-cell house with one heated room. This was probably originally a long-house, the present unheated second cell having been converted from a byre. The windows are modern enlargements.

recorded, five are of one storey, thirty-seven of one-and-a-half storeys and twenty-nine of two storeys. Single-cell dwellings form twenty-seven per cent of the sample, two-cell dwellings seven per cent, and sixty-five per cent are of the long-house family (Figs. 101 and 102). The roofs are mostly slate-covered, although a few thatched houses survive. Le Vieil Atelier 1 (Fig. 86) illustrates the regional type, the big round-arched doorway giving access to the hall, the square-headed doorway to the byre.

Walling in Quadrat 8 is entirely of granulite with a high proportion of ashlar. Many houses were rebuilt in the nineteenth century in a rather severe style, some of them on the ground plans of former long-houses, and often incorporating earlier walling, doorways and window openings in the rear walls and occasionally in the gables too. Of the fifty-four houses recorded, twenty-three are of one storey, six of one-and-a-half storeys and twenty-five of two storeys. Single-cell houses form nine per cent of the total, two-cell houses seventy-six per cent, and

thirteen per cent are of the long-house family (Figs. 101 and 102). Kermalero 3 is typical of the two-cell, two-storey house with rendered rubble walls and ashlar dressings, re-built in the nineteenth century on a former long-house ground plan. The small windows are placed to light the working space by the hearth (Fig. 87). Most of the one-cell, one-storey dwellings are associated with fishermen's homes, and the two-cell, two-storey buildings are farmhouses.

Quadrat 9 is thinly settled and poor in vernacular architecture. Nearly all the houses are built of schist with granite dressings and slate roofs. Buildings are characteristically small and undistinguished. Of the fourteen houses recorded, eight are of one storey, one of one-and-a-half storeys, four of two, and one of two-and-a-half storeys. Single-cell dwellings formed seven per cent of the total, two-cell dwellings eighty-six per cent, and seven per cent are long-houses (Figs. 101 and 102). Pennalé 2 (Fig. 88), a single-storey, two-cell house, is

Fig. 84.   Clevry 7, La Harmoye, Côtes-du-Nord
A one-cell single-storey dwelling, typical of the area. Note the well-laid schist walling, the roughly squared quoins and the severe doorway and window dressings.

typical of the area and probably represents a conversion of a former long-house, only one cell being heated.

Of the thirty-one dwellings recorded in Quadrat 10, twenty-one are of one storey, one of one-and-a-half storeys, and nine of two storeys. Single-cell dwellings constitute forty-two per cent of the total, two-cell dwellings twenty-nine per cent, and a further twenty-nine per cent are of the long-house family (Figs. 101 and 102). Walling is of Carboniferous schist, and slate-covered roofs are universal. Kernantal 2 (Fig. 89) is typical of the single-cell house, probably resulting, as in other areas, from the nineteenth- or twentieth-century conversion of a former long-house, the lower cell being unheated.

In Quadrat 11 (Fig. 90), 179 dwellings were recorded, fifteen of one-and-a-half storeys, 152 of two storeys and four of two-and-a-half storeys. Single-cell houses form forty-five per cent of the total, two-cell houses eighteen per cent, and thirty-seven per cent are of the long-house

family (Figs. 101 and 102). Significant in this area are both the low proportion of two-cell houses and the lofts a whole storey in height. Walling is of schist and sandstone, sombre in colour, with slate roofs and 'toothed' slate ridges. Lintels are all of wood and window openings small.

Of eighty-four houses recorded in Quadrat 12, three are of one storey, forty-four of one-and-a-half, thirty-six of two storeys, and one of two-and-a-half storeys. One-cell houses form thirty-five per cent of the total, two-cell houses fifteen per cent, and forty-eight per cent are of the long-house class (Figs. 101 and 102). Walling is characterized by large areas of *torchis* and by the use of purple Montfort schist and light-coloured Ordovician *grès armoricain* rubble to produce a polychrome effect. All the roofs are covered with slate. Frequently, the first metre or so of the wall is of stone, the rest of *torchis*. Front walls tend to contain more stone than rear walls, which are often almost entirely of *torchis*. Beau Normandie 9 (Fig.

Fig. 85. Le Tetre 7, Plévenon, Côtes-du-Nord
A two-cell, one-and-a-half storey long-house (first derivative) with separate entry to the byre. Characteristic features of the area are the very wide chimney-stacks, the hipped dormers and the undercut wood lintel.

91) is a typical long-house, first derivative (*see* Chapter 10), of two storeys with polychrome walling and large amounts of *torchis*. Lintels are of wood and the projecting sole-plates under the eaves are a common feature in the district.

Brioverian schists are used for the rubble walls in Quadrat 13, and roofs are everywhere of slate. In the absence of suitable stone for dressings, jambs are of schist and lintels of wood, usually undercut to give an arch. Roof pitch tends to be steep, and tiny hipped *lucarnes* are common. Of the fifty houses recorded, twenty-one are of one storey, twenty-one of one-and-a-half storeys, seven of two, and one of two-and-a-half storeys. Single-cell dwellings constitute twenty-two per cent of the total, two-cell dwellings ten per cent, and the long-house class sixty per cent (Figs. 101 and 102). Lanjuères 1 (Fig. 92) is a typical long-house, first derivative, with added outbuildings.

Granite rubble walling and dressings also of granite characterize Quadrat 14. Although there are now many slate roofs, much thatch survives. Of the forty-five houses recorded, forty are of one-and-a-half storeys, and five of two storeys. One-cell buildings form forty per cent of the total, two-cell buildings fifty-eight per cent (Figs. 101 and 102). Surprisingly, only two per cent are long-houses, but many of the two-cell houses are probably long-house conversions. The raised coping and off-set in the gable for the thatch is typical of the southern littoral (Fig. 93).

A total of thirty-two houses were recorded in Quadrat 15, three of one storey, twenty-five of one-and-a-half storeys, three of two, and one of two-and-a-half storeys. Single-cell dwellings form thirty-seven per cent of the total, two-cell dwellings fifty-six per cent, and six per cent are long-houses (Figs. 101 and 102). Once again, the high proportion of two-cell houses probably came about as the result of the conversion of the byres of long-houses to form second cells. Walling is of granite and gneiss, and thatch has almost disappeared from the area, having

Fig. 86.   Le Vieil Atelier 1, Sougéal, Ille-et-Vilaine
A two-storey long-house (first derivative). Note the double-arched multi-voussoir doorway, typical of the Saint-Malo region, and the curiously 'staggered' quoins.

been replaced with slate. Bremelin 7 (Fig. 94) is a rare example of a single-cell, gable-entry home.

Ouadrat 16 provides abundant examples of the granite rubble-walled dwellings, typically long-houses of one-and-a-half storeys with a rye-thatched roof so characteristic of southern Morbihan. Dressings are often of a very high quality. Of the thirty-five houses recorded, thirty-two are of one-and-a-half storeys, and three of two storeys. Single-cell dwellings form twenty-nine per cent of the total, two-cell dwellings eleven per cent, and fifty-seven per cent are of the long-house class (Figs. 101 and 102). The long-house and adjacent single-cell house at Lesunalec (Fig. 95), with internal communication, are excellent examples of the regional style.

Of the eighty-four dwellings recorded in Quadrat 17, two are of one storey, seventy-two of one-and-a-half storeys, nine of two, and one of two-and-a-half storeys. Single-cell houses form thirty-nine per cent of the total, two-cell houses twenty-one per cent, and thirty-seven per

cent belong to the long-house class (Figs. 101 and 102). This area shares the characteristics of the southern littoral, in that a high proportion of buildings are of one-and-a-half storeys, and many are long-houses, once thatched but now frequently slate-covered. Walls are of schist or granite rubble, with granite dressings. Ridges are usually finished in the traditional manner with 'toothed' slates (Fig. 96).

In Quadrat 18, twenty-nine dwellings were recorded, nineteen of one, eight of one-and-a-half, and two of two storeys. Single-cell dwellings form eighty-three per cent of the total, two-cell dwellings fourteen per cent, and three per cent are long-houses (Figs. 101 and 102). Walling is of Silurian schist and sandstone rubble, and roofing of slate. Much of the building in this district is too heavily altered to be worth examining, and some represents late nineteenth-century settlement on newly enclosed waste (Fig. 97).

Of the fifty-nine houses recorded in Quadrat 19, four

Fig. 87. Kermalero 3, Primelin, Finistère

'. . . typical of the two-cell two-storey house with rendered rubble walls, ashlar dressings, re-built in the nineteenth century on a former long-house ground plan. The small windows are placed to light the working space by the hearth'.

Fig. 88. Pennalé 2, Dinéault, Finistère

'. . . a single-storey, two-cell house, is typical of the area and probably represents a conversion of a former long-house, only one cell being heated'.

Fig. 89.   Kernantal 2, Plévin, Côtes-du-Nord
Typical of the single-storey, two-cell house, probably resulting from a nineteenth- or twentieth-century conversion of a former long-house, the lower cell being unheated. The large window openings are late in date.

are of one storey, forty-eight of one-and-a-half storeys, six of two, and one of two-and-a-half storeys. One-cell houses form thirty-six per cent of the total, two-cell houses fifteen per cent, and forty-seven per cent are long-houses (Figs. 101 and 102). This area shares the traditional one-and-a-half storey thatched long-house of southern Morbihan with granite-rubble walling, a type which continues into Loire-Atlantique as far south as the Loire. Some houses have the pigsty in a lateral outshot, a characteristic feature of the *pays de Guérande* and the Grande Brière (Fig. 98).

The regional house of Quadrat 20 is also built of granite-rubble walling, but the low-pitch roofs are covered with the half-cylindrical 'Roman' tiles. Chimney-stacks, and sometimes door and window dressings, are of thin red brick. Of the thirty-seven dwellings recorded, twenty-seven are of one storey, and ten of two storeys, forty-nine per cent are single-cell dwellings, nineteen per cent two-cell, and thirty-five per cent of the long-house

family, the latter all of 'long-house form' (Figs. 101 and 102). La Baulerie in Frossay (Fig. 99) is typical.

In Quadrat 21, twenty-five dwellings were recorded, three of one storey, and twenty-two of two storeys; eighty per cent are one-cell houses, and sixteen per cent two-cell (Figs. 101 and 102). The contrast of storeys compares sharply with Quadrat 20 and may be explained by the building of second storeys during the late-nineteenth and twentieth centuries. There were no two-storey houses in Frossay before 1945. Walls are of granite rubble, often rendered and whitewashed and the low-pitched roofs covered with 'Roman' tiles (Fig. 100).

The evidence of the sample quadrats finds support in the writings of several authors. Le Lannou recognizes the often sharp contrasts brought about by changing building materials: '*la ferme des pays granitiques, en beaux moëllons bleutés; la ferme des pays de schistes, en pierres plates grises dans les régions de schistes ardoisiers, rouges sur les schistes lie-de-vin qui, au Sud*

Fig. 90. La Ville Bonne 1, Taupont, Morbihan
'Significant in this area is the low proportion of two-cell houses and the lofts a whole storey in height. Walling is of schist and sandstone, sombre in colour, with slate roofs and "toothed" slate ridges. Lintels are all of wood and window openings small.' Note the exposed tie-beam ends.

du bassin de Rennes, constituent l'enveloppe du grès armoricain; la ferme de torchis du bassin de Rennes, où manque la pierre.[279] Houses are only rarely wholly built of the best locally available material. Even the greater rural buildings generally use dressed stone sparingly, confining it to the façade, and using rubble for the end and rear elevations. Much building is of poor quality, and walls exposed to the weather quickly deteriorate. Material is rarely sought from afar and walling is not infrequently of *torchis*, even when stone is available at a few metres depth, or in a quarry a few kilometres distant. In Le Lannou's view, *'le paysan breton n'est pas un bâtisseur, et jamais en Bretagne n'a prévalu, comme dans les pays méditerranéens, le souci de construire des demeures paysannes robustes et ornées . . . On pare ici au plus pressé, et la grande préoccupation est d'éviter les transports lourds'*. Other factors may explain the relative simplicity and uniformity of much peasant building. In

some areas, tenants were required to take materials from the landlord's own quarries and this may explain an unwillingness to expend more than absolutely necessary upon construction.[280] The poorest buildings were for long those in the areas of *'bail à convenant'* in which the tenant was not able to change the form, state or dimensions of his property, or reconstruct in dressed stone a wall built of rubble, or repair in slate a roof of thatch without consent. The owner often refused permission lest these improvements should make the *congéement* more costly.[281]

Roofing was once everywhere of thatch. As has already been explained, during the eighteenth century slate roofs became common in the towns, along the coast and on the islands. Only in the mid-nineteenth century, partly as a result of pressure by insurance companies, did slate begin to replace thatch in the countryside. Even in regions where houses have been slate-roofed for a

Fig. 91.   Beau Normandie 9, Paimpont, Ille-et-Vilaine
. . a typical long-house, first derivative, of two storeys with polychrome walling and large amounts of *torchis*. Lintels are of
'ood and projecting sole-plates under the eaves are a common feature in the district'.

Fig. 92.   Lanjuères 1, Saint-M'Hervé, Ille-et-Vilaine
Walling is of Brioverian schist and roofs everywhere are of slate. Lintels are of wood, undercut to form an arch. Roof-pitch
tends to be steep and tiny *lucarnes* are common. A long-house, first derivative, with later outbuildings.

Fig. 93. Kerliviou 1 Moëlan-sur-Mer, Finistère
A one-and-a-half store, single-cell house of granite rubble with some ashlar dressings. The raised coping and thatch are typica
the southern littoral.

century or more, thatch continued to be used on farm buildings until after World War II. Gautier confirms the variety of building material in interior Brittany and the essential *traits* demonstrated by evidence from the sample quadrats.[282] Le Lannou ascribes the spread of slate roofs to the period following the mid-nineteenth century and to the role of the Nantes–Brest canal and the railways in disseminating slate from the major local quarries as well as from those of Anjou, into the interior. A map of slate-roofed houses must once have closely reflected this transport net, except for those areas where local slate had previously been used within a small radius of some favourable quarry. If superficial details, rather than plan-type, be the criteria, then there is considerable variety of rural architecture in Brittany.

The great variety of superficial characteristics is also noted by J.-S. Gauthier.[283] Recognizing differences in walling and roofing material and also in size, colour and form, the variety in the size of door and window openings, and in the presence or absence of certain characteristic detail, he classifies the houses into '*le type Finistérien*' and '*le type Morbihannais*', regarded as the two fundamental types. Whilst this crude classification will not stand a moment's scientific examination, and hopelessly fails to recognize the importance of plan and evolution, it does recognize the remarkable superficial uniformity of appearance of buildings along the southern littoral, from Moëlan in Finistère to the *pays de Guérande*, brought out by the sample quadrats. It also recognizes the relative and contrasting severity of the greater slate-roofed houses of coastal Finistère. It totally disregards, however, the regional variations in Brittany at large, so clearly brought out by the sample quadrats. Vallaux also recognizes the close correlation between building material and geological outcrop in Basse-Bretagne and the fact that maximum use is made of local material, the better stone being confined to dressings except in the most expensive buildings. Only in a few

Fig. 94.   Bremelin 7, Pont-Scorff, Morbihan
'. . . a rare example of a single-cell gable-entry house'.

Fig. 95.   Lesunalec 1, 2, Grand-Champ, Morbihan
A long-house and a single-cell house, typically of one-and-a-half storeys with the rye-thatched roof, so characteristic of southern Morbihan.

Fig. 96. Les Bois, 1, 2, 3, Béganne, Morbihan
A preponderance of one-and-a-half storey long-houses, once thatched, but now frequently slate-covered. Walls are of schist or granite rubble with granite dressings. Note the finish to the ridge.

Fig. 97. Saint-Jean-Baptiste-des-Landes, Joué-sur-Erdre, Loire-Atlantique
A nineteenth-century farm on newly-enclosed *landes*. Two single-cell dwellings and outbuildings, dated 1896.

Fig. 98.   La Grande Poissevin 5, Guérande, Loire-Atlantique
This area shares the traditional one-and-a-half storey thatched long-house of southern Morbihan which continues through Loire-Atlantique as far as the Loire. Note the steep roof-pitch and the pigsty in the lateral outshot, a characteristic of the *pays de Guérande* and the Grand Brière.

Fig. 99.   La Baulerie, Frossay, Loire-Atlantique
A single-storey dwelling of long-house form, typical of the area south of the Loire. Note the granite-rubble walling, the 'Roman' tiles and red-brick chimney-stack.

Fig. 100. Beaulieu 1, 2, 3, Saint-Hilaire-de-Clisson, Loire-Atlantique
The two-storey houses contrast sharply with those of Frossay.

cases is there complete uniformity and buildings are entirely, or almost entirely, of dressed stone; '*c'est le cas des massifs granitiques du Huelgoat, de Quintin–Duault, de Guéméné–Pontivy et du Faouët; c'est aussi le cas des régions qui avoisinent les grandes veines granitiques exploitées de l'Ar-Mor, Perros, l'île Grande, l'Aber-Ildut, Kersanton*'.[284] In other regions such as the interior of the Lannionais and of Trégorrois–Goëllo, wood is used for lintels, as well as doorway and window surrounds. The older houses of Basse-Bretagne at the turn of the century had no upper storey, or if they had, it was low and hardly more than a loft. This was the general rule, except in Lannionais, Trégorrois and certain places on the coast where modernization had been accompanied by the building of an upper storey.[285] The evidence of the sample quadrats suggests that perhaps many of the two-storey houses in the western part of Brittany have thus been built upwards during the twentieth century. Two other surveys tend to confirm these observations. It was noted in 1939 that walling material in Côtes-du-Nord was still strongly correlated with geology, with much use of *torchis* in the Dinan–Loudéac–Saint-Méen triangle. Both here and in Finistère, walls were frequently lime-washed, but this seems essentially a coastal practice rarely encountered in the interior. Indeed, lime-washing seems to have become associated with the hygiene movement and it increased between the two World Wars and is reported from Loire-Atlantique after World War I along with other 'improvements'. In Finistère these improvements were sometimes accompanied by the building of a second storey and enlarging window openings.[286]

Both the evidence of the sample quadrats and the observations of other writers combine to confirm the considerable regional variation in walling and roofing material and architectural detail, as well as of colour, texture and form. The greatest area of relative uniformity is along the southern littoral from south-east Finistère to the Loire, but even within this belt there are considerable variations in form and materials. Elsewhere, size and

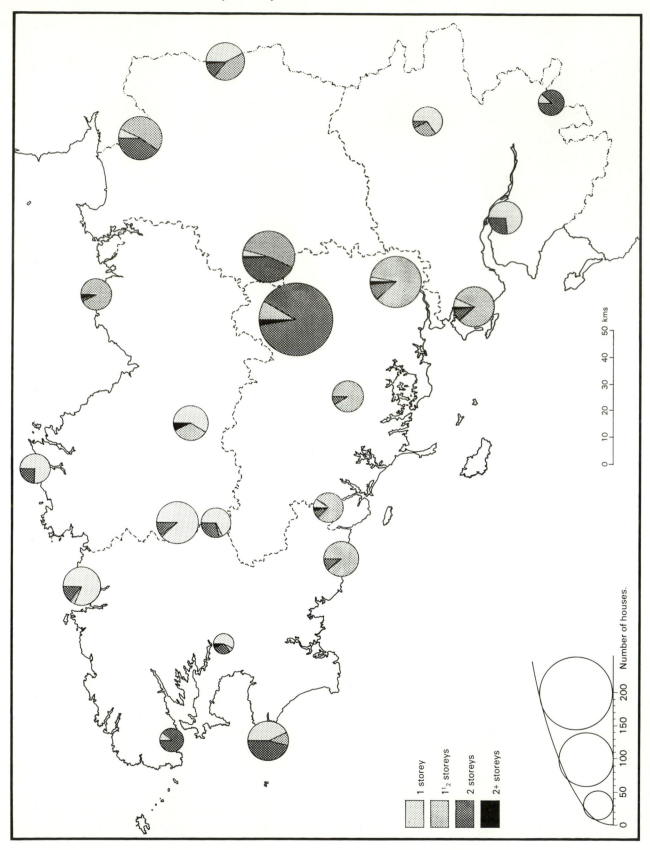

Fig. 101.   Houses: number of storeys

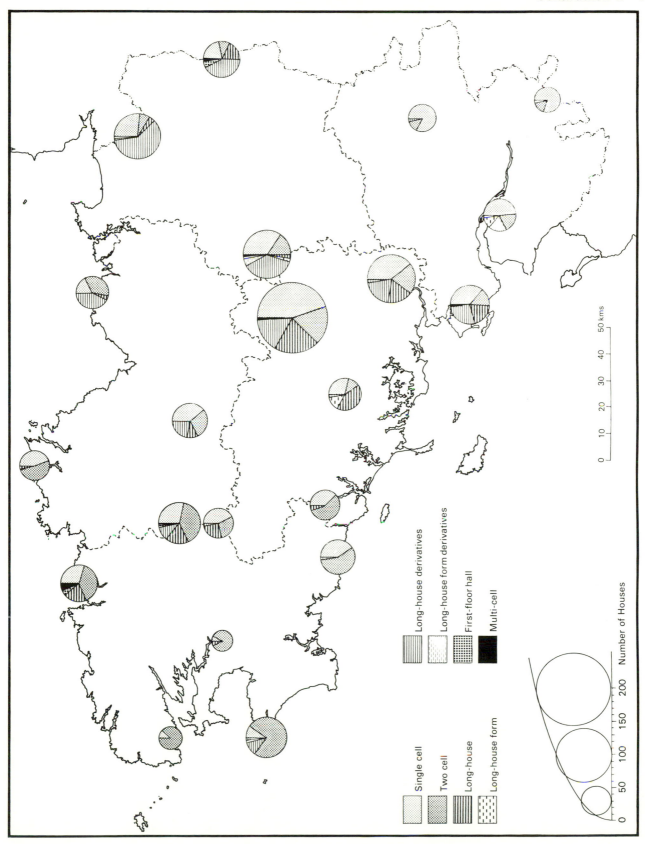

Fig. 102. Houses: plan-types

Single cell

Two cell

Long-house

Long-house form

Long-house derivatives

Long-house form derivatives

First-floor hall

Multi-cell

Number of Houses

0   50   100   150   200

0   10   20   30   40   50 kms

shape of buildings vary remarkably. The tiny huddled dwellings of the Crozon peninsula could hardly contrast more sharply with the large severe farmhouses of neighbouring Cap-Sizun, and both are totally different from the dwellings of interior Finistère. So too with Côtes-du-Nord, and whilst Ille-et-Vilaine probably provides the greatest regional contrasts, none could be sharper than the dichotomy between the unmistakably Breton rural dwellings north of the Loire, and those south of that river with their 'Roman' tile roofs and a hint of the south.

A truly 'Breton house' as a concept does not exist.

Nevertheless, the houses of Brittany, so difficult to characterize in words, engrave themselves so clearly upon the visual memory that they are instantly recognizable: they could never be mistaken for those of any other part of western Europe. It is to the combination of earth, stone, slate, wood and thatch that they owe this unmistakable character, notwithstanding wide regional variations, united by roof construction and plan. The latter, probably more than anything else, is responsible for giving the dwellings their peculiarly Breton character and it is to the consideration of plan that attention must now be turned.

SEVEN

CIRCULAR BUILDINGS

Circular building forms were widely distributed in western Europe from early times and in some areas are the earliest archaeologically known form of human habitation. Erixon has discussed at length the circular and sub-circular houses, the *capanna*, of the Roman Campagna, drawing attention to the similarity of construction to that employed in certain Palaeolithic huts in Finland.[287] Primitive circular structures without walls have survived all over Europe and were used until recent times as dwellings by charcoal burners and other woodland workers, or for the storage of tools and materials.[288] The technique of building circular huts in stone with dry-stone walling and corbelled roofs, or with roofs of timber and thatch, has been well established since prehistoric times. Welsh examples dating from the early Iron Age through to the Early Christian period are numerous and various sub-types have been recognized.[289] Circular pigsties survive in Wales, all but two or three having corbelled stone roofs. They are between three and four metres in height and of 1.50 metres to 2.00 metres diameter internally. Peate regards them as a survival of the type and technique found also in Ireland and Scotland and adapted to the accommodation of the pig, the one farm animal for which they are well suited.[290] A similar view is expressed by Evans in describing structures from the Gaeltacht where the buildings continue to be used, from Mayo to Kerry, for storing milk or turf.[291] In Lecale, County Down, large numbers of *clochans* demonstrate that an 'ancient tradition of corbelled building in stone has for centuries been kept alive through human poverty in an isolated peninsula where timber was always scarce'.[292] Henry observes that dry-stone huts are numerous in France, Spain, Portugal, southern Italy and the Balkans.[293] Many are still in use by shepherds, for storage, or as tool-sheds in the fields. Large numbers survive in France where they are usually built of limestone, with great concentrations in the Vaucluse. Their distribution extends across southern France, over the Massif Central into the south-west where they are well-known in the Causses, Périgord and

Quercy. Recent research has provided new insights into the construction and extent of dry-stone circular structures in France and has highlighted the considerable literature.[294] In parts of France there is still a memory of their being used as dwellings, and at Alberobello in southern Italy they are still extensively inhabited.[295] Walton has observed that in many areas once occupied by the Megalith builders, corbelled buildings have continued to be erected to the present day, providing examples from Africa and the Mediterranean lands: Sicily, Sardinia, Menorca and Mallorca.[296] With the survival into modern times of the circular hut, both with corbelled and other forms of roof, in the British Isles, in mainland France and around the Mediterranean, it is not surprising that circular buildings should have survived also in Brittany.

Information about early buildings necessarily depends on archaeological sources and, despite the considerable work achieved in the field of prehistoric archaeology in Brittany, evidence of dwellings and domestic arrangements is relatively slight. Perhaps the rarity of prehistoric habitation sites is to be explained by the generally unfavourable conditions, thin acid soil, absence of limestone caves, fluctuations of sea-level and the consequent erosion of the cliff-lines.[297] From the Neolithic period onwards, hill-forts and promontory-forts are found containing dwellings for a hundred to one hundred and fifty people,[298] but whether there was a considerable rural population beyond these major centres is unclear. A large number of Neolithic sites, usually strategically situated, is known, but few have been systematically excavated. Hut floors have been found around domestic hearths in various parts of the country. Dry-stone dwellings of late Neolithic date are reported on the island of Er Yoh near the Île d'Houat, Morbihan.[299] At Le Lizo, a late Neolithic site, located on a plateau overlooking the Crac'h river, an enclosure measuring 200 metres by 155 metres contained hut foundations of circular or sub-circular form with a hearth at the centre and associated ovens nearby.[300]

Fig. 103.   Barnenez, Plouézoc'h, Finistère
'The finest examples are to be found in the great Cairn de Barnenez where eleven parallel passage-graves, within one great long-barrow, each terminate in a corbelled cell entirely lined with dry-stone walling, the majority capped with a dry-stone corbelled roof,'

Belonging to a much later period, a Gaulish village near Pontivy, between Quelven and Kervan, has foundations, both round and rectangular, regularly grouped and surrounded by an enclosure.[301] The dwellings were slightly sunk into the earth and simply built of small stones, but what formerly lay above these low walls is unclear. Remains of clay found in the soil may be derived from the upper walls or from a clay roof covering. In the centre of each dwelling lay a hearth surrounded by large burnt stones as at Castel-Finans in the Sar valley, where the site proved to contain similar structures, some round, lightly sunk into the ground. These villages were originally thought to date either to the end of the Armorican Bronze Age or to the early Veneto-Gaulish period. The houses, built of small stones without mortar, had floors of a yellow beaten earth, the hearths

much reddened by fire with stones arranged as a tripod.[302] In the sand-dunes at Etel, near Kerhillio in Erdeven, two dwellings, within an extensive Veneto-Gallo-Roman settlement, had walls of different size stones mixed with clay resting on sand. The floors, circular in form and about 3.00 metres in diameter, were of *terre battue*. In the centre of each dwelling, flat stones, laid both horizontally and vertically, formed the hearths.[303] Many of the buildings, once thought to be prehistoric, are now believed to be medieval in date. The De la Grancière sites in Morbihan, for example, are mostly medieval. At many sites it is at present uncertain whether structures belong to the medieval period or whether they are earlier.[304] A recently excavated sub-circular structure, possibly belonging to the end of the Bronze Age, occurs at Brandivy.[305]

Circular building forms are not confined to dwelling sites. The great Megalithic monuments of the Neolithic period incorporate circular cellular structures. Three fine examples may be quoted: Er-mané in Quéric-la-Lande near Carnac, the cairn of Kerlévan in La Forêt-Fouesnant, and that on l'Île Carn in Ploudalmézeau. All are of the order of 2.50 to 3.00 metres diameter internally, and each has a corbelled roof. The finest examples are to be found in the great Cairn de Barnenez where eleven parallel passage-graves, within the one great long-barrow, each terminate in a corbelled cell entirely lined with dry-stone walling, the majority capped with a dry-stone roof (Fig. 103).[306] Circular grave forms, dating from the late Bronze Age to the early Iron Age, survive in Brittany. Covered with earth, and having an overall diameter of 10.00 to 12.00 metres and a height of from 1.00 to 2.00 metres, these cells are of dry-stone rising to *c*. 1.00 metres, and have an internal diameter of 5.00 to 6.00 metres. Walling is usually of schist. The great majority contain cremated remains and are located in Morbihan and south Finistère.

Other structures of circular or sub-circular form are to be found in the underground galleries, *souterrains*, found in considerable numbers and dating from the La Tène period of the Iron Age.[307] They are varied in form and although their original function is unknown, it is possible that they served for the storage of food, as cellars and grain-stores, or for other purposes. Occasionally they are provided with hearths and chimneys. Some are of only one cell, others of several, the cells being sub-rectilinear, oval or elliptical in form. Dimensions may reach 5.00 to 6.00 metres in length, 3.00 metres in width and 2.00 metres in height.[308] Although original and later functions cannot clearly be distinguished, these were probably complementary to those of the habitation sites invariably located in close relationship.

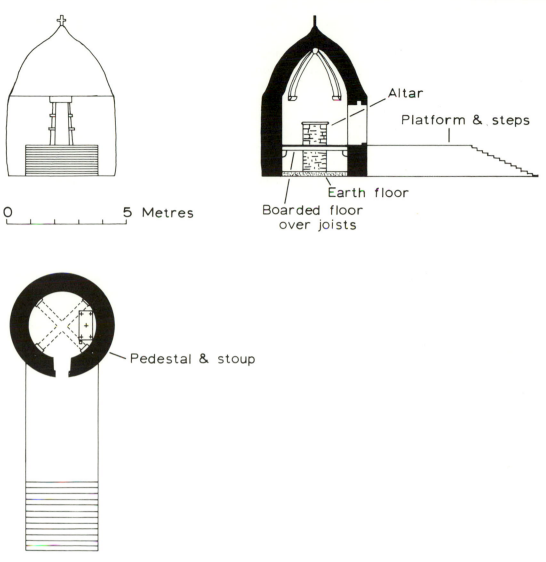

Altar

Platform & steps

Earth floor

Boarded floor
over joists

Pedestal & stoup

0   5 Metres

GIM-J   25.12.75.

Fig. 104.   Forn Modez, Île de Bréhat, Île Saint-Maudez, Côtes-du-Nord

Brittany thus had a strong tradition of circular and sub-circular building from Neolithic times at least, continuing through the Bronze Age into the Gallo-Roman period. Sufficient evidence is not yet available to indicate the proportion of circular domestic buildings compared with the rectilinear forms also well-known throughout these periods.

During the first part of the sixth century, Celtic missionaries from the British Isles established monastic settlements on the Bréhat archipelago, in the estuary of the river Trieux. St. Maudez, a follower of St. Tugdual, established his settlement on the island of that name, about one kilometre in length and *c.* 250 metres wide.

On the highest point of the Île Saint-Maudez stands the circular tower traditionally considered to have been St. Maudez' cell, much restored over the centuries (VV 990110). Known locally as 'Forn Modez', or St. Maudez' oven, the building is approached by a flight of stairs rising to a long stone platform and there is but a single entrance, a doorway of trapezoidal form (Fig. 104). Sloping jambs are often found in the oldest buildings in Ireland and Scotland and may afford evidence that in some forms of round house the walls were not upright but took the shape of a cone.[309] Walling is of grey granite rubble and the building is roofed by a stone vault of ogival form. The external diameter is 4.50 metres, internal

Fig. 105.   Le Bilou, Le Conquet, Finistère
'. . . the roof is corbelled in a manner similar to that at Barnenez'.

diameter 2.80 metres and walls *c.* 0.80 metres thick. The height from the ground to the top of the cross is 6.80 metres. Some details may be obscured by restoration at different periods, and the rendering on the walls and stone vault may mask evidence of openings. The vault, which may be corbelled, is supported by two pairs of ribs. Both date and history are disputed. The rendering also masks what evidence there may be for the former existence of a slit or window, disputed by several workers. Gaultier du Mottay says that a slit existed and Barbier quotes this as evidence, but as De la Borderie does not report its existence, Barbier takes the view that Gaultier is in error. It is likely that the rendering has been renewed from time to time and this may explain La Borderie's negative evidence. Grand appears to be quoting his own, but undated, observations when he draws attention to a blocked slit, 0.40 metres wide, and 0.50 metres high on the inside, narrowing to 0.35 by 0.15 metres on the outside. This information is too precise to be rejected, but as the exact location of the slit is not given, it is omitted from Fig. 104. The cross on the apex dates from the restoration of 1927.

Internally there are two levels, that of the chapel proper and that of a shallow crypt below, some 1.10 metres in depth. The main floor, which has now collapsed, was formerly of planks carried on joists supported at their ends by stone corbels projecting from the walls. The building has served as a chapel, and to the right of the door is an altar, of blue schist, rising from the earth floor of the crypt below. On its surface are five consecration crosses.[310] It seems likely, however, that the altar is of eleventh-century date or earlier, that the flat ribs supporting the vault are amongst the oldest in Brittany, and that the walls of the building date from the original sixth-century settlement, having been repaired in the second half of the twelfth century when the vaulting was added. This type of beehive hut is compared with the type of house commonly believed to have been inhabited by the Gauls and described by Strabo.[311] Some of the Gaulish huts shown on the Antonine column are round in form, with vertical walls and a dome-like roof. The circular form was used in later centuries for look-out posts on the Breton coastline, and examples survive like that at Le Bilou near Le Conquet (Fig. 105). It is difficult to know whether Forn Modez was always roofed in stone, for it may originally have been thatched with straw, dried seaweed or some other vegetation.[312] Some 3.00 metres east of the chapel are the remains of a second circular building with a total diameter of 7.40 metres, the walls of which stood over 0.50 metres high as late as the nineteenth century.[313] The existence of such a building suggests a grouping of cells known also to survive on the neighbouring Île Lavret and Île Verte.

Buildings on Île Verte are also thought to date from the fifth or sixth centuries, traces of fourteen circular cells having been found.[314] On Île Lavret, south-east of St. Budoc's church, itself on the site of a Gallo-Roman villa, are the remains of eight cells (Fig. 106). De la Borderie reported all to be circular, or nearly so, with lower courses built of large blocks of stone and internal diameters of *c.* 3.00 metres, occasionally approaching 5.00 metres. These he maps in a line, north-east to south-west, three huts nearly touching, others separated by distances of four, five or ten metres, the last two being forty metres apart. Crop marks betray the existence of still more huts beneath the turf. Excavations, as yet unpublished, during the summer of 1979, highlight the inadequacy of De la Borderie's map and observations and may lead to significantly different interpretations of this site. Associated pottery is of eleventh- and twelfth-century date, and although the cells may rightly be considered eremitic, they may date from a revival of eremetism during the eleventh and twelfth centuries. It is not impossible that the cells of St. Budoc's monastery were also on this site. Those now being excavated may

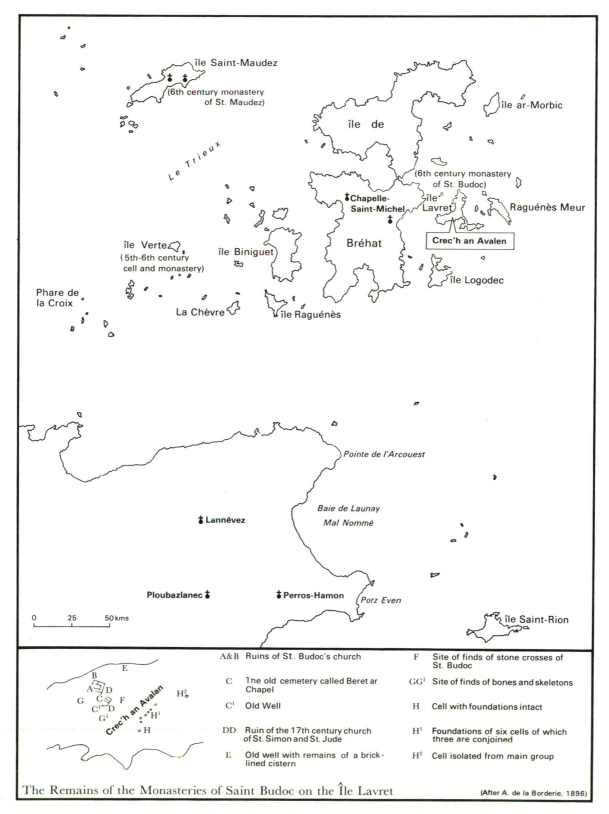

The Remains of the Monasteries of Saint Budoc on the Île Lavret

(After A. de la Borderie, 1896)

A&B Ruins of St. Budoc's church

C The old cemetery called Beret ar Chapel

C¹ Old Well

DD Ruin of the 17th century church of St. Simon and St. Jude

E Old well with remains of a brick-lined cistern

F Site of finds of stone crosses of St. Budoc

GG¹ Site of finds of bones and skeletons

H Cell with foundations intact

H¹ Foundations of six cells of which three are conjoined

H² Cell isolated from main group

Fig. 106. Monastic settlements on the islands at the mouth of the river Trieux, Côtes-du-Nord

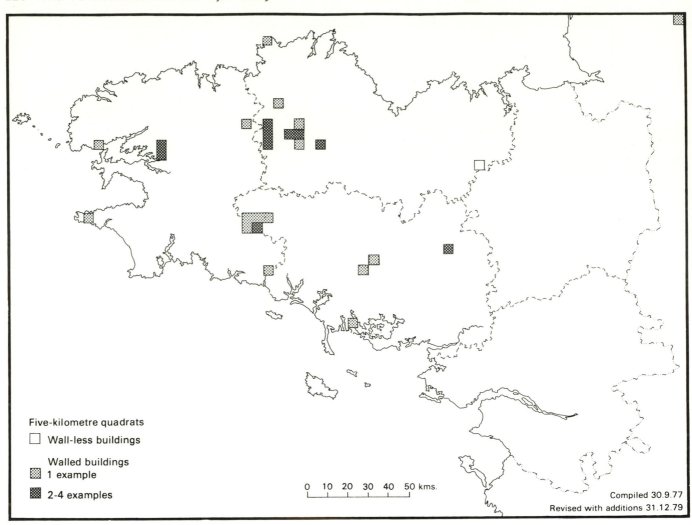

Fig. 107.   The distribution of some circular buildings in Brittany

date from the earlier period, later to be transformed or re-utilized. St. Budoc's cells, however, may equally have lain some distance away.[315]

Dating these buildings is difficult. The roof of 'Forn Modez' may belong to the twelfth century, the same period as the neighbouring rectilinear Romanesque chapel. The shallow bands of stone forming the ribs of the vault resemble those of the baptistry at Mélas, Drôme, attributed to the Carolingian or Merovingian period.[316] As in later periods, styles may have persisted here, on the western fringes of Europe and away from the main streams of cultural change, longer than elsewhere. The walling is much more difficult to date. Couffon claims it to be no older than the twelfth century, La Borderie and Grand attribute it to the sixth-century settlement, regarding the roof only as being twelfth century.[317] Barbier observes that the dimensions of these two cells

are comparable in every respect to those on Île Verte and Île Lavret, thought to have been built by the first monks, accepts the early date and suggests that the cell was then restored and converted into a chapel in the twelfth century.[318] In the absence of documentary or other archaeological evidence this seems a logical interpretation, for the restorers might well have thought this cell to be that of St. Maudez himself. Devailly and Riché express the view that the installation of hermitages is without doubt earlier than the arrival of the Bretons, as the Council of Vannes in 465 A.D. forbade monks to return to cells without the authority of their abbot.[319]

Evidence of Celtic monastic settlement is also to be found on the Île d'Indret at Basse-Indre. Here lie the remains of a monastery, destroyed by the Normans in 843 A.D., on a hillock overlooking the Loire. Twin circular cells are interpreted as dating from the foundation

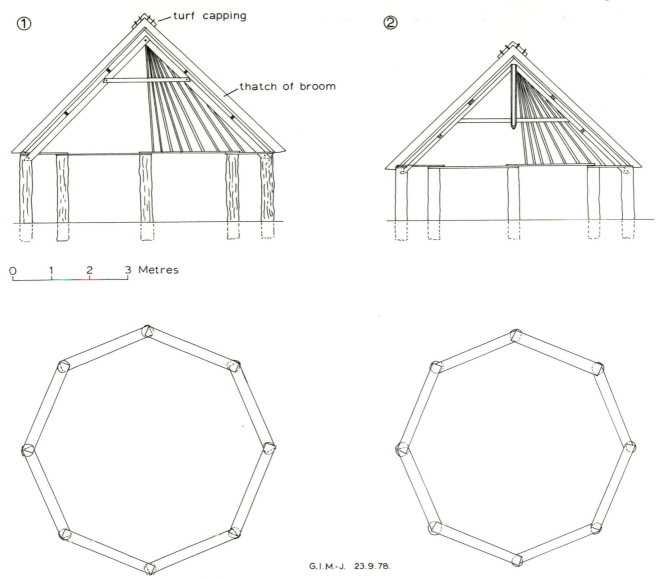

Fig. 108. Goas Henry, Carnoët, Côtes-du-Nord

by St. Hermeland in the seventh century and as deriving from a pair of beehive huts.[320] Circular huts of monastic origin are also reported on the Île d'Ouessant, the Île Tibidy and at Lampaul in Ploudalmézeau.[321]

A total of nearly fifty circular farm buildings has been recorded in Brittany. Oral evidence suggests that once they existed in large numbers, and in some regions there is evidence for there once having been one or more to each farm. The buildings at Île Saint-Maudez and Basse-Indre and the look-out huts or *guérites* at Le Bilou, Cancale, Perros-Guirec, and at a number of other sites along the north coast are essentially of the same type. Within Brittany, the distribution is essentially westerly, except for the wall-less structures in Caulnes (Fig. 107).

The principal concentrations are in the Callac region of western Côtes-du-Nord and around Le Faouët and Gourin in western Morbihan. In Hanvec, Finistère, four examples were discovered within a few hundred metres of each other. The remainder of the distribution clearly shows that circular farm buildings were once probably known over the whole of western Brittany. Further fieldwork will undoubtedly result in a filling-in of some of the gaps in the present distribution. Three circular pigsties without walls, in an advanced state of decay, and subsequently demolished, were recorded at La Haie in Caulnes, Côtes-du-Nord. The relative absence of circular buildings from the east need not surprise, for the distribution may highlight the survival of an ancient form

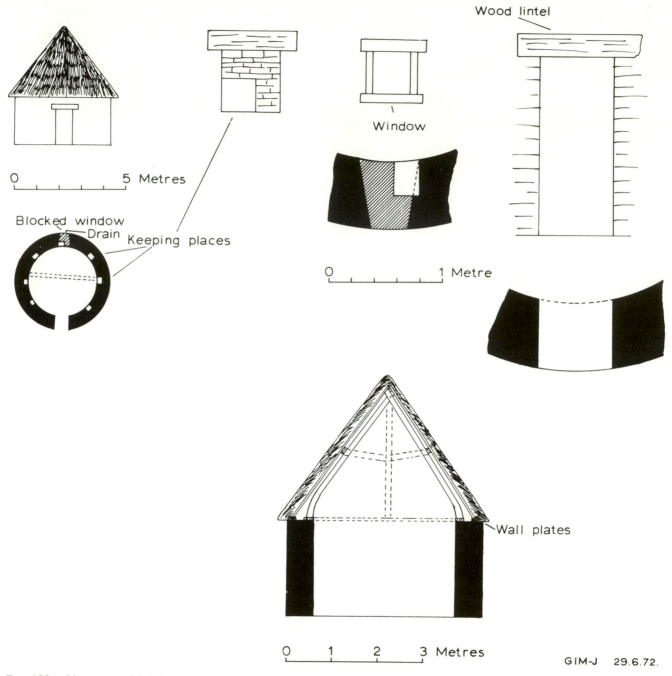

Fig. 109.   Moustoirac, Morbihan

in the more remote westerly areas, as the concentration near Callac suggests, although further intensive fieldwork may yet lead to discoveries further east. Two examples, at Ger, east of Mortain, southern Manche, and north-east of Vire, demonstrate conclusively that the form and tradition are known east of the Breton Marches. Only that near Vire appears on Fig. 107, in the extreme north-east corner of the map. A thatched circular pigsty at Ger has no principals, the common rafters, or poles, resting on its wall-heads as at Kerguestoc, below. It is surprising, however, that no examples have so far been observed in the Grande Brière or in eastern Morbihan, both areas where ancient customs are known to have survived. In Callac and the neighbouring *communes* there were large

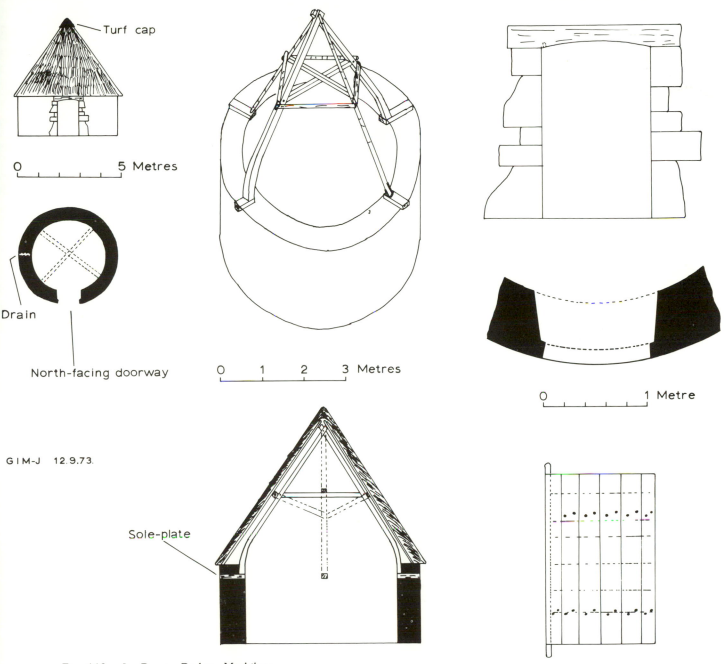

Turf cap

0   5 Metres

Drain

North-facing doorway

0   1   2   3 Metres

0   1 Metre

GIM-J 12.9.73.

Sole-plate

Fig. 110. Le Parun, Baden, Morbihan

numbers of circular pigsties until about twenty years ago, a few survive, and many a farmer will tell of the recent destruction of examples as farmyards are being modernized. Fournier leaves no doubt that the pigsty in Bulat-Pestivien frequently took a *'forme cylindrique, surmontée d'un toit de chaume conique'*. The *broyeur d'ajonc*, a building in which gorse was crushed for feedstuff, also often took a circular form in Bulat-Pestivien,[322] and what are believed to be the last two

surviving examples have been discovered at Goas-Henry in Carnoët (Fig. 108).

With the exception of the large hut at Saint-Urlo, and a building of similar size in Kernanvel, Hanvec, Finistère, the buildings are remarkably similar in size (Figs. 109-114). The two largest, at Moustoirac and Le Parun, have external diameters of 4.25 and 4.70 metres respectively. Those at Kerguestoc and Saint-Quidy are smaller with external diameters of 3.75 and 3.90 metres.

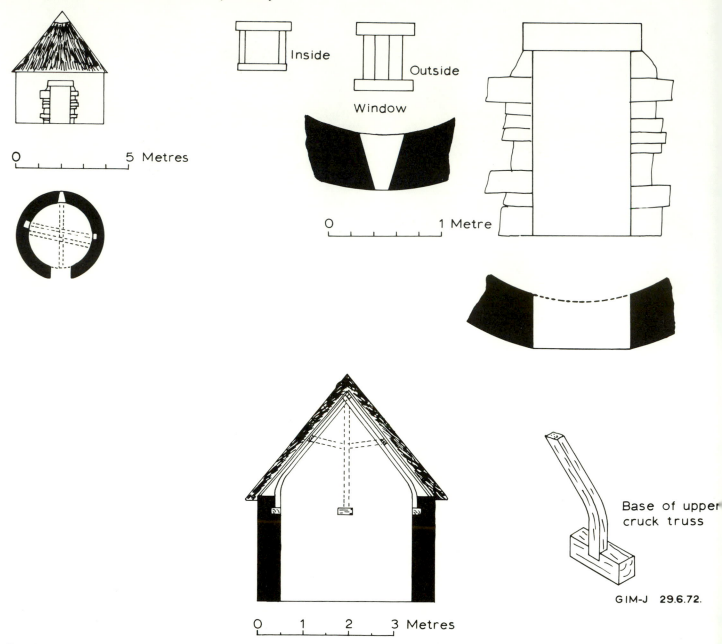

Fig. 111. Saint-Quidy: Penhoët, Plumelin, Morbihan

These compare with the external diameter of 4.35 metres at Forn Modez. Wall heights and total heights are more variable. Forn Modez has a total height of 6.80 metres and a wall height of 3.35 metres, at Kerguestoc these are 3.20 and 1.15 metres, at Le Parun 5.75 and 1.90 metres, at Saint-Quidy 5.10 and 2.35 metres, and at Moustoirac 5.30 and 2.05 metres. Saint-Urlo is of a totally different order and in some respects resembles Pen Coët Sal, below. With an external diameter of 9.95 metres, this building more nearly approaches the size of the circular Iron Age huts known from the British Isles, whilst the other buildings are more akin in size to the smaller cells associated with the monasticism of the Early Christian period.

Le Parun lies in the *commune* of Baden, Morbihan (WT 045734), and the building stands at the end of the farmyard close to the house and byre, its doorway facing north away from the prevailing wind. It is characterized by stone walls of buff-grey granite rubble laid in irregular but well-formed courses and bonded with a mortar of

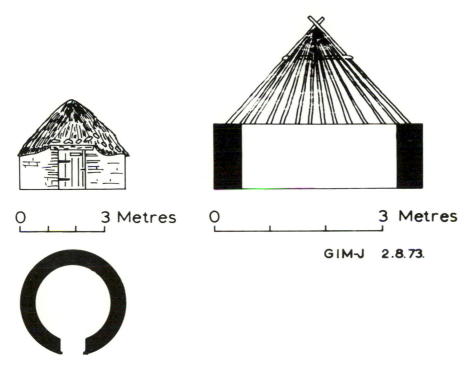

O   3 Metres   O   3 Metres

GIM-J   2.8.73.

Fig. 112.   Kerguestoc, Plouzané, Finistère

pisé. The roof is thatched with rye-straw and the apex capped with turf. The plan is slightly oval, long and short axes measuring externally 4.70 and 4.50 metres, internally 3.55 and 3.30 metres. Wall height is 1.90 metres and the total height from ground to apex 5.75 metres. The doorway is the only opening and the jambs are of roughly-dressed granite blocks and the lintel of wood, with an arched soffit. The door is made with wooden planks pegged to battens and harr-hung, holes for this purpose being provided in the floor and in the soffit of the lintel. Four sole-plates are let into the wall masonry some 0.50 metres below the wall-head and from these rise the two trusses which intersect at the apex. One truss is composed of a well-formed pair of upper-crucks and the other of straight rough chestnut poles, of a type greatly used in south Morbihan for rafters. The upper-cruck truss has a collar pegged and mortised whilst the second truss has a collar nailed to the principals. The two collars lie approximately at right angles to each other and do not intersect, the one passing over the other at the point of contact. The first truss is halved and pegged at the apex, and the chestnut poles of the second truss rest against it at this point. Four rough lateral purlins are fastened by nails to form a girdle around the two trusses, at a point some two-thirds of the way up. They serve to support the common rafters of chestnut poles which radiate from the apex to the wall-

head on which the feet of the rafters rest. There is no wall-plate. The common rafters are tied, at intervals of *c.* 0.60 metres, with straw rope and the thatch is then tied directly to the rafters. The apex is crowned with a cap of turf. A drain is provided and the floor, formerly of *terre battue*, is of concrete. It is impossible to give a date to the structure which could equally be several hundred years old or quite recent. It is well built, and from the presence of the drain it must be assumed that it was intended for the housing of animals. At present it serves as a pigsty and it is probable that it was always so used (Fig. 110).

The building at Moustoirac (WU 124005) is of similar construction to that at Le Parun, and has been demolished since it was recorded (Fig. 109). The diameter is 4.25 metres externally and 3.05 metres internally. Wall height is 2.05 metres and the height from ground to apex 5.30 metres. Walling is of granite rubble and the roof is thatched with rye-straw. Construction is very similar to that at Le Parun, but the building was in an advanced state of decay when recorded. Walls were overgrown with ivy and other vegetation and the roof in a poor state. The doorway was formed of granite rubble jambs and a plain wooden lintel, but the door was missing. There had been a small window at the back, framed in wood outside and with a wooden lintel inside, opposite the doorway, but it had been blocked. A drain lies immediately beneath and the floor is of *terre battue*.

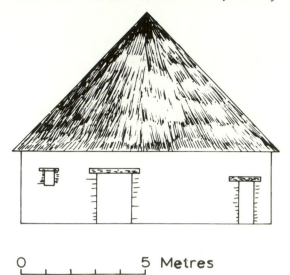

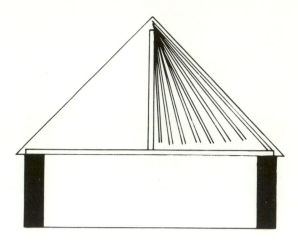

0 _____ 5 Metres

Reconstruction based on field evidence

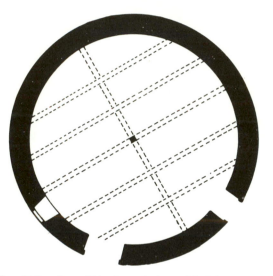

GIM-J 11.9.73.

Fig. 113.   Saint-Urlo, Lanvénégen, Morbihan

Seven keeping-places were arranged around the walls, an unusually high number for such a small building, one being provided in the blocked window opening. A simple tie-beam spanned the structure and there were two pairs of upper-cruck trusses. Unlike Le Parun, there were two circles of wall-plate on the inside and outside edges of the wall-head. The feet of the trusses rested on the inner plate, the rough chestnut poles forming the common rafters resting on or near the outer plate. Rafters radiated from the apex and were tied together with straw rope, at intervals, as at Le Parun. Thatch of rye-straw, once used throughout Morbihan, was tied directly to the rafters, and the apex was presumably once finished with a turf capping. When recorded, the building had fallen into

disuse, but from the presence of a drain it must be assumed that it was intended for animals and probably, like Le Parun, for pigs.

Saint-Quidy-Penhoët, Plumelin, Morbihan (WT 065998), within a few kilometres of Moustoirac, is also built of granite rubble bonded with a mortar of clay, but the dressings are of a higher quality. The roof is thatched with rye-straw. Internal and external diameters are 2.84 and 3.90 metres respectively. Wall height is 2.35 metres and the apex stands 5.10 metres above the ground. There is a small window for ventilation and the building was in use as a poultry-house. The floor, as in the other examples, is of *terre battue* and there is no drain. Two keeping-places are provided in the walls. The roof

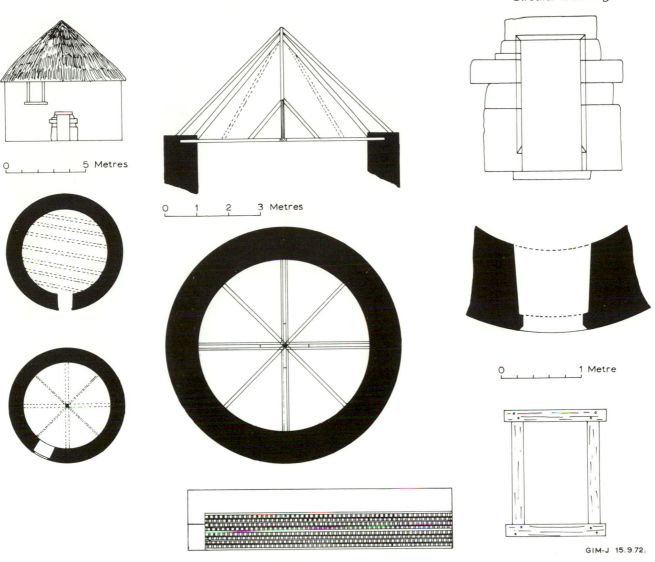

Fig. 114. Pen Coët Sal, Mériadec-en-Pluneret, Morbihan

structure is similar to that at Le Parun (Fig. 111). Two pairs of upper-cruck trusses rise from wood blocks set horizontally into the wall and flush with the inside surface. The feet of the principal rafters rise a few centimetres before curving just above the wall-head. One pair of principals is halved and pegged at the apex, and the ends of the second pair are pegged into the first pair. Common rafters, tied together with straw rope, radiate from the apex and their feet rest on the wall-head. There is no wall-plate. The trusses are girdled by collars nailed to the principals. The thatch, of rye-straw, is tied directly to the common rafters, and although the apex is now capped with a galvanized iron cone carrying a weather-vane, the original capping was almost certainly of turf. From the absence of a drain it should not be supposed that the building was never intended to house animals, for many Breton long-houses have no drain. It is probable that this cell too was intended to accommodate pigs or, as at present, poultry, but it is rather too substantial a building for the latter. Pigs were a far more valuable farm animal and it is much more likely that it was to house them, particularly when farrowing, that such buildings were constructed.

Kerguestoc, Plouzané, Finistère (UU 804587) is the smallest of the recorded buildings and, according to its owner, not very old (Fig. 112). The walls are low, rising to the lintel at the doorway, the only opening. Walling is of granite rubble bonded with *pisé*, and dressings of door and window openings are of rubble with lintels of wood. The roof is thatched with meadow grass and the thatch

Fig. 115.   Lababan, Pouldreuzic, Finistère
'A link between the Neolithic period and the present is provided by the use of corbelling in certain of the medieval churches of Brittany.'

held down by a series of wire strands weighted with stones and pieces of brick. The external and internal diameters are 3.75 and 2.65 metres respectively. Wall height is 1.15 metres and the apex stands 3.20 metres above the ground. The walls are only 0.50 metres thick and are low except where they rise to the level of the door lintel. The doorway is the only opening. There are no principal rafters, the roof being formed of rough chestnut poles joined at the apex and radiating to the wall-head on which the feet rest. These are tied at intervals with horizontally laid straw rope, and the underside surface whitewashed. One pair of rafters, only slightly more substantial than the others, serves as a truss and a rough collar is nailed to them. Thatch of *esk*, or sedge, is tied directly to the rafters and held more firmly in place by a series of wire strands, whose ends are weighted down with stones and pieces of brick. There is no window or slit, no drain, and there are no keeping-places. The building is roughly constructed, was probably a pigsty originally, but is now used for poultry.

At Saint-Urlo, in Lanvénégen, Morbihan (VU 593188) a large circular hut was recorded a month after it had collapsed and when the walls were till largely intact. It was impossible to enter the ruins but sufficient evidence remained for the chief outlines to be recorded (Fig. 113). Walling and dressings were of buff-coloured crystalline schist rubble, the same rubble being used for doorway and window dressings. Roofing was of thatch. Wall height was 2.90 metres and the total height estimated at 8.50 metres. Internal and external diameters were 8.40 metres and 9.95 metres respectively. The reconstruction is based on a careful archaeological examination of the remains. This building more nearly approaches the size of the circular Iron Age huts known from the British Isles. There are two doorways, the smaller 0.90 metres wide, the larger 1.40 metres wide, and a single window opening. All the lintels are of wood. Five joists were carried on a single tie-beam from which rose a king-post. The bracing of this and the position of the principal rafters suggested that the roof had much in common with that of

Pen Coët Sal (Fig. 114). Rough chestnut poles radiated from the apex and their feet rested on the wall-head, there being no wall-plates. They were more widely spaced than was general in the region (*c.* 0.50 metres) and the light lateral purlins appear to have been spaced also at intervals of *c.* 0.50 metres between the wall-head and the apex. Thatch was tied directly to the frame thus formed. According to the owner, there had at one time been an internal partition extending across the building, the space so formed at the back being in use until recently as a byre. Its exact position is, however, unclear, but its existence may explain the need for two doors. The building was used for the accommodation of cattle, and the large roof-space served as a hay-loft.

There can be no doubt that buildings of this kind once existed in hundreds, and probably thousands, but have now disappeared without trace. The concentration of circular pigsties in the Callac region suggests that many more remain to be discovered in that area. Oral testimony from Plumelin and Baden, Morbihan, indicates that they were more numerous there within living memory. A declaration made in 1747, in connection with a farm lease at Trouguennour in Cléden-Cap-Sizun, Finistère, records '*un soue à porsseau en forme ronde couvert de terre*',[323] confirming their former presence in far western Finistère. Whether this pigsty was stone-vaulted, or roofed in thatch, is unclear, but the practice of covering a thatched roof with *terre battue* to make it more weatherproof was formerly widely practised in exposed parts of western Brittany and may still be seen on the Île d'Ouessant. The earth covering may equally have been a rendering to a stone-corbelled roof for the same reason. At Beuzec-Cap-Sizun in 1765, at the Manoir de Kerlesque, there existed a '*soue à porceaux . . . construite de simple maconnage et couvert de pierre et terre*'.[324] The building was seven *pieds* square and four *pieds* high, and there can be no doubt that in this case the covering was intended to render the stone vault waterproof, and although there is no proof here that the building was corbelled, it seems probable that this was so.

Different in structure are the corbelled huts, the *guérites de guetteurs*, or *vigies de douaniers* at Le Bilou (Fig. 105), near Perros-Guirec,[325] and elsewhere. Another *guérite*, square in form, but with a corbelled roof, is recorded near Cancale.[326] These have walls of similar construction to the buildings described above, but the roofs are corbelled like that at Barnenez (Fig. 103). Flat pieces of stone overlap so that the inner edges of the roof become ever closer until finally they meet at the top which is then completed with a single flat slab, sometimes ornamented. This form of roofing, known from the architecture of the Megalithic period, long precedes the

Fig. 116. Le Guerno, Morbihan
'. . . a circular tower roofed with a corbelled conical structure carrying a lantern and possibly dating from the rebuilding of the church about 1580.'

development of the arch and is seen at its best in many of the great chambered tombs of western Europe. A link between the Neolithic period and the present is provided by the use of corbelling in certain of the medieval churches of Brittany. The south porch of the church of St. Paban at Lababan in Pouldreuzic, Finistère, is of fifteenth-century date and has corbelled vaulting additionally supported by two pairs of ribs.[327] The ridge is completed by bridging the last course of corbelling with a row of transverse slabs (Fig. 115). At Plovan, about five kilometres south of Lababan, the north porch is similarly vaulted, as are those at Tréogat and and Pouldreuzic nearby.[328] These examples may indicate a much more widespread occurrence, or the feature may be confined to western Finistère, where it could be explained as the product of a local school of craftsmen. At Le Guerno, Morbihan, the church of Saint-Jean-Baptiste has a circular tower roofed with a corbelled conical structure

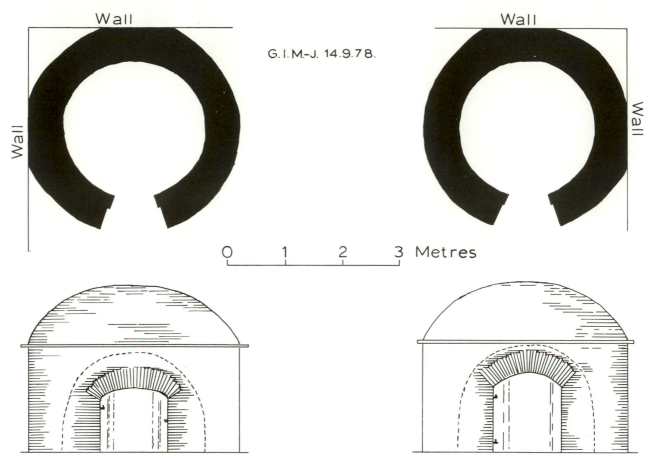

B   A

Wall   Wall

G. I. M.-J. 14.9.78.

Wall   Wall

0   1   2   3 Metres

Fig. 117.   Quéhéon, Ploërmel, Morbihan

carrying a lantern (Fig. 116) and possibly dating from the rebuilding of the church about 1580. It is worth noting here that the circular plan-form is used in two churches in Brittany: at the famous Romanesque church of Sainte-Croix at Quimperlé, and at Lanleff, now in ruins.[329]

Two remarkable buildings are to be found in the corner of a walled garden at the *manoir* of Quéhéon in Ploërmel (Fig. 117). They are the only corbelled farm buildings other than well-covers, dove-cots and bread-ovens, yet discovered in Brittany. In comparison with the thatched farm buildings they appear large but this is chiefly owing to the necessary height of a corbelled roof. Both buildings are slightly elliptical. Building A has diameters of 2.33 and 2.37 metres internally and walls 0.64 metres thick. Building B has diameters of 2.40 and 2.50 metres internally and walls 0.66 metres thick. As both buildings are integrated with the garden wall, it is not possible to give meaningful external diameters. In both cases the

total external height is *c*. 3.00 metres. The beginning of the externally domed roof is marked by a raised course some 0.05 metres deep protruding some 0.15 metres. This stands 1.90 metres above ground level in the case of building A and 1.82 metres in the case of building B. The doorway of building A is 0.72 metres wide at its narrowest and 1.40 metres high, that of building B 0.70 metres wide at the narrowest point and 1.12 metres high. Internal heights are 1.90 metres and 1.75 metres. Walls and roof are of the same thin pieces of purple schist characteristic of the region. The quality of the stonework, laid in a mortar of *pisé*, is high. There seem to be only two possible functions for the buildings: they are either tool-sheds or pigsties. Although externally they give the impression of being much larger than the other pigsties described, judged by their internal measurements they are small, and scarcely much larger than Kerguestoc. Certainly they are significantly smaller than some of the

Fig. 118.   Kerrousse, Baden, Morbihan
A corbelled well-cover.

manner in which the cover is formed, that regional variations occur. Whilst in close-knit villages and hamlets one well may serve several households or even a whole settlement, in isolated farms and in loosely scattered settlements one well per household is more usual. In such cases the well-shaft is rarely far from the doorway of the house, sometimes only a few paces across the farmyard, not infrequently sited in close proximity to the wall of the house itself and occasionally integrated with the wall, water being drawn with equal facility from inside and outside the house. In a wet and windy climate proximity to the house is even more important.

The true conical corbelled well-cover is not common in percentage terms, but occurs in some numbers and is widespread in distribution. Superficially, it is similar to the stone-vaulted cover with domed roof, the constituent stonework of which is wholly or partially supported by stone slabs laid across the drum. The true corbelled vault

Fig. 119.   La Touche, Sucé, Loire-Atlantique
A corbelled well-cover.

thatched examples. The storage function must remain a possibility, but in view of the known function of the small circular structures as pigsties all over western Brittany it seems virtually certain that this is their true function. In some areas the pig — for there was usually only one — was put into the sty every night, but in others where the pig had free access to the hall along with the chickens, the sty was used chiefly for farrowing.

The provision of a boundary wall around the top of a well-shaft, partly for reasons of safety and partly to prevent pollution of the water, is probably almost as old as the digging of wells itself. As the well-shaft is usually circular in cross-section, it is not surprising that the circular form is commonly used for the well-cover throughout Brittany. Low walls of rubble or ashlar, circular or sub-circular in cross-section, surround the head of the shaft, usually with an off-set in the wall at one point more easily to facilitate the drawing of water. This off-set is often formed by setting a slab of schist vertically. It is in the treatment of the circular drum, and in the

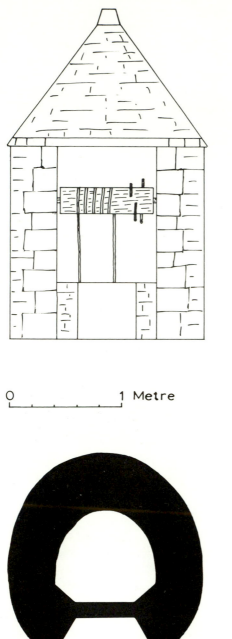

G.I.M-J. 15.7.73

0 _____ 1 Metre

Fig. 120.   La Croix Havard, Montreuil-sur-Ille, Ille-et-Vilaine

is to be seen in the magnificent example at Kerrousse (Fig. 118) and in a smaller example at Le Ter, Baden, Morbihan, where instead of rising symmetrically over the shaft, the cover leans buttress-like against the gable wall of the barn. That at La Touche, Sucé, Loire-Atlantique, is almost perfectly circular at the base, except for the off-set at the front, providing access to the well, and rises to a height of 1.50 metres before being corbelled gradually inwards (Fig. 119). The walling is of thin schist rubble and the cap is partially supported on a lintel of schist. Whilst the true corbelled vault may be found all over the country, it nevertheless appears to be more common in the south and in the west, those areas where older traditions are best preserved, and is totally absent from certain other areas. The stone-vaulted type in which the opening is bridged by horizontally laid slabs of stone is

Fig. 121.   Toulallan, Île d'Ouessant, Finistère
A corbelled well-cover with a door and a *niche* for a religious statue.

also widely distributed and is rather more common than the corbelled vault. A fine example exists at La Croix-Havard, Montreuil-sur-Ille, Ille-et-Vilaine (WU 999509) (Fig. 120). The drum, of oval cross-section, is off-set at the front and capped by slabs of granite which, in turn, support a cone of solid masonry rising to a cap, in the form of a truncated cone of dressed granite. Winding gear with two buckets attached is symmetrically placed and set into the walls of the drum. The greater part of the structure is of granite rubble but the well opening is of roughly dressed granite blocks. External diameter is 1.72 metres, the maximum width internally 0.90 metres, and the depth from front to back 0.80 metres. The walls rise to 1.70 metres and the apex stands 2.94 metres above the ground. This type is more common in Morbihan, whilst in some regions of Finistère it replaces almost all other types. In exposed situations, well-covers are sited with their backs to the prevailing wind and sometimes provided with door, as on the Île d'Ouessant, where some, rising to a height of 2.00 metres or so, are usually

semi-circular, or nearly so, in cross-section. At the base where the sides project, flat slabs of stone provide a pair of low platforms on either side of the opening. Such shelves are analogous to keeping-places and serve to support buckets and other utensils. Sometimes, as at Toulallan (Fig. 121), a small niche is provided for a religious statue, a reminder of the sanctity of wells and springs, venerated from pre-Christian times, for they frequently had their patron 'saint' or guardian to whom votive offerings of flowers were made.[330] Another fine example occurs at Kernizan, Plougasnou, Finistère (Fig. 122). Built of roughly dressed blocks and rubble, the cover rises to over 2.00 metres. Stone shelves are provided, and adjacent to the well stands the *auge*, or drinking trough for animals, which can be filled periodically without the need to carry water far. Another example, sited against the façade of a house, is that at Keravel, Crozon-Morgat, Finistère (Fig. 123).

In some areas the well-cover consists simply of a boundary wall with an off-set for access. Most of the

Fig. 122.   Kernizan 3, Plougasnou, Finistère
Stone shelves for utensils and an adjacent *auge* or drinking-trough for animals, are commonly provided.

examples observed lie in the drier areas of Loire-Atlantique, south of the Loire, as at Saint-Antoine, Frossay (Fig. 124). Further north, in Ille-et-Vilaine, a type widely distributed in the Rennes basin is that seen at La Gestinière in Saint-M'Hervé (Fig. 125). A low circular wall of rubble has an off-set for access, two posts rising from a sill carry a pair of tie-beams and a slate roof is supported on a timber frame which also carries the winding gear. Slates are nailed to the boarded rafters. The roof is asymmetrical, being shorter at the front and sweeping back at the rear to cover the well-shaft. A simpler form of cover with sub-circular cross-section and flat front, and walls rising to carry a flat sloping roof, falling from front to back (Fig. 126), has a wide distribution, especially in the three westernmost *départements*.

Examples of monumental quality are sometimes found in towns or associated with church foundations. That at Rochefort-en-Terre, Morbihan, is built of ashlar and the winding gear was formerly supported by an elegant wrought-iron superstructure (Fig. 127). At Champeaux, Ille-et-Vilaine, the canons' lodgings were supplied with water from a well with an elaborate cover dated 1601. The low wall of dressed blocks supports a wooden frame on which rests a roof of ogival form (Fig. 128). Six posts are mortised into a wooden sill and scissors-braced. These posts also support the winding gear, and are mortised into a plate, hexagonal in plan, from which rise the rafters. The slate roof is surmounted by a ball and cross. Wherever stone is good enough to be dressed, elaborate sculptured wells may be found. Often bearing nineteenth-century dates, these are not uncommon in parts of Morbihan.[331] A good example is that at Kerriec, Guern, Morbihan (Fig. 129), where a stone drum supports an elaborate pair of stone posts and transom within which is contained the winding gear.

Before World War I and the advent of the itinerant baker, every household baked its own supply of bread. Ovens are consequently ubiquitous, their density bearing some relation to the density of settlement, sometimes one oven to a household when settlement is dispersed, communal when dwellings are grouped, perhaps serving a dozen households or more. Although located at a particular farm, they were for communal use in Bulat-Pestivien. Invariably circular or sub-circular in form, ovens are built of dressed stone, rubble, brick or *terre battue*. During baking, the opening was closed with a stone slab or sheet of iron and hermetically sealed with cow-dung.[332] The vast majority, no longer used, are decaying rapidly.

Of monumental proportions is the oven at Kermadoué, Trégunc, Finistère (Figs. 130–132), rising to over 2.00 metres and built of roughly dressed granite rubble blocks. The structure is almost circular, except for the flat front, and the drum is finished with a narrow raised course, above which rises the domed roof, now covered with vegetation, but probably formerly finished with a rendering of earth. Small keeping-places are provided on each side of the recessed entrance. The interior has a plain stone vault (Fig. 132). Similar in size and form, but superior in finish, is the magnificent oven at Kermeun (VT 425970) in the neighbouring *commune* of Névez where stone is of high quality. It is curiously associated with a large number of exfoliated granite boulders and low enclosing walls, some built of orthostats (Fig. 133). Built of dressed granite, there is no flue, the opening being recessed 0.25 metres and framed by fine ashlar slabs, over which a smoke-hole is provided. The building stands 3.40 metres high at the gabled front, and

Fig. 123.   Keravel 6, Crozon-Morgat, Finistère
A corbelled well-cover built conveniently against the wall of a house.

Fig. 124.   Saint-Antoine, Frossay, Loire-Atlantique
Most of the wells observed in the drier areas of Loire-Atlantique, south of the Loire, have no covers.

Fig. 125.   La Gestinière, Saint-M'Hervé, Ille-et-Vilaine
The regional type of well-cover in eastern Ille-et-Vilaine.

Fig. 126.   La Maison Neuve, Béganne, Morbihan
This simple type of well-cover has a wide distribution in the westernmost *départements*.

Fig. 127.   Place-du-Puits, Rochefort-en-Terre, Morbihan
Built of ashlar, with winding gear formerly supported by an elegant wrought-iron superstructure.

is 4.05 metres in diameter at its widest point and 2.80 metres in diameter internally. The internal height is 1.60 metres. Ovens of this quality are common in south Finistère and especially between Pont-Aven and Concarneau.

Of similar size is the communal oven at Saint-Rivoal (VU 261557) in the Monts d'Arrée where the stone, a schist rubble, is of poorer quality (Fig. 134). The gable front of Saint-Rivoal B stands 3.00 metres high, and although the interior is roughly circular with a diameter of 2.65 metres, only the back is semi-circular in form outside. The overall length is 5.00 metres, the width 4.60 metres and the internal height 1.20 metres. The opening is recessed 0.30 metres, and formerly a flue, a pair of inclined slabs of schist forming the arch, was supported on corbels. A single keeping-place lies at ground level beneath the opening and a projecting stone forms a small shelf. The vaulting is a plain stone vault identical to that of Saint-Rivoal A, and it is possible that both these ovens were formerly given a coating of *torchis* or *pisé* to make the outer roof weatherproof. A second oven on this site (Fig. 134) is much smaller and was built for private as distinct from communal use. The front stands 4.45 metres high, has a flat monoclinal roof, is flat-fronted, nearly circular and of 1.55 metres diameter internally. The building is entirely constructed of roughly coursed schist rubble. A small projecting shelf and a single keeping-place lie to the right of the recessed opening. As with the larger example, there was formerly a flue supported on corbels, but only the latter now remain.

Whenever good building stone is available in Brittany, ovens of high quality are to be found. That surviving at Saint-Jean, Campénéac, Morbihan (WU 550150), on the western edge of the Forêt de Paimpont, is a good example (Fig. 135), built of schist rubble, and formerly served a community of three dwellings. The gabled front stands 2.60 metres high, the length is 2.90 metres, the width 2.90 metres and the internal height 1.02 metres. A flue is formed by carrying the gable across the recessed opening on a stone lintel, leaving a narrow space behind.

Fig. 128.　Maisons des Chanoines, Champeaux, Ille-et-Vilaine
Well-covers of monumental quality are often associated with church foundations. This example is dated 1601.

Only a few kilometres away in Paimpont, Ille-et-Vilaine, stone becomes scarcer and *terre battue* replaces stone for much of the walling. Whilst stone ovens are still to be found, there are also many which have a base of stone rubble above which construction is entirely of earth, except for the red-brick lining and a roof covering of slate, as at Beau Normandie 2 (Fig. 136). The roof is semi-circular in plan at the rear but has a short ridge at the front, the latter formed in the tradition of the district by raising the slates on one side so that they rise above the other, the joint beneath being sealed with earth. The oven of *terre battue* is widespread in the Rennes basin. That at Les Rues des Moulins has a base of stone rubble and an opening framed with ashlar, whilst the remainder, except for the interior lining of red brick, is of red-brown earth. The whole is covered by a slate roof, supported

around its edges, as at Beau Normandie, by projecting short timbers set horizontally in the earth covering (Fig. 137). Some of these ovens have no flue at all; others, like that at Coganne, Paimpont, Ille-et-Vilaine, have a flue of brick and walling that is an admixture of polychrome rubble and earth (Fig. 138).

Occasionally, an oven will be built into an oven-house, *le fournil*, as at Les Rues Bellay 2, Paimpont, Ille-et-Vilaine (WU 668219) (Fig. 139). This oven is almost perfectly circular in form, 3.00 metres in diameter externally and 1.70 metres internally with an internal height of 1.00 metres, lined with red-brick, with an opening framed in cast iron. The building is probably of nineteenth-century date. Walling is of well-coursed schist and rubble blocks. The admixture of purple schist rubble

Fig. 129.　Kerriec, Guern, Morbihan
Wherever stone is good enough to be dressed, elaborate sculptured well-covers may be found. These seem often to bear nineteenth-century dates and are not uncommon in parts of Morbihan.

manner as at Le Beuchet, Saint-M'Hervé (XU 422375). The oven is built of schist with some sandstone dressings around the opening (Fig. 141). The front gable stands 2.60 metres high, the diamater is 3.65 metres externally and 1.90 metres internally. The roof of the oven inside rises 1.05 metres above the base. This construction is almost perfectly circular outside and slightly pear-shaped inside. It is covered by a slate roof which rests on top of a thick *pisé* coating laid over the stonework. The oven entrance is slightly recessed and there are no keeping-places. The slate roof and curved gables may be original. A second example in the same hamlet (Fig. 141), of similar construction and materials, has a gable front rising 1.85 metres above the ground, and the diameter is 3.20 metres externally and 2.25 metres internally. The oven rises to 0.95 metres inside. There is no evidence of a slate roof in this case and it is possible that none ever existed.

Fig. 130. Kermadoué, Trégunc, Finistère
A bake-oven of monumental proportions. Small keeping-places are provided on each side of the recessed entrance.

and cream-coloured quartzite blocks creates a striking effect of some quality, the quartzite being laid in a broad band close to the top of the wall of the oven and in four or five courses over schist footings in the bake-house. The vault of the oven is of red brick (Fig. 140). A flue is provided and contained in the gable wall of the bake-house, terminating in a red-brick chimney-stack. A ridge is formed of red tiles but these are possibly of a later date as the original roof is more likely to have been finished by overlapping slates. The oven is covered by a slate roof, also with a short red-tile ridge, and the roof of the bake-house is supported partly by the gable wall and partly by two full king-post trusses. The king-posts support a ridge purlin and there is one lateral purlin on each side. The tie-beams rest on wall-plates. The rafters are covered with close-set wooden boards to which the slates are nailed.

Further east, in Ille-et-Vilaine, ovens frequently have pitched roofs rising to a ridge formed in the traditional

Fig. 131. Kermadoué, Trégunc, Finistère
The dome, now covered with vegetation, was probably formerly finished with a rendering of earth.

Fig. 132. Kermadoué, Trégunc, Finistère
The interior has a plain stone vault.

A thick covering of *pisé* rests over the stone vault and this probably illustrates the kind of roofing which was formerly extensively used before slate roofs were erected, to save having to repair the clay covering annually. Evidence suggests that, in parts of Brittany, earth was once used as a roof covering for farm buildings, the practice surviving in the far west. It is certain that the majority of the slate roofs on ovens are later in date than the ovens themselves, having been put there for better protection when the practice of periodically repairing the earth covering ceased. This was so at Bulat-Pestivien.[333] The countryside around Saint-M'Hervé is full of examples similar to these two, mostly with the slate ridge-roof. That at L'Orrier (XU 422398) is a particularly fine example of the regional type (Fig. 142). The walls stand 1.85 metres high and the front gable rises to 2.90 metres above the ground. Diameter is 3.10 metres externally and 1.50 metres internally. The internal height of the oven is 0.75

metres. The schist rubble walling rests on a foundation of *terre battue*. Sandstone dressings are used at the corner of the eaves at the front gable and for the framing of the oven opening. The plan is almost perfectly circular externally but pear-shaped internally. A slate ridge-roof now covers the oven and this is possibly an original feature. Alternatively it may have been added later to reduce the need to repair the *pisé* capping of the stone vault. The ridge line is finished by carrying the slates on one side over the heads of the other.

The free-standing sub-circular oven is also common in the south-east where examples, formerly earth-covered, may be found in the countryside around Guérande (Fig. 143) and, turf-covered, in the Grande Brière (Fig. 144). Sometimes the oven is built at the back of a *fournil* which is either an integral part of a house or a lean-to addition. An oven built on to the gable of the house, its opening in the back of the hearth of the common living room, is known in certain widely separated areas. It is common on the Île d'Ouessant (Fig. 145), in the Rennes basin (Fig. 146) and south of the Loire (Fig. 147). Such ovens are obviously intended to serve only one household and must be regarded as an improvement on the detached oven which, in a wet and windy climate like that of Ouessant, must be extremely inconvenient.

Circular dove-cots survive in large numbers and appear to be both widely and evenly distributed. Known variously as *les colombiers, les fuies* or *les pigeonniers*, they were built to house the pigeons kept as a feudal right by the larger landowners from the Middle Ages until 1789. In northern France the right to keep pigeons was *seigneurial* and was of some value as the pigeons provided meat for the household and yet fed mostly on the tenants' crops. There appears generally to have been some relationship between the number of birds and the amount of land in the estate, but the exact relationship is difficult to determine and was probably subject to regional variation. In Brittany, it is variously reported as one pigeon to every *journal de terre*, or one to every *demi-journal de terre*. Consequently the largest, and often the finest, dove-cots are associated with the more prosperous estates.[334] These examples are modest in size when compared with the *pigeonniers* of the Paris basin,[335] but that is to be expected in Brittany where estates were generally small.

No attempt has been made to map the number observed. There are regional variations of style. Some dove-cots are of simple cylindrical form, rising from an earthen floor with nesting holes arranged around the inside wall, from floor-level to the roof. Others are divided into two storeys, one for storage, the other for pigeons. Access for the birds is usually by a hole in the

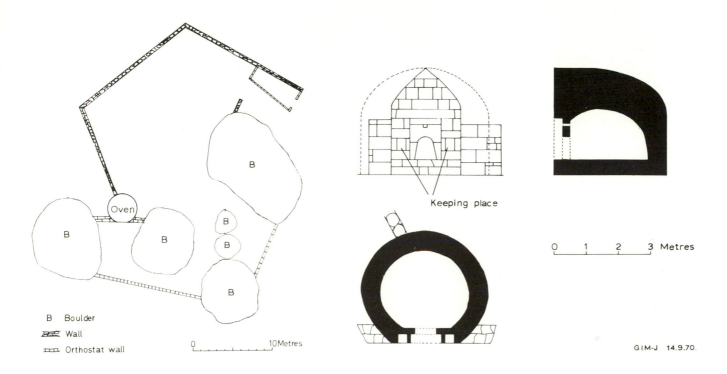

Keeping place

B Boulder
Wall
Orthostat wall

GIM-J 14.9.70.

Fig. 133. Kermeun, Névez, Finistère

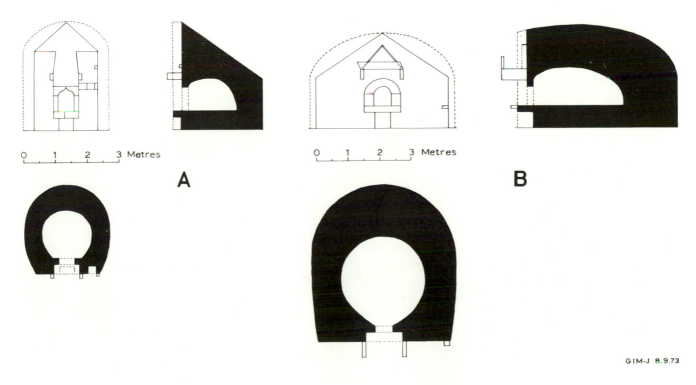

A

B

GIM-J 8.9.73

Fig. 134. Saint-Rivoal, Finistère

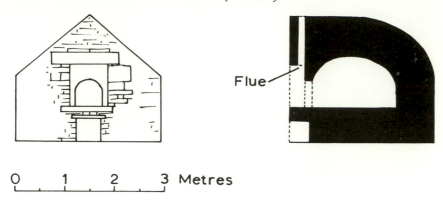

Flue

0   1   2   3 Metres

GIM-J   23.8.75.

Fig. 135.   Saint-Jean, Campénéac, Morbihan

Fig. 136.   Beau Normandie 2, Paimpont, Ille-et-Vilaine
A stone-rubble base with *torchis* above and a red-brick lining.

Fig. 137.   Les Rues des Moulins, Melesse, Ille-et-Vilaine
The oven of *torchis* is widespread in the Rennes basin and some of the slate roofs are original features.

Fig. 138.   Coganne 1, Paimpont, Ille-et-Vilaine
Some have a flue of brick and walling that is an admixture of polychrome rubble and earth.

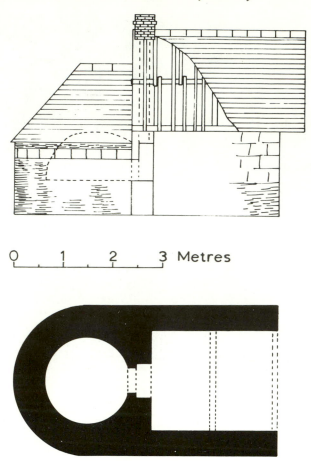

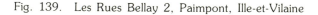

0   1   2   3 Metres

Fig. 139.   Les Rues Bellay 2, Paimpont, Ille-et-Vilaine

GIM-J 21.5.73.

roof, but sometimes in the side. A doorway at ground level is general. Some structures have a central rotating pole to which are added arms that support a ladder, used to gain access to the nesting holes for cleaning purposes.[336] Most are wholly built of stone, but examples in *torchis* must once have been common, similar to that at Quéhéon, Ploërmel, destroyed in the 1930s.

Several fine examples survive in Loire-Atlantique, notably at La Patissière in Saint-Herblain, and Les Dervallières.[337] In both cases the corbelled roof supports a cupola or lantern with four openings, and pairs of dormer window openings serve to light the interior and also provide entry for the birds. Such arrangements are not uncommon in constructions of the highest quality. The *manoirs* of Basse-Bretagne each possessed a dove-cot and many remain in Trégor.[338] Some were contained in the upper storey of a tower or were incorporated into the body of the house as a row of holes built into the façade, or into the gable wall. In other cases, as at Le Logis, Remouillé, the dove-cot is one of a number of planned farmyard buildings (Fig. 148). In general, however, '*le colombier, signe extérieur le plus marquant de la noblesse du propriétaire*',[339] is a detached building sited away from the farmyard and standing some distance from other buildings, as at Lesmoal, Plounérin, and Troas, Pleudaniel. Lesmoal is ascribed to the sixteenth century and Troas to the end of the fifteenth century, and it is probable that many of these structures are of sixteenth- and seventeenth-century date.[340] In Trégor, the dove-cot is nearly always circular, built of rubble, dressed stone, or both, and roofed with a corbelled stone vault. Many are now in a poor state of repair and some have disappeared. Frotier de la Messelière gives a list of those formerly existing.[341] A uniformity of construction is reported from central Finistère, with stone walls, corbelled roofs and simple doorway dressings.[342] Inside, walling is usually of alternate thin courses of schist and dressed sandstone blocks, set apart to form the nesting holes. An occasional raised course provides a perch for the birds.

Fig. 140. Les Rues Bellay 2, Paimpont, Ille-et-Vilaine
A red-brick lining.

Four examples, from Finistère, Morbihan and Loire-Atlantique, illustrate some of the variety of Breton dove-cots, the two from western Finistère being similar in form but of different size. That at Lesnavor in Plovan (UU 092114) (Fig. 149), 7.75 metres in diameter, externally, has walls 1.30 metres thick, rising to 5.70 metres externally, magnificently constructed of dressed granite, the social aspirations of the owner being apparent in the blank shield above the doorway. The total external height is *c.* 8.00 metres. A corbelled stone roof is pierced by a central hole, the existence of which lessens the weight of the roof and also provides an entrance for the pigeons, which roost in niches arranged in seven banks of three rows, separated by raised courses that serve as perches. Except where interrupted by the doorway, there are some thirty-two holes in each row, giving a total capacity of some eight hundred and fifty birds.

Nearby is the similar, but smaller, structure at Pouldu in Ploumoguer (UU 711603) (Fig. 150). The diameter is 7.00 metres externally and 4.45 metres internally, the walls, 1.30 metres thick, rise to 4.50 metres and the roof apex is *c.* 6.35 metres above the ground. The whole is roofed with fourteen courses of corbelled stonework, and access for the pigeons, as at Lesnarvor, is provided by leaving a circular hole some 0.60 metres in diameter centrally placed in the roof. Walls are of irregular courses of dressed granite blocks, with massive dressings to the solitary doorway, raised and moulded eaves, and a *niche* immediately above the doorway. Five banks of holes, four of four rows, and one, the top bank, of seven rows, with twenty-seven holes in each row, provide a total accommodation for some six hundred pigeons.

Some particularly fine specimens are to be found in Loire-Atlantique,[343] one of which, in Batz-sur-Mer (WT 403364), was fortified by the Germans and used as a gun emplacement during World War II (Fig. 151). Consequently, there is additional concrete facing on the inside of the walls, and the concrete ceiling is supported by steel girders. It is of two storeys and external diameter at the base is 6.75 metres, but this increases with height

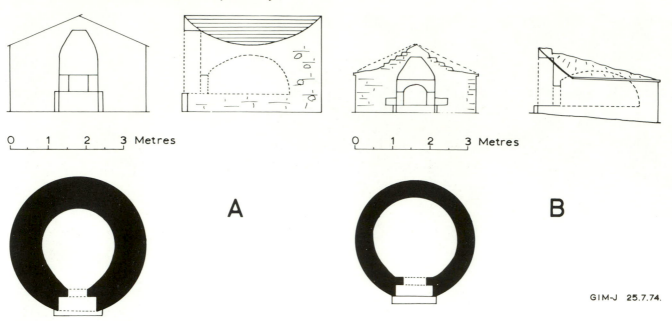

0   1   2   3 Metres

0   1   2   3 Metres

A

B

GIM-J   25.7.74.

Fig. 141.   Le Beuchet, Saint-M'Hervé, Ille-et-Vilaine

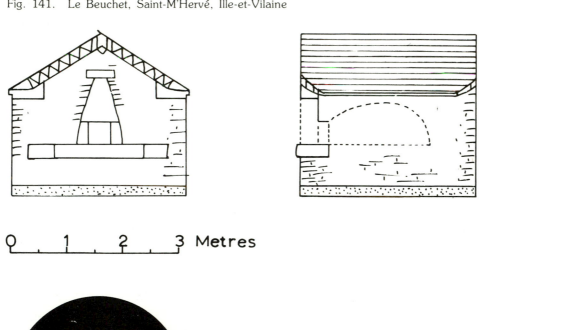

0   1   2   3 Metres

GIM-J 9.5.74.

Fig. 142.   L'Orrier,
Saint-M'Hervé, Ille-et-Vilaine

Fig. 143. Kergaine, Guérande, Loire-Atlantique
A stone-vaulted roof, formerly earth-covered.

Fig. 144. Bréca, Saint-Lyphard, Loire-Atlantique
The turf-covered roof once usual in the Grande Brière.

The stone-vaulted oven with an opening in the back of the hearth is common on Ouessant.

Fig. 146.   Le Bré, La Mézière, Ille-et-Vilaine
Such ovens are obviously intended to serve only one household.

Fig. 147.   Marie-Avé, Frossay, Loire-Atlantique
The oven built on to the gable is common south of the Loire.

to *c.* 7.00 metres at the level of the first floor, then decreasing to the eaves. The walls are 1.15 metres thick and rise 6.70 metres to the eaves. The apex stands *c.* 8.35 metres above the ground. There is no internal communication between the ground floor and the pigeon loft, and access is provided by two off-set doorways, one for each storey. A series of holes in the outer wall, built of coursed granite rubble, may be putlog holes, but as some penetrate the thickness of the wall, they may have been intended to provide further ventilation. Three raised courses provide perches inside and the rows of holes, set in the interior wall at first-floor level, can accommodate some three hundred birds. Flooring, both at ground-floor and first-floor level, is of *terre battue*, and on the first-floor a drip course, some two centimetres across, has been eroded into the clay floor by dripping from the circular opening, 1.15 metres in diameter, in the roof. The latter is constructed of corbelled stone rubble with four marked stepped courses visible to the outside. Three raised courses provide perches and the rows of holes can accommodate some three hundred birds.

Somewhat different is the dove-cot at Pen Coët Sal, Mériadec-en-Pluneret, Morbihan (WT 076819) (Fig. 114). Walling is of granite rubble with doorway dressings of roughly dressed blocks with flat-splay chamfers. The loft opening is framed in wood. External diameter is 7.35 metres and the walls, 1.00 metres thick, rise to 3.80 metres. The apex stands *c.* 7.70 metres above the ground. Walling is of coursed granite rubble and there are separate entries to the ground floor, by a solitary doorway obviously once used by both man and birds as there is no separate entry for the latter, and to the loft. Accommodation for over four hundred birds is provided at ground-floor level. The first floor is in use as a hayloft. A pair of tie-beams supports a full-length king-post from the top of which the rafters radiate. The king-post is braced four ways from a point about one-third of the way up. Common rafters are set close together in the manner usual in south Morbihan and the thatch, of rye-straw, is tied directly to them.

Windmills, important elements in the rural landscape, were once numerous. Few are now in good condition

Fig. 148.   Le Logis, Remouillé, Loire-Atlantique
The dove-cot is one of a number of planned farmyard buildings.

and even fewer in working order, but remains of large numbers survive. Some 2,175 were recorded in Finistère alone in 1848.[344] In Cap Sizun there were as many as fifty-eight windmills at the end of the nineteenth century. Gautier has plotted all windmills shown on the large-scale maps revised in 1893–5, including those then recorded as destroyed, and the resulting map gives some idea of the distribution at the end of the nineteenth century (Fig. 152).[345] East of the Trieux–Blavet line, windmills are much more numerous than to the west of that line, but the greatest concentration is south of the Rennes basin, in the *pays de Guérande,* and the *pays nantais,* and further south into the Vendée. Density increases between the Loire and the Sèvre, on the islands in the Grande Brière, along the Sillon de Bretagne and around the Lac de Grandlieu. Towards the Forêt de Paimpont, and west of the Blavet, windmills become rare and do not appear again in any numbers until the northern coastline is reached; they are strongly represented on both sides of the Rance and along the northern edge of the Marais de Dol, but in western Brittany there are large areas devoid of windmills, notably the plateaux of Léon and Cornouaille. Along the northern coast, where they might be expected to be present, they are confined to Trégor

and do not appear west of the Morlaix river. The coast of Léon is curiously devoid of them but the islands of Ouessant, Molène and Beniguet possess large numbers, as do the peninsulas of Crozon and Cap Sizun, south of the Rade de Brest. Lesser numbers occur around the bays of Audièrne and Douarnenez. History and the desire to imitate have been the essential factors leading to the present distribution, windmills chiefly having been diffused along the principal routeways of pre-1789 Brittany, from Nantes towards the Rohan estates. The part played by the landed gentry and the church in this diffusion process is yet far from clear. The distribution of windmills is not always balanced by that of watermills, whose location along the principal water courses is more easily explained. Not all mills are on elevated sites, as might be supposed, and the presence of heathland and the pattern of ancient rural trackways have played a part in their diffusion.[346]

There is some regional variation in building style. In the extreme south-east, towards the Vendée, the towers are often of several storeys, as at Saint-Hilaire-de-Clisson (Fig. 153), whilst in Cap Sizun, towers are short squat cylinders, as at Tréguennec (Fig. 154), but probably the greatest variation is between the small mills of the Île d'Ouessant and the magnificent structures of the *pays de Guérande.* The former are built on small cylinders of solid masonry rarely more than 2.00 metres in height (Figs. 155 and 156), of which large numbers now survive. On the drums were mounted small rectilinear wooden boxes with hipped roofs containing the machinery. These small mills, of which a hundred or so existed at the end of the nineteenth century, were essentially family concerns, and complemented the nine three-storey mills of the larger proprietors which existed in 1918.[347]

Among the windmills of the south-east, those of the *pays de Guérande,* between the Loire and the Vilaine, are the finest, as shown by two examples, the Moulin du Diable in Guérande, now restored (Fig. 157), and the semi-derelict Moulin de la Falaise in Batz-sur-Mer (WT 387367) (Fig. 158). The external diameter at the base is 5.10 metres, reducing to 4.40 metres and widening again to 5.40 metres at the first-floor level. The drum rises 3.55 metres above the plinth and supports the circular first floor 2.50 metres deep. The height from the base of the plinth to the eaves line is 7.15 metres and the apex stands *c.* 11.00 metres above the ground. This is an example of the regional style of windmill and is exceptionally fine. Walling is of dressed granite and the roof is covered with cleft shingles. The drum rests on a circular base with a strongly pronounced batter. Machinery was formerly housed at first-floor level and maximum power obtained

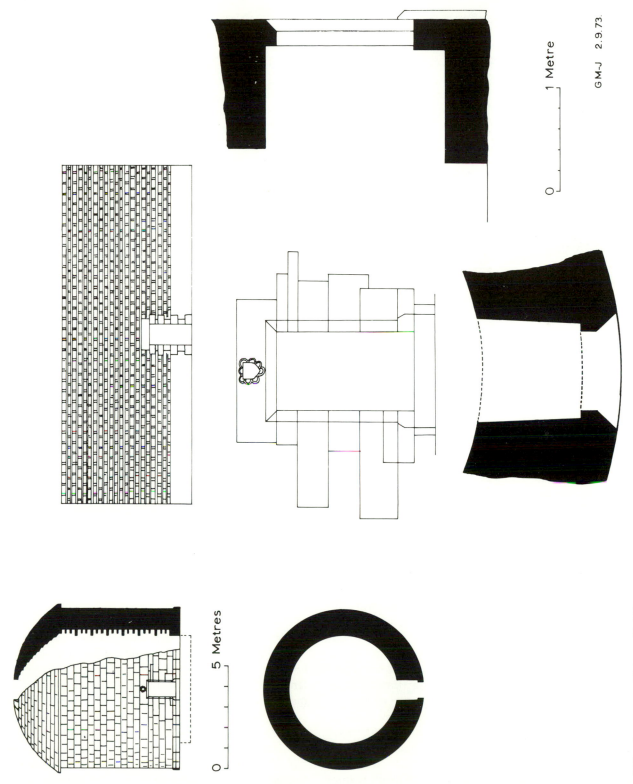

GM-J   2.9.73.

1 Metre

5 Metres

Fig. 149. Lesnarvor, Plovan, Finistère

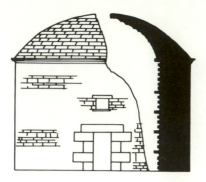

0 . . . . . 5 Metres

GIM-J   4.8.73.

Fig. 150.   Pouldu, Ploumoguer, Finistère

by turning the rotating conical roof with the aid of a long fixed pole, thereby placing the sails in their optimum position in relation to the wind. Storage was provided on the ground floor, which contains a stair with stone treads and an iron rail, curving around the inside wall. The structure is exceptionally finely built of dressed granite blocks of courses of varying widths, and doorway and window dressings are of the highest quality. The working room, at first-floor level, was formerly panelled in wood, fragments of which remain, and a wood-panelled stone bench runs around the walls. Cupboards and window fittings are of a high order. The building is difficult to date but it is likely that some at least of these windmills date from the seventeenth century, some may be earlier and others are probably of eighteenth-century date.

The *broyeur d'ajonc*, a gorse-crushing machine, was common in the nineteenth century, often powered by a horse moving along a circular track. Others were hand-operated. Although some stood in the open air, various types of building were adapted to shelter them. A circular building was in many ways ideal for the work-pattern, and the only two such structures known to survive lie

adjacent to the farmyard at Goas Henry in Carnoët (VU 604587). Both structures consist of a conical roof thatched with broom capped with turf, resting on eight earth-fast posts. The internal diameter of Goas Henry 1 is *c.* 6.00 metres and that of the second building 5.60 metres. The posts of the former building are 1.80 metres high, *c.* 0.30 metres in diameter. The second building is slightly lower, the posts being 1.40 metres high and *c.* 0.25 to 0.30 metres thick. The extent to which the posts descend below ground level is unknown, but is probably of the order of 0.40 or 0.50 metres. The roof structure of the first building is of the collar-truss type without a tie-beam. The second building also lacks a tie-beam but boasts a king-post into which the interrupted collars are tenoned. The total height of both buildings is *c.* 4.50 metres. In that the rafters are slotted into the earth-fast posts, albeit rather crudely, and that tie-beams are absent, the structure must be considered as being supported by scarfed crucks and is mapped as such on Fig. 65. Purlins are either nailed or tied to the rafters and the bundles of broom for thatch just pushed into the structure. The chestnut poles that comprise the common

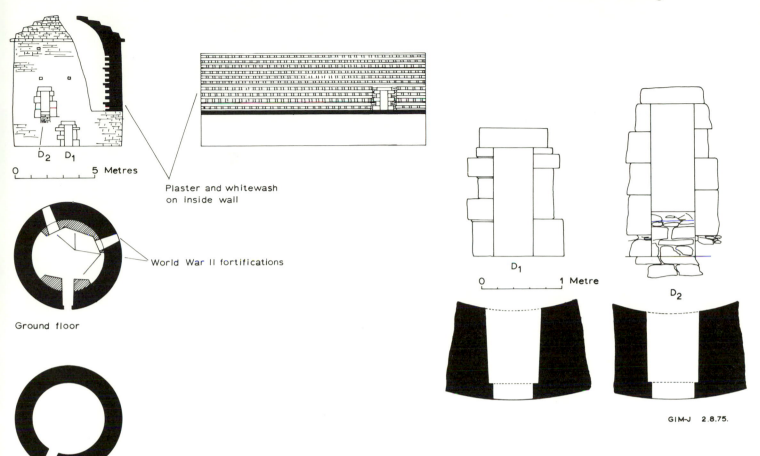

Plaster and whitewash
on inside wall

World War II fortifications

Ground floor

First floor

D₁

D₂

GIM-J 2.8.75.

Fig. 151.   Batz-sur-Mer, Loire-Atlantique

rafters rest with their feet on crude wall-plates. The age of buildings, fifty to fifty-five years, is an indication of the durability of such structures with earth-fast posts (Fig. 108).

Circular buildings are technically the easiest to construct as they require no knowledge of the art of cornering. Since they enclose the maximum area with the minimum circumference, a well-known property of the circle, the quantity of materials needed is minimum. It is unfortunate that, having thus economized, the resulting plan, difficult to subdivide, is impracticable for many purposes. To overcome this problem in early times, additional circular huts were often constructed, a solution which, unless the buildings were conjoined, resulted in the need to pass into the open air when moving from one to another. It is not surprising, therefore, that the circular dwelling came to be abandoned in favour of other ground plans. Nevertheless, it survived late in some parts of France, but there is no evidence yet for the survival of

circular houses in Brittany in recent historical times, except for the charcoal burners' huts still to be found in the forested areas. Le Braz illustrates such a dwelling, and Vallaux and Souvestre record them, as does Périer de Lahitolle.[348] Testimony to the continuation of the circular tradition is mostly to be found in the widespread distribution of well-covers, dove-cots, ovens, windmills and circular farm buildings. The circular stair-turret, commonly found in many of the larger farmhouses, is yet a further example. Many of the windmills, ovens and dove-cots are now defunct, and although some may be preserved, they are decaying fast and could disappear altogether within a generation or so. Buildings of this kind are extraordinarily difficult to date, construction is relatively simple and techniques span hundreds and probably thousands of years. Building materials are always of local provenance and reflect what is readily available: granite, schist, slate and sandstone or, where stone is absent, *terre battue* for the walls, or an admixture

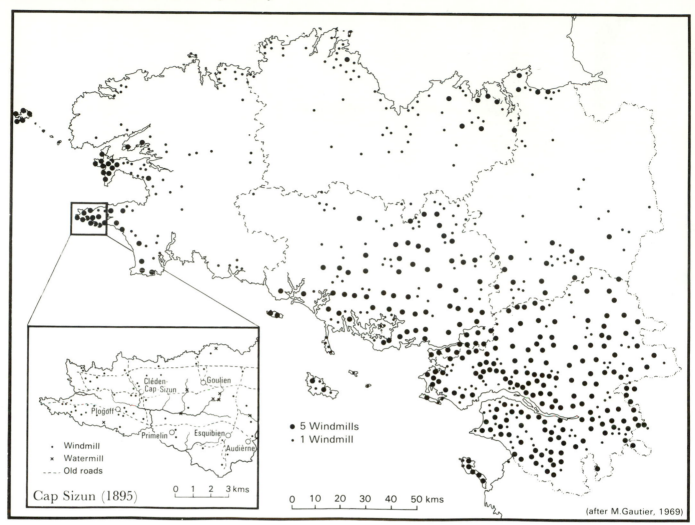

Fig. 152.   Brittany: distribution of windmills at the end of the nineteenth century

of two or more of these. Roofing is of timber and thatch, with use of the upper-cruck truss or of straight principals, or with either a plain stone vault or a corbelled vault. The latter is particularly common for the roofing of dove-cots, for which it is well-suited as it permits an opening to be left in the centre.

The circular form is widespread in Europe and the few surviving examples of farmyard buildings in Brittany most closely resemble what is known of the circular dwellings of the prehistoric period. Over the centuries the circular dwelling has descended the social scale to the point at which it has become a home for pigs and poultry, for whom its form and size are most suitable. The distribution of the surviving circular farmyard biildings in Brittany is markedly westerly, a further example of the survival of the earliest forms in the remoter parts of the Atlantic ends of Europe.

Fig. 153. Saint-Hilaire-de-Clisson, Loire-Atlantique
Towards the Vendée, towers are often tall and of several
storeys.

Fig. 154. Le Cosquer, Tréguennec, Finistère
Short squat cylinders are characteristic of the *pays bigouden*.

Fig. 155. Kerdreux, Île d'Ouessant, Finistère
The tiny windmills of Ouessant.

Fig. 156. Kerdreux, Île d'Ouessant, Finistère
The machinery was housed in small wooden structures supported on cylindrical drums of stone. Large numbers of the latter remain.

Fig. 157. Moulin du Diable, Guérande, Loire-Atlantique
The finest stone windmills are those of the *pays de Guérande* and adjacent areas.

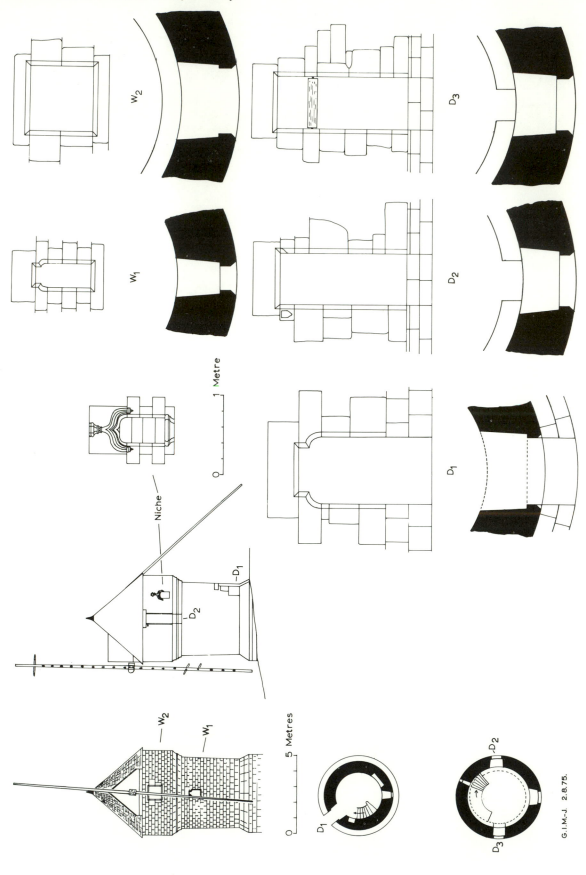

Fig. 158.   Moulin de la Falaise, Batz-sur-Mer, Loire-Atlantique

SUB-RECTILINEAR, EARLY AND PRIMITIVE RECTILINEAR BUILDINGS, AND RELATED STRUCTURES

Buildings of a primitive kind are widely distributed, and simple structures may be found standing alone in a field or occupying part of a farmyard. Although the term 'primitive' is most unsatisfactory, and may be considered to have pejorative overtones, there is no suitable alternative. It is understood to refer to those structures capable of being built without the assistance of a skilled craftsman, such as a carpenter. The necessary skills would be shared by most adult male members of rural society. With recent agrarian reforms and government subsidies for the improvement of farm buildings, the use of primitive buildings is diminishing, and repairs are not being made. Many have been swept away in recent years and few are likely to survive the next decade or so.

At Bouleguy, between Locminé and Baud in central Morbihan, and close to the Route Nationale 24, about forty-five kilometres east-north-east of Lorient, in the *commune* of Plumelin, is a group of four structures arranged around a farmyard, with the present nineteenth-century farmhouse and its adjacent stable (Fig. 159). The most interesting of these structures is Bouleguy 2 (WU 097045), a tent-like building in which the thatched roof reaches everywhere to ground level (Fig. 160). Construction is almost identical to that of the majority of the roofs of the Morbihan farms (Figs. 55, 178, 184, 185, 186, 189) and has been described in detail elsewhere.[349] Principal rafters are an inverted 'V' shape, two trusses being of chestnut poles with collars of light timber crudely fastened with nails. Lateral purlins are similarly formed and also held in place with nails, and the ridge-pole is formed of three overlapping chestnut poles. Common rafters, as in many Morbihan houses, are laid against the ridge-pole and lateral purlins and bound together with ropes made of twisted straw, their feet resting on the ground.[350] The practice of carrying the roof down to ground level in this manner may once have been widespread in Atlantic Europe, for it has been observed in circular huts in Iberia.[351] A group of circular pigsties formed of radiating chestnut poles, covered with thatch, was recorded near Caulnes, Côtes-du-Nord, in 1973 (Fig. 107). The sub-rectilinear plan is completed by carrying the common rafters around the structure and an interior wall formed by the placing of split logs one above the other, between the principal and common rafters, up to a height of about one metre. Over this framework is laid a thatch of rye straw, held down at intervals with long thin pieces of wood and in some cases with lengths of wire (Fig. 160). In its present form this building is lighted by a small window at one end only, with access by two doors, one of which is of wood and unhinged. The central doorway is framed with wood and provided with a 'rush' door. Horizontal bars fit into holes bored into the uprights holding alternating layers of rye straw tightly woven between the bars (Fig. 160). It was built as a pigsty and, when recorded, was still in use as such. The significance of this structure lies not just in survival, for similar buildings have been observed all over Brittany, but in the fact that the type was once used as a dwelling. At the turn of the century there were a hundred or so in the neighbourhood. These dwellings apparently differed from Bouleguy 2 only in that the whole structure was laid upon a low *talus* or bank of earth to give better headroom and wall space within. Heat was provided by an open fire set in the middle of the floor, opposite the door, smoke

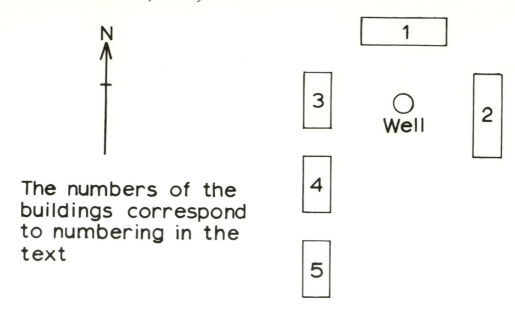

Fig. 159. Bouleguy, Plumelin, Morbihan

escaping through a hole in the roof immediately above. There was no chimney or louvre and smoke was 'guided' up to the hole by a tripod of chestnut poles upon which was suspended a cooking pot. The floor, as in all Breton dwellings before the advent of cement, was of *terre battue*, and the furniture was of the simplest kind. The inhabitants of these *loges* were very poor and, in the Plumelin area, mostly occupied with itinerant trades. Such people probably owned little or no livestock. Nevertheless some of the structures could have been long-houses, of rectangular or sub-rectangular plan, with provision for man and beast under the same roof.

Three other buildings, the construction of which is different from Bouleguy 2, lie in the yard and are numbered Bouleguy 3, 4 and 5 (WU 097045) on the plan (Fig. 159). In the case of numbers 3 and 4, the roof is formed of three simple collar trusses with their feet resting on a wall-plate supported in turn, on both sides, by three rough posts driven into the ground. Common rafters are placed at wide intervals, compared with Bouleguy 2 and the majority of Morbihan roofs, and there are five lateral purlins on each side held in place with wire. The ridge-pole is supported in the intersections of the principal rafters and one side of the building lies adjacent to an earth *talus* or field boundary which additionally buttresses this side. Earth filling is provided on the other side and the thatch covers all, descending on one side to the top of the *talus* and on the other to the

ground (Fig. 161). The walls are lined on the inside with planking formed of split logs as in Bouleguy 2. Temperature in buildings of this kind, with thatched roofs and floors of beaten earth, is remarkably even throughout the year, and is ideally suited for use as a *cave*, a cellar in which the year's supply of cider is kept.

Bouleguy 4 (WU 097045), similar in construction, has sides of vertical split logs, the structure being used as a hay barn. Bouleguy 5 (WU 097045) is different in that the upright posts support tie-beams above which rest 'wall-plates' to which the posts are braced with short struts crudely nailed on. This structure supports a 'roof' of brushwood piled up in convex form. Protection from driving rain is provided on one side by the earthen field bank, and on the other by a stack of small wood, prepared ready for use as firewood. This type of roof, formed of heaped brushwood, or sometimes of broom, has been observed elsewhere, notably in west Finistère, where there is a marked absence of timber. In spite of its appearance, it does shed water effectively and the structure is in use as a cart-shed. A similar structure has been recorded at Saint-Rivoal, Finistère (VU 261557), where the roof is supported on six rough posts slightly sunk into the ground (Fig. 162).[352] Whereas Bouleguy 5 uses reversed assembly, at Saint-Rivoal the relationship of tie-beams and wall-plates is that of normal assembly. Guilcher illustrates an example at Plouvien, Finistère, where one side is formed by a stone wall, the other, as at

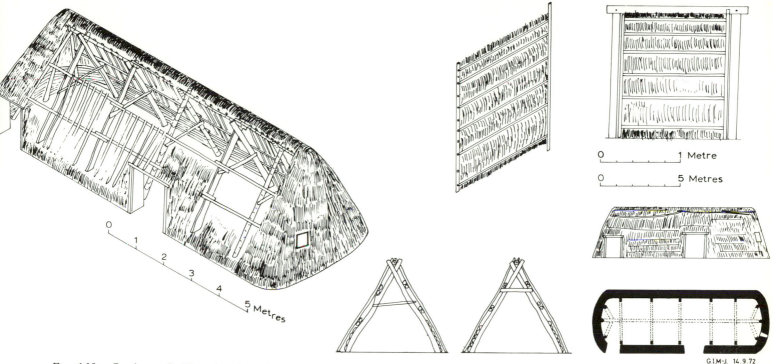

Fig. 160.   Bouleguy 2, Plumelin, Morbihan

Saint-Rivoal and Bouleguy, by posts, the brushwood and straw roofing being held securely by straw ropes carried over and secured to the wall-plates.[353] Structures of this kind, with the roof supported either on stone walls, or posts, or a mixture of the two, have been widely observed in Finistère and Morbihan where they serve a multitude of purposes including the storage of root crops, carts and farm implements. This type of structure may well once have been common in Britain and seems to fit the idea put forward for the roofing of crew yards at Goltho and Barton Blount.[354]

At La Grande Noë, Saint-Molf, Loire-Atlantique (WT 473487), a field barn built for essentially similar purposes is of rather superior construction (Fig. 163).[355] Essentially, the structure consists of six posts, two only having their feet on stone pads, and three tie-beams, from which rise full king-posts in turn supporting a ridge beam. Wall-plates rest on the tie-beams in reversed assembly and the principal rafters support one lateral purlin. Common rafters are again of chestnut poles, spaced at about 0.50 metre intervals, in turn supporting thatching spars to which the thatch is tied directly. Spars of this kind are used whenever the common rafters are widely spaced as at Bouleguy 3 (Fig. 161). Where, as at Bouleguy 2 (Fig. 160), the common rafters are closely spaced, thatching spars are unnecessary and thatch is tied directly to the common rafters. This structure is a good example

of a field barn of higher quality and shows how the king-post roof, almost universal in better quality vernacular buildings throughout France, has been utilized in conjunction with reversed assembly.

In the Grande Brière, large numbers of field buildings survive and two from Bréca (WT 516459) are illustrated (Figs. 164 and 165). Posts rest on stone pads, proving that buildings of this kind will stand for thirty years or more, withstanding storms, without the need to sink posts into the ground. Both the buildings at Bréca were built during World War II, have only required the usual annual repairs to their thatch, and are likely to last for another decade or so. Reversed assembly is used on both buildings. The common rafters and thatching spars are arranged as at La Grande Noë (Fig. 56), and the ridge is finished in a manner common in southern Brittany and universal in the Brière. Longitudinally, the roof is scissors-braced, a common feature in many of the higher-quality vernacular buildings both in Brittany and elsewhere in France. The quality of the carpentry in all these buildings is low, and although occasionally a pegged mortise and tenon, or a halved, joint may be found, mostly the timbers are nailed in place, as in both the examples at Bréca. In the Brière, where reeds are available in large quantities, reed thatch is used instead of the more common rye thatch, and screens or curtains of reed are used to cover the 'walls' of the field buildings,

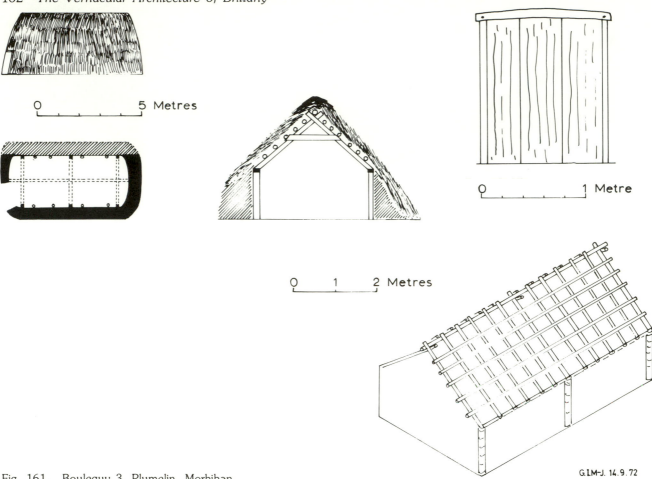

Fig. 161.   Bouleguy 3, Plumelin, Morbihan

G.L.M-J. 14.9.72

providing protection from driving rain, and to a certain extent from the wind.[356]

Passing-braces appear to have been introduced to provide lateral strength, primarily to resist wind pressure, and their existence in north-west France together with reversed assembly is of great interest. Some English examples of passing-braces are of thirteenth-century date,[357] and the continued use of the technique in rural France six hundred years later is remarkable. The survival of reversed assembly is no less remarkable, and has been observed all over Brittany in primitive farm buildings of twentieth-century date. Hewett has described its use in Essex, where the barn at Belchamp St. Paul's Hall, dated 1400, is regarded as one of the last survivals of a long tradition,[358] although Roberts finds its continued use in Lincolnshire in the seventeenth century.[359] Whether or not the use of reversed assembly was necessary because of the poor alignment of the posts in these early buildings is perhaps arguable.[360] The rearing of pairs of tied posts was perhaps the easier task, the wall plate being laid on top afterwards.

Unfavourable natural conditions, poor, thin and acid soils, variations in sea-level, and the erosion of cliff-lines are held to be responsible for the rarity of prehistoric habitation sites,[361] but a number of excavations have yielded valuable information concerning dwelling sites and have shown the former existence of rectilinear and sub-rectilinear buildings. These have been referred to in more detail elsewhere[362] and many of the so-called Bronze Age and Iron Age dwellings are now regarded as being probably medieval. This applies also to some of the rectangular houses on promontory hill-forts, as at Castel-Coz and Castel Meur. The houses of the central pound on the Île Guennoc, Landéda, are certainly medieval and the De La Grancière sites in Morbihan are mostly medieval.[363]

These sites include Perros-Kergalen, Morbihan, with remains of walls of dry-stone and earth, and a former hearth, betrayed by reddened soil, in the centre of the living area on the *terre battue* floor. A similar site is known as Brennilis, Finistère, in the heart of the Monts d'Arrée.[364] Rectilinear buildings are also associated with

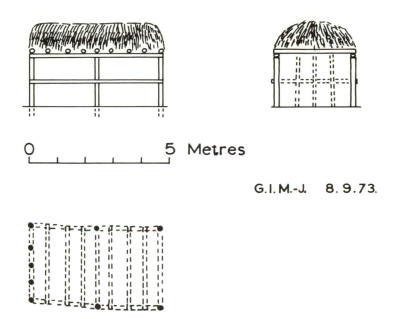

0 _____ 5 Metres

G.I.M.-J.   8.9.73.

Fig. 162.   Saint-Rivoal, Finistère

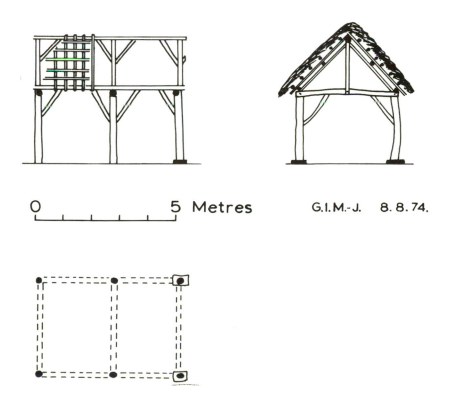

0 _____ 5 Metres   G.I.M.-J.   8.8.74.

Fig. 163.   La Grande Noë, Saint-Molf, Loire-Atlantique

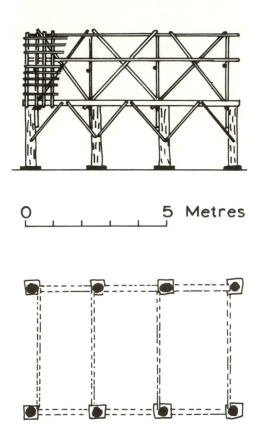

0   5 Metres

G.I.M.-J. 15.8.74.

Fig. 164.   Bréca 1, Saint-Lyphard, Loire-Atlantique

fortified hill-top camps[365] and other naturally defended locations. The houses, known from several sites, are small, often rectilinear, built on wide foundations of dry-stone, and have floors of *terre battue*, sometimes with traces of stone paving. Superstructures may have been of wood and thatch, but in other sites baked clay debris has been found with traces of clay and vegetable matter, which suggests that the superstructures may have been covered with *torchis*.[366] The practice of covering a thatched roof with *torchis* or *terre battue* to make it more weatherproof was formerly widely practised in exposed parts of western Brittany, and may still be seen on the Île d'Ouessant (Figs. 53 and 54). On mainland Finistère, buildings are recorded in the eighteenth century as having their roofs covered with clay,[367] such a covering presumably being intended to make the thatch more waterproof and at the same time providing weight on a roof exposed to a wet and windy climate. The use of clay on the ridge, eaves and the gables is also known from Ireland,[368] its use in layers in stapple thatch from northern Ireland[369] and as clay thatch in Scotland,[370] and this seems the most probable explanation of similar debris at a site in Jersey.[371] On the Île Gaignog, Landéda, Finistère,

rectilinear houses, with walls nearly 2.00 metres thick, were built of dry-stone, the inside walls being lined with vertically placed slabs of stone. There is no evidence of the former roofing, but the structure resembles the huts of the seaweed collectors of northern Finistère, formed until quite recently of an old boat upturned and placed over low walls.[372] Excavated houses near Pontivy[373] and Castel-Finans[374] were built of small stones without mortar, the hearth in the centre of each house surrounded by three stones arranged as a tripod and burnt by long usage. Rectilinear buildings, perhaps built of rough stone and turf on low foundation walls, are sometimes found in groups, but there is doubt whether they are pre-medieval.[375] Undoubted medieval structures have, however, recently been excavated at two sites in Morbihan and, although they have been fully described elsewhere,[376] their importance justifies repetition of the details.

At Pen-er-Malo in Guidel, three buildings were brought to light in 1970 (Fig. 70). Building A is elliptical in form, aligned at eleven degrees to the east–west axis, and measures 11.75 metres by 6.70 metres. The surviving walls, rising to 0.60 or 1.20 metres but with certain

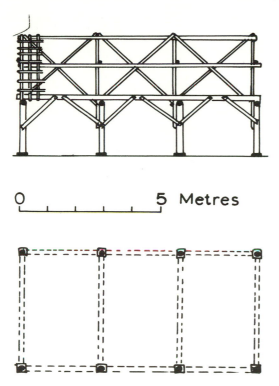

0 _____ 5 Metres

G.I.M.-J.   15.8.74.

Fig. 165.   Bréca 2, Saint-Lyphard, Loire-Atlantique

stretches much reduced, are of granite rubble with large blocks at the base, set in a sandy clay mortar. From the northern wall projects a low dividing wall. There are two doors. That on the south side, marked by a sill, is 1.25 metres wide and has a cavity some 0.15 metres in diameter, enclosed by three blocks of stone, undoubtedly a hole for the pin of a harr-hung door. Opposite, in the north wall, is a blocked doorway formerly 1.20 metres wide. Ground level inside falls from west to east and from north to south, and there is no trace of paving, the floor being formed of *terre battue*. East of the dividing wall, the black soil contains rare charcoal pieces, the southern part being occupied by a large granite block resting on the ground. West of the dividing wall there are two central hearths, H_1, roughly circular, 0.72 to 0.74 metres in diameter, delimited by four and two vertically set slabs respectively. The western hearth, H_2, is simpler and bounded by five blocks of granite. Around these hearths the earth is very black and rich in charcoal. A post-hole sited at the extreme south end of the dividing wall undoubtedly contained a roof support, but there was no trace of tile, slate or any other form of roof covering. Two coins of Conan III (1112–1148) date the house securely to the first half of the twelfth century, in accordance with a C14 dating of charcoal remains.[377]

Building B is oval in form and built on the side of a hill,

the walls of granulite and schist being of similar construction to building A, but thinner.[378] There is a single entrance, 1.10 metres wide, and a drop of 0.41 metres to the *terre battue* floor inside, with post-holes suggesting that formerly there were some steps. Zones of cinders along the walls suggest that the roof may have been destroyed by fire, and several post-holes lie just inside the walls, inclined at forty-five degrees, one containing a piece of burnt wood. Several large flat stones served as seats or work benches. The main hearth is 0.80 metres in diameter, and has a pyramidal stone placed at the centre, presumably to act as a support for a cooking pot too small to rest on the bounding stones. The irregular depth of cinders seems to indicate that the hearth was not used all over, but that the fire lay off-centre and was proportional to the heat required. The form of the hearth is very similar to that of building A.

Building C is of a different shape, being oval at one end and rectilinear at the other. The open central hearth is bounded by four fine pieces of mica-schist embedded in the earth, between which was a layer of white kaolinitic clay, blackened and hardened in the centre by fire. The entry on the south side was 1.10 metres wide, and there may have been a second entry in the north wall where several steps give access to the yard.[379]

Two oval buildings excavated in 1973–74 at Kerlano in

Plumelec, central Morbihan, on the Landes de Lanvaux, formed part of a deserted village (Fig. 71).[380] Building A is 11.60 metres long and 5.00 metres wide, and is aligned almost exactly east–west. Walls of granite rubble are *c.* 0.70 metres thick and are marked by a curious break and slight off-set where they curve round to form apsidal ends. The walls stand about 0.50 metres high, but may have been somewhat higher to judge by the amount of debris left. There was no trace of a former roof covering, and no more than a square metre of slate was found. Of the two openings, one in the south side perhaps gave access to the dwelling end. The other, 1.40 metres wide, in the northern wall, is reinforced by large blocks and may have been the entrance to a byre. The lower end is floored with *terre battue* spread over large paving blocks, an unusual arrangement, and the ground is concave, rising to the walls and reaching its lowest point near the northern wall, such as one might expect with heavy wear. The hearth has not been located.

Building C is oval, being formed of two semi-circular gables, the eastern one 2.90 metres, and the western 2.60 metres, in diameter. Between the two a space of 2.00 metres served as an entry. There was no evidence of a hearth and the building may have served as a shelter or workshop. No artifacts were discovered except for abundant and highly fragmented pottery, which, together with similarities to the Guidel site, have led excavators to suggest tentatively a mid thirteenth-century date.

Recent archaeological discoveries of oval houses, both dispersed and grouped in hamlets, have been made at Berné, Morbihan, in the Forêt de Pont-Calleck. Dry-stone walls rise to *c.* 0.50 metres and dimensions average *c.* 13.00 by 8.00 metres. A late-medieval to early-modern date was provided by a solitary piece of pottery.[381] Similar discoveries have been made at Kervini in Poullan, Finistère.[382] An elliptical building, possibly a house dating from the end of the Bronze Age, was recently excavated at Kerlande in Brandivy.[383] At the base of the feudal motte of Leslouch, in Plouédern, Finistère, an open hearth, of some 0.50 metres diameter, was uncovered close to a wall.[384] The open hearth of a house at Coat-mocun in Brennilis, Finistère is recorded by Du Châtellier.[385] Another medieval fortification, that at Le Coudray in Bain-de-Bretagne, has revealed a house plan with a lateral hearth.[386] Several other sites, currently being excavated, are revealing oval, semi-oval and rectilinear structures.[387]

The records of the E.A.R. for Morbihan contain information about three houses, all simple structures, now demolished, from the *commune* of Plumelin in which Bouleguy lies. Two were long-houses of the simplest kind, with man and beast housed at opposite ends under one roof with entrance by a common lateral doorway. There is no physical division inside, the functional separation being outlined by the location of furniture. In one case, an extra entry for the cattle has been made in the gable wall. The investigator has marked on the measured drawings not only the individual pieces of furniture, but also the cattle in the byres, so that there can be no doubt about the function of the lower end, or that the buildings were true long-houses. Large numbers of simple long-houses have been recorded in Brittany, but nearly all have a wooden partition dividing hall and byre, probably not an original feature, but one inserted as an improvement during the eighteenth or nineteenth century.[388] Like most of the Breton houses, there is in these examples only one doorway, and not, as in the case of the excavated buildings at Pen-er-Malo and Kerlano, pairs of opposed doorways. The cross-passage thus exists only in embryo form. Both long-houses lay in the hamlet of Talforest, and one retains, even as late as the 1940s, its open hearth, although a hood and chimney have been built, probably as a later addition. These houses have been described in detail and fully illustrated elsewhere, together with a third building at Kerspec.[389] The latter had no window, light entering only by the open doorway, nor a hole in the roof for smoke to escape. These buildings are important evidence for the evolution from the open hearth to a hearth set in the gable with a chimney-stack, outlined in detail elsewhere.[390] All three buildings are roughly rectilinear with walling of stone set in a clay matrix. Koh-Coët is an example of such a settlement where, *c.* 1900, some fifty families lived, each having a few small parcels of land near their *hutte*.[391]

Four other surviving primitive buildings, all found in that same area between Baud and Locminé from which so many examples in this chapter are drawn, provide a considerable insight into the construction of *loges*. This category of buildings lies between the more flimsy primitive structures that might last anything from a generation to fifty years or so, and the 'permanent' vernacular building that might be expected to stand upwards of four or five hundred years. In this sense, it is a 'bridging' category that shows there can be no clear divide between the 'primitive' and the 'vernacular' in architecture. The one merges into the other as skill improves and the tradesman, be he carpenter or mason, is increasingly brought into the construction process.

At Botcol in Guénin (WU 048056) stands a small long-house which has recently been acquired for use as a folk museum and restored *in situ* (Fig. 72).[392] Until about twenty years ago it was occupied as a long-house with a cow the sole occupant of the lower end beyond the flimsy

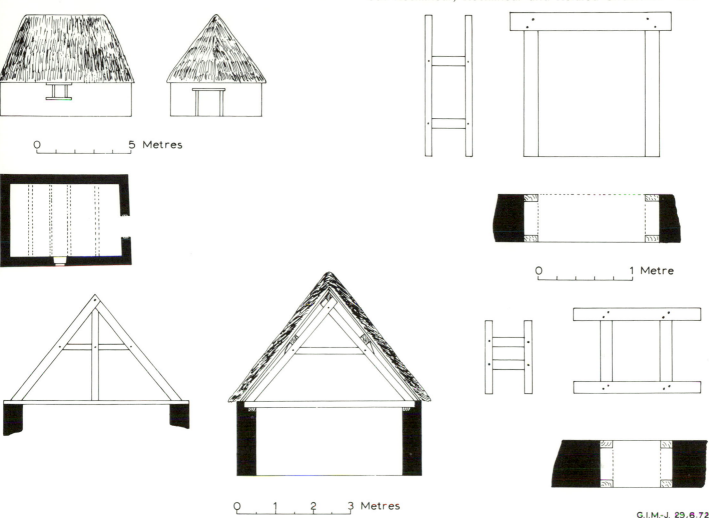

Fig. 166. Pon Digeu, Plumelin, Morbihan

G.I.M.-J. 29.6.72

wooden partition, itself probably a later insertion, the original house being open from end to end, giving the animal a sight of the hearth. The building is roughly rectilinear and its length *c.* 8.90 metres externally and *c.* 7.60 metres internally. It is *c.* 6.40 metres wide externally and *c.* 5.10 metres wide internally. Height from ground to eaves is 1.80 metres and the ridge rises to 4.85 metres. Walls are of stone rubble set in a coarse matrix of clay, the high clay content being a characteristic of this class of building. The timber posts embedded in the front elevation are regarded as a relic of former timber-frame construction in the countryside and here suggest that the builder was less than wholly confident in the mechanical strength of his stone walling. There is a single doorway giving access for man and beast and a glazed window lights the hall. Two unglazed and unshuttered openings ventilate the byre. The hearth stands against the upper gable and the wattle-and-clay chimney hood rests on a

wooden breastsummer which is not corbelled out, but supported by a pair of vertical posts. This hearth represents an intermediate stage in the evolution of the hearth from an open hearth to one fully integrated with the gable wall (Fig. 73). There are five tie-beams and the roof is supported on slender collar and tie-beam trusses. The thatch of rye-straw is tied directly to the closely spaced chestnut common rafters lashed together with straw rope. A clay capping completes the ridge.

Nearby Koh-Coët 1, a *loge* occupied until 1976, is now in an advanced state of ruin, the roof having collapsed (WU 062055) (Fig. 167). It too may well originally have been a long-house but was not so used latterly when the lower end served as a store. The windows are probably original but that at the lower end, now glazed, may formerly have been merely a ventilation hole as at Botcol. A stage in the evolutionary sequence between oval and rectilinear plans is illustrated by the

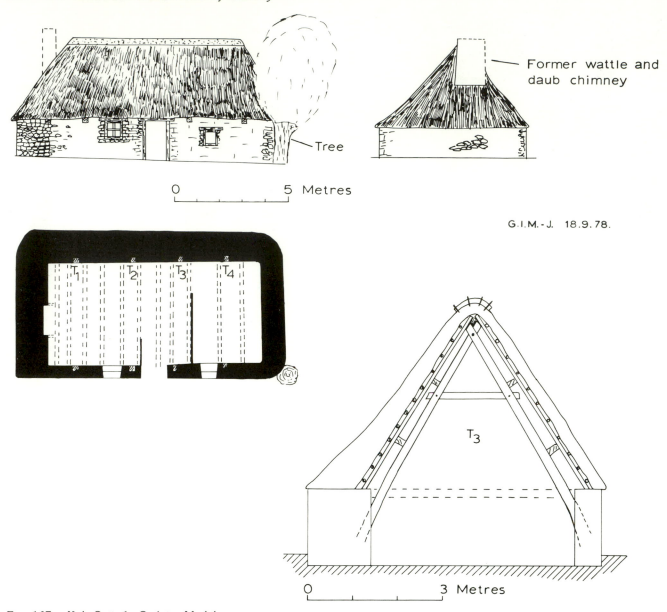

Former wattle and daub chimney

Tree

0   5 Metres

G.I.M.-J. 18.9.78.

T₁ T₂ T₃ T₄

T_3

0   3 Metres

Fig. 167. Koh-Coët 1, Guénin, Morbihan

curvature of three of the corners. Walling of stone rubble, set in a thick matrix of clay, is irregular in thickness, varying from 0.55 metres to 1.45 metres, and a tree grows out of one corner. The structure has a hipped roof, as at Botcol, and the hearth is just incorporated into the upper gable. The building measures *c.* 11.90 metres by *c.* 6.50 metres externally and *c.* 9.50 metres by *c.* 4.50 metres internally. The ground slopes slightly towards the lower end and the wall-head stands 1.85 metres above the ground by the single doorway. At the centre of the building, the ridge rises *c.* 5.50 metres above the ground. The chimney-stack, of wattle-and-clay, or daub, rises

through the upper hip. There are four roof trusses all of the full-cruck type. This is the second-best example of the full-cruck truss discovered in a dwelling, the other being in a now demolished house, at Talforest, in the same area, recorded by the E.A.R., which has been illustrated elsewhere.[393] It is of the collar type, there being no tie-beams. Ceiling beams are entirely independent of the trusses and one supports a loft platform. Rye-straw thatch is tied to the closely spaced common rafters of rough chestnut poles tied together with straw rope.

The third *loge*, Koh-Coët 2 (Fig. 168), inhabited until recently, is now also in an advanced state of decay (WU

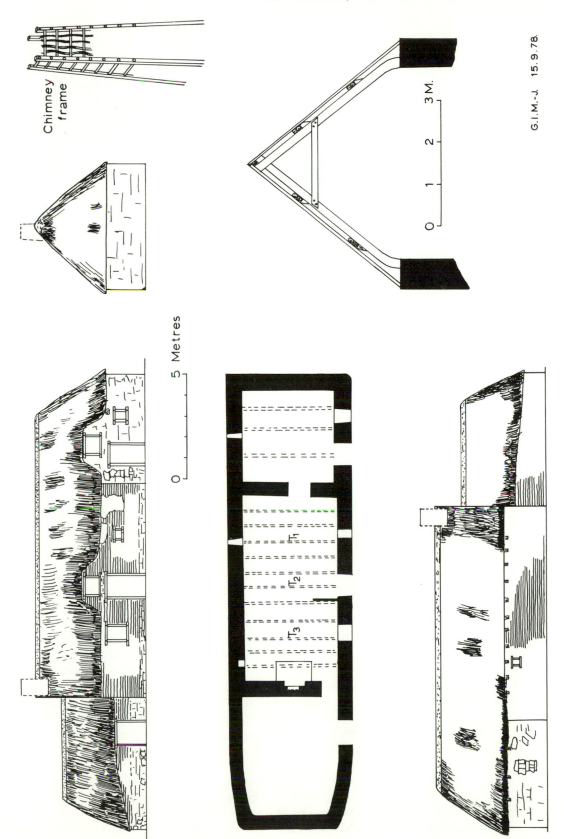

Chimney frame

G.I.M.-J. 15.9.78.

3 M.

2

1

0

5 Metres

0

T_1

T_2

T_3

Fig. 168. Koh-Coët 2, Guénin, Morbihan

Fig. 169. Koh-Coët 3, Guénin, Morbihan

052057). Walling is entirely of unbaked clay bricks. There are two courses of stone footings rising to *c.* 6.30 metres followed by 1.80 metres of clay bricks formed of sixteen courses. The bricks, *c.* 0.12 metres thick, were laid wet with layers of straw between the courses and the whole façade is rendered with *pisé*. The original building is of long-house form with a central doorway and two asymmetrical window openings. The lower end, also ventilated by a slit in the rear wall, was probably originally a byre. Lean-to additions have since been made at both ends and doors inserted in the original gable walls to provide access. The original length was *c.* 10.45 metres externally and *c.* 9.05 metres internally. Width is *c.* 5.90 metres externally and *c.* 4.50 metres internally. There are three trusses of the upper cruck, collar and tie-beam type. Thatch is of rye-straw tied directly to the closely set chestnut poles that constitute the common rafters, tied together with straw rope. The hearth is set 0.20 metres into the upper gable and surmounted by a wattle-and-clay chimney hood.

Also at Koh-Coët is a small timber-frame house, almost certainly the last inhabited *loge* in the area (WU 055055).

The timber-frame structure, of pine, was constructed in 1924 by the husband of the present occupant, a carpenter by trade, one year after his marriage. The frame has a clay infill and the outer surface is covered by weather-boarding. Recently the materials have so deteriorated as to require a sheathing of galvanized iron (Fig. 169)! Assuming the structure to be at the end of its useful life, its exact date of construction permits a life expectation of this type of building to be given as *c.* fifty-five years. This tallies with the life of the circular structures for the *broyeurs d'ajonc* at Goaz-Henry in Carnoët, with their earth-fast posts, and the other primitive buildings described in this chapter and dating from the years after World War I. The timber-frame building at Koh-Coët has an earth floor and a chimney-stack constructed of wooden boards nailed to a frame. The plan is that of a long-house, first derivative, with a byre and store at the lower end with its own doorway and internal doorway permitting direct access from the hall. Recently, a clay *loge* with a clay-and-wattle chimney has been discovered in Maxent, Ille-et-Vilaine.

A farm building at Pon Digeu (WU 084043) in the

nearby *commune* of Plumelin (Fig. 166) is of a form of construction very similar to the stone houses described above. Walling is of granite rubble and roof covering of rye-straw thatch. The building is approximately 6.80 metres long and 4.85 metres wide externally and internal measurements are 5.80 metres by 3.80 metres. The eaves line is 1.80 metres, and the ridge 5.50 metres, above the ground. Rubble walling is bonded with a thick matrix of *pisé* such that the resulting wall represents a transitional stage between an earth wall containing small quantities of stone and a stone wall bonded with earth. This 'compromise' is not as strong as either a stone or an earth wall and this may explain the need to protect the doorway with a double frame of timber. A timber frame with elongated sill and lintel is also provided for the window opening. The floor is of *terre battue* and the tie-beams are irregularly spaced. Roof trusses are of the collar and tie-beam type supporting a ridge purlin and a pair of lateral purlins which rest on cleats. Common rafters of rough chestnut poles rest with their feet on the wall-heads and it is to these that the thatch of rye-straw is tied directly. The building has a roof fully hipped at both ends. This is not a house and there is no evidence of a chimney or any form of heating. The significance of this building lies in the rather primitive walling which has been recorded elsewhere in the area and in the survival of the fully hipped roof associated with more primitive housing before the development of stone gables incorporating a chimney-piece and stack.

The survival of such simple houses at the mid-twentieth century is remarkable and was not confined to this part of Morbihan. They certainly survived late in Loire-Atlantique, as evidenced by a photograph of an open long-house in Guérande in 1938,[394] with a cow staring across to the hearth from a byre, enclosed by a low partition of the kind referred to by Cambry.

Several writers have referred to the simpler buildings of the past. Cambry, travelling in Finistère to record the state of that *département* shortly after the Revolution, regarded the dwelling of the poorer classes to be much the same throughout Brittany. He describes the simple long-house as an ill-lit hut, full of smoke, with only a light partition to divide it into two parts, one occupied by the master of the house, his wife, children and grandchildren, the other containing the oxen, cows and all the animals of the farm. '*Les exhalaisons réciproques se communiquent librement, et je ne sais qui perd à cet échange.*' The houses were about thirty *pieds* long and fifteen *pieds* wide with a single window eighteen *pouces* high.[395] A chimney existed, presumably in the upper gable wall with *lits clos* placed on both sides, a table, two benches and very little else. This furniture compares with

that in the three houses at Plumelin recorded by the E.A.R. In the two dwellings with the central open hearth, at Kerspec and Talforest, the *lits clos* are placed against the wall of the upper gable. At Kerspec, there is no window, nor is there a table, whilst in the second, the table is found in the 'classic' position, placed in front of the window, perpendicular to the wall, the place it came to adopt in most Breton houses after the abandonment of the central open hearth and the acceptance of the hearth and chimney into the upper gable wall. With the hearth in this position, the *lits clos* formerly placed against the gable have moved to make way for the hearth and a frequent arrangement is for them to stand on either side of the hearth, as Cambry describes. Invariably, the conjugal bed is found on the northern side opposite the window and in the corner next to the hearth. Sometimes this is the only bed, but more usually there are others, especially if the family is large. It is on the side opposite the window, however, that the continuous range of *lits clos*, *armoires* and other pieces are found. The significance of the arrangements of the furniture in the houses in Plumelin, with their open hearths, is that they give a clue to the positions of the beds before the migration of the hearth to the upper gable.

Guilcher, describing the rural habitat at Plouvien in north Finistère, refers to the type of farmyard building recorded at Bouleguy and known in Breton as a *lokenn*.[396] At Plouvien, dimensions varied, 5.00 metres by 2.50 metres being an average. The *lokennou* were used for a variety of farm purposes, as worksheds, and for the storage of crops and implements. Of the farms in the *commune* in the late 1940s, 32.6 per cent had one *lokenn*, 14.2 per cent had two and 4.60 per cent more than two. The temporary dwellings of the *sabotier* and other woodland workers survived in small numbers until after World War II, and that recorded in Plouvien was regarded as being of a type adapted to semi-nomadism, '*une hutte de chaume et de fougère, sans cheminée (la fumée passe à travers le toit) avec deux petites fenêtres pouvant être adaptées à une nouvelle hutte. C'est une survivance d'un passé bien mort . . .*'.[397]

Nomadism, both temporary and permanent, has long been a factor among the Breton population. Numerous small trades were practised in the countryside by a class apart from the settled agriculturalists. Inevitably this group included vagabonds, the extreme poor as well as those temporarily unemployed. These numbers had decreased by the beginning of the twentieth century but still formed a significant proportion including *sabotiers* and charcoal burners. Principal locations included the woods of Camors, Floranges and Lanvaux, the *pays vannetais*, and Huelgoat, Beffou, Coat an Noz and

Duault in the north-west. '*Les sabotiers mènent une existence très primitive. Leurs campements ressemblent à des villages indiens. Ce sont des huttes rondes en branchages avec portes basses et trou pratiqué dans le haut. Une hutte plus grande que les autres sert d'atelier. Les cabanes d'habitation contiennent pêle-mêle quelques meubles et des lits faits de grosses branches non travaillées; au milieu, un foyer sans cheminée, dont la fumée sort par le trou du toit.*'[398]

Similar farm buildings of simple construction were recorded in Bulat-Pestivien, Côtes-du-Nord.[399] Not only farm buildings of this kind exist in Basse-Bretagne but simple houses also, in the very region, around Locminé, where the Bouleguy, Talforest and Kerspec structures occur, thus confirming the widespread survival of these primitive buildings in that part of central Brittany. '*Les huttes de domaniers — on ne peut les appeler maisons — sont nombreuses en particulier aux environs de Remungol, de Locminé et de Moustoirac.*' Some had walls of stone, apparently without corners, others were of timber frame and planks, or of *torchis*, and covered with thatch. Chimneys were also of *torchis*, or of old pieces of zinc, in both cases presumably applied to a wooden frame. Such buildings may well have retained a central hearth as at Talforest, the former hole in the roof having been replaced by a simple chimney. Alternatively, the hearth may have been located against a gable, but gables would be unlikely if the walls were not cornered, and it is more probable that these houses had roofs hipped in the manner of Bouleguy. In this region, not only were such houses kept carefully in repair, but also newly built during the first decade of the twentieth century. '*Non seulement on ne démolit pas ces cabanes, mais on les entretient telles quelles avec un soin jaloux, et il y a des points, heureusement rares, comme Moustoirac, où même aujourd'hui on en fait de nouvelles sur le même modèle.*'[400]

A remarkable example of a pauper settlement occurred on the grand massif of Quintin-Duault, in Saint-Nicholas-du-Pélem, an area of large estates and great poverty. A wealthy landowner, *c.* 1860, in charity, provided a small plot of land for any landless and homeless person who cared to build a *cabane*. By the turn of the century a group of some hundred families were established, without any means of existence save alms and marauding. The former common lands were also favourable to the establishment of squatter settlement. In this way the *penty* were first established, as a transitional phase before the building of permanent *penty*.

In Trégorrois, Le Braz found '*une chaumière qu'on eût plutôt prise pour une hutte de sauvage*'.[401] It too had a 'rush' door, '*la claie de genêt tressé qui lui servait de*

porte'. Many examples then existed in *Arcoët*, some in the Forêt de Porthuault, where he found '*ces logis de paille et de boue épars dans les solitudes des monts*'. These too were '*ronde, ventrue, amincie seulement en haut, la hutte, avec ses cloisons de branchages et de genêts entrelacés, semblait moins une cabane humaine qu'une ruche énorme disposée au bord de la sente pour recevoir un essaim géant*'. The door was *bourrée de paille*, presumably like that at Bouleguy 2 (Fig. 160). A fire of chippings burned in the middle of the room on a circular hearth, formed of a primitive masonry of stone and clay. It was possible to see only by the light of the fire until one's eyes became accustomed to the poor light. Three wooden posts supported the roof and on a shelf fixed against one of them stood a statue of the Virgin. Against a wall were the tools of the sabotier's trade and the remaining furnishings consisted of a heavy cupboard on which stood a cooking pot, a dresser with a dozen earthenware bowls, four or five stools cut out of oak trunks and a cage containing a sleeping owl! '*Je cherchais du regard les lits: le sabotier me montra une rangée de piquets plantés dans le sol et que des ramilles de bouleau, tordues comme des câbles, reliaient entre eux. C'étaient les bordures des couchettes. Quant aux couchettes elles-mêmes, rien de plus agreste, en vérité: des jonchées de fougères sèches en guise de sommiers et des couettes de balle de seigle pour matelas. . . . Ce ne sont pas les lits les plus moelleux qui donnent les meilleurs rêves, prononça notre hôte en son parler sentencieux . . . Et puis, ajouta-t-il, on repose ici, veillé par les astres. Il nous indiquait, du doigt, au-dessus de nos têtes, une ouverture béante ménagée dans la coupole de la hutte pour laisser passage à la fumée, et où s'encadrait un pan de ciel nocturne, un champ d'azur sombre semé de froides lueurs d'étoiles*'.[402] These examples provide further proof of the survival of the open hall with central hearth and a hole in the roof for smoke to escape. In Briec in 1818, 232 *sabotiers'* huts are recorded.[403]

The writings of several authors provide insights into the widespread survival into the nineteenth and early-twentieth centuries of primitive dwellings. Souvestre describes a *cabane* at Kerity-Penmarc'h in Finistère, which had a roof thatched with seaweed held in place by heavy stones.[404] There was obviously a 'rush' door as at Bouleguy 2, made of broom and willow, for '*une claie de genêts verts tournant sur des liens d'osier tenait lieu de porte*'. A narrow window, unglazed and without shutters, let out the smoke from the, presumably, open hearth. *Cabanes* of a more substantial kind were seen at Kerlern in Crozon.[405] A hamlet of woodland workers, in the Forêt du Gavre, is described in some detail. All the *huttes* were round, '*bâties en branchages dont on avait garni les interstices avec du gazon ou de la mousse, et recouvertes d'une toiture de copeaux'*. Opposite the door was a big *'cheminée en clayonnage'*, presumably wicker-work. This was an improvement on the simple hole in the roof, but the hearth remained in the centre of the floor. *'A l'aspect étrange du lieu, on eût pu se croire dans un wigwam de Peaux-Rouges sans la conversation bruyante des fileuses réunies près de l'âtre'*. Furniture was of the simplest kind.[406]

In several *communes* of the *canton* of Châteaulin, *huttes* of *mottes*, or turf, covered in straw or heath were the only new buildings in the early-nineteenth century.[407] These dwellings were homes of the poor and destitute as well as of forest workers, and it is possible that their numbers increased during the nineteenth century as population grew. There can be no doubt that they represent the continuation of a long tradition of primitive buildings.

Not far from Plumelin, on the borders of the *communes* of Grand-Champ and Brandivy, during the mid-nineteenth century, a group of five or six dwellings stood on the *landes*. Each consisted of a *hutte*, almost circular, of which the long axis was barely 4.00 metres. Walls, *c.* 1.00 metres high, were of earth bounded externally by brushwood. The roof was of close-set common rafters rising to a cone some 2.00 metres above the ground. A little off-centre, a hole had been cut to allow smoke to escape. The hearth was a simple slab of granite. Furniture consisted of a box-bed, and pieces of roughly squared oak served for table and benches. These dwellings were known as *loges* in the district. In 1858, Grand-Champ boasted twenty-five to thirty of them inhabited by 384 individuals.[408] Primitive buildings certainly survived late in central Morbihan and the last but one surviving example of a *loge* in the *pays de Baud* ceased to be inhabited only in 1974 (Fig. 167). They were essentially squatter settlements, the houses measuring *c.* 12.00 by 5.00 metres, occupied either by forest workers or by the destitute who sought to eke out a living by enclosing and cultivating a few small parcels of *landes*.[409] Three writers, Choleau,[410] Le Bourhis,[411] and Picard,[412] concerned with the landless peasants and the rural poor, provide illuminating insights into the humbler dwellings and their construction. Du Châtellier describes a chance encounter with a primitive long-house at Loqueffret, Finistère, during the last decade of the nineteenth century.[413] A detailed commentary on Du Châtellier's observations has been published elsewhere and further reference to the interior is made below.[414]

The reports of the *Comités d'Hygiène* for Côtes-du-Nord, by *canton*, from 1852 onwards, are greatly concerned with the housing conditions of the poor, frequently referring to sub-vernacular buildings. Turf seems to have been widely used for walling. In Rostrenan, the *cabanes* were for the most part *'en gazons superposés, surmontés d'un méchant toit de chaume, percé d'un trou pour l'évaporation de la fumée, et d'une porte, qui donne à ces asiles de malheureux l'aspect de l'entrée d'une caverne'*. At Saint-Nicholas-du-Pélem, the number of *cabanes* in the *canton* that were *'occupées par les classes pauvres'* had risen to 180. They were built of earth and *'gazon mélangé de quelques pierres, couvertes en chaume ou bruyère'*, and normally sited on the verge of a road or track or on a *lande*. Furniture was virtually non-existent save for *'quelques morceaux de bois et de paille sur lesquels couchent ces malheureux'*. At Maël-Carhaix, *logettes* were built of *terre et mottes*, and in Bourbriac there were as many as four hundred of these *huttes* in 1852. In Loudéac, *cabanes* were built with walls of earth and of schist orthostats. On *'un talus de terre sont appuyés deux murs latéraux en branchages. Le devant en de même construction; une claie sert de porte, quatre poteaux, deux aux angles de la façade et deux près de la porte, soutiennent le toit en fougères qui repose de l'autre côté sur le fossé. Ou bien, de grandes plaques de schistes dits ardoises du biscuit, sont dressés entre des poteaux avec lesquels elles sont plus ou moins jointives. On met, par dessus, quatre pants de mur ainsi faits, un toit en fougère'*.[415] These orthostat dwellings are similar to those recorded by the E.A.R. at Pont-Rot in Plounévez-Quintin.[416]

These examples show how the long-house in its simplest form has survived to the mid-twentieth century, and also how early techniques of timber building have survived long after they have disappeared elsewhere.

The sub-rectilinear building, Bouleguy 2, seems without doubt to be a survival of a type once used as a dwelling-house which, as its owner has testified, existed in large numbers before World War I, and only differs from the houses in that the latter were built on low banks of earth and stone. Such walls are evident in the excavated buildings at Kerlano and Pen-er-Malo as well as in the prehistoric buildings outlined above. Bouleguy 2 has the type of roof which would fit the medieval buildings. Its principal rafters, whilst they cannot be called crucks, must be regarded as the immediate antecedents of the cruck, for with a slight curve and some lengthening these trusses could be placed on, or their feet incorporated within, a low wall. As wall height increases, a tie-beam could be introduced, as in the fine example recorded by the E.A.R. at Talforest.[417] Whether the excavated buildings were long-houses or not is unclear. Absolute proof of the occupation of the lower end of these dwellings by animals is lacking. Nevertheless, from what is known of the Breton house and the fact that the long-house was a standard form of dwelling until recent times, it is highly probable that animals were so accommodated. It would seem prudent, however, to use the term 'long-house form' for these buildings in the absence of such complete proof.[418] The survival of the elementary long-house in the examples described by Cambry and in the examples recorded by the E.A.R. also helps interpret the plans of the excavated houses. The medieval structures show the form with pairs of opposed doorways, which is interesting in that so many surviving Breton long-houses have only one doorway. Firm proof of the plans of the *sabotiers'* houses described by Le Braz, Guilcher[419] and others is also lacking, but it seems probable that they were not dissimilar to the *lokennou*. Certainly the three posts supporting the roof in Le Braz' example suggest a sub-rectilinear rather than a circular building. This being so, the *huttes des sabotiers* are likely to have resembled the *lokennou* and, if so, provide further evidence of the survival of the primitive house with the open central hearth. The oval form was common throughout western Europe in medieval times and it is interesting that a memory of it survives in other rectilinear houses with rounded gables. Examples occur all over Brittany but they tend to be localized, as around Saint-Thégonnec in Finistère, Saint-M'Hervé in Ille-et-Vilaine, Saint-Joachim and the Grande Brière, where corners are rounded without practical reason. Fox has observed similar features in Wales.[420]

The examples given also show considerable variation in their dimensions. The prehistoric buildings are much smaller than the medieval and modern ones. Bouleguy 2, however, is of similar length to, if somewhat narrower than, building A at Pen-er-Malo.

These structures are notable for their simplicity, for the fact that they have survived into the twentieth century and in that they illustrate the link between buildings whose plans can only be determined by excavation and buildings of similar form, once used as dwellings and for other purposes, but now found, if at all, only in the farmyard. The buildings at Bouleguy and Bréca are all about thirty years old, and can reasonably be expected with proper maintenance to last another decade or so, at least. Rebuilding would thus be necessary every generation or so, and in the absence of prepared foundations which might have been re-used, any rebuilding is unlikely to have been on the same plan precisely, the earlier structures leaving little surface trace of their former existence. In an area known for the extreme fragmentation of land holdings, they were probably occupied by the perhaps numerous families low in the social scale, some of which might be landless.

A further class of primitive building is that of the sunken-featured building.[421] Evidence of sunken-featured buildings in England has been summarized by Hurst[422] and Addyman.[423] Following first recognition at Sutton Courtenay in the 1920s, sunken-featured buildings or *Grubenhäuser* have been found at a large number of widely separated sites. They are by far the commonest known type of Anglo-Saxon timber building, probably because they are often easier to identify than other types.

Suggestions that dwelling houses must always have been above-ground structures, and that the sunken-featured buildings were used only for ancillary purposes, is now difficult to accept when evidence from West Stow and Mucking shows by far the largest number of structures to be *Grubenhäuser*. The implication must be that some, at least, of these buildings were dwelling-houses. It is probable that others were adapted to a number of industrial, storage or other ancillary functions, and evidence clearly shows that some sunken buildings were used for weaving. Excavations on the European mainland have shown the type to be present over wide areas, and they continued in use in the Harz until the thirteenth and fourteenth centuries. Twentieth-century examples, known once to have been inhabited, are reported from Somerset[424] and Ireland.[425] English examples, known from excavation, are commonly rectilinear, of *c.* 3.00 metres by 2.00 metres on average, and varying in depth from 0.20 metres to 1.00 metres or more. Reconstruction of the former superstructure, walls and roof, is very difficult as the evidence is generally meagre. Usually there is a single post-hole in the centre of each short side and, at some sites, rows of stake-holes around the edge which may be either vertical or sloping, suggesting a flimsy tent-like structure. Evidence from West Stow suggests that some examples may have had quite substantial timber structures resting on sill-beams. In the light of this uncertainty examples of the considerable number of sunken-floored huts that have survived in Brittany to the late-twentieth century are of the greatest interest.

These are all used for storage and there is yet no record of the *Grubenhaus* ever having been used as a dwelling in Brittany, nor is any example yet known from excavation. This is not surprising as medieval archaeology has only recently made an impact on the Province. Insofar as so many sunken-floored huts survived until recently, it would be surprising if medieval examples were not eventually discovered, and given the extreme poverty of many primitive dwellings in Brittany even in recent times, proof that some sunken-floored huts were inhabited may eventually be forthcoming.

The sunken-floored hut is particularly common in parts

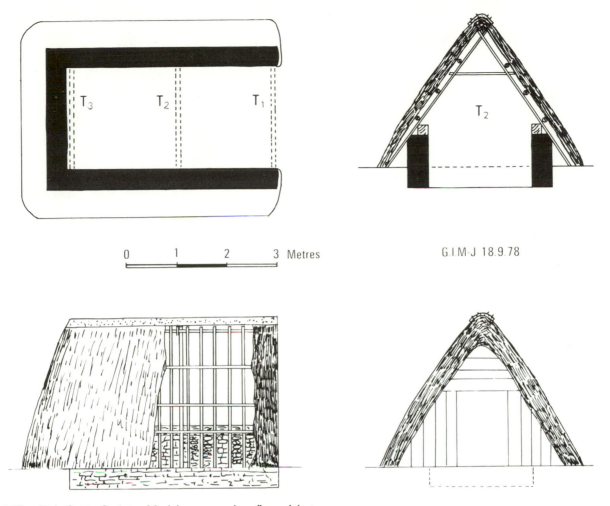

0   1   2   3 Metres

G.I.M-J 18.9.78

Fig. 170.   Koh-Coët, Guénin, Morbihan: a sunken-floored hut

of Morbihan and of Ille-et-Vilaine, and two examples have been recorded in the *commune* of Guénin, Morbihan. That at Koh-Coët (WU 061055) measures 3.90 metres long by 2.60 metres wide internally, and 5.50 metres long by 4.40 metres wide externally, and has a floor beaten earth sunk to a depth of 0.20 metres (Fig. 170). The internal height of the structure from floor to ridge beam is 2.50 metres and the walls rise to 0.60 metres above the floor. Internally, the example at Botcol is 4.15 metres long by 2.00 metres wide at the rear, 2.05 metres at the front, and 5.20 metres long by 3.80 metres wide externally. The floor of beaten earth is sunk to a depth of 0.40 metres. Internal height from floor to ridge-purlin is 2.70 metres and the walls rise 1.05 metres from the floor. Unlike that at Koh-Coët, whose walls internally are of earth, those at Botcol are revetted by a stone wall 0.40 metres thick, on top of which rests a wall-plate 0.20 metres square. The wall rises 0.65 metres from ground-

level and the thickness of thatch on the outside adds a further 0.50 metres to the width.

The hut at Botcol (WU 048056), with its stone walling, is the better construction of the two (Fig. 171). There are three collar-trusses, one in the middle, the others at the ends. These are formed of roughly-cut chestnut poles, the collars being nailed on. Between the trusses, chestnut poles, closely laid at intervals of 0.15 to 0.20 metres or so, form the common rafters. There are nine such poles in the rear gable and fifteen along each side. Their feet rest on the ground outside the walls, and the upper ends rest against the ridge-purlin. Three pairs of lateral purlins are tied by straw rope to the outside of the principal and common rafters. The ridge-purlin is carried in the 'V' of the intersecting principal rafters which differ from the common rafters only in that they are of slightly greater diameter. Their function is to support the ridge-purlin. Some practical benefit is derived from the presence of the

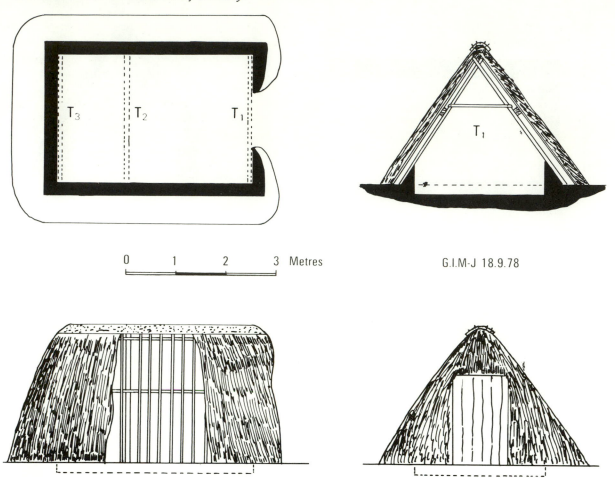

0   1   2   3 Metres

G.I.M-J 18.9.78

Fig. 171.   Botcol, Guénin, Morbihan: a sunken-floored hut

collars across which are laid plank shelves, on which are stored baskets and other equipment. The common rafters are stabilized by being tied at intervals with straw rope, and the thatch, traditionally of rye-straw, is tied directly to the rafters and descends to the ground, wholly masking the walls on the outside. A capping of turf pegged into the thatch finishes the ridge. This roof differs from the traditional roof construction of south Morbihan only in that the principal rafters are of similar scantling to the common rafters and the lateral purlins rest on the outside of both principal and common rafters. Whilst in vernacular buildings the principal rafters and often the purlins are carpentered, here there is no attempt at carpentry. Walls are of rubble laid in a coarse matrix of clay-mortar, the simple *terre battue* with which the floor is also covered. The inside wall-head, with its plate, provides a narrow shelf around three sides of the structure. The door-frame and front end of the hut are of wood and the surface covered with boards. It is reasonable to suppose that this is a relatively late

arrangement and that similar structures would once have been finished, as at Koh-Coët, by bringing the thatch roof round the front gable, leaving only a rectangular doorway. Traditionally the door would almost certainly have been a harr-hung rush-door, similar to that previously described at Bouleguy.

The somewhat inferior hut at Koh-Coët has three trusses, one of which, a roughly carpentered affair, is placed about one-third of the length from the rear gable. It is of the collar-truss type with a ridge-purlin supported in the intersection of the rafters and one lateral purlin in each side nailed to the outer side of the principal rafters. Rough chestnut poles are again closely spaced and rest with their feet on the ground and the upper ends against the ridge-purlin. They are tied at intervals with straw rope and the whole structure is thatched with rye straw tied directly to the common rafters. The ridge is finished with turf pegged into the thatch. Like the hut at Botcol nearby, the interior is almost rectangular, but on the outside, corners are rounded. The thatch curves round at the front to form the gable, leaving only a space 1.80 metres high and 1.10 metres wide for the doorway, closed by a door of rough planks. The step from the ground-level outside to the floor-level within is too shallow to require an additional step as is provided at Botcol.

At the time of recording these huts were used for storage. That at Koh-Coët contained a miscellany of tools for field and garden use, whilst the Botcol hut was in use as a cellar for the storage of cider, and contained four barrels, in addition to a number of tools which lay on the ground and on the shelves. A fully thatched building is surprisingly cool in summer, conserving warmth in winter. When the floor-level is sunk and covered with beaten earth, the interior is remarkably temperate, remaining cool even during the hottest weather. In a region where cider has been the staple drink, the ability to construct at negligible cost undoubtedly explains why such buildings have continued in use. They are difficult to date, and seem to have a life of from twenty to fifty years providing the timber is of good quality and the thatch is repaired annually. Most of those that survive were built between the two World Wars, and as the present oldest generation passes, they are likely to be swept away or simply left to decay. At the present rate of destruction, it is unlikely that more than a few will be left in twenty years' time.

Until recently, there has been a tendency to assume that European village plans of the twentieth century are little changed from those of the Middle Ages, save perhaps for some addition and infilling. Recent work by medieval archaeologists in Britain is showing how considerably village plans have changed during historic time, and how little trace has been left by earlier buildings. The danger of basing theories of house development on evidence derived solely from surviving buildings of the last three of four centuries has also been brought out by recent work.[426] There is a similar temptation to imagine that the small but substantial Breton stone houses, however simple in plan and function, are little changed from their predecessors of the Middle Ages, but primitive structures of timber and that like those described in this chapter undoubtedly existed in large numbers in earlier centuries. At what period more substantial building in stone began is not yet known, but stone houses must gradually have superseded the flimsy type of structures seen at Plumelin and elsewhere. By the early-twentieth century these had been largely, but not entirely, relegated to the farmyard, being used as dwellings in only a few areas. It may be that the plans of Breton hamlets, like those of English villages, have also changed with time, taking on a relatively permanent form only with the advent of more durable building material.

NINE

THE SINGLE-CELL HOUSE

Fieldwork shows single-cell houses to exist in large numbers (Fig. 102). Although the numbers diminish proportionately in some coastal areas where the two-cell house predominates, in the interior and in the eastern districts single-cell houses usually exceed twenty-five per cent of the sample. In Plougrescant (Quadrat 1, Fig. 80), thirteen of the twenty-nine houses examined were of one cell only, representing forty-five per cent of the total. In Plougasnou (Quadrat 3) twenty-nine per cent were single-cell dwellings, whilst in Quadrats 2, 8 and 9 the proportion fell to eleven, nine and seven per cent respectively. Along the southern littoral numbers increased. In Quadrats 14 and 15, forty and thirty-seven per cent were single-cell dwellings. Numbers dropped slightly to twenty-nine per cent in Grand-Champ (Quadrat 16), but increased to thirty-nine percent in Béganne (Quadrat 17), where thirty-three of the eighty-four houses were of only one cell. The proportion was approximately the same in Guérande with thirty-six per cent (Quadrat 19), but rose to forty-nine per cent in Frossay (Quadrat 20), and to eighty-three and eighty per cent in Quadrats 18 and 21. In the interior, in Quadrats 4, 5, 6, 11 and 12, twenty-eight, thirty-nine, eighteen, forty-two and forty-five per cent of the total number of recorded houses, respectively, were single-cell houses. Probate inventories, together with the evidence of travellers and others, demonstrate conclusively that the greater part of the Breton population traditionally lived in one room (see Chapter 15). This, however, includes all the dwellings of the long-house category, also present in substantial numbers, in which the family dwelt in a single cell at the upper end, the animals occupying the lower end. First-floor halls also constitute a small but significant portion of the total.

It is difficult to assess accurately the proportion of single-cell dwellings present at any given period in the past, and those mapped (Fig. 102) represent only the survivors in the 1970s. Numbers are shown to be highest in the interior and in the east, in those areas where land holdings were small and fragmentation greatest, and

where there were fewer opportunities to engage in a second occupation. The single-cell house is less well represented in the coastal and other historically more prosperous areas. The common living-room, known variously in Brittany as (Br) *kegin*, (Fr) *la cuisine, la salle, la pièce, la pièce unique*, is referred to throughout this work as the 'hall', in accordance with English practice. Travellers and writers, although frequently referring to the hall, rarely say whether it adjoined a byre, as in the long-house, or some other farm building. Certainly in Côtes-du-Nord, until after World War II, the *pièce unique* was virtually the rule[427] and it is probable that a high percentage of these dwellings was of one cell, most of the remainder being long-houses. Colin expresses the view that in Porzay, Finistère, the single-cell house gave way to dwellings of two cells during the nineteenth century, except for the dwellings of poorer people.[428]

The *penty* was a cottage occupied by an agricultural worker, either landless, or possessing only one or two fields, barely sufficient for domestic needs. Where a small amount of land was attached, the term *penty* was sometimes applied to the holding and not simply to the house. Economically, the *journalier* was dependent on one or more farmers for his employment, cultivating a little for himself. *Penty,* whose place-names often begin with the element *ty-, loch-* or *menez-*, seem to have been rare in some parts of Finistère, but more common elsewhere. Their numbers increased with the colonization of the waste in the nineteenth century when they became very numerous in the form of squatter settlements on the waste and on the margins of the road. In Cléden-Cap-Sizun, *penty* were believed to be very rare.[429] The single-cell house was only one of several types present in Bulat-Pestivien, normally about 5.00 to 7.00 metres in length, and 4.00 to 5.00 metres in width, either with or without an *appentis de branchages*.[430] Writing of Basse-Bretagne, Vallaux, by implication, clearly regarded the single-cell house as being widespread and confined to the poorer classes.[431] Even after World War I, the countryside seems to have supported almost as many *penty* as farmsteads,

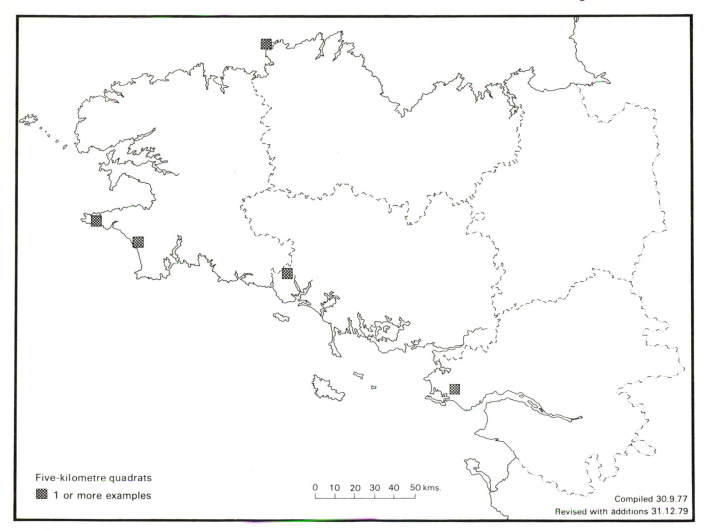

Fig. 172. The distribution of gable-entry houses

and field evidence indicates that these cottages could only have been single-cell dwellings.[432]

Examples of single-cell houses from the sample quadrats illustrate the variety of size and form. Trovern 1 and 2 (Fig. 82) are excellent examples of very small dwellings, one dated 1712. Built of *granit rose* with slate roofs, these houses are of one storey with very limited storage space in the roof. Clevry 7 (Fig. 84) is somewhat larger, and although the loft is still used for storage as evidenced by the ventilation slit in the lower gable, space is still limited. The position of the doorway, *c.* 1.00 metre from the lower gable, leaves only a little space at the lower end. Kerliviou (Fig. 93) is of similar dimensions but of one-and-a-half storeys, offering considerably more roof storage space, with access to the loft by a small lateral door. Bremelin 7 (Fig. 94) is of similar size, and again of one-and-a-half storeys, with a loft door. This house is distinguished by its gable-entry, the doorway being set in the upper gable alongside the stack. Five examples of gable-entry houses have been recorded (Fig. 172), all but one in the south. Although the distribution is sufficient to indicate that the type exists widely distributed in Brittany, there are as yet insufficient numbers to indicate its origin and mode of diffusion. It cannot, however, be derived from the long-house, as suggested for Welsh examples,[433] for the cross-passage of the Breton long-house was not structurally defined in its elementary form. The Welsh long-house, however, often had a doorway into the hall, adjacent to the hearth which backed on to the cross-passage. The gable-entry house is known from excavation[434] and it seems probable that its origin lies in prehistory, that it may derive from the simple tent-like dwelling without walls but with a doorway in the gable.

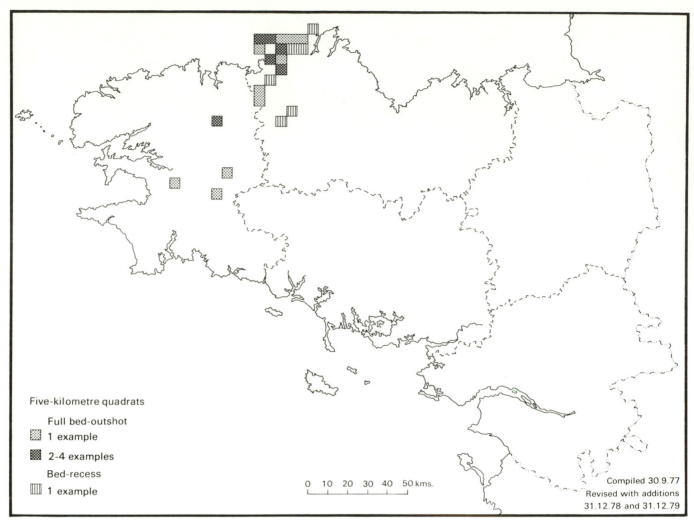

Fig. 173.   The distribution of the bed-outshot

Lesunalec 1, 2 (Fig. 95) is a single-cell dwelling conjoined with another house. Many examples of such rows or *rangées* exist, often with internal communication between the independent units. Single-cell houses forming part of a row occur in Les Bois (Fig. 96), Saint-Jean-Baptiste-des-Landes (Fig. 97) and Beaulieu (Fig. 100). South of the Loire, houses were almost all of one storey until the twentieth century, when the need for further space was satisfied by the addition of upper storeys. An interesting case of two adjacent single-cell dwellings is provided by Fresnay Normandie (Fig. 52). Superficially resembling a long-house derivative, this type of arrangement, which occurs also in western Normandy, is probably to be interpreted as a pair of houses for families related by blood, or by economic arrangement. Thus they might be occupied by two generations of the same family, by a landowner and a working tenant or servant, or by the families of two brothers working the farm jointly. In buildings of this kind, one doorway is nearly always larger than the other, suggesting seniority, or greater social importance.

Numerous examples of single-cell houses are provided by the E.A.R. Some are only of one storey, as at Miné-Tréouzal in Scaër, Loguivy in Ploubazlaˑ c, Le Rhun in Plougrescant and Kermenech in Prat. Others like Le Drenec in Sizun and La Mellerie in Cuguen are of two full storeys. Roof structures include upper cruck, tie-beam, collar and tie-beam, and upper king-post trusses, and coverings include slate, thatch and tile. Considerable variations in size occur. In general, lengths average 7.00 to 9.00 metres, and widths 5.50 to 6.50 metres, externally. Miné-Tréouzal measures 8.90 by 5.70 metres, Loguivy 8.40 by 5.60 metres and Le Rhun 7.70 by 6.10 metres.[435] All the 'primitive' houses at Loc-Envel and Pont-Rot, referred to earlier, are single-cell dwellings. Three houses in Morbihan have similar dimensions. The open hall at Kerspec in Plumelin is 8.00 by 5.50 metres, and the houses at Radenac and Bruneton measure 7.30 by 5.70 metres and 8.50 by 5.00 metres, respectively. In the east, single-cell houses are often very short, and this is an especially noticeable characteristic of those houses arranged in rows. L'Alleu in Pipriac is 5.50 metres wide, but only 4.70 metres long. The three dwellings, Île de Mazin 17, 18, 19 in Saint-Joachim, are 6.65 metres wide and have a total length of only 19.30 metres. All have pairs of opposing doorways but number 19 has no windows. Île de Fédrun 60 in the same *commune* is 6.60 metres wide but only 4.26 metres long.[436] Elsewhere, single-cell houses of fine build are by no means to be construed as the homes of the rural poor. La Mellerie in Cuguen, 8.35 metres wide and 8.10 metres long, is an extremely fine structure of two storeys. Le Drenec in Sizun measures 10.30 by 8.20 metres, the great width being explained by the existence of the table outshot, (Br.) *kuz-taol*, containing table, benches and also, usually, a bed.[437] This form of outshot will be discussed in Chapter 10, but although frequently containing a bed, it must be distinguished from the bed-outshot. The former is invariably a projection of the south elevation, the side opposite that traditionally associated with the conjugal bed. The bed-outshot, which is not confined to single-cell houses, and may be found in long-houses, two-cell houses and multi-cell *manoirs*, is associated with the conjugal bed itself and is thus accommodated in the north wall of a south-facing house. Normally it projects from the corner by the hearth, but at Quimill, Châteaulin (Fig. 176), it is at the lower end of the hall. Bed-outshots, located at the upper end of the hall on the side opposite the window, and obviously intended to contain the conjugal bed, are to be found in two locations in Ploulec'h. The wall is recessed some 0.35 metres, partly to receive the bed, and projects externally as a true outshot with slated roof. In several other houses there is a wall recess intended partially to accommodate the bed, but without an outshot.[438] All known bed-outshots and wall recesses are shown on Fig. 173. Five different types of bed-outshot and bed-recess have been distinguished: the bed-outshot, either with its own slate or tile roof, or alternatively roofed continuously with the house; the bed-outshot built so as to appear like a buttress, with a corbelled or vaulted roof; the bed-outshot carried up through two storeys to provide for both first- and second-floors; the bed-outshot concealed in a larger contemporary outshot complex; and the bed-recess, that is a shallow recess in the wall intended to accommodate only some 0.10 to 0.20 metres of the bed

and not requiring the outward projection of the wall. A detailed account of the bed-outshot in Brittany has appeared elsewhere[439] but Fig. 173 includes some more recently discovered examples. The greatest concentration of bed-outshots is in the area around Lannion where they occur *'dans presque toutes les maisons de cette région'*.[440] The bed-outshot is known in widely separated parts of north-west Europe,[441] and it may have been introduced into Brittany from the sea by way of the Lannion region from which it was diffused. The distribution of the feature in Brittany coincides with no other significant cultural distribution, and yet the examples mapped on Fig. 173 are confined to an area north-west of a line from Tréguier to Carhaix-Plouguer.

Whilst further fieldwork will no doubt strengthen and extend the distribution, extensive fieldwork has failed to produce any examples outside this area. There can be no doubt that the true bed-outshot, both the type with a roof continuous with that of the house, and the buttress-type, are found in houses of seventeenth-century date with which they are contemporary. Some examples may date from the late-sixteenth century but surviving examples earlier than this are unlikely, for there is little vernacular building surviving from before c. 1550. It would therefore seem that the bed-outshot dates from the early-sixteenth century at the latest. The bed-recess, already known by the seventeenth century, can be said with certainty to have continued to be built into new houses of eighteenth- and nineteenth-century date, and possibly even of twentieth-century date. It is typologically descended from the true bed-outshot, of which it must be regarded as a degenerate version. Possible factors leading to the development and survival of the bed-outshot are discussed elsewhere.[442] Its survival may be ascribed partly to innate conservatism and partly to the fact that the great majority of Bretons continued to inhabit a single room. The alignment of furniture against the rear wall of the hall may also have been a contributory factor to its late survival. It permitted the bed, that item of furniture of greatest width, partly to be recessed in the wall, thereby reducing the amount of space the whole row took out of the room, and also keeping the box-bed and its chest free of the hearth-stone. It is interesting that the bed-recess continued to be built so late, long after there was any possible need for it, and often so shallow as to be ridiculous. It may be no accident that the earliest known examples occur in houses of the upper rural social classes. It is more than possible that their persistence and survival owes something to the 'ceremony of the bed'.[443]

Interior arrangements of single-cell houses are discussed in Chapter 15, and examples of furniture layout shown in Figs. 237 and 238. Some houses with

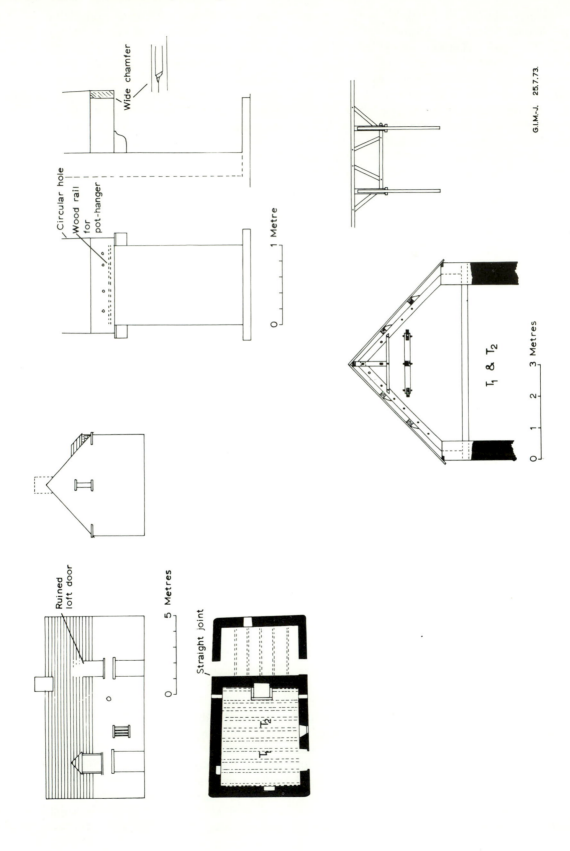

Fig. 174. Les Landes de l'Etriac 1, Lamballe, Côtes-du-Nord

symmetrical plan, central doorway and two windows, which appear from the outside as two-cell houses, consist of one long room occasionally arranged without subdivision, a variation well illustrated by the three examples from Basse-Bretagne,[444] and that from Huelgoat.[445] These are classed as single-cell houses in this work, but could be regarded as 'open' two-cell houses.

Fieldwork has brought to light a variety of examples of single-cell houses. Some are constituent parts of *rangées* of two or more dwellings, others are detached. Those at Les Landes de l'Etriac, Tréubert and Tréberouan (Figs. 48, 49 and 174) have already been mentioned. The hamlet of Kervaly, Morbihan, provides several examples. Kervaly 1 (Fig. 178) is a single-cell house, attached to a long-house, with an original internal communicating doorway. Kervaly 5 has a similar relationship to Kervaly 6 (Fig. 180) but without internal communication. Kervaly 8 (Fig. 181) appears to have been added to Kervaly 7, when a communicating doorway was provided. Kervaly 11 and 14 (Figs. 183 and 184) are similarly related to other dwellings, one with, the other without, internal communication. All these buildings are of one-and-a-half storeys, *c.* 7.00 to 8.00 metres long and *c.* 6.00 to 7.00 metres wide. The variety of roof trusses demonstrates various stages in the evolutionary sequence of carpentry postulated earlier, including upper-cruck tie-beam trusses, upper-cruck collar and tie-beam trusses and collar trusses. All the roofs are thatched except for Kervaly 7 which has a slate covering.

At Kerhaliou in Spézet, Kerhaliou 2 (Fig. 196) may be a single-cell house, but the lower end is long enough to have accommodated at least one cow and possibly two. This *rangée* is clearly of three separate builds. Kerhaliou 1, a long-house, is probably of seventeenth-century date, Kerhaliou 2 having been added in 1800 and Kerhaliou 3, a two-storey single-cell house, in 1907. *Rangées* existed both with and without internal communication, and with communication between some, but not all, of the constituent houses. The *village rangée* has been noted by several authors and is particularly well-developed in certain areas.[446]

The single-cell lower end at Mériadec-en-Plumergat is 5.50 metres long and 5.00 metres wide and is later in date than the long-house of 1689 against which it is built. It is provided with a drain and a hearth. The possibility exists that the hearth was intended for the preparation of animal foods, the cell really being a byre, but the design of the window suggests that this is unlikely. More probably it was designed to provide for use by either humans or animals as necessary (Fig. 185).

Kermorfezan 6 and 7 (VU 393939) are located in a hamlet formerly of eleven dwellings dominated by a *petit manoir* (Fig. 175). Walling is of granite rubble (*granit rose*) with dressings of the same material for doorway and window openings. Roof covering, formerly of either slate or thatch, is now of corrugated asbestos. Total length is *c.* 15.60 metres and the width *c.* 5.90 metres. Kermorfezan 6 measures *c.* 6.00 metres long by 4.45 metres wide internally; Kermorfezan 7, 7.35 metres long by 4.60 metres wide internally. Wall thickness varies from 0.50 metres to 0.85 metres. Height from ground to eaves is 2.35 metres for Kermorfezan 6 and 2.10 metres for Kermorfezan 7. Dimensions are typical for single-cell houses in this district. The rubble walling is bonded with a mortar of *pisé* and the floor is of *terre battue*. There is no loft flooring and the interiors are open to the roof. The roof structure of Kermorfezan 7 consists of four tie-beam trusses supporting ridge purlins and two pairs of lateral purlins resting on cleats. There are no collars. The roof in Kermorfezan 6 is entirely modern. The chimney-pieces are entirely of granite, breastsummers resting on two pairs of corbels in each house. Door and window openings are of dressed stone, D1 being square-headed with a flat-splay chamfer, D2 round-headed with no chamfer. Window W2 displays a feature commonly encountered, jambs with mouldings that do not match, in this case a flat-splay moulding coupled with a cavetto moulding. There is an intercommunicating doorway between these two houses suggesting occupation by related families. Variations in wall thickness indicate that the history of the two houses is not straightforward and there may be more than one phase of building confirmed by the straight joint between the two houses. The style of doorway D2 suggests that Kermorfezan 7 is the older house but as styles persisted late, the possibility that Kermorfezan 6 may be the older must not be discounted. Although there is room in Kermorfezan 6 to keep a cow tethered at the lower end, it seems more likely that this was a single-cell house. Kermorfezan 7, however, is unmistakably a long-house with a pair of doorways not opposed. The pair of windows W2 and W3 suggests a two-cell house, but symmetry of windows can often be misleading and the lower one is often intended to light a byre, giving the impression externally of a two-cell house. Doorway D2 and a former small window opening alongside it are now blocked. The house is an excellent example of a *penty* of substantial build, sited close to the *petit manoir* to which it belongs.

Quimill in Châteaulin (VU 199385) is built of schist rubble with wood lintels in a district devoid of ashlar (Fig. 176). Roof covering is of slate and the ridge of red tiles. Maximum length is 11.90 metres and maximum width 6.70 metres, but the total length of the house alone is 8.30 metres. The dwelling is 6.10 metres long internally,

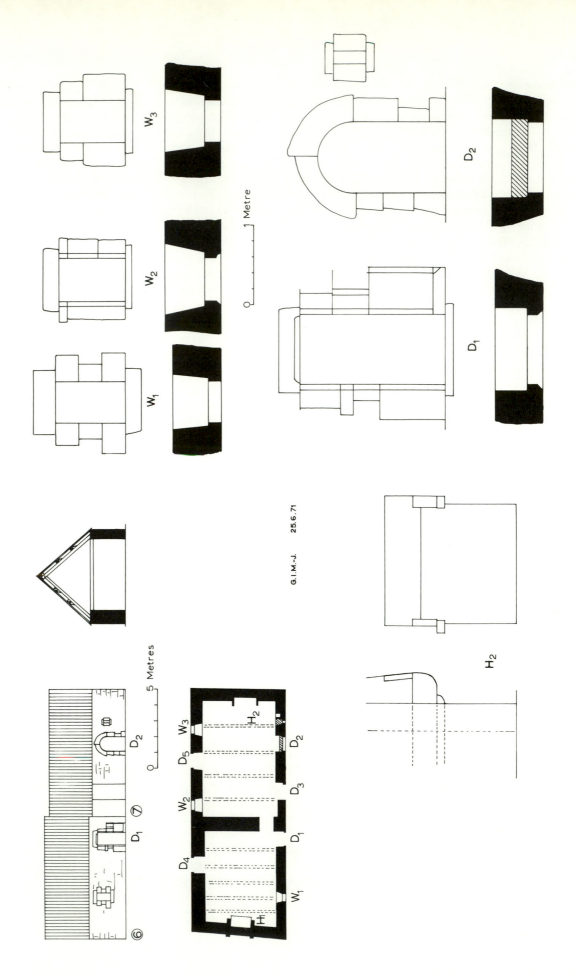

G.I.M.-J.   25.6.71

Fig. 175.   Kermorfezan 6, 7, Plougasnou, Finistère

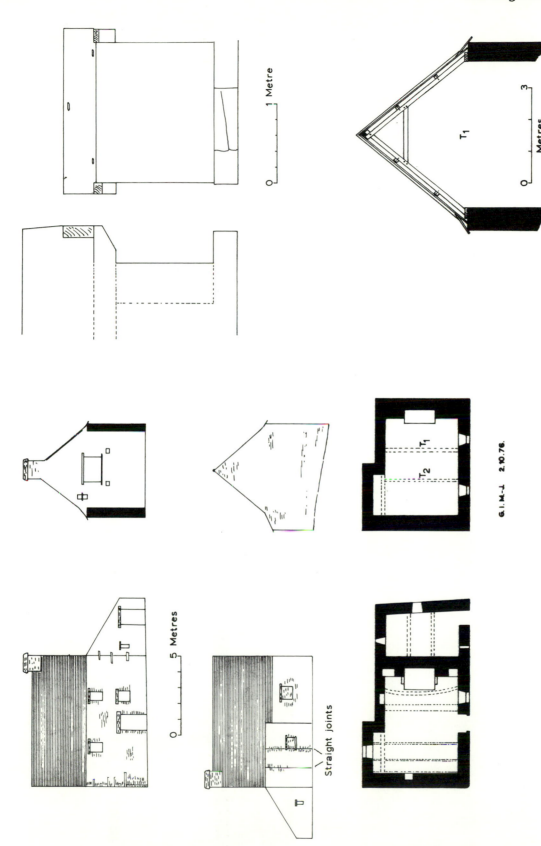

Fig. 176.   Quimill, Châteaulin, Finistère

13

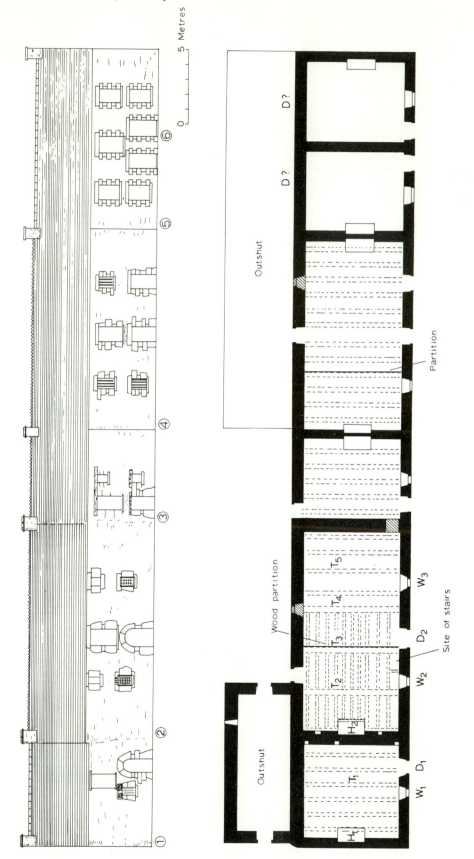

Fig. 177a. La Ville des Nachez 1-6, Taupont, Morbihan

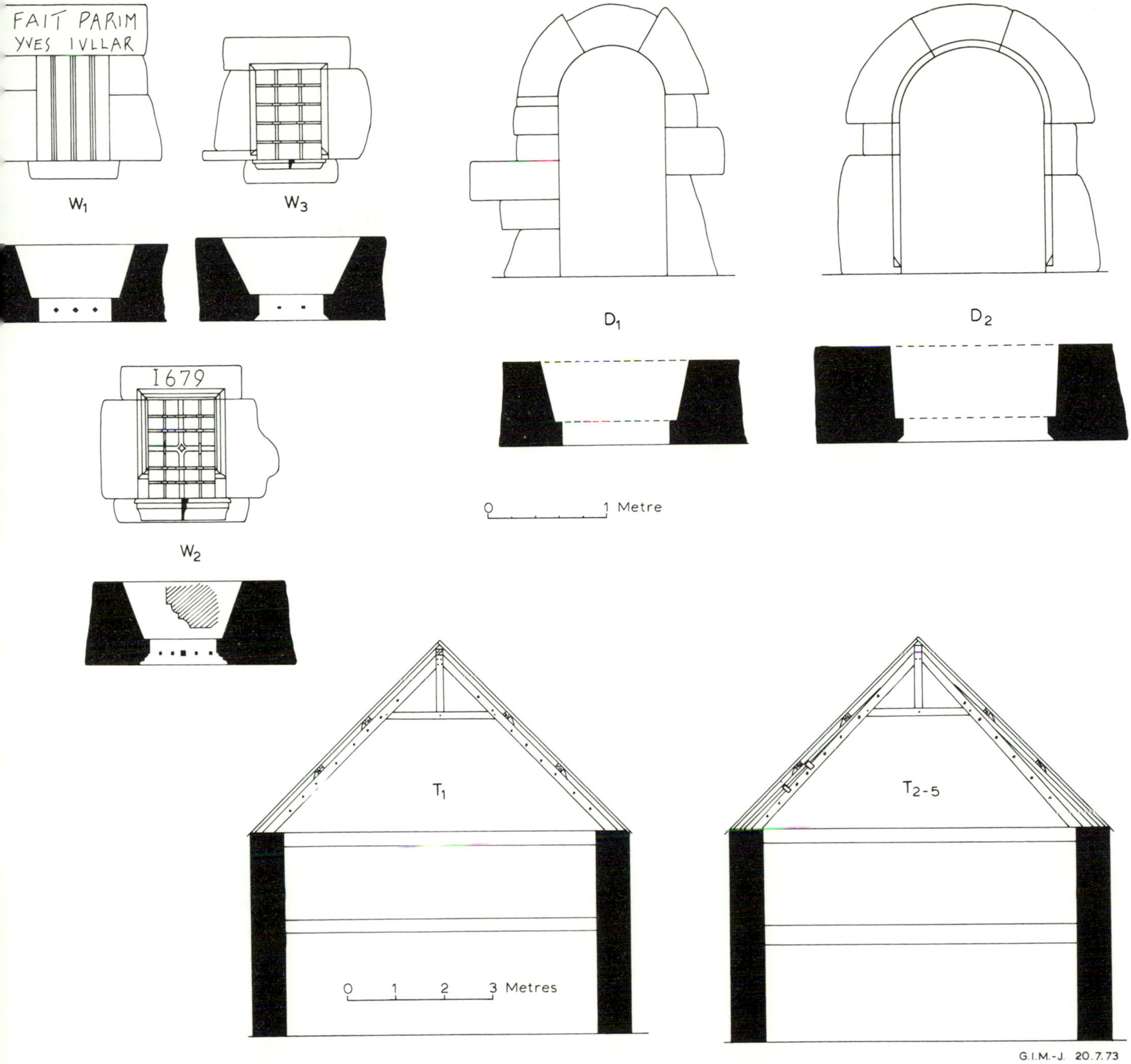

FAIT PARIM
YVES IVLLAR

W₁

W₃

1679

W₂

D₁

D₂

0   1 Metre

T₁

T₂₋₅

0   1   2   3 Metres

G.I.M.-J. 20.7.73

Fig. 177b.   La Ville des Nachez 1-6, Taupont, Morbihan

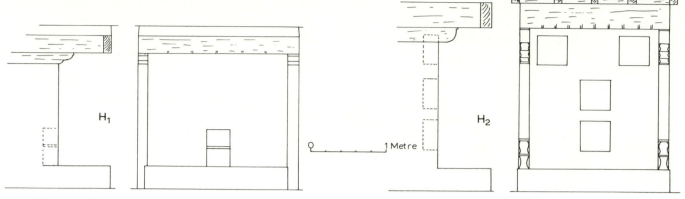

Fig. 177c. La Ville des Nachez 1-6, Taupont, Morbihan

4.60 metres wide at the upper end and 5.30 metres wide at the lower end. Wall thickness varies considerably from 0.60 metres to 1.20 metres. At the front the eaves rise 3.75 metres above the ground and at the lower end the ridge stands approximately 7.30 metres above ground level. Schist rubble walling is laid in a mortar of *pisé*. The structure is of two full storeys, the upper storey being used as a loft. The floor is of *terre battue* and the loft floor is of boards nailed to the ceiling beams. These have been subject to alteration. That nearest the hearth is curved, that by the door is of the order of 40 centimetres square. At the lower end are three modern beams, but that spanning the outshot appears original. There is no tie-beam at wall-top level. Two collar trusses support a ridge beam and two pairs of lateral purlins are fastened to the rafters with pegs. The feet of the principal rafters rest on wall-plates. Common rafters of roughly sawn timber are staggered at the apex and rest with their feet on the wall-heads, their lower ends sprocketed out. Small slates are nailed to the close-set boarding. The hearth is deeply recessed into the gable wall and the rubble chimney-hood is supported on a wooden breastsummer resting on wooden corbels. There are three large keeping-places in the upper end and one in the lower gable wall. The hall was originally lighted by a window at the upper end with a second window in the outshot. Door and window openings are framed with schist and all the lintels are of wood. A few longer pieces of schist appear in the quoins linking the house with the present lean-to. The appearance of the upper gable wall with a hearth at first-floor level and a keeping-place suggests that the present-day lean-to may originally have been a first-floor hall. In the rear wall are two problematical straight joints and what appears to be a blocked window, the latter matching one of the keeping-places in the hall. This building is very narrow at the upper end and there is scarcely enough space for the conjugal bed alongside the hearth opposite

the window. The doorway is also located so close to the hearth as to leave little room for the table by the window. The outshot at the lower, end can thus only have been intended for a bed and the house must be interpreted as a single-cell house with bed-outshot.

Tréubert 1, Trégunc, Finistère (VT 393956), is built entirely of stone, the biotite-granite of the area south of Trégunc (Fig. 50). The chimney-gable is of dressed stone and rubble and the lateral walls are of orthostats. The outshot is of granite rubble. Thatch is of rye-straw and the ridge is finished with a turf capping. Externally the house measures 7.70 metres by 5.00 metres and internally 6.85 metres by 4.45 metres. Height from the ground to the eaves is 2.20 metres and to the ridge 4.85 metres. The gable wall and chimney are of dressed stone and rubble with a mortar of *pisé*, and the chimney-stack has a plain cap. Lateral walling is of orthostats with a *pisé* filling between the joints. The dwelling is a single-cell house but there is sufficient space at the lower end to accommodate a cow and it is not beyond the bounds of possibility that this was formerly a very short long-house. The hall is lighted by a single plain window, and a small plain light is provided for the loft. There are six tie-beams, one of which supports the collar and tie-beam truss, a ridge purlin and two lateral purlins. At the lower end, the house abuts a house whose gable serves to terminate Tréubert 1. The chimney-piece is entirely of granite, a pair of granite corbels projecting through the gable wall and supporting a single piece of granite forming the breastsummer, and the chimney-hood is of granite rubble. The outshot, entirely of rubble, is irregular in shape, and thatched with rye-straw held down by spars pegged into it.

Les Landes de l'Etriac 1, Lamballe, Côtes-du-Nord (WU 356716), has walling of *torchis* (Fig. 174). Eight 'lifts' of *torchis* are visible in the gable-end, the rendering having mostly fallen away. Height to the apex is *c*. 6.25

metres, giving a rise for each 'lift' of *c.* 0.80 metres. Chimney-hood and stack are of *torchis* and the floor is of *terre battue*. There is evidence that the walls were formerly plastered internally with *pisé* and whitewashed. The structure is *c.* 7.75 metres long externally and 6.50 metres wide; 6.30 metres long internally with a maximum width at the lower end of 5.00 metres. Length, with added byre, is 11.60 metres at maximum and the internal dimensions of the byre are 3.10 metres long by 5.00 metres wide. Wall height to eaves-line is 3.30 metres and to the apex 6.25 metres. The house is of one-and-a-half storeys and living accommodation confined to the ground floor. Access to the loft-space used for storage is by the opening immediately over the door to the house.

Wall thickness varies from *c.* 0.55 metres to 0.60 metres. Access is by a single doorway and the room is lighted by one window and two small circular 'port-holes', one on each side of the house at the upper end along the line of the hearth. It is probable that these were inserted as much to provide extra draught for a smoking chimney as to provide light. The lower and rear walls at the lower end of the house are provided with keeping-places. That in the lower wall is 0.30 metres deep and 0.68 metres wide, and contains two wooden shelves and a wooden door. The second keeping-place in the rear wall is also 0.30 metres deep, 0.62 metres wide and 1.02 metres above the ground. Door and window frames are of wood and the window entirely unglazed, the space being sub-divided by two plain mullions. The ceiling is formed by nine common beams, each *c.* 0.20 by 0.20 metres, some decorated with rough chamfers. In addition there are two short beams, on either side of the chimney-piece, carrying the loft flooring of simple planks. The chimney-piece is of wood, the wooden frame being laid over a pair of short wood corbels which pass through the gable wall behind. There are four empty pegholes in the breastsummer, formerly containing pegs on which were hung domestic utensils. There is a circular hole in the right-hand side of the chimney-hood and it is presumed that this formerly carried the flue of a coal-fired stove that stood alongside the original hearth. A feature, not unusual, is a wooden rail laid across the opening inside the hood from which was formerly suspended the pot-hanger. As in many of these wooden-framed chimney-hoods, the inside of the breastsummer is cut away in a crude chamfer bearing a chamfer stop. The carpentry is of high quality for a small *torchis* house, the trusses being of the upper king-post and collar type. Principal rafters have holes to carry the pegs formerly used as an aid to climbing the roof during the building process. The upper king-post carries the ridge beam and the side purlins rest

on cleats. Between the feet of the principal rafters, which rest on the wall-heads, are placed wooden posts, presumably so that the weight of the roof will not rest directly on a rather fragile clay wall. Wall-plates lie on the outside edge of the walls, carrying only the common rafters. Common rafters carry close-set boarding into which are nailed the roof slates. Two trusses are braced on their outsides to the ridge beam and also carry an under-ridge purlin which is itself braced to the ridge beam. The loft opening is crowned by a small hipped gable. There are straight joints at the upper end of the house at the junction with the byre, showing that this was a later addition. The roof of the byre is supported by purlins laid gable to gable, the length of the byre being so short as not to require a truss. There are five beams 0.20 by 0.07 metres laid longitudinally. This is a single-cell house with a later byre.

Two conjoined houses of some importance are centrally situated in the hamlet of Kervorn in Laz (Fig. 216). They are of different builds, Kervorn 2 being later than Kervorn 1. Both are distinguished by a complex system of outshots, the large bed-outshot at the upper end of Kervorn 1 having been used within living memory. These houses will be discussed more fully later but it should be noted that Kervorn 2 is basically a single-cell house with a heated chamber above. The function of the room in the outshot is unclear; it is not a *kuz-taol*, or table-outshot, and although it might have served as a bed-chamber, it is more likely that it was a pantry or a dairy. The lateral hearth is a rare feature observed in only a few houses in the whole of Brittany (Fig. 74).

A group of houses, La Ville des Nachez 1–6, well illustrates the growth of a *rangée* including single-cell dwellings. Numbers 1 and 2 are the earliest in date, 2 pre-dating 1 which is built against it (Fig. 177). The round-headed doorways of both these dwellings suggest a seventeenth-century date, borne out by the figures 1679 on a window lintel. The vertical joints show that numbers 3, 4, 5 and 6 were all later additions. All these houses, as is general in this district, have full loft-storeys and numbers 1, 3, 5 and 6 are single-cell dwellings; numbers 2 and 4 are long-houses and will be discussed later. Number 1 is almost a perfect square in plan with sides of 6.25 metres internally, one doorway and a hearth of some quality. Number 3 has a pair of opposite doorways at the lower end, and is 6.50 metres wide but only 5.30 metres long internally. Numbers 5 and 6 were not fully surveyed but clearly date from either the late-nineteenth or the early-twentieth century and form a pair of 'semi-detached' single-cell dwellings with a common loft space. Each is 5.30 metres long internally. The only internal communication in this *rangée* is provided between numbers 2 and 3. There can be little doubt, however, that the row was occupied by a kin group and displays growth in response to population increase between the seventeenth and early-twentieth centuries. Oral evidence confirms this. The outshots are later additions.

The single-cell dwelling with hall on the ground floor and a storage loft above, and of one, one-and-a-half or two storeys, appears to be the standard form of dwelling throughout Brittany for the rural classes who were either landless or who did not own livestock. They were thus mostly the homes of poor people, but other groups of higher social status and not directly engaged in agriculture might also have occupied a single-cell house, as is suggested by the survival of dwellings of considerable quality. Examples have been found with bed-outshots, lateral chimney-stacks, and with gable entry, features known in the British Isles and which are thus now confirmed in Brittany, albeit as yet in small numbers. The table outshot is so far unknown outside north-west Brittany, except for isolated examples in Ulster and south Wales.

TEN

THE LONG-HOUSE AND ITS DERIVATIVES

The long-house, a dwelling in which man and beast are housed under the same roof, is named after the Welsh *tŷ hir*.[447] In its simplest form, a two-unit structure, it has internal access from the dwelling at one end to the byre at the other, the two units being separated by a cross-passage. This cross-passage need not be structurally defined and there may be either one or two doorways, often of considerable width, used by both man and beast. The type has also been recognized in Monmouthshire where it appears in the 'three compartment and passage' plan, inner room, living room, cross-passage and cowstalls, the feeding walk being an essential feature of the economy of the farm related more closely to the working than to the family portion. In many Welsh examples cowstalls are provided in the byre, and the cross-passage, which is up to three metres wide, allows cows, whose spines are laterally inflexible, to turn.[448] More recent work has shown the long-house to be widespread in Breconshire, the type surviving in a variety of modified forms.[449] The long-house has also been identified in England[450] (notably in Devon,[451] in Cornwall,[452] in Cumberland and Westmorland[453]), in the Hebrides,[454] and widely in Ireland.[455] Doubts cast on the origin and distribution of the long-house in Britain have been dispelled by Peate,[456] drawing on the documentary evidence for the *domus longa* in medieval England, and by Hurst,[457] who summarizes the now impressive body of archaeological evidence for what appears to have been the normal type of dwelling in many deserted medieval villages. The known distribution of surviving buildings, essentially west European and Celtic, led Smith to suggest it was 'a late manifestation of Celtic culture'.[458] Evidence for the long-house has also come to light in Brittany and the type is now known to occur across the whole of northern and western France.[459]

Smith has defined the long-house as a 'rectangular aisleless house in which, at an early stage in its history, a cross-passage divided the human occupants from their animals and served both as entrance and feeding walk',[460] emphasizing as Peate[461] had done that the byre was intended for cows, and milking cows particularly, without special provision for other stock. These definitions were based on English and Welsh buildings that were in some cases relatively sophisticated. There are repeated references to long-houses of three-unit form and Hurst several times refers to the lower end as the third room beyond the cross-passage.[462] There has also been a tendency to assume that because cattle, and particularly dairy cattle, are the sole occupants of the lower end of surviving long-houses, this was always so. However, Peate quotes seventeenth- and eighteenth-century examples of the type housing all the animals of the farm, and there is now sufficient evidence to show that this was formerly the case in Brittany.[463]

The crux of the problem, however, is that all the published definitions have taken account of both form and function without allowing for the possibility that evidence may be forthcoming for the one and not for the other. From an examination of surviving buildings it may be possible accurately to record the form of a structure and the archaeological evidence of change. If animals no longer occupy the lower end, or if there is no archaeological evidence to show that they formerly did, oral or documentary evidence may establish that fact. The archaeologist, however, attempting to interpret excavations, is faced with a particular problem in that although he may clearly be able to establish the form of a building, there may be no evidence whatsoever to enable him to interpret the functions of the rooms. Stalls, tethering rings and drains may never have existed in many long-houses, and large numbers of Breton farms, for example, have no such provision to this day. The problem of function is one which arises not only in the case of excavated buildings. In a number of Breton long-houses, the function of the lower end has manifestly changed from time to time. What may have been a house and byre during the lifetime of husband and wife may cease to be so upon the death of the husband if the stock are sold off and the widow continues to inhabit the upper end of the dwelling, using the lower end for storage purposes. Upon her death new occupants may restore the lower end to its function as a byre. Again, around the coastal lowlands of Brittany fishermen have been found living in dwellings of long-house form, using the lower end for the storage of garden implements and fishing tackle, insisting, in reply to enquiry, that animals were never kept there. Yet in *every such case*, known long-houses survive only a few kilometres away. The example at La Ville des Nachez (Fig. 177) in north Morbihan further illustrates this problem of interpretation where evidence of function is unclear. Number 4 is a long-house with separate entry to a byre provided with hearth and chimney. Enquiry ascertained, however, that the lower end had always been a byre and that when the house was built in the nineteenth century a hearth had been inserted in case at some later stage the occupant wished to eject the livestock and use it as an additional room for his family. This practice seems to have been widespread in western Brittany, at least, for Vallaux reported that '*ce qui dure toujours, c'est la déplorable facilité avec laquelle, dans nombre de localités, on change une étable en habitation et réciproquement, après un nettoyage sommaire ou même sans nettoyage aucun: au Faou "on déménage des hommes pour mettre des vaches, et des vaches pour mettre des hommes"* '.[464]

On the basis of this evidence an attempt was made to refine the definition of the long-house and widen it slightly, taking into account both form and function. The long-house is simply a rectilinear or sub-rectilinear aisleless dwelling in which man and beast are housed at opposite ends, under one roof, with entry by a common lateral doorway.[465] In the French literature, the long-house is variously referred to as *une maison rudimentaire* or *la maison élémentaire*, without defining the precise relationship between man and beast and relating it to house plan. The terms, equally applicable to cohabitation of man and beast in the very different alpine house-types, must be discarded as essentially unscientific. Flatrès, in his revue of Peate's work, translates 'long-house' as *maison-longue*, as does Pesez, establishing the practice followed by French medieval archaeologists.[466] The recent use of *maison-longue* for a *rangée* which may include not only one or more long-houses, but single-cell dwellings and even occasionally a first-floor hall, has further confused matters.[467] The term *maison-en-longueur* (or *longère*), widely used by French geographers from Brunhes and Demangeon onwards, is generally employed to describe a row of farm buildings in line, including one or more dwellings. It is imprecise, unscientific and best avoided. The problem of terminology may be resolved by confining the use of 'long-house' to buildings where both form and function are

proven, and by using the term 'long-house form' for those structures in which the use of the lower end is either unclear or is demonstrably for farm purposes other than the housing of animals. Care has been taken in arriving at the above definition to avoid specifying the number of rooms in the domestic end of the building, as these are an unreliable guide, confuse the issue, and may even lead to the byre or lower end being referred to as the 'third room'. In most Breton examples the long-house is of two cells only — hall and byre — whereas in many English and Welsh examples the domestic accommodation often comprises additional rooms. Likewise, the 'pure' long-house has been defined only with one doorway. A long-house built with, or altered so as to provide, separate entry to both dwelling and byre, but retaining internal communication, may then be regarded as the first derivative of the 'pure' long-house. When internal communication is finally discarded the second derivative has been reached. Both the 'pure' long-house and the two derivatives will have sub-classes according to the number and disposition of additional rooms, the position of the hearth and whether the cross-passage is present with a pair of opposing doorways, or in embryo form with only one doorway.

For the purpose of mapping, although further subdivisions are suggested, the buildings have been grouped into pure long-houses, dwellings of long-house form, and their derivatives. The pure long-house occurs in each of the sample quadrats (Fig. 102) except numbers 2 (Plouzané, Locmaria-Plouzané), 8 (Plogoff, Primelin), 14 (Moëlan-sur-Mer), 18 (Joué-sur-Erdre), 20 (Frossay) and 21 (Saint-Lumine-de-Clisson, Saint-Hilaire-de-Clisson). Long-house derivatives occur in most sample quadrats in addition to the pure long-house, and houses of long-house form and their derivatives are particularly conspicuous in the east, where only Quadrat 21 failed to produce any examples. Quadrats 2 and 21 provided no trace whatsoever of any member of the long-house family. In Quadrat 2, there has been much re-building following war damage, and as the long-house is known once to have been common in Léon, this negative evidence may be set aside. That the true long-house almost certainly once existed south of the Loire is suggested by the survival of houses of long-house form in Frossay, and consequently the negative result of Quadrat 21 may not be representative of extreme south-eastern Brittany.

The distribution of the main classes of the long-house is illustrated in Fig. 102. Percentages of dwellings in the long-house family vary considerably, from zero in Quadrats 2 and 21 to sixty-five per cent of the sample in Quadrat 7 (Sougéal, Antrain, La Fontenelle). High

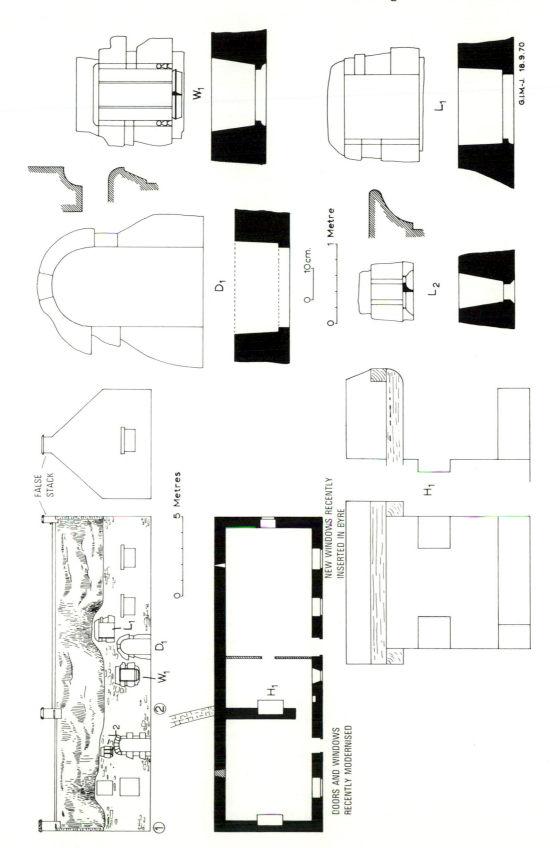

Fig. 178.   Kervaly 1, 2, Plumergat, Morbihan

percentages are also recorded in Quadrat 6 (Plévenon) with forty-five per cent, Quadrat 12 (Paimpont) with forty-eight per cent, Quadrat 13 (Saint-M'Hervé) with sixty per cent, Quadrat 16 (Grand-Champ) with fifty-seven per cent, and Quadrat 19 (Guérande) with forty-seven per cent. In Quadrat 20 (Frossay) thirty-five per cent of the sample belonged to the long-house family, all of long-house form. The proportion was thirty-seven per cent in Quadrat 17 (Béganne), as it was in Quadrat 11 (Taupont). In Quadrat 10 (Plévin) it was twenty-nine per cent, thirty-two per cent in Quadrat 5 (La Harmoye, Le Haut-Corlay), twenty-eight per cent in Quadrat 4 (Carnoët) and twenty-one per cent in Quadrat 3 (Plougasnou). Low percentages were recorded in Quadrat 1 (Plougrescant) with three per cent, Quadrat 8 (Plogoff, Primelin) with thirteen per cent, Quadrat 9 (Dinéault) with seven per cent, Quadrat 14 (Moëlan-sur-Mer) with two per cent, Quadrat 15 (Pont-Scorff) with six per cent, and Quadrat 18 (Joué-sur-Erdre) with three per cent. These low proportions are nearly all in coastal areas where the two-cell houses first became popular in the eighteenth and nineteenth centuries. The samples show the survival of the long-house and dwellings of long-house form in almost every quadrat, often amounting to an extraordinarily high percentage of the total sample.

Outside these areas, in addition to the concentration of long-houses in south Morbihan, like those at Kervaly, below, the type has been recorded near Plougasnou, Audièrne, Trégunc, Carhaix-Plouguer, and the Monts d'Arrée, all in Finistère. It is widely distributed in Côtes-du-Nord, and occurs throughout Morbihan and Ille-et-Vilaine as well as in many parts of Loire-Atlantique where it is particularly strongly represented in the Grande Brière and around Guérande. Only south of the Loire is it notably absent and then only locally. The distribution is thus sufficient to permit the inescapable conclusion that the long-house is widely distributed over the whole of Brittany, the type being found from the Normandy border to farthest Finistère, that it probably once existed in much greater numbers, and that most of the surviving examples are now to be found in areas of relative poverty. In spite of recent agricultural reforms and improvements in the standard of living, some long-houses are still occupied as such, others have only recently ceased so to be used, and numerous farmers tell of how their parents lived with the animals in a former long-house now given over entirely to stock. Further evidence for the former existence of the long-house is presented below.

The wide distribution of the long-house in Brittany, already noted, is accompanied by considerable variations in size and materials. Granite walls are associated with thatched roofs in south Morbihan, whilst in north Morbihan, dwellings are of two full storeys capped by slate-covered roofs. In Finistère and in parts of Loire-Atlantique the houses are frequently only of one storey. Some long-houses are very short, capable of accommodating only a single cow at the lower end, whilst others are sufficiently large to house ten or more. Given that families lived entirely in one room (see Chapter 15), the size of a long-house is more a function of the agricultural requirements and the wealth of the owner than of the demands of a family for multi-cell or specialist accommodation. A number of widely drawn examples illustrate the variety of size, form and building materials.

The hamlet of Kervaly, Plumergat, Morbihan, consists of fifteen former dwellings of which ten are long-houses, two still in occupation as such, the other eight now given over entirely either to man or beast. Five dwellings are single-cell houses. All the buildings are arranged in rows of two or three houses, an arrangement characteristic of many Breton hamlets. In some hamlets up to a dozen houses may be seen in a single row, many of the dwellings clearly always having been single-cell houses, but others are either long-houses or probably were long-houses now converted to near-symmetrical, two-roomed dwellings with a central doorway. Most Breton long-houses are considerably shorter than the Welsh examples discussed by Peate[468] and Fox and Raglan.[469] In general length varies between 9.00 and 13.00 metres, the majority being between 10.00 and 12.00 metres.

Kervaly 3 and 4 (Fig. 179) (WT 075867), a pair of long-houses, have recently been re-roofed and the walls heightened to carry the straight lines of corrugated asbestos which replaces thatch. The houses stand on a site with no perceptible slope, the two byres abutting each other with the halls at the outer ends. They are clearly of separate build, for although of similar size, Kervaly 3 is slightly longer than Kervaly 4 against which it is built, and is probably the later of the two. Walling is entirely of granite rubble, dressed stone being used for door and window surrounds and larger blocks of rubble for some of the quoins. Roof covering was formerly of rye-straw with a turf ridge. Kervaly 3 and 4 form a small row with total length of 21.90 metres externally. Kervaly 3 is 6.20 metres wide, and Kervaly 4, 6.75 metres wide, externally. Kervaly 3 is 11.25 metres long and 4.85 metres wide internally and Kervaly 4, 8.45 metres long and 5.30 metres wide internally. The old eaves line is 3.15 metres above the ground and the ridge *c.* 6.85 metres above the ground. Walling is laid in a mortar of *pisé* and the floors of both houses are of *terre battue*. The original doorway and window dressings are extremely fine. Doorway D1, round-headed, is quite plain, but

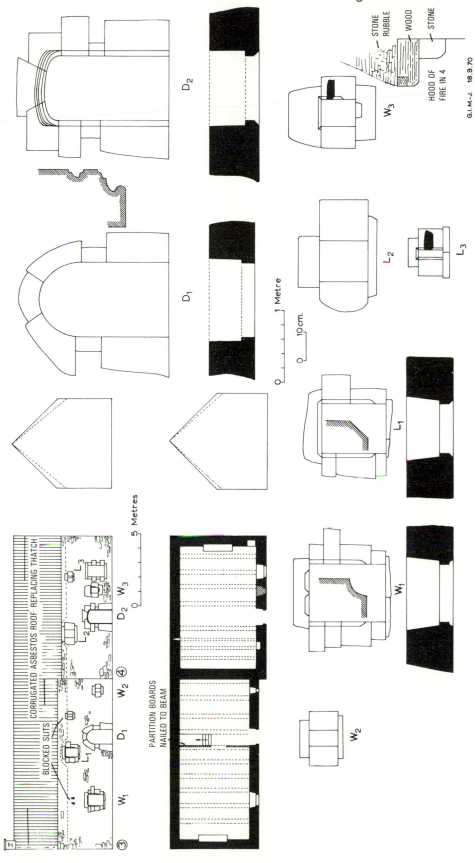

Fig. 179. Kervaly 3, 4, Plumergat, Morbihan

doorway D2 with flat-splayed chamfers on the jambs, has a three-centre door-head with elaborate mouldings. Windows W1 and W3 are probably original, but W3 is now blocked and Kervaly 4 has a large modern window placed alongside W3. Other original openings are the loft doorways L1 and L2, the byre slit or small window W2 and the loft slits, one of which, L3, has flat-splayed chamfers. The tiny window, W3, gives a very good indication of how small the windows of many of these houses formerly were. Window W1 with its cavetto moulding has probably been widened at some stage. Kervaly 3 has no openings at the rear but Kervaly 4 is provided with a slit at the lower, or byre, end. There are no keeping-places in Kervaly 3 but two are provided in Kervaly 4, one in the upper gable and one in the lower end. The original roof structure of both these houses consisted of trusses of the upper-cruck type, their feet set in the wall-heads with collars and tie-beams. The ridge purlin and lateral purlins were of rough chestnut poles, as were the common rafters. Thatch of rye-straw was tied directly to these common rafters held together with straw rope. Both hearths are of the traditional type, the chimney-hood of stone rubble resting on the wooden breastsummer supported by wooden corbels. In the case of Kervaly 4 these are supported by stone corbels. Loft floors are of a type traditional in southern Brittany and consist of slender poles of hazel or chestnut rolled in *pisé* and laid close together, the upper surface being finished off with *pisé* to form a floor effectively of *terre battue*. These loft floors rest on common beams with scantling of *c.* 0.30 metres, except at the lower end of Kervaly 4 where the beams are of lighter scantling. There is no trace of any partition in Kervaly 4 and it is probable that this house represents the original arrangement with the animals in the byre separated from the family in the hall only by pieces of furniture. In Kervaly 3 a wooden partition is nailed against the beam nearest the doorway at the lower end of the hall. This is probably a late modification to the interior and may well be as recent as the twentieth century. A flight of stairs placed against this partition provides access to the loft from inside the house. The halls are lighted by a single window, and ventilation for the byres is provided by slits framed with dressed stone. Neither of these byres has any fittings. Indeed, stalls are a rare feature in Breton long-houses and the only fittings found in Kervaly are iron tethering rings set in the inside wall of two of the byres. Although the byres are occasionally provided with a drain, this is not always so, and the presence of a drain must not be used as a criterion for determining the function of the lower end of the long-house. Drainage, as in some Irish long-houses, appears to be by the doorway but there is no evidence of

a channel for this purpose. Dung must formerly have accumulated in large quantities. Nor are the Breton long-houses always aligned down slope with the byre at the lower end: the byre is not infrequently at the upper end and such drainage as there is must pass the hall on the outside.

The regional house in Morbihan is commonly of one-and-a-half storeys, the half-storey and roof space serving as a loft. Thus the ceiling beams, as in the Kervaly houses, also serve as tie-beams, and are closely set and of the order of 0.25–0.30 metres square. Often these have simple chamfers, usually in the hall only, but occasionally in the byre too, and the ends of the beams are frequently exposed in the lateral walls, in some cases being protected from running water by flat projecting stones set in the wall immediately above. The beams carry longitudinally a cover of closely set *batons* of chestnut or hazel rolled in *pisé*. A further layer of *pisé* is applied to form the smooth loft floor, a covering which is both warm and serviceable. Although still commonly found, the beaten-earth floor has in some cases been replaced by one of boards. Access to the loft is by an opening set in the front elevation and frequently framed with dressed stone as in Kervaly houses. Occasionally a staircase or ladder from the hall is provided in addition, perhaps placed, as in Kervaly 3, next to the partition and opposite the doorway. This arrangement is rare in Kervaly and a ladder is mostly necessary to gain access to the loft from outside.

Practically all the houses are gable-ended, and the hipped roof, although not unknown, is certainly rare, having been encountered in small numbers in only a few locations, notably in the Névez–Trégunc area with its orthostat-walled houses (Figs. 47–50) and in the primitive houses around Plumelin (Figs. 72, 167–169). In the Kervaly houses the principal rafters rise out of the tie-beams, there being generally two, or occasionally three, trusses between the gables. The trusses in many of the dwellings examined appear to have been re-used. They are morticed into the beams and halved and pegged at the apex. Lateral purlins are usually rough chestnut poles joined by a simple overlap against the trusses into which they are either notched or supported on cleats pegged into the trusses. Not infrequently they are supported by a solitary peg. A ridge-beam, usually a rough chestnut pole, is carried in the 'v' of the intersecting principal rafters. Common rafters, like the loft floor, are formed of close-set chestnut poles, laid alternately along the ridge-pole, with their feet resting on the wall-heads, for wall-plates are an unnecessary luxury rarely encountered. On this base is laid the thatch, which extends to the gable walls, off-set to receive it, in most of the Morbihan examples. A curious feature is the frequent occurrence of long stout pegs projecting at close intervals from both sides of the principal rafters (Fig. 182). Whilst these are aids to climbing the hay when it is piled high, they were undoubtedly intended to be used as 'ladders' during the building of the roof. Elsewhere, tie-beam trusses with the upper king-post rising from the collar, not the tie-beam, are common. Hybrids are found, notably the upper-cruck truss with an upper king-post rising from the collar and supporting the ridge-pole.

Terre battue is a particularly good insulator and this covering both of the hall floor and of the loft above results in a room that is both warm and dry, particularly with a load of hay in the loft, for with only a single doorway and a solitary small window there are few draughts. Keeping-places are frequently provided, as in Kervaly 4 (Fig. 179), not only within the chimney back, but also in the walls of both hall and byre. These are characteristically 0.30 to 0.40 metres wide and about 0.30 metres deep but larger places are also found, some with arched lintels and a dividing stone shelf. Lofts are used for the storage of hay, but sometimes also for grain, and occasionally for other farm purposes, the storage of potato seed, or of simple farm implements. In some areas they are used also to provide additional sleeping accommodation, as in Finistère where lofts provided with a hearth have been recorded, but there is little evidence for this in the Morbihan houses so far examined.

In Kervaly 2 (WT 074866) the hall is remarkably short and the byre twice as long. Kervaly 1, adjoining, is a single-cell dwelling (Fig. 178). Walling is entirely of a fine-grained granite rubble, larger pieces being used for the quoins and also in other places to assist bonding. Total external length is 19.95 metres and width 6.90 metres. Kervaly 1 measures 6.45 metres long and 5.50 metres wide internally, whilst Kervaly 2 is 11.30 metres long and 5.50 metres wide internally. The walls rise 3.00 metres from the ground to the eaves line and the ridge is approximately 6.20 metres above the ground. Granite rubble walling is laid in a mortar of *pisé* and floors are entirely of *terre battue*. Roof trusses are of the upper-cruck type, the feet of which are embedded in the wall-heads. These intersect at the apex and carry ridge and lateral purlins of rough chestnut poles. From the ridge-pole to the wall-head lie the common rafters consisting of close-set chestnut poles lashed together with straw rope. Thatch of rye-straw is tied directly to these common rafters, and although the ridge was formerly finished with turfs held down by wooden pegs, it is now covered with galvanized iron. The hearths are of 'standard' construction. That in Kervaly 2, H1, is illustrated. A wooden breastsummer is supported on a pair of wooden

corbels and these in turn support the chimney-hood of granite rubble. A pair of keeping-places is provided in the hearth-back and the hearth-stone is formed of large granite slabs. Doorway- and window-surrounds display a variety of periods. Doorway D1 is round-headed and probably contemporary with window W1 and loft opening L1. Dressings are plain but W1 has a cavetto chamfer and decorated stops together with a dressed lip on the sill. Loft opening L1 has a cavetto chamfer on one jamb only. Loft opening L2 has a dressed lip and a flat-splay chamfer. The doorway of Kervaly 1 appears to be of twentieth-century date and the windows are modern. Following its conversion to a byre, Kervaly 2 has recent windows inserted, two in the façade and one in the lower gable. A doorway is provided for internal com-munication. Kervaly 2 is clearly formerly a long-house and there is a slit in the rear wall at the lower end. A single keeping-place is provided in the front wall at the upper end. The dividing partition is formed of wooden planks nailed to one of the beams. It is probable that this house was originally open from end to end without separation between man and beast and this partition represents a late nineteenth- or early twentieth-century improvement. It divides the interior space, house to byre, in the ratio of approximately 1:2, thus making this one of the larger long-houses. Kervaly 1 has recently been considerably modernized but Kervaly 2 retains the traditional loft over the house supported on heavy common beams. The loft floor is formed of thin poles rolled in *pisé* and smoothed over with the same material to form a floor largely of *terre battue*. It is possible that these two houses are not of the same date and that Kervaly 1 is a late nineteenth- or early twentieth-century addition to Kervaly 2, but there is no clear indication of jointing in the walls. Another possibility is that the door dressings were renewed during the earlier part of the twentieth century in Kervaly 1. The whole building, seen from a distance, has the appearance of a *petit manoir* of the three-unit form, an impression furthered by the presence and position of the three chimney stacks. The third of these, at the gable end of the byre, is false, such stacks, more slender than the true stacks, being common in both Morbihan and Finistère.

Kervaly 5 and 6 (Fig. 180) (WT 075867) are somewhat enigmatic. Walling is of granite rubble which is also used for the quoins and chimney-stacks and for some of the door and window dressings. Dressed stone is used for the majority of door and window openings. The roof is covered with a thatch of rye-straw but the original ridge covering of turf has been replaced by strips of galvanized iron. Kervaly 5 and 6 form a row with a total external length of 30.05 metres and width 6.75 metres.

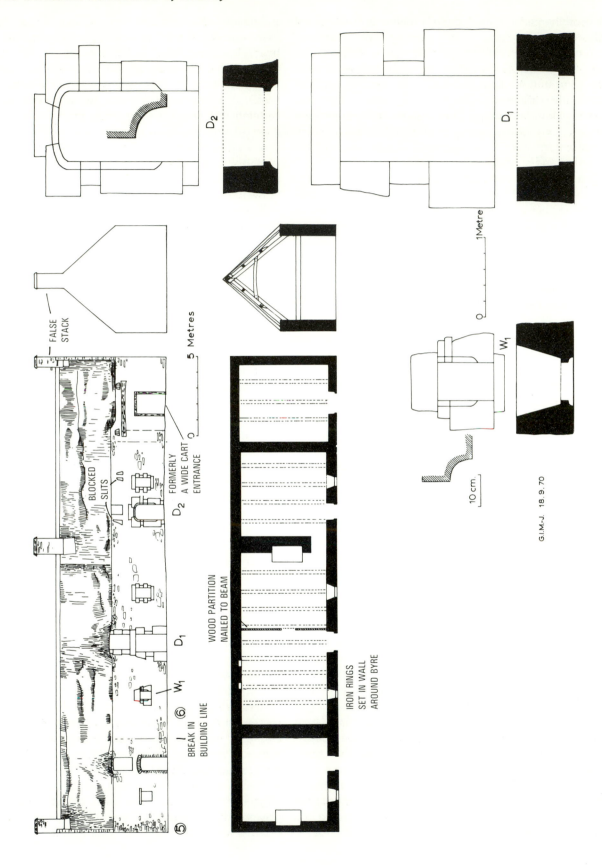

Fig. 180. Kervaly 5, 6, Plumergat, Morbihan

The row is made up of four cells whose function is not entirely clear. Kervaly 5 is an almost square single-cell house 5.35 metres long and 5.37 metres wide internally. Kervaly 6 is 10.75 metres long and 5.35 metres wide internally and the two additional cells are 5.25 metres long and 4.85 metres long and approximately 5.40 metres wide internally. There is no communication between Kervaly 5 and 6 internally but Kervaly 6 communicates with the adjacent cell which has a separate outside doorway, D2.

The granite rubble walling is laid with a mortar of *pisé* and the floors are entirely of *terre battue*, the loft floors resting on the common beams, most of which have a scantling of *c.* 0.25 metres, being of the traditional type. Roof trusses throughout are of the upper-cruck, collar and tie-beam type. In the case of Kervaly 6, one of the trusses with a very high collar has an upper king-post. There are two pairs of lateral purlins and the intersecting cruck blades carry a ridge purlin. Purlins and common rafters are all of chestnut poles, the rafters being closely set and bound together with straw rope. There are no wall-plates and the feet of the rafters rest on the wall-heads. Thatch of rye-straw is tied directly to the common rafters. Chimneys are of stone rubble and the chimney-hoods rest on wooden breastsummers which in turn are supported by wooden corbels. Hearth stones are of granite slabs. Doorway and window dressings vary considerably in quality. Doorway D2 has a three-centred arch and cavetto moulding. The earliest-looking window, W1, also has a cavetto moulding, but these features are associated with windows, and doorway D1 and its adjacent loft opening are of regular square-cut granite dressings. These suggest at the earliest a late eighteenth-century date and are more likely to belong to the later nineteenth century. The doorway to Kervaly 5 is dressed entirely with rubble. The upper cell formerly had a wide entrance but this has partly been blocked and provided with a much narrower wood-framed doorway.

Kervaly 5 is clearly a small, single-cell house and, as the vertical joint suggests, is a later addition to Kervaly 6. The latter building is a simple long-house but with internal communication to an upper chamber which has a much earlier looking doorway, D2. This upper chamber or cell may have originally been a house provided with a hearth which was demolished when the end cell, most likely constructed as a cart shed, was added. An alternative explanation is that the upper cell with its doorway, D2, is an original feature and was unheated from the beginning, but in view of the general housing arrangements in the area this seems extremely unlikely. The long-house Kervaly 6 has a wooden partition probably of nineteenth-century date nailed to the beam next to the doorway at the lower end of the hall. The byre end is provided with two keeping-places and iron tethering rings are set at intervals around the wall. This long-house was still in use as such with man and beast at opposite ends, both in 1970 when the original survey was made and again in 1972. Entry to the hall, however, was generally made through doorway D2 rather than through doorway D1, although this remained open, as did the doorway in the wooden partition separating the hall from the byre. Of the three chimney-stacks, the one at the gable end over the cart shed is false.

Kervaly 7 (WT 075866) is also a long-house to which is attached a single-cell dwelling (Fig. 181). Although here there is a communicating doorway, it is doubtful whether the two dwellings are contemporary and more likely that the smaller is the later of the two. This building is exceptional in Kervaly in that it is of two full storeys, with a slate roof, and is provided with a pair of opposing doorways. The byre, whose gable is asymmetrically placed, is rather longer than the hall from which it is separated by a stone partition. Walling is entirely of granite rubble but dressed stone, also granite, is used for door and window details. The roofs are slate-covered with red tiles on the ridge. The buildings are not regular in shape and the total external length is approximately 20.70 metres. Kervaly 7 is *c.* 11.00 metres long and 5.70 metres wide internally. Kervaly 8 is *c.* 6.50 metres long internally and averages about 5.00 metres wide. Granite rubble walling is laid with a mortar of *pisé* and the floors in both houses are of *terre battue*. The loft flooring, laid on common beams with a scantling of approximately 0.30 metres, is of a type traditional in south Morbihan. Thin poles or *batons* of chestnut or hazel are rolled in a mixture of *pisé* and the resulting strips laid side by side on top of the common beams. The surface is finished with an additional layer of *pisé* to form a floor several centimetres thick. Both roofs have been subject to change, and although the old roof line is difficult to see, the elevation of these houses was almost certainly similar to those of the other houses in the district, with a low eaves line over-sailing the loft openings. The present roof probably dates only from the twentieth century when the thatch covering was replaced with slate. The present roof trusses have no tie-beams and are of the collar type, the principal rafters being braced downwards into the wall-head by sling-braces which are tied to the wall-heads with spurs. These roof trusses almost certainly replace trusses of the upper-cruck type and the wall height was raised to provide a uniform eaves line capable more easily of taking the new slate roof. There are two pairs of lateral purlins over which boards are laid and the slates are nailed directly to these boards. The chimneys are of stone rubble but that

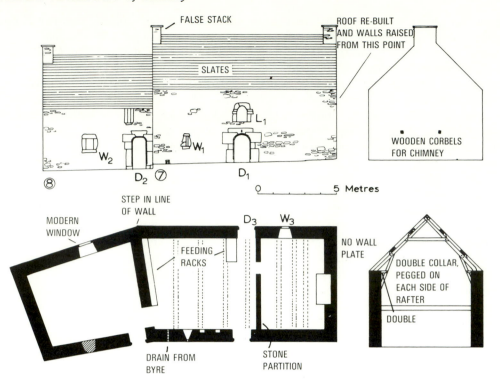

FALSE STACK

ROOF RE-BUILT
AND WALLS RAISED
FROM THIS POINT

SLATES

L₁

WOODEN CORBELS
FOR CHIMNEY

W₂

W₁

D₂ ⑦

D₁

⑧

0   5 Metres

STEP IN LINE
OF WALL

MODERN
WINDOW

D₃   W₃

FEEDING
RACKS

NO WALL
PLATE

DOUBLE COLLAR,
PEGGED ON
EACH SIDE OF
RAFTER

DOUBLE

DRAIN FROM
BYRE

STONE
PARTITION

Fig. 181a.   Kervaly 7, 8, Plumergat, Morbihan

at the lower end of Kervaly 7 is false. The hearth at the upper end has a chimney-hood of stone rubble supported by a wooden breastsummer, in turn supported by wooden corbels. The hearth in Kervaly 8, not shown in the drawings, is similarly constructed and the chimney-hood of stone rubble rests on a wooden breastsummer and wooden corbels. Both hearths are provided with massive granite hearth-stones. Door and window dressings are extremely fine. Doorways D1 and D3 are round-arched and have ovolo mouldings. Doorway D2 is three-centred with flat-splay mouldings on the jambs and a fluted moulding on the door-head. Carvings on door-heads or jambs are often encountered, such as the cider bottle on Kervaly 8 (D1). Flat-splay mouldings are used on loft opening L1 and window W2. Kervaly 7 is a long-house with a pair of opposed doorways at the ends of an embryo cross-passage defined on the upper or hall side by a stone partition. The use of a stone partition is relatively rare but it is probably a later insertion and not an original feature. The hall is lighted by window W3 and feeding racks or mangers are now located in the byre. A drain is provided. Kervaly 8 is a single-cell house communicating internally with Kervaly 7 but served by a separate doorway D2. The original window W2 is blocked and the cell is now lighted by a modern window. This house is very irregular in shape and the vertical joints and inset wall line suggest that it is a later addition to

Kervaly 7. At the time of the survey, September 1970, this pair of houses was occupied by three generations of one family. Kervaly 8 was used as a common hall for living, cooking, eating and sleeping and Kervaly 7 was still in use as a long-house, entry for man and beast being by either doorway D1 or D3, but the hall of the long-house was in use only for sleeping.

Kervaly 9 and 10 (WT 075866) are also a pair of long-houses sited where the ground slopes from right to left (Fig. 182). The byre of Kervaly 10 has neither drain nor ventilation slits, supporting the contention that drains appear to have been provided in only a minority of byres. Walling is of granite rubble and some dressed granite is used for door and window surrounds. Roof covering is a thatch of rye-straw. The buildings are not quite in line and measure approximately 24.30 metres in length externally. Kervaly 9 is 9.65 metres long and 4.50 metres wide, internally. Kervaly 10 is 7.40 metres long and 4.85 metres wide, internally. The two houses are separated by a byre approximately 3.80 metres long and 4.55 metres wide internally. The eaves line is not at a uniform height above the ground level. At its lowest point it is 2.80 metres above the ground and its greatest height at the lower gable of Kervaly 9 is *c.* 3.20 metres above the ground. The ridge line is also not uniform. The apex of the lower gable is 6.00 metres above the ground and at the upper gable 6.55 metres. Rubble walling is bonded

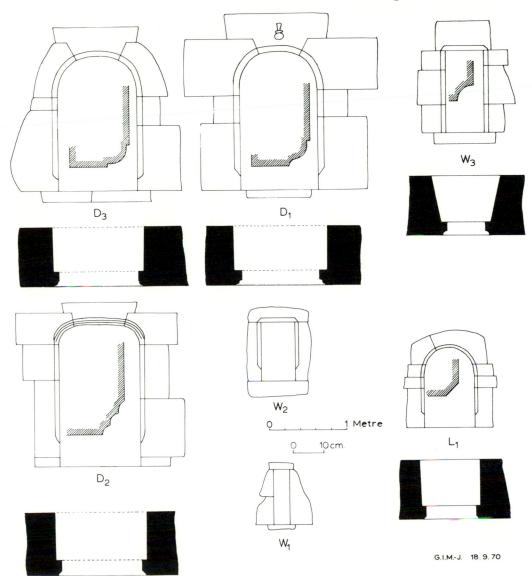

Fig. 181b. Kervaly 7, 8, Plumergat, Morbihan

with a mortar of *pisé*. Slightly larger rubble blocks are used for quoins and at intervals in the walling. Several doorways have jambs of rubble and wood lintels. Doorway D1 and loft opening L1 are of dressed granite blocks, as are three of the window openings. Roof trusses are of the upper-cruck type, two of them being upper-cruck and tie-beam trusses, the third an upper-cruck, collar and tie-beam truss. The roof of Kervaly 10 has two pairs of lateral purlins and a ridge purlin, that of Kervaly 9 only one pair of lateral purlins and a ridge purlin. Common rafters are provided with 'climbing' pegs. Purlins and common rafters are of rough chestnut poles. These are close-spaced, never more than 1.00 metres apart and bound with straw rope. It is to this framework

of common rafters that the rye thatch is tied directly. The ridge was formerly of turf. The loft floor is formed of *batons*, the surface finished with a further layer of *pisé*. Both hearths are provided with rubble chimney-hoods resting on a breastsummer of wood which in turn is supported by wooden corbels. The massive hearth stones are of granite slabs. The three doorways are all flat-headed but only D1 is of dressed stone. The small window openings W1, W2 and W3 are almost certainly original and have a variety of chamfers; in addition W1 is provided with a dressed lip. Both these houses are long-houses with a single doorway for both man and beast. Kervaly 9 remains in its elementary form without a physical separation between hall and byre. In Kervaly 10,

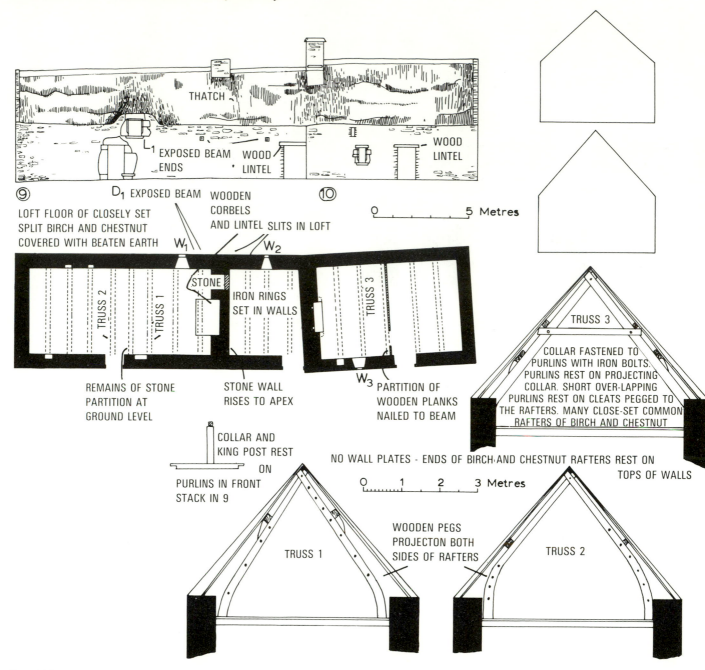

THATCH

EXPOSED BEAM ENDS

WOOD LINTEL

WOOD LINTEL

⑨   D₁ EXPOSED BEAM   WOODEN CORBELS AND LINTEL SLITS IN LOFT   ⑩

0   5 Metres

LOFT FLOOR OF CLOSELY SET SPLIT BIRCH AND CHESTNUT COVERED WITH BEATEN EARTH

W₁   W₂

STONE

TRUSS 2   TRUSS 1

IRON RINGS SET IN WALLS

TRUSS 3

REMAINS OF STONE PARTITION AT GROUND LEVEL

STONE WALL RISES TO APEX

W₃   PARTITION OF WOODEN PLANKS NAILED TO BEAM

TRUSS 3

COLLAR FASTENED TO PURLINS WITH IRON BOLTS. PURLINS REST ON PROJECTING COLLAR. SHORT OVER-LAPPING PURLINS REST ON CLEATS PEGGED TO THE RAFTERS. MANY CLOSE-SET COMMON RAFTERS OF BIRCH AND CHESTNUT

COLLAR AND KING POST REST ON PURLINS IN FRONT STACK IN 9

NO WALL PLATES - ENDS OF BIRCH AND CHESTNUT RAFTERS REST ON TOPS OF WALLS

0   1   2   3 Metres

TRUSS 1

WOODEN PEGS PROJECTON BOTH SIDES OF RAFTERS

TRUSS 2

Fig. 182a.   Kervaly 9, 10, Plumergat, Morbihan

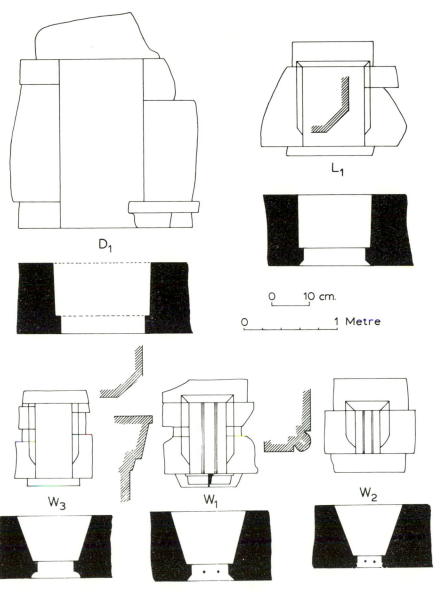

Fig. 182b. Kervaly 9, 10, Plumergat, Morbihan

however, a wooden partition has been added by nailing planks to the common beam next above the doorway. Kervaly 9 has keeping-places in the walls of both the hall and the byre and in the upper gable lies a now blocked doorway leading into a byre or stable which has iron tethering rings set into the walls. The relationship of this house to Kervaly 10 shows that it is not of the same date and it seems likely that Kervaly 10 is the later of the two, having been added to the original structure. The hall of Kervaly 10 is provided with only one keeping-place.

Kervaly 11 and 11a (WT 075866) consist of a long-house with an adjacent single-cell house, probably of later date (Fig. 183). The partition has been moved recently, and this house must once have been open from end to end, the first partition perhaps being inserted during the nineteenth century. Walling is of granite rubble with some dressed stone used for door and window surrounds. Thatch is of rye-straw. Kervaly 11 and 11a form a short row *c.* 16.75 metres long and 6.00 metres wide externally. Kervaly 11 is 8.85 metres long and 4.65 metres wide internally, while Kervaly 11a is 5.85 metres long and 4.65 metres wide internally. The eaves line is

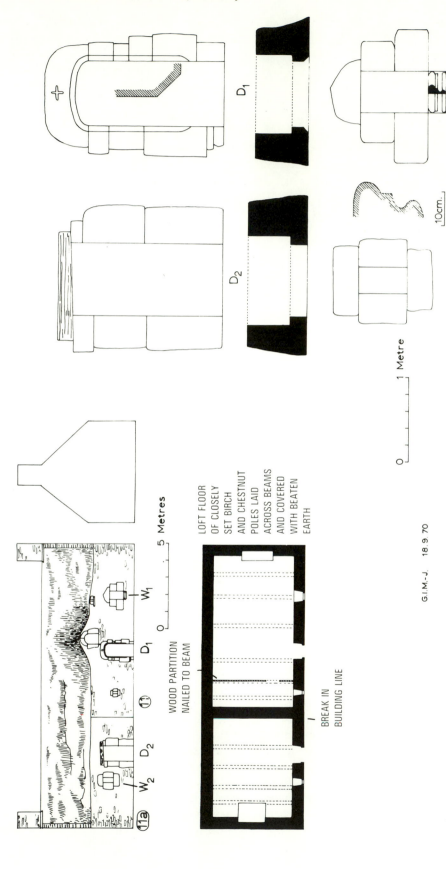

LOFT FLOOR
OF CLOSELY
SET BIRCH
AND CHESTNUT
POLES LAID
ACROSS BEAMS
AND COVERED
WITH BEATEN
EARTH

WOOD PARTITION
NAILED TO BEAM

BREAK IN
BUILDING LINE

G.I.M.-J.   18.9.70

Fig. 183. Kervaly 11, 11a, Plumergat, Morbihan

variable in height, but *c.* 2.50 metres above the ground and the ridge rises 5.50 metres above ground level. Rubble walling is bonded in a mortar of *pisé* and larger rubble blocks are used both in the quoins and within the main body of the walling. Floors are of *terre battue* and the loft floor is made of *batons* of chestnut or hazel strips rolled in *pisé* and laid side by side across the common beams, finished with a further layer of *pisé*. Doorway D1 has a three-centred monolithic door-head bearing a cross, and both the door-head and the jambs have flat-splay chamfers. Doorway D2 has plain stone jambs and a wood lintel. Windows W1 and W2 have plain stone dressings except that W1 is provided with a sill bearing an elaborately dressed lip. The roof trusses in both houses are of the upper-cruck, collar and tie-beam type and support ridge and lateral purlins of rough chestnut poles. Common rafters, also of chestnut poles, are tied together with straw rope. Thatch of rye-straw is tied directly to this roof. The houses are not of the same date and the position of the vertical joints suggests that Kervaly 11a is a later addition to Kervaly 11. There is no internal communication between the two houses. Kervaly 11a is a single-cell house with sufficient space at the bottom end of the hall to accommodate at least one and possibly two cows. The possibility that it was so used as a small long-house cannot be dismissed. Kervaly 11, however, is clearly a long-house with a slit provided to ventilate the byre. The wood partition nailed to a beam is of very recent date and this long-house was almost certainly formerly open from end to end.

Kervaly 12, 13 and 14 (WT 074866) comprise the longest row in the hamlet (Fig. 184). Apart from an additional byre and pigsty, it consists of two long-houses and a small single-cell house. Walling is of granite rubble with dressed stone for door and window surrounds. Roof covering is of rye-straw thatch. Kervaly 12, 13 and 14 form a row which, together with the lean-to pigsty, is *c.* 35.65 metres long and 6.50 metres wide externally. The pigsty is 1.90 metres long and 3.65 metres wide internally. This is followed by a byre, or stable, 3.65 metres long and 5.15 metres wide internally. Kervaly 12 is 10.70 metres long and 5.15 metres wide, Kervaly 13 is 10.20 metres long and 5.15 metres wide, and Kervaly 14 is 5.15 metres long and 5.15 metres wide, internally. The eaves line of Kervaly 12 and 13 is approximately 3.90 metres from the ground, that of Kervaly 12 is 7.20 metres, and that of Kervaly 13, 7.45 metres above the ground. The eaves line of Kervaly 14 is 2.65 metres, and the ridge line 5.70 metres above ground level. Rubble walling is bonded with a mortar of *pisé*. Larger pieces of rubble are used for the quoins and occasionally in the main body of the walling. Most of the door and window

dressings are of cut granite blocks. Floors throughout are of *terre battue* and the loft floors are formed in the traditional manner. Roof structure is supported on trusses of the upper-cruck, collar and tie-beam type. These carry a ridge purlin and two pairs of lateral purlins. Rough chestnut poles tied together with straw rope at close intervals form the common rafters, and to these the thatch of rye-straw is tied directly. The ridge was originally finished with a capping of turf pegged to the thatch, but is now covered with galvanized iron strips. All the chimney-stacks are real and built of granite rubble. Hearths have granite rubble hoods resting on wood breastsummers in turn supported by wood corbels. Hearth stones are of large granite slabs. Doorway and window dressings are elaborate and sometimes extremely finely cut. Doorway D2 bears a cross on the left-hand jamb. The doors and windows of Kervaly 13 and 14 appear to be original but Kervaly 12 has a window W1 which appears to be much later than its doorway D2, and a modern window has recently been inserted into what must have been the byre end. Vertical joints are in evidence between Kervaly 12 and 13 and again between Kervaly 13 and 14. It is probable that Kervaly 13 is the earliest of the three buildings, that Kervaly 12 was added to this and at a later date Kervaly 14 added at the other end. Internal communication exists throughout the length of these three houses. There is no evidence of vertical joints between the byre or stable at the lower end of Kervaly 12 and this may or may not be a later addition. It should be noted that the ends of the common beams are visible in the rear walls of these houses and that to protect these beam ends from the weather flat stones placed immediately above them project slightly. These houses have no keeping-places whatsoever and only one wooden partition is in evidence, in Kervaly 12 which is also provided with an internal wooden staircase giving access to the loft. This must be presumed to be of very recent date. Kervaly 14 is a small single-cell house. Kervaly 13 is a classic long-house of elementary form and one of the finest surviving examples in the area. Kervaly 12 is likewise an extremely fine long-house but it seems probable that the window W1 is a nineteenth-century insertion replacing a much smaller original window and that the large modern window at the lower end is a recent insertion made when the byre was converted into a sleeping chamber. The building below was probably a stable or alternatively a second byre and the small lean-to certainly a pigsty.

Other examples illustrate the long-houses of south Morbihan. At Mériadec-en-Plumergat (WT 076829) a short row consisting of a long-house and a single-cell house results from an addition to the original house of

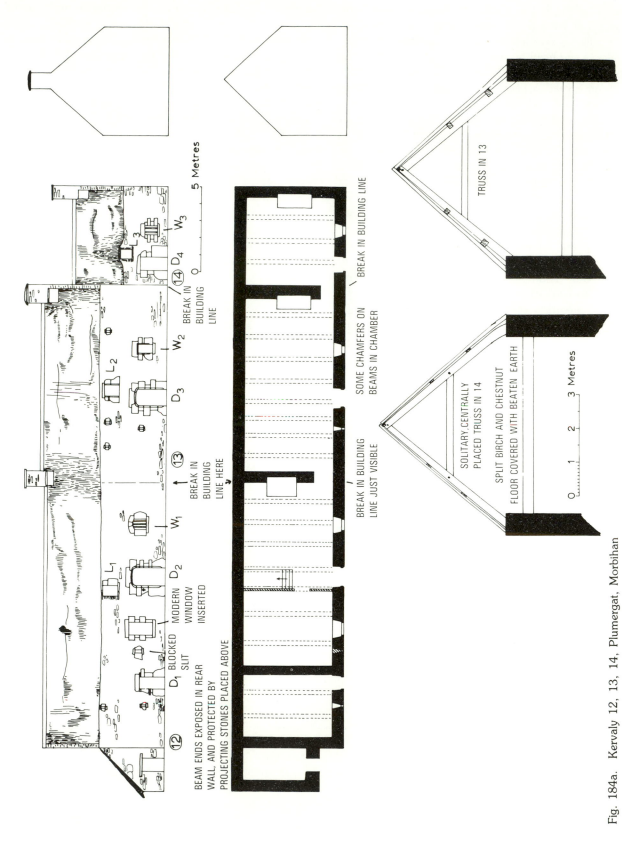

Fig. 184a. Kervaly 12, 13, 14, Plumergat, Morbihan

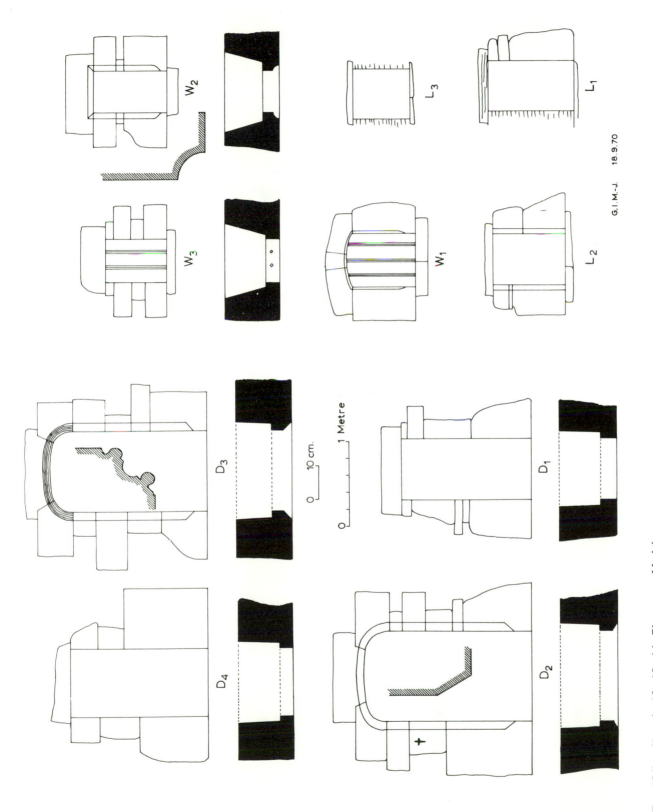

W₂

W₃

L₃

L₁

W₁

L₂

D₃

D₁

D₄

D₂

1 Metre

10 cm.

0

G.I.M.J.   18.9.70

Fig. 184b.   Kervaly 12, 13, 14, Plumergat, Morbihan

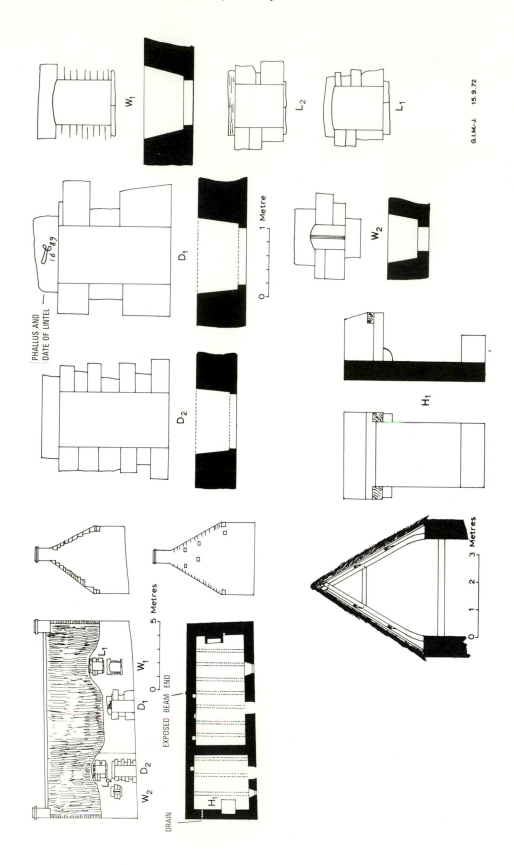

PHALLUS AND DATE OF LINTEL

1689

W₁ L₂ L₁ D₁ W₂ D₂ H₁

EXPOSED BEAM END

DRAIN

1 Metre

5 Metres

3 Metres

G.I.M.-J. 15.9.72

1689 (Fig. 185). Walling is of granite rubble and door and window dressings are of cut stone. Larger blocks of rubble, roughly trimmed, are used in the gables. Roof covering is of rye-straw thatch. This building consists of two dwellings with a total length of *c.* 14.50 metres and a width which falls from 5.30 metres at the lower end to 4.90 metres at the upper end. The eaves line is approximately 2.30 metres above the ground and the ridge rises to 6.70 metres above ground level. The lower dwelling is 4.05 metres long and *c.* 4.00 metres wide, and the upper dwelling 8.10 metres long and *c.* 3.60 metres wide, internally. Rubble walling is bonded with a mortar of *pisé.* Floors are of *terre battue* and the loft floor is formed of *batons.* Common beams are *c.* 0.20 metres square and one is exposed in the rear wall. Roof trusses are of the upper-cruck, collar and tie-beam type carrying a ridge purlin and two pairs of lateral purlins supported on cleats. Common rafters of rough chestnut poles are placed close together and tied with straw rope. Thatch of rye-straw is tied directly to this. Formerly the ridge was finished with turf but is now capped with a strip of galvanized iron. Chimney-stacks are of granite rubble and rubble also forms the chimney-hoods which are supported on a breastsummer of wood in turn resting on wood corbels. Doorways D1 and D2 have plain granite dressings. Window W1 has a stone-arched lintel and rubble jambs, whilst window W2 with its iron bar is of plain dressed stone. Loft openings L1 and L2 have dressed stone jambs and wood lintels. The two dwellings are not of the same date, as is evident from the vertical joint. It is probable that the lower dwelling is a later addition to the upper which bears the date 1689 and a phallic symbol on the door lintel. The lower dwelling is of one cell only. It is provided with a drain, and although this suggests that it may have been in use as a byre or stable, the hearth being used simply for the preparation of animal food, it is more likely that it has also served at some time as a dwelling. The upper house is a long-house of the classic type, open from end to end with no trace of any former partition between hall and byre.

Coët Cunec 2, Plumergat (WT 073859) is one of the shortest long-houses recorded (Fig. 186). The building is approximately rectangular and measures *c.* 7.30 metres long and 6.25 metres wide externally, 5.75 metres long and 4.85 metres wide internally. The walls are *c.* 0.70 metres thick. The height from ground to the eaves is 3.10 metres at the front, and 2.65 metres at the rear. The height from ground to ridge is *c.* 7.20 metres. Walling is of granite rubble with door and window openings of dressed stone bonded with a mortar of *pisé.* Gable walls are off-set to receive the rye-straw thatched roof. The coping is of roughly dressed granite blocks. The floor is of

terre battue and the loft floor is supported on five beams 0.30 metres square. The loft floor is formed in the traditional manner with *batons* of chestnut. There is one roof-truss of the upper king-post and collar type, the rafters being upper-crucks. Carpentry is of good quality and the purlins are properly cut squared timber. There is a ridge purlin and there are two pairs of lateral purlins. Common rafters are staggered at the apex and their feet rest on the wall-heads; they are of close-set chestnut poles tied with straw rope and the thatch of rye-straw is tied directly to them. The roof is finished with a turf capping. One of the ceiling beams projects through the front elevation so that its end is exposed alongside the doorway, a common feature. A hearth is recessed into the gable wall. The chimney-hood of stone rubble rests on a wooden breastsummer which, in turn, rests on wooden corbels. The chimney-stack is also of granite rubble and at the lower end of the house there is a further, but false, chimney-stack. Doorway and window dressings are of good quality but plain except for an opening in the lower gable which has a chamfered round-headed arch. A window lighting the hall is now blocked, as is the rear door. In its original form a pair of opposing doorways lay at opposite ends of the embryo cross-passage. To the left was the hall and to the right the byre. The house is thus an extremely short long-house, with room for two, or even three, cows to be tethered at the end wall. There is no reason to believe that the date 1805 on the lower gable is not that of first building.

Lopabu 5, Grand-Champ (WT 101909), is only slightly longer. The building is approximately rectangular and measures 8.20 metres in length and 6.00 metres in width externally and 6.70 metres in length and 4.65 metres in width internally. The walls are *c.* 0.70 metres thick. Height from ground to eaves is *c.* 3.30 metres and from ground to the apex of the gable 6.80 metres (Fig. 187). Granite rubble walling with an occasional dressed block is bonded in a mortar of *pisé.* Granite dressings are used for part of the door and window surrounds. Thatch is of rye-straw. The floor is of *terre battue.* There is one roof-truss of the upper king-post type, the feet of the rafters being embedded in the wall-heads. It is probable that the feet are curved and descend into the tie-beam as upper crucks. There is a ridge purlin and two pairs of lateral purlins. These in turn support close-set common rafters of chestnut to which the thatch is tied directly. The ridge was undoubtedly once finished with turf but is now capped by a sheet of galvanized iron. The hearth is recessed into the gable wall, a hood of rubble is supported on a breastsummer resting on wooden corbels and there is one small keeping-place. A single doorway opens into the embryo cross-passage. To the right is the

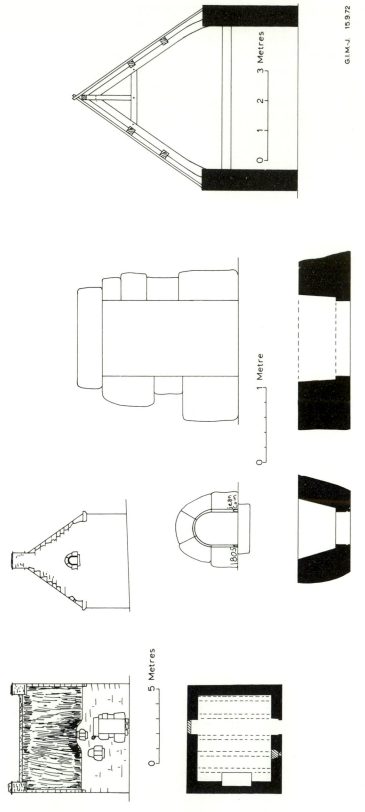

Fig. 186. Coët Cunec 2, Plumergat, Morbihan

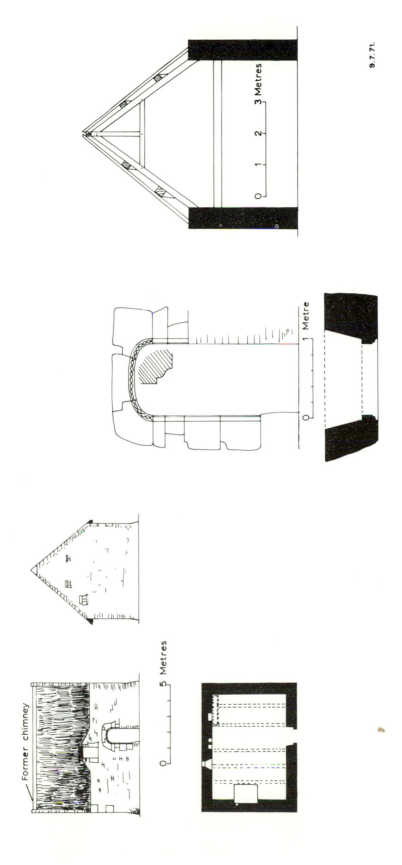

9.7.71.

Fig. 187. Lopabu 5, Grand-Champ Morbihan

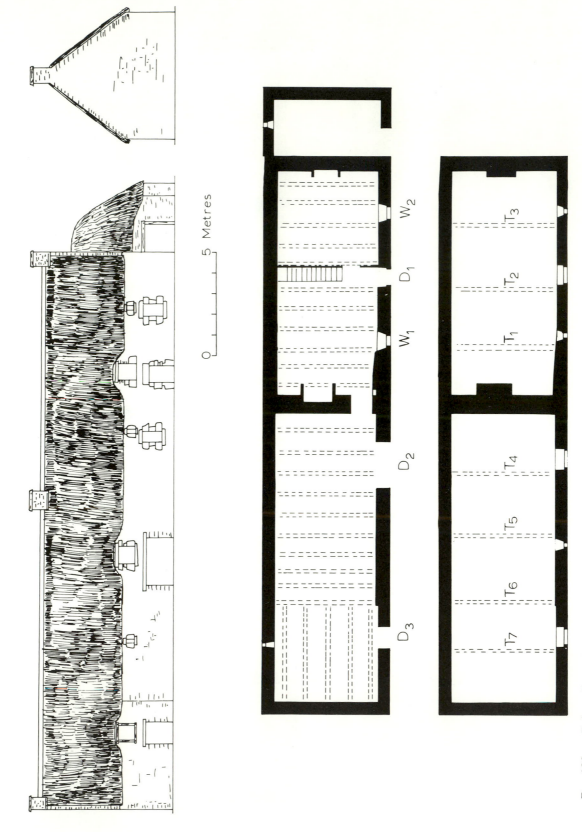

5 Metres

0

Fig. 188a.   Rulano Bras, Grand-Champ, Morbihan

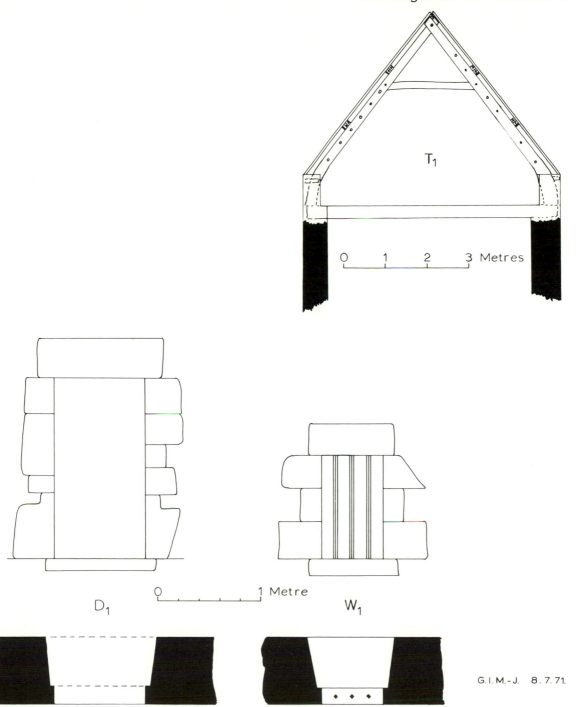

T₁

0   1   2   3 Metres

D₁   0   1 Metre   W₁

G.I.M.-J.   8. 7. 71.

Fig. 188b.   Rulano Bras, Grand-Champ, Morbihan

former byre with a trough or manger against the back wall, and to the left the hall is lighted by a small window in the rear wall. Also in the rear wall are three small keeping-places. The doorway and window openings are largely of dressed stone except where blocks of stone appear to have fallen away. There is some chamfering and the door-head, a three-centred arch, has a cable moulding. This building is a very short long-house but obviously of some quality judged by the fittings and the fact that the walls are given a certain amount of batter at the base.

Rulano Bras, Grand-Champ (WT 119922), provides an example of a long-house of exceptional length (Fig. 188). Externally the total length, including the lean-to outshot, is 30.40 metres and the width 6.20 metres. Internally the total length is 25.60 metres and the width *c*. 4.80 metres. The eaves line is *c*. 2.50 metres, and the ridge *c*. 6.50 metres, above the ground. Wall thickness varies from *c*. 0.60 metres to *c*. 0.90 metres. Walling is of granite rubble with granite dressings to some of the windows and doorways laid in a mortar of *pisé*. Roof covering is of rye-straw thatch. The ridge was formerly finished with turf but is now covered with strips of galvanized iron. The floor is of *terre battue* and the loft floors, for the greater part, are formed of *batons* of chestnut or hazel. Roof trusses are of the upper-cruck type with collar and tie-beam, the curved feet of the crucks having holes formerly occupied by the pegs which projected to form a ladder for use during construction. Many of these holes are now empty. The ridge-purlin rests in the intersection of the principal rafters, and two pairs of lateral purlins are supported on pegs driven into the rafters. Common rafters are of rough chestnut poles laid close together and tied with straw rope, their feet resting on the wall-heads, and they are staggered at the apex. Thatch of rye-straw is tied directly to this bedding of common rafters. There are two hearths, one with a chimney-hood of stone rubble supported on a wooden breastsummer which, in turn, rests on wooden corbels. The second is a poor and obviously late nineteenth- or early twentieth-century insertion to provide heat for the second cell. Although the doorway and windows are framed with dressed stone, this is not of particularly high quality and the building may well be as late as nineteenth century in date. One window, W1, retains its three iron bars, and although these windows are now glazed they were unglazed in their original state. There are changes in wall thickness which betray more than one phase of building. The lean-to outshot is clearly an addition and the straight joint at the far lower end, together with a change in direction of the common beams, betrays an addition to that end also. This far end is provided with a

false chimney-stack. Door D2 is wide enough to take a cart and this must be regarded as a late insertion. The presence of a relatively modern hearth in the second cell may also be regarded as a late addition and it seems likely that the original house was a simple long-house of the south Morbihan type, later converted, by the addition of a hearth, to a two-cell house, and at that stage a byre was built at the upper end. The thickening of the wall here and its subsequent thinning into the byre provides a clue to this extension and it seems likely that the communicating doorway was driven through the upper gable wall at this stage. There would seem to be, therefore, as many as four stages of growth. In its present form this is one of the rare examples of a two-cell long-house with a byre at the upper end adjacent to the hall, but this is to be regarded as the result of freak growth rather than as representative of a widespread plan-type.

Vieux Coët Sal, Pluneret (WT 079824), is an excellent example of a 'gentry' long-house (Fig. 189). Substantially bigger in its original form than most long-houses, the total length of this irregular building is approximately 20.05 metres and the width of the older part 7.70 metres externally. The original house measures approximately 13.50 metres in length and 6.30 metres in width internally. The added chamber is *c*. 4.60 metres long and 6.50 metres wide. The eaves line is *c*. 4.40 metres above the ground and the ridge rises 7.90 metres above the ground. Walling is of granite rubble with door and window dressings of cut stone bonded with a mortar of *pisé*. Roof covering is of slate. Larger rubble blocks are used for the quoins and at intervals within the walling, but door and window dressings are of finely cut granite. The floor is of *terre battue* except for the later chamber where concrete is used. The loft floor is of wood planks nailed to the common beams. Roof trusses are of the upper king-post and collar type braced downwards into the walls with sling-braces which are also tied to the wall-heads with spurs. This type of roof truss seems to be late in date and almost certainly represents a rebuilding. It is certain that this building was thatched until at least the later nineteenth century, the wall-heads being lower and the thatch roof oversailing the loft opening in a half-dormer. Chimney-stacks are also of granite rubble, that at the lower end being false. Hearth H1 at the upper end of the house is an extremely fine structure with a granite breastsummer resting on dressed corbels partly supported on granite posts. The chimney-hood is of granite rubble and there is a large hearth-stone, also of granite. Hearth and chimney-piece in the later chamber are of a debased form. This chamber could well be of the twentieth century and is accessible only from the upper end of the house. The original building is clearly a long-house of considerable size and fine quality. It consists of hall and byre and there is no evidence to suggest that there was ever any partition to separate man and beast. The present partition is of concrete blocks and very recent in date. Doorway D1 is a fine structure in the Flamboyant style with magnificent chamfers, foliated decoration and an animate form, probably a monkey, incorporated. The original window, W1, is now blocked and there is no evidence of the form of the lintel. Cavetto chamfers on the jambs remain, however. Three modern windows are now provided in the rear wall of this building. The original slit to provide ventilation for the byre rests *in situ* and there is a small keeping-place at the byre end close to the door. This long-house was still lived in as such at the date of the survey in August 1972, and access to the hall was by doorway D1, also used at that stage by a herd of about a dozen cattle.

La Ville des Nachez 1-6, Taupont, Morbihan (WU 407149), is a row of six dwellings (Fig. 177). Walling is almost entirely of Brioverian schists and sandstones, the latter, chiefly the Grès de Gourin, used for doorway and window dressings. The schist walling is very dark and sombre in hue but the sandstones are of a much lighter colour. Roofing in this district is almost entirely of small slates. Whilst some of the ridges are finished with red tiles, the traditional method is to project the slates either continuously from one side, or alternating, so as to leave a tooth-like effect. The six houses form a continuous row, or *rangée, c.* 53.00 metres in length. The external width is *c.* 7.95 metres. Internal dimensions are as follows:

Number 1: length   6.25 metres, breadth 6.35 metres
Number 2: length 13.20 metres, breadth 6.40 metres
Number 3: length   5.30 metres, breadth 6.45 metres
Number 4: length 12.50 metres, breadth 6.50 metres
Number 5: length   5.25 metres, breadth 6.50 metres
Number 6: length   5.40 metres, breadth 6.50 metres

There are two outshots at the rear, only one of which was measured. Both seem to be later additions.

Walling is laid in a mortar of *pisé*. The six houses all rise to a full two storeys, a feature characteristic of this part of north Morbihan. This results in loft space a full storey in height with additional roof space above. Wall thickness varies from *c.* 0.60 metres to *c.* 0.90 metres. Flooring is entirely formed of *terre battue*. Not all the roof structures were examined but those of numbers 1 and 2 are of the upper king-post, collar and tie-beam type. There is a ridge-purlin and two pairs of lateral purlins associated with these roof trusses. Holes, formerly fitted with long pegs, survive in the principal rafters and were provided for use as a ladder by the carpenter during the construction of the roof. The sawn common rafters are staggered at the apex and to these are nailed wooden

boards to which, in turn, the slates are nailed. Construction of the hearths and chimney-pieces is the same in each house although the quality varies. Breastsummer and corbels are all of wood and these support a chimney-hood of schist rubble. Hearth-stones are usually provided and there are frequently keeping-places in the hearth backs. The row is not all of one date and the oldest house appears to be No. 2. This is a long-house of the classic type and a building of some quality. The façade is apparently symmetrical, the window opening to the byre being comparable in size to the hall window. This, however, is deceptive and there is no doubt that the left-hand end provided with a hearth was formerly the hall and that the lower end served as a byre. Today, a wooden partition is nailed to the beam next to the doorway on the upper side but this is undoubtedly a later addition. It is significant that the better or hall end of the house has joists as well as beams, a relatively rare feature in Brittany except in buildings of the highest quality. The lower or byre end is provided simply with common beams. There is an additional doorway to the hall in the rear wall but this may be a later insertion. A window in the rear wall of the byre has been blocked. The hearth-back is amply provided with keeping-places and the breastsummer bears curious short flutings along its bottom edge, a feature also present on the breastsummer in house 1. A communicating doorway with house 3 is now blocked. There seems little doubt that the date 1679 on one of the window lintels is that of first building. It is probable that the second house to be built was number 1, a single-cell structure with only one doorway and a window. There is no date on this house but it is unlikely to be much later than the date of number 2. The wood lintels of number 3, also a single-cell house, suggest a building of poorer quality but give little indication of date. As the row now grew continuously towards the right, it seems likely that an eighteenth-century date would be probable. Number 3 has a pair of opposing doorways and a single window. Number 4 is of the type here defined as long-house, first derivative, that is, a separate doorway has been provided for the byre end. There is still a pair of opposing doorways and an embryo cross-passage, and although a wooden partition now exists nailed to one of the beams, this is obviously a later addition and the house, like number 2, would originally have been open from end to end. Oral evidence puts a mid to late nineteenth-century date on this house and confirms that the hearth and chimney at the byre end were original features put there in case at some future date the occupant wished to convert his hall and byre into a two-cell house. Houses 5 and 6 were not investigated internally and there is some doubt as to whether there are

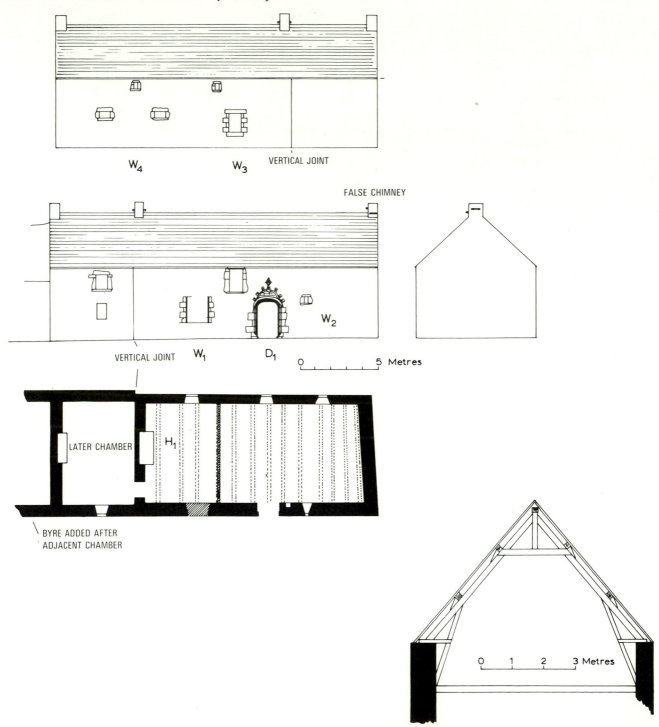

VERTICAL JOINT

W₄   W₃

FALSE CHIMNEY

VERTICAL JOINT   W₁   D₁   0   5 Metres

W₂

LATER CHAMBER   H₁

BYRE ADDED AFTER
ADJACENT CHAMBER

0   1   2   3 Metres

Fig. 189a.   Vieux Coët Sal, Mériadec-en-Pluneret, Morbihan

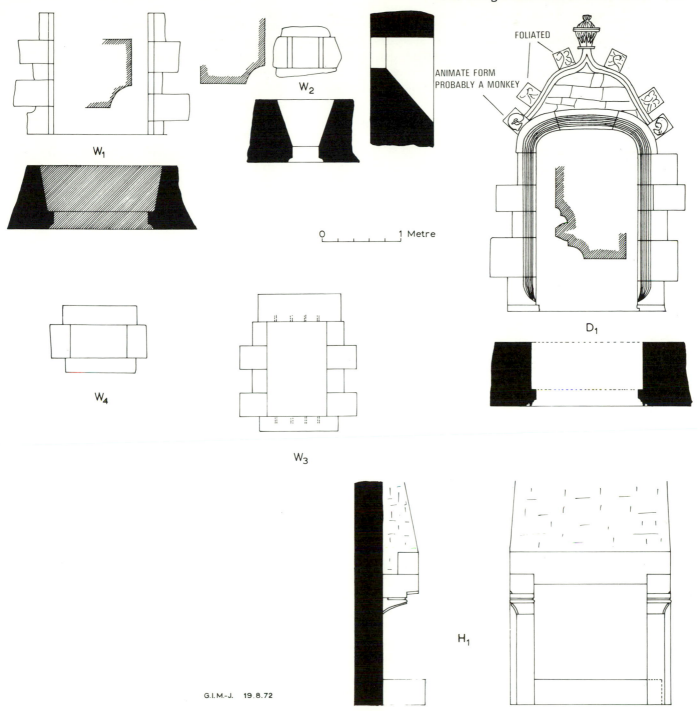

FOLIATED

ANIMATE FORM
PROBABLY A MONKEY

W₁

W₂

0   1 Metre

W₄

D₁

W₃

G.I.M.-J.   19.8.72

H₁

Fig. 189b.   Vieux Coët Sal, Mériadec-en-Pluneret, Morbihan

doorways providing direct access to the outshot. This seems probable. This pair of houses is interesting because it is of late nineteenth- or early twentieth-century date, and although the façade suggests a building of some pretension, it is in fact a pair of single-cell dwellings with loft space above.

This row is an excellent example of the growth of *rangée* over the period of some two hundred and fifty years. Unlike some of the examples in south Morbihan, there is here internal communication between only one house and the next. La Ville des Nachez illustrates extremely well what has been observed throughout Brittany, namely that no *rangée* is ever composed wholly of houses of one date. The *rangée* always represents evolution over a period of time, often three or four centuries.

Kermorfezan 6 and 7 have been described earlier and are good examples of the small houses often found in association with a *petit manoir*. Number 7 is probably a former long-house of one storey (Fig. 175). Tréberouan 1, Trégunc, Finistère (VT 379955) is another excellent example of a short long-house (Fig. 49). Walling is entirely of granite, rubble and dressed stone being used for the gable wall and the rear wall and granite orthostats for the front wall and the lower gable. Thatch is of rye-straw and the ridge was formerly finished with turf. Externally the building measures 8.60 metres by 5.70 metres and is almost perfectly rectangular. Internally the measurements are 7.70 metres by 4.80 metres. The height of the walls to the eaves is 2.20 metres and the height of the ridge above the ground is 6.00 metres. Two walls, the upper gable and the rear wall, are of dressed granite and granite rubble, the dressings being used for the quoins and the coping of the gable as well as the chimney-stack which is finely cut and finished with a plain cap. Orthostats set into the ground *c.* 0.50 metres form the façade, except for the wide doorway, and total fifteen. There are a further fourteen orthostats in the lower gable. At the time of recording, the building was in a ruinous condition and the roof had collapsed. The drawing is therefore a reconstruction based on the surviving evidence which was substantially complete. It was clear that the building formerly had one hip at the lower end. Lighting is provided by a small window in the wall opposite the door, and in the same wall at the bottom end there is a keeping-place. There were five tie-beams and one of these, that immediately to the left of the doorway, supported a collar and tie-beam truss. There was a ridge beam and two lateral purlins supported on cleats. The chimney-piece is built of massive slabs of granite typical of the region. A pair of granite corbels passing through the walls support a granite breastsummer

and these support the chimney-hood of granite rubble. The hearth-stone projects *c.* 1.00 metre; there are no keeping-places but a cinder hole is provided in the back of the hearth immediately above the granite hearth-stone. Although the house appears to be a single-cell building, there is sufficient space at the lower end to accommodate at least one cow, and it is extremely probable that there was a wooden partition nailed against the tie-beam immediately to the left of the door. The building may thus be regarded as a short long-house, typical of the region.

Saint Philibert 1, Trégunc, Finistère (VT 378954), is a classic long-house of the first derivative type, formerly having a byre with its own doorway separate from that of the hall. The outshot would have provided additional storage space and was formerly of the lean-to type. The building is dated 1867 on the chimney-stack and this is almost certainly the date of first building (Fig. 50). Walling is entirely of calco-alkaline biotite-granite. The gable walls and the outshot are of roughly squared blocks of granite whilst the lateral walls are of orthostats. The orthostats measure *c.* 0.40 metres wide and 0.30 metres deep. Their total length is often in excess of 2.00 metres but they are embedded in the ground to a depth of 0.40 to 0.60 metres. The outshot is entirely of stone rubble. The chimney-stack is of dressed stone. The roof, newly thatched, is of reed. Externally the house measures 11.40 metres by 5.55 metres, internally 9.95 metres by 5.05 metres. It is almost perfectly rectangular. The outshot increases the length of the building to a total of 14.90 metres. The gable walls of the house are 0.70 metres thick and the lateral walls rather less than 0.30 metres. The walls of the outshot are *c.* 0.65 metres thick. The gable walls of the house are built partly of dressed stone and partly of rubble and they rise above the line of the roof, being offset to receive the thatch. Orthostats are used for both the lateral walls and are extremely accurately cut so that little filling is necessary in the joints. They rise to 2.15 metres above the ground and support a wall-plate on which rest the eleven tie-beams of light scantling. Roof structure is entirely modern and dates from a recent reconstruction. The two *lucarnes* probably also date from this reconstruction, as does the outshot in its present form. Thatch is of reed and the ridge is completed with clay and turf. The chimney-stack is terminated by a finely moulded cap. The hearth is set into the gable wall *c.* 0.30 metres and the hood is supported on fine, but plain, granite corbels, and the breastsummer is also of a single slab of granite. The floor was formerly entirely of *terre battue* and the house is divided into two parts by a wooden screen let into a stone sill. The window to the left-hand side of this screen occupies the site of a

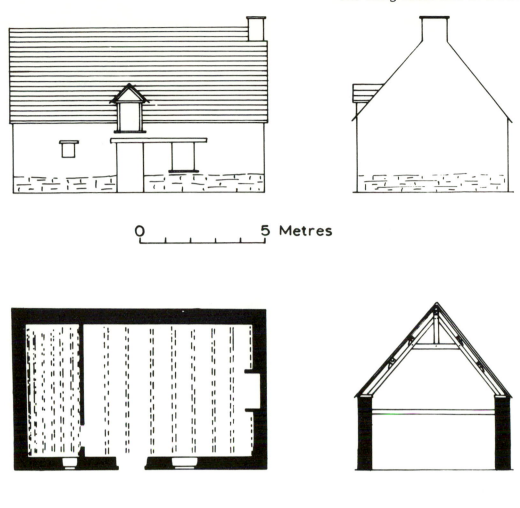

Fig. 190.   Le Courtil, Paimpont, Ille-et-Vilaine

former doorway. Twenty-six orthostats form the rear wall.

Le Courtil, Paimpont, Ille-et-Vilaine (WU 675208), was a pure long-house and the living area was probably always separated from the byre by a wooden partition placed originally against the beam immediately to the right of the doorway. This partition has twice been removed and at present separates the living area from the store-room at the lower end of the house. The building is typical of the small, pure long-house type and is of no great age. It probably dates either from just before World War I or from the early 1920s (Fig. 190). Walling is of *torchis* except for the footings which are of stone rubble and rise to a height of rather less than 1.00 metre. Doorway and window lintels and the framing of the loft opening are of wood, and roofing is of slate with a red-tile ridge. The chimney-stack is of stone rubble rising from

the *torchis* wall. The structure is not a perfect rectangle and measures externally *c.* 10.10 metres by 6.40 metres and internally 9.00 metres by 5.50 metres. Height from the ground to the eaves is 3.00 metres and to the ridge 6.70 metres. Walls are a simple rectilinear shell of *torchis* rising from stone footings. The ceiling is of wooden planks nailed to the ceiling beams. There are seven beams *c.* 0.10 by 0.20 metres over the living area and, in addition, a pair of half beams on either side of the chimney-hood. At the lower end of the house are seven closely spaced and rather flimsy beams. The chimney-piece is formed in the traditional manner, a wooden frame supported on wooden corbels and supporting a chimney-hood of stone rubble plastered over. The floor was formerly of *terre battue* but is now concreted. Door and window details are extremely simple and there is no ornamentation. The loft-opening is a half-dormer with a

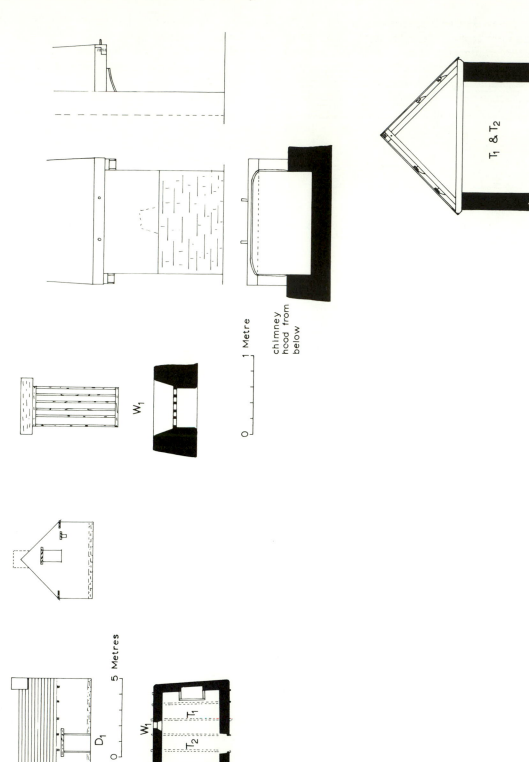

chimney hood from below

W₁

T₁ & T₂

D₁

D₂

W₁

T₁

T₂

1 Metre

5 Metres

G.I.M-J. **25.7.73.**

Fig. 191.   Les Landes de l'Etriac 2, Lamballe, Côtes-du-Nord

ridge roof and slated cheeks. The roof truss rests on sole-plates and is of the upper king-post and collar type. Two pairs of lateral purlins are carried on cleats.

Les Landes de l'Etriac 2, Lamballe, Côtes-du-Nord (WU 356716), was a simple open cell at the time of recording but the presence of a second lower door and formerly of a slit in the lower gable strongly suggests that livestock were accommodated at the lower end. Whether or not there was a partition dividing the hall from this very small byre at the lower end is impossible to say. There is no evidence of such partition and it is highly probable that the building was never structurally subdivided. Nevertheless, it is of long-house form, being a first-derivative type with a second entry at the lower end (Fig. 191). Walling is of *torchis*. Shallow foundations and footings are of roughly coursed rubble rising to *c.* 0.25 metres above ground level. Seven 'lifts' of *torchis* are identifiable in the gable, each of *c.* 0.65 metres. There is a slate roof and red-tile ridge. Doorway, window frames and doors are of wood. The house is 7.50 metres long at the greatest extent and 4.75 metres wide, externally. Internally, it measures 6.20 metres by 3.60 metres. The height to the eaves is 2.20 metres and to the ridge 4.60 metres. At the time of recording it consisted of a single open cell with two doorways, D1 and D2, lighted by a solitary window, W1. A blocked slit lies high up in the lower gable. There is no hearth-stone, but the hearth-back is faced with coursed stone rubble to a height of 0.80 metres. The chimney-hood of *torchis* is supported on a wood frame, in turn resting on a pair of crudely chamfered wood corbels. Both the side pieces of the frame and the corbels pass through the earth wall and are visible on the outside of the building. There are two peg-holes in the breastsummer, and the pegs, intended for hanging utensils, remain *in situ*. At the back of the hearth there appears once to have been an opening which can only have been an access to an oven built against the upper gable of the house. There are now no traces of this oven and it was presumably also built of earth. The window was unglazed and there are four light wood mullions. The floor is entirely of *terre battue*. The six ceiling beams are *c.* 0.20 by 0.10 metres and carry the loft floor of plain wooden boards nailed to them. Those beams which serve as tie-beams for the roof trusses are slightly longer than the others and bear simple decoration on their ends. There are rough wall-plates in pairs, resting on the inner and outer side of the wall heads respectively. A tethering block, with a circular hole 0.08 metres in diameter drilled in it, projects from the lower gable. There are two tie-beam trusses, carrying the ridge-purlin, and two pairs of side-purlins resting on cleats. These purlins in turn carry the roughly sawn common rafters on to which

is nailed a covering of close-set wooden boards which carry the slates. The principal rafters, 0.15 by 0.07 metres, are halved and pegged at the apex. The common beams all project through the lateral walls and are visible from the outside. Access to the loft is by an entrance door set in the lower gable.

Botcol, Guénin, Morbihan (WU 053053), is a very good example of the simple long-house (Fig. 171). The hall is separated from the byre by a crude wooden partition nailed against the beam immediately to the right of the doorway. Until the 1950s this house was in use as a long-house and two cows were kept in the lower end. The byre is lighted and ventilated by two small windows, neither of which originally had any form of glazing. The hall measures approximately 5.30 metres by 5.10 metres and is lighted by a single window, large by Morbihan standards. Brackets on the beam immediately to the left of the doorway formerly supported a wooden shelf. There are no keeping-places or any other fittings. Walling is of stone rubble set in a heavy clay matrix, *pisé*, with wooden posts set within the body of the wall. The roofing is of reed thatch or *roseau* and the ridge was formerly finished with turf. The building is only roughly rectilinear and the lower gable wall is considerably bowed out. Externally the building measures *c.* 8.90 metres by 6.30 metres and internally 7.55 metres by 5.10 metres. The hearth is asymmetrically placed. The height from the ground to the eaves is 1.80 metres and to the ridge *c.* 4.70 metres. This house is a very good example of relatively late primitive construction, typical of this poor part of north Morbihan. Walls are characterized by a large amount of *pisé* used as a mortar for the rubble walling. The building is particularly important because two timber posts have been set within the body of the stone walls in the front elevation to provide added strength. This is probably a vestige of former timber-frame construction in the countryside and in this case also indicates a lack of confidence on the part of the builders in the strength of their rubble walling. An additional timber post is placed on the front inside wall as a support for one of the beams. The floor is of *terre battue*. There are five beams *c.* 0.20 by 0.10 metres laid flat side down. Three of these support trusses of the collar and tie-beam type. There is a ridge-beam and the lateral purlins are supported on cleats. The carpentry is pegged but is of very slender scantling. The common rafters are of rough chestnut poles laid close together and bound with straw rope in the manner common in south Morbihan. On to these the thatch is tied directly, and originally the ridge would have been finished in clay and turf. At the time the house was recorded, the thatch was in a poor state of repair and a corrugated iron roof had been placed on top of it. The

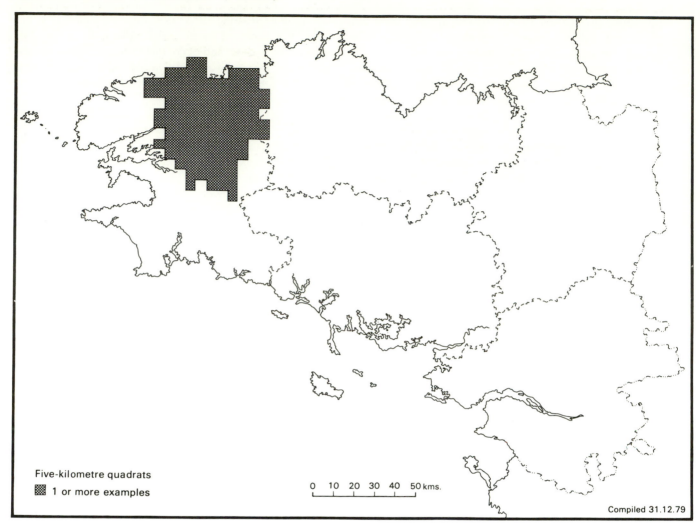

Fig. 192.   The table-outshot, or *apoteiz*, in north-west Brittany: 5 km quadrats

Five-kilometre quadrats

1 or more examples

0 10 20 30 40 50 kms.

Compiled 31.12.79

hearth rests against the gable wall which is not off-set to receive it. The hood is supported on two posts and rises through the roof in the form of a clay and wattle chimney-stack. This stack is of extreme importance as one of the few surviving examples in Brittany. The four circular posts have horizontal ladder-like pieces dowelled into them and between these are woven sticks of hazel, on to which a daub of *pisé* has been laid. The roof is fully hipped at both ends.

A feature widespread in north Finistère is the table-outshot, (Br.) *kuz-taol,* or *apoteiz*. It is generally accepted to be a Léon feature, its distribution extends southwards into northern Cornouaille and eastwards into the borders of Cornouaille and Trégorrois (Figs. 192 and 193), and it is unknown in Brittany outside this region. The type is particularly common in the rich agricultural area around Saint-Pol-de-Léon, with many of the earliest and finest

examples surviving in the *communes* of Pleyber-Christ, Saint-Thégonnec, Guimiliau, Loc-Eguiner and Commana; parishes heavily involved in the linen trade during the sixteenth and seventeenth centuries. All periods from the seventeenth century to the twentieth are represented by dated buildings and a number of architectural variations which include single- and two-storey types, with both gables and oversailing roofs. Dimensions vary considerably. From this apparent core area it spreads southwards over the Monts d'Arrée, where it is well represented, to the valley of the Aulne, with only a few outlying examples so far recorded south of this river. The western boundary of the distribution, except for a few substantial isolated examples, is remarkably clean and nowhere extends further than Lesneven. The eastern boundary is more ragged and characterized, unlike the west, by a scatter of poor single-

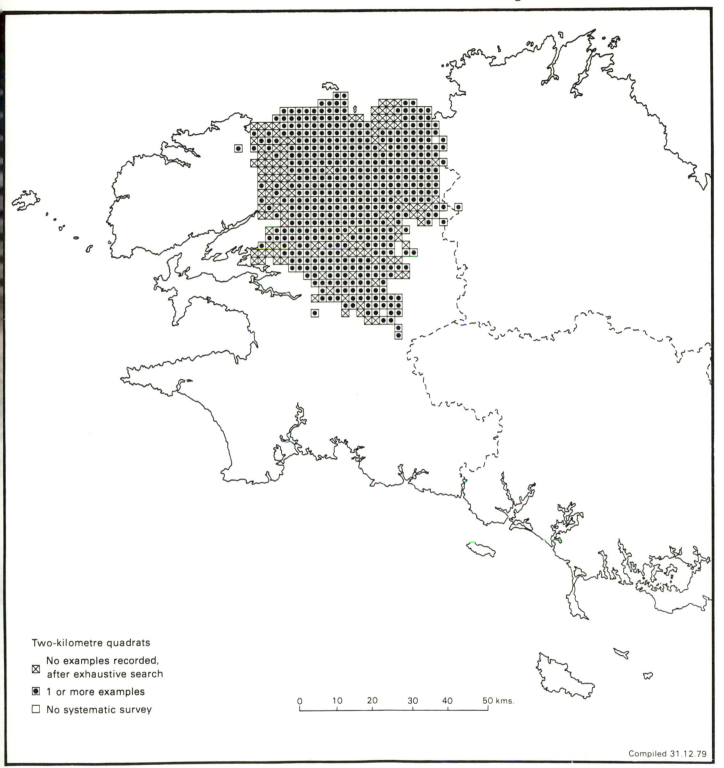

Two-kilometre quadrats

⊠ No examples recorded,
    after exhaustive search

◉ 1 or more examples

□ No systematic survey

0   10   20   30   40   50 kms.

Compiled 31.12.79

Fig. 193.   The table-outshot, or *apoteiz,* in north-west Brittany: 2 km quadrats

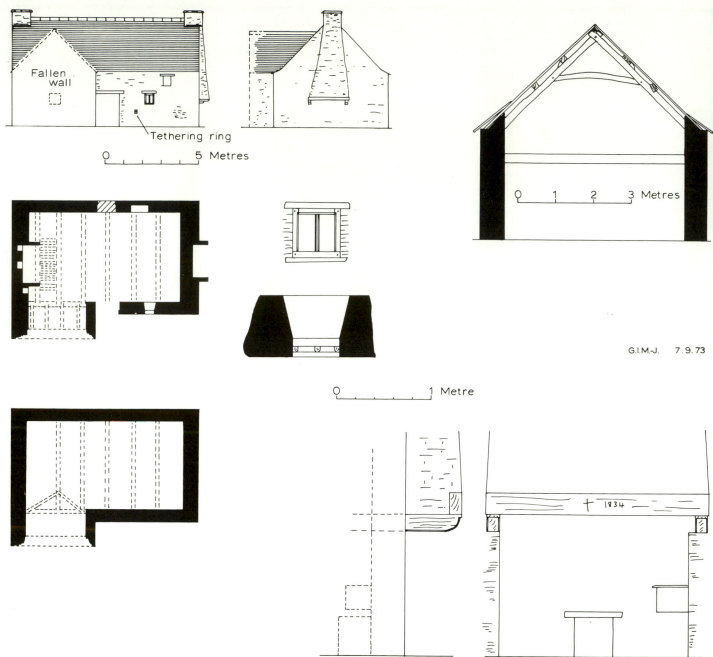

Fig. 194.   Glugeau Bras 3, Lopérec, Finistère

storey examples, notably in the south-east. It is difficult to escape the conclusion that the table-outshot has its origins to the south of the fertile plain of Léon, in the foothills of the Monts d'Arrée, probably during the later sixteenth century, and that it spread outwards from there. Fieldwork is still in progress here and it is almost certain that the distribution will grow, particularly in the east and south. The area north of the Monts d'Arrée was, in early-modern times, a great flax-growing area and the spinning and weaving of linen was an important industry. The spinning particularly was undertaken in countless farmhouses around the hearth. It seems probable that the table-outshot was an architectural response to the need for further work space around the hearth and that the cash income derived from the growth of flax and spinning provided the means to build. Once established, the table-outshot proved so useful an innovation inside the house, and so ornamented the outside, that it continued to be built long after the linen industry had passed its zenith. Twentieth-century vernacular examples are not uncommon, and since World War II it has found a new expression in the modern houses now being built in large numbers. As an extension of the hall it normally accommodates the table and benches and often a box-bed, the *banc* of which serves as seating for the table (see Chapter 15). Two long-houses illustrate this feature, the *kuz-taol* being contained in a structural cross-wing in both cases.

Glugeau Bras 3, Lopérec, Finistère (VU 242543), one of several examples in that hamlet, measures 10.10 metres long externally, 6.00 metres wide at its narrowest and 7.35 metres wide at its widest. Internally the building measures 8.10 metres long, 4.75 metres wide at the lower end and 6.20 metres wide at the upper end. The eaves are 3.00 metres and the ridge 5.90 metres above the ground (Fig. 194). Walling is of Brioverian schist. Roof covering is of slate, with a red-tiled ridge. Flooring is of *terre battue* and the loft floor is formed of wooden boards nailed to the common beams. Roof trusses are of the collar-truss type and it is probable that the feet of the principal rafters are simply embedded in the wall-heads. The tie-beam lies at a slightly lower level, and although it is possible that the rafters curve in the manner of upper-crucks, this seems unlikely in this case. A ridge-purlin is carried by the intersecting rafters, and two pairs of lateral purlins are borne either on cleats or in slots in the rafters. Common rafters, resting with their feet on the wall-heads and staggered at the apex, are sprocketed out and support wooden boarding on to which the slates are nailed. There are two chimneys, but one belonged to a house built against the lower end and now demolished. The chimney at the upper end is built of schist rubble and the chimney-hood is supported on a wooden breastsummer, in turn resting on wooden corbels. These are decorated with flat-splay chamfers, and the breastsummer, marked with a cross, bears the date 1834. There are two keeping-places in the hearth-back. Doorways and windows are framed with schist rubble and lintels are all of wood. The windows were never glazed and the house must represent one of a number of surviving examples of unglazed houses lived in within recent memory. Window openings have wooden frames with wooden mullions closed at night by inward-opening wooden shutters. The doorway at the rear of the house is now blocked and there is a large keeping-place at the lower end and a small one at the upper end adjacent to the hearth. The house is a good example of the type found in northern Finistère with a table-outshot, *cache-table*, *kuz-taol* or *apoteiz*. This is formed within a structural outshot which rises to the full height of the main

walls but whose roof is slightly lower than that of the longitudinal part of the building. The common beams are carried on a transverse beam at the opening of the outshot and the loft is then formed by four smaller beams embedded in the gable wall. The latter has now completely fallen away and the building is ruinous. The main part of the house is a medium-sized long-house of classic form and there is no evidence that there was any internal division between the hall and the byre. The hall is fitted with horizontal rails between the two beams nearest the hearth and it must be supposed that these were intended for the storage of foodstuffs and possibly the suspension of meat. The other feature of interest, quite common in Brittany, is the tethering ring formed by piercing a piece of schist with a circular hole and building it into the body of the wall. There was no evidence of these tethering rings on the inside of the house.

The much larger house of the same type at Saint-Rivoal, Finistère (VU 261557), is dated 1702 (Fig. 195) and well illustrates the contrast between the detail and planning of a 'gentry' house in the Monts d'Arrée and the complete absence of privacy. Although the house has been lived in as a long-house within living memory, there has never been any separation between man and beast, nor have the windows ever been glazed. Total external length is 19.00 metres including the two outshots. The house measures 11.30 metres long and 8.00 metres wide externally. Internal length is 9.50 metres and the width 6.50 metres at the upper end of the hall and 4.60 metres at the byre end. Walling is formed of blocks of schist of varying size laid in a mortar of *pisé*. Larger blocks of stone are used for the doorway dressings at the front of the house but all the other door and window dressings are of wood. Flooring is of *terre battue* with the addition of patches of stone paving in the byre end and of a continuous row of stones covering the water course which enters the house at the upper end of the hall. The floor of the loft is formed of wooden boards nailed to the common beams. The difficulty of obtaining suitable timber is well illustrated by the fact that forked timbers have had to be used in three cases for common beams in order to gain sufficient length. Roof trusses are of the collar and tie-beam type, the principal rafters intersecting to support a ridge-purlin. Two pairs of lateral purlins are fastened to the principal rafters with pegs. Roughly cut common rafters are laid across the purlins and are staggered at the apex. Wooden boards are laid across these and the slates nailed to them. The ridge is finished in the traditional manner by projecting one of the slate courses above the other and across the top of the ridge. Some of these slates are cut into patterns or animal forms as a decorative feature.

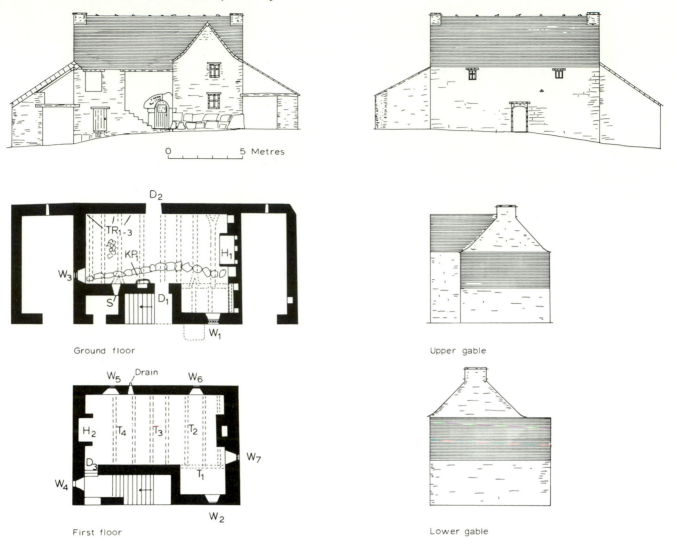

0 ___ 5 Metres

D₂

TR₁₋₃

KP₁

H₁

W₃

S

D₁

W₁

Ground floor

W₅   Drain   W₆

H₂   T₄   T₃   T₂

D₃

T₁

W₄

W₂

W₇

First floor

Upper gable

Lower gable

G.I.M-J.   29.7.73.

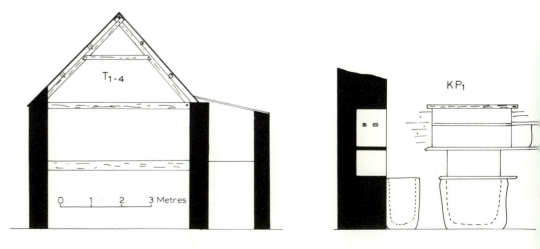

T₁₋₄

0   1   2   3 Metres

KP₁

Fig. 195a.   Saint-Rivoal, Finistère

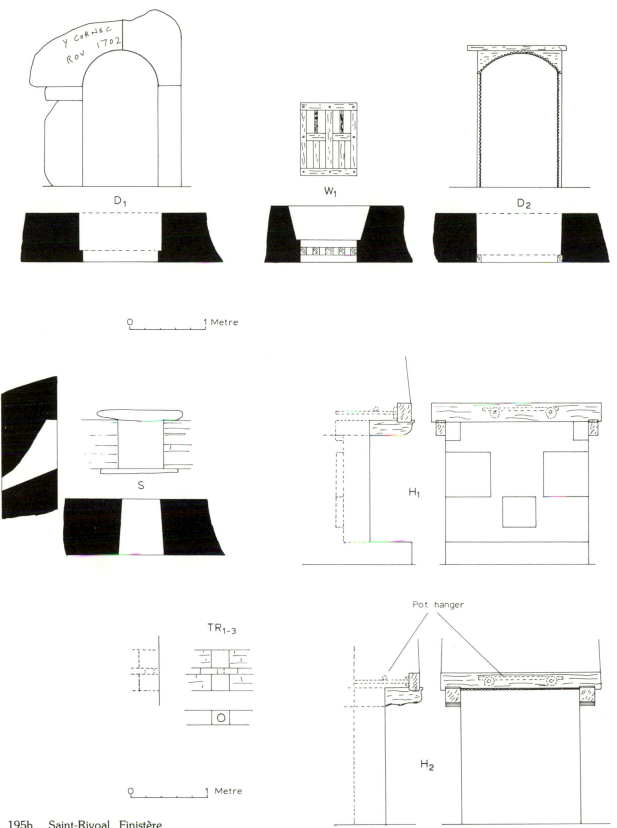

Fig. 195b.   Saint-Rivoal, Finistère

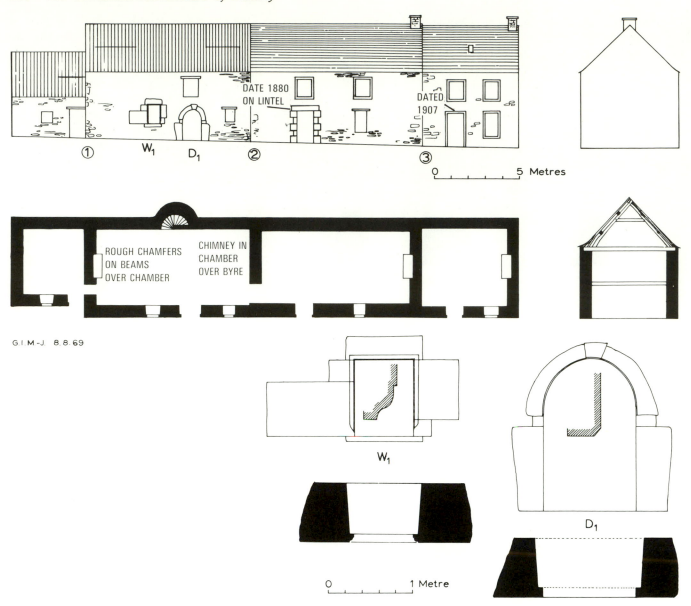

DATE 1880
ON LINTEL

DATED
1907

①   W₁   D₁   ②   ③

0   5 Metres

ROUGH CHAMFERS
ON BEAMS
OVER CHAMBER

CHIMNEY IN
CHAMBER
OVER BYRE

G.I.M-J. 8.8.69

W₁

D₁

0   1 Metre

Fig. 196.   Kerhaliou 1, 2, 3, Spézet, Finistère

This house, dated 1702 on the door lintel, is a building of considerable social standing for its period. In plan it is an open long-house and continued to be lived in as such for much of its history. During the nineteenth century a partition was inserted between the hall and the byre. There are two doorways, D1 and D2 not quite exactly opposite. Doorway D1 was always used by man for access to the hall, and the cattle were always led into the house from the back entrance, doorway D2. The table-outshot is wide enough to contain also a box bed. In this case the outshot is continued at first-floor level as well, providing an additional space at the lower end of the

upper room. The house is extraordinarily well planned for a building of the period. There is an abundant supply of keeping-places, and a spring which rises above the house is brought in under the upper gable wall and flows the length of the house underneath a series of paving stones. Water can thus be drawn at a point close to the hearth and drainage was provided by the lower part of this water course. In the gable end of the table-outshot, a stone bench is built into the wall to provide seating for the table which was placed longways on to the window opening. The byre end is fitted with three tethering rings formed of pieces of schist with holes in them, built into the rear wall of the byre. A window, W3, provides ventilation for the byre and a chute enables the pigs in the pigsty built underneath the external stone stair to be fed directly from the byre. A large keeping-place between the doorway, D1, and the chute is the *laiterie*, or dairy, the place where milk products were stored. Immediately in front of this is the *charnier* or *saloir* in which was kept the salted meat supply. An external stone stair leads by doorway D3 to an upper room, also heated and provided with window openings and a drain. The presence of the drain strongly suggests that this was a dwelling quite separate from that in the long-house below. In effect, this seems to have been a first-floor hall perhaps providing accommodation for the landowner and his family. The long-house below would then have been inhabited either by a relative or by a tenant farmer. Alternative arrangements are possible with the upper room, for example, perhaps being reserved for occasional visits by an absentee landlord. That it was an independent dwelling seems extremely likely. Hearths and chimney-pieces are of good quality in an area devoid of building stone suitable for dressings. Chimney-hoods of schist are supported on breastsummers of wood, which in turn rest on wooden corbels. There is some attempt at decoration, particularly in the case of hearth H2 at first-floor level. This further emphasizes the social superiority of the upper room. In both cases the hearths have retained their wooden pot hangers resting on a pair of wooden rails let into the back of the breastsummer and set into the stone hearth-back. The window openings of this building were never glazed and all retain the wooden window frames with their wood mullions and transoms. The rear doorway D2 bears decoration similar to that on the breastsummer of hearth H2. This building is a magnificent example of the regional house with table-outshot. It was clearly the home of someone of considerable wealth and importance. Nevertheless the elementary long-house arrangement existed at ground-floor level but with an upper chamber or first-floor hall for the landowner or head of the family.

Kerhaliou (VU 462352), near Spézet, Finistère, on the northern slopes of the Montagnes Noires, consists of a row of three houses which, with the addition of an outbuilding, measure 29.90 metres in length externally and *c.* 5.85 metres in width (Fig. 196). The outbuilding is *c.* 3.55 metres long and 3.80 metres wide. Kerhaliou 1 is 9.05 metres long and 4.40 metres wide internally; Kerhaliou 2, 8.65 metres long and 4.25 metres wide internally and Kerhaliou 3, 5.00 metres long and 4.55 metres wide internally. The buildings lie on falling ground so that the eaves line, which is 4.00 metres from the ground at one end, is 4.50 metres from the ground at the other. The ridge line is 6.85 metres from the ground at the upper end of Kerhaliou 1 and 7.35 metres from the ground at the lower end of the row. Walling is of extremely finely laid schist bonded with a mortar of *pisé*. Door and window dressings are sometimes finely cut but in other cases windows have rubble jambs and wood lintels. Floors are of *terre battue* throughout and the loft flooring is of wooden planks nailed to the common beams. The buildings rise through two full storeys and the original roof trusses are of the collar and tie-beam type with a ridge-purlin and two pairs of lateral purlins. The original roofing seems to have been of slate nailed to boards fastened directly to the common rafters. Recently some roofing has been replaced by corrugated asbestos. The chimneys are also of finely coursed schist rubble, the same material being used for the chimney-hoods supported by wooden breastsummers resting on wooden corbels. Some of these corbels and breastsummers bear simple carving. Kerhaliou 1 has a stair turret at the rear. The three buildings form a row and Kerhaliou 1 and 2, along with the outbuilding at the end, have continuous internal communication. Kerhaliou 3 does not communicate internally with Kerhaliou 2. The latter is dated 1800 and Kerhaliou 3, 1907. There is no date for Kerhaliou 1 but the round-arch doorway suggests a seventeenth- or possibly an early eighteenth-century date. It is thus possible to trace the growth of this particular row. Kerhaliou 1 is unmistakably a long-house but clearly one intended for a person of some substance, for the loft above the byre end is provided with a hearth. There is no evidence of any internal partition between hall and byre at the lower end. In 1800 Kerhaliou 2 was built and internal communication provided. It too was probably originally a long-house but the hall is particularly long; the openings to the loft are more recent and these may have been rebuilt in 1907 when Kerhaliou 3, a single-cell house, was added at the lower end. Heated lofts are common and it is probable that parts of such lofts were used for sleeping by farm servants or junior members of the family who could not be accommodated in the hall. The interconnecting doorway is an early feature probably dating from the addition of the later of the two dwellings.

Two small long-houses in Côtes-du-Nord which are similar in dimensions to the smallest in Finistère and Morbihan are Gollot La Rivière 4 and 5, Carnoët (VU 617548) (Figs. 197 and 198). Gollot La Rivière 4 is 8.85 metres long and 6.95 metres wide externally, 7.45 metres long and 5.55 metres wide internally. Walls are *c.* 0.65 metres thick. The eaves line is 3.00 metres above the ground and the ridge 6.90 metres above ground level. The carboniferous schist walling is laid in a mortar

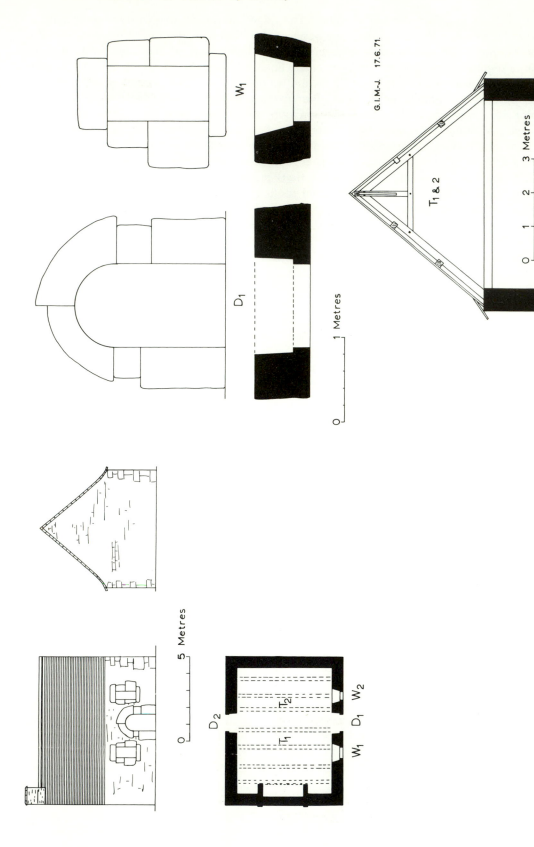

Fig. 197. Gollot La Rivière 4, Carnoët, Côtes-du-Nord

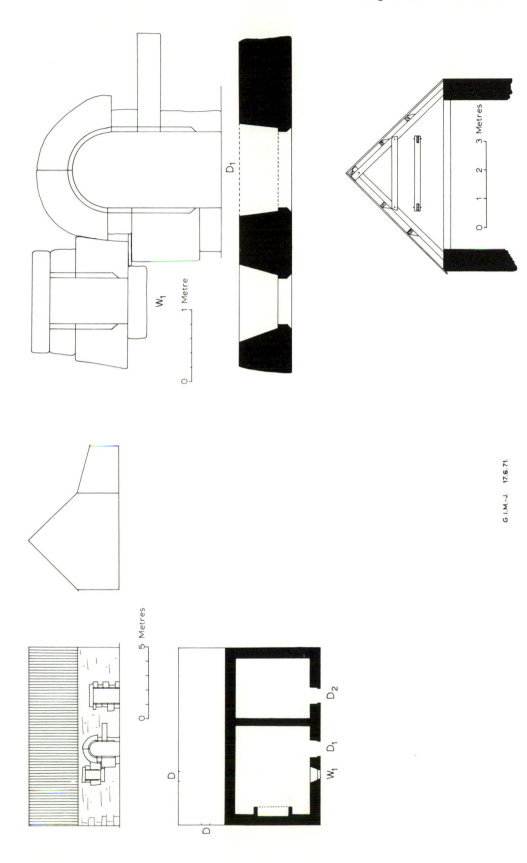

Fig. 198.   Gollot La Rivière 5, Carnoët, Côtes-du-Nord

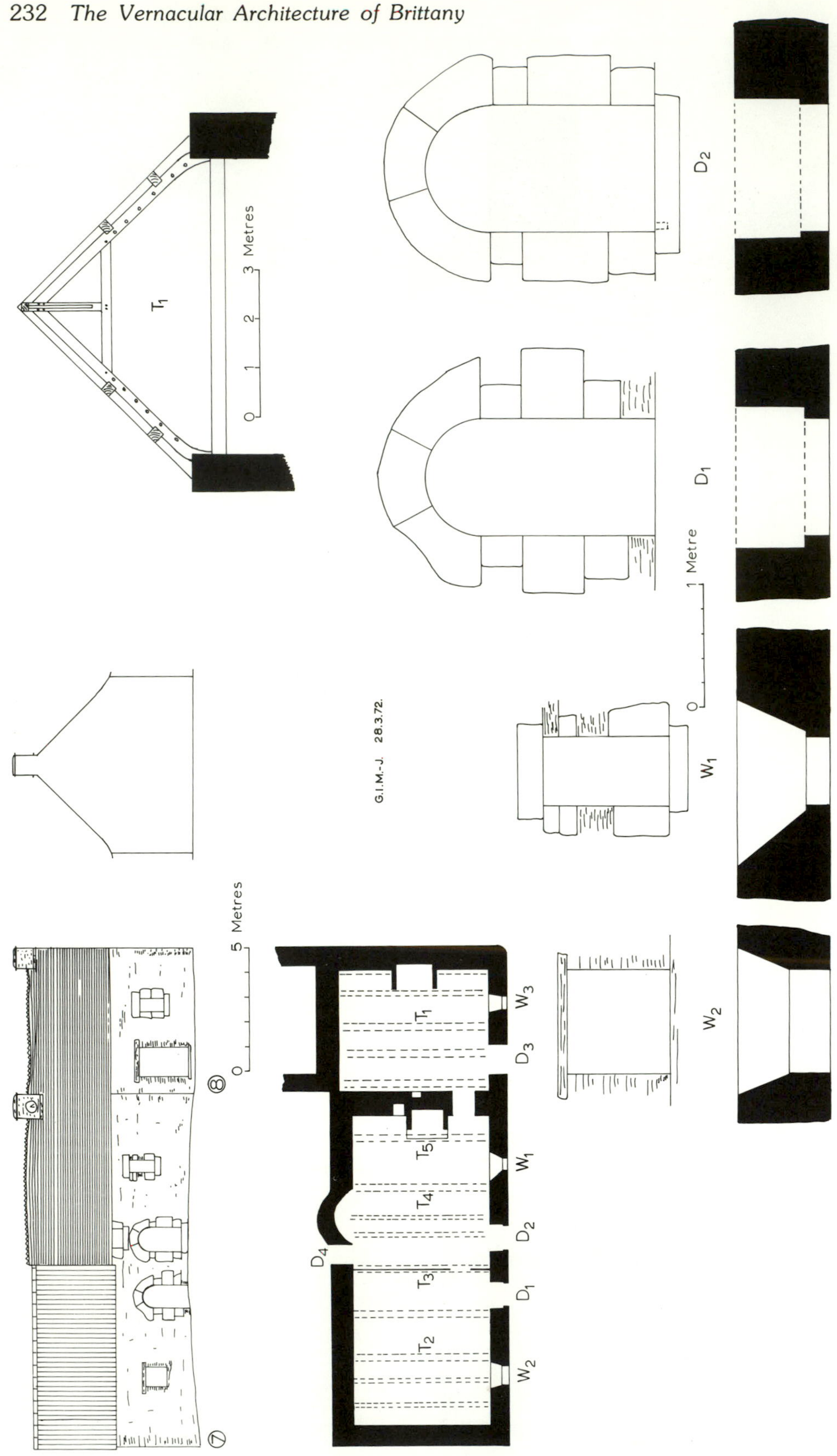

G.I.M.-J. 28.3.72.

Fig. 199. Les Portes, 7, 8, La Harmoye, Côtes-du-Nord

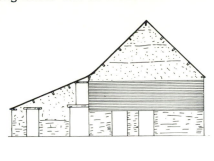

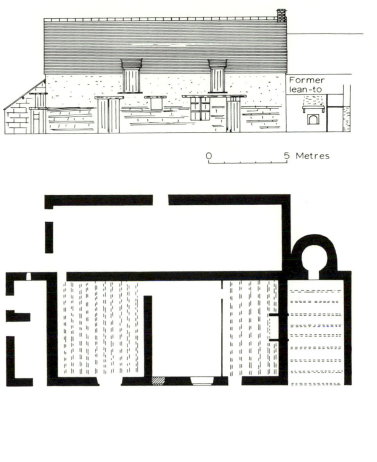

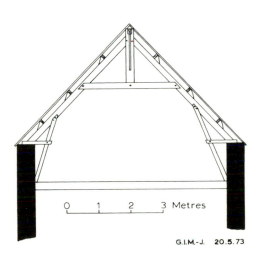

Fig. 200.   Beau Normandie 10, Paimpont, Ille-et-Vilaine

of *pisé*. There are two roof trusses, both of the upper king-post, collar and tie-beam type. The king-post supports a ridge-purlin and there are two pairs of lateral purlins slotted into the principal rafters. Common rafters rest on the wall-heads and are staggered at the apex. Boards are nailed to these and the slate roofing is in turn nailed to the boards. The building is of one storey only and the only storage space lies in the roof. There is a pair of opposing doorways, D1 and D2, at the ends of the embryo cross-passage. Two windows, of unequal size, light the interior. The building is undoubtedly a short long-house with a heated hall above the cross-passage and a byre at the lower end. The round-headed doorway suggests a seventeenth-century date. There are no keeping-places and fittings are extremely simple. This is a good example of a small long-house in a relatively poor part of the interior of Brittany.

Gollot 5 is a rare example of the long-house with separate entry to the byre and no internal communication between byre and hall. Externally the building measures 12.50 metres in length and 6.75 metres in width. Internally it is 5.20 metres wide, the hall is 6.25 metres long and the byre 4.15 metres long. The walls are *c.* 0.75 metres thick. The eaves are *c.* 2.90 metres and the ridge *c.* 6.30 metres, above the ground. Carboniferous schist rubble walling is laid in a mortar of *pisé* and the granite dressings of the window and the two doorways are of similar quality. The round-headed doorway suggests a seventeenth-century date. The floor is of *terre battue* and the loft is not boarded in its present form. It is quite possible that the building was always open to the roof. The roof trusses are of the collar and tie-beam type, the ridge-purlins being supported by the intersecting principal rafters on which also rest two pairs of lateral purlins supported on cleats. The collar, as is quite common in Breton buildings, is slotted to take the principal rafters. The house is extremely plain inside and there are no keeping-places. It appears to be all of one build and there

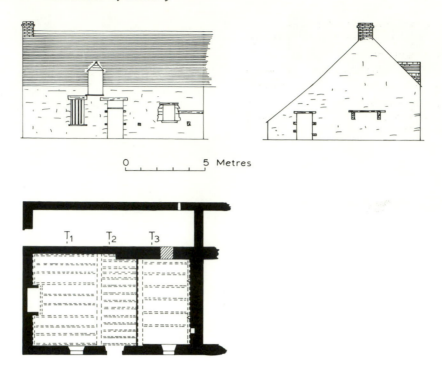

Fig. 201a.　L'Orrier 1, Saint-M'Hervé, Ille-et-Vilaine

is a continuous stone wall dividing the hall from the byre with no internal communication between the two. This may be a later insertion but in its present form the structure represents one of the few examples of the long-house, second derivative, i.e. a long-house in which the byre has become completely separated from the hall and access to the byre is solely by an external doorway.

Les Portes 7, La Harmoye (WU 012537), illustrates a somewhat larger house with separate entry to the byre (Fig. 199). The total length of the two houses is 20.50 metres; number 7 is *c.* 7.25 metres wide externally and number 8, 7.80 metres wide externally. House 7 is 12.70 metres long and 5.55 metres wide internally. House 8 is 4.90 metres long and 6.05 metres wide internally. Ground level varies somewhat and the eaves lie *c.* 3.20 metres from the ground and the ridge *c.* 7.00 metres above the ground. Wall thickness varies from 0.70 to 1.00 metres. Schist walling is laid in a mortar of *pisé* and in house 7 the two doorways and the principal window have granite dressings, the round door-heads suggesting a seventeenth-century date. The window to the byre, W2, has schist jambs and a wood lintel, as has doorway D3 to house 8. The window of house 8, W3, has granite dressings. The floors of both houses are of *terre battue* and the chimneys and chimney-hoods are of schist. The roof trusses are of the upper-cruck type, with an upper king-post which supports the ridge-purlin. Lateral purlins are slotted into the principal rafters which also contain

holes for the pegs which formerly served as ladders during the roof construction. The common rafters rest with their feet on the wall-heads and are staggered at the apex. Slates are nailed to boards laid across the common rafters and the ridge is finished by carrying the slates over the ridge and finishing them to give a serrated appearance. This type of ridge finish is widespread and probably dates from the introduction of slate during the late-eighteenth and early-nineteenth centuries. House 7 is a long-house, with hall and byre divided by a wooden screen slotted into a beam and also into a wooden sill. This partition may possibly be original and is, in any case, a rare example of a partition that is properly fitted and not simply nailed on to a convenient beam. The house is probably of seventeenth-century date, and as the partition has every appearance of being original, it constitutes important evidence for the existence of this type of long-house at that date. A separate doorway, D1, which appears to be original, provides access to the byre from outside. A further doorway, D4, provides access to the hall from the rear, so that the hall is served by a pair of nearly opposing doorways, D1 and D4, and the screen separating hall and byre is therefore on the lower side of this embryo cross-passage. The house is therefore a long-house, first derivative. A stair-turret exists at the back of the hall, although all trace of the staircase, presumably a wooden newel stair, has gone. House 8 is a single-cell dwelling clearly added at a later stage to the upper end of

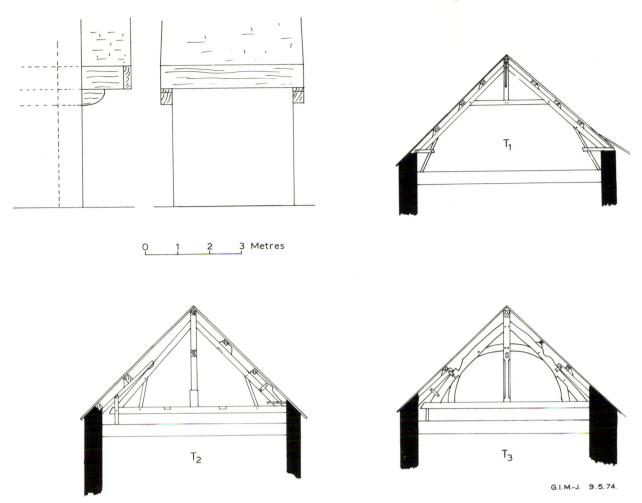

0   1   2   3 Metres

Fig. 201b. L'Orrier 1, Saint-M'Hervé, Ille-et-Vilaine

the hall. The communicating doorway was presumably driven through the upper gable of house 7 at the time of the addition. The most likely interpretation is that the two houses were occupied by related families. Two features of note are the circular corner on house 8 and the sundial placed on the chimney-stack of house 7.

The eastern *départements* also provide excellent long-house examples. Beau Normandie 10, Paimpont (WU 673212), is a good example of the standard type of accommodation in that area, built in the early-twentieth century (Fig. 200). The total length, including the outshots, is 21.90 metres externally, and the total width including the rear outshot, 12.05 metres. Straight joints suggest that the three outshots are later additions to the original building. The latter measures 15.20 metres long and 7.20 metres wide externally. Internally it is 6.05 metres wide and the hall is 8.00 metres long and the byre 5.45 metres long. The eaves rise 3.80 metres, and the ridge 7.45 metres, above the ground. Wall thickness

varies slightly but is *c.* 0.65 metres. Walling is of stone and *torchis*. The purple schist (from Montfort) and the *grès amoricain* are laid in bands to provide a striking polychrome effect. The upper part of the walling is of *torchis* and the roof is covered with slates. The ridge is of red tile and the chimney-stack of red brick. The first metre or so of wall is of alternating bands of polychrome stonework, laid in a mortar of *pisé*. Above this the wall is of *torchis* and the courses or lifts of *torchis* each some 1.00 metres high can best be seen in the lower gable. There is more *torchis* and less stone in the walls at the back of the house than in the front. Flooring is of *terre battue* and the roof is supported on trusses of the upper king-post and collar type, the principal rafters being sling-braced downwards to the tie-beam through the spars. King-posts carry the ridge-purlin, to which they are braced upwards. Three pairs of lateral purlins rest on cleats and support the common rafters. These in turn carry wooden boarding on to which the slate roof is

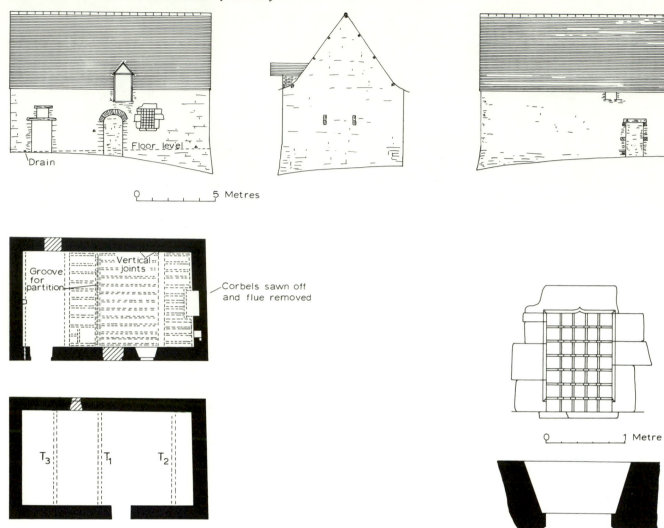

Fig. 202a.   L'Orrier 3, Saint-M'Hervé, Ille-et-Vilaine

nailed. This roof structure is of late appearance and oral evidence suggests that the house was built *c.* 1910. A red brick chimney-stack rises from a stone rubble chimney-hood which, in turn, rests on a wooden breastsummer supported by wooden corbels. Doorways and window openings are large, again indicative of a late date, and the windows were probably glazed from the start. Doors and window fittings therefore are almost certainly original. All the lintels are of wood and two dormers provide access to the loft. The rear outshot provides additional byre accommodation: that at the lower end serves as pigsties and that at the upper end is a bake-house at the end of which is the oven lined with red brick. The core of the house is a long-house with a large hall and byre separated by an original wall, containing a communicating doorway. The byre, however, is provided with its own

entrance from outside and the long-house is thus of the first-derivative type. A later outshot, bake-house and pigsties complete the ensemble.

Although the elementary long-house is known in Saint-M'Hervé, the type with two doorways is almost universal. L'Orrier 1 (XU 422398) is an example of the former (Fig. 201). Externally the building measures 11.45 metres long and 6.80 metres wide but the outshot extends this width to 9.60 metres. Internally the building is 10.00 metres long, 5.75 metres wide at the upper end and 5.35 metres wide at the lower end. Wall thickness varies from 0.50 metres to 0.85 metres. The eaves stand 3.35 metres and the ridge 6.90 metres above the ground. The Brioverian schist walling is laid in a mortar of *pisé* and the door and window lintels are of wood. The only granite dressings are those of the window jambs. Several

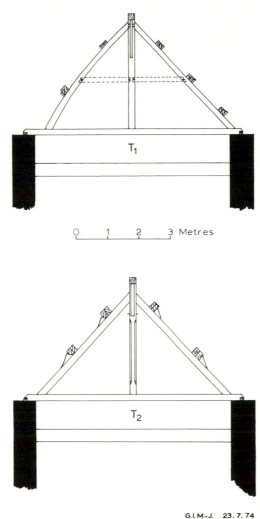

T₁

T₂

0   1   2   3 Metres

G.I.M.-J.   23.7.74

Fig. 202b.   L'Orrier 3, Saint-M'Hervé, Ille-et-Vilaine

blocks of wood are laid in the body of the wall usually to carry door hinges or fastenings. The floor is of *terre battue*. There are three trusses, all completely different and of such extraordinary construction that T2 and T3 can only be heavily and rather crudely adapted second-hand features. Nevertheless in their original form they are fine pieces of carpentry indicative of high quality. This is particularly true of T3 which has curved braces and a chamfered king-post of the kind normally associated with the barrel roofs of ecclesiastical buildings. Truss T1 is of the upper king-post and collar-type with short spurs braced down to the tie-beam with sling-braces. This roof illustrates the juxtaposition in the region of the full king-post truss and the upper king-post truss. King-posts carry a ridge purlin and the lateral purlins are fastened as well as possible on to various forms of cleat and secondary principal rafters in order to support the common rafters.

These, in turn, are boarded and the slates nailed to the horizontal boards. Also arising from the second-hand use of trusses is the existence of a double tie beam. The hearth lies at the upper end and supports a chimney-hood of stone rubble resting on a wooden breastsummer which in turn rests on wooden corbels. The chimney-hood terminates in a red-brick stack. Common beams are of good quality and, as is not uncommon in this district, support also common joists to which the loft floorboards are nailed. A partition fastened against the lower beam separates the hall from the lower end of the house. The hall window is fitted with four iron bars and a gabled dormer provides access to the loft. Externally the need to hold down the chimney corbels with a horizontal piece of wood should be noted and is probably indicative of the relatively low mechanical strength of the schist walling. Also to be noted is the rather high doorway with a light

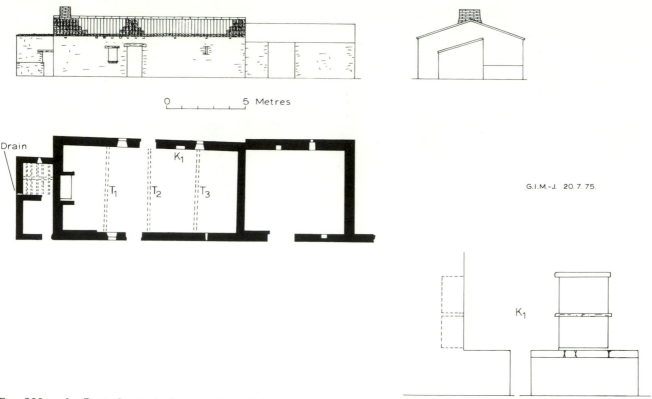

G.I.M.-J. 20.7.75.

Fig. 203a.   La Petite Louinais, Frossay, Loire-Atlantique

above the door, suggesting a rather late date. There is no suggestion that the outshot is other than an original feature but variation in wall thickness at two points does indicate a rebuilding and perhaps the present house should be regarded as dating from the later nineteenth century. It lies at the end of a row of two houses and outbuildings. In its present form it is undoubtedly a long-house of the elementary type with a single doorway for man and beast.

L'Orrier 3 (XU 422398) is *c.* 12.50 metres long and 7.70 metres wide externally. Internally, it is *c.* 10.80 metres long and 6.00 metres wide. Ground level drops sharply from right to left but the eaves rise 3.90 metres above ground-floor level and the ridge stands 8.85 metres above ground-floor level. Wall thickness varies from 0.80 to 0.90 metres (Fig. 202). The Brioverian schist walling is laid in a mortar of *pisé*, and dressed stone, in this case granite, is used only for the solitary window which lights the hall. The floor is of *terre battue* and the loft floor of wooden boards nailed to the common beams and joists. The roof is supported on three trusses of the full king-post type, the king-posts supporting the ridge-beam and resting on tie beams, which stand only a little distance above the common beams. Truss T2 shows a particularly fine king-post with

flat-splay chamfers. King-posts are braced upwards to the ridge-beam and truss T1 has a false collar. There are two pairs of lateral purlins which overlap at the trusses and are either supported on cleats or on pegs driven into the rafters. The roughly sawn common rafters overlap at the ridge and rest with their feet on the wall-heads. At this point the common rafters are sprocketed out. The roof slates are nailed to boards laid horizontally across the common rafters. The purlins and the wall-plate, a rare feature, are exposed in the upper gable. Access to the loft space is by a doorway in the form of a dormer which carries a projecting gable roof and has slated cheeks. The house is a long-house, first derivative. Formerly there were two doorways giving access to the byre end which is provided with a drain. The floor level rises from the byre through the hall up to the upper gable in opposition to the ground level outside which falls away. The main doorway giving access to the lower end of the hall is now blocked and has a circular head formed of stone rubble. The window which lights the hall has fine quality dressings with flat-splay chamfers and retains its original iron grille. The chimney and chimney-hood have entirely disappeared, only the wooden corbels remaining embedded in the wall. This is a house of some importance, as exemplified not only by the fine quality

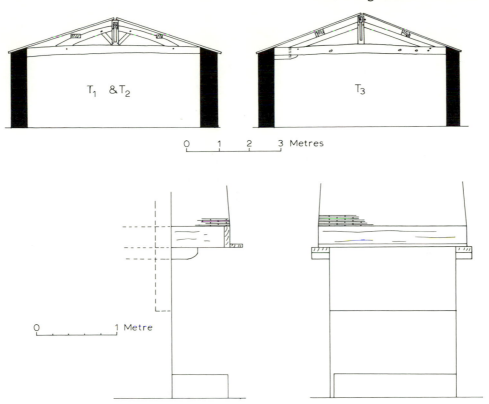

Fig. 203b.   La Petite Louinais, Frossay, Loire-Atlantique

and large size of the window but also by the high quality beams and the presence of common joists, a relatively rare feature in Brittany as a whole, but much more common along the eastern Marches. The hall and byre were formerly separated by a wooden board partition slotted into a groove in the beam immediately to the left of the doorway. It seems possible, however, that this was a later insertion, for the joists continue to the next beam, suggesting that they were once meant to be visible from the hall. A further factor here is the presence of a stair-well in the loft floor. Quality is also evidenced by the strongly marked batter at the upper end of the house and on the down-slope side. The outside wall near the main doorway is fitted with an iron tethering-ring, and another tethering-ring exists near the upper front corner. The blocked rear doorway has a wood lintel and is provided with wooden blocks in the wall to take the door hinges and fastenings.

From the area south of the Loire, in Loire-Atlantique, there is as yet no proof that houses were once occupied by man and beast. However, houses there are often of long-house form, with both one and two doorways. La Petite Louinais, Frossay (WT 824317) is an example of the former, with a pair of opposed doorways (Fig. 203). Total external length, including the two outbuildings, is 21.45 metres. The house measures *c*. 12.25 metres long and 6.50 metres wide externally, and 10.15 metres long and *c*. 5.30 metres wide internally, narrowing towards the lower end from 5.35 metres to 5.20 metres. The eaves stand 2.60 metres and the ridge 3.90 metres above the ground. Walling is of granite rubble and the roof covered with 'Roman' tiles. Thin red bricks are used for the chimney-stack. Flooring is of *terre battue*. The house is entirely open to the roof. The roof structure is supported on three trusses of the short king-post type. King-posts receive the ridge-purlins which are tenoned into them. Thick principal rafters carry one pair of lateral purlins which are either slotted into the rafters or supported on pegs. The king-posts are braced upwards both to the ridge-purlins and also to the principal rafters. Common rafters are staggered at the apex and rest upon the wall-heads. Wooden boarding is laid on these and the boarding, in turn, supports the half-cylindrical 'Roman' tiles known as *tuiles creuses* or *tiges-de-bottes*. The hearth and chimney-piece are of the construction widespread in Brittany. The hearth-stone stands against the hearth-back which is offset at a height of about 1.00 metre. This offset feature is not confined to the area south of the Loire and has been observed elsewhere in north and central Brittany. A chimney-hood of thin red bricks

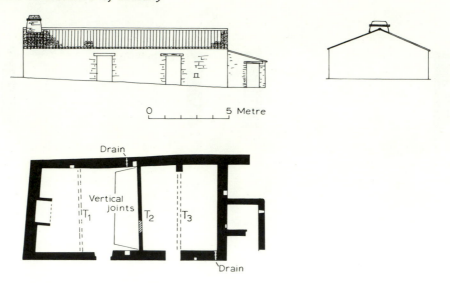

0 ⸺ 5 Metre

Drain

Vertical joints

T_1 T_2 T_3

Drain

Fig. 204a.   Le Bois Rialland 2, Frossay, Loire-Atlantique

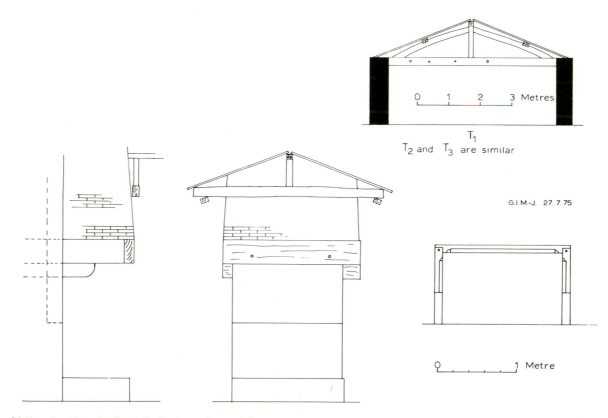

T_1

T_2 and T_3 are similar

0   1   2   3 Metres

G.I.M.-J. 27.7.75

0 ⸺ 1 Metre

Fig. 204b.   Le Bois Rialland 2, Frossay, Loire-Atlantique

rests upon a wooden breastsummer, in turn supported by wooden corbels. The plan of the house is of the long-house type but there is no proof that the lower end was used to house animals. In the absence of such proof it is best regarded as being of 'long-house form'. There is a pair of nearly opposite doorways and the hall or upper end is lighted by two windows. The lower end below the embryo cross-passage is lighted by a window on one side and a slit on the other. This end is also provided with a substantial keeping-place, K1, containing two shelves and a stone bench standing in front. This type of keeping-place is usually associated with the storage of milk and other dairy products. The doorway and window dressings are of the simplest. Jambs are of granite rubble, lintels of wood, and only the sill of the window is of red brick. The two outshots are later additions, that at the lower end being a byre and that at the upper end a pigsty with a small yard in front.

Le Bois Railland 2, Frossay (WT 801303), is irregular in shape. Maximum external length including the outshot is 15.35 metres, and the maximum external width 6.75 metres. The house is wider at the lower than at the upper end and the maximum internal measurements are 11.45 metres by 5.45 metres. The ground falls sharply from the upper to the lower end and the maximum height of the eaves above the ground is 2.50 metres. The ridge rises 1.30 metres above the eaves line. Wall thickness varies a little from 0.50 metres to 0.75 metres (Fig. 204). Granite rubble walling is laid in a mortar of *pisé*. The floor is of *terre battue* throughout and the building is entirely open to the roof. Roof structure is supported on three trusses of the short king-post type. King-posts rest on the tie-beams and carry the ridge-purlin. Lateral purlins overlap at each truss and are slotted into the principal rafters. Common rafters rest with their feet on the wall-heads and are staggered at the apex. Close-set wooden boarding is laid on these and in turn supports the red-tile roof. An additional 'truss' stands immediately in front of the chimney-hood and consists simply of a collar and short king-post resting on the lateral purlins. There is only one chimney, provided for the hearth at the upper end. Chimney-stack and hood are both of thin red bricks and are supported on a wooden breastsummer which in turn rests on wooden corbels. Two empty peg holes in the breastsummer formerly contained pegs for the suspension of household articles. The hearth-back is offset at a height of about 1.00 metre to provide a ledge which serves as a keeping-place. The undersides of the breastsummer and corbels are chamfered. Doorway dressings are of the simplest. The jambs are of granite rubble and both lintels were formerly of wood, but the doorway to the hall now has a new concrete lintel. There

are no window openings and this must once have been common to many houses of the district. Both the upper and the lower end are provided with drains and there is some doubt as to whether these are original features. Keeping-places occur in several places, including a spot on the outside wall below the door to the lower end. The presence of vertical joints suggests that the stone wall now separating upper and lower end is a later insertion. The doorway that once provided communication is now blocked. It cannot be proved, but it seems very likely that the lower end originally served as a byre, and this would explain the presence of a drain. At the time of survey, however, it was in use as a *cave*. The drain at the lower end of the hall is more difficult to explain and may date from the conversion of the hall to a byre. A pigsty forms an outshot at the lower end and formerly there was a bake-house at this end as well. That the lower end was used for the accommodation of animals cannot be proved, but remains highly probable. In the absence of absolute proof, however, the house is best regarded as of 'long-house form'. The separate entrance to the lower end puts it into the first derivative category. The roof structures with their short king-posts are typical of the area (Figs. 62 and 63).

Abundant evidence for the survival of the long-house at the end of World War II was collected by the E.A.R., especially in Morbihan and Loire-Atlantique, where the elementary long-house existed as late as the 1940s, man and beast being housed under one roof in an open rectilinear cell. Two primitive houses at Talforest, in Plumelin, already established as a culturally retarded *commune,* are both long-houses, with no separation between man and beast, *c.* 1945. Detailed drawings have been published elsewhere.[470] The first of these, whose *stridsuler*-type roof-truss has already been referred to (Chapter 6), is a 'platform' house, cut into the slope of the ground, the earthen bank forming the lower part of the rear lateral wall. Smoke from the central hearth is guided upwards through a flimsy hood, probably of wickerwork. The relative positions of the furniture are described further in Chapter 15. The functional division between the upper, or hall, and the byre, or lower, end, is approximately along the line of the central truss which lies close to the lower end of the doorway. Two *armoires* partially obscure, from the hall, the three cows, shown by the surveyor on the drawing, tethered to the front lateral wall. In the far lower corner is an enclosure for the solitary pig. This house is provided with a gable entry to the lower end for use by the animals, a rare feature. The dwelling has a total length of 8.85 metres, and a width of 4.00 metres, internally. Walling is of rubble blocks laid in a thick matrix of clay, or *pisé,* as found in the surviving building at Pon Digeu in the same commune (Fig. 166), and varies in thickness from 0.50 to 0.70 metres. The second house at Talforest has a cruck-trussed roof. It too is an elementary long-house, open from end to end, some 10.50 metres long and 4.70 metres wide internally. Walls, *c.* 0.70 metres thick, are of stone rubble set in a matrix of *pisé*. Entry for man and beast is by a common lateral doorway opening into an embryo cross-passage. *Armoires* define this cross-passage by the doorway. A *banc-coffre* and a longcase clock, opposite the doorway, complete the 'partition' between the hall and byre. The hearth, located against the upper gable, is not recessed into the wall and is covered by a wickerwork chimney-hood. The whole is strongly reminiscent of Botcol (Fig. 72) in the nearby *commune* of Guénin. Two cows are shown tethered to the lower gable wall and the 'calf-box', containing a solitary calf, is bounded by the *banc-coffre* and clock. These two houses show not only the survival of the elementary man-animal relationship into the mid-twentieth century, remarkable in itself, but also that three or four animals, and possibly more, can be accommodated in a building some 9.00 or 10.00 metres long internally, in addition to the family. In both these examples the interiors are entirely open to the roof.[471]

Other examples of the long-house in various stages of development are included in the Morbihan survey. Kernegan, Moustoir-Remungol, a first-floor hall of 1760, is integrated with a one-a-half storey long-house. Both have stair-turrets and there is a communicating doorway from one to the other. The hall of the long-house, 6.00 metres long and 5.25 metres wide internally, is separated from the byre, 9.50 metres long, by two non-aligned stone partitions, one of which contains keeping-places and stone shelving on the hall side. At Brenec in Plumelin, a long-house abuts a heated cell, to which there is internal communication, and which was probably originally a separate single-cell house. The long-house has a stair-turret, and the heated cell a circular stone stair in one corner. The hall of the long-house is 4.90 metres long, and is separated by a wooden partition from the byre, 14.10 metres long. An irregular vertical joint suggests that this exceptionally long byre was originally shorter. A round-headed doorway opens into the byre just below the dividing partition against which is placed the manger. Another doorway also provides entry to the byre at the lower end. Metairie du Frotage, Pluherlin provides yet another example of a long-house to which additions have been made at both ends. The original single doorway opens into an embryo cross-passage, at the opposite end of which is the stair-turret. A short stone wall, containing shelves, provides some privacy so that the hearth cannot be seen from the doorway. On the byre

side is a wooden screen with an open doorway at the end. The byre has been lengthened so that it is now 6.30 metres long, but originally it was less than half this length. The surveyor has carefully marked in the positions of the animals: five cows tethered to the gable wall, three heifers and a pair of working oxen to the wooden partition. Ten animals thus virtually filled the byre to which an inserted doorway now provides direct access from outside. Other similar examples of long-houses occur in the Morbihan survey, nearly all with a wooden partition separating hall and byre. In many cases a second doorway provides access to the byre from outside, whilst internal communication is maintained through the partition. This second doorway is in some instances a later insertion but in others it is original. At La Vallée, Pluherlin it is placed at the back of the house, whilst entry to the hall is at the front. Kerberon, Quistinic provides several examples of long-houses. A long-house of 1863 comprises hall and byre separated by a stone wall containing a communicating doorway. Each cell has separate access from outside. A separate single-cell dwelling and a *cave* lie at the upper end. In the same yard a second long-house also consists of a hall and byre separated by a stone wall. Both have hearths and it is clear that the present byre, 7.45 metres long, was formerly a hall and byre and that the present *cuisine,* or hall, was once a single-cell house with a communicating doorway to the original long-house.

The ease with which a long-house may be disguised is shown by an example from Bruneton in Guiscriff. A house of one storey has a hearth and chimney built into the upper gable and a fully hipped gable at the lower end. The building is apparently a one-cell house with internal measurements of 7.55 by 4.15 metres. Oral evidence, however, permitted the surveyor to reconstruct the interior *c.* 1900, showing the lower end, from the doorway to the gable, given over to cattle. There was then no chimney-hood against the wall, but a fire, presumably open, seems to have lain close to the upper gable. The furniture consisted simply of a table and benches by the window, a box-bed, an *armoire* and a *charnier.*[472]

Further examples of the elementary long-house were found in Loire-Atlantique, notably in the Grande Brière. At Quebitre, La Chapelle-des-Marais, a long-house, 11.00 by 5.70 metres internally, had a pair of opposed doorways at the ends of the embryo cross-passage. The latter was bounded on the lower, or byre, side by *armoires* and by the circular stair set partly in the wall, and on the hall side by the centrally placed table. Beyond the *armoires* was a corridor-like space containing the *crèche* and an 'open' partition to which cattle could be tethered. Entry to the byre, 4.00 metres long, was by a separate doorway. Space for the pig was partitioned off in a corner. Île de Mazin 13, in Saint-Joachim, is a similar example with a pair of opposed doorways at the lower end of the hall and an additional doorway for entry to the byre separated from the hall by an open partition, the vertical posts of which rise from the manger to a ceiling beam. Between these posts the heads of the cattle could pass to feed from the manger. Other examples were found at Mayun, La Chapelle-des-Marais, again with separate entry to a byre completely open to the hall. A lateral outshot served as a pigsty. Another example, at Quebitre, was almost identical but had the pigsty outshot at the rear. This practice of putting the pigs in an outshot projecting usually from the front of the house, but sometimes also the rear, is a characteristic of the houses of the Grande Brière. It was also found in Finistère, associated with houses having the table-outshot. At Le Bas Hoscas in Herbignac, a long-house 9.20 metres long and 5.80 metres wide had no separate entry to a byre completely open to the hall except for tethering posts and manger. The byre was only 2.70 metres long but would accommodate at least four cows. Somewhat different was the house and byre at Clis. Although 6.30 metres wide internally, the lengths of hall and byre were only 3.07 metres and 2.80 metres respectively, the two cells being separated by a stone wall containing a communicating doorway. The main doorway led into the upper end of the byre, close to the doorway into the hall. At the rear was a second doorway into the byre. A small 'box' was provided in the corner for the pig. Several houses had wooden partitions separating house and byre, as in Morbihan. That at Villeneuve in Le Gâvre had a separate entry to the byre, as had Île de Fédrun 43 in Saint-Joachim, and La Croix in Queniquen. The last two both had pigsty outshots. Another example at Queniquen had a wooden partition to separate byre from hall, and the manger was placed against the lower gable.

Two more groups of houses must be noted. In one, the lower end is not a byre but a compartment separated from the embryo cross-passage by furniture and called the *derrière*. Its function seems to be partly for storage, and occasionally a bed is found there. Examples occurred at La Rouardière, Saint-Père-en-Retz and Les Hauts Pilorgères, and a similar example at Mayun, La Chapelle-des-Marais. These are similar to the houses recorded in Frossay, above. It is highly probable that the lower ends were once byres and that they became extensions of the hall after cattle were transferred to separate buildings. Proof is lacking, however, and they are best described as being of long-house form. Into another category fall the few houses of which La Grande Île, Saint-Père-en-Retz,

is an example in which the byre, although still under the same roof, does not communicate internally with the house. This represents the final stage of the development of the long-house, before the house and the accommodation for animals became separated.[473]

The survey of Finistère contains proportionately fewer long-houses. That at Drollou-Vihan has a byre and hall separated by a wooden partition, a 'box' for the pig, and separate entrance to the byre. The hall is 6.00 metres long and 5.20 metres wide, and the byre 4.00 metres long. At Le Drenec in Sizun, a hall with table-outshot has a curious arrangement by which the byre is housed in a second lateral outshot in front of the house at the lower end. The lower end of the hall may well once have been a byre, but of this there is no proof. Another house in the same hamlet has the pigsty in a lateral outshot at the lower end. An original arrangement is better shown at Lestrevignon in Bodilis. This house, like the previous two, has a table outshot at the upper end and a *crèche,* in this case for calves, in a lateral outshot at the lower end. This lower end, separated from the hall by a wooden screen, serves as a byre and has a manger against the rear wall. Entry for man and beast is by the only doorway set in the front wall between the two outshots.[474]

Several dwellings recorded in Côtes-du-Nord are of the long-house type. That at Talen, Saint-Gilles-Vieux-Marché comprises a long range of buildings under one roof. The hall communicates with a dairy, at its upper end, from which it is divided by a stone wall. Bounding the lower side of the embryo cross-passage is a wooden screen shutting off the byre which also has a separate entrance. Beyond the byre is the *grange* with a pair of pigsties in a lateral outshot. A long-house at Villeneuve, Plédran has a stone wall with central doorway separating house and byre. Another doorway gives access to the byre from outside. A similar arrangement is found at Le Foeil in Saint-Launec. At Eglise Blanche, Maël-Pestivien, the original single-cell house appears to have been lengthened in both directions, with a byre on one side and a stable, cellar and *grange* on the other. Nowhere is there internal communication. A good example of an elementary long-house is that at Kerguistiou, La Chapelle-Neuve, where a wooden partition has been placed diagonally across the entry cross-passage from the upper side of one doorway to the lower side of the other. One doorway thus serves the hall, the other the byre. Internal communication is maintained by a door in the partition.[475]

The survey of Ille-et-Vilaine provides some examples of long-houses. That known as Le Marquidoin, Bazouges-la-Perouse is of two cells, a *cellier* and the byre under one roof, but with no internal communication. A smaller house, of long-house form, is La Vignonais, Saint-Jean-sur-Couesnon. What was once almost certainly a byre, and now a store, is divided from the hall by a stone wall containing a doorway. Both hall and former byre have pairs of opposing doorways. Several complex arrangements exist in which buildings have been added to an original nucleus to give, as at La Clairejaudière, Melesse, byres, hall, second cell, store-room and *grange,* all in line. This is not a true long-house, but nevertheless within the long-house tradition. Although the majority of Breton houses are only one room deep, many have had an outshot, used as a dairy or store, added to the back. Some possess such an outshot as an original feature, particularly those houses built during the nineteenth century. Thus in La Clairejaudière the *cellier* and dairy are in rear outshots. An excellent example of the short long-house is Petit Chevrigné, Saint-Hilaire-des-Landes. There are separate doorways to house and byre which are separated internally by a wooden partition. There is no internal communication. This house is 6.50 metres wide and 8.10 metres long internally, the hall occupying about two-thirds of this space. Grand Chevigné in the same *commune* provides a similar example but with a communicating doorway in the partition.

One of the smallest houses of long-house form, but lacking that absolute proof that the lower end was ever used as a byre, is La Mellerie in Cuguen. The dwelling is 6.65 metres wide and 6.45 metres long internally. The lower end is under 2.00 metres long and served by a pair of opposing doorways. There is a doorway in the wooden partition and another doorway at the rear giving separate access to the hall. Further excellent examples of short long-houses are the two dwellings at La Theberdais in Pipriac. One is 5.45 metres long and 5.70 metres wide internally, with a pair of opposing doorways and embryo cross-passage dividing the space into two roughly equal parts. There is no partition in this elementary long-house. The second house has doorways in the front only, one to the hall, the other to the byre. This house, 5.25 metres long, is shorter but 6.30 metres wide. A partition of vertically set slabs of schist separates hall and byre and there is a space by the doorways to get through from hall to byre.[476]

A complete range of examples of the long-house, from the simple elementary space with only a functional division into hall and byre, to the point where although the byre is still under the same roof as the hall it is not accessible from within, is illustrated by the E.A.R. These examples also demonstrate the great variety of dimensions, with the smallest long-house capable of accommodating only one or two cows. Indeed such houses are easily confused with single-cell houses and it must be wondered how many of the latter formerly accommodated a cow tethered simply to a ring in the wall at the lower end of the hall, in the 1.00 metre or so of space between the gable wall and the doorway. A distinction between the single-cell house and the simplest and smallest of the long-houses is thus very difficult if not impossible to make. The one gradually merges into the other as the practice of keeping one or two animals at the lower end increases.

The earliest written account of life in a Breton long-house is that by Cambry, who, though writing specifically of Finistère, was of the opinion that in Brittany '*l'habitation des laboureurs est à peu près partout la même*'.[477] The typical dwelling, a '*cahutte sans jour, est pleine de fumée; une claie légère la partage: le maître du ménage, sa femme, ses enfans et ses petits enfans occupent une de ces parties; l'autre contient les boeufs, les vaches, tous les animaux de la ferme. Les exhalaisons réciproques se communiquent librement, et je ne sais qui perd à cet échange. Ces maisons n'ont pas trente pieds de long, sur quinze de profondeur; une seule fenêtre de dix-huit pouces de hauteur, leur donne un rayon de lumière . . .*'.[478] This picture of an 'open', or elementary, long-house, the family at one end and the animals at the other, with only a low partition to make the functional subdivision, is mirrored by literary descriptions of the elementary long-house in Wales during the seventeenth and eighteenth centuries.[479] Fifty years later, a similar description of the houses of the Monts d'Arrée by Bachelot de la Pylaie confirms Cambry's evidence. Here the villages were composed of houses '*couvertes en paille, à peine closes par leur porte unique, et dont la fenêtre sans vitres, et à peine haute de deux pieds, donne encore plus d'accès dans l'intérieur au froid et à l'humidité. C'est là que vit comme pêle-mêle une famille . . . Un bout de la maison est pour l'espèce à figure humaine; l'opposé pour les moutons, sans autre séparation qu'un treillis peu élevé fait avec des branches de chêne entrelacées; quelquefois on y loge encore des vaches, d'où il résulte qu'une partie de l'intérieur n'est que boue et fumier, comme la cour qui est au-devant de la chaumière. La saleté des meubles se joint encore à celle de la famille, qui offre sous ce rapport la plus complète incurie, sans que la santé paraisse en souffrir manifestement, ce qui me semble le phénomène hygiénique le plus inconcevable. Fait-on de feu, c'est-à-dire, allume-t-on deux ou trois mottes de l'herbe desséchée qu'on enlève avec sa racine dans les landes d'alentour, il en sort une fumée épaisse, lourde, qui retombe en partie dans la maison et noircit meubles, plancher, etc. Autour de ce feu, qui n'est que visible, se* groupe la famille assise sur l'âtre de pierre qui élève le foyer à dix pouces au-dessus du reste de l'appartement . . .'.[480] Bachelot de la Pylaie visited several of these *tristes cabanes* which appear to have been little better than the medieval long-house and perhaps similar to Botcol or the dwellings at Koh-Coët (Figs. 72, 167, 168, 169). Notable are the existence of but one doorway, and the unglazed windows. Nor was the lower end used for cattle only, and here in the Monts d'Arrée, with their extensive *landes,* sheep were an important element in the rural economy. The lower end housed all the domestic animals. Comfort and privacy were unknown, as in Kerveden du Fret, where Bachelot de la Pylaie found '*ces chaumières misérables où l'homme n'a que de la paille encaissée pour reposer son corps fatigué, où il passe sa vie au milieu d'une lueur crépusculaire et de la fumée, entouré de la boue produite par ses fumiers et l'écoulement de ses étables*'.[481] In eighteenth-century Ouessant the houses were '*hutes dispersées dans la campagne sous lesquelles les habitants couchent pêle-mêle avec leurs bestiaux*'.[482]

Writing of Finistère during the first half of the nineteenth century, Souvestre thought that Cambry had exaggerated, and that, in some two-thirds of Breton farms, the animals were housed in byres separated from the house.[483] Field evidence alone shows that total separation, i.e. in detached buildings, cannot have been possible except on the biggest farms, and Souvestre is clearly referring to byres separated from the hall by a partition of wood or stone. Internal communication, the chief criterion of the long-house, would have remained. He admits, however, that '*dans les montagnes, chez les cultivateurs pauvres, on voit encore parfois les vaches et les moutons habiter le même corps-de-logis que les fermiers, dont ils ne sont séparés que par une claire-voie à hauteur d'appui; mais généralement les bestiaux ont des étables separées adossées au pignon de la maison principale. Ces étables sont basses, humides et n'ont aucune ouverture*'.[484] It is more likely that the 'open' elementary long-house survives in the interior parts of Finistère rather than simply 'in the hills'. Coastal areas responded much earlier to improvements in housing conditions, and contrasts between the extremes were often most marked in Finistère. Souvestre's evidence shows, not that the long-house was disappearing, but rather that it was evolving.

Two English travellers provide glimpses of rural life during the nineteenth century. In north Morbihan, around Ploërmel, the inhabitants dwelt 'in huts' where 'men, pigs and children live all together, without distinction, in these cabins of accumulated filth and misery', and 'It is absolutely a common thing, in Britanny

(sic), for men, women, children and animals, all to sleep together in the same apartment, upon no other resting place, than that of the substantial earth, covered with some straw. We once saw, near Josselin, a man drive into his cabin a cow, and a horse, followed by a pig, and afterwards entering himself, he shut the door'.[485]

During fieldwork in 1971, oral evidence was adduced for the long-house, Héréot 2 in Carnoët, Côtes-du-Nord which had been so inhabited until *c.* 1950. Later in the nineteenth century Blackburn observed the farmhouses with 'one living and sleeping room — kitchen, sitting-room, bedroom, all in one . . . There is often a dung heap outside, and a shed for cows opening into the living room, which is common alike to pigs, fowls, and children. We see the women coming out of their dark, unhealthy dwellings . . . We see them thrashing corn and scattering the grain wastefully on the ground, and farming on a small scale in primitive fashion. But the Bretons who live thus are nearly all prosperous and thrifty in their own way . . . .'.[486] Even after partitions fully separating house and byre had become common, the domestic pig was a frequent visitor to the hall and was often fed there, as shown in several prints of Breton interiors.[487] Hens may still be seen in and out of the open doorway, feeding on scraps thrown on to the hall floor. Formerly they roosted on a ledge near to the ceiling, sometimes across the doorway as described at Pouldreuzic in the 1920s.[488] That prejudiced observer, Roger, scarcely able to find a good word for the Bretons, is undoubtedly correct when he writes of the '*gens qui sont aussi peu soigneux de leur toilette ne peuvent avoir pour maisons que des taudis d'une saleté repoussante. Et c'est le cas de ses habitations qui servent à loger à la fois la famille et les animaux. Sous le même toit, côte à côte, vivent les enfants et le bétail. Les appartements ne sont séparés des écuries que par des minces cloisons qui laissent filtrer les odeurs de purin et de fumier. Quelquefois même ses cloisons n'existent pas, et seul, un meuble établit la séparation*'.[489] Thus by the end of World War I, in Finistère at least, the 'open' or elementary long-house remained, but many seem to have been functionally sub-divided by a wooden partition.

Several major works in human geography contain references to the rural house. Le Lannou was of the opinion that, in the period immediately following World War II, only a few dozen *maisons rudimentaires*, i.e., long-houses as described by Cambry, then remained in the more remote *cantons* of Arcoët.[490] Most had by then been converted to farm buildings. This, whilst in one sense true, fails to grasp the significance of the long-house as a type. Writing of the same period, Guilcher thought that the '*promiscuité des bêtes et des gens*' had perhaps been exaggerated in Brittany, existing only in backward areas. In the post-World War II period not a single farm in Plouvien, Finistère survived in which man and beast were separated by only a wooden partition, least of all a half-partition. A wall of stone always separated them. Separation, however, was not absolute. Six farms had a communicating doorway and in four other cases a former doorway had been blocked. In general, a small proportion of farms had internal communication with the byre and stable. It seems probable, however, that hall and byre separated by a wood partition existed up to the eighteenth century. The farm at Le Guen, Kerglien, Plouvien (Fig. 237) is simply a hall and byre, with a pair of opposite doorways at the ends of a cross-passage, and a communicating doorway to the byre which also has a separate doorway from the outside.[491]

In the *commune* of Bulat-Pestivien, Côtes-du-Nord during the 1930s, there were still four examples of the elementary long-house with a low partition of planks separating man and beast. Other examples existed in which the animals had been expelled from the lower end, a low partition remaining to form a sort of entry-corridor. The solitary doorway lay at the lower end, beyond the partition. In addition, houses existed in which internal communication remained, although a separate doorway to the byre from outside had been provided.[492]

In Basse-Bretagne at the turn of the century, byres and stables, in general, were built continuously with the house, and even c. 1900 there was sometimes no separation between the two. The example of the farm at Trouguennour in Cap-Sizun (Fig. 237) shows the persistence of internal communication from house to byre and stable.[493] Several other authors record the existence of the long-house at various periods. During the eighteenth century Bagot, quoted by Sée, considered one of the principal causes of the epidemics of 1744 to be *'l'usage où sont les paysans d'avoir leurs bestiaux sous le même toit sans cloison qui sépare les hommes des animaux et des fumiers'.*[494] Dupuy thought that in the eighteenth century it was the small farmers who shared their houses with animals, separated by only a low thin partition.[495] Inventories for the *pays de Quimper*, however, contain no evidence of this cohabitation, which is hardly surprising as they are chiefly the records of the better-off classes (see Chapter 15).[496] In eighteenth-century Côtes-du-Nord, when a farmer owned stock, *'une des pièces dont leur habitation est formée, soit réservée a leur "cheptel", parfois limité à un cochon ou à une coche et ses petits. Il s'agit alors de "chaumières [qui] ne comprennent qu'une seule pièce, qu'une mince cloison peu élevée partage en deux compartiments, dont*

l'un est réservé au bétail, l'autre forme la demeure du paysan et de sa famille . . ."'.[497]

In the interior of the *pays vannetais,* at the end of the nineteenth century, the dwelling was used as house and byre except where the occupant practised a trade or kept a shop, in which case the lower end served as a shop or workshop.[498] In mid-nineteenth century Côtes-du-Nord, a report on the rural house draws a distinction between the coastal areas where housing standards had evolved and the interior where it was normal to live in one room and where *'Chez les pauvres gens, cette même pièce n'en forme qu'une seule et unique avec l'étable et l'écurie',* i.e. the 'open', elementary long-house.[499]

Evidence of the long-house is still plentiful in the twentieth century. Although in Morbihan the byre and hall are now generally separated by a wooden partition or wall, this was not always so, and there was a time when no separation existed.[500] Pieces of furniture were used in some houses to delimit the functional division of house and byre. The *auge,* or feeding trough, also served to delimit the byre, where there was no partition.[501] The existence of the 'open' long-house, with only a half-partition, is shown by an illustration of the interior of a small long-house at Kerbourg in Guérande in 1938. The cow stares across the hall at the hearth, over a low wooden partition. This arrangement was once common and a few examples still remained near Guérande in 1956.[502] Hélias describes such a house in Pouldreuzic, Finistère in the 1920s, *'une pièce réservée aux humains et un réduit plus petit où créchaient la vache et le cochon. Entre les deux appartements, une cloison à claire-voie, établie en mauvaises planches d'écorce, n'empêchait pas les animaux de réchauffer les gens'.* In other houses with internal communication from hall to byre, the door was left open in cold weather so that the warmth from the byre could heat the hall.[503] Giese also reports the survival of the elementary long-house in the Monts d'Arrée between the Wars.[504] This close juxtaposition of man and beast survived well into the twentieth century in Côtes-du-Nord, and one enquiry reports a few cases where *'gens et bêtes vivent ensemble. Là une cloison serait très nécessaire'.*[505] At the beginning of the twentieth century Vallaux observed in La Feuillée, Le Conquet, Lochrist and Névez that *'les porcs ont libre entrée partout dans les habitations pauvres'.* In Locminé peasants continued to build long-houses with only a partition between kitchen and byre, to be regarded as progress compared with the half-partition described by Cambry.[506]

The 'open' long-house was probably much more common in the years before World War I, the hall separated from the byre by a trough formed of a hollowed oak. On one side the animals, *'vaches, bœufs, porcs, moutons, volailles, sont parqués. De l'autre côté les lits-clos à la mode bretonne et les armoires sont dressés parallèlement à une table-huche et à ses bancs . . . Presque toutes les métairies morbihannaises offrent ces représentations de l'arche de Noé, car les espèces vivantes et germantes sont enfermées sous leur toiture de chaume'.* In some houses a partition separated hall and byre. Occasionally, circular holes in the wooden partition allowed the animals to pass their heads through into the embryo cross-passage to feed from the trough and see the fire. *'Le laboureur gallot voit plusieurs avantages à cette promiscuité, et le plus certain, c'est le chauffage économique produit par la chaleur de ces animaux, pendant l'hiver.'* [507] The embryo cross-passage thus took on the characteristics of a feeding walk.

Whether or not some authors have exaggerated the proportion of dwellings of the long-house type, particularly the elementary long-house, with no separation between man and beast, the fact remains that it existed, in large numbers in some areas and before the present century, and that a few surviving examples remained locally until the mid-twentieth century. Long-houses with a wooden partition or a low stone wall, with interior communication, survive still in large numbers although many are today uninhabited or the animals have been expelled and the former byre used for storage or converted into a second room.

The earliest evidence for the existence of the long-house is that presented for Pen-er-Malo and Kerlano (Figs. 70 and 71; see Chapter 8). Although absolute proof of the existence of a byre at the lower ends of these buildings is lacking, it remains highly probable that they were occupied as 'open' long-houses, the family at one end, the stock at the other, with no physical partition between them. These sites provide evidence for dwellings both with a single doorway, and a pair of opposed doorways. There is no evidence that the cross-passage was structurally defined, although there can be little doubt that the space connecting two opposing doorways, or leading back to the rear wall from a single doorway, performed the function of a cross-passage in that it saw the 'to-ing and fro-ing' of the inhabitants, and served to separate man and beast. In the absence of a physical partition, however, it is best referred to as an embryo cross-passage. There is as yet no evidence for the development of the long-house between the earliest known example of twelfth-century date at Pen-er-Malo and the oldest surviving vernacular buildings. Further possible medieval sites with oval buildings and lateral doorways, suggestive of long-houses have, however, been discovered but not yet excavated.[508] The earliest known vernacular long-houses date from the sixteenth

and seventeenth centuries and, apart from the occasional rounded corner, they are rectilinear in form. Evolution from the primitive to the vernacular thus resulted in the abandonment of the oval shape in preference for the rectilinear, although primitive houses survived well into the twentieth century, in decreasing numbers. Literary and field evidence, as well as oral testimony, demonstrates beyond doubt that the 'open', or elementary, long-house survived in great numbers until World War I, continued to exist in remote and poorer areas until World War II, and a few examples survived into the post-World War II period until *c.* 1950. Segregation of man and beast at opposite ends is undoubtedly of great antiquity and arose from the need to provide shelter for domesticated animals. Thus the long-house came into being as a result of segregation within the family cell itself, and not as a consequence of combining two separate buildings.

Physical separation between man and beast first took the form of a low partition like that illustrated by Gauthier in the *pays de Guérande*[509] and by the E.A.R. in the Grand Brière.[510] This is undoubtedly similar to the *claie légère* observed in late eighteenth-century Finistère.[511] This partition bounded the cross-passage on the byre side and, as has been shown, often had a manger placed along its length, either within the byre or in the embryo cross-passage. The latter thus also took on the function of a feeding walk, and in some instances a second trough may have been provided for the crushing of gorse, an activity which otherwise normally took place in an outbuilding. This low partition seems later to have developed into a full partition in Haute-Bretagne, but with circular holes so that the cattle, tethered with their heads towards the hearth, could still feed from the manger places against the partition in the cross-passage. Full partitions recorded are either of wood or stone and invariably divide hall and byre at a point above the cross-passage, so that the latter is bounded physically on the hall side, but is quite open to the byre on the other. No long-house has yet been encountered in which the cross-passage is bounded by screens on both sides. Stone partitions are impossible to date and the existence of straight joints in some cases suggests that many were later insertions to pre-existing houses. Few wooden screens can with confidence be described as original features (Fig. 199). Large numbers of screens have been observed which have all the appearance of a nineteenth-century date, and are nailed to the beam closest to the doorway on the upper side. It thus seems possible that in most of the long-houses the wooden screen is a nineteenth- or twentieth-century insertion, a response to demands for privacy, greater comfort and perhaps also a response to health hazards arising from sharing an open cell with animals. A further development, difficult to date, is the provision of a separate doorway to the byre whilst maintaining the convenience of internal communication between hall and byre as well (Figs. 51, 91, 92, 188, 191, 200, 202). This development is certainly later in the evolutionary sequence, though not necessarily chronologically later. It is more common in the east and rarer in the conservative interior and the west. However, it is never found to the total exclusion of the pure long-house. A few examples are known in which interior communication no longer exists — the final stage in the development of the long-house — before the total separation of house and byre (Fig. 198).

There can be no doubt both from the distribution of surviving examples outlined, and from oral and literary evidence, that the long-house was formerly the standard type of dwelling over the whole of Brittany for families owning stock. The division between hall and byre was of a flimsier nature than the board partitions now to be found in surviving examples. This evidence may help further to clarify problems arising from studies of the long-house in Britain.[512]

Hearths and chimneys of the type now found probably became common from the sixteenth and seventeenth centuries onwards (see Chapter 6), but it would appear that the hall was previously heated by an open fire and smoke had to find its way out via the window and door openings. It seems likely, however, from dated long-houses, that the chimney was widely known in the seventeenth century, even if it was then only found in a minority of dwellings. Houses illustrating a transitional form, with a byre and hall open to the roof, but with the hearth and chimney at the gable, survived for a long time as at Talforest, above. The introduction of a half-loft marks the evolution towards a fully-ceiled hall and byre with storage loft above.[513] The false chimney stack is also a widespread feature and the explanation that it was erected above the byre gable to provide symmetry purely for decorative purposes is possible. The long-house with byre equal in length to the chamber is a remarkably symmetrical structure all too easily disguised by the conversion of the byre into a second chamber. Furthermore, the distribution of false chimney-stacks is not confined to Brittany, for they have been observed in north Wales.[514] The traditional beliefs that cows must see the fire[515] and that 'warmth increases the yield of milk'[516] are present in Brittany and may explain the practice, but most of the stacks must have been in existence before partitioning became common. Whether they represent a means of providing a 'hearth' for the cattle is uncertain. However, several Breton farmers have confirmed that

this practice as a superstition was held to be beneficial to the cattle. There is sufficient oral evidence to confirm that the sight of the fire was believed to be beneficial to cattle and to increase milk supply. This was probably an important factor in explaining the persistence of the half-partition between hall and byre and the reluctance in some areas to shut off the byre completely. The false stack, once built, gives many a long-house (Fig. 180) a symmetrical look and others the appearance of a *petit manoir* of the three-unit plan (Fig. 178). This pleasing improvement to the elevation may have helped to sustain the practice, but it may not have been the cause of it.

Smith regarded the long-house as a Celtic form, a view he no longer holds.[517] Invoking the concept of cultural mingling and arguing that a recessive material culture will occur whenever economic circumstances allow, his hypothesis was supported by the close relationship between the known distribution of the long-house and that of Celtic place-name elements. If the type is of late Celtic origin it is likely to have been taken to Brittany by British migrants from the fourth century A.D. onwards. But it is also widely distributed across northern and western France.[518] The maximum easterly limit of the Breton language in the ninth century may be regarded as marking the extent of the Breton settlement, but examples of long-houses already found lie well to the east of this line (compare Figs. 27 and 102). It seems probable, therefore, that the long-house is an earlier west European, rather than a late Celtic type, but this does not exclude the possibility of its being Celtic in the wider sense, for it could be a survival of the Gallo-Roman period in France. In this respect, the interesting alleged Romano-British example reported at Iwerne in Dorset may prove significant. It is considerably longer and wider than most modern long-houses, with a lateral doorway only probable and not proven. Although the whole building displays features of other traditions, exemplified by the porch and entry in the lower gable, it does appear to be more like a long-house than anything else known from Roman Britain, the stone-lined drain providing indisputable evidence of the former presence of cattle.[519] It would seem more probable, however, that the type is much earlier, dating perhaps from the domestication of animals during the Neolithic. Proof of this must await archaeological evidence.

Work by British scholars has placed great emphasis on the cross-passage as a feeding walk and on the housing of cattle, principally dairy cattle.[520] That this should be so in certain areas of Atlantic Europe, particularly in parts of Wales and Ireland, is understandable. 'The custom of providing space for cattle under the family roof . . . occurs in areas of heavy rainfall where the emphasis is on dairy produce rather than crops',[521] yet there seems to be no reason why the long-house should be associated solely with a pastoral economy. On many of the small and fragmented Breton land holdings there may be considerable emphasis on the growing of crops. Families have often been too poor to own more than one, two or three beasts, and some byres, to judge from their size, are scarcely capable of containing more than one or two animals. The long-house occurs widely in areas of mixed farming economy and there can be little doubt that the byre formerly housed not only the family cow but occasionally a horse as well, or indeed, as Cambry has said, all the animals of the farm.

The single-cell units attached to the long-houses (Figs. 178, 181 and 196) have been referred to above as separate dwellings, but the possibility that these may be additional heated chambers must now be considered. If this be so, it is difficult to understand why each is provided with an outside doorway. Some of the units are long enough to have had a byre or at least space for a single animal to be tethered at the lower end (Kervaly 1 and Kerhaliou 3, Figs. 178 and 196). Where a communicating doorway to the adjacent house exists, it may in a few cases be of recent origin, dating from the conversion of the two dwellings into a single living or farm unit, or it may be an original or a long-standing feature, as would appear to be so in the majority of cases. Although a few of these single-cell units may simply be additional chambers, it seems more than just coincidental that they have direct access from outside without exception. This interpretation is supported by the very strong tradition of living entirely in one room until relatively recently (see Chapter 15).

The occupation of adjacent dwellings by kin groups undoubtedly provides the explanation, although it is nearly impossible to prove. A recent study of the several *rangées* in north-west Morbihan attempts to relate the multiple dwellings to the extended family, mostly based on twentieth-century data.[522] However, there seems to be a clear relationship between many *rangées* and former common fields (Chapter 3), and most examples also betray organic growth and extension over the centuries. A communicating doorway would be consistent with the presence of the second and third generations in the larger house, with perhaps the elderly first generation in the single-cell dwelling, living independently, but easily accessible. A similar explanation may well account for the grouping of these dwellings in twos and threes even where no such communicating doorway exists. The so-called unit system, with two or more adjacent farms sharing land as well as a common yard, has been recognized in Wales[523] as well as in north-west England.[524] Undoubtedly similar practices existed in Brittany but the precise nature of these, and any possible relationship with the practice of partible inheritance, must await further investigation. Oral evidence for the occupation of rows by related families is forthcoming from several areas, including the Grande Brière, and an almost tyrannical relationship in some areas between the rows and former openfield has been observed (see Chapter 3; Figs. 31 and 32).

ELEVEN

THE FIRST-FLOOR HALL

The first-floor hall is a dwelling in which the hall, or common living room, is located at first-floor level over a ground-floor room used for storage, for the accommodation of animals, or as an additional, or an independent, dwelling unit. Access to the hall is normally by an external staircase, but internal stairs are not infrequent. Over one hundred and seventy examples have now been recorded in Brittany, and the distribution shows that they are present from the eastern Marches to farthest Finistère (Fig. 205). Proportionately, however, first-floor halls are few. Eight of the sample quadrats contained examples, one in each of Quadrats 4, 7, 8, 12 and 20, two in each of Quadrats 3 and 17 (Plougasnou and Béganne) and three in Quadrat 13 (Saint-M'Hervé) (Fig. 79). They appear to be rarest in the economically poorer areas. Where a region has been economically prosperous, they occur in greater numbers. Thus in Plougasnou, an area in which agriculture has been prosperous for several centuries and where the vernacular architecture is of high quality, three examples were found close to, but outside, the sample quadrat. The countryside south of Guérande grew rich in the sixteenth and seventeenth centuries as a consequence of the trade in salt, and the three first-floor halls recorded around the Marais Salant suggest that many more examples in that district await discovery. The three examples in Saint-M'Hervé, an area of good soil and small prosperous farms, are a probable indication of large numbers waiting to be discovered on the Breton Marches. The distribution suggests that the type is widely known in Brittany. It occurs south of the Loire, along the whole length of the southern littoral, in the north and the interior. Gaps in the distribution must in part be attributed to lack of fieldwork. A large percentage of the total number of first-floor halls recorded is derived by interpretation of photographs in the archives of the Commission d'Inventaire de Bretagne. First-floor halls are relatively easy to identify and any error incurred in the interpretation is felt to be small. Just as intensive fieldwork in Plougasnou and Saint-M'Hervé threw up

numerous examples, so the published inventories for the *cantons* of Carhaix-Plouguer, le Faouët and Gourin include many examples of undoubted first-floor halls within the confines of relatively small areas. They also include examples of unproven first-floor halls, in which an upper room is nevertheless of undoubted importance, a category that will be discussed later.[525] The unpublished records of the Commission d'Inventaire contain many photographs of first-floor halls, but these, like the author's fieldwork, result from work in discrete areas. The total resulting distribution does therefore tend to show considerable concentrations. Nevertheless, subjective observation during travel in Brittany tends to confirm the large number of first-floor halls to be found, for example in north-east Morbihan and around Fougères in the eastern Marches of Ille-et-Vilaine. Notable for their concentration of first-floor halls are the *communes* of Saint-Ouen-des-Alleux in Ille-et-Vilaine, and Pontivy, Bubry and Langoëlan in Morbihan. The relatively poor agricultural area around Callac has also produced a high proportion.

The first-floor hall is known in adjacent parts of western Europe. In the British Isles it is found all over England, with examples from town and country as early as the twelfth century. It occurs in a purely military context, as the hall of a castle, but its relationship to cellared houses may suggest that its origin was not defensive. The illustration of the type on the Bayeux tapestry shows that it was known in England before the Norman Conquest.[526] In country areas it persisted throughout the Middle Ages at the social level of the manor house, and although its origin may not have been defensive, there can be no doubt that many first-floor halls did fulfil defensive requirements, providing dry and secure accommodation. Surviving examples are almost all of stone, suggesting that they were homes of socially important people, landowners, merchants and clerics.[527] The tower houses of northern England, Scotland and Ireland where there are great concentrations, are a variation of the first-floor hall.[528] The castles of the Anglo-Scottish Border region,

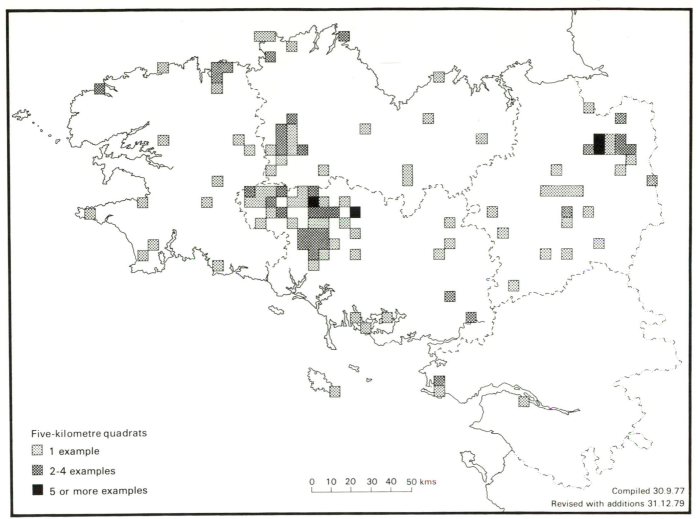

Fig. 205.   The distribution of first-floor halls in Brittany

fortified or defensible farmhouses of the sixteenth and seventeenth centuries, are local variants of the first-floor hall tradition, adapted to the needs of a turbulent area.[529] In south Wales, the type is associated with the upper classes. Notable are those of Pembrokeshire of which four sub-types have been recognized: the unfortified first-floor halls, the first-floor hall with a small element of fortification, the tower-house, and the houses of townsmen. Whilst the first-floor hall is widely distributed in Wales, it is in the south-west, north and east that it is most numerous.[530]

Dwellings with the principal room at first-floor level are common in the Mediterranean areas and occur throughout France. Rabelais' house, La Devinière, near Chinon, is an excellent example of the small first-floor hall, with an external staircase and a secondary living-room, probably a kitchen, at ground-floor level. Such a kitchen, in addition to its primary function, would have

provided living accommodation for the domestic servants. Similar buildings are recorded in central France in the Grande Limagne. Here the hall, and sometimes the bedroom when one exists, is at first-floor level. The ground-floor is reserved for animals, or use as a cellar, the *cuvage* or wine-making process, or for storage. Such houses are neither necessarily those of wine growers, nor of persons high in the social scale. Although the origin of the type may lie in the Mediterranean lands, there is yet no proof of this.[531]

Several authors have observed the existence of the first-floor hall in Brittany. Le Lannou refers to the type as the *maison en hauteur* and claims that, whilst it is not common, examples are to be found more or less everywhere, particularly around the Golfe du Morbihan, in the Pontivy area, and in northern Cornouaille, especially the south-west Côtes-du-Nord, and also in the Monts d'Arrée.[532] Characteristically, the type has an

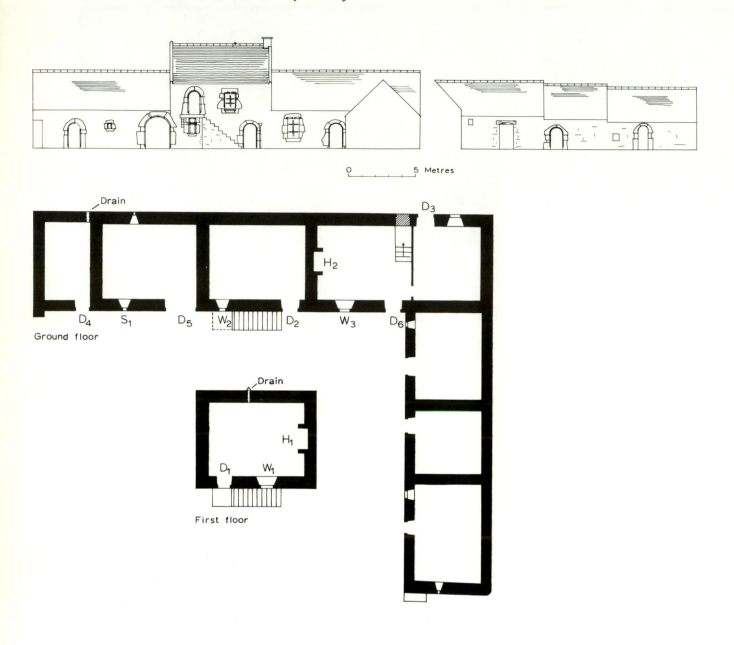

0   5   Metres

Drain

D₃

H₂

Ground floor

D₄   S₁   D₅   W₂   D₂   W₃   D₆

Drain

H₁

D₁   W₁

First floor

G.I.M.-J. 29.6.72.

Fig. 206a. Keradour, Plougasnou, Finistère

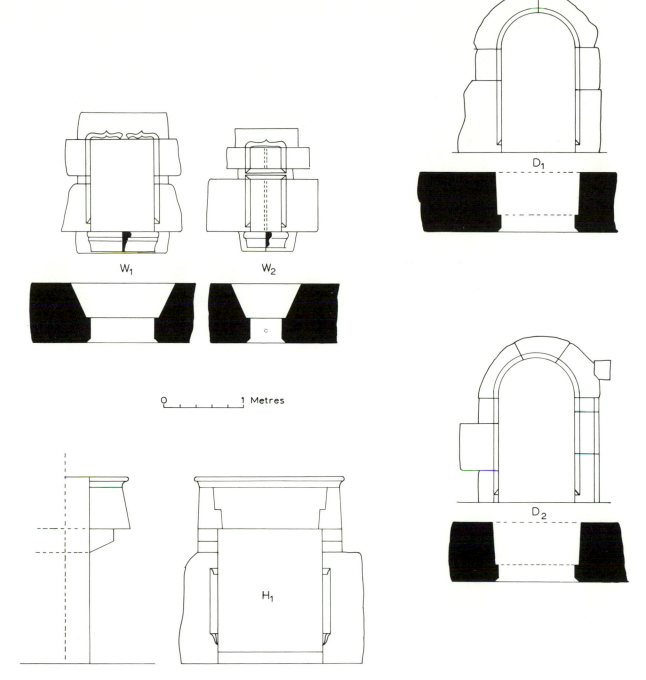

Fig. 206b. Keradour, Plougasnou, Finistère

external staircase of stone giving access to the first floor, and the doorway is sometimes sheltered by a porch. A convincing example from Lanrivain, Côtes-du-Nord is illustrated, but a second example, claimed as a variant of the type, is a house with table-outshot at Botmeur in the Monts d'Arrée. The house is similar to the long-house at Saint-Rivoal (Fig. 195), and the upper room is served by a stone stairway under the cover of the projecting roof. These upper rooms may have been first-floor halls in some instances, but until proof is forthcoming, they are best regarded as possibilities to be treated with caution. Buildings of this type are not plotted as first-floor halls on Fig. 205. First-floor halls are generally among the best constructed buildings of their locality, and finely carved doorway and window detail, together with monumental chimney-pieces, indicates a certain social superiority. Dating from the seventeenth and eighteenth centuries, these buildings had external stone stairways, many of which have fallen, only to be replaced by internal wooden stairs. They rarely occur in isolation and nearly always dominate a group of obviously humbler dwellings. Many of these *maisons en hauteur* may have been some kind of *manoir* and they are frequently associated with land holdings of thirty to fifty hectares. Whether the *seigneur,* living at first-floor level, would better have been able to survey the work of his tenants as Gautier and Le Lannou suggest, is doubtful. More likely the type was a status symbol with the added advantage of greater cleanliness and comfort, being separated from the animals. The ground floor often served as a stable or byre. Gautier's claim that the type is particularly common west of Pontivy is entirely supported by the distribution on Fig. 205. The first-floor hall has all the appearance of dignity and status and may have been modelled on the town houses of the wealthy.[533]

One or two first-floor halls with an external staircase and a stable on the ground floor existed in Bulat-Pestivien, Côtes-du-Nord in the 1930s.[534] At Keraredeau in Plouvien an example, inhabited until 1926, stood adjacent to a single-cell house from which the hall was accessible by an internal stone stair. There was no external staircase. Others also appear to have existed.[535] Souvestre writes of a *manoir* at Kerneïs in Trégorrois, in which two rooms were reserved for the seigneur and *'C'etait là que le nouveau propriétaire venait passer quelques jours chaque année pour recevoir ses fermages, chasser son gibier et surveiller ses plantations'.*[536] It is possible that the principal room here was at first-floor level. The reservation of an upper room in an otherwise multi-cell house for the occasional visits of an absentee landlord was a widespread practice. There is oral evidence for this from Le Cosquer, Guérande, Loire-Atlantique, where in the 1970s the lease of the house specifically excluded one of the first-floor rooms, kept by the proprietor for himself although he had no need of it, nor had he ever used it. Such a practice can only bespeak a long-standing tradition. Similar oral evidence explains the first-floor room at Les Hauts Talus, Montgermont, Ille-et-Vilaine (Fig. 44). Indeed, located so close to Rennes, halls of this kind might well have served as weekend homes for rich *bourgeois* who had chosen to invest their money in land. The existence of *métayage* may also have been a factor encouraging this type of arrangement, with the landlord, either permanently resident, or an absentee paying only occasional visits, living in the upper hall, and the working farmer living at ground-floor level in an adjacent house. Finally there is the testimony of oral evidence from all parts of Brittany, that in former times the *seigneurs* lived at first-floor level.

Gauthier records the existence of the *maison en hauteur* near Pontivy, in the *pays d'Arrée*, Trégorrois and north Léon.[537] He illustrates a first-floor hall at Locmalo, Morbihan and several other farms with an outside stone stair leading to the *grenier* or loft. The latter are unheated and should not be confused with the first-floor hall. In some the loft rises a full storey as at Lesunalec 3, Grand-Champ. Le Lannou may have confused the two.[538] His observation that the first-floor hall is common around the Golfe du Morbihan is unsupported, and considerable searches in that area have produced few examples, although the external staircase associated with a storeyed loft is widespread.

Five examples give some idea of the great variety of form, texture, colour and ornament in Breton first-floor halls. At Keradour, Plougasnou, Finistère (VU 408934) a first-floor hall is associated with another dwelling and a range of outbuildings (Fig. 206). Formerly, the courtyard, with buildings bounding two sides, was closed by a high wall pierced by a gateway and a doorway. Overall length of the domestic range is 28.95 metres and of the range of outbuildings set perpendicular to the domestic range, c. 17.60 metres. The two dwelling houses have a total length of 18.65 metres and a width of 6.20 metres, externally. The first-floor hall measures 6.10 metres by 4.55 metres internally and the adjacent long-house, 10.20 metres by 4.55 metres internally. Walling is chiefly of granite rubble laid in a mortar of *pisé*. Dressed granite blocks, also of *granit rose*, are used for doorway and window dressings and occasionally for quoins. The roof covering is entirely of slate, the lower part of the roof of the first-floor hall being covered with the rather chunky local slates. It is probable that the outbuildings were originally thatched and that the present covering is of imported Anjou slate. All the ridges are finished with red tile. The two dwelling houses each have one hearth, hearth H1 being in the upper chamber of the first-floor hall, and hearth H2 at the upper end of the hall in the long-house. They share a common stack. The construction of both chimney-pieces is monumental but that in the first-floor hall is of very high quality. In both cases the granite breastsummers are supported on granite corbels which pass through the thickness of the walls. Doorway and window dressings are of a high order. All the chamfers are flat-splay and nearly all the door-heads are round. Only the cart-shed doorway, D5, has a slightly flattened arch. The windows of the dwelling houses formerly had stone mullions and transoms but these have now disappeared from both the long-house and the upper chamber of the first-floor hall, having been replaced by wooden casement windows. Only the narrow window to the ground floor of the first-floor hall, placed beneath the staircase, retains its original stone transom. The first-floor hall has a doorway and a window opening for each storey and there is no internal communication between ground and first floors. Access to the first-floor hall, still lived in as such at the time of survey, is by an external stone staircase. The long-house originally had a pair of nearly-opposite doorways, but one of these is now blocked and a partition has been erected on the lower end of the embryo cross-passage and an extra doorway, D3, inserted to provide access to what was formerly the byre. A wooden staircase provides access to the loft. The window, W3, and the principal doorway, D6, are the original openings to this long-house. There is no internal communication between the ground floor of the first-floor hall and the long-house, nor is there any internal communication anywhere throughout the length of this range of buildings. The buildings are not all of one date but it seems probable that the first-floor hall and the long-house are contemporary, and it may be that the outbuildings to the left of the first-floor hall are also contemporary, but the range of buildings at right angles to the long-house, three separate byres, were clearly added at three different dates and represent growth of the original nucleus. In the absence of a date-stone, the round-headed doorways suggest a late sixteenth- or, more probably, a seventeenth-century date. The yard here appears once to have been walled and provided with a pair of entrance doorways but this wall has been demolished.

This is undoubtedly the home of an important local landowner in an area noted for its agricultural prosperity. It is one of a number of first-floor halls in the district. The ground floor beneath the hall is unheated, and whilst it may once have been used as a byre, it seems likely that it has been a store for the greater part of its history. The quality of the window dressings and the hearth, together with the provision of a drain at first-floor level, leave no doubt whatever that it was the upper hall which was the common living room. The group appears to have grown with time, and the building of a wall enclosing the courtyard may have been the final stage of development. A kin- or working-relationship is the most likely explanation of the domestic arrangements. The head of the family might have occupied the first-floor hall, with a married son or younger brother in the long-house. Alternatively the landowner could have occupied the hall, with the working farmer or tenant, in the adjacent long-house.

A small, simple and probably rather late example of the first-floor hall is that at Tréubert 2, Trégunc, Finistère (VT 393956), built entirely of granite rubble with only the occasional piece of dressed stone. Externally the building measures 4.35 metres by 5.00 metres and internally 3.20 metres by 3.75 metres. It is thus shorter than it is wide, and of one-and-a-half storeys, the upper storey being reached by an external stone staircase (Fig. 48). The gable walls are offset to receive the slate roof and a half-dormer accommodates the entrance doorway to the first floor. The plain rubble chimney-stack belongs to a hearth on the first floor. There is no heating at ground-floor level.

An example of a first-floor hall located in the centre of a group of lesser dwellings is provided by Le Beuchet 3 (XU 422375), Saint-M'Hervé, Ille-et-Vilaine (Fig. 207). The house measures 5.70 metres long and 9.40 metres wide externally. Internal measurements are 4.55 metres by 8.35 metres respectively. Wall thickness is c. 0.60 metres. The height from ground to eaves is 3.50 metres at the upper end and the ridge stands 7.00 metres above the ground. Heights at the lower end are approximately 0.50 metres greater. Walling is of schist rubble and the roof is covered with slate. Lintels are of wood. The schist rubble walling is laid with a mortar of *pisé*. Walls are surprisingly thin for a building of this kind and this suggests a rather late date. The ground floor is covered with *terre battue*. At first-floor level the beams are covered by wooden boards and the upper surface of these is plastered with a layer of *pisé*. The presence of joists as well as beams is an indication of quality. Interior wall surfaces are also plastered with *pisé*. The roof structure is supported by only one truss of the full king-post type. The king-post carries a ridge-purlin, to which it is braced, and there is a pair of lateral purlins supported by cleats. The tie-beam rests on wall-plates, the latter being visible in the gable ends of the building. The house is very much wider than it is long and at first-floor level the end of the truss proper rests on a joist into which a

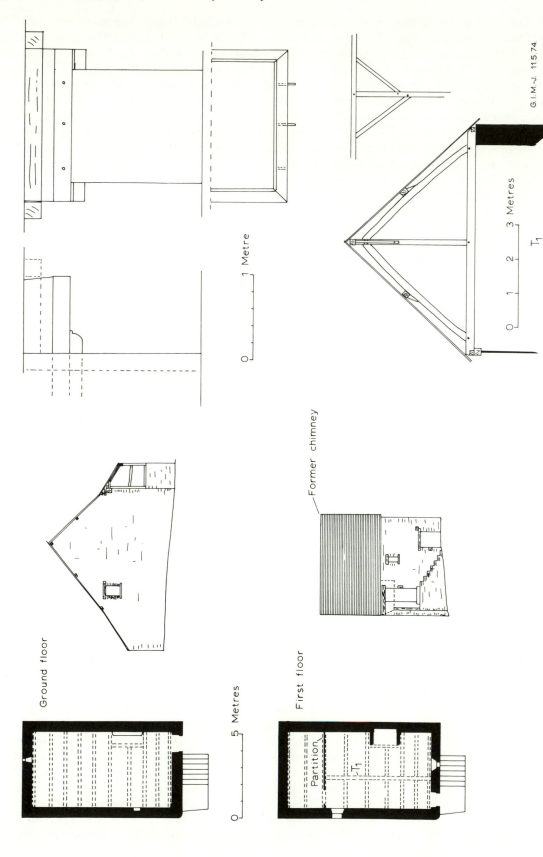

Ground floor

First floor

Partition

T₁

Former chimney

G.I.M.-J. 11.5.74.

1 Metre

0

Metres

0 1 2 3

T₁

5 Metres

0

Fig. 207. Le Beuchet 3, Saint-M'Hervé, Ille-et-Vilaine

wooden partition is slotted. The base of this partition is slotted into the sill. Purlins carry the common rafters, staggered at the apex, and to these are nailed wooden boards spaced a few centimetres apart. It is to these boards that the roof slates are nailed. Along the front elevation the roof line is sprocketed out and carried over the head of the stone stair. At the rear of the building the common rafters are carried over from the end of the line of the truss to the rear wall. The only hearth is at first-floor level but the ground-floor ceiling beams are arranged to carry the weight of the hearth-stone and the wall is corbelled out to provide additional support. The chimney is now demolished, but a chimney-hood of stone rubble is carried on a wooden breastsummer which in turn rests on wooden corbels. Three pegs formerly projected from the breastsummer, and household items were hung on these. One peg is now missing. Door and window openings are of simple construction. Jambs are of the same schist as the walling but wooden blocks are set into the jambs at those points where door fastenings are required. Lintels are of wood and it is a characteristic of the area that the lintels are in many cases under-cut to provide a low, rounded arch. This house is a small first-floor hall. At the time of survey the ground floor was used for storage but it is possible that it may once have served as a byre. There is no evidence of a drain. The hall is approached by a flight of external stone stairs terminating in a small landing protected by an oversailing roof supported on a light wooden framework. The hall is heated by a hearth in the upper gable and lighted by two small windows. A wooden partition separates the hall from a small store room in the outshot beyond. Le Beuchet 3 is not as finely built as Keradour, but dressed stone is rare in Saint-M'Hervé, and most of the lintels are of wood blocks undercut to provide a decorative arch.

At Tronoën, in Saint-Jean-Trolimon, Finistère (VU 007015), between a chapel and another house stands a first-floor hall, once the home of the priest (Fig. 208). The ground slopes steeply from the back of the building towards the front so that laterally the house is cut into a slope, the first-floor level at the rear being only slightly above ground level. The house measures externally, from the upper gable to the wall of the chapel, 8.85 metres. Width is 4.65 metres externally and 3.15 metres internally. The eaves are 3.80 metres and 2.40 metres above the ground at the front and the back respectively. The ridge rises 6.55 metres above the level of the ground floor.

Walling of dressed granite, with a rubble core and rubble for the inside facings of the walls, is set in a mortar of *pisé*. Roof covering is of *roseau*. The roof structure consists of a collar-and-tie-beam truss which carries a ridge-purlin and two pairs of lateral purlins set on cleats. Common rafters are spaced at intervals of *c.* 0.50 metres and are staggered at the apex. Thatching spars are laid horizontally at approximately the same interval and it is to these that the thatch is tied. At the time of survey the roof had decayed and collapsed. The gable wall at the upper end is offset to receive the thatch roof and the coping finished with triangular-shaped blocks. The floor at ground-floor level is of *terre battue* but at first-floor level is formed of wooden boards nailed to the common beams. The doorway has a flat-headed key-stone and circular arches so that is not quite a three-centred doorway. Window openings are small. The ground floor is lighted by windows W1, W2, W3 and W4, all of them little more than slits with flat-splay chamfers. W3 and W4, at the rear of the building, are at ground level. The first floor is lighted by windows W5, W6 and W7, of which W7 is little more than a slit and W5 is clearly the most important window in the house, placed at the end near the hearth and intended to provide light for a table which must once have lain adjacent to it. A garderobe also formerly existed at first-floor level, but the opening for this has been blocked and only the corbels now remain. The chimney-piece is formed of a breastsummer, a single piece of granite resting on plain granite corbels.

This house is the former chaplain's residence belonging to the chapel of Tronoën. It appears to have been built at a later date than the chapel and arranged to fill the space between two of the buttresses in the east wall of the chapel and a pre-existing house further to the east. The two buttresses form part of the lateral walls and the roof line formerly ended against the east wall of the chapel. The building is of generous length for a single-cell house but very narrow. It is clearly a first-floor hall but there is no evidence of a stair and there was once a doorway, now blocked, from the ground-floor cell into the chapel. Access to the first floor, in the absence of a doorway at first-floor level, must have been by way of doorway D1 and an internal staircase. The elaborate window, W5, and the existence of a garderobe, pointed to the high social status of the occupant. It is undated, and although a seventeenth-century date is possible, the doorway could be as late as eighteenth century.

At Languivoa in Plonéour-Lanvern, Finistère (VU 058073), another priest's house, lay until recently in ruins but has now been restored (Fig. 209). It stands on the south side of the ruined chapel with which it communicates directly by doorway D3 at ground-floor level. The building is integrated at one end with the walling of the adjacent chapel. Externally the structure measures 9.60 metres by 6.40 metres. The ground floor measures internally 7.80 metres by 4.85 metres, and the

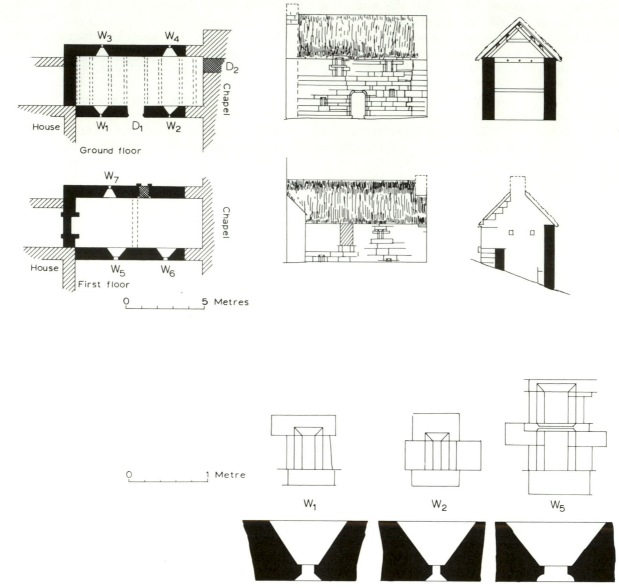

Fig. 208a.   Tronoën, Saint-Jean-Trolimon, Finistère

first floor 8.00 metres by 4.90 metres. The lateral walls are 0.75 metres thick. At ground-floor level one gable wall is 1.00 metres thick and the other 0.75 metres thick. The building rises two full storeys and the height from ground to eaves at the lower end is *c.* 5.00 metres, and the ridge stands *c.* 8.50 metres above the ground. Walling is of granite rubble carefully coursed and laid in a mortar of *pisé*. Quoins, door and window dressings are of cut granite. The roof is slate-covered. Flooring at ground-floor level is of *terre battue* and the first floor is formed of wooden boards nailed to the six common beams. There are also six common beams serving as tie-beams at first-floor level and two of these support upper king-post,

collar and tie-beam trusses. These carry a ridge purlin and two pairs of lateral purlins resting on cleats. Common rafters, staggered at the apex, are sprocketed out over the wall-heads. Although the roof structure is new, as surviving buildings of this quality in Finistère nearly always have an upper king-post truss, the reconstruction is plausible. The slate covering is nailed to wooden boarding fastened in turn to the common rafters. A dormer window is built into the hipped end of the roof and provides lighting for the roof space. There is a hearth at first-floor level. A massive granite breastsummer rests on granite corbels and carries the chimney-hood of stone rubble. The latter rises through the roof to finish in a

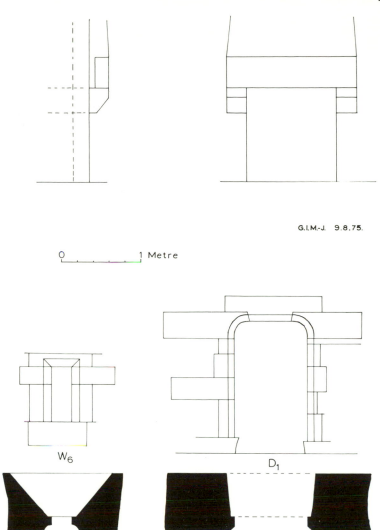

G.I.M.-J. 9.8.75.

0   1 Metre

W₆   D₁

Fig. 208b. Tronoën, Saint-Jean-Trolimon, Finistère

simple ornamented chimney. Door and window openings are of dressed granite blocks and these are mostly chamfered; the most common chamfer is the flat splay but doorway D2 bears a cavetto chamfer. Window openings W2 and W3 have plain jambs, lintels and sills. Window W6 retains its central iron bar, window W4 is plain but is associated inside with a keeping-place provided with a drain which finds its outward expression in a lip on the outside wall surface. Immediately below this drain is a similar feature provided for the ground-floor level. The eaves line is characterized by a moulded cornice. The most elaborate feature of the building is the square-headed dormer window with an elaborate Renaissance hood.

The building is a first-floor hall of considerable quality, intended as accommodation for a priest attached to the adjacent chapel. Access to the hall is by an external staircase rising to doorway D1. The hall is lighted by four windows and a keeping-place is provided next to the hearth; it is large and well-lighted. There is no internal communication between the first and the ground floors and the latter is provided with two doorways, one centrally placed in the lower gable, and a second in the upper gable providing direct entry from the ground floor into the chapel. There is no evidence of the former function of this ground-floor level. It may have been used as a store but it could also have served partly or wholly as a byre or a stable. By the mid-1970s the building had been reduced to a ruin with the walls only partly standing. Restoration and reconstruction were complete by 1975. As the rear wall had been almost completely destroyed there was no evidence of a former garderobe. None has

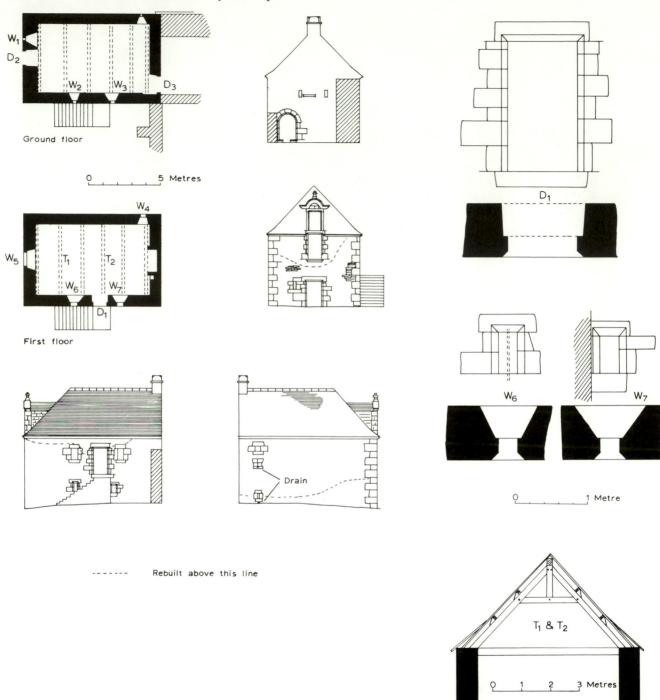

Ground floor

0   5 Metres

First floor

Drain

- - - - - -   Rebuilt above this line

D₁

W₆   W₇

0   1 Metre

T₁ & T₂

0   1   2   3 Metres

Fig. 209a.   Languivoa, Plonéour-Lanvern, Finistère

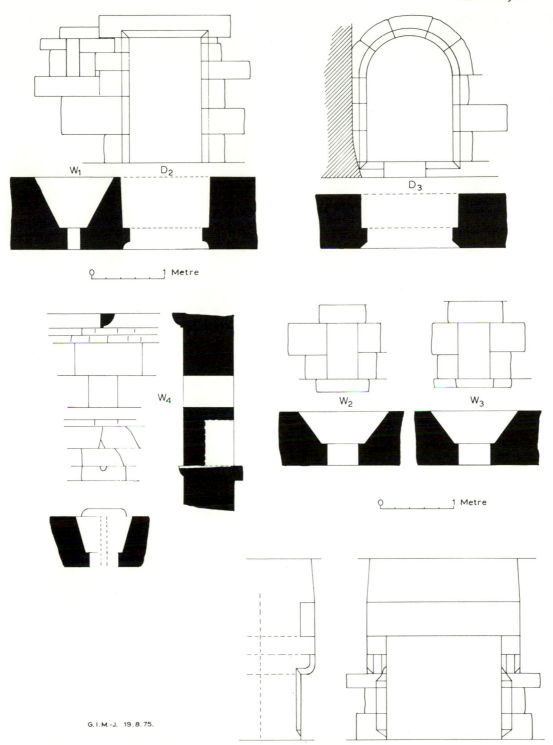

G.I.M.-J. 19.8.75.

Fig. 209b. Languivoa, Plonéour-Lanvern, Finistère

therefore been incorporated in the reconstructed building. It would, however, be surprising if a garderobe had not been provided at first-floor level in a building of this quality and it is not unreasonable to assume that one formerly existed but that all trace of it had disappeared before plans for reconstruction were made. Although undated, the building is probably of late sixteenth- or early seventeenth-century date.

Houses, not all first-floor halls, were once attached to many of the chapels in the Breton countryside. That at Saint-Héleau, in Plogonnec, was a long-house, but at Saint-Jean, Campénéac, the priest's house, now in ruins, was a first-floor hall. Other first-floor halls have been observed attached to, but not communicating internally with, adjacent manor houses. Two examples, at Kermorfezan and La Salle, are illustrated (Figs. 217, 222). Both lie over cells used for living purposes, probably, but not necessarily, by another family. External stone stairs, now demolished, gave access to these first-floor halls, each provided with a fine chimney-piece, showing, together with the garderobes and superior window dressings, that they must have been intended for families of some social status.

First-floor halls are found amongst the buildings recorded by the E.A.R. in all *départements* except Finistère. In Côtes-du-Nord, Ker Yagu Bian on the Île Grande is a row of dwellings and farm buildings which includes a first-floor hall over a ground-floor living room. Access to the hall is by a stairway contained in a rear outshot. There seems little doubt that the upper room with its monumental chimney-piece is the most important of the two rooms, and the building is dated 1613. High quality is apparent throughout, ceilings are fitted with joists as well as beams and the roof truss is a plain but solid upper king-post truss. Including the contemporary outshot, the building measures 8.70 by 7.75 metres externally, and the hall is 7.00 metres long by 3.75 metres wide internally. There is a wall recess of *c.* 0.30 metres in the hall to accommodate the bed, and the room below has a more pronounced bed-recess of *c.* 0.75 metres.[539]

Kernegan in Moustoir-Remungol, Morbihan, consists of a two-storey building attached to a one-and-a-half storey long-house with internal communication from the hall of the long-house to the ground floor of the two-storey end building. Both units have stone staircases built into stair turrets at the rear. The two-storey building, dated 1760, measures 8.75 metres long by 6.95 metres wide externally. The ground-floor was recorded as a *chambre* and by 1946 had assumed the function of a bedroom for the adjacent long-house. Whatever function this cell originally performed, there seems little doubt that

the first-floor room was the hall, an arrangement with an adjacent long-house, similar to that at Keradour, above.

A detached first-floor hall, still occupied as such in 1946, occurs at La Vallée in Pluherlin. The ground-floor cell, although provided with a hearth, served as a *cave* and store, a wooden partition dividing the room into two parts. A circular stone stair turret is built into one corner and this provides access to the first floor furnished in the traditional manner, with benches on either side of the hearth, table by the window and box-beds ranged round the walls. The building, of fine construction with much dressed stone, measures 9.20 by 7.50 metres externally and the hall is 7.70 metres long and 6.10 metres wide internally. The ceilings have beams and joists and there is storage space in the roof loft. As in other houses of fine build, the roof is supported by an upper king-post truss. A second first-floor hall in the same hamlet is of inferior construction. This hall, approached by an external stone stairway, stands over the byre. Externally it measures only 5.85 metres long and 4.45 metres wide. Another first-floor hall, of moderate quality, stood at Kerbillio in Gourin. There is no indication of the function of the unheated ground-floor room, but it was probably a byre. This hall, contained partly in the roof-space, has a monumental chimney-piece, but is little more than a loft with walls rising to less than 1.00 metre in height. Nevertheless it is an undoubted first-floor hall, 5.00 by 5.00 metres internally.[540]

A pair of adjacent dwellings at Clis in Guérande is dated 1699 and each has its principal doorway at first-floor level, approached by an external stone stairway. There can be little doubt that originally the main accommodation was the first-floor hall in each house.[541] In Ille-et-Vilaine a fine but undated example occurs at La Pierre de l'Ane, in Poilly. Built of schist with some ashlar courses and dressings, the house has a hearth in both first- and ground-floor rooms. Although at the date of the survey the ground floor had become the common living room the monumental character of the chimney-piece in the upper-room, together with the provision of a garderobe built into a corner, leaves no doubt that this was a first-floor hall. Carpentry is of a high order with joists and beams and an upper king-post truss. A wooden staircase is provided inside the house which measures 9.40 by 7.90 metres, externally, and the hall 7.60 metres long and 6.65 metres wide, internally.[542]

The first-floor hall is widely distributed in Brittany, and although many examples have now fallen into disuse or have become storage rooms or barns, others continue to perform their original function. Apart from the true first-floor halls, there are a few heated upper rooms associated with ground-floor rooms also used for living.

Where there is no internal communication between the two and the upper room can only be reached by an external stone stairway it seems probable that two entirely separate units of accommodation were intended originally for two families, the upper unit being a first-floor hall. Where, however, as at Ker Yagu Bian, or Kernegan, access to the first floor is by an internal stairway and the ground-floor cell is heated and used for living, then an alternative explanation must be considered. In this case the upper room may not have been a true first-floor hall, but a superior room used by senior members of the household as a private withdrawing room and perhaps also for sleeping. Here the function is that of a solar rather than of a first-floor hall. It is often very difficult to distinguish the two types on the basis of field evidence alone. The criteria of an internal stairway and heated ground-floor cell cannot be infallible, as many an intended ground-floor store may have been provided with a hearth as a provision for possible future change of function, as was done with the byres of some long-houses.

First-floor halls with separate dwelling units beneath are sometimes encountered attached to houses of the social level of the *manoir*. Examples at Kermorfezan (Fig. 222) and La Salle (Fig. 217) have been cited. There can be little doubt that these were true first-floor halls, for they communicate neither with the adjacent upper rooms of the *manoir*, nor with the separate single-cell dwelling beneath. They were accessible only by an external stone stairway and they were furnished with garderobes, a symbol both of independence and high social status. The other category of building with external stone stairway referred to by Le Lannou, very common in south Morbihan, is that with lofts often a full storey in height. These are not *maisons en hauteur*. The heated *chambre* over hall or long-house, common in the Monts d'Arrée, may not always have been a true first-floor hall. The example at Botmeur is a dwelling of the long-house and table-outshot type like that at Saint-Rivoal (Fig. 195). Although the upper room may have been a separate first-floor hall, this is not proven, and it may be that it served a function more akin to that of the solar. More oral and documentary evidence is required before this problem can be solved, but it is possible that uniformity of usage did not exist, that one such house may have been utilized differently to another, and that there may also have been changes with time.

A chronology of Breton first-floor halls is difficult to establish at this stage of research. That at La Salle may belong to the sixteenth century. Those with date-stones are of either seventeenth- or eighteenth-century date, and such halls may well have continued to be built into

the nineteenth century. The greatest concentrations of first-floor halls seem to occur in areas where land holdings have been small. It follows that they do not occur in the same number in those districts where large landowners were established by the end of the Middle Ages. The implication is therefore that they were favoured as the homes of a small landowning class who, because their land holdings were small, occurred in fairly large numbers. Where holdings had become engrossed, then large estates and *châteaux* to match were the rule. This liking for the first-floor hall during the sixteenth and seventeenth centuries was shared by the more prosperous *bourgeoisie*, as is evident from the examples in the towns and in prosperous areas like the Marais Salant. It is no accident either than some of the finest examples to survive were priests' houses, for many of the clergy were drawn from the sons of the gentry who might be expected to uphold some of the social values of their forebears. Certainly there is nothing yet known convincingly earlier than the sixteenth century, although further work may yet establish that earlier houses survive. It seems probable that the type derives directly from the first-floor halls of the medieval castles.

The link may well be provided by examples of the scale of Kerbiguet in Gourin, illustrated by the Commission d'Inventaire.[543] This is truly monumental, with an arcaded and pillared ground-floor, part of which might be considered to be a *salle de garde*, the main quarters being above, approached directly from outside by a flight of stone stairs. An even closer link may be provided by the hall at Le Fretay, in Pancé, Ille-et-Vilaine, which lies in the shadow of a medieval *motte*. There is the distinct possibility that the first-floor hall here was the first residence after the abandonment of the *motte*. The influence of the towns must not be overlooked. Well-known houses in Dol-de-Bretagne are essentially first-floor halls. That known as Les Petits Palets is strongly reminiscent of the Jew's House at Lincoln, has romanesque details and is attributed on stylistic evidence to the eleventh or twelfth centuries. Aristocratic and merchant classes modelled their town dwellings on the most socially advanced buildings of the day, and although the rural first-floor halls probably have a direct link with the medieval castles, the rural first-floor tradition was undoubtedly stimulated by the example of the towns. Indeed, it may wholly derive from urban influence which in turn may derive its inspiration from the Mediterranean. The surviving rural first-floor halls of Brittany represent a flowering of the type during the sixteenth and seventeenth centuries, when the lesser gentry and small landowners were building new houses in the aftermath of Union with France and the more prosperous times it brought. By the eighteenth century, the type was outmoded and ground-floor living became fashionable for the wealthy. Conservative ways persisted, however, in remote areas, and although the upper classes discontinued the practice of building such halls, many families continued to live in them. Eighteenth- and even nineteenth-century examples are known, presumably built by the conservative at heart, or by persons lower down the social scale who sought, belatedly, to imitate their superiors. Those families who abandoned their first-floor halls for larger buildings with ground-floor accommodation were replaced by tenants. Many such halls continue to this day to be occupied by peasant families.

The association of these buildings with houses of superior social status, or pronounced economic prosperity, together with the generally high quality of workmanship which they display, leaves little doubt that they were built for persons high in the rural hierarchy. It is no accident that the clergy chose first-floor halls for their own accommodation, but it would probably be wrong to associate them with any one section of the upper classes. Those persons who regarded themselves as being socially superior, or who were accorded such status by their fellows, and who also had the means to build, often favoured the first-floor hall. The fact that when they occur in a hamlet, there is rarely more than one of a type, suggests that they were intended for use by either the landowner or his representative, perhaps a bailiff or steward charged with the supervision of an estate. This would be a plausible explanation at La Salle where the first-floor hall is adjacent to the solar, and although it does not communicate directly with the latter, both share the same garderobe, surely sufficient indication that the occupants of the first-floor hall were of comparable social status to those of the solar.

The first-floor halls so far recorded are late in date and lack overt defensive characteristics. The type may have originated in the Mediterranean lands and been brought northwards before the present millennium. Whether the original halls were defensive or not, they certainly came to be favoured by the upper rural social classes so that by the seventeenth century in Brittany they were widely diffused although proportionately few. No doubt in a country where most peasants lived cheek to jowl with their livestock, the elevation of the living room provided a degree of cleanliness and comfort valued by the few who could afford it.

TWELVE

THE TWO-CELL HOUSE

The two-cell houses occur in each of the twenty-one sample quadrats (Fig. 79), and have been observed in every part of Brittany, but proportions, compared with other types, vary considerably. In general, the highest percentages were encountered in the coastal areas. In Quadrat 1 (Plougrescant) fifty-two per cent fell into this category, eighty-nine per cent in Quadrat 2 (Plouzané/Locmaria-Plouzané), seventy-six per cent in Quadrat 8 (Plogoff/Primelin), eighty-six per cent in Quadrat 9 (Dinéault), and fifty-eight per cent in Quadrat 14 (Moëlan-sur-Mer). High percentages were also encountered in some interior areas, as in Quadrat 5 (Carnoët) with fifty-one per cent and Quadrat 15 (Pont-Scorff) with fifty-six per cent. Only slightly lower were the figures encountered in Quadrat 3 (Plougasnou) with forty-per cent, Quadrat 5 (La Harmoye/Le Haut-Corlay) with twenty-nine per cent, Quadrat 6 (Plévenon) with thirty-six per cent, Quadrat 10 (Plévin) with twenty-nine per cent and Quadrat 17 (Béganne) with twenty-one per cent. The remaining quadrats yielded figures below twenty per cent. Quadrat 11 (Taupont) had eighteen per cent, Quadrat 12 (Paimpont) fifteen per cent, Quadrat 18 (Joué-sur-Erdre) fourteen per cent, Quadrat 19 (Guérande) fifteen per cent, Quadrat 20 (Frossay) nineteen per cent, and Quadrat 21 (Saint-Lumine-de-Clisson/Saint-Hilaire-de-Clisson) sixteen per cent. The lowest percentages were in Quadrat 16 (Grand-Champ) with eleven per cent, Quadrat 13 (Saint-M'Hervé) with ten per cent and Quadrat 7 (Sougéal/Antrain/La Fontenelle) with seven per cent. These percentages, summarized cartographically (Fig. 102), show the predominance of the two-cell house on the western and northern littoral and adjacent areas. Proportions fall in the west-central interior and are lower still in east-central areas. The lowest proportions are in Morbihan, the south-east, and along the eastern Marches, the very areas in which the survival of large numbers of long-houses and one-cell dwellings has been observed. Not surprisingly, these are the agriculturally retarded areas with a predominance of small farms.

Many two-cell houses were obviously built as such, whilst others appear to result from modernization and adaptation. Castel 6, Plougrescant (Fig. 80), is a good example of a two-cell single-storey house in which both cells are heated, and one, presumably the hall, lighted by two windows, is considerably larger than the other. The building appears to be of nineteenth-century date. Locmaria 2, Locmaria-Plouzané (Fig. 81) is a symmetrical two-cell two-storey house probably of eighteenth-century, or earlier, date. Both ground-floor cells are heated, and although the upper rooms are large enough to have been used as additional *chambres*, it is likely that they were originally intended for storage. Reference has already been made to the conversion of long-houses to two-cell dwellings, and field observation suggests that very large numbers of two-cell houses originated in this way. Such conversions are frequently betrayed by the existence of a large modern window-opening at the former byre end, not matching the original window dressing of the hall. In other cases completely new, and larger, windows have been inserted into an older house, giving an appearance of symmetry. Such appears to have been the case at Quinquis Simon 2, Carnoët (Fig. 83). Here the lower room is unheated, another indication that it may once have served as a byre. Pennalé 2, Dinéault, and Kernantal 2, Plévin (Figs. 88 and 89) fall into the same category. Both are single-storey dwellings with an unheated lower end. Whilst the window openings in both houses are probably original, ideas about symmetry may well have led to long-houses being built in this way during the nineteenth century. As Vallaux has pointed out, the lower ends of many long-houses were often converted to second rooms if needs dictated, only to revert to a byre at a later date.[544] Two-cell houses combined with a byre are long-houses. It is necessary here only to recall their existence and draw attention to the example at Le Tetre 7, Plévenon (Fig. 85). Of the large two-cell houses of Cap-Sizun, below, the example at Kermalero 3, Primelin should be noted (Fig. 87). There is evidence that some of these dwellings

265

18

were re-builds of former long-houses on the same ground plan.

Not surprisingly, in a country with such a large proportion of one-cell dwellings and long-houses, the two-cell dwelling was the expression of wealth and social position before the nineteenth century when it came to represent the home of those lower down the social scale whose lot was improving. In earlier centuries, dwellings of the *manoir* class were frequently of the two-cell type. Les Hauts Talus, Montgermont, and Fresnay Normandie, Melesse (Figs. 44 and 52), are indicative of the relative prosperity of the Rennes basin and display varied regional styles. Les Hauts Talus is a large courtyard farm associated with a first-floor hall. The principal house is a two-cell dwelling, probably of late seventeenth-century date and essentially Gothic in feeling. Like Fresnay Normandie it may well have been built by a *bourgeois* from Rennes anxious to invest money in land. Fresnay Normandie represents a category of two-cell house widely distributed in north-east Ille-et-Vilaine. Most examples are of two storeys, with the ground-floor cells, which communicate internally, being heated and having separate access from outside. The type may be compared with the long-house, first derivative, in which the byre has a separate entrance from outside, and from which it may derive. Usually one of the doorways is larger and more elaborately treated than the other as if to imply seniority or social superiority. Several interpretations are possible. The second cell may have been a store, derived from the byre of a long-house, with direct access from outside. Alternatively, the type may have housed a landowner living in the 'upper' end with his family, whilst the farmer occupied the lower end. Such an arrangement would accord with the *métayage* system once much commoner in Brittany. It would also be consistent with the almost universal practice of families living in one room (see Chapter 15). Other possibilities are that the two cells served as separate dwellings for two related families, father and son, or two brothers, working a farm in common, or for two families, one of servant status. Alternatively, but perhaps less likely, the plan exhibits a desire to create a second living room, the beginnings of specialization of function. If this is so, it is difficult to understand why a second outside doorway was needed.

These examples from sample quadrats and elsewhere serve to illustrate the variety of two-cell houses, large and small, of both one and two storeys, and displaying considerable variation in building material and regional style. The subjective impression gained from the survey is that apart from the minority of large houses that are unmistakably of seventeenth- or eighteenth-century date,

the large majority of the smaller two-cell houses have a distinctly nineteenth-century air about them. They appear either to have been built, or largely rebuilt, during that century, or the first part of the twentieth century, or they represent former long-houses whose byres were converted to form a second cell, often remaining unheated.

Several authors have commented upon the existence of the two-cell house. Le Lannou describes a 'typical' interior as consisting of a central corridor with two opposed doorways, one leading to the *cuisine*, the common living room or hall, the other to the *salle*, a room used only on special occasions.[545] The traditional furniture and layout associated with the hall (see Chapter 15) is not found in the *salle*, which often has a smaller chimney-piece, modern furniture, and frequently also performs a storage function. Gautier observes a second room, *'une petite pièce, en "salle" '*, generally paved, to be found in *'les fermes les plus importantes'*.[546] Serving mainly to receive visitors, it might also contain an ordinary bed and a sewing machine. There is no doubt that the *salle* served for only occasional use and played a minor role to that of the hall. Fournier makes similar observations of Bulat-Pestivien, Côtes-du-Nord.[547] It was in the larger farms and *manoirs*, between the two World Wars, that a second cell, *'une salle à manger de parade'*, was to be found. Vallaux observed, at the beginning of the twentieth century, that whilst the practice of living entirely in one room still reigned supreme over most of Brittany, a second room had made its appearance in many parts of Basse-Bretagne. The arrangement was always the same: central cross-passage serving as a vestibule, bounded by wooden partitions, at the end of which a staircase led to the first floor. On one side of the cross-passage was the hall, on the other the *'salle'*. The hall was the heart of the house, the *'salle'* a reception room *'constamment déserte; l'homme, la femme, les enfants, les serviteurs vivent et mangent dans la cuisine'*.[548]

Gauthier illustrates numerous examples of the two-cell house, of both one and two storeys, from places as far apart as Essé, Ille-et-Vilaine, Guilers, and Plozévet, Finistère, Quiberon and Bieuzy, Morbihan.[549] Two-plan variations are regarded as being typical, but essentially very simple. In small dwellings, two rooms existed, one by the entry serving as a store-room, the other a *salle commune*. or hall, For 'middling' houses, the doorway opens on to a central corridor bounded by wooden partitions. Two rooms are both heated, one serving as a hall, the second as a *salle réservée* or occasional room. The first of these types is in reality a single-cell dwelling with storage space at the lower end, the hall having been separated from the entrance by a partition. Gauthier's view of the Breton house is a romantic one, disregards the existence of the long-house, and pays scant attention to the possibility of other plan-types. Nevertheless, he draws attention to the fact that both one and two-roomed dwellings were extremely common by the mid-twentieth century.

Writing of Plouvien, Finistère, Guilcher demonstrates that the two-cell house was known in the area in the eighteenth century, in only a minority of farms.[550] Inventories show that seventeen farms in Plouvien then had a second ground-floor room and twelve others a second room of uncertain function. The two-cell dwelling might then have represented about ten per cent of the total if the inventories are representative, which they are almost certainly not (see Chapter 15). The increase in numbers of the two-cell house appears to have accompanied the building of a second storey, from 1845–1850 onwards in Plouvien, where some forty-five per cent of storeyed houses date from before 1900, the chief period being 1880–1900. Often the new house was built on the same site, and even on the same foundations. Many of these houses were still of only one storey, or perhaps one-and-a-half storeys, the *grenier*, or storage loft, also being used for extra sleeping accommodation. This *grenier habité* represents an intermediate stage between the one-storey and the two-storey house. The late development of the two-cell house, of both one and two storeys, is confirmed by evidence from Côtes-du-Nord. A greater degree of comfort was general on the littoral where *'les chambres à lits des maîtres de la maison sont communément placées au premier étage; quelquefois on a une salle ou un cabinet isolé: c'est la qu'on reçoit les étrangers'*, contrary to the interior of Brittany where the one-cell house reigned supreme.[551]

Evidence from the *pays de Quimper*, at the end of the eighteenth and beginning of the nineteenth centuries, suggests that the two-cell house was then known.[552] The houses of Cléden-Cap-Sizun were all built on the same model, only the dimensions varying.[553] The central doorway opened on to a cross-passage at the end of which a stairway provided access to the first floor. On one side was the *cuisine*, or hall, on the other a room often divided into two parts, one serving as a reception room for special occasions, the other used for the heavy household work such as the preparation of animal feed, and also as a dairy. In the eighteenth century most houses seem to have been of only one storey but of two-cell plan.[554] The majority of farmhouses in the *commune* of Goulien, also in Cap-Sizun, were built before 1857.[555] House-types changed little from the end of the eighteenth

century to the beginning of the twentieth. In the seventeenth century they were of only one storey, but by the nineteenth century a fully developed second storey was common. The plan, from the seventeenth century onwards, consisted of a cross-passage separating two cells, one the hall, the other a store. In storeyed houses, the second ground-floor cell served as a *salle à manger* for special occasions. At the end of the cross-passage a stairway, beneath which was a store, gave access to the first floor, the rooms of which were becoming true bedrooms.

Transition from single-cell to two-cell houses is evident in the *pays de Porzay* during the nineteenth century. The former hall was divided, except in the poor *penty*, and wooden partitions separated the new hall from the *'salle'* used only on special occasions. Storeys were added and bedrooms established.[556] In the *arrondissement* of Quimper in 1801, the two-cell house was common and in 1829 *'la maison d'habitation mesure . . . 12 à 15 metres de long pour 6 à 7 metres de large. Elle se compose de 2 pièces séparées par un mur de refend . . . La maison est percée de 2 portes, une dans chaque façade et de 2 ou 3 fenêtres . . .'*.[557] Both one- and two-storey, two-cell houses became common during the nineteenth century.[558] In the early-nineteenth century, two-cell houses were rare in the *arrondissement* of Morlaix, but in Brest two rooms separated by *'une mauvaise cloison'* seem to have been more common.[559]

This general trend towards the two-cell house with the hall retaining all its basic functions, but with the development of a second cell, used mainly for housework, but serving also as a reception room for special occasions, increased and it was recognized, along with the single-cell house, as being a dominant type by the mid-twentieth century. Whilst the single-cell house remained on small farms, many in Côtes-du-Nord were by then divided into two rooms. The same was true of Finistère, Loire-Atlantique and Morbihan.[560]

Seven buildings were surveyed in detail as representative of the two-cell house. Classification is based on ground-floor plan only, although in some instances upper rooms were used for purposes other than storage. Trévinou in Saint-Jean-Trolimon, Finistère (VU 041011), is a large house with a total external length of *c.* 21.00 metres and a maximum width of 11.45 metres (Fig. 210). The external width of the hall is 6.55 metres. Internal length is *c.* 18.55 metres and the internal width of the principal rooms 5.20 metres. The height of the eaves above ground level is 5.80 metres and the ridge rises to 6.90 metres above the ground. Wall thickness varies considerably but the original front and rear walls are 0.65 metres thick, the hall gable is 1.35 metres thick

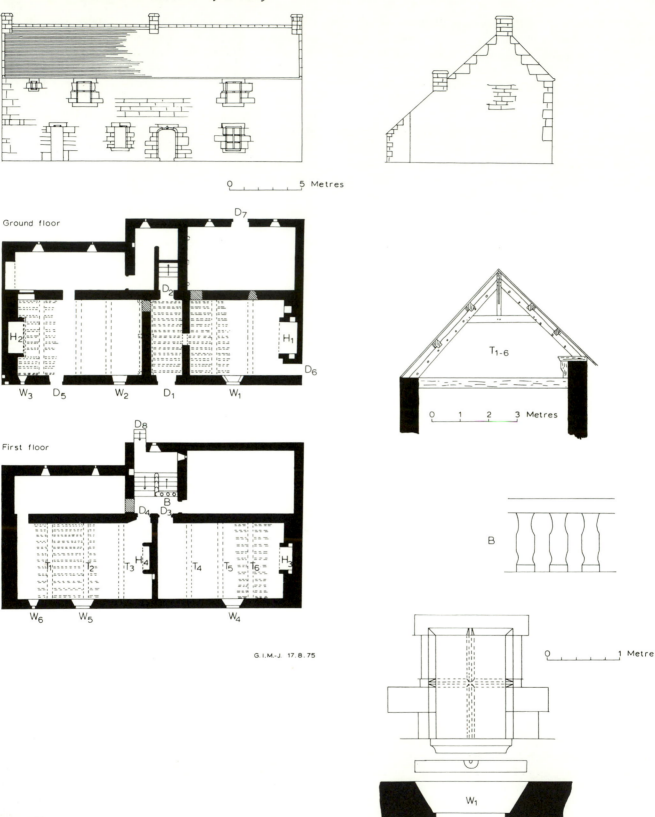

0 —————— 5 Metres

Ground floor

D₇
D₂
H₂   H₁
D₆
W₃   D₅   W₂   D₁   W₁

T₁₋₆

0   1   2   3 Metres

D₈
First floor
B
D₄ D₃
T₁ T₂ T₃ H₄ T₄ T₅ T₆ H₃
W₆   W₅   W₄

G.I.M.-J. 17.8.75

B

0 —————— 1 Metre

W₁

Fig. 210a. Trévinou, Saint-Jean-Trolimon, Finistère

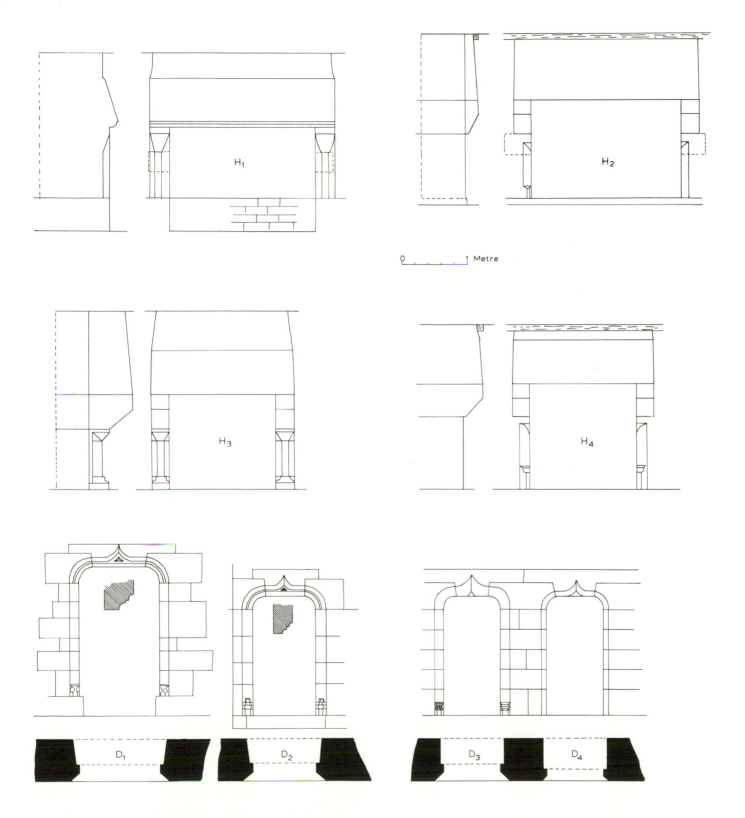

Fig. 210b. Trévinou, Saint-Jean-Trolimon, Finistère

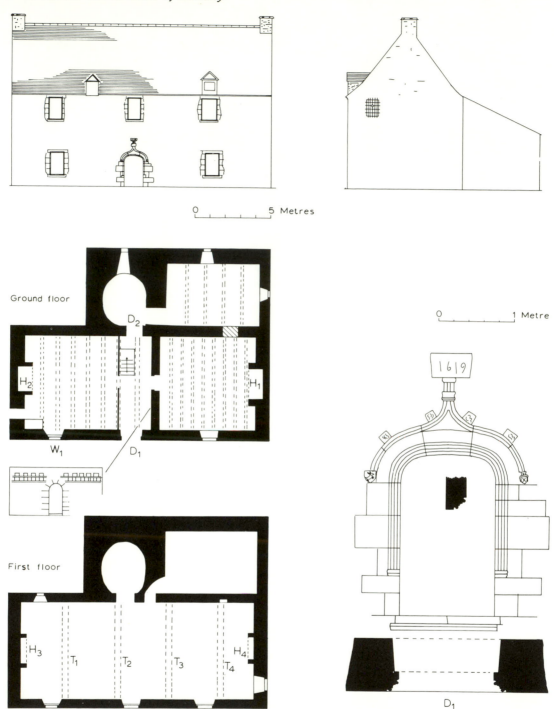

Fig. 211a.   Kerrio 5, Grand-Champ, Morbihan

and the lower gable wall 1.15 metres thick. Walling is entirely of granite. The front elevation and all doorway and window dressings and the chimney-piece dressings are of granite ashlar. So too are the chimneys and the copings. Gable walls and much of the rear of the building are of granite rubble. The roof is slate-covered and the ridge finished with red tiles. Walling is laid in a mortar of *pisé*. The floors of the hall, cross-passage and the second cell were all formerly paved with granite slabs, a sure indication of affluence as well as of the availability of

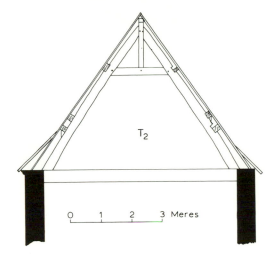

T₂

0 1 2 3 Meres

G. I. M.-J. 8.7.71

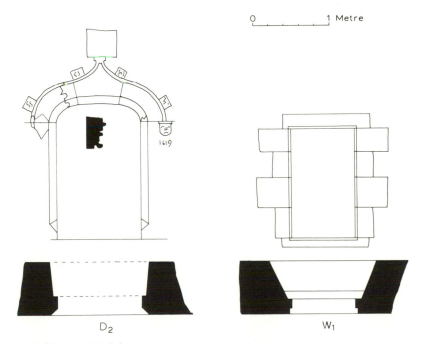

0   1 Metre

1619

D₂   W₁

Fig. 211b. Kerrio 5, Grand-Champ, Morbihan

suitable stone. First-floor rooms had their floors boarded over the ground-floor ceiling of common beams and joists. The loft floor, over the first-floor rooms was of *pisé* rolled over *batons* of chestnut in the manner once widespread in Brittany. It seems possible that the rooms at first-floor level were also originally floored in this manner. Roof structure is asymmetrical, resulting from the need to carry the roof line over the rear outshot; this confirms the observation that the smaller of the rear outshots is an original feature, for there is no straight joint in the gable wall. The rear wall of the two principal rooms thus rises over a metre higher than the front wall and the principal rafter rests on a sole plate which is, in turn, supported by a post whose foot rests on the tie-beam.

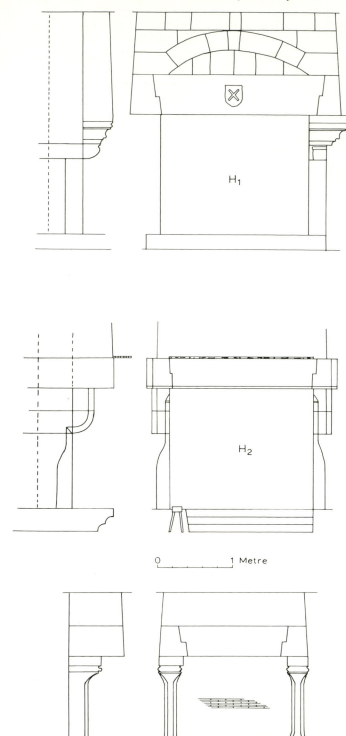

H₁

H₂

0   1 Metre

H₃,₄

Fig. 211c.   Kerrio 5, Grand-Champ, Morbihan

The remainder of the roof trusses are entirely typical of the better quality housing of Brittany. Principal rafters carry a collar which supports an upper king-post which in turn carries the ridge purlin. King-posts are braced upwards to the ridge purlin and the principal rafters are slotted to carry two pairs of lateral purlins which are also supported, in part, by pegs driven into the principal rafters. Common rafters rest with their feet on the heads of the front wall but are carried over the rear wall of the two upstairs rooms and over to the rear wall of the outshot and stair turret. The common rafters are boarded over and the slates nailed directly to these boards.

There are four chimney-pieces of high quality but each is different in design and, in some cases, left-hand and right-hand jambs differ as in H1 and H2. The finest chimney-piece, entirely of granite, is H1 serving the hall, with a particularly high hearth-stone. The breastsummer, as in all four chimney-pieces, is of a single massive slab of granite. Whilst the hall is provided with the finest of all four chimney-pieces, that in the second cell is only slightly less grand. Upstairs the two chimney-pieces are somewhat smaller in dimensions and significantly shallower, as it was presumably not intended that they should be used for cooking purposes. Chimney-pieces H3 and H4, notwithstanding their slightly smaller dimensions, are nevertheless of high quality. It is interesting to note that neither of them bears any trace of ever having been used, unlike the two downstairs hearths. The axial chimney-stack on the dividing wall gives the building, along with its gable stacks, a false appearance of having a three-unit plan.

Doorways are all fundamentally of the same style with ogee heads in the flamboyant style; the rather severe outline suggests a late date and the whole building could be as late as the eighteenth century. The principal entrance doorway D1 is the largest and finest of the group but that to the stair-well, D2, is only slightly smaller in dimensions and scarcely less fine. At the head of the stair-well, doorways D3 and D4 give access to the two upper rooms and, from the size of D3 and the width of its chamber compared with that of D4, there is no doubting which of the two rooms was the more important. This observation is confirmed by the chimney-piece, H3, being significantly finer than H4. It would thus appear that the upper room above the hall was the more important of the two upper rooms. Doorway D6 is a late insertion to give access to a modern outbuilding, D7 is also provided to give access to an outshot added later, and D8 is a recent insertion in the rear of the stair turret. Doorway D5 is not original and results from the probably recent alteration of a window-opening. Several doorways, including that from the cross-passage into the second cell, are now blocked. Windows W1, W4 and W5 are substantially in their original condition except that in the case of W5 both the mullion and transom have been removed and the mullions are missing from the upper windows W4 and W5; they were presumably fitted with wooden shutters. The hall is thus marked out by having a window of the same size and importance as those of the two upper rooms. The second cell, however, was originally provided with two long, narrow windows, the lintels and one of the jambs of which survive. The second of these windows was probably quite recently turned into a doorway at the same time that the door opening into the second cell from the cross-passage was blocked. A small slit, W3, provided additional light to the hearth end of the second cell, and a small slit above provides additional light to the upper room. The staircase is fine in its way but the granite has been worked in a somewhat clumsy manner; the balustrade at the head of the stairs is supported on three massive granite columns.

This was the home of someone of considerable wealth and social position in the rural hierarchy but it remains nevertheless basically a two-cell house with additional rooms above. Like Kerrio 5, below, it is probable that the cross-passage originally opened directly into the hall and was not bounded physically by a partition on the hall side. The present stone wall separating the cross-passage from the hall is only 0.50 metres thick, has straight joints at its junctions with the lateral walls, and is pierced by a doorway of rather poor quality. It is also built underneath a ceiling beam. Thus it is virtually certain that the original cross-passage opened directly into the hall and that, at the end of the passage, doorway D2 provided access to the stair turret which was a ceremonial way up to the two upper chambers with their fine doorways D3 and D4. The blocked doorway in the hall was effectively the way out into the yard at the back, for the rear outshot here, with its doorway D7, is clearly an addition as betrayed by the straight joints and the thinner walls. The hall was also provided with a small window on this, the yard, side. At the end of the cross-passage a doorway, now blocked, gave access to the second cell which also, as in the case of Kerio 5, probably served as a kitchen, providing sleeping and other accommodation also for the domestic staff. It was lighted by a small opening, W3, and two long narrow windows, now replaced by W2 and doorway D5, the chamfers on the lintels betraying the original lights. The window pattern would appear to suggest a function quite different from that of the hall, with W3 intended to light the working area around the hearth. The room is provided with a large keeping-place in one corner, and a doorway provides access to an original outshot which communicates, in turn, with a store-room beneath the

staircase. This outshot was heated, the chimney-piece now being demolished, and lighted by two small slits. It seems probable that the second cell served as a kitchen, additionally providing all necessary living accommodation for domestics. The outshot and the small room under the stairs would thus most likely have been for the storage, and perhaps even the preparation, of food. This interpretation is consistent with the architectural and archaeological evidence. Hearths H1 and H2 are both massive but H1 is the more elaborate and the hearth-stone set high. Hearth H2 is plainer, and the hearth-stone set lower, suggesting that it was designed more as a working hearth, whilst H1 was primarily for heating and display. The hall would thus have been a true common hall, the senior members of the family withdrawing to the upper rooms for privacy. The importance of the staircase here is not in doubt. The entrance doorway is fine. An attempt is made to decorate the staircase itself, at the head of which two three-centred ogee-headed doorways give access to the upper rooms. The relative importance of these is betrayed by the larger and more elaborate doorway D3. Hearth H3 in this room is also considerably finer than H4. Thus the upper room above the hall is the more important of the two. A second upper room has direct access to the loft over the original outshot. The fact that the upstairs hearths have never had a fire lit in them may indicate that they were never occupied as heated chambers but perhaps were used as rooms for sleeping purposes only. The evidence suggests that it may be unlikely that they ever performed the function of a solar and certainly not of a first-floor hall. Perhaps this is a case of the architectural provisions never being put to their intended purpose. A doorway from the top of the stairs to the loft over the lower outshot is late in date. The present doorway, D8, to the stair turret from outside, is recent and it is probable that the stair turret was originally higher and crowned with a conical roof, providing access to the loft in the roof, but it is now partly demolished and reduced in height. The house is difficult to date. Three-centred doorheads are recorded in each century from the sixteenth to the nineteenth (Fig. 80). A date in the seventeenth or early-eighteenth century seems the more likely in view of the severe style of doorway and window openings.

Kerrio 5 in Grand-Champ, Morbihan (WT 108919), is also a large house of two full storeys and a loft (Fig. 211). The house measures 17.20 metres long and 7.55 metres wide externally, 15.30 metres long and 6.15 metres wide internally. A stair turret and rear outshot further extend the building. Wall thickness is c. 0.70 metres with the end walls increasing to 1.00 metre and the stair turret with walls of variable thickness. The straight joints between the house and the outshot show that the latter is an addition, and the doorway from the base of the stair turret was presumably driven through the wall at the time the addition was made, as was the entrance to the loft above from the first floor. The eaves rise 6.15 metres above the ground and the ridge stands 10.90 metres above ground level.

The granite walling is laid in a mortar of *pisé*. Roughly dressed granite blocks are used for the doorway and window openings as well as for the hearths and some of the doorways inside the house. One of the dormer windows is framed with granite rubble, the other with wood. Chimneys are of granite rubble. The roof is slate-covered, with a red-tile ridge. The floor is of *terre battue* in the hall but the kitchen is paved with stone. Flooring at first-floor level is of wooden boards nailed to the closely spaced common beams; above this are the four tie-beams which almost certainly once supported another floor forming a loft served by the two dormer windows. There are four hearths, all of fine quality dressed stone. The hall is heated by hearth H1, with its magnificent chimney-piece of granite bearing a shield of arms with the cross of St. Andrew. Chimney-piece H2, serving the kitchen, is only marginally less fine. The hearth-stone here is curiously under-cut, presumably to allow easier access for cooking, and is offset at one side, permitting the insertion of a wooden bench of the traditional Breton type. This chimney-piece has the traditional wooden shelf set above the breastsummer. Chimney-pieces serving what may once have been two separate cells at first-floor level are identical, and the chimney-backs here are formed of small red tiles, possibly imported from the Nantes area. All these chimney-pieces are of first-class workmanship and set the house apart as being the home of a considerable landowner. This impression is furthered by the magnificent flamboyant-style doorway at the front of the house, a feature which is repeated at the entrance to the stair turret. The date 1619, certainly that of the building of the house, appears on both doorways. The cross-passage which now holds a wooden staircase (the original stone stair having fallen in), is bounded by a stone wall on one side and a wooden partition on the other. It is possible that this stone wall is an original feature but it seems more likely that it is a later insertion. It would accord more closely with observations elsewhere if the cross-passage had originally been bounded physically on one side only and had opened directly into the hall on the other. The stone wall, however, be it original or not, contains nesting-holes for pigeons, a curious feature.

There is a blocked doorway between the hall and the rear outshot, and another doorway, not marked on the plan, exists in the gable wall of the kitchen, giving access from the kitchen to a byre added later. The windows are large and moulded to receive wooden shutters. At first-floor level the original shutters remain *in situ* and this house was almost certainly not glazed in its original form. The first-floor window in the upper gable with its iron *grille* is a good indication of the way in which windows were originally finished. The survival of large areas of rendering on the exterior walls shows beyond question that the rubble walling was originally rendered with a covering of *pisé*. A similar coating of *pisé* remains in places on the interior walls and has been whitewashed. Roof structure is typical of houses of this quality. From the tie-beams rise the principal rafters which support the collar on which stands an upper king-post supporting a ridge-purlin. Lateral purlins are either slotted into the principal rafters or they rest on cleats. Common rafters, with their feet resting on the wall-heads, are sprocketed out at the base and support wooden boarding into which the slates are nailed.

An interpretation similar to that for Trévinou is possible. The hall was the common living room, designed for show, and the second cell, probably the working kitchen, also providing living accommodation for domestics. Hall and cross-passage are paved with *terre battue*, the second cell with stone. That the hall, the most important room, was not similarly treated may be explained by the fact that *terre battue* is warmer and more comfortable, but the stone harder wearing and perhaps more suitable for the working kitchen of a large house. A later byre now adjoins the house on the left, and a doorway in the gable of the second cell provides direct access. It is difficult to say whether this doorway is an original feature intended from the start to connect with a byre on that side. The upper floor must originally have been subdivided, perhaps into three cells, two heated. The hearths are of identical construction, are of fine quality and have brick firebacks. Kerrio 5 is conceived on a slightly more modest scale than Trévinou. There was no original outshot for storage and the upper rooms are less elaborate. Ceilings are supported by common beams, joists — always a sign of wealth and quality — being absent. Such an arrangement is typical of Morbihan.

This is an important two-cell house clearly designed as such from the start. The outshot was probably added to serve as a food store or a dairy, and the loft over the outshot provides storage for grain. The fact that the upper rooms are heated suggests that they were either used originally for sleeping, or more likely as a solar within the house. One or more of them may even have performed the function of a first-floor hall. The association of the most magnificent hearth, H1, with an

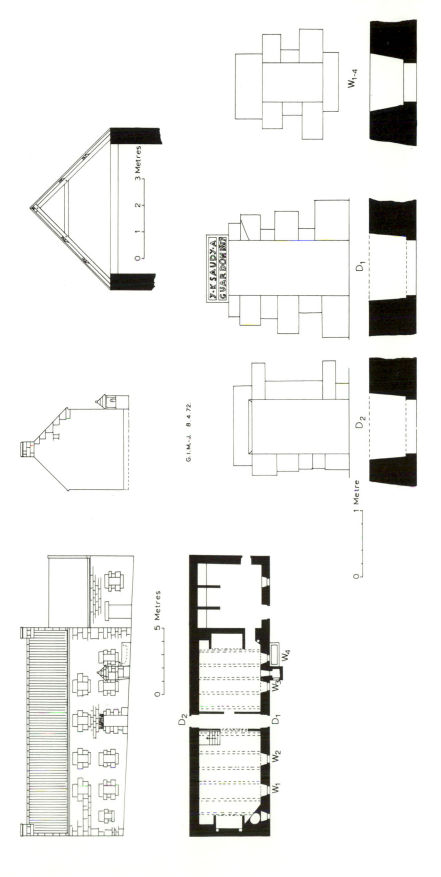

Fig. 212. Landrer 1, Plogoff, Finistère

earth floor and the somewhat less splendid hearth, H2, with a stone floor need not surprise. The earth floor would have been more appropriate for the common hall, even though provided with the finest hearth, whilst the stone floor would have been appropriate for a working kitchen, which the second cell almost certainly was from the beginning. This kitchen would also have served effectively as a single-cell dwelling for some of the domestic staff whilst the senior members of the family could have withdrawn from the common hall to the upstairs chambers. Kerrio 5 thus probably represents the house of an early-seventeenth century landowner of modest means.

Reference to the large two-cell house of the Cap-Sizun region has already been made. These buildings, identified in sample Quadrat 8, have been described by Pelras[561] and Bernard[562] and possess characteristic interior arrangements (see Chapter 15). The examples observed in Quadrat 8 nearly all bear date-stones and some are clearly rebuilds of earlier houses on the same site and, occasionally, the same ground-plan. Dates start at the end of the eighteenth century and continue to the early twentieth, but the majority fall between 1800 and 1840, indicating a considerable phase of building and re-building (Fig. 78). Most of these houses are also inscribed with the names of the builder and sometimes that of his wife. Landrer 1 in Plogoff, Finistère (UU 776215) is a good example, dated 1817 (Fig. 212). Walling is entirely of granite, with ashlar used for the front elevation and rubble for the end and rear elevations. The roof was formerly slate-covered but was probably originally thatched. It is now covered with asbestos sheeting and has a red-tile ridge. The total external length of the house is 15.80 metres and the width 6.10 metres. Corresponding interior dimensions are 14.00 metres and 4.70 metres. The byre extends the length of the house by a further 5.50 metres. Lateral walls of the house are 0.70 metres, and the end wall *c.* 0.90 metres, thick. The walls of the byre are 0.65 metres thick. Maximum height of the eaves above the ground is 4.90 metres and the ridge rises to 8.00 metres above ground level. The ground drops from left to right, about 0.80 metres, and from front to back.

Stone walling is laid in a mortar of *pisé*. The grey granite of the district is an excellent building stone and cuts readily into rectangular blocks. It also takes bold but simple detail well, as in the case of the chimney-capping and cavetto moulding of the cove. Doorway and window dressings are plain and simple and give the house a somewhat austere appearance. As is customary in this district, the name of the original builder or inhabitant is carved on the doorway lintel together with the date of

building, in this case 1817. Flooring is entirely of *terre battue*, except for the cross-passage which is paved with stone. The passage is physically bounded on both sides by partitions of wooden planks set into a stone sill. This finish is of high quality and relatively rare in Brittany, being confined to a few prosperous regions. Loft flooring is of wooden boards nailed directly to the common beams. The chimney-pieces are a variant on the normal Breton pattern, for instead of the breastsummer being supported on single or double corbels, these corbels extend vertically downwards to form what are effectively stone screens on both sides of the hearth. The hearth of the principal room is provided with two keeping-places, but the only keeping-place in the second cell is that provided in the corner of the wall by the doorway leading to the byre. A *charnier* is built in to one corner of the hall. Access to the first floor is by a wooden stairway at the lower end of the hall. This room is lighted by three windows, the smallest of which provides light for the working area close to the hearth. The existence of straight joints between the house and the byre shows clearly that the latter was an added feature, but whether the communicating doorway formerly led into a byre already in existence when the house was constructed in 1817 must remain doubtful. The building is of two full storeys in height and the roof truss is of the collar and tie-beam type supporting a ridge-purlin and two pairs of lateral purlins held by cleats. Common rafters are staggered at the apex and their feet rest on the wall-heads. Slates were formerly nailed to boarding fixed to the common rafters.

The house illustrates the extraordinarily high level of construction in this district. Great attention was given to detail and the well was dug close to the front wall of the house and the well-cover built against this wall so that water could be drawn directly from inside the house as well as outside. A stone spout at the back of the well allowed water to be poured directly into the stone drinking trough also placed against the wall of the house. The fittings in the byre, with stone partitions separating the three places served by a manger, are again a relatively sophisticated feature for Brittany at that date. The house is a good example of the two-cell house that spread into the rural coastal areas, particularly of Finistère at the end of the eighteenth and the beginning of the nineteenth century. The hall, in this case the room to the left-hand side of the passage, remained the principal dwelling room but a secondary room had come into existence on the lower side of the passage, and this amongst other functions served for the preparation of food for animals and for domestic work of a heavier nature. Although the first floor is fully developed, it was initially a storage loft and not intended for sleeping,

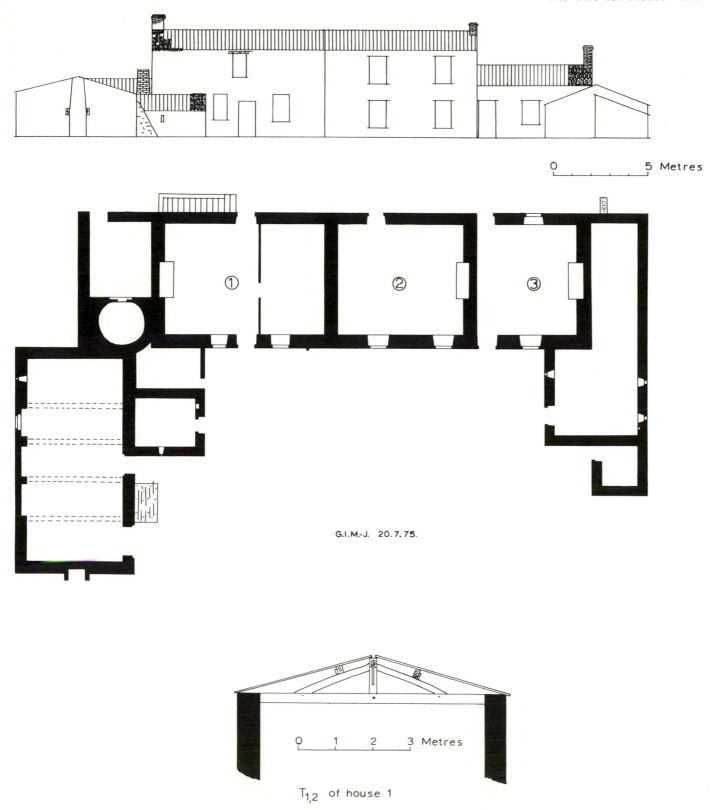

0   5 Metres

G.I.M.-J. 20.7.75.

0   1   2   3 Metres

T$_{1,2}$ of house 1

Fig. 213. La Masse 1, 2, 3, Frossay, Loire-Atlantique

although it gradually came to be used for the latter purpose.

A sharp contrast is provided by La Masse 1, Frossay, Loire-Atlantique (WT 823311). Walling is entirely of granite rubble with doorway and window dressings of the same material. Wood lintels are general. The roof covering is of 'Roman' tile and chimney-stacks are of small red bricks. The three houses form a line at the head of a courtyard and are integrated with farm buildings which line two sides of the yard. Only the dimensions of the houses are considered here. The total external length of the three dwellings is 23.20 metres and the width 7.15 metres. Internally, house 1 measures 8.35 metres by 5.80 metres, house 2 measures 6.65 metres by 5.80 metres, and house 3 measures 5.25 metres by 5.80 metres. Wall thicknesses are *c.* 0.70 metres. La Masse 1 and 2 are of two full storeys and the eaves line is *c.* 4.65 metres above the ground, the ridge rising to 5.75 metres above ground level. La Masse 3 is a single-storey structure with walls 2.80 metres in height and the ridge rising to 3.90 metres above the ground (Fig. 213).

Rubble walling is laid in a mortar of *pisé*. Granite dressings are conspicuously absent and rubble is used for doorway and window surrounds. The ground floor was formerly of *terre battue* but has now been concreted. Loft flooring is formed of wooden boards nailed to the common beams. Chimney-pieces are formed in the traditional Breton manner, the breastsummers being supported on projecting corbels, in this case all of wood. Chimney-stacks and the flues are built of the small red bricks common in the area around Nantes. Houses 1 and 2 rise to two full storeys and the upper storey is used entirely for storage. That of house 1 is approached by a flight of external stairs rising to a doorway in the rear wall. House 3 has no loft storage space. It is clear from the well-marked straight joints between each of the three houses that they belong to different phases of building, the group having grown over a period of time. An oven and oven-house are built into the gable end of La Masse 1, and against the oven at right-angles to the axis of the house is a barn with pigsties in front. A byre is built against La Masse 3 with a pigsty added to its lower end. The evidence of a former hearth on the end wall of the barn suggests that there was once another dwelling down-slope of the barn.

Roof structure of all these buildings is identical. A substantial tie-beam supports a short king-post into which ridge purlins are tenoned. Purlins are braced downwards to the king-posts and principal rafters support lateral purlins often held in place only by a peg. Irregular common rafters are laid across the ridge and the lateral purlins, their feet resting on the wall-heads. Boards are nailed to the common rafters and the half-cylindrical 'Roman' tiles are laid on the boarded surface.

These dwellings represent the homes of a small community. La Masse 1 is a two-cell dwelling, the second cell being unheated. It is important in that it represents a transitional stage in the development of the two-cell house. La Masse 2 is a large single-cell dwelling and La Masse 3 a small single-cell dwelling such as might have been occupied by elderly members of the family.

La Vieuxville 1, La Harmoye, Côtes-du-Nord (WU 019549), is a late nineteenth-, or early twentieth-century, dwelling representative of the kind that followed an agricultural revolution which led to the development of better, and often detached, farm buildings (Fig. 214). Severe in outline, it is a two-cell structure with a doorway opening into a lobby. Walling is of schist rubble with doorway and window dressings of sandstone. The house measures 14.10 metres long and 7.00 metres wide externally and 12.65 metres long and 5.75 metres wide internally. Walls are *c.* 0.70 metres thick. The ground slopes from left to right and the height of the eaves above the ground at the greatest point is 3.65 metres, the ridge rising to 7.20 metres above ground level. Walling is laid in a mortar of *pisé*, and clearly marked courses are visible. Sandstone dressings of ashlar are used for the doorway, windows and loft opening. These are very evenly cut and suggest a nineteenth- or even an early twentieth-century date. Roughly squared rubble blocks are used to a certain extent in the corners. Chimneys are of schist rubble capped with a projecting course. Roof covering is of slate, as is the roof of the dormer, the cheeks of which are of schist. Floors are of *terre battue* and the loft is formed of wooden boards laid across the common beams. Chimney-hoods are formed in the traditional Breton manner, in this case with a wooden breastsummer laid across wooden corbels projecting from the end walls. The house is of two cells, the rooms being divided by wooden partitions, and the window at the rear provides lighting for the small storage room at the back. Along with the outbuildings, the house forms an incomplete courtyard and there is every indication of its having been built later in the nineteenth century when the need for separate accommodation for cows, horses and farm implements was recognized.

La Ville Bonne 2, Taupont, Morbihan (WU 402134), is a rare example of a house of two-and-a-half storeys (Fig. 215). Undercut lintels were known as early as the eighteenth century (Fig. 78), but a nineteenth- or early twentieth-century date more likely accords with the form of the house. Whilst several features — size, height, and roof structure — point to a building of some quality, others are poor. Walling is of pre-Cambrian schists and

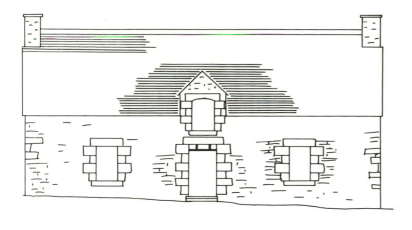

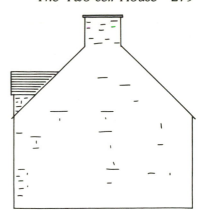

G.I.M.-J. 14.6.71.

0   5 Metres

Fig. 214. La Vieuxville 1, La Harmoye, Côtes-du-Nord

sandstones, the schist rubble very dark in colour with lighter sandstone ashlar for doorway and window dressings. Roof covering is of slate. Externally the building measures *c.* 11.50 metres in length and *c.* 7.20 metres in width. Internally, measurements are *c.* 9.70 metres by *c.* 5.75 metres. The hall is *c.* 4.80 metres in length and the unheated second cell *c.* 3.50 metres in length. The lateral walls are *c.* 0.70 metres thick and the gable walls 0.90 metres thick. The eaves stand 5.90 metres, and the ridge 9.70 metres, above ground level.

Walling is laid in a mortar of *pisé*. All the door and window dressings have ashlar dressings but the loft opening is framed in wood. A feature often encountered in Breton houses is the relieving arches of rubble built above the lintels to lessen the weight falling on them. This is a sure sign that the sandstone lacks great mechanical strength. The ground floors are of *terre battue* but the first floor is formed of wooden boards nailed to the common beams. A characteristic of this house is the existence of joists as well as beams, a sure indication of quality. Loft flooring is also of wooden boards nailed to the common beams, all three of which project through the front wall of the house so that the beam ends are visible from the outside. This, too, is a common feature in Brittany. The other floors are approached by a flight of wooden stairs rising at the end of the cross-passage, bounded, in this case, by wooden partitions. There is a fine wooden staircase. At first-floor level it opens into a lobby with a small room on the front side of the house and a single large chamber with a hearth at one end and a small unheated room at the other. This pattern mirrors the ground-floor arrangements where the hall is heated from a substantial hearth but the second cell is unheated. The loft is used entirely for storage. It is surprising that a house with many high-quality features should have such poorly developed secondary rooms. Whilst from the outside this is an important-looking two-cell house, in fact the second chimney is false and the whole of one end of the building

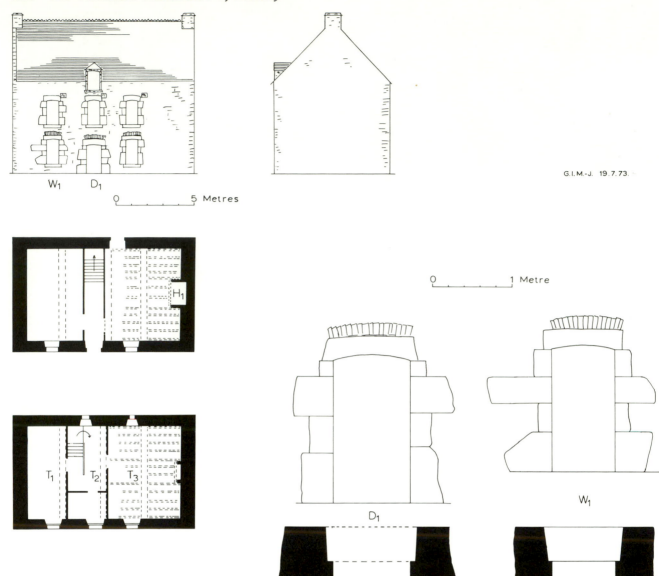

G.I.M.-J. 19.7.73.

Fig. 215a. La Ville Bonne 2, Taupont, Morbihan

is unheated. The undercut lintels and the general appearance of the building suggest an eighteenth-century date, but in view of the general conservatism the structure might be nineteenth century or even as late as the early-twentieth century. Roof trusses are of the upper-cruck type rising from tie-beams, but most of the curvature of the feet of the crucks remains hidden in the wall-heads. The collar supports a king-post on which rests the ridge-purlin, and a second purlin, or under-ridge purlin, is butted into the base of the king-posts and braced crosswise to the ridge-purlin with scissors braces. The ridge-purlin is also braced downwards to the king-posts. Principal rafters are slotted to receive three pairs of lateral purlins and the principals also have holes which formerly contained pegs used as a ladder during the roof-building process. Common rafters rest over the purlins with their feet on the wall-heads, and boarding is fastened to these common rafters, the slates being nailed directly to the boards. As is usual in this district, the chimney-pieces are of wood, the wooden frame supporting a rubble hood resting on a simply carved pair of wooden corbels. This is a late two-cell house, and as there are no attached farm buildings it must be supposed that it was the home of either a small landowner, himself not directly engaged in agriculture, or of someone with commercial interests. The building certainly has rustic pretensions.

Kervorn 2, Laz, Finistère (VU 356335), is a single-cell house with a lateral chimney-stack. Kervorn 1,

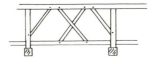

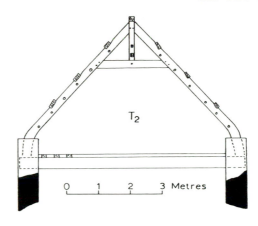

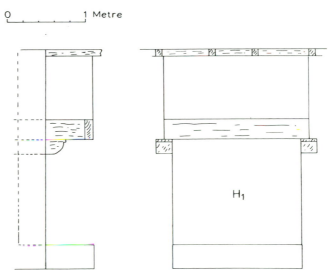

Fig. 215b.   La Ville Bonne 2, Taupont, Morbihan

conjoined, is a two-cell house of some quality, as displayed by the joints and common beams (Fig. 216). Total external length is 19.90 metres. Widths vary considerably. The maximum width of Kervorn 1 is 9.10 metres and of Kervorn 2, 10.10 metres. Internally, Kervorn 1 is 9.05 metres long and Kervorn 2, 7.75 metres long. Maximum height of the eaves above the ground is 5.20 metres and the ridge rises 4.75 metres above the eaves. The ground falls from right to left so that the walling of Kervorn 1 is somewhat higher than that of Kervorn 2. Wall thickness varies considerably from *c.* 0.70 metres to *c.* 1.10 metres. Walling is of schist rubble with doorway and window dressings of granite, laid in a mortar of *pisé*. Ground floors are of *terre battue* but the

first floor is formed of wooden boards nailed to the common beams and joists. Loft flooring is similarly formed of wooden boards. Roof structure varies. In Kervorn 1 the roof is supported on two trusses of the upper king-post, collar and tie-beam type. The upper king-post carries the ridge-beam and there are two pairs of lateral purlins resting on cleats. In Kervorn 2 there is only one truss of the collar and tie-beam type, the ridge-purlin resting in the intersecting principal rafters, and there are two pairs of lateral purlins resting on cleats. Common rafters rest with their feet on the wall-heads, in both cases, and are staggered at the apex. They are sprocketed out over the wall-heads and covered with wooden boards on to which the slates are nailed. The

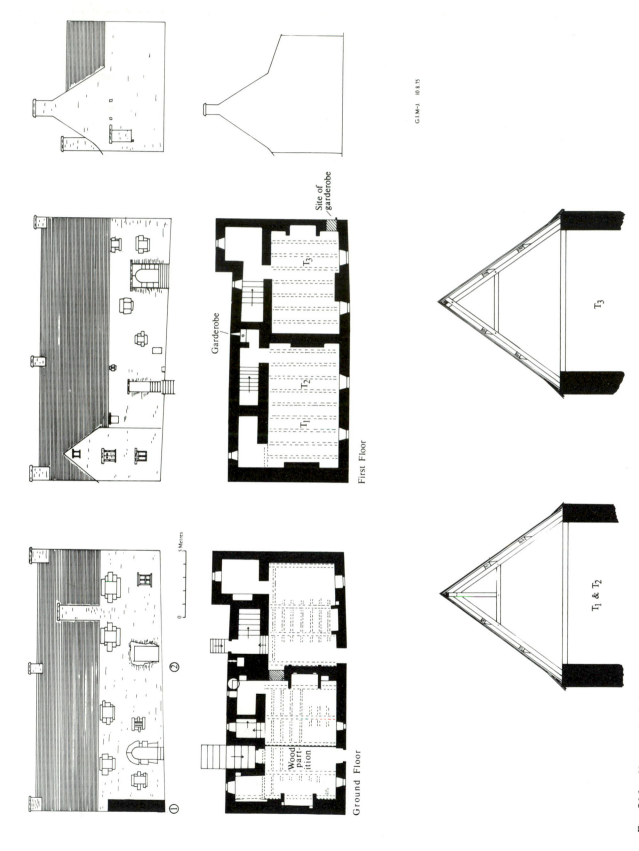

Fig. 216.   Kervorn 1, 2, Laz, Finistère

ridge is finished by projecting one row of slates across the top of the other. Chimneys and chimney-hoods are also formed of schist rubble, set in a mortar of *pisé*. The hoods rest on wooden breastsummers which in turn are supported on wooden corbels. Doorway and window dressings are of good quality, but somewhat plain, and there is an absence of chamfering. The principal doorway to Kervorn 2 has fallen away but that of Kervorn 1 suggests a seventeenth-century date. Some of the windows may be later insertions but others are clearly original and still have their unglazed wooden frames with wood mullions and transoms. In the rear gable of Kervorn 2 the original wooden shutters survive.

It seems likely that the buildings are not contemporary and that one was added to the other. If this is so, then it is more likely that Kervorn 2 is the later in date and that Kervorn 1 was the original dwelling. Both are complex houses. Kervorn 1 has a pair of opposing doorways, one of which, at the rear, is approached by a stone staircase which gives access to a deeply set round-headed doorway. On one side of this entrance-porch is an outshot which oral evidence proves conclusively was a bed outshot within living memory. The other side of the porch contains a stone staircase rising to first-floor level under which is a small room that probably served as a pantry or dairy. Deeply embedded in the wall is a cylindrical stone container, probably a *charnier*, visible from the outside and placed in this position because it was cool. The interior is divided into two parts by a wood partition which, although nailed to one of the beams, may be an original feature. That neither of these rooms was originally intended to be a byre is suggested by the adjacent outshots and by the presence, in a poor part of Brittany, of high-quality beams and joists. This then appears to be a two-cell house, each cell being provided with a hearth. Kervorn 2 is also approached from the back by a flight of stairs which open on to a second flight giving access to first-floor level. A structural outshot at the rear contains a room of doubtful function. It seems too small to have served as a living room and the presence of a large keeping-place in the wall suggests that it, too, must have been a dairy or pantry. This house has a lateral chimney-stack, a very rare feature in Brittany. It was originally provided with a communicating doorway to Kervorn 2 but this is now blocked. The existence of such a doorway suggests that the two dwellings were occupied by related family groups. Kervorn 2 is provided with a heated chamber at first-floor level but there is nothing to suggest that this was a separate first-floor hall, although it may possibly have been so. In the structural outshot a small secondary room is again provided but its function is unclear. Archaeological evidence shows beyond question

that a garderobe was formerly sited on the gable end. This room, then, was either a separate first-floor hall, or alternatively an upper chamber or solar. Kervorn 1 also has a large unheated upper room. A curious outshot exists over the entrance staircase and there is an outshot in the hall. A garderobe is provided in a small cubicle at the head of the staircase and this feature is curious in that the shute, and part of the garderobe chamber itself, is within the confines of Kervorn 2. The shute has an opening at the base of the wall. It seems likely that the garderobe was constructed at the time of building of Kervorn 2. Alternatively, and if this interpretation is wrong, then the two houses must be regarded as being contemporary. This pair of houses is of high quality in a relatively poor and backward part of Brittany and must represent the homes of substantial landowners. The function of some of the rooms and spaces is uncertain. The houses, which communicated at ground-floor level, were almost certainly originally occupied by related families of some social standing and are by far the finest in the hamlet.

A number of two-cell houses are to be found in the survey of the E.A.R. The Cap-Sizun style is present at Pont-Croix where Kervillou, dated 1884, is of two full storeys. A cross-passage separates hall and *salle*, the latter, used only rarely, having been subdivided so that the hearth end, with a doorway replacing the original window, may serve as a *cuisine des animaux*. A finely built single-storey house at Kerfland in Plomeur is dated 1818. There is no rear doorway, the staircase at the end of the cross-passage giving access to the loft. Part of the hall is partitioned off to form a *laiterie* and the second cell, the *belle pièce*, provided sleeping accommodation for the parents. Kerlaboussec in Lanvéoc is a similar, but much smaller, house with a cross-passage and opposing doorways, built in 1856. Pors-Driou in Saint-Nic, dated 1888, is a large house of two storeys with contemporary lateral outshot for the *cuisine animaux* and a gable outshot for the *cave*. The hall has been subdivided to form a *cuisine, laiterie* and *lingerie*. Pen-ar-Menez in Combrit is a much smaller house dated 1853. A thatched single-storey structure, it consists of hall, *salle* and cross-passage, with a *reserve* at one end. The parents slept in the hall, their daughters in the *salle*. In Penandreff, Pouldreuzic, a similar structure, dated 1870, the parents slept in the hall, the *salle* containing beds for the children in addition to a heap of potatoes and barrels of cider.

Lezanquel in Cléden is dated 1887. The *pièce* has been subdivided to form a *cuisine animaux* at the hearth end and the first floor has two heated rooms and a small third room. All three contain beds, as does the hall. In many of these houses there is no doorway at the rear of the cross-passage. Instead, a staircase gives access to the first floor, as at Celeriou in Scaër. This house, undated but obviously of the nineteenth century, has two rooms — hall and *chambre* — both containing beds. Keranguen in the same *commune*, dated 1868, is composed of two cells — hall and *salle* — the latter containing only a table, dresser, *armoire* and spinning wheel. Beds are found in the hall and the heated upper rooms. Additional rooms — *cuisine* and *laiterie* — are contained in the contemporary rear outshot. In Penty Lanneon, Pont-Croix, dated 1850, the hall occupies about two-thirds of the space. Below the cross-passage is an unheated room used as a dairy and potato store.[563]

Le Grand Moustoir in Theix, dated 1880, is of two storeys. Only the two ground-floor rooms are heated and the arrangement is unusual in that the hall stack is axial rather than at the end gable. The *salle* contains beds. A similar plan, with an axial stack in the hall, occurs at Brouel on the Île aux Moines, a much older house surely formed by the combining of two single-cell houses with internal communication. A two-cell house, Metairie du Frotage, in Pluherlin, with an unheated lower end, looks like a converted long-house. The small *chambre* contains three beds, there being only one in the hall.

The Manoir de Brecehan in Saint-Gravé is a superb example of the two-cell house with stair turret. Unfortunately, peasant occupation makes it impossible to determine the original room functions. At ground-floor level the hall continues to fulfil its historic function, but the second cell has been converted into a byre, one of the windows having been replaced by a doorway. Here is an example of a two-cell 'gentry' house being converted to a long-house first derivative. There are two contemporary outshots, one now a byre, the other a *cave*. The latter has a hearth as at Trévinou, above. An integral outshot provides two rear rooms at first-floor level. Of the two other first-floor rooms, one, always unheated, is used as a hay barn, the other is a bedroom. The second floor also has two rooms, one formerly with a hearth. Detail and finish of this house are magnificent.[564]

La Croix Moriceau in La Haie-Fouassière provides an example of the single-storey two-cell house south of the Loire. A wide cross-passage separates hall and *chambre*, the latter containing two beds. Oven and bake-house are contained in a rear outshot. Several houses have a symmetrical façade behind which lies a continuous room. In the absence of structural sub-divisions, functional divisions are marked by pieces of furniture. Thus, at Les Hauts Pilorgères in Saint-Père-en-Retz, the area below the embryo cross-passage, the *derrière*, is marked off by *armoires*. Whilst these houses are of long-house form, and may be derived from the long-house, they are nevertheless embryo two-cell houses.[565]

The *minutes notariales* provide further evidence for the two-cell house. In 1782, Pierre Coail of the Métairie de Kermeno in Plougonver, Côtes-du-Nord has goods worth 2950 *livres*, chiefly made up of livestock including six large oxen, sixteen small oxen, fifteen cows and five horses. It was a farm of some size and importance. Furniture and utensils were, however, very limited. The *cuisine* contained four beds, two *mayes à patte*, a *vesselier*, a *table coulante*, three oak *armoires*, a chest, and three *huges bois de chesne* in the entry passage. In the *chambre* were four more beds, numerous chests, two *armoires*, two tables and a miscellany of implements.[566]

Some farms appeared to be making use of another single-cell house as a second cell, illustrating the adaptation of a second dwelling in the absence of a house with two rooms. At Keruzec in Pommerit-de-Vicomte in 1838, Francois Le Fur, whose estate totalled 4054 *francs*, occupied a house consisting only of a *cuisine* with *grenier* above. On the ground floor of the adjacent *petite maison* was a miscellany of furniture and implements, including a bed '*à gauche du foyer*', a spinning wheel and other tools. This was a farm of some wealth, engaged, as were many others of the period, in the linen trade, about half the total value being made up of livestock and implements.[567] In 1835, Jacques Le Page of Kerhenry in the same *commune* lived in the hall, but '*dans l'appartement appellé Ty Traou*' were to be found a collection of implements, a small table, items used for preparing linen thread, and '*les fus . . . de cidre*'.[568] The relative prosperity of these examples is shown by the fact that Le Page and Le Fur both had forks to use at table as well as other utensils of high quality.

A similar example occurs at La Gaudais, Sougéal, in 1845. Louis Bounissant left an estate worth 4768 *francs* of which household goods amounted to only about 1200 *francs*. The *cuisine* was the most important room with beds on both sides of the hearth. Wealth is displayed by a longcase clock. There was, however, a '*maison de decharge*' containing various utensils, a stone *charnier* full of *lard*, a bed and several other items of furniture.[569] Pierre Fauger of La Gaullairie, in Pocé, left an estate of 855 *francs* in 1806. His house was of two cells. The *chambre* contained a bed, *charnier*, a *boutique* and tools for preparation of linen thread. Iron forks supplemented the wooden spoons used at table.[570]

The strong tendency for wealth to be in livestock and implements rather than household goods is brought out by the inventories for Loire-Atlantique when draught oxen always carried high values. At the Métairie de la Maindonière in Saint-Hilaire-de-Clisson in 1818, Pierre Pouvuais had a two-cell house, the hall containing a longcase clock. Jean Perraud of La Maindonière in the same *commune* also had a house of two *chambres*. In both cases the hall contains all the essentials for living, whilst in the second *chambre* there is always a bed, together with a miscellany of tools and implements, some other items of furniture and barrels of wine. One has a *charnier*.[571] Claude Glanaud of Pontchâteau, a *cordonnier* by trade, had his hall on the ground floor, but above was the *chambre haute* with a bed, two chests and a small table.[572] In 1804, Jacques Bernier of the Metairie de la Bironnerie in Sainte-Reine lived in a *chambre basse* at the end of which was the byre. This long-house was insufficient for his needs, for another *chambre* next to the house contained a bed, a spinning wheel and a miscellany of implements.[573] Jean Crahé of Beaulieu, Pontchâteau, in 1824 had a hall with a bakehouse above which was a *chambre* containing several beds and chests. His needs were such that another house adjoining the first contained further beds and a spinning wheel and yet another house was needed for the accommodation of light chests, a table and two benches.[574]

A similar picture of multi-purpose second cells is evident in Finistère. Claude le Cloquer of Guern, Plougasnou, in 1803 had, in addition to the hall, a *maison manelle*, a *chambre* in which were contained *armoirs*, *barriques*, a bed, numerous farm implements and tools for the preparation of linen.[575] Jean Le Front of Quilimesier, Plouzané, had a hall with a *chambre* above in 1801. The latter contained a bed, two chests, bedding, numerous implements and a pair of scales.[576] Marie Eon of Kerenpellan, Moëlan-sur-Mer, in 1845, lived entirely in the hall, the *chambre* being used solely to store potatoes.[577]

Field evidence and the writings of travellers and other workers, together with that of the E.A.R. and documentary evidence, point to the same conclusions. The two-cell house of symmetrical, or near symmetrical, 'Renaissance' plan, with or without rear outshots, is present from the early-seventeenth century onwards. The type first found its expression at the higher social levels in the *manoir* class, and such examples usually have heated upper rooms intended to provide sleeping and 'withdrawing' accommodation for the senior members of the family. To this extent these rooms are the lineal descendants of the medieval solar (see Chapter 13). At ground-floor level, the hall retains its historic function, but a second cell, not present in the medieval house, appears to be connected with the work of the household, particularly cooking, and provides accommodation also for domestics. There is usually also a storage loft and the outshots may rise to give additional rear storage rooms at first-floor level. Ground-floor outshots served for the storage of food, especially drink, and for dairy functions. The wealth of the owner usually found expression in the stonework and detail: a stair

turret, often furnished with a magnificent and sometimes vaulted stairway, chimney-pieces, doorways and window dressings are of high quality.

There is no evidence for the existence of the two-cell dwelling at the level of the middling and lower peasantry before the end of the eighteenth century. A few examples of the 1780s and 1790s are to be found in Cap-Sizun. It is with the onset of the nineteenth century that the two-cell house gains favour, firstly in the coastal areas, notably in Finistère and along the north coast where today it predominates. In a few areas, as in Cap-Sizun, there appears to have been a considerable building and re-building during the nineteenth century both of one- and two-storey, two-cell houses. Further evidence suggests that many were re-builds of long-houses on the same ground plan. Ironically, whilst this was happening, many of the two-cell *manoirs* were descending the social scale so that they came to be occupied by a peasant family content to live entirely in the hall, using the other rooms only for storage. Numerous examples remain in this state. Greater economic prosperity in *Armor* certainly made possible the introduction of the second cell, which by implication required the erection of farm buildings to house the stock once kept in the long-house. The origin of the style is unclear. It did not come from interior Brittany, for the areas where it first took root are the ones where the two-cell house is today most strongly represented. As the type is still also poorly represented in the eastern and south-eastern parts of the Province, it seems unlikely that it was diffused from metropolitan France by land. Probably it was introduced by sea, either from France or from other countries. South-west Britain could have provided many models. Except in Cap-Sizun where two-storey houses were built from the end of the eighteenth century, the second storey was rare until the later nineteenth and twentieth centuries when many houses were raised in height. It is also clear that the two-cell peasant house was not modelled on the two-cell Renaissance *manoir*, for the second cell of the latter performed an entirely different function to the ill-developed second cell of most of the two-cell peasant houses. As inventories, the E.A.R. records and field observations show, the second cell of peasant houses never acquired a specialist function. In a sense it was a parlour reserved for special occasions, used also for overflow sleeping accommodation, for the storing of implements and frequently for an 'industrial' function. The spinning wheel and accessories of the linen trade were kept there. Once the fashion was established, the two-cell *manoir* may have been an influence, reinforcing the trend, a reminder of the mode of life of a higher social class and something to be emulated. It is unlikely to have provided the stimulus for the new fashion.

Many of the new two-cell houses were converted, rather than completely rebuilt, long-houses. Some, like Kervaly 12 (Fig. 184), with their asymmetrical window openings, betray the fact to this day. Others had two windows refashioned at the same time and may be less obvious. Frequent unheated second chambers may reflect this long-house origin, and in any case represent a transitional stage in the development of the type. The two-cell house can thus be seen in one sense as a long-house derivative. Certainly the facility with which a byre was converted to a chamber and *vice versa*, before World War I, shows how close the two types were. Rather, it was the form of the Breton long-house with the byre often roughly equal in length to the hall which made such a change so convenient and the result symmetrical. The change, once made, is often very difficult to detect, particularly when window openings are greatly enlarged, fittings modernized and outside walls rendered. Sufficient proven examples exist, however, for the generalization to hold. There are thus three categories of two-cell house: the symmetrical *Renaissance* manoir, the new two-cell house of the coastal areas introduced from the late-eighteenth century onwards, and dwellings converted from pre-existing long-houses. The first of these stands apart as having important functional differences in its original form.

THIRTEEN

MULTI-CELL HOUSES

Multi-cell houses are defined as those containing more than two cells used wholly, or largely, for living, as distinct from storage or the accommodation of animals. The cells may all be on the ground floor, or some may lie at first- or second-floor level. Most of these buildings are of the *manoir* class, an ill-defined term, but one generally understood to refer to the chief house of an estate, built for, and possibly occupied by, the landowner. Frequently these houses constitute one of a number of buildings in a hamlet, others being occupied by tenants or employees. Elsewhere, they stand isolated. As soon as buildings appear to belong to the supra-vernacular category, they fall outside the scope of this work. The boundary is not a sharp one, but it is usually possible subjectively to recognize whether a building falls into the vernacular category or not. It was often in the construction of supra-vernacular buildings that new ideas, styles and techniques were introduced into an area, later to be copied and diffused down the social scale.

The sample quadrats have produced very few multi-cell buildings, hardly surprising as the quadrats have sides of only 2.5 kilometres and the bulk of the population lived in small houses. However, the relative prosperity of some areas is reflected in the greater frequency with which multi-cell houses are encountered. Three were recorded in Quadrat 3 (Plougasnou) and many more survive in the countryside around. Carnoët (Quadrat 4), Paimpont (Quadrat 12), Saint-M'Hervé (Quadrat 13), Guérande (Quadrat 19) and Saint-Lumine-de-Clisson (Quadrat 21) each produced one example. In no other quadrat was an example recorded. The detailed examples, below, are thus largely taken from outside the sample quadrats.

La Salle, Plurien, Côtes-du-Nord (WU 436863), is one of the few recorded buildings truly medieval in concept, though not necessarily in date (Fig. 217). The total external length of the buildings, including the lean-to outshot at the lower end, is 41.50 metres and the width *c.* 8.00 metres. The ground falls *c.* 0.20 metres from right to left and the height of the eaves above the ground at the

upper end is *c.* 5.50 metres, the gable rising to 9.80 metres above ground level. The house can be divided into four cells, excluding the outshot, the lowest of which measures *c.* 7.75 metres by 5.65 metres internally, the second 4.65 metres by 6.20 metres internally, the hall 12.40 metres by *c.* 6.30 metres and the upper cell 6.65 metres by 6.40 metres internally.

Walling is entirely of Brioverian schist rubble laid in a mortar of *pisé*. Doorway and window dressings are of ashlar, as are the raised copings at the gable ends and at the junction between the hall and the upper cell. The chimney-stacks are of rubble, that at the lower gable being of rectangular, the other two being of circular, cross-section. That to the hall, now demolished, was circular. The roof is slate-covered and the ridge of red tile. The ground floors were all originally of *terre battue* but only in the hall and the upper cell do these survive, the other two cells now being floored with concrete. The upper floors are of boards laid across the beams and common joists. Roof structure is uniform throughout the length of the building, differing only in detail. Roof trusses are of the upper king-post, collar and tie-beam type, the king-post supporting a ridge-purlin, and two pairs of lateral purlins being slotted into the backs of the principal rafters. Common rafters rest with their feet on the wall-heads and they are staggered at the apex. Slates are nailed to wooden boarding laid across the common rafters. As there has been some outward movement of the walls at wall-head height, adjustment of the roof-line has been necessary. Over the solar, for example, the principal rafter has been sprocketed out and one of the lateral purlins placed on cleats, leaving an empty trench. This truss was formerly braced upwards both ways to the ridge-purlin but the braces are no longer in position. The principal rafters were also arch-braced, both to the collar and to the tie-beam, but the two lower arch-braces are also now missing. Over the hall there has been considerable outward movement of the walls so that the original tie-beam at the rear side has come completely away from the wall-head. The tie-beam has also been cut

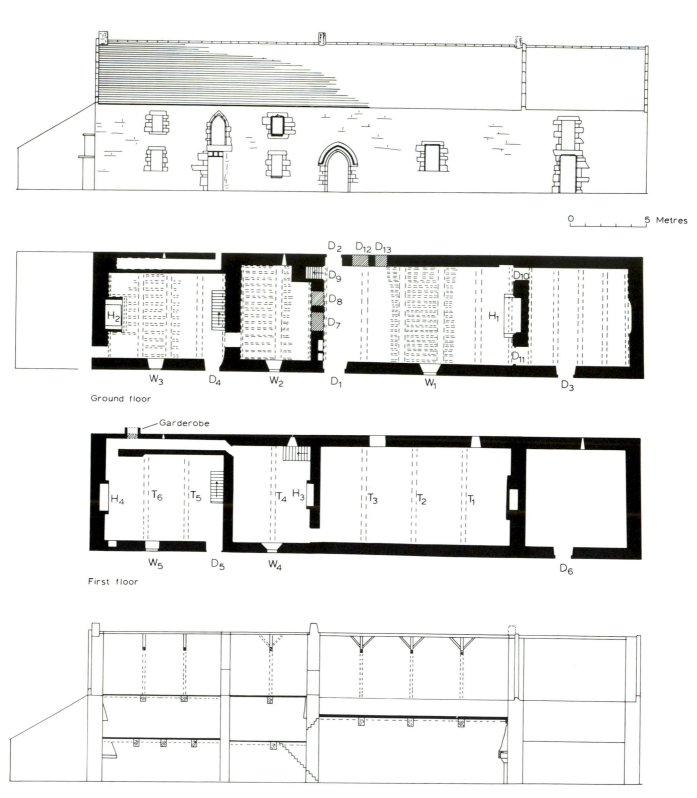

0 _____ 5 Metres

Ground floor

First floor

Fig. 217a.   La Salle, Plurien, Côtes-du-Nord

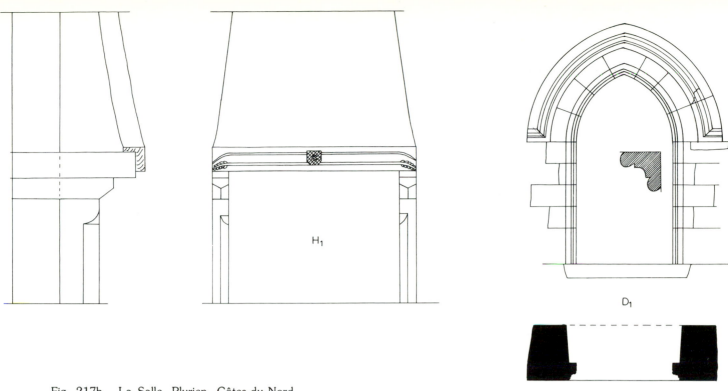

H_1

D_1

Fig. 217b. La Salle, Plurien, Côtes-du-Nord

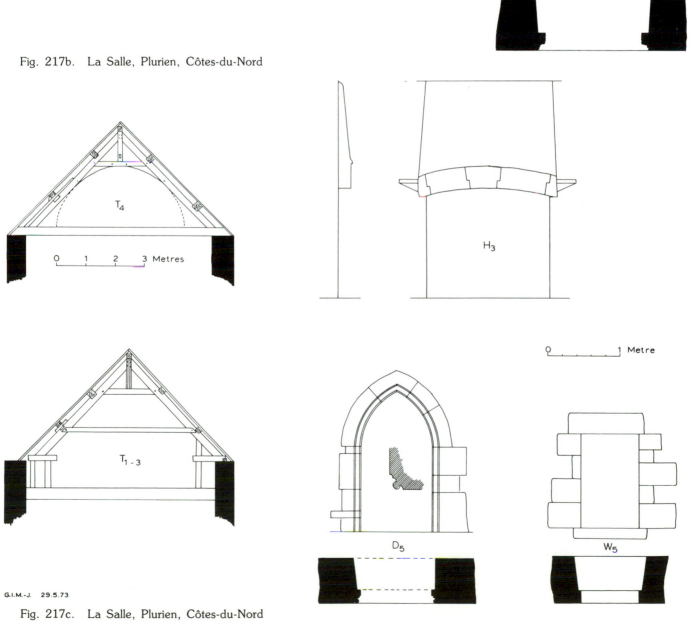

T_4

0   1   2   3 Metres

H_3

T_{1-3}

0   1 Metre

D_5

W_5

G.I.M.-J. 29.5.73

Fig. 217c. La Salle, Plurien, Côtes-du-Nord

away and, in order to strengthen the truss, a secondary collar placed at a low level has been bolted to the principal rafters. The truss is also now supported by vertical posts descending to the level of the heavy beams spanning the hall. Upper king-posts are braced both ways to the ridge-purlin.

There are four hearths, in the hall, solar, and in both the ground- and first-floor cells at the lower end. Construction is identical except for the solar. H1, H2 and H4 have wooden breastsummers supported by stone corbels. Chimney-hoods are of stone rubble plastered with *pisé,* as were all the walls originally. Some of this *pisé* rendering remains and the hood above H1 retains its complete coating of *pisé.* H1 and H4 are plain in finish but H1 has ornamentation on the wooden breast-summer. A shield of arms is centrally placed and ears of wheat, a fertility symbol, decorate the ends of the breastsummer. The chimney-piece in the solar, H3, is of entirely different construction and here the breastsummer is formed by a stone arch, and stone shelves are placed immediately on either side. This hearth is now blocked but it was formerly relatively shallow, clearly not intended as a working hearth as were the others. Doorway and window dressings are occasionally of fine quality, notably the principal doorways, D1 and D2. Doorway D5 is also of fine quality but the stone is now much weathered. The finest window is that to the solar, W4, and the hall window originally had mullion and transom but these have been removed. The remaining door and window openings are relatively plain. Doorway D3 giving access to the upper cell has a flat-splay chamfer interrupted on the left-hand jamb.

The plan of this building is of the greatest interest. The hall is of the classic medieval type; doorways D1 and D2 opening on to an embryo cross-passage, closed on the lower end by a stone wall but open to the hall on the upper side. A pair of doorways, D7 and D8, can only have been service doors, now blocked, but once opening into the service rooms underneath the solar. These now form one complete cell with access from the lower ground-floor cell and with a later window, W2. A pair of large keeping-places is also provided in the wall close to doorway D1. The hall is lighted by a large window, W1, and the hearth lies at the upper end. Doorways D10 and D11 give access to the upper cell which in recent times has been used as a stable. The former presence of a hearth in this upper gable may suggest that its original function was different, but this must remain problematical. It may have been built as a provision lest its function change. Alternatively, it may have been intended to provide warmth for farm servants sleeping within the house, though this seems unlikely. Doorway

D10 is extraordinary in that it rises to a great height for which there is no immediately obvious explanation. It appears to be an original feature, for the rear lateral wall is recessed in order to receive the open door. Doorway D11 on the other side of the hearth is a conventional round-headed doorway with cavetto moulding. Two doorways, D12 and D13, now blocked, are also problematical; they are placed very close to the rear doorway D2, and it can only be assumed that they formerly led into another building, perhaps a lean-to outshot, built against the rear wall of the hall. This was possibly a *cellier* or *cave,* long since demolished. There is no trace of such building on the external wall. Alternatively, they may have led to a kitchen. Doorway D9 gives access to a staircase rising to the solar at first-floor level. The hall is of exceptional height for a Breton house and is out of phase with the ceiling levels of the other three cells which accord closely. The result is that the loft over the hall has to be approached by a flight of stone steps set within the wall dividing it from the solar. These are probably a late insertion and a ladder is necessary to gain access to the first step. There is also a suggestion of a break in the walling, the upper courses appearing to be of later date. If this is correct, and the walls have been raised, there is a possibility that the hall was originally open to the roof, had a central hearth, and that the present ceiling is a later insertion, the chimney built, and perhaps the upper cell or stable added, at the same time. Much of this, however, is conjecture pending further archaeological investigation. Roof trusses T1–3 have certainly been disturbed but there is no trace of soot blackening nor any reason to believe that these trusses are not original. The tie-beams were at some stage cut away, when it was desired to make use, or greater use, of the loft for storage. Wall-heads have moved outwards, so that the tie-beam stubs have come away and vertical posts to transmit the weight to the ceiling beams have been introduced along with additional cross-bracing and the jacking-up of purlins at the rear. The other cells at first-floor level are those over the stable and at the lower end. Originally there was no communication between these end cells at first-floor level except that the solar and the upper cell at the lower end share the same garderobe and communication is possible via the intra-mural passage. The plan of this complex is thus basically the classic one of hall and service rooms with solar above, to which are added, at the upper end, a cell, formerly heated but in recent times used as a stable, with a hayloft above and at the lower end a pair of completely independent single-cell dwellings communicating neither with each other nor with the adjacent solar and service rooms in their original state. This arrangement can only be satisfactorily explained by interpreting these end cells as independent single-cell dwellings. That at first-floor level is effectively a first-floor hall; and that the social status of the occupants must have been similar to those of the solar is shown by the fact that they shared a common garderobe. It seems likely, therefore, that this first-floor hall was intended either for a near relative of the landowner whose family occupied the solar or for a steward or bailiff of comparable social status. The ground-floor dwelling beneath could then have been occupied by a working farmer. The entrance doorway, D5, of the first-floor hall must formerly have been approached by an external stone staircase, but all trace of this is now gone. It is likely, however, that it rose from a point close to the present window of the former service rooms, W2, for it is the right-hand jamb of doorway D4 which shows the greatest sign of disturbance; furthermore, doorway D4 is late in style, probably eighteenth or nineteenth century at the earliest, and this doorway must replace the original entrance to the ground-floor cell. Windows W3 and W5 are almost certainly enlargements of the original window openings. It is probable too that doorways D3 and D6 are late in date and either represent alterations to the original doorway or indicate that the stable at the upper end of the building is a later, perhaps eighteenth-century, addition to the hall. This idea would be further supported by the presence of the raised coping at the end of the hall. Doorway D11 does, however, look an original feature, and if the present upper cell is a later addition, then it is possible that there was always some sort of stable or byre at this end of the hall. The thick wall at the lower end of the service rooms also suggests that the first-floor hall and the room below may represent additions to the original hall, service rooms and solar complex. If this is so, then the garderobe and intra-mural passage would have been built at the same time and this may explain the curious twist in the intra-mural passage at the point where it enters the solar. The solar doorway to the intra-mural passage is also awkwardly placed at an angle, suggesting that it too may be an insertion. These additions, however, must have been made at a fairly early date, for not only is doorway D5 of Gothic form, but the doorway from the solar into the intra-mural passage is round-headed, and this would suggest that this end of the building was complete not later than the end of the seventeenth century.

If these interpretations are correct, the original building may have comprised a hall, possibly open to the roof, either with or without service rooms and a solar. The end cells may then have been added, that at the upper end possibly as late as the eighteenth century. It is impossible to give a date to the hall except to indicate that it must be earlier than *c.* 1650. The Gothic doorway suggests a sixteenth-century date, but the possibility that the building may be fifteenth century must not be discounted, pending further detailed archaeological study. In its developed form the structure provides accommodation for three families, the *seigneur* in the hall and solar, one family in the first-floor hall, and one beneath. The fact that the garderobe is shared by the solar and the first-floor hall suggests that the occupants of the latter were of similar social status to the *seigneur*, perhaps related, or the steward of the estate, with the working farmer living beneath.

Kerpontdarms, Guérande, Loire-Atlantique (WT 404427), is another Gothic *manoir* with similarities to La Salle (Fig. 218). Externally the building measures a total of 27.00 metres long and 8.10 metres wide. All the outside walls are 0.80 metres thick. The building is divided into three cells of which the hall is 11.70 metres in length including the area below the cross-passage, and 6.50 metres in width. The cell at the lower end is 4.50 metres long and that at the upper end 7.55 metres long. The house stands on a nearly level site, the eaves being 5.35 metres and the ridge 9.90 metres above ground level. Walling is of granite throughout, rubble for the greater part, with ashlar for door and window dressings, laid in a mortar of *pisé*. The ground floor, throughout its length, is of *terre battue* and the flooring at first-floor level is of boards laid across the beams and common joists. The roof is covered with slate and the exposed parts of the chimney-stacks are of the thin red bricks characteristic of the Nantes region. All the roof trusses are of the upper king-post, collar and tie-beam type. King-posts carry a ridge-beam and two pairs of lateral purlins are carried on cleats. The king-post is braced upwards to the ridge. Three trusses above the hall, T1–3, are braced as if to take a barrel vault, and the king-post descends below the level of the collar which is interrupted and morticed into the post. Trusses T4 and T5 have no curved braces. The wall-heads have moved outwards with time, and adjustment of the roof to this shift has been necessary. Consequently, the lateral purlins no longer rest in the trenches cut into the principal rafters but are supported by cleats placed over the former housing. Common rafters rest with their feet on the wall-heads and are staggered at the apex. Slates are nailed to boards resting on the common rafters. There is a red-tile ridge. The hall is provided with a massive hearth, H1, in which the wooden breastsummer, with its three empty peg-holes, is supported on stone corbels, bearing flat-splay chamfers. Two stone shelves are built into the angle between the corbels and wall. Originally there was no other hearth at

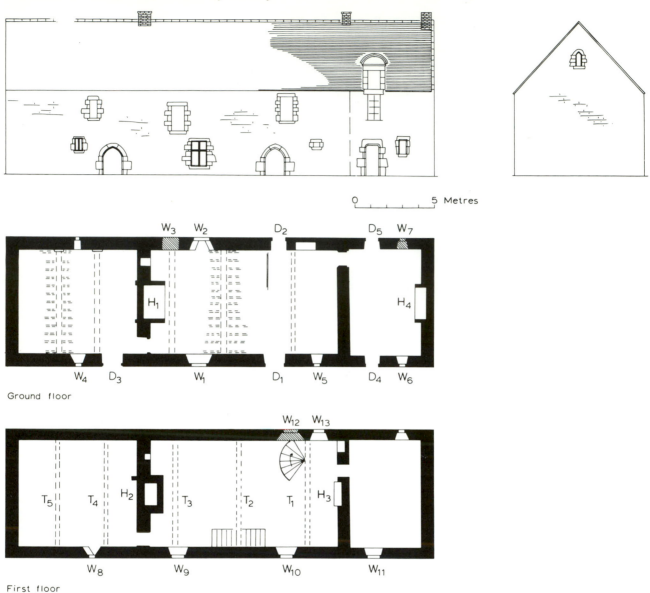

Ground floor

First floor

Fig. 218a. Kerpontdarms, Guérande, Loire-Atlantique

ground-floor level, but the solar was formerly provided with a hearth, H2, now demolished. Hearth H3 in the loft over the hall is a small and late insertion and the small end cell, also an addition to the original building, is provided with a fine chimney-piece, H4. There are three original Gothic doorways, D1, D2 and D3. Original, too, are windows W1 and W2 with their stone mullions and transoms and the large slit, W4, with a stone mullion. W5 is also probably original. The former window, W3, is now blocked. Doors D4 and D5 to the extension are also contemporary with the building of that extension, as are probably its window, W6, and the blocked opening, W7. At first-floor level window W11 and the loft opening

above are almost certainly contemporary with the extension. Window W8, providing light for the solar, is also contemporary and provided with the window seat on one side. At ground-floor level window W2 is the only one provided with window seats and is additionally provided with a drain. Mouldings on these doorways and windows are either of the flat-splay type or cavetto. The hall is provided with a large keeping-place to the right of the hearth and an even larger one, round-headed, in the lateral wall just below doorway D2. An inserted wooden staircase provides access from the present hall to the loft space above and a part-circular stair gives access from the first-floor to the former loft over the hall. Window W12

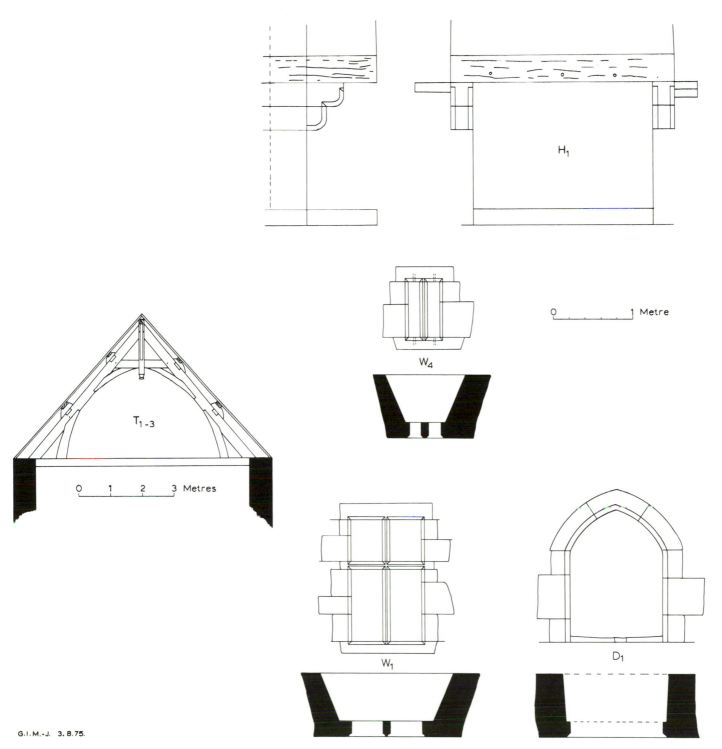

Fig. 218b.   Kerpontdarms, Guérande, Loire-Atlantique

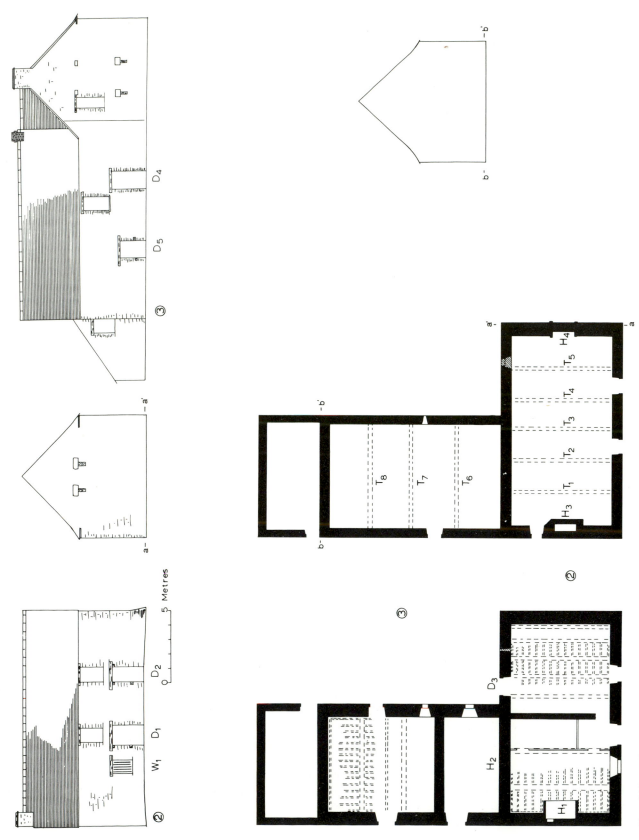

Fig. 219a.   Beau Normandie 2, 3, Paimpont, Ille-et-Vilaine

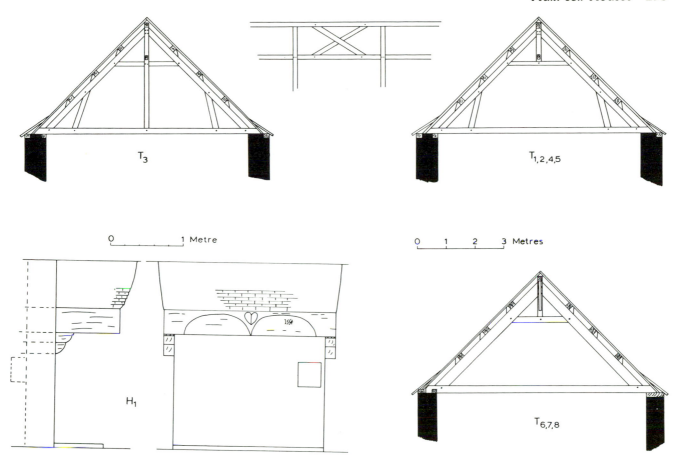

Fig. 219b. Beau Normandie 2, 3, Paimpont, Ille-et-Vilaine

was presumably blocked when this circular stairway was inserted. There is no evidence of the original stairway from the hall to the solar.

The original house consisted of the medieval hall, together with the cell at the upper end beyond hearth H1. The lower cell with obviously later details probably belongs to the late-seventeenth or early-eighteenth century. It is impossible to date the original house but it could be of any period up to about 1600 and may even belong to the early-seventeenth century. Doorways D1 and D2 define the embryo cross-passage which appears never to have been physically bounded on either side in its original form. There is no trace of original partitions, but fragments of a later screen survive. It seems probable that the cross-passage remains in its original state without physical boundaries. Even the service end, with its large *garde manger* in the wall, is open to the hall, unlike that at La Salle, and true service rooms seem never to have existed. The doorway into the cell at the lower end was presumably made at the time of the extension. The hall was lighted by two large original windows, both closing with wooden shutters. A doorway in the upper wall of the

hall gives access to the cell approached also by the Gothic doorway, D3. This was never heated and it seems likely that it was intended for occupation by animals, either horses or cattle, but more likely the former. Immediately above it is the solar, but how this room was reached originally is difficult to say. There have been several modifications to the building, and windows W9 and W10 certainly represent later alterations, for they are considerably larger than would have been expected in the original house. Window W9 is the loft entrance and its sill is level with the floor of the room over the hall. There is the possibility that this level was originally approached by an external stone stair but there is no archaeological evidence of such a feature. A doorway in the lower wall now provides entry to the cell over the ground-floor cell at the lower end. There is no trace of a garderobe. The upper cell at the lower end was probably a *chambre* used for storage and sleeping. In its present form, Kerpontdarms provides accommodation for two families, that of the *seigneur* in the hall and solar, and that of a relative, steward or other employee in the later addition. There is no evidence of the roof-line ever having been

0   1 Metre

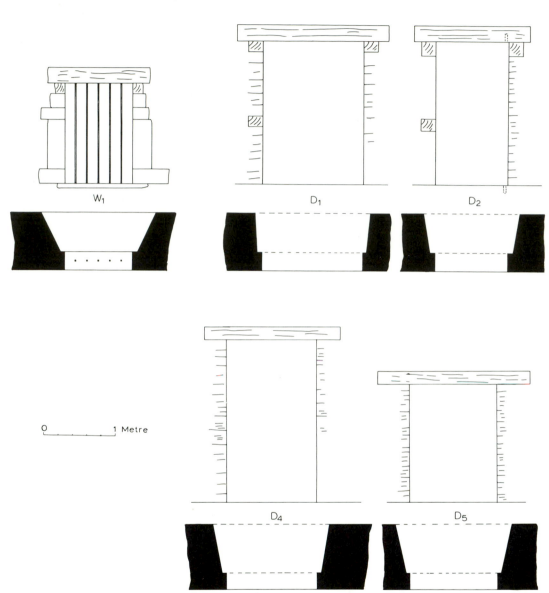

0   1 Metre

Fig. 219c.   Beau Normandie 2, 3, Paimpont, Ille-et-Vilaine

raised and it is probable that the house was built with chimney-stacks. It represents, with its 'open' service end, an earlier stage in the evolutionary sequence than La Salle, but it may not be earlier in date, perhaps belonging to the later sixteenth century. A further example of a medieval *manoir,* not yet examined in detail, is Kerat, Baden, Morbihan. Like La Salle, it has small chimney-stacks of circular cross-section. Kerpontdarms thus appears to have been the home of a substantial landowner who provided himself and his family with an

upper withdrawing room. At some later stage the house was extended, presumably to provide accommodation for an additional family.

Beau Normandie, 2, 3, Paimpont, Ille-et-Vilaine (WU 669211), consists of two dwellings (Fig. 219). Externally, Beau Normandie 2 measures 15.00 metres long and 8.50 metres wide. The internal measurements are 13.15 metres by 6.90 metres. The hall is 6.60 metres long and the byre 6.15 metres long. Gable walls are 0.90 metres thick and lateral walls 0.80 metres thick. The eaves stand *c.* 4.70 metres and the ridge *c.* 8.60 metres above ground level. Beau Normandie 3 has a total external length, including the outshot, of 16.80 metres and a width of 8.50 metres. The hall is 3.75 metres long and 6.65 metres wide internally, and the byre 7.35 metres long and 6.65 metres wide internally. Walls vary in thickness from 0.75 metres to 0.90 metres. The ground slopes from left to right and at the upper end of the slope the eaves stand 4.60 metres and the ridge 8.75 metres above ground level.

Walling is of the Ordovician *grès armoricain,* or sandstone, with occasional pieces of the purple Montfort schist rubble, laid in a mortar of *pisé.* There is no evidence of ashlar, and door and window surrounds are formed of rubble, as are the quoins, although here a few larger blocks are occasionally used. Roofing is of slate with red-tile ridges. Chimney-stacks are of the same material except for one stack which is of red brick. The ground floor is of *terre battue* and the loft floors are of boards nailed to the beam and joists. Roof structures are similar. In Beau Normandie 3 there are five trusses, the centre one of which is of the full king-post type, the remaining four having upper king-posts. King-posts support a ridge-beam and there are three pairs of lateral purlins supported on cleats. Principal rafters are braced down to the tie-beams. There are wall-plates, two at the front of the house and one at the back. Common rafters are sprocketed out over the eaves. There is an under-ridge purlin scissors-braced to the ridge-purlin. In Beau Normandie 3, the three roof trusses are of the upper king-post type, the king-posts being braced upwards to the ridge-purlin. Again there are three pairs of purlins supported on cleats and the common rafters are sprocketed out over the wall-heads. Slate roofs are nailed to boards laid across the common rafters in both cases. Beau Normandie 2 originally had three hearths, one in the hall and two at first-floor level, but both the latter have now been demolished. Hearth H1 is a fine structure displaying some attempt at decoration. Construction is in the usual manner, and in the absence of suitable building stone a wooden breastsummer is supported on wooden corbels and in turn supports a chimney-hood of stone rubble, also corbelled out in a rather unusual manner (Fig. 219). There is no reason to believe that the date 1554 carved on the breastsummer is not the date of building. In Beau Normandie 3 there was formerly a hearth, H2, in the tiny hall but this was demolished about sixty years ago and only the red-brick chimney-stack now remains as evidence of its previous existence. All the doorway and window lintels are of wood and a feature of this district is the wooden blocks set transversely in the walls and intended to be used to hold door fastenings.

Window W1 retains its original five iron bars. Another local feature which is characteristic is the placing of two very large rubble blocks in the body of the wall over the chimney corbels, to weigh them down.

Beau Normandie 2 is a long-house, first derivative, with separate doorways, D1 providing access to the hall, and D2 and D3, almost opposite each other, to the byre. Both hall and byre are finely ceiled with both beams and joists. This evidence, together with that of the hearth, of high quality for the district, indicate that the building was originally intended for someone of fairly high social status. This is further emphasized by the fact that the loft was provided with hearths. There is no proof that either of these upper rooms was used as a solar or indeed what their function was, but there were clearly three heated cells. Beau Normandie 3 appears to be of much later date and the red-brick chimney-stack suggests that it perhaps belongs to the nineteenth century. It appears to be all of one date and it is possible that the stone partition wall now dividing the hall and the byre is a later insertion. Certainly that in the older house is an insertion, for the straight joints are very clear to see. In its present form Beau Normandie 3 is a long-house of the second derivative with no internal communication between hall and byre. The outshot at the end is probably a still later addition with a clearly marked straight joint. A problem in the evolution of these two buildings is the position of the straight joint in the gable wall of Beau Normandie 2. This is offset from the end of Beau Normandie 3 and it must be supposed that part of the gable of Beau Normandie 2 was demolished before Beau Normandie 3 was built. As the gable wall of Beau Normandie 3 rises from the lateral wall of Beau Normandie 2, there seems little doubt that it is the later of the two houses, quite apart from the evidence of the late chimney-stack. Beau Normandie 3 is a good example of a long-house in which the byre is upslope from the hall and must have drained past the open door of the hall. The light wooden partitions within the hall of Beau Normandie 2 are a recent feature. There is no internal communication between the two houses and number 3 must have been occupied by a second family, perhaps related by kinship or work.

Le Beuchet 1, Saint-M'Hervé, Ille-et-Vilaine (XU 423375), is also a long-house, second derivative, hall and byre being separated by a stone partition (Figs. 220 and 234). Externally the house measures *c.* 13.90 metres long and *c.* 8.45 metres wide. Internally, it is *c.* 12.00 metres long and *c.* 6.80 metres wide, the hall being *c.* 6.50 metres, and the byre *c.* 5.10 metres, long. The eaves stand *c.* 5.40 metres, and the ridge *c.* 10.70 metres, above ground level and the ground falls about 0.20 metres from left to right. The gable walls are 0.90

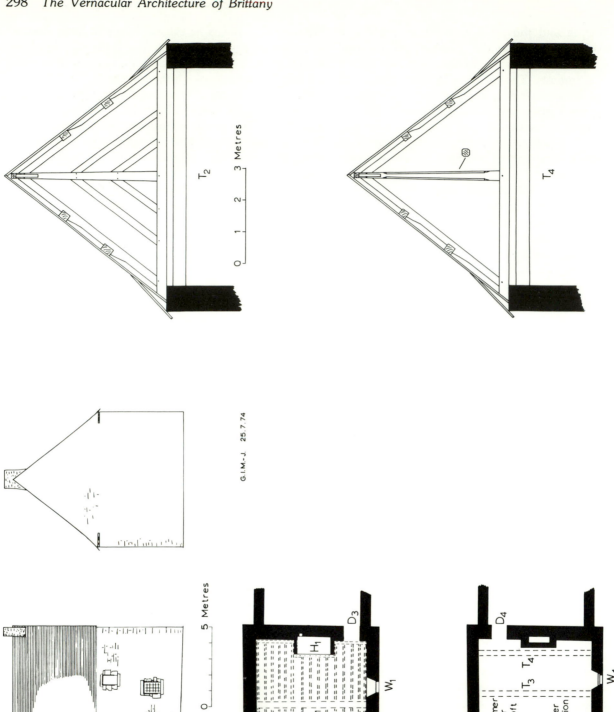

T₂

3 Metres
0 1 2 3

T₄

G.I.M.-J.   25.7.74

5 Metres
0   5

D₃
H₁
W₁
B₁
D₁
W₂ D₂
H₂
Ground floor

D₄
Former stair to loft
T₄
T₃
T₂
Former partition
W₄
W₅
T₁
W₃
H₃
First floor

Fig. 220a. Le Beuchet 1, Saint-M'Hervé, Ille-et-Vilaine

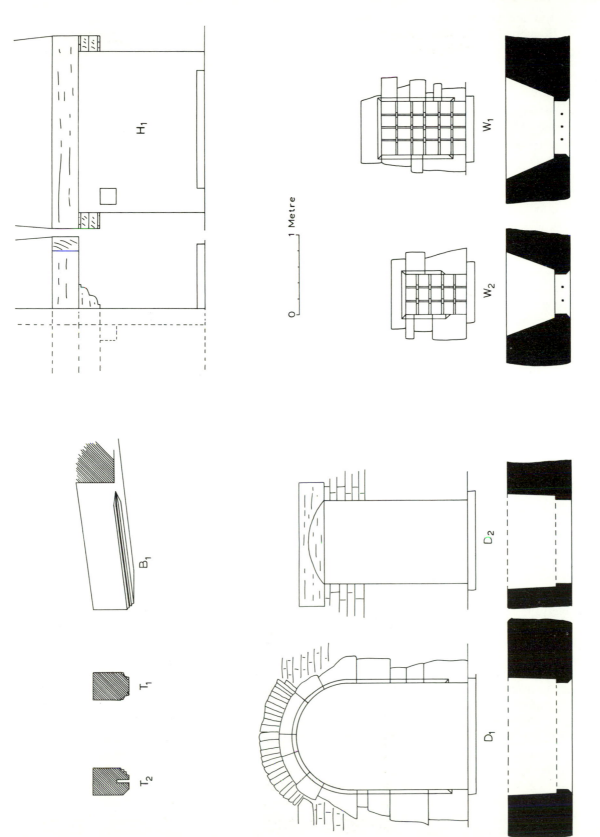

Fig. 220b. Le Beuchet 1, Saint-M'Hervé, Ille-et-Vilaine

metres thick and the lateral walls 0.80 metres thick. Walling is of Brioverian schist rubble with dressings for doorway D1 and all the windows. The roof is covered with slate. Doorway D2 has a wood lintel and rubble jambs. The walling is bonded in a mortar of *pisé*. Flooring in the hall and byre is of *terre battue* and that of the first floor consists of wooden boards laid on the beams and joists. The ceiling of the hall is finely built. One massive beam, B1, has an elaborate chamfer, and common joists are laid across it. A similar, but plainer, ceiling is provided for the second cell at ground-floor level, now the byre. At first-floor level there were formerly two chambers, one heated by hearth H3, the other unheated. There is a change of floor level, the space above the hall being *c.* 0.25 metres higher than the chamber above the byre. This change of floor level coincides with the stone partition wall separating hall and byre. The two upper rooms were formerly ceiled but all trace of this is now gone and they stand open to the roof. A stairway which once provided access from the unheated chamber to the loft in the roof space is also missing, only the circular cavity in the wall remaining as witness to its former existence. Roof structure is of the full king-post type, some of the king-posts being chamfered and all tapered. King-posts support a ridge-purlin and there are two pairs of lateral purlins slotted into the principal rafters which are shaped to form cleats. Common rafters are sprocketed out over the wall-heads. A curious feature is the presence of a double tie-beam; the tie-beam of the roof truss rests on the wall-heads, but some 0.20 metres below lies a secondary and heavier tie-beam. Roof truss T2 has its king-post braced down to the tie-beam and this was formerly contained in the partition wall separating the two first-floor cells. Remains of the clay-and-lath partition survive.

Originally there were three chimney-pieces, but H2 has been demolished, as has the chimney at the lower end of the house. Hearth H1 provides heat for the hall and H3 for the principal upper room immediately above the byre. All these chimney-pieces are of wood, there being no suitable building stone available in the district. The principal doorway is round-headed, bearing a flat-splay chamfer, and has a relieving arch in schist immediately above. All the windows are of the same pattern and those at ground-floor level retain their original iron *grilles*. The doorway to the byre, with its wood lintel, is very much simpler and obviously less important. There is a possibility that this represents a later insertion but there is no evidence that the stone wall dividing the hall and byre is anything but original, and so it seems more likely that doorway D2 is an original feature. The first floor is lighted by windows W3 and W4 and the heated cell by window W5 which is provided with window seats. The walling below window W4 is off-set to permit close access but not provided with seating. Doorways D3 and D4 at the upper end of the building now provide access to the adjacent long-house, a building of recent date, and it seems likely that doorway D3 is a fairly recent insertion, perhaps dating from the late-nineteenth or early-twentieth century. Doorway D4, however, appears to have been the loading doorway giving access to the unheated first-floor room which must have been used as a storage loft, either for hay or grain.

Fundamentally this building could be regarded as of two-cell plan but the second cell, although heated, does seem to have been intended as a byre, as there are slits in the rear wall and the chimney-piece, H2, is relatively poor in quality. In addition to the two slits at the rear, ventilation is provided by window W2 which, like W1, retains the original iron *grille*. It is unusual for a byre to be so finely ceiled, and the size and quality of window W2 is surprising. This cell may have been provided with a hearth in case it was subsequently desired to expel the cattle and convert to a dwelling, as was reported at La Ville des Nachez. Alternatively, it may have been built as a stable, with a hearth for the farm servants who slept with the horses, or it may have been originally a dwelling, having later been converted to a byre. The ceiling is considerably lower than that of the hall in order to provide the first-floor room above with adequate headroom. A wooden newel stair in a corner of the byre leads to this upper room heated by hearth H3. At the time of survey, a bed stood in the corner between window W5 and the gable wall, the traditional position of the conjugal bed. Although the present occupants live entirely in the hall, the upper room may once have been a first-floor hall, occupied by the *seigneur,* leaving the lower hall for his farmer, or it may have served a function closer to that of the medieval solar, or it may simply have been an extra room used for additional sleeping accommodation. The house, therefore, remains problematical and is difficult to date, and whilst it is probably of seventeenth-century origin, it may be as early as the sixteenth century. The hall is an extremely fine room with some magnificent detail, as is the cell over the byre. The poor quality of the building stone reflects availability of material in the district, and the chimney-pieces do not match in quality the superb carpentry in the roof and on the ceilings. There can be no question that the two important rooms are the hall and the first-floor heated chamber. An alternative explanation is that this house was formerly open to the roof and the ceiling over the hall represents an insertion. This, in the absence of supporting evidence, seems extremely unlikely. The hall ceiling is a massive affair which shows *every* sign of being original, there is no trace of smoke blackening anywhere in the roof and it is unlikely that the hearth, H1, is anything but original too. The change in floor level is, therefore, more easily explained by the desire to give greater headroom in the first-floor chamber at the expense of the byre where it was not necessary.

Goasven, Plougasnou, Finistère (VU 408936), is also a problematical building (Fig. 221). Its two wings, at right angles, enclosing a stair turret, are probably of different dates, the turret having been added when the cross-wing was built. The total length of the building is *c.* 16.20 metres externally and the maximum width of the cross-wing *c.* 11.20 metres. Internally, the principal room measures 8.65 metres by 5.30 metres and the total length of the cross-wing, internally, is *c.* 9.00 metres and the width 5.20 metres. The ground drops sharply from back to front and from right to left. Close to the main doorway, D1, the eaves stand 7.00 metres, and the ridge 10.80 metres, above the ground. Wall thickness varies considerably but most of the lateral walls are *c.* 0.75 metres and the thickest gable wall 1.15 metres thick. Walling is of *granit rose*, mostly rubble, but with coping, doorway and window dressing of ashlar, and roughly squared blocks for the quoins laid in the mortar of *pisé.* Roofing is entirely of the chunky local slates, capped with red-tile ridges. The ground floor is entirely of *terre battue* and the surface of the first floor is formed of wooden boards nailed to the beams and joists. The loft-space in the roof is also floored with wooden boards. Roof trusses are of the upper king-post, collar and tie-beam type, the king-posts supporting a ridge-purlin and two pairs of lateral purlins resting on cleats. The king-post is braced upwards both ways to the ridge-purlin. Common rafters rest with their feet on the wall-heads and are staggered at the apex. Slates are nailed to boarding laid across the common rafters. Hearths, four in number, are entirely of granite, and as this material in this district is mechanically very strong, the breastsummers are formed of huge slabs of stone. The quality is monumental, and although H1 is the finest, the other three are of a similar order. The chimney-hoods are of rubble, as are the chimney-stacks. Doorway and window dressings are also of fine quality, the principal doorway, D1, having a Gothic arch, D2 being round-headed and the two doorways at the head of the stone stair, giving access to the upper rooms, both being shouldered. Most of the windows have either flat-splay or cavetto mouldings and some originally bore mullions and transoms, although these have now been removed. All windows would originally have been closed by wooden shutters opening inwards. Window W2 is now blocked. Doorway and window dressings are typical of the high quality to be expected in this district.

The L-shaped plan is unusual. A trace of a straight joint close to doorway D7 at the rear of the building, together with the differences in doorway heads, suggests that the two limbs of the building are of different date. Proof of this is, however, lacking. If this suggestion is correct, then the hall is the earliest part of the building with access by the Gothic doorway D1. At a subsequent stage the cross-wing was added, together with the stair turret. Although the Gothic doorway may be sixteenth century, the possibility of its being as late as early-seventeenth century must not be discounted. The round-headed doorway, D2, could also be late-sixteenth century but a seventeenth-century date for this is much more likely. It is surprising that doorway D7 was thought necessary, and it may indeed be a later insertion. The cross-wing has the appearance of a long-house but the cell at the lower end may be the result of a later insertion of the stone partition. If it is original, then use as a *cellier,* pantry or — less likely — a dairy, may be suggested. Doorway D2 is too narrow for a long-house and it is unlikely that cattle were led in via D1 and D6. Even if the original building was used as a long-house, it thus seems unlikely that the cross-wing was ever so used. At first-floor level, doorways D3 and D4 give access to the two large upper rooms, both provided with hearths. Formerly the newel stair rose further, as the archaeological evidence indicates, and the most likely interpretation of this is that access was provided as far as the loft in the roof space. The stair turret presumably ended in a conical roof but all trace of this has now disappeared and the loft is accessible only by ladder from the first floor. The thin concrete partitions in the hall are of very recent date. The house thus appears to comprise four large rooms, one of them, in the cross-wing, subdivided to make a small end cell. It is also noteworthy that the most important window in the cross-wing is at first-floor level. The communicating doorway, D6, suggests that the two parts were occupied by related families. The upper room in the cross-wing, subdivided by a later partition, was of some importance to judge by window W6. Access was by the stair turret and the shouldered doorways D3 and D4. This room could have been a separate dwelling, a first-floor hall or, as suggested for Le Beuchet, a solar. The other upper room may be similarly explained. Accommodation certainly existed for two families, probably related, with, additionally, the upper rooms. Certainly the cell over the cross-wing looks more like a residence than the other upper room which may just have been a heated *chambre*. There is a tradition in Brittany of the *seigneur,* when letting a house

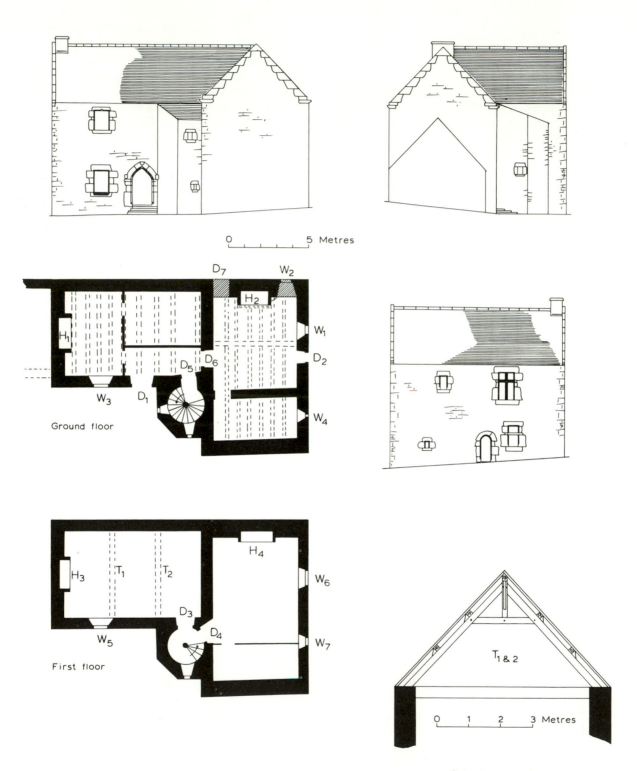

0 _____ 5 Metres

D₇   W₂

H₂

W₁

D₂

H₁

D₅ D₆

D₁

W₃   D₁

Ground floor

W₄

H₃   T₁   T₂

H₄

W₆

D₃

D₄

W₅

First floor

W₇

T₁ & ₂

0   1   2   3 Metres

G.I.M-J. 14.9.72

Fig. 221a.   Goasven, Plougasnou, Finistère

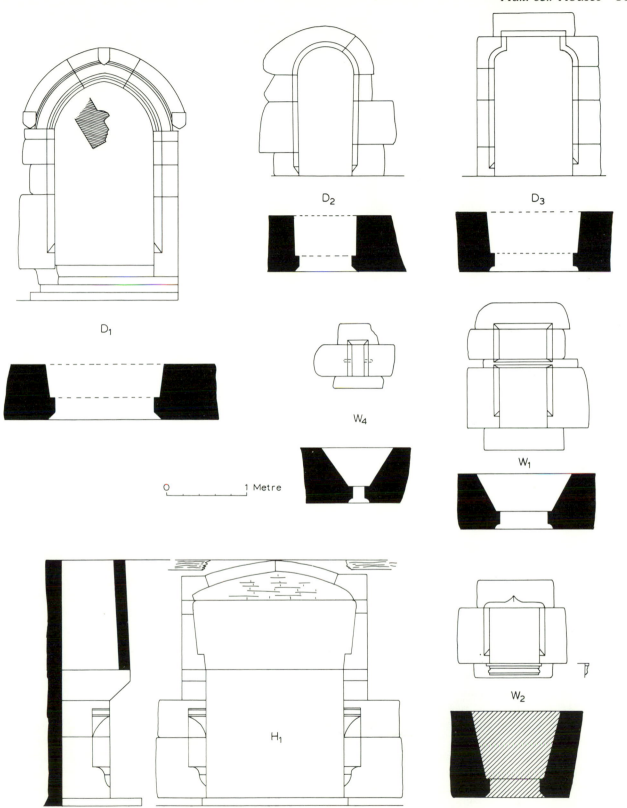

Fig. 221b. Goasven, Plougasnou, Finistère

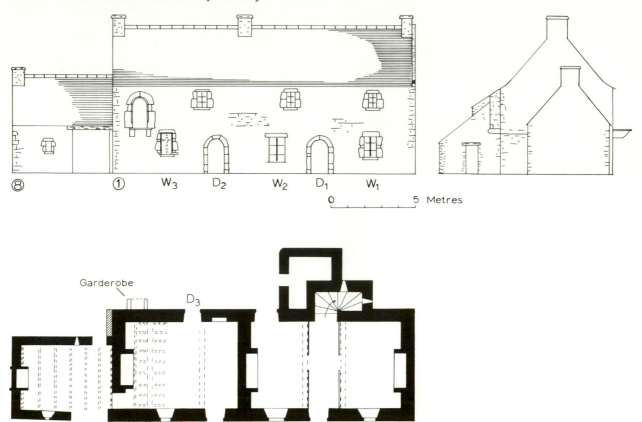

W₃ D₂ W₂ D₁ W₁

0   5 Metres

Garderobe

D₃

G.I.M.-J. 25.6.71.

Fig. 222a Kermorfezan 1, 8, Plougasnou, Finistère

or making provision for a farmer, keeping a room for himself. So strong is the tradition that the practice continued at Cosquer in Guérande, where a first-floor room is still reserved by the absentee proprietor although he has never used it and is never likely to. The practice seems to stem from the former need of the *seigneur* to visit all his *manoirs*, to collect rents and dues, hunt game and partake of the fruits of his property. This was the case at Kerneïs in the *pays de Treguier* which the *seigneur* visited once a year *'pour recevoir ses fermages, chasser son gibier et surveiller ses plantations'*.[578] A similar arrangement would fit the *métayage* system. Many of the *petits manoirs* have long been inhabited only by a peasant family, the proprietor being absent, and it may be doubted whether the *seigneurs* ever lived long in some of them. Certainly many of the hearths in upper rooms appear to be unmarked by fire. It may be that large numbers were built only for status, of a size in keeping with the area of the estate.

Kervorn 1, 2, Laz, Finistère (VU 356335), has already been referred to, for it consists of one- and two-cell dwellings, with a communicating doorway, now blocked (Fig. 216). Kervorn 2 has a heated upper room approached by a stone stairway, and Kervorn 1 has both a bed-outshot and a storeroom on the ground floor in addition to the two cells. The first floor is here unheated, but may well have been used for additional sleeping accommodation, judging by the provision of an elaborate stairway. There is no loading door. Kervorn 1, 2, may thus be regarded as two separate multi-cell houses of an elaborate kind not observed elsewhere. The use of the upper room as a solar rather than a first-floor hall has been suggested for some of the more elaborate long-houses in the Monts d'Arrée (Fig. 195).

Kermorfezan 1 and 8, Plougasnou, Finistère (VU 396932), provide another excellent example with accommodation for more than one family (Fig. 222). Externally, Kermorfezan 1 measures 18.05 metres long

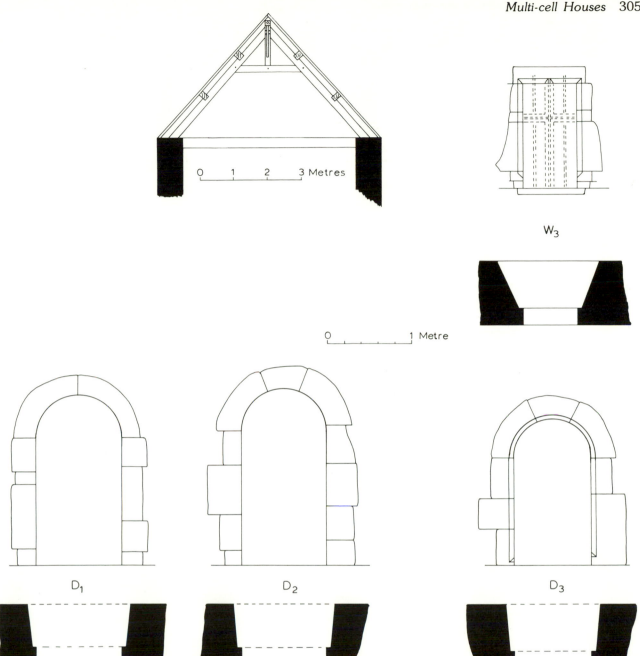

0   1   2   3 Metres

W₃

0 _____ 1 Metre

D₁   D₂   D₃

Fig. 222b   Kermorfezan 1, 8, Plougasnou, Finistère

and 6.60 metres wide with the stair turret and rear outshot increasing the width to 10.20 metres. The single-storey building, Kermorfezan 8, adds a further 5.60 metres to the total length, externally. Kermorfezan 1 is a complex of three dwellings. The two-cell house on the right measures internally 8.80 metres long and 5.10 metres wide. A single-cell dwelling to the left and the first-floor hall immediately above are 6.60 metres long and 5.10 metres wide internally. The small single-cell dwelling, Kermorfezan 8, measures *c.* 5.30 metres long and *c.* 3.90 metres wide. The eaves stand *c.* 5.20 metres, and the ridge *c.* 8.85 metres, above ground level. The lateral walls of Kermorfezan 1 are 0.75 metres, and the gable walls 0.80 metres, thick. Those of Kermorfezan 8 are 0.50 metres thick. Walling is of *granit rose* rubble with some ashlar for doorway and window dressings laid in a mortar of *pisé*. The roof is of slate, mostly of a chunky local variety but with some imported

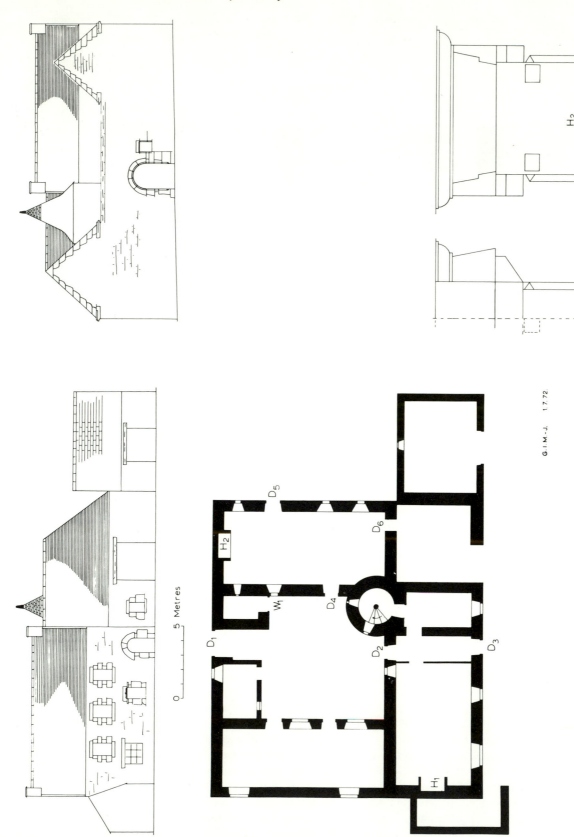

Fig. 223a   Traon-ar-Run, Plougasnou, Finistère

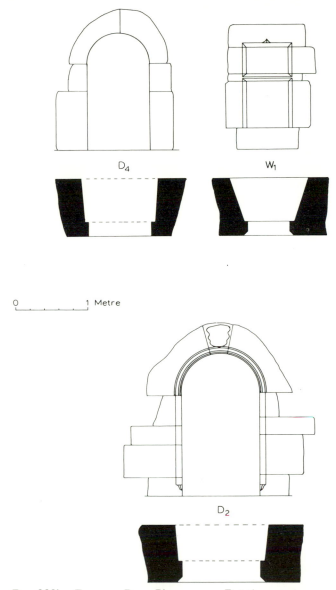

D₄   W₁

0 _____ 1 Metre

D₂

Fig. 223b   Traon-ar-Run, Plougasnou, Finistère

slate near the ridge, which is completed with red tiles. Flooring at ground-floor level is of *terre battue* and at first-floor level of wooden boards nailed to the beams and joists. The loft floor is also of wooden boards. Roof trusses are of the upper king-post, collar and tie-beam type. King-posts carry a ridge-purlin and two pairs of lateral purlins are trenched into the back of the principal rafters. Common rafters are staggered at the apex and rest with their feet on the wall-heads. Slates are nailed to boarding fastened to the common rafters. The complex contains a total of seven hearths: one in Kermorfezan 8, and three on each of the ground and first floors of Kermorfezan 1. Construction of all these hearths is similar: granite corbels support a granite breastsummer

on which the rubble chimney-hood is supported. The chimneys themselves are also of granite rubble. All the doorways are round-headed and mostly plain, exceptions being the doorway to the first-floor hall and doorway D3, the rear entrance to the single-cell dwelling underneath the first-floor hall. The quality of the masonry is high and typical of the area.

Kermorfezan 8 is clearly a single-cell house formerly occupied by a family dependent upon the larger house which was the focus of a small estate. Kermorfezan 1 can be divided into three distinct parts. To the right is a two-cell dwelling with central cross-passage and doorways opening left and right into the hall and the smaller second cell which also has a doorway leading into the yard at the back. It is probable that this second cell performed the function of a kitchen in a manner similar to that at Kerrio 5. At the end of the cross-passage a staircase rises within a stair turret to first-floor level where there is a pair of rooms, each heated. The stair rises further to give access to the loft-space within the roof. The outshot beyond the stair turret was probably a pigsty. Next to this two-cell dwelling is a pair of single-cell dwellings, that on the ground floor having two doorways, D2 and D3, not quite opposite each other, and a ceiling of some quality with massive beams and common joists. A doorway next to the chimney-breast now provides access to Kermorfezan 8, but it is doubtful whether this is an original feature. There is no communication between this single-cell dwelling and the two-cell dwelling to the right. Above it is a first-floor hall, also without any means of communication with the first floor of the two-cell dwelling. Access was formerly by a stone stairway leading to the platform supported on massive granite corbels. The stairway has gone, but platform and corbels survive. Immediately opposite at the rear of the building the garderobe is preserved *in situ*. This is a good example of a first-floor hall with a relationship to the rest of the house similar to that at La Salle. Archaeological evidence in the form of the continuation of the 0.75 metres thick wall at the front elevation and a remnant of wall at the rear of the house, together with the very thin walls of Kermorfezan 8, suggests that the latter dwelling may replace an earlier building which formed the continuation of Kermorfezan. A seventeenth-century date seems likely. Kermorfezan 1 thus provided accommodation for three families under one roof, the *seigneur* in the two-cell dwelling and someone of high social status, as at La Salle, in the first-floor hall, with perhaps a farmer in the ground-floor cell. The remaining tenants and dependents were housed in nearby single-cell dwellings and long-houses.

Troan-ar-Run, Plougasnou, Finistère (VU 411958), is a courtyard farm with a layout once common in the *commune* (Fig. 223). In recent years the enclosing walls of many farms have been demolished to make yards more accessible to machinery. Only the ground-floor level of Troan-ar-Run was surveyed. Two separate dwellings are evident with buildings around an enclosed courtyard. Maximum length of all conjoined buildings is 30.60 metres and maximum depth from front to back 20.60 metres. The principal residence is *c.* 15.00 metres long and 6.90 metres wide externally and is divided into two cells and a cross-passage. The larger cell, the hall, is 8.55 metres long and 5.25 metres wide internally. The ground falls from front to back and the present dwelling is the tallest building, the eaves standing 4.70 metres and the ridge 8.50 metres above ground level, although the top of the cone over the stair turret rises to 9.70 metres. Walls are all *c.* 0.70 to 0.80 metres thick, except for those of the small barn outshot and the modern pigsty in the courtyard. Walling is entirely of *granit rose* rubble with ashlar of the same material for doorway and window dressings. Roughly dressed blocks are used for the quoins. Most of the roofing is covered with a local chunky slate, but there is some use of Anjou slate. All the ridges are finished with tile. Floor covering was formerly entirely of *terre battue* but the house has been extensively renovated and concrete flooring laid over the whole of the ground floor of the present dwelling and over the floor of the byres as well. Only the single-storey dwelling with hearth H2, now uninhabited, is still floored with *terre battue*. Floor covering in the upper rooms is of boards laid across the common beams. Chimney-pieces are constructed in the traditional manner with massive granite breastsummers supported on granite corbels. Hearth H2 is typical of the quality in this house. Doorway and window dressings are of good quality, although many of the original window surrounds have been destroyed. W1 is a good example of an original window opening formerly closed by wooden shutters. Only one small window in the front elevation of the house remains of the original windows. Doorways are all round-headed, with the exception of doorway D6 which is shouldered. Some, like D4, are plain, others like D2 have flat-splay chamfers on the jambs and more elaborate mouldings on the arch. Doorway D2, presumably the original main entrance to the house, approached via the large doorway D1 in the wall enclosing the courtyard, bears an empty shield of arms, an indication of the social aspirations of the builder.

This group is one of the few surviving examples of the once many courtyard farms of the district. The presence of straight joints suggests that it is not all of one build. Although the present dwelling appears at first sight to be the principal structure, the now empty single-cell dwelling

of the right-hand side of the courtyard preserves more original features; above it is another single-cell dwelling which may have served as a first-floor hall. The present dwelling has clearly been considerably altered and three large modern windows inserted at first-floor level. It may always have been of two storeys but the ground-floor plan is difficult to interpret. The small cell at the end may have been a service room but it is doubtful whether there was a partition on the hall side of the cross-passage which, in its original form, probably opened directly into the hall. The remaining buildings around the courtyard consist of byres and pigsty. The well, not shown in the drawing, is a plain but well-constructed stone structure just beyond doorway D1 and outside the confines of the courtyard. The position of the doorway is unusual and the service end may be an addition, perhaps dating from the building of the stair-turret, as may be the upper storey, with its later window dressings. The wing at right angles, heated by hearth H2, retains its original doorways, D4, D5, and D6, and transomed window openings. Above is another room, of uncertain function, but probably a first-floor hall or solar. There is no communication with the cell below and access is via the stair-turret. There was accommodation here for at least two households and possibly three if the upper room was used solely as a dwelling. The straight joints suggest that the group evolved over a period of time. A similar observation was made in connection with Keradour in the same *commune* (see Chapter 11), and as a generalization it probably applies to most of the courtyard farms of the area, many of which would have accommodated several families. It will be shown in the next chapter, on the basis of documentary evidence, that the oldest part of this house is the wing on the right, the Ty Coz, or old house, with its two superimposed cells, rather than the present two-storey front elevation.

The only multi-cell *manoir* recorded by the E.A.R. is Keranvern in Ploumilliau. Elaborate ranges of farm buildings enclose three sides of a courtyard, the dwelling closing the fourth side. The drawings are inadequate for detailed analysis, but the dwelling appears to consist of two houses of different builds. The lesser of the two has hall at the front and a second heated cell at the rear. The principal house, of two-and-a-half storeys, consists of cross-passage, hall, *cellier,* and *bucher* on the ground floor. Upper floors, for which no details are available, are approached by a stair-turret at the end of the cross-passage.[579] Recent observation suggests that a type of multi-cell house with cross-wing exists in Kerity-Penmarc'h, Finistère, and that mariners' houses near Brest may also be complex multi-cell structures.

Illustrations of multi-cell houses appear in the works of

the Commission d'Inventaire. In general, in the *canton* of Carhaix-Plouguer, the *manoirs* are one room deep with the cross-passage leading to a stairway. The *manoir* at Kerniguez is of two builds, a single-cell dwelling of one-and-a-half storeys, of sixteenth-century date, and a later building of three cells and cross-passage. Various outshots at the rear are additions. At the upper end, an unheated cell was presumably a byre or stable and has no communication with the hall. The cross-passage, with the stair-turret at one end, is defined in stone on both sides but there is no evidence to show whether these walls are original. The lower cell, now a byre, has a hearth and may once have contained service rooms. Langautec, a *manoir* of *c.* 1600, has an added wing at the rear. The building is of two cells, each with a separate doorway, and a full storey above. Le Ster is a two-cell sixteenth-century house, the cross-passage being defined on one side only and open to the hall on the other. The lower end has no hearth and the outside doorway is probably a late insertion. Whether this cell was originally a service room is difficult to say, but the two-storey house has preserved its primitive aspect. The stair-turret provides access to a heated upper room, probably a solar. Kerligonan and Le Stanger both illustrate sixteenth-century plans in which the cross-passage opens directly into the hall. In both cases the cell below the cross-passage seems to have been a byre, suggesting a close relationship with the peasant long-house. The other plans are too inadequate to permit interpretation, beyond observing the almost universal presence of a stair-turret and the fact that the cross-passage is open to the hall on one side, as at Penayeun and Coat Quévérand.[580]

Similar *traits* are in evidence in the *cantons* of Le Faouët and Gourin. Kerbiquet appears to be a complex multi-cell structure, with a first-floor hall of some size. At Minguionet the cross-passage formerly opened directly into the hall, and the stair-turret stands at the upper end of the hall at the junction with an unheated cell. The upper floors, out of phase, have important heated cells and the structure may originally have been two adjacent first-floor halls of early sixteenth-century date. Kermain is a three-cell structure with two stair-turrets, none of the cells communicating internally. An embryo cross-passage in the central cell divides it into hall and service ends as at Kerpontdarms, above. The other two heated cells were presumably separate dwellings. Penguily is a multi-cell building, possibly of one date, forming two separate dwellings. The original house consisted only of a hall with a stair-turret, leading to the heated upper room, below the embryo cross-passage in what was presumably the service end. The principal room here seems to have been at first-floor level. The other wing, which may not be

contemporary, is of unclear function and has a separate stair-turret. In this area, during the sixteenth and early-seventeenth centuries, there seem to have been important first-floor halls, usually with other halls beneath. Probably many of these were true first-floor halls, the lower hall being used for cooking and the accommodation of servants. Whether the multi-cell houses with no interior communication were meant to be lived in as one house, as official opinion seems to imply, is doubtful. More likely they housed separate families, different branches of the same family, or families related by work.[581]

The various works of Frotier de la Messelière contain large numbers of line drawings illustrating *manoirs* of various sizes, plans and periods, the variety illustrated being too confusing to be of value other than as a starting point for a detailed survey beyond the scope of the present work.[582] The *manoir* of Côtes-du-Nord was distinguished generally by an enclosed courtyard surrounded by stables, byres, bakehouse, dairy, barns, cider-presses, dove-cot and, often, a chapel. Of the house itself, the ground floor normally consisted of two great rooms sometimes separated by a corridor at the end of which was the stair-turret. One room served as the dwelling of the *seigneur* and his family, the other for the domestics. Such a description fits the interpretation already advanced for Kerrio, above. Upper rooms, sometimes inhabited, often served as stores or workrooms, perhaps for the processing of flax. Furniture was similar to that found in peasant houses, except that it would be bigger and of higher quality: large tables and benches by the window, pious images, family portraits, old arms and hunting equipment hung on the walls, and spinning wheels and dressers with their complement of crockery.[583] Useful line drawings, from which it is possible to gain some idea of the size and extent of buildings, illustrate the somewhat romantic works of Louis Le Guennec. Particularly useful are his illustrations of the manorial *ensembles* with enclosing walls. Certain of the buildings shown have since suffered partial or total demolition.[584]

The occasional exhibition catalogues produced by the Commission d'Inventaire frequently illustrate multi-cell houses. Those of the *châteaux* and *manoirs* around Guingamp, and of the *Malouinières,* are especially useful.[585] Plans of the Breton *manoirs* find parallels in those of other parts of France, notably in Perche where the two-cell ground-floor plan, kitchen and hall, is common,[586] and also in the Soissonnais.[587]

In 1801, François Gourvil of Keramouzel in Plougasnou left an estate worth 4348 *francs*. The house consisted of a *'cuisine ou manelle',* a room, *'en bas de la cuisine en dehors du cloison'* and *'la chambre sur terre aboutissante du midi à la dite manelle'*. Whether the latter was a separate single-cell house or not is unclear. The *cuisine* was fully equipped as a common hall with box-bed, table, chests and a *'fauteuil de bois près le feu'*. The room at the lower end beyond the partition had the characteristics already outlined for the second cell of a two-cell house: bed, chests, *armoire,* barrels and implements. The third cell contained two box-beds, *armoires,* and a *charnier.* This accommodation was insufficient, however, and the *grange* contained a miscellany of chests, *armoires,* bed, barrels, tools of the flax trade, spinning wheels and implements.[588] In the same year, Hervé le Flammanc of Kerdiez in the same *commune* left an estate of 1802 *francs.* His home consisted of *'la maison manalle'* or hall, a second *'maison'* adjoining it to the west and a *'petit chambre à l'orient de la dite manalle'*. Apart from three beds, a table and an *armoire,* the hall contained a large collection of household utensils and implements. One of the adjoining cells had an *armoire,* chest, *charnier,* and various utensils, the other a spinning wheel, tools for preparation of flax, two chests, barrels and a ladder. Another bed was to be found in a *'maison en appentis'*.[589] Guillaume Tallegas of Kerdiez in Plougasnou in 1848 had two houses, each of three cells. The first house consisted of hall and *chambre sur terre,* both containing beds and *armoires,* and the *petite maison,* a store. The second house, at Kerbignon, had a hall, *petite maison* and *chambre.* There were five beds in the hall and two in each of the *petite maison* and *chambre.*[590] François Keraudy of Kerdalidec Ty Nevez, Plougasnou had a hall, *la manale,* with an entry, at the bottom end, containing a chest; a *'maison dite Ty Isella'* containing a whole range of implements, spinning wheels, and chests, together with the *charnier* and a bed; an *'arrière cuisine'* containing two chests; a *chambre* above the *Ty bian* with a *pétrin,* a bridle and a flax comb; a *chambre* above the kitchen with a bed, table, *armoires* and other furniture, obviously a bedroom; another *chambre* over the kitchen with two beds and a range of furniture; a *grande chambre* with a bed, *armoires,* equipment for processing flax, various utensils and tools; and the *Ty Bian* with a bed and some implements. There thus seem to have been two houses, the *Ty Bian* of two rooms, one over the other, and the principal dwelling with a hall, outshot at the rear, and rooms above.[591] Armel Le Reun of Neis-Vran in Locmaria-Plouzané in 1803 had a *cuisine* with three box-beds, dresser, table, *armoire,* chests and a longcase clock; *la salle,* with two box-beds, and chests; a *chambre* with an *armoire* and a chest; and a *chambre basse* with two box-beds and various chests.[592] One of the wealthiest

houses recorded was that of Charles Balanger, a merchant of Lampaul, Ouessant, who in 1822 left an estate valued at 4123 *francs.* He had a *chambre à coucher,* another *chambre,* a *cabinet,* a *salle* and a *cuisine.* All contained beds except the *cabinet.*[593]

The home of Jean-Marie de Gaudemont, of La Monforière, Côtes-du-Nord, is a good example of the home of a *seigneur* in 1781, before the Revolution. There was a *cuisine, la salle,* and a *cuisine* above with a *cabinet* adjoining. All contained beds and the house appears to have been of two-cell plan with the two first-floor rooms. As the first-floor rooms in many noble houses later came to be used for storage when they passed to peasant occupancy, it is instructive to note the contents. The *chambre* contained two beds and an *armoire,* the *cabinet* a bed, *table de toilette* and mirror, some clothing and jewellery. The upper rooms thus appear to have been true bedrooms, indicating the degree of specialization in a noble house towards the end of the eighteenth century.[594]

No multi-cell houses were described in the inventories examined for Ille-et-Vilaine and only three in Morbihan, two of three cells and one of five cells. The latter, in Ploëmeur, had a *cuisine* and a second room on the ground floor, and three rooms above. All contained beds except the second ground-floor cell.[595] Three large houses in Loire-Atlantique were recorded, one in a town house of ten rooms in Guérande, excluded from the analysis of inventories (Fig. 239). Jean Brebien had a six-cell house at Herbignac in 1825 consisting of a *salon, salle, cuisine, chambre à coucher,* two other *chambres* and a *cave,* the latter probably in an outshot. There were no beds in either the *salon* or the *salle,* but they were to be found in the *cuisine* and the two *chambres.* There was much high quality furniture and the estate, in a poor area, was valued at 2041 *francs.*[596] In 1802, Julien Rousseau of La Metairie de la Nourissonière in Boussay left 3274 *francs.* The four-cell house consisted of hall, a second ground-floor room containing a bed, circular table and two chests, and two rooms above. There were three beds in the hall; apart from one bed in an upper room, they were used entirely for storage. The presence of equipment for the processing of flax is again noteworthy.[597]

Probate inventories include examples of houses with from four to ten rooms with their relative positions often stated. The paucity of large houses in the sample quadrats is a function of the sample rather than an indication that few such houses existed, for they survive in large numbers, but remain proportionately few, so numerous are the small dwellings. Frotier de la Messelière claims that Côtes-du-Nord alone contained over 1700 *manoirs,* and if this density were repeated over the whole of the historic Province, there must have been over 8000 such houses, most of which survive.[598] Detailed examples illustrate considerable variety. The medieval hall with service rooms and solar exists at La Salle, Plurien. There is no proof as yet, however, of there ever having been a central open hearth with the hall open to the roof, in a surviving *manoir.* At La Salle, the mixture of Gothic and Renaissance style doorways, together with other evidence, suggests that the original building may have consisted simply of a single hall, i.e. a large single-cell dwelling, the late medieval equivalent at *manoir* level of the large number of single-cell peasant dwellings. Evidence at the Manoir de Quéhéon, Ploërmel, points in the same direction. Whilst otherwise less elaborate, Kerpontdarms is also representative of the late medieval hall with service end and solar. The stable at the upper end may here be original, but that at La Salle could be later. Other houses, like Goasven and Traon-ar-Run, illustrate the complexity of multi-cell relationships suggested by the inventories for the *commune* of Plougasnou. Both La Salle and Kermorfezan illustrate the close juxtaposition of totally independent multiple cells, some providing discrete living accommodation at first-floor level. At Cosquer in Guérande there remains the practice of the owner retaining for his own use an upper room, a relic of the days when the *seigneur* kept an upper room, whether a true first-floor hall, or a solar, for his own occasional use. Fournier quotes the example of the Métairie de Bodellio, the lease of which, in 1931, included a provision for the reservation of two rooms.[599]

Evidence from the Commision d'Inventaire suggests that some of the earliest medieval *manoirs* may have been large first-floor halls. Further work is needed to verify this, but if it is so, then such buildings may provide the link between the first-floor halls of the medieval castles and the multitude of small surviving first-floor halls. Inventories provide evidence of beds in almost all rooms. Only in a few instances, however, are the upper rooms true bedrooms, but a degree of specialization had been achieved by the nobility before the Revolution. Many gentry families abandoned their homes during the eighteenth century to pursue their social aspirations in Paris and elsewhere. This *trait,* already well advanced before the Revolution, was further accelerated afterwards. Their *manoirs* were taken over by peasant tenants and so descended the social scale, for the peasant families lived in one room and used the remainder for storage.

The multi-cell houses, in spite of their size and pretensions compared to the humble peasant dwellings that surround them, were built, and in many cases inhabited, by noble landowners whose attachment to the soil was real and whose wealth was often little greater than some of the neighbouring non-noble farmers. Such men took a direct part in the cultivation of their soil and compare with the Welsh lesser gentry, status-conscious of ancestry, title and armorial bearings, often poor but anxious to play a lead in the public and cultural affairs of the Province. Such were the *'gentilshommes-laboureurs qui conduisaient la charrue l'épee au côté, et siégeaient, en sabots, aux états de la province'.* [600]

FOURTEEN

FARM BUILDINGS

Farm buildings reflect the size of a holding, the type of agriculture practised and, to a certain extent, the nature and quality of the soil. Both Le Lannou and Gautier discuss farmyard form. The simplest consists of house and outbuildings, byre, stable and a *hangar* or small barn, arranged in a line, twenty to thirty metres in length. A *cellier* may take the form of an outshot at the rear of the house. The remaining elements, the heap of straw, the hay, the wood supply and the manure, are arranged either in front of the house on the *aire à battre*, or threshing yard, or in the *courtil*. This type of arrangment is frequent over the whole of Brittany, especially in the interior, and some two-thirds of farms are claimed to fall into this category. The long-house and its derivatives, or the single-cell house with the added byre, are found where holdings are small. The constituent houses of a *village rangée* or *rue* are usually long-houses, often converted to farm use. Where up to a dozen families once lived, now only two or three may survive, the abandoned houses having been transformed into byres, barns and pigsties. The line of buildings has often resulted from the progressive growth of the simplest long-house. Other farms demonstrate the various stages, real or imagined, in the development of a 'courtyard farm' with buildings arranged around two, three or four sides of a yard. This arrangement is frequent in the Rennes basin and in Trégorrois where a prosperous agriculture has long existed. Sometimes a completely enclosed yard is encountered, but gaps in the angles between gables usually permit access to other parts of the holding. Such a plan might have houses and byres on one side, stables opposite, and a *cellier* and pigsties facing each other to complete the *cour*. The *aire*, always kept clean, would lie beyond, close to the *hangars*. Occasionally, a farmyard with double courtyard is encountered. Frequently, a new house was erected at right angles to the old home, a phenomenon observed especially from the nineteenth century onwards, the old dwelling being relegated to occupation by animals. In other cases, new stables and byres were erected opposite the old house and byre, a

process that was extended to farms with buildings around three or four sides of a yard.

The stable was given most care, often being the first building to be renovated, for the horse was the most valuable animal of the farm. Here, too, the farm servants slept, if unmarried. Small barns of simple construction covered with a thatch of broom or buckwheat straw served to protect implements and vehicles. Straw was rarely protected but left in stacks about the yard. In the *cellier*, often an outshot at the rear of the house, were stored the cider, potatoes and other root crops destined for animal feed. Dairies are rare, and milk and dairy products were stored in the hall, usually in a keeping-place. The making of butter and cheese also took place there. Other common buildings are the bake-oven, the well and sometimes the shelter for the crushing of gorse, the *broyeur d'ajonc*. A manure heap stands in the yard. Traditionally the manure is left to lie in the byre for four or five months and reaches a considerable depth.[601]

Vallaux confirms that in Basse-Bretagne, stables and byres were, in general, aligned with the house.[602] Only *crèches*, buildings for pigs and other small animals, were separate. It will be demonstrated, below, that a large number of byres and stables were once dwelling houses, and that over much of Brittany the purpose-built farm building appears to be of nineteenth-century date or later. De Cambry observed that '*Un appenti couvert de chaume conserve les charrues et les instrumens du labourage; une aire découverte, sert à battre les grains. On n'y voit point de granges, les blés battus se déposent dans les greniers de la maison principale, ou se conservent en mulon*'.[603] As all the animals occupied the lower end of the long-house, there was no need for other buildings. The extent to which the 'typical' Breton farm consisted simply of a long-house and a few other buildings will be examined later.

Four writers provide case-studies of individual *communes*, containing, *inter alia*, information about farm buildings. In Bulat-Pestivien, Côtes-du-Nord, the long-house was the general type, but one or two first-floor halls existed, with a byre beneath the hall. The simplest open long-houses had a lean-to of wood. Structures some fifteen to twenty metres long consisted of house, i.e. the hall, byre, stable and barn. In other farms, there were two rows of buildings, one a new dwelling, the other a former house converted to accommodate animals. A few larger farms of the 'type manoir' consisted of a storeyed house, with a full range of farm buildings, usually arranged around a courtyard. Apart from byre, stables, henhouses, barns and shelters, buildings comprised pigsties, frequently circular, the *broyeur d'ajonc*, a shelter for vehicles, a well, and a bake-oven. There was usually only one oven per hamlet, the property of one of the farms but with rights for all the inhabitants. Conditions for animals were poor. Improvements consisted of temporary structures, *crèches* and *hangars*, of wood, earth and thatch, quickly erected, costing nothing, and easily pulled down. Such buildings were of no value at the end of the lease.[604]

For Plouvien, Finistère a variety of farmyard plans has been recognized, including that with 'open' yard, the most common type. Buildings were dispersed around the dwellings. More regularly planned examples were recorded with parallel rows of buildings, or a line of byre and stable set at right angles to the house. The single line of farm buildings was not well represented and the completely enclosed courtyard rare. Of the latter, four of the six examples were *manoirs*.[605] Farm buildings reflected the tendency towards stock-rearing and dairying. Stables and byres were the most important and stone-built, with roofs of slate or thatch, the larger farms also having a separate byre for the heifers, one for the calves, and sometimes a separate lodging for the bull. Barns were small and numerous. Eighteenth-century inventories show that farms had insufficient permanent outbuildings. Instead, *logettes* were constructed and dismantled when a farmer moved to a new farm. By the mid-twentieth century, outbuildings were nearly always of stone, although lean-to shelters and henhouses were often of wood. A shelter with one wall of stone, the other 'open' with four wooden posts, is illustrated. Tie-beams support brushwood covered with straw, the whole held down with straw rope. They were used for a variety of purposes including the storage of root-crops and the housing of carts. The insufficiency of buildings in which to store root-crops is one reason why *lokennou, loges,* or *logettes* have survived. Their dimensions average 5.00 by 2.50 metres (see Chapter 8), with an entrance either in a gable or a lateral wall. In 1948, 32.6 per cent of farms had one *lokenn*, 14.2 per cent had two, 4.2 per cent had three, and 0.4 per cent, four *lokennou*. They were not only found on the poor farms; frequently they

were found in the yards of the most up-to-date farmers. The bakehouse, another characteristic building, with its oven at one end, ceased to be used for the baking of bread in many farms before World War II, although many continued in use for the preparation of animal feed. The cereal crop was kept in the *grenier* or loft above the hall. When the house had a second storey and no loft, or hall open to the roof, the loft of another building might be used, or grain kept in chests, either in the hall or in another building.[606]

These scattered references appear to point to a wide variation in the provision of farm buildings. At one end of the scale there is the long-house with perhaps an outshot and a lean-to, whilst in the richer areas, and especially near the coast, purpose-built outbuildings of some quality may be found. Such is the case in Cap-Sizun, where the houses, mostly of late eighteenth-century or early nineteenth-century date, are of fine build, with outbuildings in a similar style. Those of Cléden-Cap-Sizun have the stable built at one end of the house, the *hangar* stands on one side of the *aire à battre*, and the byre and pigsty are variously placed.[607] In the adjacent *commune* of Goulien, plans and styles are similar. Pelras illustrates several examples showing how buildings are grouped around a yard with two entries.[608] The stable lies against the gable end of the house, the byre across the yard and a barn variously placed.[609] Nomenclature of farm buildings and their constituent parts, in the Breton language, is occasionally given in the E.A.R. survey.[610]

Farm buildings were excluded from data obtained from the sample quadrats except when contained within a long-house. Their observation and recording has therefore been limited and choice is more subjective. Nevertheless, a good idea of the size, variety and functions of various farm buildings may be obtained. Numerous examples have already been noted, amongst which are the circular pigsties particularly common in south-west Côtes-du-Nord (Fig. 109). The circular byre at Saint-Urlo (Fig. 113) is the only building of its kind so far discovered, and several of the circular pigsties, e.g. Kerguestoc (Fig. 112), are now used as henhouses. It is not altogether clear why the circular form remained popular for pigsties long after it had fallen out of use for other buildings. Their size and form is uniquely suited to the pig which has a tendency to root in the corners of rectilinear buildings and perhaps break out of weaker structures. It seems probable that in many cases they were used only by farrowing sows. Most pigsties, however, are rectilinear structures, some integrated with the house, and others, standing apart, are sometimes of very high quality. The majority of farm buildings of the Cap-Sizun district date from the late-eighteenth or

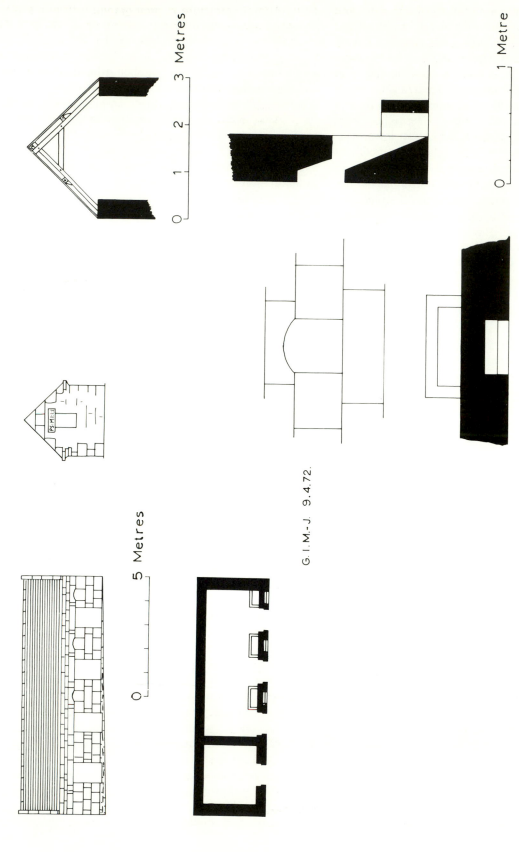

G.I.M.-J. 9.4.72.

Fig. 224   Kerodeven, Primelin, Finistère

nineteenth century. Rarely are they all of one date, and several periods of replacement and renewal are represented. Generally the house is the earliest building, followed in turn by stable and byre, and then by the lesser buildings, pigsty, oven and well-cover. The pigsty at Kerodeven, Primelin, Finistère (UU 787217), is not dated, but is a particularly fine example with façade, quoins and coping of finely cut granite blocks, the remainder of the walling being of rubble (Fig. 224). Roof covering is of slate with a red-tile ridge. Externally the building measures 10.00 metres long and 3.00 metres wide. It is divided internally by a stone wall into two unequal parts, the larger of which is 6.10 metres long by 2.15 metres wide and the smaller 2.45 metres long and 2.15 metres wide. The ground slopes so that the lower gable is 0.30 metres higher than the upper gable. At the upper end the eaves stand 1.70 metres and the ridge 3.35 metres above ground level. Walls are 0.50 metres thick at the gables and 0.40 metres thick elsewhere. The larger cell is served by three doorways and the interior was presumably sub-divided in its original state by wooden partitions, no trace of which now remains. There are three 'windows' which, in addition to providing ventilation, serve as chutes enabling feed to be poured directly into the three troughs from the outside. Construction of these chutes is such as to prevent an animal getting out of the building by the window opening. The small cell has no such arrangement. It may be that the original building was floored to create a loft space but no trace of this floor now remains. A loft door, however, survives in the upper gable. Roof structure is of the collar-truss type, the intersecting principal rafters supporting the ridge-purlin and the lateral purlin being supported by cleats. Slates are nailed to boards laid on the common rafters. The single cell at the lower end may have been intended either for the boar or for the farrowing sows. Pigsties are built as a lateral outshot on the front of many of the houses in the *pays de Guérande* and the Grand Brière Fig. 98) and integrated with the long-houses of the Monts d'Arrée and northern Finistère. That at Saint-Rivoal, built under the stone stairway, is a particularly fine example (Fig. 195).

Circular well-covers vary in form and regional distribution (see Chapter 7). Occasionally they are square in form, nearly all those of Cap-Sizun being of this type and of nineteenth-century date. That at Landrer 1, Plogoff (Fig. 212), built against the wall of the house, is typical. Here, water may be drawn from both inside and outside the house and a spout permits the adjacent trough to be filled directly. Bake-ovens, nearly always circular or sub-circular, are sometimes combined with a bake-house as at Les Rues Bellay 2, Paimpont (Fig.

139). A larger structure in grey granite with fine ashlar dressings occurs at Kerodeven, Primelin, Finistère (UU 787217), its oven now largely destroyed (Fig. 225). Walling is entirely of grey granite, mostly of rubble but with ashlar for the quoins, door and window dressings and the coping. The roof is covered with slate and has a red-tile ridge. Externally the building measures c. 10.00 metres long and 5.94 metres wide. Internally the length is c. 8.75 metres and the breadth c. 4.75 metres. Wall thickness is c. 0.60 metres and the eaves rise 2.20 metres and the ridge 5.20 metres above ground level. Rubble walling is laid in a mortar of *pisé* and the floor is of *terre battue*. The roof truss is of the collar and tie-beam type, the intersecting principal rafters supporting the ridge-purlin and the lateral purlins held on cleats. Slates are nailed to boards laid over the common rafters. There was originally a bake-oven contained in the upper gable but this has now largely been demolished, all that remains being the entrance on the inside wall of the building. A window and doorway are provided in the lateral wall and a cart entrance exists in the gable opposite the hearth. The building is dated 1859. There are three keeping-places. Construction is of high quality, typical of nine-teenth-century building in Cap-Sizun. Whilst this structure was undoubtedly intended to serve both as a bake-house and for the storage of farm vehicles and possibly implements as well, it is probable that it housed a family of servants during the population peak at the end of the nineteenth century. The lateral doorway and window, and the presence of a hearth, provide a 'hall' of much higher quality than many of the structures then being lived in. Dove-cots (see Chapter 7) are almost exclusively confined to the homes of landowners. Many stand detached from the main buildings (Fig. 150), but others are closely related to the yard (Fig. 148).

Examples of former dwellings now converted to byres occur at Kervaly (Figs. 178–184). Kervaly 12, 13 and 14 once consisted of two long-houses and a single-cell house. Now, Kervaly 12 is a two-cell dwelling, the remaining buildings all being given over either to stock or storage. Apart from the byres at the lower ends of the long-houses, original accommodation here consists of a stable and an adjacent lean-to pigsty. Kervaly 9 (Fig. 182) likewise has a cell added between its hall and the adjacent house. Iron rings in the wall betray its function, and although it may have been a byre, it could also at some stage have served as a stable. The small building adjacent to Kerhaliou 1 (Fig. 196) is in the same category. These buildings are the only stone-built accommodation for animals in substantial hamlets. Whilst *lokennou* may have once existed in larger numbers, it seems likely that virtually all the stock were contained in

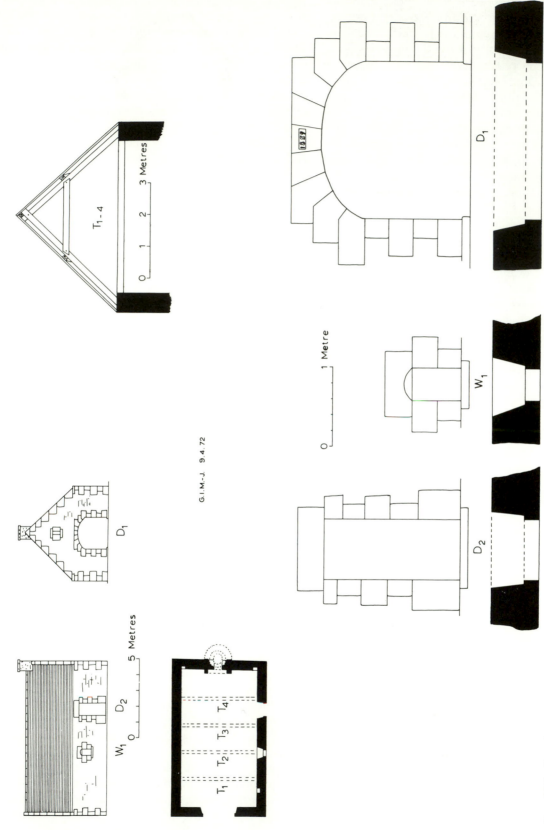

G.I.M.-J. 9.4.72

Fig. 225 Kerodeven, Primelin, Finistère

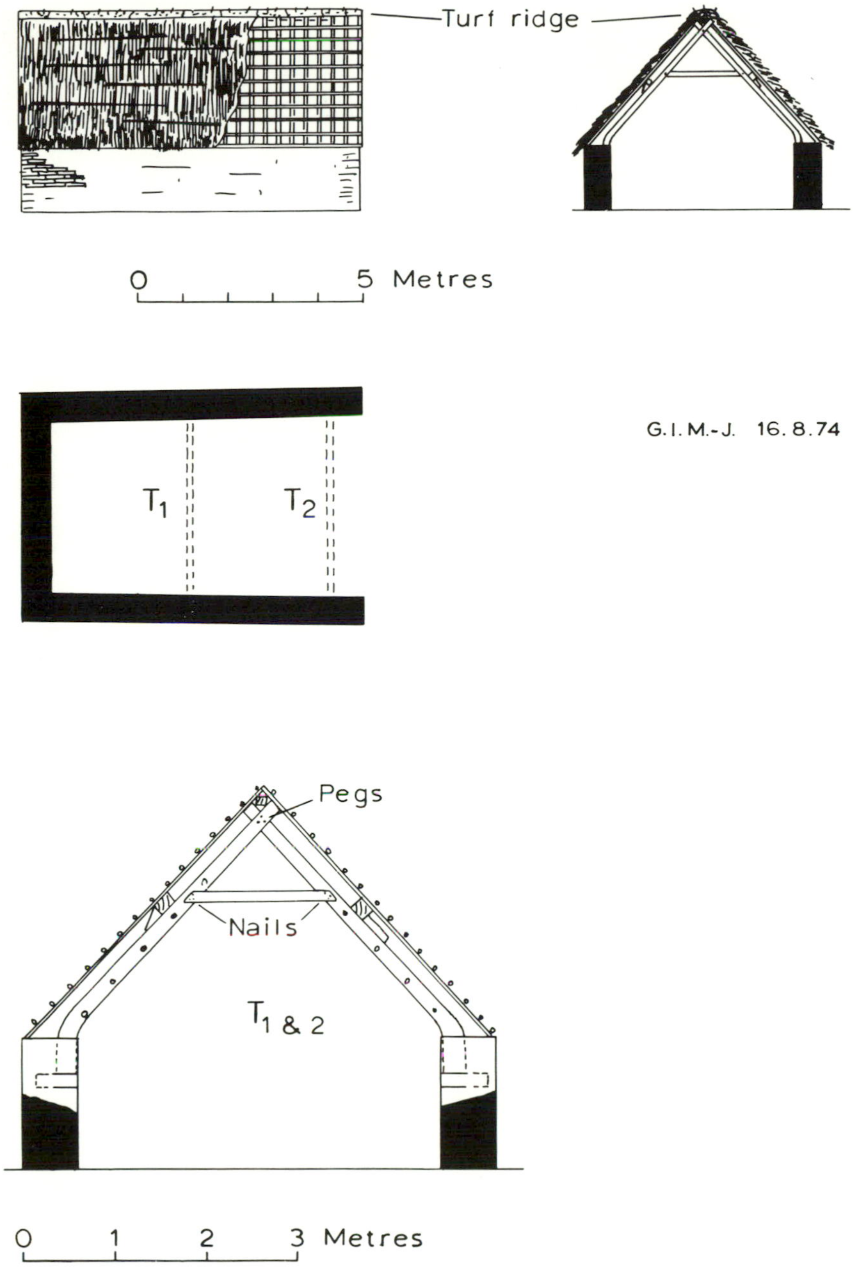

Fig. 226 Penhap, Marzan, Morbihan

the 'permanent' buildings. The possibility that there were always abandoned houses to be used for accommodation of stock must be discounted in places like Kervaly and Kerhaliou, where it is a recent phenomenon. These hamlets are representative in areas of very small farms and high population where all forms of life were accommodated within the long-house, with little need for additional buildings. This was true over large areas of the interior, and in some places near the coasts additional accommodation, where needed, took the form of *lokennou* and other temporary buildings illustrated at Pon Digeu (Fig. 166), Bréca (Figs. 164, 165), La Grande Noë (Fig. 163), Saint-Rivoal (Fig. 162), Bouleguy (Figs. 159-161), and already described (see Chapter 8). The *rangée* at La Ville des Nachez (Fig. 177) falls into the same category, as does that at Linsard, Taupont (Fig. 31).

The house of 1702 at Saint-Rivoal (Fig. 195) also entirely accommodated the livestock as well as one, or possibly two, families. Byre and pigsty have already been

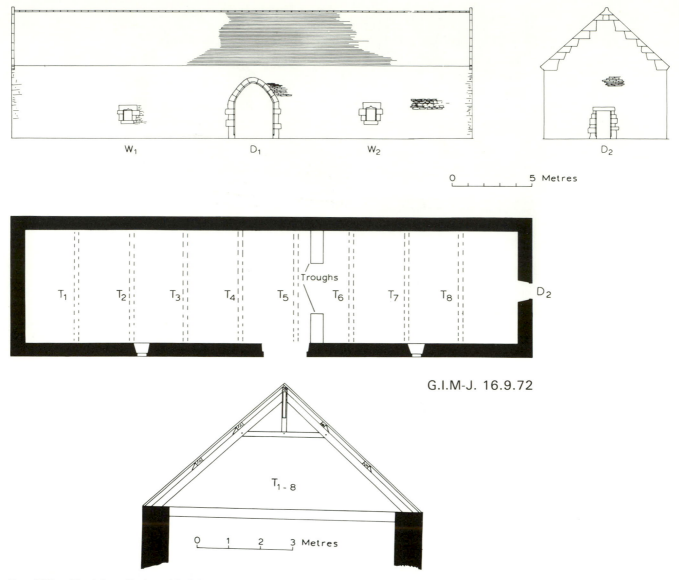

W₁   D₁   W₂   D₂

0   5 Metres

T₁ T₂ T₃ T₄ T₅ T₆ T₇ T₈   D₂

Troughs

G.I.M-J. 16.9.72

T₁₋₈

0   1   2   3 Metres

Fig. 227a   Kerdelan, Baden, Morbihan

noted, the gable outshot would have accommodated vehicles and implements, two ovens stand close by and *lokennou* and field shelters provided additional storage. Small farms south of the Loire were similarly all-accommodating. La Petite Louinais (Fig. 203) has an adjacent byre and a pigsty, with a well opposite the house and a now ruinous oven close by. In agriculturally more prosperous areas, farms appear to have had stone outbuildings for several centuries, as around Plougasnou where Keradour (Fig. 206) provides an example of a courtyard farm until recently completely enclosed by a boundary wall. Byres, stables and cart-house are arranged around two sides of the yard, but the straight joints and breaks in the roof-line betray its accretion over

a period of time. As in other examples of courtyard farms, Keradour is not the result of a single build.

Large barns are rare and generally confined to the bigger *manoirs*. Hay and straw were normally stacked in the farmyard and *lokennou* provided additional storage for crops where necessary. The structure at Penhap, Marzan, Morbihan (WT 515646), illustrates a building intermediate in size between the *lokennou* and the larger barns, which could be used equally for hay, straw or the storage of implements and vehicles (Fig. 226). Walling is of granite rubble, the roof covering of *roseau*, or reed, ridged with turf pegged down to the thatch. The building measures 7.50 metres long externally and is 5.00 metres wide at the lower end and 5.20 metres wide at the upper

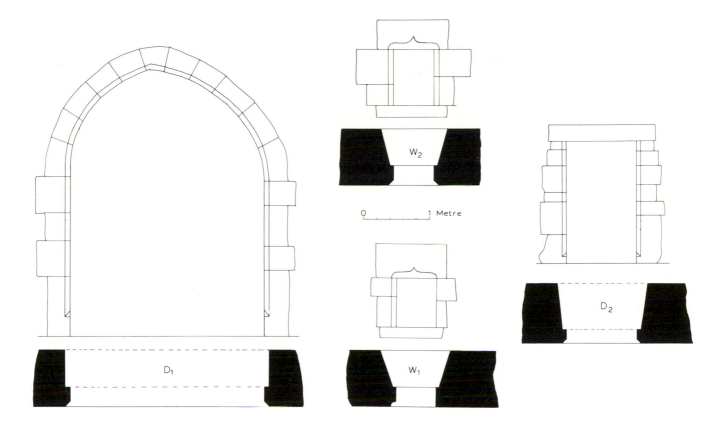

Fig. 227b   Kerdelan, Baden, Morbihan

end. Internally the length is 6.80 metres. The eaves stand 1.45 metres, and the ridge 4.50 metres, above ground level. Walling, 0.60 metres thick, is of granite rubble laid in a mortar of *pisé*. There is no dressed granite. Lateral walls are low, the front is entirely open and the rear gable is built of stone rubble. Flooring is of *terre battue*. Roof construction is of a kind typical in south Morbihan. Two roof trusses, T1 and T2, consist of pairs of crucks with collars, but without tie-beams. Intersecting crucks carry a ridge-purlin, and lateral purlins are supported on cleats. Common rafters of chestnut poles are laid at intervals of approximately 0.20 metres along the length of the building with their feet resting on the wall-heads. Across these are laid, also at intervals of *c.* 0.20 metres, spars to which the thatch is tied. Reed thatch is tied directly to this roof structure and held down with thatching spars. The ridge is covered with turfs pegged down to the thatch. The crucks have holes formerly holding the long pegs used as a ladder during the process of roof construction. The elbow in the crucks is sharp and occurs just above the

level of the wall-heads, and the feet of the crucks are let into wooden blocks set in the thickness of the wall. The crucks are secured by pegs at the apex but the collars are simply nailed on with no attempt at making a proper joint. This building is a field barn of a type once very common in Brittany but it is distinguished by being one of the few examples using the full cruck truss, as distinct from the upper-cruck truss common in the houses of the area. In dimension and form these crucks are not greatly dissimilar to the upper-crucks.

The barn at Kerdelan, Baden, Morbihan (WT 093724), is the only recorded example of a large tithe-barn (Fig. 227). Walling is of granite rubble with dressings of ashlar. The roof is slate-covered, with a red-tile ridge. Externally the building measures 32.80 metres long and 8.80 metres wide. Internally the dimensions are 31.00 metres by 7.05 metres. The gable walls are 0.90 metres thick and the lateral walls 0.85 metres thick. The eaves stand 5.30 metres, and the ridge 9.30 metres, above ground level. Walling is entirely of granite rubble with rubble also largely used for the quoins. Dressed stone is used only for the coping and for the door and window surrounds. The floor is of *terre battue*. The eight roof trusses, of the collar, tie-beam and upper king-post type, are identical. King-posts support a ridge-purlin and there are two pairs of lateral purlins held on cleats. Common rafters are boarded over and the slate roof nailed to the boards. The king-posts are braced both ways to the ridge-purlin. This building is a large barn of a type only to be expected in association with an estate, perhaps a manor, or a church possession. An asymmetrical Gothic doorway in one side is provided as a cart entrance and a small flat-headed doorway for everyday use is provided in a gable wall. There are two small windows with ogee heads, the dressings of W1 being asymmetrical. Ventilation is provided by two series of holes placed in the rear lateral wall. Whilst the date of the building is uncertain, the Gothic doorway probably places it in the seventeenth century.

The E.A.R. contains much detailed information on farmyard plan, construction and the interior arrangement of buildings. A variety of plans is illustrated for Finistère, ranging from the rectilinear incomplete 'courtyard' plans at Pont-Croix, Plomeur, Lanvéoc, Combrit and Cléden, to the irregular layout at Scaër, and the amazing jumble of tiny farms, most forming a line, in Kerhaliou-Goëlet, Spézet. The Finistère survey shows many purpose-built farms where there can be no question of the stables and byres having been converted from former dwelling houses. Many resemble the fine nineteenth-century farms of Cléden-Cap-Sizun. Indeed, one of the characteristics of Finistère is the co-existence of farms and buildings of advanced design, at all periods from the seventeenth century to the twentieth, together with those that have scarcely changed since medieval times. At Kerhaliou-Goëlet all the farms appear to be long-houses, and expansion has taken place both by the building of additional byres against the gable walls, and by the conversion of abandoned houses. At Miné Tréouzel, in Scaër, what was obviously a small long-house was extended by the addition of a byre at the upper end. Both the byre and a separate stable are built of stone rubble and *pisé* matrix incorporating a timber-frame. Whilst the big farm complexes of Finistère may reflect an increasing prosperity during the nineteenth century, accompanied by an agricultural revolution, the use of improved rotations and, gradually, of machinery, large numbers of small farms survived into the 1940s and beyond. Dwellings were often rebuilt first, older outbuildings continuing in use, or even newly constructed by more 'primitive' methods. Penty Lanneon, in Pont-Croix, is an example of what was almost certainly once a simple long-

house. The lower end was converted to a dairy and potato store, and a byre established in an entirely separate building, whilst the pigsty was built against the upper gable. Development of the farm at Celeriou in Scaër between 1828 and 1943 is admirably shown. A former long-house became a stable and byre when a new house was built, whilst a second byre and pigsty later came to be a vegetable store and yet another byre was used as a wood store.

The simple row of buildings is not well represented in the Finistère survey which is weighted to the larger farms, but Penandreff in Pouldreuzic is a good example: a two-cell house with a byre built against one gable and pigsty against the other. There is no throughway from house to byre and the straight joints show them to be of different dates. Lestrevignon, Bodilis is a long-house with table-outshot. Cattle had to cross the lower end of the hall, partitioned off from the byre, to pass from the single doorway to the byre. A calf 'box', projected laterally, balanced the table-outshot. The stable was built against the upper gable and was approached only from the outside.[611]

The survey of Côtes-du-Nord shows a similar range of plan development. Le Bot in Saint-Martin-des-Prés is a fine *manoir* completely closing three sides of a courtyard, with a full range of buildings: pigsties, stable, *cellier*, cart-sheds, stable and dairy. The provision of a separate dairy is a rare feature. Ker Anvern, Ploumilliau is a *manoir* almost completely enclosing the yard, with a full range of buildings and a dove-cot. Many houses recorded are either long-houses or were so until relatively recently when animals were expelled to other buildings and either the byre converted to a second room, or the hall extended to the full length of the house. A simple 'house and byre' is that at Crec'h Negaret, Plougrescant. This was probably always a single-cell house, with a tiny pigsty built into the lower gable, and two small byres built at 120 degrees to the hall. Le Guyandet in Ploulec'h provides a good example of the 'double' yard resulting from change, demolition, the building of a new house and the conversion of the old one into a barn. Here the new house has a dairy at the lower end. Against the lower gable is accommodation for sheep and pigs. Apart from the cart-shed and barn, there is a stable, byre and a *cuisine*, another former house. Talen, Saint-Gilles-Vieux-Marché is a good example of a row of buildings in line: barn, cart-shed, pigsty in a lateral outshot, stable, hall and dairy. Horses occupy the byre end of the long-house and cattle are housed in a separate and larger byre. Need for space may not have been the only factor here, for horses were more valuable and the farmer may have wished to keep them nearer at hand. Villeneuve, in

Plédran, is a small farm with buildings in line: cart-shed and *cellier* abut the first-derivative long-house, even the domestic rabbits being kept in a corner of the byre. A few farms show the development of the lateral outshot at the rear, as at Le Foeil, Saint-Launeuc, used largely as a *cellier*, or as at Kerouzan in Pleumeur-Bodou, used as a barn.[612]

A similar range of plans and buildings is found in Morbihan. Brouel on the Île des Moines is a large long-house, the only other building being a barn and pigsty, both detached. Morbihan probably shared with Côtes-du-Nord the greatest number of surviving long-houses still providing almost all the accommodation required for the farm. That at Kernegan, Moustoir-Remungol is such an example, as is Brenec, Plumelin, with its *cave* built on to the upper end. There are plenty of examples of abandoned houses being used for storage, or to house stock. The survival of the simple row of buildings, perhaps with an additional detached building, is common, and the developed courtyard farm rarer than elsewhere. Converted dwellings at the Metairie du Frotage, Pluherlin, form a loose courtyard grouping, and the Manoir de Brecehan, Saint-Gravé, has a walled yard, but with few buildings.[613]

Ille-et-Vilaine provides further examples of plans already noted. Particularly conspicuous is the row of buildings in line at Le Marquidoin, Bazouges-la-Perouse: pigsty, house, *cellier* and byre. The henhouse is in a rear outshot and the stable is a detached building. A similar arrangement existed at La Vignonais, Saint-Jean-sur-Couesnon. Use of converted buildings is evident at La Guibougère, Billé, with house, *pressoir* and byre, the latter a converted house, all in a row. The pigsty, barn, sheephouse and bake-house are all detached buildings. La Clairejaudière, Melesse, is an excellent example of a line of buildings. Rear outshots accommodate dairy, *cellier* and store. Numerous small long-houses survived, that at Petit Chevigné, Saint-Hilaire-des-Landes, being typical, having additionally only a henhouse, well and oven.[614]

In Loire-Atlantique, the principal *traits* outlined above are also in evidence. Notable are the tiny long-houses of the Grand Brière and the small farms of the Brière and the *pays de Guérande*, with a pigsty in the front lateral outshots. South of the Loire, the one- and two-storey houses with 'Roman'-tile roofs are universal. The tendency to develop accommodation in the rear outshot is widespread. At La Sauzaie, La Haie-Fouassière, the main axis accommodates bake-house, hall, *pressoir* and a small enclosed yard, whilst in the outshot are found the oven and two *celliers*. Pigsties abut the walled garden. Incorporation of the bake-house within the row of

buildings is characteristic south of the Loire, and La Grande Île, Saint-Père-en-Retz, has a small byre and pigsty at one end, followed by two single-cell houses and a bake-house with its oven in the gable wall.[615]

Much detail about farm buildings may be found in the *minutes notariales*, in probate inventories, farm leases and declarations. The declarations usually made in connection with the *domaine congéable*, include descriptions with measurements of all the buildings. Inventories, which show that ancillary buildings were in existence from the seventeenth century onwards, are chiefly concerned with the possessions of the better-off classes, those who might be expected to own the best and biggest farms (see Chapter 15). It is also apparent from many inventories that when only a byre is named, this refers to the lower end of a long-house. Sometimes the reference is implicit rather than explicit, a list of animals following the description of belongings in the hall, as at Kerguelen, Brasparts, in 1799.[616] In a rich area such as Plougasnou, by the end of the eighteenth century, farm buildings were constructed of granite. Field observation and inventories support each other in testifying to this. At Penantrez in 1802 there was both a stable and a *loge* containing the carts.[617] Trevenannou, in 1802, had a bake-house, *loge*, stable, and a barn,[618] whilst at Kerverrot in 1852 there was a *loge à charrette*, a stable and a *crèche à vaches*.[619] Many of the Plougasnou inventories list animals without specifying where they were kept, as at Corn-a-Lou in 1851.[620] There was a *loge à charrettes*, a *crèche à vaches* and a stable at Corvez in 1850, but in Petit Tregastel in 1849, only a *crèche à vaches*.[621] Some inventories also specify a pigsty.

Many of the Côtes-du-Nord inventories fail to list outbuildings although in some cases they must have existed. The noble house of La Monforière, in 1781, however, had a stable at the end of the yard, a second stable in the yard, a second byre, and a pigsty.[622] There was a stable, byre, pigsty and two barns at Keruzec, Pommerit-le-Vicomte in 1838.[623]

A similar picture emerged from Ille-et-Vilaine. A farm in Erbée in 1810 had a stable, a byre, and a barn.[624] Most of the inventories, however, make no mention of buildings, and where the number of animals is few, perhaps two or three cows, a horse and a few pigs, it is reasonable to suppose, in the light of field evidence, that they were kept in a long-house. A similar observation would be valid for most parts of Loire-Atlantique, where occasionally there is mention of the byre which housed the draught oxen as well as cows. Even in the crowded years of the nineteenth century when new houses were built, the old house was often turned into a byre. It is possible that in many of the *rangées* the houses were never lived in all at one time, but that some were always in use as byres, supplementing the space at the lower end of the long-house. Thus in Grand-Champ in 1828, two small houses were recorded as 'servant d'écurie'.[625] The facility with which a dwelling could be turned into a byre and back again as necessary has already been commented upon.

Three declarations for Côtes-du-Nord in 1776 give an indication of the number and size of farm buildings. The 'grande maison du lieu noble de Locmenar' consisted of a cuisine, chambre et grenier at the head of the yard, another house adjoining the first, also with a grenier, and a small stable adjoining the house, with another against it. A byre and a small pigsty adjoined the main house. Kernéun in Gommenec'h consisted of a house and chambre in the same line, 34 pieds long, 17 pieds wide and 9 pieds high. A doorway in the north wall had stone dressings, and a second doorway lay in the south wall. A chambre had a separate doorway. The description is long and detailed. Ceilings were of beams and joists and the roof thatched. There was a stable, 14 pieds by 17 pieds, a pigsty 9½ pieds long, 5 pieds wide and 5 pieds high. In a similar description for Tromeuret in Goudelin, the house was 33½ pieds long, 9¼ pieds high, and 16 pieds wide. At the western end lay a ruined stable, 9½ pieds long, 16 pieds wide and 7 pieds high. At the southern end of the yard stood a bake-oven of stone with a clay capping, 4½ pieds in diameter. A small loge, 12 pieds long and 5 pieds high, stood against the oven. At the western end of the yard lay a pigsty, 8 pieds long, 6 pieds wide and 3½ pieds high. The well in the yard had a depth of 4 pieds 4 pouces.[626]

Evidence for the number and quality of buildings is forthcoming from Finistère. Many are long-houses with no outbuildings. Others are substantial farms. Ty Coz at Kerbabu, Plougasnou, in 1803 consisted of a house, a chambre, byre, a small house, a stable, two pigsties, and a loge à charrettes.[627] Penpoul, Plougasnou, in 1781 consisted of a house, 28 pieds long, 14 pieds wide and 8 pieds high. A three-storey house at the western end measured 28 pieds long, 15 pieds wide and 15 pieds high. Another house against the eastern end was 16½ pieds long, 14 pieds wide and 14½ pieds high. A crèche on the eastern side of the yard measured 26 pieds long, 9 pieds wide and 7 pieds high. On the other side of the yard, towards the west, lay two more byres and a pigsty. There was also a bake-house and a grange. Full measurements are given.[628]

Two farms are recorded in long and detailed accounts at the end of the eighteenth century and the descriptions may be compared with the field evidence. Troan-ar-Run (Fig. 223) was declared in 1774 (see Chapter 13). The

house was of trois étages, showing that the present two-storey house, with loft over, was then in existence. It was 44½ pieds long, 12 pieds wide and 16 pieds high. There were two windows 'à carrée de Bois', a doorway on the south side, and a second doorway in the northern wall, together with 'une dalle et fenêtre de pierres vertes'. At the lower end of the house, or la manelle, a stairway of fourteen steps led to the chambre, over the hall. The chambre had two large windows, with wooden shutters, in the south wall, and one in the north wall, with a stone chimney-piece at the western end. A grenier above had three roof-trusses. At the eastern end was a second chambre, separated from the first by a wooden partition. A house 'nomme La Grange sous même couverture', 19 pieds long, 16 pieds wide and 12 pieds high with a doorway opening on to the threshing yard, and a large window, lay at the eastern end of the maison principale. Another 'maison a trois étages nommée le Ty Coz' and formerly the cuisine joins the others on the eastern side opening on to the yard. It was 28 pieds long, 15½ pieds wide and 16 pieds high with a doorway and three windows on the eastern side and a doorway and window on the western side. Another window and blocked doorway lay in the north wall, along with the chimney-piece. Above was a chambre approached by the stone stairway from the main house, with a window overlooking the yard. There was a chimney in the northern wall and three windows in the eastern wall. Access to the grenier above was by the stone stairway in the turret which has two small windows. At the junction of the chambres was a 'voute ou caveau' and a 'vollière à pigeons soutenue par un pillier et croisière de Bois'. At the western end of the yard lay the stable, 38 pieds long, 12 pieds wide and 14 pieds high. Two doorways and two windows opened on to the yard. Over the stable stood the cabinet, with access from the chambre of the house. A pigsty en appenty, 9 pieds long, 6 pieds wide and 4½ pieds high, lay against the side of the house. Another pigsty, 11 pieds long, 6½ pieds wide and 5 pieds high, stood against the Ty Coz in the corner by the yard wall. The enclosing wall had two doorways. A well and washplace lay against the north wall of Ty Coz. The bake-oven, in the north of the yard, was 26 pieds long, 19 pieds wide and 7 pieds high. On the aire a small loge stood against the wall of the grand clos, with a loge à charettes against the same wall. Against the western end of the house another loge en appenty was used to store the grain in August. The clos was bounded by a wall. Much of this building remains, as described above, but the aire and basse cour are now largely built over with later buildings and the clos has gone. Although there have been some changes in door and window openings, the house remains essentially the same. Ty Coz, both by its name and by its former function as *cuisine*, would seem to be the oldest part of the farm.[629]

The state of Kermorfezan (Fig. 222) was recorded in 1780. The *maison manalle* and *chambre* at the western end were 47 *pieds* long, 15 *pieds* wide and $7\frac{1}{2}$ *pieds* high. There were two chimney-pieces, three windows and two doorways. At the eastern end of the *manelle* was a crèche 19 *pieds* long, 15 *pieds* wide and $6\frac{1}{2}$ *pieds* high, with a doorway and a window 'à carré de bois'. To the east of the *crèche* stood a *loge* for crushing gorse, 10 *pieds* long, 13 *pieds* wide and $5\frac{1}{2}$ *pieds* high. There were two pigsties in the yard, $22\frac{1}{2}$ *pieds* long, 6 *pieds* wide and 5 *pieds* high. The yard, containing a well, was enclosed. The bake-house was $24\frac{1}{2}$ *pieds* long, 9 *pieds* wide and $5\frac{1}{2}$ *pieds* high. A *loge à charette* was $22\frac{1}{2}$ *pieds* long, $16\frac{1}{2}$ *pieds* wide and 5 *pieds* high. The *aire* lay south of the house, the garden south of the *chambre*. There is no mention of upper rooms or of the first-floor hall and garderobe, and it must be wondered whether these were added later.[630]

Field and documentary evidence, together with the observations of other writers, suggest that farmyard plan-types are too many for a meaningful classification to be made. The simplest is the long-house which, by the addition of byres and stables, grew in length. Sometimes buildings were erected at right angles, producing an L-shape. Further growth may have led to the enclosure of a rectilinear space. Whilst some factors in the development and planning of a farmyard may be apparent, others are not. Human decision-making processes are too little understood to permit a meaningful explanation, but there was probably a basic desire to enclose space and protect the yard. The tiny enclosed courtyards of western Léon and Crozon illustrate this, as do the larger enclosed yards of Plougasnou, of which that at Traon-ar-Run is one of the finest surviving examples. Many of these show, by their vertical joints, that they were the product of growth and not the work of a single build. No courtyard farm of one build has yet been encountered. Field evidence and documents support each other to show that farm buildings were few and, in many cases, non-existent before the end of the eighteenth century. The building of permanent separate byres and stables, as distinct from *lokennou*, began in the nineteenth century and only slowly filtered down the social scale. The smallest and poorest farms never had permanent outbuildings save perhaps for a pigsty, the lower end of the long-house being sufficient to accommodate all the stock. Even when rural wealth increased and the need for more accommodation became apparent, it was the houses that were often rebuilt and the old dwellings turned into byres. In other cases the principle of alternate rebuilding is evident. Homes were rebuilt first, byre and stables later, the latter sometimes left permanently in their primitive state. This may well explain many of the straight joints.

Permanent farm buildings first developed at the upper end of the social scale and had still not reached the lower end by the 1920s when vernacular buildings ceased. Just as the bulk of the Breton population of the nineteenth century lived in long-houses and single-cell dwellings, so too they lived without permanent outbuildings. The few domestic animals, one or two cows, a horse and a pig, together with a few chickens, could all be accommodated in the long-house. *Lokennou* provided any additional accommodation and *loges* or cart-sheds could be constructed as at Bouleguy (Figs. 159-161). At the middle and lower social levels, permanent farm buildings only became numerous as the nineteenth century progressed.

FIFTEEN

HEARTH AND HOME

In France, a *foyer* symbolizes more than 'hearth' in the restricted sense and is commonly used to designate a kin-group, or a community, the number of households in a settlement being equated with the number of *'feux'*. As late as 1975 the writer was informed near Laz, Finistère that the hamlet of Kervorn then contained only four *feux*, whereas formerly there had been twenty-four. Hearth and fire, until the economic changes that followed World War II, were tended with great care and the fire allowed rarely to die out. Where for some reason this happened, live embers were sought at the one fire in the hamlet tended with special care. This was all the more important before the advent of the safety match, for fires could not be so easily re-lit. These practices are confirmed by Sebillot, who likens the hearth to the family altar upon which the sacred flame burns.[631] To facilitate the preservation of fire throughout the night, some hearths of superior construction were provided with an ash-hole in the chimney back (Figs. 228 and 229). Hot embers were placed in the hole and covered with a slate or other flat stone. When a special keeping-place was not provided, embers could be kept alive by covering with a heap of ash or, more effectively, with an overturned cooking-pot.

The importance of fire is illustrated by the part it played in the celebration of the summer solstice, in France Christianized as the Feast of St. John, which survived in a few areas until recently.[632] Remains of the fires of St. John were accorded mysterious properties and the cinders piously kept as talismen against ills that might befall man and beast. The firebrands were said to preserve houses from thunder, and the ashes, spread over the fields, assured an abundant harvest. Farm servants were also hired on this day, for the year, and had to enter the home of their new master before the traditional fire died out.[633] Bachelot de la Pylaie describes how the branch of box was fastened behind a cross on the box-bed and *'Ce précieux talisman préserve la maison du tonnerre, des maléfices, des sorciers; conjure le malin esprit, etc. . . . On se couche ainsi sous l'influence des sentiments religieux, et jamais on ne fait de mauvais rêves'.*[634]

Traditions concerning the departed are strong and formerly influenced the conduct of the hearth. Souls were believed to return after sunset to those places on earth with which they were once familiar. A fire was sometimes left for them and the practice of leaving food continued until recent times.[635] Hence the practice of each person present at the fire of St. John throwing a stone into the hot ashes of the dying fire, the stones being called (Br.) *anaon*, the deceased. On the eve of All Souls, a meal was laid out and a large fire left.[636] Food was left by the hearth for the 'wee-folk' and sometimes additionally in a furrow in the fields.[637] The association of the hearth with the departed is brought out in the tale of *Les deux vieux arbres*. Hervé Mingam, lying in his box-bed, turning to his wife Radegonda, draws her attention to the hearth: *'Regardez. Quoi? Où? Là, dans le foyer, ces deux vieux. Ne les reconnaissez-vous pas? . . . Dieu pardonne aux défunts! . . . Mais c'est votre père et votre mère! . . . Dans l'âtre, le vieux disait à la vieille: Êtes-vous assez réchaufée, Maharit? Voici bientôt notre heure. Et la vieille disait au vieux: Oui, je n'ai plus si froid, Jelvestr. Mais il me tarde bien que ma dure pénitence soit finie. . . .'.*[638]

Over the greater part of Brittany wood has been abundant throughout historic time. Even in the 1970s, notwithstanding the diffusion of oil- and gas-fired kitchen ranges among an increasingly affluent peasantry, large numbers of Breton peasants continue to burn wood cut from the pollarded trees of the *bocage*. Neat stacks of *fagots* stand ready for use. The open fire continues to be the chief source of heat. In thousands of homes, especially those of older people, it remains the sole source of heat for cooking. In some areas, however, wood was always scarce, notably along the littoral and in the western peninsulas. Where wood was in short supply alternative fuels were used. Even in well-wooded areas, the poorest peasants with no rights and without means to purchase wood resorted to alternatives. In Cap Sizun, *landes*, generally synonymous with gorse, although sometimes referring also to heath, and *genêt*, the common broom, were burnt. Near Morlaix it was *genêts*, *landes* and *mottes,* green turf stripped off the commons and not to be confused with *tourbe,* or peat. Turf and cow-dung were burnt in Crozon, whilst near Lesneven, in western Léon, the peasants burned only broom, gorse and *de la paille.* On the Île de Batz and in Landevenez, fire was made with cow-dung and sea-weed, fuels also recorded on the Île d'Ouessant,[639] where, as abundant oral evidence testifies, these fuels continued to be used, alongside peat and turf, until after World War II. Hélias records the use of cow-dung in the *pays bigouden* in the 1920s.[640] Dung was peeled off the ground when dry and stacked alongside the hearth. It seems probable that the practice of burning cow-dung was once widespread in the poorer parts of Brittany. In some areas peat was available. Near Châteaulin, it was used to supplement wood, charcoal and coal, and also used by the smiths to heat their forges, but the greatest centre of peat production, continuing until recent times, was the Grande Brière from which it was exported to the surrounding towns, notably Nantes.

Further written evidence about fuel is available towards the mid-nineteenth century. Near Saint-Nic, turf cut with a spade on the mountain, and gorse cut from the *terres incultes,* were used. The latter gave '*un feu vif, mais c'est un feu de paille quant à sa durée; tant qu'on en a besoin, il faut l'alimenter sans cesse. Cette lande brûle en pétillant et donne une flamme élevée qui jette beaucoup de clarté: c'est là le grand combustible, le gros bois du pays*'.[641] Clean fuels such as these were used to heat bake-ovens. The use of seaweed was not unknown along the coast and Souvestre records a *cabane* at Kerity-Penmarc'h, Finistère, where a woman '*était à genoux sur le foyer, occupée à allumer un feu de goémon*'.[642] In the *arrondissement* of Morlaix, fuel consisted of wood, with peat near Ponthiou and Sizun, wood and gorse at Landivisiau and, on the coast, gorse and seaweed. The ashes of the latter were conserved and sold, at a high price, as fertilizer. In the *arrondissement* of Brest, oakwood, broom, gorse, peat and heath are cited, with marine plants on Ouessant. In the *arrondissement* of Châteaulin, gorse and broom were taken from the field-banks, but in the *canton* of Crozon, the inhabitants '*qui sont à peu près privés de bois font sécher au soleil la fiante de leurs bestiaux et s'en servent pour leur chauffage*'. Around Pleyben, Châteauneuf and Huelgoat, turf and peat were common. In the *arrondissement* of Quimper, wood, turf, broom and gorse are cited.[643]

At the turn of the century these traditional fuels were still in use. Le Braz records at Saint-Jean-du-Doigt, Finistère, an almshouse in which '*la cheminée monumentale de la cuisine . . . brûtaient d'immenses*

flambées d'ajonc dont la clarté était à elle seule une joie et un confort'.[644] Even after World War I, the turbaries of the *marais* in the uplands were exploited, notably near Callac, Loguivy-Plougras, Plounérin, Plougonver and Pont-Melvez, in Côtes-du-Nord. Peat was dug with a spade and then left to dry.[645] These examples serve to emphasize the strong traditions and archaic practices which have influenced and sometimes governed human activity around the hearth, (L.) *focus* of life in the Breton house.

The *régime alimentaire* is of considerable importance to the understanding of the house, for it influences the range of cooking equipment and provisions required as well as the number and type of storage facilities. These in turn, influence the form and extent of the living accommodation which finds its ultimate expression in the architecture, development and organization of the house.

Much has sometimes been made by British scholars of the alleged practice of cooking outside, in a separate, and often detached, kitchen. The practice of the great houses is cited as evidence, as are the excavated remains of detached kitchens in manor houses.[646] There is yet not a shred of evidence from Brittany to suggest that cooking took place other than at the hearth within the house, except for the baking of bread. A second hearth sometimes came later, to be used also for cooking purposes, but this was always within the same house. The very names of the principal, and generally only, room in the house, (Fr.) *cuisine,* (Br.) *kegin,* confirm this, one of its most important functions. Not even in the temporary dwellings of the woodland workers is there evidence of outdoor cooking.

Cambry's account of Finistère at the end of the eighteenth century contains numerous references to diet, emphasizing the dependence of the population on cereals. On the Île de Batz, the peasantry fed on *bouillie, far de blé noir,* potatoes, bread of barley and rye, milk, butter and *soupe au lard.* In Crozon, barley furnished the basis of diet. Wheat, barley, rye, buckwheat, oats and *métail* (a mixture of wheat and rye) were the chief crops in Pont-Croix, together with beans, peas, turnips and parsnips. Potatoes had been known in the district for only one year. This is not surprising, for although the potato was known as early as 1740, it was not grown widely until after 1816-17.[647] On Ouessant, where fuel was so scarce by the twentieth century that fires were lit only for cooking, the houses remaining otherwise unheated, bread was made by placing the dough on the hearth-stone and covering it with hot cinders, a process even more rudimentary than the Irish pot-oven. Around Lesneven, in addition to *crêpes* and *galettes,* milk, butter, *lard* and salted meat are cited. In the Morlaix district the farmers ate little meat, pork being served only twice each week with *far de blé noir*, a baked pastry containing a filling of flour, eggs and milk, and sometimes dried plums or raisins. Milk was a staple drink, and butter and *bouillie* were eaten in large quantities.[648] *Crêpes* and *galettes* are an important part of the diet throughout Finistère at this period, and although universally eaten on Fridays, they appear on other days as well, in addition to, and as a substitute for, bread. The other staple cereal food is porridge, or *bouillie*, made from either oats or buckwheat. Salted meat, especially pork, was eaten two or three times a week, but the poorest classes scarcely ever tasted it. Other foods, eggs, fruit and vegetables, were sold in the towns for cash, as was also most of the fish, to be consumed as regular diet only by the well-to-do. On Ouessant, eggs were eaten only at Easter, and for the remainder of the year they were sent to Brest for sale. Local variations inevitably occurred, as around Saint-Pol, an area rich in vegetables. Little alcohol was consumed in Léon, and then mostly on Sundays and feast-days. Cider was imported from other districts, and wine consumed on special occasions. On feast-days and for marriages, veal, beef and *le far du four* were served, with all kinds of wine and *l'eau-de-vie*. In contrast, the poor cultivator in the Carhaix district had only a coarse diet: *le gros pain de seigle* and *bouillies de sarrasin*.[649]

At Corréjou, although the farmers had grown prosperous by selling seaweed, horses, barley and flax, their diet varied little from that already outlined. Bread was made from a mixture of barley, rye and wheat and commonly baked in an oven, usually free-standing in the yard, but sometimes built on to the gable wall of the house. Bouët and Perrin give a vivid account of the making of bread in such an oven.[650] *Bouillie* was eaten twice a day, except on Sundays, Tuesdays and Thursdays when salted meat, *lard* and *soupe de graisse* were served. In Pont-Aven, where the cider, that of Riec, was reported to be excellent, the inhabitants were just getting used to potatoes.[651] In the poorer areas of the Mont d'Arrée, wheat had to be imported, for only rye, buckwheat, summer oats and *pilat*, a mixture of oats and wheat, could be grown. *Bouillie* was the staple dish. *Crêpes*, rye bread and milk formed the remainder of the diet, with *lard* on feast-days. Even on the islands, and near the coast, little fish was eaten, the catch being sent to market.[652]

Beehives, on average seven per farm, were noted in Cap Sizun, presumably in the homes of the better off. The inhabitants lived on bread, *bouillie*, *crêpes* and milk. Most farms had a store of pork. Water was the chief drink and there is no mention of wine, cider, *l'eau-de-vie*, or other spirits.[653] In 1788, buckwheat formed two-thirds of the food intake of the people of the *pays de Morlaix*; they ate it in *crêpes*, *galettes* and *bouillie* and even put *crêpes* into their *soupe* in preference to bread. Butter was more an item of commerce than of consumption. Eggs and poultry are curiously absent from accounts and reports. They, too, must largely have been items of commerce, and fowls were used to pay *seigneurial* dues in Montfort at the end of the eighteenth century. The poverty of the great mass of the peasantry and the insufficiency of their food was of concern to the *sub-délégués* in 1774-5. A poor diet, uniform and unbalanced, is reported, not only in the interior, but also in the east and west of Brittany. The *gens de journée* of the south-east, who formed there the greater part of the population, were unable to feed their families adequately by their work alone. Reports from medical practitioners and clergy accord with this evidence. Hunger, poverty and the poor quality of the cereals were strong contributory causes to disease, epidemics and death.[654]

The nineteenth century brought little change in diet. Meals in Finistère were of '*bouillie de blé noir, de froment ou d'avoine*', *crêpes*, potatoes and milk. Only the better off could afford *lard* two or three times a week and *far de blé noir*, but never beef, veal or mutton. Near the coast, sardines were consumed in small quantities. The normal drink in Cornouaille was water and cider.[655] Vegetables were generally consumed in *soupe*. A *sabotier* and his wife, in the *pays de Vannes*, were observed eating a *soupe* of black bread and salt water out of the same wooden bowl, with a spoon which they passed alternately to each other.[656] The basis of peasant food had remained unchanged since the eighteenth century in the *pays de Porzay*, Finistère, except for the introduction of the potato and the change to wheat-bread. Bread was home-baked, wine was rare, but coffee was widely known among the better off.[657]

Wild fruits and nuts constituted a significant part of the diet, especially of the poor. The sweet-chestnut tree was widespread, 'supplying a means of subsistence for the poor during the greater part of the year. The people collect the chestnuts in sacks and pile them up within their cabins: several families are even so needy that they seldom taste the luxury of bread; but these are among the children of wretchedness in the extreme degree . . . in the neighbourhood of Brest, the lower orders resort to acorns, as well as chestnuts for food, which have some nutritious quality when boiled with milk'.[658] Chestnuts formed an important element in diet during the eighteenth century, in Montfort, Rennes, Redon and Vitré.[659] Fruit and nuts, especially chestnuts, remained important until World War II.[660] Another nineteenth-century English traveller found 'black bread, made with buckwheat, or rye, oats or barley, boiled with milk', and potatoes for a change.[661]

Surveyed by *arrondissement*, Châtellier's *Recherches statistiques* appear to give a reliable guide to the food of the late 1830s. Throughout Finistère it was the rule to eat three meals a day in winter and four in summer. *Soupe* with potatoes, morning and evening, *bouillie d'avoine* or *crêpes* at midday and a little bread for *casse-croute*, were the rule in the *arrondissements* of Châteaulin and Morlaix. In Châteaulin, rye bread was general except in Crozon where barley bread was the rule. The better off ate pork or salted meat once or twice a week, usually in the *soupe*. Two or three times a week in Morlaix, pork, beef or salted meat were served in *soupe* with black barley bread. The consumption of potatoes was reported greatly to have increased. In the *arrondissement* of Quimper, the main foods were rye-bread, *bouillie d'avoine*, *crêpes* and *galettes* of buckwheat, milk and potatoes, with *soupe de graisse ou de beurre*, or *soupe de viande ou de lard*, once or twice a week. Several coastal *communes* made barley bread, but everywhere the potato was gaining ground. Similar régimes were reported from Quimperlé and Brest.[662]

Evidence from the Comités d'Hygiène for the five Breton *départements*, c. 1850, essentially confirms this *régime alimentaire*. Most reports indicate some improvement during the previous twenty years or so. Considerable variations in quality were reported from Ille-et-Vilaine. Food was stated as being good in the *canton* of Vitré, with water and cider as the main drinks. Wheat-bread, *galettes* of buckwheat, fresh and salted meat and vegetables were reported in Saint-Malo, with cider and water to drink and salt and pepper for seasoning, but more fresh meat was considered necessary for the well-being of the people. The ordinary farmer ate little meat. *Galettes* of buckwheat formed a third of the food intake in the *canton* of Retiers, and bread made with *métail* and *lard salé* was eaten but little butchers' meat. In Redon, many people lived solely on *galettes de blé noir, groux* or gruel, bread and *soupe* with no meat. A similar pattern is reported from Rennes, with salted fish, but rarely meat. Pepper occurs frequently as seasoning in these eastern *cantons*. Salt was universal, and indeed essential for the preservation of the meat. That fish was not unknown in the interior is borne out by the report for Grand-Fougeray where, in addition to salted pork, salted sardines were eaten. A fuller account is available for Fougères, where the landless labourers ate a *maigre soupe de beurre rance, de galettes de sarrasin, de sardines. Lard* formed almost exclusively the only meat eaten by the poor. Better-off peasants ate it at least once a day. Only in the *canton* of Antrain, on the Normandy border, is there

report of a considerable consumption of butchers' meat, and this is ascribed to the increased prosperity of agriculture.[663]

The picture in Côtes-du-Nord is less satisfactory. *Bouillie*, of oats or buckwheat, was common everywhere. Water and cider were the usual drinks. Many families in Rostrenen never ate meat, and vegetables were general in the town but not in the country. Well-to-do farmers of Saint-Nicholas-du-Pélem ate two or three meals of salted meat per week with a *soupe* made with oat flour, butter and milk. *Bouillie d'avoine* was served once or twice a week. The poorer classes hardly ever ate meat and their food consisted chiefly of rye bread, *bouillie d'avoine, galettes,* and *soupe de graisse ou de farine d'avoine* in which butter was occasionally put. At Callac, Bourbriac, Guingamp and Belle-Isle-en-Terre things were much the same, with only the better off eating meat once or twice a week. At Bégard, turnips, carrots and cabbage were known. In the more prosperous areas around Dinan, food was reported to be good, and fresh meat was on the increase. In several *communes* of the *arrondissement* of Loudéac, food was insufficient, and happy were the families who could find enough not to go hungry. Sometimes meals were of 'la soupe faite soit avec un peu de graisse salée, soit avec du beurre rance, on y ajoute des choux, des navets ou des pommes de terre lors qu'on peut se procurer ces légumes, ce qui n'arrive pas une fois la semaine. Souvent, tant la misère est grande, la soupe se compose d'eau chaude dans laquelle on ne peut pas toujours jeter un peu de sel'. At Mur, nine-tenths of the *canton* did not eat fresh meat as much as six times a year, having to be content with salted meat, and half the population had neither fresh nor salted meat more than twenty times a year.[664]

By the eve of World War II, ninety years later, the quality, quantity and variety of food had improved, although the basic pattern of dishes, and their method of preparation, remained fundamentally unchanged. Cider was still the universal drink in Finistère, except in Léon where water or milk were the common drinks, with wine on Sundays. In Ille-et-Vilaine, although cider again reigned supreme, coffee had made headway. In Loire-Atlantique, cider was universal north of the Loire, and wine to the south.[665]

Improvement in the quality and variety of drink is perceptible in Côtes-du-Nord, and three *régimes alimentaires* stand out. Meat was exceptional and butter rare in the interior. In the eastern coastal region butter was common and meat rare, and then only in the form of *lard*. On the richer western coast butter and meat were general, meat being eaten once a day. Improvement was

Fig. 228   Troinguy 2, Lopérec, Finistère
A modernized traditional interior in the Monts d'Arrée. Note the shelf suspended from the ceiling, the *banc* by the hearth, the box-bed with its chest in front, and the *terre-battue* floor.

very slow during the nineteenth century. Certain regions showed marked improvement at the turn of the century, but the main changes came after 1918, with the increased consumption of fresh vegetables, fruit, fresh meat and fish.[666] A detailed description of the food at Goulien, Cap-Sizun, before and after 1914, leaves no doubt about improvements.[667]

The poorest people had few belongings and only the barest of utensils. Cutlery was a luxury until recent times, and even in the 1970s many country people ate with only a spoon and a pocket knife. There are oral reports of people so poor in twentieth-century Côtes-du-Nord that they possessed not even a plate, eating directly off the table. *Bouillie,* probably one of the oldest of cooked dishes, was traditionally eaten, not out of a wooden bowl, but by all out of the common pot, a practice continued in the more conservative areas until World War II. At Poullaouen, between Huelgoat and Carhaix, *boullie d'avoine* was eaten communally from the *chaudron,* or three-legged pot placed centrally on the

terre battue floor. Those present sat around the pot, each person using his own wooden spoon. Taking turns, the spoon was dipped into the pot, usually after first taking a little butter. Oral evidence shows this practice to have been widespread in the years before World War II. The custom has a twofold significance. The method of consumption has probably remained unchanged from the Neolithic, and the leaving of the table in order to consume the dish suggests strongly that the former was introduced into the house relatively late. In other districts the eating of the *bouillie* from a common pot took place at the table where '*tous les jours on mange la bouillie de froment ou de blé noir, dans les écuelles de bois, jadis sculptées, ou dans les terrines en faïence de Quimper, décorées de types bretons, et que le vendredi on mange les crêpes. La bouillie est servie dans une grande terrine; au milieu, on a fait un trou, dans lequel on a mis du beurre; les convives se servent sur les bords, avec leur cuiller, qu'ils trempent ensuite dans le beurre, à tour de rôle*'.[668]

Fig. 229 Troinguy 2, Lopérec, Finistère
A modernized table-outshot.

At the end of the eighteenth century, it is possible to detect a social hierarchy based on food intake: an élite always well fed, a minority capable of sustaining itself adequately even though the quality of the food left much to be desired, a majority divisible into two unequal parts, one living adequately in some years and struggling to survive in others, the other poor and wretched most of the time and seriously affected by the bad years to the point of sickness and death.[669] There is also a clear distinction between the more favoured littoral zones where quality and variety were greater, and the interior where the *régime* was worst. This subdivision remains true throughout Brittany until the end of World War I. The *seigneur,* amply fed, enjoyed not only the traditional cereal dishes but a whole range of dairy products and animal foods, including fowl and game. The small *seigneur,* and the better-off farmers, fall into the category of the adequately fed. The remainder form the vast majority of the population, of which a considerable section was extremely poor and highly vulnerable to the variations in weather and harvests. There are also marked regional variations in the quality and quantity of the food. The northern littoral was much better off than the western peninsulas, whilst the whole of the interior and the poorer areas of Morbihan and Loire-Atlantique seem to have been the worst off.

The two great regional divisions of Brittany, Basse-Bretagne and Haute-Bretagne, are both reflected in furniture styles. Léon, Cornouaille and the Vannetais produced distinctive types, with centres of production at Pontivy, Hennebont, Auray and Guémené. Character, form, ornamentation and process of manufacture change subtly with the regions. Regions around Saint-Malo, Dol, Fougères and Vitré displayed distinctive variations, different, in turn, from Rennes, the pays de la Mée or Guérande.[670]

The box-bed, (Fr.) *lit-clos,* (Br.) *gwele-kloz, gwole-cloz,* once in use nearly all over France, especially in Rouergue and Savoie, persisted longest in Brittany where a few are still in use (Figs. 228, 230). The earliest surviving examples are of seventeenth-century date, and they continued to be made until the twentieth century.

Whilst normally having two doors, those of Léon have only one. Box-beds with curtains in place of doors, (Fr.) *lits mi-clos*, are found notably in Haute-Bretagne (Fig. 230). A chest in front of the bed is used for storage, seating during the daytime, and as a means of getting into the bed, a process requiring some skill and agility (Figs. 228, 230, 235, 236). The four-poster bed, (Fr.) *le lit-à-colonnes*, (Br.) *gwiléou-steng*, is not uncommon in Ille-et-Vilaine and Loire-Atlantique. The chest, (Fr.) *coffre*, (Br.) *coufr, arc'h*, is one of the oldest pieces of furniture. A grain chest may be as much as 2.00 metres long and 1.50 metres high. Examples from the fifteenth century onwards are common. Smaller chests were used for clothing and linen. From the end of the seventeenth century the chest was gradually replaced by the (Fr.) *armoire*, (Br.) *armel*. The latter, without a precise English equivalent, performs the functions of both cupboard and wardrobe. The (Fr.) *presse-à-lin*, used by weavers for storage, evolved in Léon towards the end of the seventeenth century, a region renowned for the manufacture of linen. Milk, other dairy products and utensils were stored in the (Fr.) *armoire-à-lait*. *Armoires-de-mariage* were often newly purhcased at the time of marriage and intended for the large quantities of clothing which both bride and bridegroom brought with them to the new home. Each member of the family had his own *armoire*, and this helps to explain the large number often found in a household. The *buffet* (Fr.) appeared at the end of the seventeenth century in the homes of the wealthier classes and became particularly common in the eighteenth and nineteenth centuries. It appears in various forms. The simple buffet, not unlike a small *armoire*, is a piece of furniture for the storage of household items, with several cupboards and drawers. Combined with a chest used for seating, and placed close to a table, it is known as (Fr.) *banc-trustel*. It is also found in the form of a (Fr.) *buffet vaisselier*, equivalent to the English dresser, with cupboards below and open shelves for the storage of pottery above. Nineteenth-century examples from the regions of Plouay and Scaër incorporate a longcase clock, the (Fr.) *buffet-vaisselier-à-horloge*.

The table, (Fr.) *table*, (Br.) *taol*, appears in two forms, the simples table (Fig. 228) and the (Fr.) *table-huche* (Figs. 230, 236). The latter had a sliding top opening to reveal a large chest, or *huche*, which served as a food-container or *garde-manger*. It is often described in inventories as a *table-coulante*. Bread, cold meat and butter were items typically stored in it. Seating was provided on benches, chairs and chests (Figs. 228, 235). Bench and chest were often combined, as in front of the box-bed. Individual seats were rare, except for the great wooden chair with arms by the fire, (Br.) *an gador*. Long

benches with backs, (Fr.) *banc-dossier*, were not uncommon, and in Cornouaille the high-back bench or *banc-tossel*, reaching almost to the ceiling, was known. The *banc-coffre* was a storage chest provided with a back to form a long seat. When placed next to the box-bed, the latter provided support at the back, giving the *banc-coffre-de-lit*.

Two other forms of chest are common, both supported on legs to keep its contents out of reach of rats, mice and larger animals. The (Fr.) *pétrin* is a kneading trough, often approaching two metres in length, whilst the (Fr.) *maie* (or *mé, mée, met, metz*) was intended for the storage of the bread.

During the eighteenth and, more especially, the nineteenth century, the longcase clock, (Fr.) *horloge*, found its way into the farmhouses, very slowly at first, for it was not common until *c.* 1850. Often combined in a row of furniture with a box-bed or an *armoire*, it was known as (Br.) *trustel*. Other common items of furniture included the spinning wheel, (Fr.) *rouet*, the small (Fr.) *vaisselier-égouttoir*, and the (Fr.) *porte-cuillers*, small square or circular frameworks with holes in which hang the wooden spoons, one for each member of the household. Spoon-holders generally hang over the table (Fig. 236). The cradle, (Fr.) *ber, berceau*, was an item found in many households (Fig. 230).

Travellers have described, sometimes in astonishment and amusement, the interiors of houses encountered on their travels. Accounts tend to be either romantic, or written with an aggressive superiority. Noël du Fail, in the earliest known description, tells of the hall with a fine table 'sur le bout de laquelle la touaille ou nappe, ce m'est tout un, estoit encore du reste du dîner'. By the hearth, a chest, 'auquel estoit en élégante disposition les hardes du villageois comme chapeau, gibbessière, sa ceincture bigarrée et demy ceinct de sa femme, entremeslée l'odorante marjolaine'. Also by the fire, the box-bed and 'des selles et chaises de bois tortu et les pièces toutes bien rapportées'. There were also numerous utensils: bowls, a pot and a *tranchoir*.[671] These interiors appear to belong to the better-off classes of the mid-sixteenth century, a happy people, satisified with their condition, living in an agriculturally fertile area. Many of the peasantry at that date, however, almost certainly lived in poorly built single-cell houses with floors of *terre battue*, lighted by small unglazed windows. Sée considered damp and dirt to be the cause of the frequent and murderous epidemics, the inhabitants living 'dans l'eau et la boue, dans la malpropreté la plus repoussante, sans aucun souci des règles les plus élémentaires de l'hygiène'.[672]

Cambry found the single-cell house universal in the Morlaix region. Light from a small window illuminated 'un bahu, sur lequel une énorme masse de pain de seigle est ordinairement posée sur une serviette grossière; deux bancs, ou plutôt deux coffrets sont établis le long du bahu, qui leur sert de table à manger. Des deux côtés d'une vaste cheminée, sont placées de grandes armoires sans battans, à deux étages, dont la séparation n'est formée que par quelques planches où sont les lits dans lesquels les pères, les mères, les femmes et enfans entrent couchés, car la hauteur de ces étages n'est quelquefois que de deux pieds; ils dorment sur la balle d'avoine ou de seigle, sans matelas, sans lit de plumes, sans draps; beaucoup d'entr'eux ne sont couverts que d'une espèce de sac de balle, très peu se servent de couvertures de laine, quelques-uns en possèdent de Ballin: c'est une espèce d'étoffe tissue de gros fil d'étoupe. Ils emploient aussi quelquefois des couvertures de poil: si par hasard, ils ont des draps, à peine atteignent-ils les deux extrémités du lit'. The remainder of the furniture consisted of earthenware bowls, some pewter plates, a dresser, a griddle for making *crêpes*, some cauldrons, a pan and several milk pots.[673] His description is probably that of the home of a middling peasant, for, as probate inventories show, the poorest people were unlikely to have possessed pewter plates. The house was dirty, but elsewhere the furniture was washed, cleaned and waxed, 'mais ces maisons sont rares, et sont toujours sans air, étroites et privées de lumière'.[674] Floors were rarely flagged or boarded and were almost universally of *terre battue* which wore unevenly. Blocks of wood are commonly placed under the legs of the furniture to level them, but the unwary visitor was unlikely to fall into a deep hole and break his leg as Cambry suggests. The interior seems to have been dirty enough: 'la mal-propreté, l'odeur, l'humidité, la boue . . . l'eau de fumier, qui souvent en défend l'entrée, qui, presque toujours, y pénètre'.[675] Half-a-century later, De Freminville claimed that Cambry's description remained true to reality.[676]

Stothard found the people 'dirty to a loathed excess' and the inns, in which she was compelled to seek accommodation, devoid of comfort. At Plélan-le-Grand, she found 'faggots blazing in the chimney' and a 'slush pool in the centre of the room', a 'hole for foul water and a pond for ducks, who enjoyed themselves paddling about in it. A hen-roost stood above a larder of viands, beneath which a fowl was hatching her young upon a sort of dung-hill . . .'.[677] At another inn, the 'kitchen or common hall' had 'no flooring but the substantial earth. When it rains the kennel from the street runs over through the door, and makes a soft mud carpeting . . . Near the fire-side stands the landlady's bed, supported by a hen-coop full of little chickens. In the centre of the

room, there is, as usual, a convenient slush pool, and close to it a long oak table, black from grime and grease . . . The solitary window retains but two unbroken panes of glass'.[678] The slush pool in the centre of the room probably originates in a practice associated with the construction of the house. After the priest had blessed the newly built house with holy water, the soil so dampened was dug and placed in a small bag, to be kept as a talisman against illness. The hole so formed grew larger with time, with sweeping, and with the practice of throwing waste into the centre of the room.[679]

Bachelot de la Pylaie, accustomed to the mid-nineteenth century Breton environment, was nevertheless greatly impressed. At Saint-Nic, in western Finistère, unable to find an inn, he was shown 'la demeure du paysan qui reçoit les étrangers' but 'si son extérieur était déjà capable de refroider le zèle d'un ardent touriste, l'intérieur était complétement déconcertant; tout y était aussi noir que l'âtre de la cheminée. Quoique l'on y fût aveuglé et presque suffoqué par l'épaisse fumée . . .'. A table stood next to the bed of the 'maîtres du logis' and by the hearth. Benches and chests placed in front of the beds were the only seats. Light entered by a small window and the open doorway.[680] He passed the evening at his host's house, seated in the place of the 'maître de maison', (Br.) *ar gador*, the seat usually at the right of the hearth. In the house of a neighbour the family was seated around the hearth, also lighted by 'une chandelle de résine'. The window, through which a little light entered by day, was unglazed, and at night closed by a shutter. He found the house as cold inside as outside and attributed to this fact the reason that the inhabitants all slept in box-beds. 'Ces lits sont farcies de paille jusqu'aux deux tiers environ de la hauteur de l'ouverture; par-dessus cette paillasse monstre est une ballière épaisse de douze à quinze pouces, qui tient à la fois lieu de matelas et de lit de plume; les draps, fort grossiers, sont par-dessus celle-ci, et comme fort souvent les couvertures manquent, on les remplace par une seconde ballière d'un pied environ d'épaisseur. Je ne dois pas omettre que le traversin est encore rempli avec de la balle, ainsi que l'oreiller, quand il y en a un'.[681] The remainder of the furniture consisted of a chest by the bed, serving for storage, as a seat, and as a means of getting more easily into bed. The conjugal bed, as always in the traditional Breton house, was placed in the corner by the hearth opposite the window (Figs. 228, 232, 234, 235). A sliding top to the table revealed another chest in which was kept the butter, cooked meat and any vegetables remaining after a meal, thus serving as both table and *garde manger*. Above the bench, which provided seating on the gable side of the table, was the dresser. A few

Fig. 230   Niou, Île d'Ouessant, Finistère
A traditional Ouessant interior. Note the *table-huche,* the box-bed, chest, clock and *vaissellier.*

forks and the wooden spoons hung in dove-tail cuts in the shelves. The big utensils stood on top of the dresser and, if the household was wealthy enough, some glasses. On the other side of the table, seating was provided by the *banclet* of another box-bed, that of the older children, or of the son and his wife should they remain in the house after marriage. In Finistère this bed makes an alcove, (Br.) *leur gwele tol,* for the table which is then hidden from the doorway. Where the alcove is contained in an outshot it is called (Fr.) *cache-table,* or (Br.) *cus-tol* (Figs. 229, 236). A horizontal plank suspended from the rafters above the table serves as a store for bread and meat, out of reach of cats, rats and mice (Fig. 228). Behind the second bed stood another large chest, (Fr.) *l'arch,* (Br.) *an arc'h,* containing a supply of grain for family use. The *grenier* was thus left free for the storage of turf or gorse for the fire. It was also in the *grenier,* the *cellier,* or the byre or stable, that young boys, and particularly the servants, slept, often together in the same bed. *Armoires* were always big, that of the master of the house and his

wife standing next to their bed. That of the children followed between the grain chest and the doorway.[682] This picture is substantially true of all the traditional houses of Basse-Bretagne, particularly of Léon, the interiors differing only in degree according to the wealth of the occupant. The beds often lacked covers, having instead a *ballière,* were suffocatingly hot in summer, inadequately aired and unhealthy. Layers of straw at the base were renewed only once a year, after harvest, and the straw *'se remplit bientôt des légions de ces insectes parasites, parmi lesquels l'espèce humaine ne peut goûter de repos que par la rusticité du corps, jointe à l'habitude d'en être la pâture . . . Et le fond du lit, en même temps, devient un domicile où les souris, à l'abri de tout ennemi, se multiplient dans le même rapport'.*[683] The villages of Raguénez, Kerglintin and Vénioc, Finistère, all consisted of single-storey houses with a single room which served as a kitchen, bedroom and living room, lighted by a small unglazed window.[684]

Souvestre considered Cambry's description exaggerated and thought the absence of bed linen rare and exceptional, but confirms the solitary room and tiny windows, most of the light and air entering by the doorway, ever open during the day. Irregularity of the earthen floor, oak furniture darkened by time and smoke, box-beds and *armoires* all struck the visitor. Benches stood on either side of the hearth. Several farm implements, the churns, a *buie* and some piles of grass completed the picture. Families were large, never less than eight, and the hall was consequently crowded, but for most of the day everyone was outside. Box-beds were of two tiers each often sleeping two people; brothers slept over sisters, children over parents.[685] His description is illustrated by two 'typical' interiors. In 'Hospitalité bretonne' the hearth is furnished with a pot-hanger and cauldron. To the left stands the box-bed with its bench; to the right, the *cache-table*, probably in an outshot, with its *banc-vaisselier* against the gable wall. The table is perpendicular to the window, and seating on the other side is provided by the bench of a second box-bed. A spoonholder hangs from a beam above the table and a cradle stands in the centre of the floor. 'Les enfants de la ferme' shows the conjugal box-bed to the left side of the hearth, the pot-hanger and a cauldron. In a later work, Souvestre confirms that all Breton farms were single-cell dwellings. In one such, on the floor of *terre battue*, stood four box-beds, blackened by time, and ranged on both sides of the room. Beneath were oak cupboards. A carved high-backed seat was pushed into a corner of the vast chimney. On the table stood a loaf of rye bread, covered by a cloth and basket. Copper basins stood on the dresser and tools were thrown into a corner on a heap of grass. The owner, Jean Maugueron, was marked as one of the richer farmers of the area, not by his furniture, but by the quality of the food hanging from the beams, and by the large heap of manure standing in the yard![686]

In stark contrast, the interior of a clog-maker's house in the Forêt de Paimpont shows how few belongings the poor could possess. A single stool, a chest and a bed formed of '*une paillasse, d'un seul drap de toile rousse et d'une de ces couvertures fabriquées avec des lisières tressées*'. The remainder of the *hutte* was occupied by a heap of clogs in various stages of manufacture. Near Mamers, the home of a mole-catcher was little better, '*une porte conduisant dans une petite pièce . . . dont les murs lézardés disparaissaient sous un rideau de plantes potagères conservées pour graines . . . suspendues à des os de mouton fichés dans la muraille en guise de clous. Une huche à blé, deux barriques défoncées, un banc et un lit complétaient l'ameublement*'.[687]

A group of circular huts in the Forêt du Gâvre, Loire-Atlantique, provide further evidence. Lighted only by the

Fig. 231   Niou, Île d'Ouessant, Finistère
The traditional hearth of Ouessant with its doors to close when not in use. Fires were lit only for cooking, so scarce was fuel in the nineteenth century.

open door and the flames of a fire of heath plants, a huge '*cheminée en clayonnage*' occupied the side opposite the doorway. Box-beds were ranged around the hut, together with other indescribable items of furniture. In another hut, the hearth was centrally placed. There seems to be little doubt that many houses during the nineteenth century were extremely simply, and indeed poorly, furnished. Whilst this may be spontaneous expression of poverty resulting from population increase and economic hardship, it seems far more likely to represent the survival, at the lowest social levels, of types of furniture known from prehistoric times. An interior at Loqueffret, furnished in stone, similar to the Neolithic houses at Skara Brae, has been described elsewhere.[688]

An English traveller of the third quarter of the nineteenth century was struck by the 'old farmhouses

Fig. 232 Île de Fédrun 306, Saint-Joachim, Loire-Atlantique
La maison briéronne. Note the traditional hearth, the *vaissellier* suspended on the chimney-hood, the ledge and keeping-places, pothanger and tripod. The small benches are characteristic of the Brière. The conjugal bed stands in the traditional position as does the centrally-placed table.

with their one living-room and massive furniture and mud floors'. Between Carhaix and Huelgoat, the 'aspect of the people and their dwellings . . . is more simple and primitive than we have seen; and the features of the peasants are more strongly marked with the privations of generations'. The poorest people had no beds but slept on the floor and ate chestnuts boiled in milk as their principal food. The better-off had farmhouses of 'one living and sleeping room — kitchen, sitting room, bedroom, all in one; the bedstead of carved oak, the cupboards and chests with brass handles and bosses, the copper cooking utensils bright and shining, the floor at the same time being of bare earth'.[689]

The relative wealth of *bourgeoisie malouine* of the seventeenth century contrasts sharply. The principal room was at first-floor level, other rooms having specialist functions: *cabinet de toilette, cuisine, salle à manger*. Beds existed in the hall as well as in the kitchen, the servants sleeping in the latter. Specialization at the highest social levels was thus incomplete, notwithstanding the wealth to be found in post-medieval times in a town like Saint-Malo. The country residence of the same family displays a more subdued affluence but the same *traits* are present: rooms in which specialization is incomplete.[690]

Arrangement of the furniture was nearly always the same in the nineteenth-century interiors of the *pays gallo*. All the farms had only one room: the hall in which all activity took place. Two or three box-beds aligned against the wall opposite the window, the great chimney, the table with sliding top, a longcase clock and the *armoires*, one for each person, although some members of the family made do with a chest, were universal.[691] The table attracted the attention of many travellers. Either close to it, or above, hung a wooden frame from which were suspended the wooden spoons, for '*la cuiller en bois, autrefois sculptée, est essentiellement bretonne: elle a un nom breton, er loâ, tandis que la fourchette, presque*

Fig. 233. Le Plessis, La Chapelle-des-Fougaretz, Ille-et-Vilaine
A traditional hearth in a house of *manoir* class in the Rennes basin. Note the ledge on the breastsummer, for candlesticks and other items, and the centrally-placed table.

inconne, n'a qu'un nom simplement transcrit du français.[692]

Roger, writing of Finistère at the end of World War I, observes essentially the same *traits* but draws particular attention to the '*petit corps de bâtiment construit en saillie*', the (Br.) *kuz-taol*, (Fr.) *cache-table*, which he found to be widespread in Léon. Containing table, benches and dresser, and sometimes also a box-bed, the *kuz-taol* formed a dining annexe and extension to the common living room. In contrast to the relative prosperity of Léon, he found Cornouaille untidy and dirty, the interiors lacking air and light. '*On ne peut pénétrer, sans des nausées . . . et si on s'y aventure, on est donné de la misère qu'on y découvre.*' The houses had only one room and no flooring save *terre battue*. Some transformation was then taking place, however, although furniture was nearly everywhere similar: '*une table, un vaissellier, des bancs de bois, des lits-clos, une planche à pain, une armoire, constituent toute la richesse d'un intérieur breton*'. Box-beds were often of two storeys

'*dans laquelle couchent pêle-mêle les enfants, les pères, les mères, les nouveaux mariés. Et l'on ne s'étonnera pas, connaissant ce détail, de l'immoralité des habitudes bretonnes*'.[693] The *cache-table* of Léon has been commented upon by a number of writers.[694]

These accounts, whilst undoubtedly clouded by the prejudices and prior conceptions of the authors, agree on a number of facts. The vast majority of the Breton peasantry, at least up to the end of World War I, ate, cooked, slept and lived in one-room dwellings. Floors were almost universally of *terre battue* and furniture was basic and functional: box-beds, cupboards, chests, benches, a table, a dresser and perhaps a few stools and chairs, all of wood. Material possessions were few. The poorest people had even less, and some very little indeed.

During the latter part of the eighteenth, and during the nineteenth century, travel and topographical books were frequently illustrated by engravings of country scenes, a few of which show house interiors. Whilst the people,

Fig. 234   Le Beuchet, Saint-M'Hervé, Ille-et-Vilaine
Note the traditional hearth, the conjugal bed in the corner opposite the window and the table and benches centrally placed in the room. The doorway on the right leads to a byre.

scenes and interiors so illustrated are undoubtedly the better examples of their kind, there is no reason to believe that these engravings, drawn often in great detail, are other than accurate representations. The engravings of Olivier Perrin are amongst the best. In 'Le berceau' a wood fire burns on the hearth, under a vast chimney-piece of stone. There is a *cremaillère*, and the fire-back is off-set to make a low stone shelf on which stands a pot. A keeping-place holds one or two items. A ham hangs within the chimney and a tripod rests on a hook on the side wall. To the right of the hearth, a few utensils rest on shelves, and beyond, standing against the lateral wall, facing the window (not shown), is the box-bed, its doors slid back to reveal the bedding. Immediately in front is a chest on which a woman sits, spinning with a distaff. A child rests in a cradle. The master of the house reclines in his great wooden chair, to the right of the hearth, clogs on feet, pipe in hand and hat firmly pulled down over his head. Hats appear continually to have been worn, even at the table, indoors as well as out. Oral evidence

suggests that they were removed only to go to bed, when in church, and before the clergy and the *notaire*. The position of the seat of the most senior male member of the household seems always to have been to the right of the hearth. Field observations suggest that this position was almost invariable. The woman may sit on the left of the hearth, but not necessarily so when she is working. A widow sometimes assumes the seat at the right of the hearth after the death of her husband, or a spinster upon the death of her father. On the extreme left of the engraving is the table. In the centre of the floor, two pigs feed from a circular wooden trough. A three-legged cauldron with a wooden lid stands by the box-bed. The presence of the smaller animals of the farm is not uncommon — chickens, ducks, pigs and sheep commonly found their way into the hall, as the fowls still do!

'Le maillot' also illustrates a hearth scene, with only slight variations in the positions of the utensils. The principal box-bed is in the same position *vis-à-vis* the

Fig. 235 Saint-Rivoal, Finistère
This hearth with its pothanger, *bancs*, and keeping-places is typical of the Monts d'Arrée. Note the shelf suspended from the ceiling beams, intended for the storage of bread and other items. The conjugal box-bed stands in the traditional position.

hearth. 'Passage de l'enfant par dessus la table' permits a clearer view of the side of the hearth by the window. The latter is unglazed, and has four wooden shutters. The table stands perpendicular to the window. A highbacked wooden bench provides seating on one side, and behind this, towards the door, stands the chest. The great wooden seat by the hearth, on the right, and some three-legged stools complete the picture. A great cauldron hangs from the *cremaillère* and a pot rests in the keeping-place to the left of the hearth. 'La fin du sevrage' provides a similar picture, but with another bed to the left of the hearth, and two simple benches provide seating for the table. An old man sits in *an gador* to the right of the hearth and a gun hangs upon the chimney hood. A similar picture, again with the old man in *an gador*, is illustrated by 'La bouillie'. The cradle stands on the chest in front of the conjugal box-bed, a position it frequently occupies when not in use, or when the child is left in the house alone during the day.[695]

A miscellaneous collection of engravings provides confirmation of the type and disposition of the furniture and utensils. 'Les ages de la vie', *c.* 1800, shows a man sitting in *an gador*, a woman on the hearth-stone and the cradle on the floor. Two pigs feed from a trough immediately in front of the box-bed.[696] 'L'hospitalité bretonne', of nineteenth-century date, shows the conjugal box-bed to the left of the hearth and the window on the right. Table and benches are placed close by, and perpendicular to, the window. A cauldron stands on the hearth-stone and a cradle in the middle of the floor. The pot-hanger hangs on the hearth-back. A shelf is fastened to the front of the breastsummer and a wooden rack for food storage is suspended horizontally from the beams, between hearth and table.[697] 'La veillée' (1868) illustrates a similar arrangement of the hearth.[698] Whilst the above examples are obviously the homes of well-to-do farmers, the lower end of the social scale is represented by a *sabotière* (*c.* 1840), with its centrally placed open hearth and a cradle and bed to the left. On the floor is a three-legged pot and a ladle. A basket suspended from the

Fig. 236   Saint-Rivoal, Finistère
The table outshot so characteristic of north Finistère. Note the stone bench built into the wall, the *table-huche*, the box-bed, suspended spoon-holder, and the unglazed window.

rafters and a rough *vaisselier* hanging to the left of the bed complete the picture.[699]

Over forty works dealing with various aspects of rural life in Brittany pay some attention to house interiors: official reports concerned with rural conditions from the point of view of agriculture or public health, studies by geographers and historians of *l'habitat rural*, and some articles by amateur workers. A number of authors attempt to generalize for Brittany as a whole. Le Lannou, at the end of World War II, regards the two-cell house, with *cuisine* and 'salle' separated by a corridor bounded by two wooden partitions, as typical. The former is the true salle, or hall, the latter a room reserved for special occasions. Traditional order reigns in the hall: a large hearth, monumental chimney, table and benches by the small window and a range of *armoires*, box-beds and

chests, perhaps also a longcase clock. A dresser holds all the crockery. Suspended from the ceiling may be the bread board and the spoon holder and the sides of smoked pork. The 'salle' is much less rigidly organized, the beds may be modern and a circular table with several chairs often occupies the centre of the room. This serves as a living room for special occasions and provides sleeping accommodation for visitors.[700]

Writing of interior Brittany at the same period, Gautier reports that in the biggest farms, a small room, the *salle*, separated from the hall by a wooden partition, was used to receive visitors, containing perhaps a modern bed as well as a sewing machine, whilst the hall, whitewashed with lime, preserves its ancient range of furniture, often standing on a low platform of wood.[701] Several farms in the most advanced areas then boasted kitchen, dining room and bedrooms. Specialization is thus apparent in some farms by the mid-twentieth century, and partial specialization in others.

At the turn of the century the traditional house had only a single large living room on the ground floor, serving all purposes, with its box-beds, *armoires*, benches, dresser and the colossal chimney-piece, the great majority of the houses being also without rooms upstairs. This arrangement was then universal over the whole of Basse-Bretagne except in coastal regions showing signs of change. The *pièce unique* dominated in Châteauneuf-du-Faou, Gourin, Scaër, Saint-Renan, Belle-Isle-en-Terre, La Feuillée, Plouescat and Lesneven. In some houses, however, several additional rooms had evolved. A transverse corridor in the middle, bounded by wooden partitions, with a stair at the end, separated the *cuisine*, or hall, from the *salle*, '*mais cette distribution est presque toujours purement illusoire et ne modifie en rien l'ancienne promiscuité de la vie domestique. La salle est constamment déserte; l'homme, la femme, les enfants, les serviteurs vivent et mangent dans la cuisine; ils y couchent tous, lorsque l'étage fait défaut. Aussi les progrès de la distribution intérieure n'ont pas eu sur l'hygiène sociale un effet sensible*'. The floor is rarely boarded and hardly ever paved and the ground-floor walls were very damp.[702]

Writing in general terms, J.-S. Gauthier considered the Breton interior to be very simple, a single large room formerly occupying the whole space between the two gables, but which was later divided into two approximately equal parts by a wooden partition. Houses of two storeys were sometimes found near the coast.[703] Two interior layouts were representative. For the small house, two cells, one the hall, the other much smaller and used mostly as a store and, in the larger houses, two rooms of roughly equal size were common, a hall and a room set aside for special occasions. An example from Penmarc'h, Finistère, illustrates this (Fig. 238). The hall is filled with box-beds, table and benches. One bed, two *armoires* and a table occupy the second cell. Whilst in general terms Gauthier's example appears accurate, the total absence of *armoires* and chests from the hall is surprising.

Writing generally of Basse-Bretagne, Rosot illustrates a 'typical' interior (Fig. 238). The apparently symmetrical two-cell house has no interior subdivision, as Gauthier implied above. Four box-beds and a longcase clock line the back wall, and the embryo corridor is demarcated by two *armoires*. A table and benches, one a *banc-trustill*, stand perpendicular to the window.[704]

Marchal reports the house of Haute-Bretagne as commonly of one cell, with a door situated at the lower end (Fig. 238).[705] His example is more than one room deep, however, with a *cellier*, probably a lean-to outshot, extending across the rear. The hall walls are plastered with *torchis* and limewashed. In a number of aspects this interior differs significantly from the general descriptions of Basse-Bretagne so far encountered. The table is centrally placed, and a *dalle*, with shelves of wood or stone, is built into the lower wall. This *dalle*, a place for the storage of utensils for household and dairy activity, is essentially a place of work and a wash-place. In Marchal's illustration, a doorway formerly existed by the side of the *dalle*, giving direct access to the byre. Examples recently examined in the region of Bécherel, Côtes-du-Nord, show this arrangement there to be widespread. Where a byre lies adjacent to the hall, the *dalle* drains to the byre. Where a second living room is provided here, there is no drain. The *dalle* is a feature formerly widespread in the *pays de Rennes* and survived *c.* 1920 in Porhoët and Goëllo.[706] A number of beds are ranged along the back wall, and one stands between the door and the window. No bed occupies the classic position of the conjugal bed, for that would obstruct the doorway to the *cellier*.

Buffet describes the general interior arrangement in Haute-Bretagne, noting the persistence of the *dalle*, once widespread in eastern Côtes-du-Nord and Ille-et-Vilaine. *Armoires* were ranged against the wall opposite the window along with box-beds and a longcase clock, occasionally leaving a narrow passage between the row and the wall, the *venelle* or the *ruelle aux charniers*. Whenever the room was big enough, and family size required it, a second bed was placed on the side of the hearth opposite the conjugal bed. Several items, including a bed and an *armoire*, frequently stood between doorway and window. In western Haute-Bretagne the table is placed against, and perpendicular to, the window opening, as in Basse-Bretagne, but in

Fig. 237 Beau Normandie, Paimpont, Ille-et-Vilaine
A wooden breastsummer is used even in houses of the highest quality when no stone is available. This example is dated 1554. Note the keeping-places, crane or pothanger and tripod.

eastern Haute-Bretagne it stood centrally placed in the room with its axis perpendicular to the gable.[707]

Sebillot, also writing of the houses of nineteenth-century Haute-Bretagne, notes the presence of the *dalle*. Along the northern wall, beds and *armoires* were placed so as to leave a narrow passage. The *huche* or *met*, in front of the bed, also traditionally served for laying out the corpse after death. A bed, perpendicular to the wall, an *armoire* and a dresser were often placed between doorway and window. Generally, another bed stood between window and hearth, that of '*des bonnes gens*'. In well-to-do houses, a *buffet*, dresser or *armoire* stood perpendicular to the window. The table was always centrally placed and well-lit. From the beams hung the bread rack and other shelves, as well as the *lard fumée* and the salted meat.[708]

Several writers give glimpses of house interiors, modes of living, cooking and diet, and social and economic life generally.[709] During the eighteenth century, when small farmers had only single-cell dwellings, poverty was widespread and the landless classes appear to have lived from day to day, famine and disease taking their toll in bad years. In 1772, the rector of La Chapelle-Janson was able to write that only five to six persons in the parish were in a position to give alms. Of 2,200 souls, 1,800 were in need of bread and when unable to find it, '*la plupart mangent des troncs bouillis, et à leur défaut des herbes*'. In 1771, the greater number of the inhabitants of Fougères were without resources, '*nus, couchés sur de la paille, malades et manquant de pain*'. Other reports for the same period are couched in similar terms. In the homes of such poor people, furniture was of the most rudimentary kind, a bed without a mattress and a simple covering of straw. In bad years even the straw was too expensive to buy, being replaced by bracken or dry grass, '*quelquefois même par de la cendre ou du fumier*'. In 1774 in Plénée-Jugon, 320 poor people slept on straw only. Where a box-bed existed, frequently not less that two or three slept in it at one time. In 1767, the rector of Trigavou found a mother and four children all dying in the same bed. From the beginning of the eighteenth century descriptions of property become more numerous. In the *pays de Quimper* dwellings of both one and two cells are found, the second cell being used chiefly for reception.[710] At Plonivel in Cornouaille during the eighteenth century, the house often seems to have had two rooms, on each side of the entry corridor. Several box-beds generally stood in the second cell.[711] During the second half of the eighteenth century, the poorest people of Montfort-la-Cane had goods valued at only fifty *livres*, and lived wholly — families of five, six or more — in a house of one room. Furniture was of the poorest and bed-linen scarcely existed.[712] In eighteenth-century Pleugueneuc, the peasants lived in *mazières* as often as in houses. Around Saint-Brieuc, most of the houses were built with only one room. When they possessed large animals, often only a pig or two, these lived at one end of the dwellings; frequently only a low partition divided man from beast. At Montfort-La-Cane, it was rare to find a second bed in the homes of the poorest. The whole family slept in one bed, or on straw or just on the floor, conditions which gave rise to concern, not least in connection with disease.[713] The chief items in eighteenth-century inventories in the *pays de Porzay* were the *table coulante*, plates of pewter or faïence, box-beds, *armoires, huches, buffets-vaisselliers, bancs* and *escabeaux*.[714] By the nineteenth and twentieth centuries, some amelioration in living conditions is

discernible, although the old basic items survive, except that the box-beds tend to have been replaced by modern beds, but many nevertheless remained into the inter-war period. The *chaise-de-paille* came to be replaced by the wooden chair, especially after 1900. Longcase clocks, once found only in the homes of the rich, are first noted in 1844, become common after 1854 and are found virtually everywhere by 1875.[715]

In Cap-Sizun the interiors hardly changed until World War II. A doorway opened into a corridor, at the end of which a stair led to the first floor. Beneath this was the *cabinet noir,* a dark store in which stood the *charnier* containing the supply of salted meat, a vessel of wood, granite or earthenware. The hall lay either to the left or the right, with perhaps a preference for the right. A second cell, mostly given over to storage, lay opposite. In houses with a developed first floor, where the *grenier* had given way to bedrooms, or multi-purpose rooms containing beds, the second cell on the ground floor had become a dining room, reserved for special occasions. In addition to large rooms upstairs, there may also be a *cabinet* above the corridor. In houses with an open *grenier,* the latter is still likely to be used for supplementary sleeping accommodation. The smallest houses had only one room either with the corridor at the lower end, or entry direct into the hall, and the stair to the *grenier* replaced by a ladder. Floors were always of *terre battue.* Traditional interior arrangement consisted of a hearth, with benches and *étagère* over the chimney hood. The hall had two windows, one lighting the table, the other a small working space between the high-backed bench and the chimney gable. A table, along with a box-bed and chest, was placed perpendicular to the larger window. Opposite the window were ranged the conjugal box-bed, the *armoires* and the dresser (Fig. 238). Furniture in the other rooms comprised box-beds, *armoires* and chests, but there appears to have been no regular pattern of arrangement. There is uniformity in the arrangement of the hall, not only throughout Cap-Sizun, but also throughout the greater part of Cornouaille, including the *pays bigouden.*[716] These descriptions should not obscure the possibility that simpler houses and arrangements may previously have existed, or may long have survived alongside these more developed examples. Bresson hints at the presence of houses simpler than the majority in Cap-Sizun.[717]

In the 1830s, two separate cells were rare in Finistère. '*La pièce qu'occupe la famille est encombrée de lits clos, dont les battants sont à coulisses, d'armoires, de bancs, servant à la fois de siège pour la table et de coffre pour les hardes; de grandes huches ou coffres dans lesquels sont renfermés les grains de la récolte. Un chaudron, quelques trépieds, des poëles à crêpes, des écuelles grossières, une collection de cuillers en bois, ordinairement placées debout, dans une chopine de terre vide, quelques assiettes étalée dans un vaisselier, et plusiers images grossières en luminées des plus fortes couleurs, forment l'extérieur d'une famille Léonaise. Depuis quelque temps ils y ajoutent une pendule de bois, meuble de luxe qui dénote des habitudes plus confortables . . .'.* The interior arrangement varied little, *'mal aérée, malsaine sous tous les rapports, cette habitation est encombrée de meubles qui empêchent la circulation de l'air'.* Eight or ten people often slept in the one room, ventilated by one or two small unglazed windows eighteen or so *pouces* wide, the door being left open for light and air during the day.[718] In the Monts d'Arrée, the single-cell dwelling was still almost universal after World War I. The interiors at Saint-Amboise and Restidou (Fig. 238) conform to a plan already shown to be widespread.[719] At the other extreme, an inventory of 1510 shows how wealthy a farmer could be, with several furnished rooms.[720]

Interiors certainly lacked comfort and the only decoration was that of the *armoires* and the box-beds, often richly carved. The longcase clock became common between 1840 and 1850.[721] Where two rooms existed in Finistère, the second was little utilized in daytime but it was often used for overflow sleeping accommodation for farm servants and domestics. Senior members of the family retained a preference for sleeping in the hall,[722] and farm servants slept in the stables near the animals.[723] An inventory of the family of Liscoët, *c.* 1712, records beds for the servants in two of the stables.[724]

At the end of the nineteenth century in Finistère, the poorer classes lived much as Cambry has described, even in newly built houses. A relatively advanced interior is shown at Trouguennour (Fig. 238). This house, dated 1835, and the home of a well-to-do farmer, was built when houses in that area were just beginning to be erected with an upper storey. The owner slept upstairs in 1905. This move to sleeping upstairs was noted in the *pays julot* at the start of the twentieth century, the box-beds in the hall being left for the servants.[725] At the end of the nineteenth century in the almshouse at Saint-Jean-du-Doigt, Finistère, the poor slept in a dormitory without beds, *'une épaisse paillée de froment en tenait lieu, à moins que ce ne fût de la fougère sèche peut-être un peu rustique: mais quoi! le Christ naissant n'en avait pas en d'autre . . . Et puis, ce n'est pas le coucher qui importe, c'est le sommeil'.*[726]

A survey of Plouvien, Finistère during the 1940s showed the older houses to be generally of only one room, but farms with one or two extra rooms were not unknown. A second storey was still extremely rare. Some of the extra rooms did not always contain a bed and many were undoubtedly storerooms. Shopkeepers were better housed than the peasantry, often having an upper room, circular tables and *lits d'alcôve*, in place of, or in addition to, box-beds. The *presbytère* of Plouvien contained a *cuisine*, oven-house, an upper room and a *bureau*, that at Bourg-Blanc, a *cuisine* and an upper room. This presence of upper-rooms in clergy homes is a good indication of the social position they occupied. The ordinary house was *'vraiment de triste aspect; elle est plus basse et plus misérable que celle du Vannetais . . . c'est une maison basse sans grenier. Il y a seulement parfois une sorte de plafond de planches sur la pièce unique; plus souvent, ce plafond n'existe que près de la cheminée'.* This is a reference to a half-loft as found in the Welsh house. The *kuz-taol* makes its appearance in a number of Plouvien houses, the wall towards the doorway being provided with a small window, (Br.) *toull ar fuzuilh*, (Fr.) *trou de fusil*, through which visitors could be seen. The interiors were arranged in the 'classic' Breton manner, save for a modern cooker to the right of the hearth (Fig. 238).[727]

The extent to which these simple interiors survived into the inter-War period is graphically portrayed by Hélias, who lived in the *pays bigouden*, with *'terre battue, grande cheminée, petite fenêtre à barreaux. C'est le seul endroit où il m'ait été donné de voir et d'expérimenter un lit-clos à deux étages et quatre places. Une couche de genêts tenait lieu de sommier et les couettes étaient garnis de balle d'avoine. Au-dessus de la pièce, un grenier auquel on accédait par une échelle et qui servait à tout, y compris à dormir'.*[728]

In Ouessant, by the nineteenth century, interiors had evolved to a unique pattern. Most of the houses, whether of one or two storeys, were roughly symmetrical, and divided into two cells, with centrally placed doorways and a cross-passage structurally defined by the furniture (Fig. 238). The furniture of painted wood (Fig. 230, 231) gives an appearance of the interior of a ship of the eighteenth or nineteenth century. There is a main axial throughway, both sides of which are continuously lined with furniture. The hall, (Br.) *penn lous*, dirty end, or *penn kuisin*, kitchen end, was complemented by the (Br.) *penn brao*, the *salle-de-réception* where visitors were received, especially the clergy and the doctor, and where corpses were laid out before burial. The hearths are closed by wooden doors, painted in the same style (Fig. 231). Apart from the staircase leading to the *grenier*, furniture consists of four tables symmetrically placed, one of which, the *table-pétrin*, served for making bread (Fig. 238). Box-beds, closed by curtains, open on to the

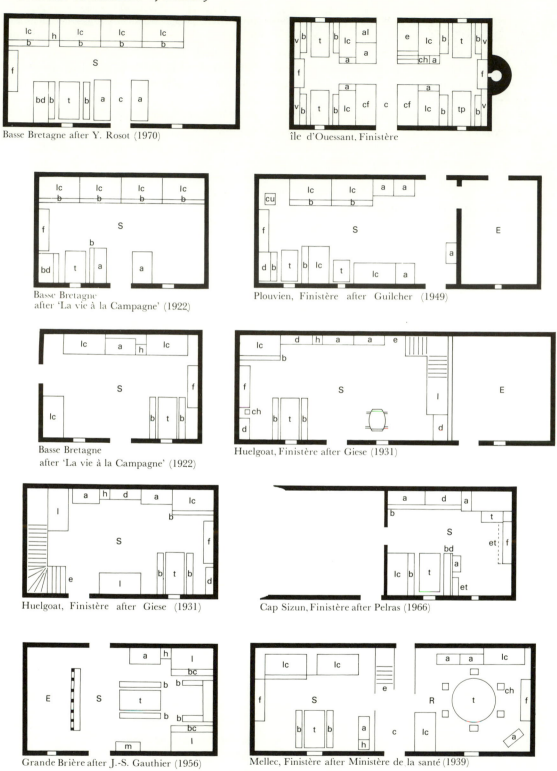

Fig. 238a   The arrangement of interiors (from published literature)

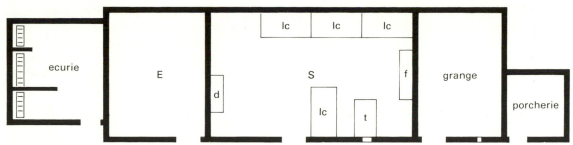

Tréflez, Finistère after Fleury (1899)

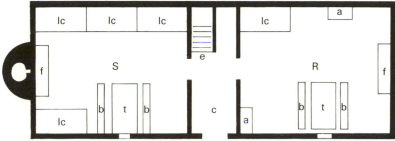

Penmarc'h, Finistère after J.-S. Gauthier (1965)

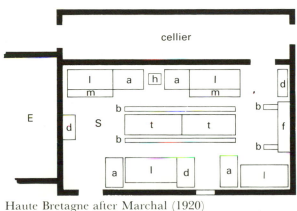

Haute Bretagne after Marchal (1920)

Not to scale

Hall	S	Salle
Byre	E	Étable
Second cell/parlour	R	'Salle' réservée
Cross-passage	c	Couloir
Stair	e	Escalier
Wardrobe/cupboard	a	Armoire
Milk store	al	Armoire à lait
Bench	b	Banc
Bench/chest	bc	Banc coffre
Bench/dresser	bd	Banc trustel/drustilh
Chest	cf	Coffre
Chair	ch	Chaise
Chest/commode	cm	Commode
Meat store	cn	Charnier
Cooker	cu	Cuisine
Dresser	d	Buffet-dressoir
Stool	es	Escabeau
Shelf	et	Étagère
Hearth	f	Âtre
Longcase clock	h	Horloge
Bed	l	Lit
Box-bed	lc	Lit-clos
Chest	m	Huche/maie
Chest	p	Pétrin
Table	t	Table
Chest/table	tp	Table/pétrin
Dresser	v	Vaisselier

Fig. 238b   The arrangement of interiors (from published literature)

tables, the bed being made on a layer of straw or seaweed. In front of each is the (Br.) *bank tosser*. Some of the *armoires* are integral with the *lits-clos*, others separately built. One serves as a small 'dairy' for the storage of milk. Implements and utensils are stored beneath the furniture. The remainder consists of *banc-coffres*, the *coffres-à-grains*, the *bancs*, simple benches, dressers and the *charnier* for the salted meat supply. There can be little doubt that this furniture is late in date. There is no reference in any of the Ouessant inventories to it, the impression in them being of traditional Breton furniture. The paint was obviously used to disguise driftwood and the fashion is probably a late nineteenth-century or early twentieth-century introduction. The relative scarcity and costliness of the material explain the need to paint it. Poverty and the absence of wood for fuel were notable. *'Dans une immense cheminée . . . brûle un maigre feu de branches d'ajonc, de bouse de vache et de mottes de gazon désséché. Tout cela incommode, sans lumière, suant l'humidité. Une odeur caractéristique saisit à la gorge, due à l'entassement de tant d'êtres humains, car souvent cette pièce sert d'abri à deux familles à la fois. Chez les plus pauvres, le même lit sert à toute la famille'.*[729] Bohéas considered the interior and the ways of life unhealthy, with six children sometimes sleeping in one bed.[730]

Writing of Bulat-Pestivien, Côtes-du-Nord, between the two World Wars, Fournier notes that the *pièce unique* still served for all. From the ceiling hung the provisions, clothes, harness, small implements and bicycles if they had them, *'c'est un logis universel'*. In the bigger farms and *manoirs*, even where there were several rooms, one still preserved this essential quality, Besides the *salle-à-manger-de-parade*, a dairy and perhaps a bedroom, the other rooms served as granaries.[731] At the end of World War I it was still possible to write of Côtes-du-Nord that the *'mobilier breton original était rudimentaire'*.[732] A mid nineteenth-century survey of the agriculture of Côtes-du-Nord observes that in the interior generally there was only one cell *'qui forme cuisine, chambre à coucher, salle à manger'*. Greater comfort was apparent by the littoral, where *'les chambres à lits des maîtres de la maison sont communément placées au premier étage; quelquefois on a une salle ou un cabinet isolé'*.[733] Furniture consisted of benches by the hearth, the *'fauteuil en bois, réservé au doyen de la famille'*, box-beds, often two storeys high, placed along the wall opposite the entry, chests in front, table and benches placed against the solitary window. A dresser, cupboard at the base, open dresser above, is sometimes found as a *meuble-de-luxe*.[734]

The reports of the Comité d'Hygiène et de la Salubrité around the 1850s and 1860s throw considerable light on domestic conditions. In Maël-Carhaix, for the greater part of the population, conditions were unhygienic, whilst in Bourbriac, the houses of the poor left much to be desired. Sad in appearance from the outside, inside there reigned *'la plus profonde obscurité, le jour n'y pénétrant que par la cheminée, ou par les feutes de mauvaises planches qui en bouchent l'entrée. Des pièces, plantés en terre, quelques branches d'arbres recouvertes d'un peu de paille, telle est souvent leur couche. Aussi, le voit-on aller en foule, réclamer gîte au cultivateur aisé qui leur offre son étable et de la paille fraîche'.* Around Dinan many houses had only one door and a small opening for a window, the whole family slept in the one room, and the floors, of *terre battue*, were often lower than the ground outside, so that water seeped in when it rained. This latter point is a frequent source of complaint everywhere, as around Guingamp, where conditions of hygiene were deplorable. Houses were small, low, overcrowded and the windows much too small. There was constant dampness. Near Loudéac, floors were everywhere of *terre battue*, paving being unknown, and often the loft was unboarded. Sometimes a few planks were placed across the beams on which to store firewood and provisions. Poor ventilation was again a source of complaint, for the air *'est introduit par une seule porte et par une énorme cheminée'*. Glazed windows were not universal and it may be likely that many houses had no windows at all. In each *arrondissement* it is either specifically stated or implied that the single-cell house was the rule.[735]

Even in the twentieth century the single-cell dwelling was virtually the rule in Côtes-du-Nord. Dwellings of more than one room were not unknown, however, and in some areas were becoming common by the mid-nineteenth century. More than two rooms were rare. *'Ordinairement les gens ne sont pas très bien logés, mais progrès immense depuis 1920. La maison comporte deux pièces séparées par une cloison de planches ou un corridor: l'une sert de cuisine et laiterie; l'autre mieux tenue, est la salle de réception et la chambre des parents'.* A second storey was exceptional before the nineteenth century, except in the biggest farms and manor houses. Even in the richer agricultural areas, the *pièce unique* existed in thirty to forty-five per cent of the houses as late as the 1950s. Elsewhere, some *communes* were made up entirely of single-cell dwellings.[736] Nor was there generally a dairy set apart. Dairy functions were performed in the hall where a keeping-place in the wall was often set aside for the vessels. In a two-cell house, dairy functions were sometimes carried out in the second cell or in an outshot at the rear. It was in the second cell that animal food was prepared. Conditions were often very crowded. *'Si dans certains foyers à pièce unique, il n'y a que deux ou trois personnes, dans d'autres, vivent entassés, une famille de huit, dix enfants'*, and *'10 maisons, presque toutes n'ont qu'une pièce, dont une loge 10 personnes'*. Near the borders of Méné, *'à la campagne, il y a 8 et 9 personnes par pièce'*. Many more instances of the crowding of single-cell houses are cited.[737] Proof of the strong tradition of living in one room is also shown by the fact that even when a peasant family lives in a house with many rooms, they frequently confine themselves to one. At Kerminguy, Grand-Champ, Morbihan, the whole family still lived in one ground-floor room as late as 1971. Other rooms were either empty, or in use for the storage of potatoes and the hatching of young chickens. Many other examples have been observed during fieldwork. Gautier confirms this observation: *'dans une maison où il y a plusieurs pièces au rez-de-chausée et plusieurs chambres à l'étage, on ne se sert que d'une seule pièce en bas. Elle est à la fois cuisine, salle-à-manger, chambre-à-coucher. Les autres pièces de rez-de-chaussée servent de débarras, les chambres sont vides.*[738]

The reports of the Comités d'Hygiène for mid nineteenth-century Ille-et-Vilaine tell a sad tale. Over-crowding was a common complaint around Vitré, as was the habit of living wholly in one room. In the *arrondissement* of Mordelles, the houses *'se composent souvent d'une seule pièce mal aërée, et mal éclairée'*, whilst around Grand-Fougeray dwellings were usually small, low and cluttered, *'la moité est situé au dessous du sol, l'autre moitié au niveau du sol; elles sont toutes très humides'*. There were few openings, no means of ventilation, and *'on ne peut diviser les chambres en 2 ou plusieurs pièces, de sorte que tous les habitants de la maison, quelquefois 6, 8, 10 couchent dans la même chambre et plusieurs dans chaque lit; il n'y a aucune propreté, aucun renouvellement de literie'*. A similar complaint about bedding is made in Fougères where it was *'très défectueuse'* and made up only of *'une paillasse et d'une ballière trop rarement renouvelées'*. Generally here there was only a single room to each farm, too often very crowded, so that some members had to sleep in other buildings: barns, byres and stables. Low floor levels, constant damp and lack of air were considered in Antrain to be a source of danger to the health of children and to engender illness.[739]

At the end of the nineteenth century, in all the houses in the region of Vannes life was confined to one cell.[740] Houses in Bas-Léon were also of one cell, although the centrally placed doorway (Fig. 238) suggests similarities of form with the long-house. A table was placed by the window and the conjugal box-bed opposite.[741] The Morbihan interiors accord closely with those of Basse-Bretagne. The chair of the eldest male member of the family was by the fire, almost always on the right hand side, (Br.) *é korn an tan*, the hearth also being equipped with two benches. Except in the extreme east of the *département*, the table stands against the window and, as elsewhere, the range of box-beds and *armoires* occupies the wall opposite.[742]

In Loire-Atlantique, many of the *traits* hitherto described for Haute-Bretagne are to be found. North of the Loire, *'à part quelques rares exceptions les habitations se composent généralement d'un rez-de-chaussée. L'usage est presque général de loger tous les habitants dans une seule pièce, les domestiques derrière les armoires. La commode est garnie de bibelots, verroterie, colifichets ainsi que la couronne de mariée et quelques photographies de famille. Deux lits encadrent généralement cette commode et faisant face à la cheminée se trouvent des armoires bien rempli de linge. Il y a deux armoires quelquefois trois, plusieurs grands coffres, une table avec ses deux bancs et suprême luxe: une buffet vaisselier'*.[743] The old houses had only one cell, the hall, the greatest number of these surviving in the *pays de Guérande*. Now there are generally two rooms, hall and *salle reservée*. The conjugal bed stands in the corner by the hearth with *armoire* and clock ranged along the rear wall. A table invariably stands in the centre of the room and a second bed is sometimes placed in the opposite corner (Fig. 238).

Reference has already been made to the conclusions of authors whose work rests, wholly or in part, on the examination of probate inventories, *les inventaires après décès*, for small regions: Cap-Sizun,[744] the *pays de Quimper*[745] and the *pays de Porzay*.[746] These documents are a rich source for the student of vernacular architecture and may be utilized in an attempt to cast light on spatial and temporal variations for Brittany as a whole. Probate inventories are rare before *c.* 1750, scarce until the late-eighteenth century, and become commoner after 1800 and frequent *c.* 1850. In view of the uniformity of household equipment that has become apparent from other evidence, together with the conservatism of the Province, this late availability of inventories is not a serious problem. It seems probable that the *notaires* not only specialized by area, but also to a degree by social class, one perhaps being more favoured by the better-off farmer, another by poorer folk. Personality was another factor which may have influenced choice. An examination of surviving inventories strongly suggests that they are a record of the chattels of the better off. Few appear to survive for the really poor whose conditions of

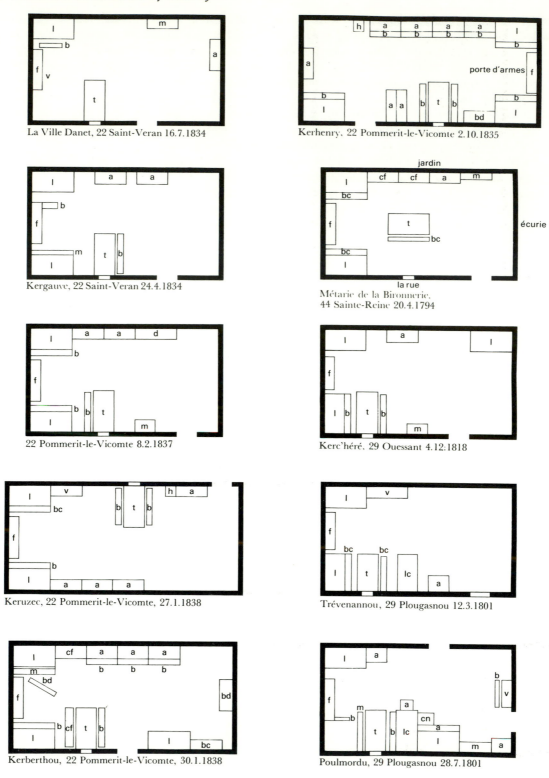

Fig. 239a   The arrangement of interiors (from probate inventories)

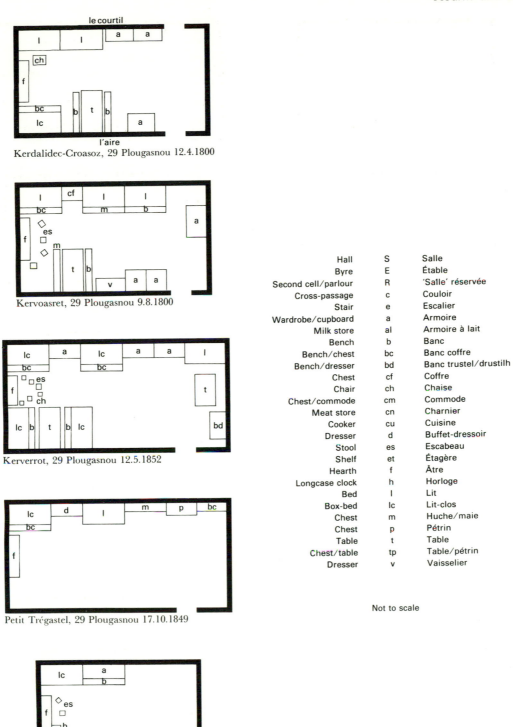

le courtil
l'aire
Kerdalidec-Croasoz, 29 Plougasnou 12.4.1800

Kervoasret, 29 Plougasnou 9.8.1800

Kerverrot, 29 Plougasnou 12.5.1852

Petit Trégastel, 29 Plougasnou 17.10.1849

Menemarzin, 29 Moëlan c.1794

Hall	S	Salle
Byre	E	Étable
Second cell/parlour	R	'Salle' réservée
Cross-passage	c	Couloir
Stair	e	Escalier
Wardrobe/cupboard	a	Armoire
Milk store	al	Armoire à lait
Bench	b	Banc
Bench/chest	bc	Banc coffre
Bench/dresser	bd	Banc trustel/drustilh
Chest	cf	Coffre
Chair	ch	Chaise
Chest/commode	cm	Commode
Meat store	cn	Charnier
Cooker	cu	Cuisine
Dresser	d	Buffet-dressoir
Stool	es	Escabeau
Shelf	et	Étagère
Hearth	f	Âtre
Longcase clock	h	Horloge
Bed	l	Lit
Box-bed	lc	Lit-clos
Chest	m	Huche/maie
Chest	p	Pétrin
Table	t	Table
Chest/table	tp	Table/pétrin
Dresser	v	Vaisselier

Not to scale

Fig. 239b   The arrangement of interiors (from probate inventories)

life have been described above. There is no clue as to why the inventories were made, beyond the obvious fact that they were needed for the fair division of property among heirs. They do not seem to have been required by law, or by the custom of the Province when there were no direct heirs, as in Normandy.[747] Strong bias thus creeps into any sample. The contents of the surviving inventories certainly do not accord with the architectural and archaeological evidence for the housing of large numbers of poor people. The inventories are of excellent quality, give considerable detail, and occasionally permit the reconstruction of the interiors of the houses. Other interiors may be partially reconstructed. The greatest care needs to be exercised, however, each inventory being interpreted on its merits. Collectively, they can be seriously misleading if not handled with extreme caution, and only the most tentative general conclusions may be made. The sample that follows is far from random and must eventually be assessed along with other evidence. A total of 325 inventories for the five *départements* have so far been examined: Finistère (85), Côtes-du-Nord (41), Ille-et-Vilaine (44), Loire-Atlantique (75) and Morbihan (80). In a few cases it was possible to examine inventories for areas studied in detail in the field. Mostly this was impossible, and recourse was had to other areas with similar geographical characteristics.[748]

The inventories vary little from one to the other in presentation. After the preliminary statement giving the name, occupation (not always) and address of the person whose goods are to be listed, there follows the list itself, nearly always starting with the hearth and its equipment. Each item is named and its value given, both in writing and in figures. Where there is more than one room in a house, the number of rooms is pointedly, sometimes pompously, stated, for to have more than one room was considered a status symbol. In a few examples, goods are so listed as to make the accurate reconstruction of a room possible. From others a partial reconstruction may be made. All the furniture is listed, clothing is sometimes given as a total value, and often itemized. Also listed in detail are the foods in store, bed linen, utensils, cutlery, dairy equipment, tradesmen's tools, farm implements, animals, crops in store, and crops sown in the fields. The total value of all these thus represents, according to the *notaire's* estimate, the value of a man's 'moveables'.

Only a brief treatment of these inventories is attempted. In order not to obscure the many *lacunae*, no attempt has been made at detailed statistical analysis, for it is felt that the distribution is too uneven in time and space for such treatment. The 325 inventories are examined graphically first to see whether there exist any *traits* so strong that some tentative conclusions may be

drawn. Consideration is then given to the numbers of rooms shown by the inventories and to the furniture in those rooms, and finally to an examination of the rarer items in the lists to see to what extent 'luxury' and 'ease' may be detected.

A series of six graphs have been prepared showing the total values of each inventory, in *francs* or *livres*, against the *étude*, or office location, of the *notaire*, for the periods 1650–1700, 1701–1750, 1751–1790, 1791–1810, 1811–1830 and 1831–1852. A seventh graph, showing the total for each of these periods, is plotted against the values of the inventories. The values plotted are crude totals, no correction being made for inflation either within the time intervals, or over the 150-year period. Any attempt at such a correction would, by its nature, be open to dispute, quite apart from the extreme difficulty of making it. The *franc* is also assumed to be of the same value as the old *livre*, and no account is taken of any national or regional variations in value. Should clear variations in time and space exist, they might be expected to override the finer variations of money values. If such variations are barely perceptible or in any way doubtful, the very nature of the sample, outlined above, will make it impossible to draw conclusions.

For the period 1701–1750, there is remarkable uniformity, all except the values being under 400 *livres*, and most lying between 200 and 400 *livres* (Fig. 240). For the period 1751–1790, fifty-two inventories are available. The majority of the totals are under 800 *livres*, but the range is greater than during the earlier period, and one or two relatively well-to-do farms are recorded. There is a big variation in wealth, but only for Plougonver and Pont-Scorff are there sufficient numbers to show that the great majority of the totals lie below 800 *livres*, with occasional higher values. For the period 1791–1810, seventy-five totals are shown. The range of wealth is again greater than in the previous two periods, but several *études* are not represented in either of the earlier periods. However, there seems to be a greater range at the lower end of the range. Over half the totals are under 600 *livres/francs* and a further nineteen between 600 and 1,200. Six *études* are represented in the 1811–1830 period, one being the Île d'Ouessant. Of the seventy-five totals shown, two high values exist at Pontchâteau and Clisson respectively, and one of over 400 *francs* at Ouessant. All the others are below 3,000 *francs*, but the range is again greater than in the previous periods, all but thirteen of the total being below 2,000 *francs*, but fourteen between 1,200 and 2,000. Pontchâteau and Saint-Joachim have fairly uniform distributions. Both are in areas where farms were small, and the numbers of low values is therefore not surprising. Grand-Champ registers eight totals between one and three hundred, with nine more between 300 and 1,000. Nearly all the houses there are one-cell long-houses, the values being largely made up of animals and implements. For the period 1831–1852, one hundred and four values exist for nine *études*, of which five are in Finistère. Saint-Renan, Châteaulin and Plougasnou show some very high values and there is now, with this higher number of available values, a clear contrast between these areas of Léon, where some farms were known to have become prosperous through the linen trade in the seventeenth and eighteenth centuries, and areas of small farmers like Merdrignac, Pleine-Fougères and Pontchâteau, known to have been relatively poor and backward, with large numbers of small farms. The contrast is sufficiently striking to show a clear regional variation, notwithstanding the defects of the sample.

Total values are now plotted against period. Weighting at the lower end is clear, the bulk of the values lying below 1,000 *francs* for all periods. There is, however, a tendency for range to increase with time. The last period shows a greater spread of small values upwards towards 1,000 *francs*, and a more uniform spread between 1,000 and 10,000 *francs*, and for a greater number of high values.

Notwithstanding the uneven sample, there is a temporal variation showing a general improvement in wealth. A number of regional variations have also become apparent; Pontchâteau and Merdrignac show a high proportion of relatively poor households. In contrast, several regions in Léon show comparative wealth and prosperity.

When more than one room existed in a house, the inventories state this. In the absence of such information, the way in which household equipment and furniture is listed, together with an absence of reference to a second room, are sufficient to assume a single cell. In Ille-et-Vilaine, only two *études* were examined, Vitré and Pleine-Fougères. Vitré provided nine inventories for 1806–10 and Pleine-Fougères thirty-four, of which half were for 1845. Forty-two of these were for single-cell dwellings, one for a single-cell household which also used a cell in another building. One house only, La Gaullairie in Pocé, had two rooms. Côtes-du-Nord is little different, and of forty-one dwellings, one had four rooms, the noble house of Lamonforière in Plénée-Jugon, three were single-cell dwellings using also a cell in another building, and the remaining thirty-eight were all single-cell dwellings. In Loire-Atlantique, a house in Herbignac had six rooms, and one in Clisson, four. There were five two-cell dwellings and one three-cell. Five households made use of a cell in another building, and sixty-six houses were of only one cell. Of the eighty-five inventories for Finistère, sixty-three are of single-cell dwellings, fourteen of two-cell, three of four-cell and one of a five-cell dwelling. The latter makes use also of three additional cells in other buildings. One of the four-cell dwellings also uses additional chambers elsewhere. These additional rooms presumably accommodated farm servants or members of extended families. Of the inventories for Morbihan, one was of five cells, two were of three cells and thirteen of two cells. The remaining sixty-four were single-cell dwellings. Many of these would be long-houses for, notwithstanding the small amount of furniture possessed by some farms, the value of implements and livestock was high, notably in Grand-Champ.

The evidence of the inventories shows, overwhelmingly, that the greater part of the population, approaching a hundred per cent in some areas, lived in single-cell dwellings. Only a few of the houses with more than one cell are other than of nineteenth-century date, but the temporal distribution of these inventories is such that it would be wrong, at this stage, to assume an increase in multi-cell houses during the first part of the nineteenth century. This must, however, remain a possibility. Field evidence shows that multi-cell houses did exist from medieval times onwards.

Most inventories begin with a listing of the equipment of the hearth. Except in the poorest households, the pot-hanger, (Fr.) *crémaillère*, sometimes two, is always found. So too is the tripod, (Fr.) *trépied*. Turnspits and similar ironmongery are rarely encountered and then only in the wealthiest farms, such as at Montdevert, Ille-et-Vilaine in 1806 and Saint-Broladre in 1804, where there were (Fr.) *landiers*, or fire-dogs. Cooking pots were relatively simple. The three-legged cauldron was common, as was the *marmite*. The poorest farms often had only one of each, or just one cooking pot. The (Fr.) *crepière* or *galetière*, a griddle, was almost universal, hardly surprisingly considering the quantity of *crêpes* that were eaten, and many homes had a frying pan. Sometimes a (Fr.) *casserole* is encountered. These utensils are often stated to be of cast iron, but earthenware pots undoubtedly survived late. Lids were of iron, earthenware or wood. They reflect the relative simplicity of the cooking methods in a country where the diet, for the greatest part of the population, was predominantly cereal-based. The Breton peasant had no need of spits to roast his meat; such little as he ate was either stewed in his *soupe* or eaten cold.

Eating utensils were of the simplest. Wooden and earthenware bowls predominate in the inventories. Many

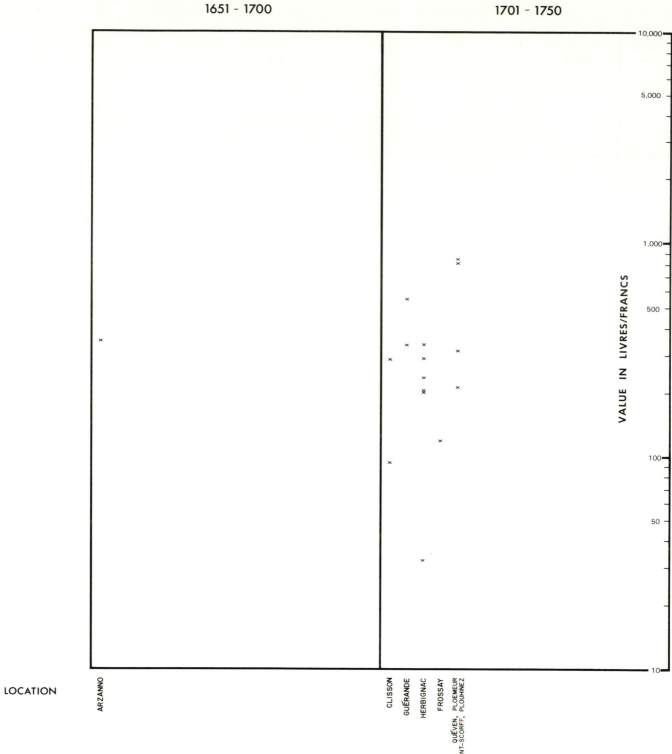

Fig. 240a   Value of furniture, livestock and crops by period (from inventories)

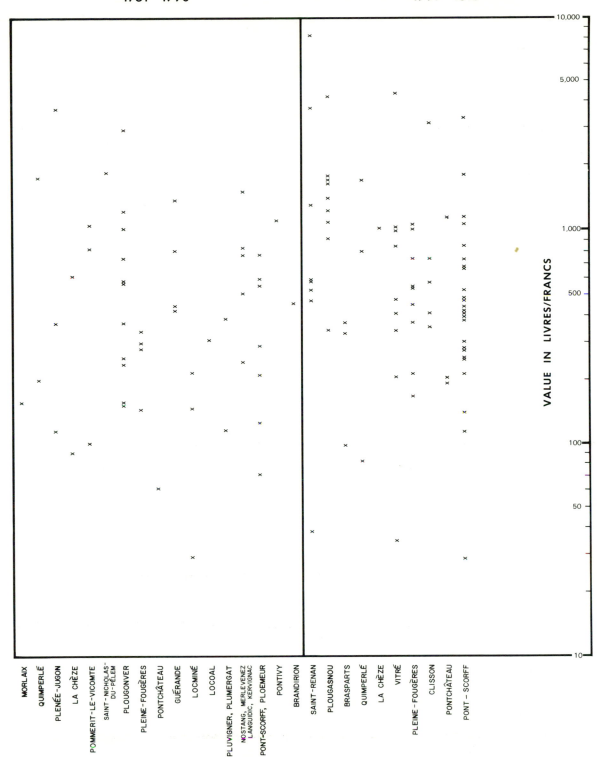

Fig. 240b Value of furniture, livestock and crops by period (from inventories)

352 *The Vernacular Architecture of Brittany*

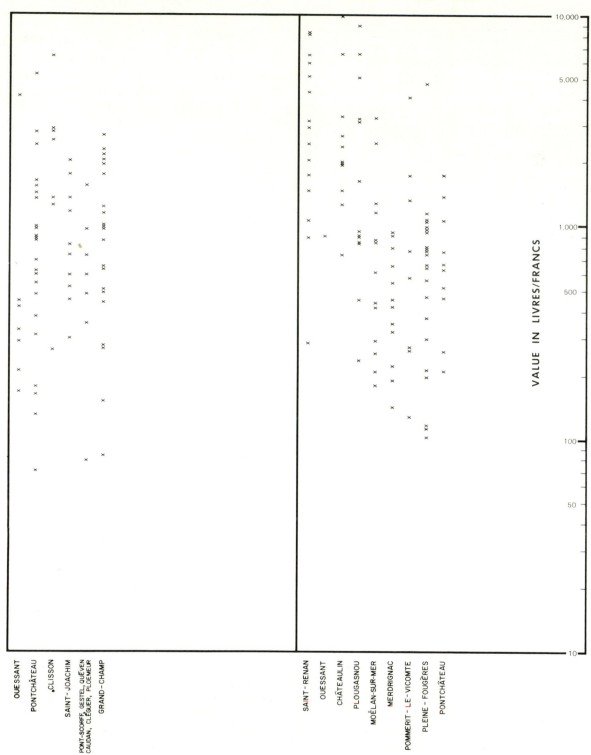

Fig. 240c   Value of furniture, livestock and crops by period (from inventories)

SUMMARY BY PERIOD

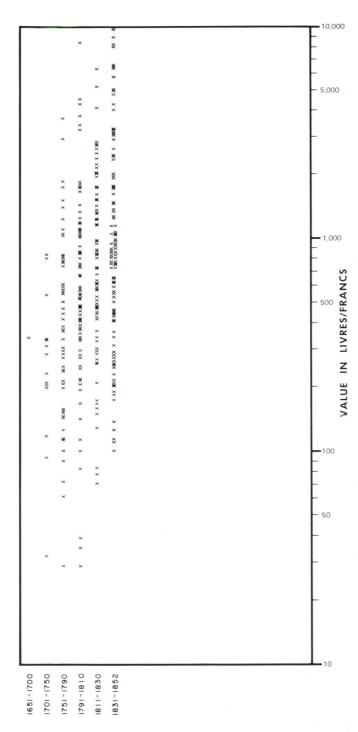

VALUE IN LIVRES/FRANCS

1651–1700 1701–1750 1751–1790 1791–1810 1811–1830 1831–1852

Fig. 240d Value of furniture, livestock and crops by period (from inventories)

households having nothing else. Others boast, in addition, a few earthenware plates. In 1841, Pierre Pornic of Cartudy in Merdrignac, Côtes-du-Nord, whose goods totalled 972 *francs*, had '*deux pots à lait, une ribotte, un bassin en terre, six ecuelles*' (worth 1 fr. 50), '*trois bouteilles de verre et une de terre, un plat et une assiette*' (worth 1 fr.). As there are no eating implements, he presumably ate with his fingers and pocket knife. A wooden spoon for each member of the household is usual, however, as at Saint-Veran in 1835 when Jean Dormet had four bowls and two spoons. Sometimes a spoon-holder is named. The wealthiest occasionally had pewter plates, but rarely more than one or two as at La Chèze in 1796, where there were brass basins and individual forks. The latter are extremely rare and appear only eight times. They are always of iron and on two occasions were found in the company of iron spoons. There is not a single reference to personal knives, confirming that the pocket knife, the universal working tool, was used. There can be no doubt that some households lacked some or even all of these implements and must have eaten with their fingers. Recent oral evidence confirms this interpretation for the smallest households. Utensils of brass or bronze, (Fr.) *airain*, were not uncommon in the larger farms.

Items of furniture accord very closely with the observations of travellers, with only the occasional mention, in the wealthiest farms, of exotic items. Beds are mostly accompanied by details of bed-linen, especially towards the mid-nineteenth century. Positions are frequently either stated or implied. Mathurin Gherieux, of La Gols Bourdière, in 1841 had '*un bois de lit à droite près le foyer . . .*' with '*une mei audevant*'. Additionally, there were four *armoires*, another *mée*, a *table à pain*, a *porte vaisselle*, '*une bois de lit à gauche pris le foyer . . .*' with '*une mé au devant*', a cradle and a chair. In 1775, Jean Henri of Kerdech, Plougonver had goods made up of '*une ronce de fer*' (a pot-hanger), two iron pots, a *crêpe* pan, three beds, an *armoire*, a poor table, a six-year old horse, a supply of rye, buckwheat, oats and hay, flax and hemp, a sickle, a slice, three beehives and two very poor chests. The total was valued at 151 *livres*. Gilles Le Haneff of Plougonver in 1789 was little better off with goods valued at 156 *livres*. The livestock consisted of two small pigs, a cow '*hors d'age*' and four hens. There were three beds, a *table coulante*, various chests and a small dresser. With five bowls and a dozen spoons his table was well equipped. Livestock often accounts for the greater part of the total value of the goods, but the mention of hens, geese and other fowl is rare and one must suppose that mostly they had taken wing before the *notaire* arrived. The high value of livestock is especially noticeable in regions where oxen are used as draught animals, for they fetched a high price. In 1829, Jean Guigand of Ros, in Crossac, had goods totalling 874 *francs*. His two oxen were worth 250 *francs*, and the two cows and a heifer, 65 *francs*. A bed, two chests, a table, an *armoire* and a *buffet* comprise all his furniture. The cart was worth 60 *francs*. A large number of inventories for Pontchâteau, 1829-1831 show that wealth was very much dependent on the number of livestock. When without land and stock, people could be very poor indeed, as was Pierre Danais of Le Rocher in Pontchâteau, worth only 70 *francs* in 1830. Apart from his clothes and those of his widow, there was one bed, two sheets, a chest, a *vaisellier*, a pot, a basin, a spade, a scythe, a fork, a cow and a calf. Although poor by the standards of the inventories, he must have been far from being among the poorest members of the community, whose wealth, or lack of it, was never documented.

Inventories at the other end of the social scale are too long to list, but they are characterized generally by duplication of the traditional items of furniture, more of the same thing, rather than by items unknown among the poorer classes. Luxury items appear. Whilst lighting in the poorer homes was provided by the light of a fire, or by a resin candle (never mentioned in the inventories) fixed to the breastsummer, or to the side of the hearth, *chandelliers*, in copper, are sometimes cited. The longcase clock also marks out the more prosperous farms in the nineteenth century. The earliest reference is at Saint-Renan in 1801, but they do not become frequent, and never common, until mid-century. Watches and other items of silver occasionally appear, and pewter is not uncommon, but usually limited in a given household to an individual plate. Among the exotic foods, evidence of the diffusion of coffee and tea appears in a few cases towards mid-century, and, as condiments, salt is common, pepper rare. Tools and industrial equipment form an important element. Farm tools are listed, sometimes showing just how few were really essential. Most inventories list the items connected with the spinning of hemp and flax. Spinning wheels are common, and there was often a considerable stock of fibre being processed, especially in Léon which had long specialized in the trade and had grown wealthy on it. Books are mentioned only twice.

In some inventories, the furniture is so described that plans of the interiors may be reconstructed with some confidence. Not every item is accurately located. Most frequently a *notaire* will describe a bed as being to the right or the left of the hearth, to the north or the south. Generally, the *armoires*, dressers and chests follow in order, one side at a time, with items at the bottom end being so described. There is rarely a mention of a door or a window and the position of these must be conjectural, but as the vast majority of the houses faced south, with doors and windows on that side, the plans shown in Fig. 239 can be claimed to have a high degree of accuracy.

The common factor in all is the proximity of the conjugal bed to the hearth. Where there are several beds, one nearly always lies on the other side of the hearth. The remainder are variously placed. Close to the table is a favourite position where a chest may serve both box-bed and table as a seat. Where a large number of beds and *armoires* are present, it is the common practice to range these along the wall. The other striking feature of all these interiors is the relatively small number of items. Utensils and farm implements are not shown on the plans, but the impression confirms the opinion, already given, that variation in wealth made little difference to the living patterns, at least until a fairly high wealth point was reached.

The drawings of the E.A.R. contain, *inter alia*, reference to the furniture, positions of which are accurately located on the plans and provide evidence of the survival of the traditional arrangements into the mid-twentieth century. Of the thirty-one houses recorded for Ille-et-Vilaine, furniture positions exist for eight. In every case there is a bed on each side of the hearth and the table is in the middle of the room. The remaining furniture is either along the back wall or at the bottom end. Of the thirty plans for Loire-Atlantique, furniture appears on thirteen. In ten of them there are beds on both sides of the hearth, either with small benches within the hearth itself or, when the beds are box-beds, with chests to serve as hearth seats. The tables are all in the centre of the room. In two plans, at Saillé and Queniquen, there is no table, whilst at La Haie-Fouassière in a house two rooms deep — no doubt a southern influence here — the interior is completely exotic. The evidence for both Ille-et-Vilaine and Loire-Atlantique confirms previous observations that the table in eastern Brittany is centrally placed. In Côtes-du-Nord the position of the beds in relation to the hearth is maintained, but of the twenty-one examples, every single one has the table against the lateral wall, by the window. In some it stands perpendicular to the wall, in others parallel to the wall. Only in one house, at Locenvel, is there no table. For Morbihan there are twenty-six plans, of which two have open hearths that will be referred to later. Three show no furniture, and ten have a table by the window. There is always at least one bed by the hearth. In three examples, two at Pluherlin and one at Saint-Gravé, both near Rochefort-en-Terre in eastern

Morbihan, the table stands in the middle of the room. In seven cases, there is a second room, a *'salle'* or *chambre*, and an adaptation of the hall. The latter appears to have lost some of its functions to the second room. This is particularly so in a house at Moustoir-Remungol where all the beds lie in the second room, only the table remaining in the first.

A cultural division between east and west Brittany is thus reflected in table position, the examples in eastern Morbihan, cited above, belonging to Haute-Bretagne. The precise boundary remains unknown, and must await further detailed fieldwork, but it seems likely that it will accord fairly closely with the linguistic divide (Fig. 27). Of the twenty-four records for Finistère, six have no interior details, three in Léon show the *cache-table,* containing not only the table, two of them circular with 'built-in' curved benching, but in each case with a box-bed as well. One dwelling, at Beuzec, is double-fronted, two rooms deep, dated 1911, and showing an arrangement relatively debased. The hall has become a kitchen with no bed, but two of the other rooms contain beds as well as other items, including tables. Only the *pièce*, obviously the main reception room, has no bed. There are, additionally, four bedrooms upstairs. Here is a case where specialization has advanced to the point where sleeping has been abandoned in both the kitchen and the best room, and where fully developed specialist bedrooms exist on the first floor, a rare but advanced example. Of the remaining plans, five show one-room dwellings with the beds by the hearth and the table by the window. In one there are no fewer than seven box-beds, four ranged down one side of the hall, one in the lower end beyond the cross-passage. Nine have a second cell, in each case imperfectly developed. If reserved for the reception of visitors, it serves other functions too. Most commonly, there is at least one bed. That at Pont-Croix has a false chimney. At Cléden there is a table, an *armoire* and chairs, and a door leading through to the *cuisine animaux*, which in turn connects with the byre. At Pouldreuzic, apart from two beds, a table and barrels of cider, nearly a quarter of the room is occupied by a heap of potatoes. At Combrit the *'salle'* contains a bed, chest, two *armoires* and a longcase clock. At Plomeur there are no beds in the hall, but two, together with table and chairs, in the *'belle pièce'*. At Lanvéoc beds and *armoires* occupy the second cell, whilst at Saint-Nic it has been divided up into two bedrooms. These records illustrate admirably the fact that although the concept of a second room is present in Finistère, probably more so than in the other four *départements*, specialization is imperfect. In a few cases only has it become purely a bedroom. Mostly it is used to receive visitors but the storage function is ever

present, and frequently the hearth is used for the preparation of animal feed. In a sense it is thus a spill-over from the hall when the need for more space is recognized. It provides a house with an additional architectural status symbol in the form of a symmetrical façade with two window openings, central doorway and two end chimney stacks, the classical Renaissance plan, but without showing interior specialization. This failure to develop specialist rooms by the mid-1940s is further clear proof of the long-standing tradition of the practice of living entirely in the common hall.[749]

The inventories provide further testimony of this incomplete specialization. At La Gaullairie, Pocé, in 1806, there was a bed in the second cell, along with a spinning wheel, an earthenware *charnier*, two oak chests, a barrel and a pair of scales, a room with both an industrial and a storage function.[750] At La Gaudais, Sougéal, in 1845, in addition to the hall, use was made of *'la maison de décharge'* in which were a small *armoire*, a bed, a wash bowl, a stone *charnier* with twenty-four kilogrammes of *lard* and a number of tools and utensils including those for the processing of flax and hemp.[751] La Maindonière and La Métairie de la Maindonière, in Saint-Hilaire-du-Bois, were both two-cell houses in 1818. In the former, the second cell contained two beds, a *charnier*, a saw, a pick, spades and wood and iron as well as four bushels of flax seed and numerous other agricultural and industrial implements. The second cell in the latter house contained a similar but larger collection of equipment, and a bed.[752] Gervaux, Clisson, in 1818, was a three-roomed house; in addition to the hall, the ground floor had *'une petite chambre'* containing a bed, three oak planks, two brass cauldrons, nineteen bushels of buckwheat seed, various tools and a pig![753] At Pont-château in 1803 there was an upper room with a bed, two chests and a small table, *'le tout mauvais'*.[754] At Herbignac in 1825, Jean Brebien had a house of six rooms. Neither the *salon* nor the *salle* contained beds, but there was one each in the *cuisine* and bakehouse, presumably for servants, for the late Jean Brebien had a *'chambre à coucher'* with a four-poster bed, a table, a desk and one hundred and thirty books, an umbrella and a large quantity of clothing. There were beds in two other rooms and one in the *grenier*.[755] In Côtes-du-Nord a house of four rooms, Lamonforière, Plénée-Jugon, had beds in all rooms in 1781. There were two in the hall, one in *'la salle'*, two in an upper room, and one in a second upper room. In the stable, in addition to the horse, was *'un vieux lit où couche le domestique'*.[756] There was also a bed in the stable at Pors an Licon, Plougonver, a single-cell house, in 1788. It has already been established that farm servants and children often slept in the second cell, or in the loft or in a subsidiary building when families were large. There is oral evidence for servants sleeping with the animals, but most of them would certainly have slept on straw. Here is clear proof of the provision of beds in the stables.

Finistère provides similar evidence for beds in secondary rooms and for incomplete specialization. At Keramouzel, Plougasnou, in 1800, the second ground-floor room contained two box-beds, several chests and *armoires* and a *charnier*. The *grange* contained two beds, numerous *armoires* and chests and a miscellany of equipment connected with the processing of flax.[757] At Trévenannou, also in Plougasnou, in 1801, there was a bed in the room above the hall, together with several *armoires*, chests and a bushel of peas, the remnants of a spinning wheel, a leather apron, hemp and flax *en baton*, and two iron tyres for a cart-wheel.[758] In the bakehouse at Kerahven, Châteaulin, in 1845, there was '*un lit clos avec accoutrements*', an '*armoire à lait*' and a granite trough as well as the normal equipment of a bakehouse.[759] At Kerenpellen, Moëlan, in 1845, the *chambre* contained nothing but potatoes.[760] At Longuenoi, Erbée, in 1810, the byre contained two cows, a heifer, two calves, several tools and '*une couchette banc garni d'une Ballière un traversin de Balle deux draps et une mauvaise couverture de Berne*'.[761] In Kerferverliat, Plésidy, in 1790, there was a bed '*dans l'aire*', from its context presumably in an outbuilding with the farm vehicles.[762] This practice of the servants sleeping in farm buildings and lofts has already been observed: '*C'est dans quelque coin de ce grenier, dans les celliers ou les étables, que sont les grabats où couchent les jeunes garçons et le plus ordinairement les domestiques, souvent ensemble!*'[763] Recent field evidence also confirms the continued existence of beds in the strangest of places, some obviously still slept in.

Evidence for multi-purpose use of the hall, the use of all other rooms for sleeping, sleeping with animals and the incomplete specialization in other rooms is thus firmly established. The lack of complete specialization indicates that the use of those extra rooms is still in a transitional evolutionary stage, and this in turn underlies, if that is needed, the fact that the people were really only used to living entirely in one room. The evidence of the E.A.R. shows that this continued to be the case up to the mid-twentieth century, and the current survey has shown the tradition still to persist, although the increased prosperity during the last twenty years has seen the gradual breakdown of the system. In newly built farmhouses the old people continue often to sleep in the kitchen.

Finally some consideration must be given to the changes to furniture positions following the migration of the hearth from the centre of the hall. There is no evidence for the furnishing of the peasant house in the Middle Ages. The interiors of the homes of woodland workers perhaps give some idea of what they might have been like. Three valuable documents, however, show the interiors of open halls at Plumelin that survived until 1945.[764] In a hall at Kerspec, the hearth lies in the centre of the room with a small wooden bench on each side. Two box-beds lie against the upper gable, and a third between them and the door, against the lateral wall and facing the fire. The remaining furniture consists of three chests, one of which stands against the presumed conjugal bed. The second house is an open long-house at Talforest, with the hearth somewhat off-centre, and on the byre side of the central truss. Beds are placed in the same relative positions as at Kerspec, and there are three *armoires* and two tables, one of which assumes the 'classic' position perpendicular to the window opening. There is also a clock. In the third example, also at Talforest, the hearth is at the gable end and the box-beds stand on either side of it, with table and benches by the window. One side of the hearth is served by a *banc*, and on the other the *coffre* to the *lit-clos* serves as a *banc*. A three-legged pot stands upon the raised hearth. The table has now assumed its traditional position in front of the window and at right angles to the lateral wall, with an *armoire* to screen the entry. The functional division of this long-house is formed by the furniture. Two cows are tethered to the wall at the lower end, and a calf stands in the space beyond a longcase clock.

This sequence provides an indication of what might have happened following migration of the hearth, and it may be that beds were commonly placed across the gable end of the hall with open hearth and that they 'parted' to make way for the hearth when it moved to the upper gable. It may be, equally, that many different arrangements existed. The date at which the 'modern' arrangement came into being is unknown, but its consistency throughout Brittany is almost tyrannical, the chief variation being the position of the table in Haute- and Basse-Bretagne. It is unlikely to predate the appearance of the chimney at the social level of the better-off peasant, but the evidence of the travellers, sixteenth to eighteenth century, shows that it was fairly established by that date. It seems probable, then, that it was widespread by the seventeenth century.

Concepts of hygiene, standards of cleanliness and the provision of washing and sanitary facilities are of fundamental importance to the full understanding of the house and its organization. Cambry took a poor view of what he saw: '*Imaginez . . . la mal-propreté, l'odeur, l'humidité, la boue . . . l'eau de fumier, qui souvent en défend l'entrée, qui, presque toujours, y pénètre: ajoutez-y . . . la mal-propreté d'individus qui ne se baignent, qui ne se lavent jamais . . . et vous aurez l'idée d'un paysan breton'.*[765] Stothard's views, quoted above, were not dissimilar. Bachelot de la Pylaie observed that in Finistère *'les pots de nuit sont comme inconnus. S'il survient un besoin nocturne quelconque, en quelque temps que ce soit, il faut se lever et aller à la cour, contre les fumiers ou le long des murailles, les hommes ainsi que les femmes. Alors, pour peu que l'ont eût chaud, se trouvant en transpiration, une pleurésie en devient la conséquence inévitable'.*[766] In mid nineteenth-century Finistère, chamber pots were largely unknown and lavatories non-existent. Field evidence shows that garderobes had existed at first-floor level in some houses of the manor-house class from medieval times. At the lower levels of society they remained largely non-existent until recently. The E.A.R. drawings show only one lavatory, in the whole of Brittany in the mid-1940s, an earth closet at Carnac, actually built on to the house. The reports of the investigators, which accompany some of these drawings, are most illuminating. For Côtes-du-Nord there is little comment, but in six cases the lack of a lavatory is specifically noted. At Saint-Gilles-Vieux-Marché it was reported that *'les besoins naturels se font en plein air ou dans l'étable quand il fait froid'.*[767] No lavatory is specifically reported for thirteen farms in Loire-Atlantique, and at La Haie-Fouassière there was *'pas d'installation spéciale. Le coin situé entre le mur de clôture et l'extrémité du petit hanger à bois semble réservé à cet usage'.*[768] Occasionally a free-standing wooden structure at the back of the house served as a lavatory, as at Le Palais in Morbihan, where there was *'une sorte de guérite en planches meublée d'une planche à trou — sous laquelle se trouve un trou, sert de lieu d'aisance'. 'Lieux d'aisance inexistants'* is twice specifically reported in Morbihan.[769] Few lavatories were reported in Finistère. At Plomeur it was *'les champs pour les hommes, les écuries pour les femmes',* and at Lanvéoc, Combrit, Pouldreuzic and Cléden there was *'rien organisé'.* Again at Saint-Nic there was *'rien organisé': l'écurie ou les champs'.* At Pont-Croix there was a *'vague caisse entre une petite cabane de planches dans le jardin. Mais c'est un net progrès sur bien des maisons du pays où il n'y a que les champs et l'étable'.* In another house at Pont-Croix there was *'un abri de perches et tôles derrière l'étable: un trou en terre'.* At Beuzec it was simply *pour les femmes l'étable, pour les hommes les champs'.* There is no report for Ille-et-Vilaine, and comments for Loire-Atlantique are entirely in the negative.[770] The 1939 survey provides confirmatory evidence. In Côtes-du-Nord, lavatories either did not exist, or were very rudimentary: *'elles consistent généralement en un petit appentis en bois placé sur une fosse creusée à même le sol: la fosse étant pleine on la recouvre et on change l'appentis de place'.* In Finistère *'il y a beaucoup de feuillées. Quand les latrines existent elles sont écartées de la maison, installées sommairement avec tinettes au fond du jardin ou sur la fumière'.* In Loire-Atlantique *'les latrines n'existent pas dans toutes les exploitations et là où elles existent, elles sont généralement séparées de la maison, situées assez loin dans une cour ou un jardin et très mal entretenues'.* In Morbihan there was occasionally some provision, but mostly just *'vagues feuillées dissimulées dans un enclos voisin de la maison'.*[771]

Dupuy, writing in Brittany in the eighteenth century, reports that in Landerneau, where the townspeople *'jettent bravement "leurs ordures et vilenies" par les fenêtres, ou bien vont les déposer "le long des murailles du cimetière de Saint-Houardon et du jardin de M. le recteur . . . ce qui cause une infection très grande" ',* latrines were completely unknown. Sanitation in the countryside was even worse than in the towns.[772] In eighteenth-century Porzay the *'table de nuit'* was unknown and chamber pots figure only rarely in the inventories.[773] The recent investigation of inventories has produced only one reference to a chamber pot and a *'table de nuit',* at the home of a wealthy merchant of Ouessant.[774] Fieldwork also failed to produce any evidence except for the medieval garderobe, the free-standing earth closet and arrangements of very recent date. In the mid-1970s, probably the majority of the traditional Breton farmhouses were without lavatories.

Concepts of cleanliness were almost non-existent until the twentieth century, and then slow to spread. Roger, admittedly a prejudiced observer, noted after World War I that the inhabitants of Finistère cared little for *'leur toilette',* sleeping together in one room, assisting the spread of disease.[775] In the congested living conditions, under-fed, poorly clad poor were a constant problem. Disease and epidemics spread rapidly, and the custom of *'la veillée des morts'* did not help.[776] The guarding of the body, *'pour tenir compagnie pendant toute une nuit, dans les logements très petits et dépourvus d'air, à un cadavre gangrené et déjà prodigieusement enflé'*[777] was a health hazard, but the practice of receiving visitors for the purpose of embracing the body, continuing into the 1920s in Finistère, made things worse.[778]

Many factors contributed towards ill-health, including infected wells placed too close to dung-hills, and the cohabitation of long-houses with little or no separation between man and beast. Overcrowding, dirt, squalor and disease are all referred to by the Comités d'Hygiène.[779] At

Saint-André-des-Eaux, in 1777, there were families so poor that some had to remain at home naked, covered with straw, in order that others in the family might go to church fully clothed. Their homes were of one room only, '*véritable taudis humide, boueux, sans air, où toute la famille grouille et croupit dans la malpropreté et dans la fange. Dès que survient la dyssenterie, ce qui arrive presque tous les ans, "les enfants, continuellement pressés de dévoiements, infectent la maison des excréments liquides et muqueux qui en sont le produit"*'. Lack of clothing and linen was regarded as a principal cause of disease, often only old clothes were available, and children were '*couchés sans chemise, sans linceul, sans couette et sans paillasse; point d'autre couverture qu'un tas de vermine qui les dévore et menace ceux qui veulent les approcher*'. On the death of a member of a household, his bed was immediately taken over by another without any attempt to wash or clean it. Utensils were not washed, the peasants '*ont la mauvaise habitude de se servir, pour boire et manger, des mêmes vaisseaux, qui sont ordinairement en bois, sans les avoir lavés, et même de boire et de manger les restes des aliments que les malades ont souvant maniés pendant longtemps . . .*'.[780] Clothes were washed only infrequently, which helps to explain why even very poor people often had large numbers of shirts, inventories often listing two or three dozen per person. In the *pays bigouden*, even as late as the 1920s, washing was done only twice a year, in spring and autumn, and dirty clothes lay in a heap for up to six months.[781] The washing of the body was not a regular practice, even well into the twentieth century. There is not a scrap of evidence in the inventories, or in the E.A.R. records, or from field observation, for a wash-place within the house. The portable wash-stand came to be used in the nineteenth century, as in Côtes-du-Nord, where people — a minority — washed in a bowl at the '*table de toilette*'. Elsewhere, in probably the vast majority of cases, they washed at the well, and in a bucket, only once a week. For privacy, recourse had to be made to the byre, stable, or an outbuilding.[782]

A remarkable uniformity and conservatism characterize the interior of the Breton house. The principles of construction of the hearth are *everywhere* the same. Materials, stone or wood, change with availability, and with the wealth of the builder, but the principles of construction are consistent: wood or stone corbels carrying a breastsummer of wood or stone and the whole supporting the chimney flue. The number and positioning of the keeping-places vary a little, and the gable is usually off-set by 0.20 to 0.30 metres to receive the hearth-stone, itself nearly always raised above the floor-level about 0.10 to 0.40 metres. This gable hearth is

virtually universal, only a few lateral hearths having been encountered during fieldwork. The open hall and centrally placed hearth appears first to have gone out of fashion at the social level of the middling peasant not later than the sixteenth century, but its disappearance was gradual and the last surviving open halls were to be found in Morbihan in the 1940s. Ancient traditions govern the conduct of the hearth. The continuously burning fire was a symbol of the continuity of life in the house; it provided warmth, and heat for cooking. Foods were relatively simple and confined to a few basic dishes, diet being almost entirely cereal-based for the greater part of the population, which ate meat only once or twice a week. Interiors displayed marked individuality, distinguishing them from those of Normandy and Anjou. Evidence of travellers and others shows a remarkable uniformity throughout Brittany during the eighteenth, nineteenth and twentieth centuries. The position of the table marks out eastern Brittany from the west, and Léon, Cornouaille and Ouessant provide regional variations. Regional furniture styles also occur, many of them only subtly different from each other, but with those of Ouessant and Guérande strikingly so.

The accounts of travellers, evidence of prints and drawings, popular and scientific descriptions all agree that the vast majority of the Breton peasantry, at least until World War I, lived entirely in single-cell dwellings. This is confirmed by the evidence of inventories which confirm relatively few material possessions and show that, even where other rooms were available, there was little specialization in room use. Although field-evidence shows that multi-cell houses existed from medieval times onwards, they were confined to a small fraction of the population. It is probable that the practice of using a second cell, by the better-off peasantry, developed only in the late-eighteenth and nineteenth centuries, and the failure to develop this cell as a specialized room, even by the mid-twentieth century, is a clear indication of the tenacity of the tradition of living entirely in one room. The inventories also show an improvement in material wealth during the first part of the nineteenth century, as well as regional variations.

Several writers, notably Gautier and Le Lannou, characterize the 'typical' traditional house as a two-cell dwelling.[783] Not only do they largely ignore the dwellings of the poor, who formed the greater part of the population, but also the overwhelming body of evidence which shows, beyond question, the strength of the practice of living in one room. Nevertheless, a degree of specialization, no more, had become apparent by the mid-twentieth century. Inventories also show that stock and agricultural implements often formed a higher proportion of the total wealth than the household goods, and that the better-off farmers lived in much the same way as the poorer ones. As Bachelot de la Pylaie has pointed out, their greater wealth was expressed in the quality of food on their tables, and the size of their manure heaps, rather than in any sharp difference in the organization of their houses, although they might have been expected to own rather better furniture than the poor, and to sleep more comfortably. They thus had no need of a larger house with more rooms. The quality of life of the very poor, of whom there seem to have been large numbers in the nineteenth century, almost defies

description, and there is no reason to believe that the picture outlined is other than accurate. Hunger, dirt, squalor, cold and disease were their lot. The absence of washing and lavatory facilities, however, extends high up the social scale. In not a single house is there evidence of lavatory or a wash-place, save for an occasional garderobe. It is in the light of these facts that the lesser rural domestic buildings must be examined. The vast majority of them were single-cell dwellings, with life confined to the common hall, and any interpretation of the field evidence must take this into account.

SIXTEEN

THE VERNACULAR ARCHITECTURE OF BRITTANY: CONCLUSIONS

This study of the traditional rural domestic buildings of Brittany has depended on an approach which goes some way towards attempting a total history of the house, and the principal characteristics of materials, construction, plan and function, with their respective evolution, have been outlined. During the last fifteen hundred years, the Breton landscape has witnessed colonization by peoples from south-western Britain whose descendants, along with those of the pre-existing population, continued the slow process of settling and cultivating the land. Houses were constructed, farms and hamlets created, woodland cleared, the soil tilled, fields demarcated, banks and walls built, and patterns of roads and tracks established. In earlier centuries the common openfield and the small enclosed parcels, held in severalty, co-existed. With the gradual enclosure of openfield, *bocage* became dominant and was to reach its fullest development in the late-nineteenth century, when population density was greatest and most of the *landes* had been enclosed.

Evidence for the choice of building materials before the late medieval period is meagre. Stone walling laid either as dry-stone or with a clay mortar was certainly used, and in Finistère there may have been a continuous tradition of building in stone from the prehistoric period to the present, but the most striking example is the use of orthostat walling. Elsewhere, evidence for this continuity of building in stone is not yet forthcoming. The building of walls with stone was common for public buildings in medieval times and for the houses and castles of the leaders of society. It seems probable, however, that a tradition of timber-frame building existed in the countryside, for relics are widely distributed, with a concentration in the eastern areas, and most towns retain timber-frame buildings. Yet there must remain some doubt as to whether the rather primitive timber framing of the nineteenth and twentieth centuries is any more than a function of extreme poverty. There is a growing evidence for the survival of large numbers of primitive houses in the nineteenth and early-twentieth centuries. The

Comités d'Hygiène report the existence, during the 1850s, of hovels built of turf, or a mixture of turf and stones, although whether these buildings represent the end of a tradition universal in the Middle Ages is uncertain. The probability is that they do, and that the technique of building in turf is an ancient one, descended by the mid-nineteenth century to the social level of the poorest classes. Whilst most peasant buildings during modern times have had walls of stone rubble, the use of dressed stone is also known from the Middle Ages onwards. In areas where it is locally available, ashlar is used not only for door and window dressings, but also for walling, especially of front elevations, but in those regions where only rubble is locally available, ashlar was imported chiefly for doorway and window dressings. Most peasant houses in schist areas made do with lintels of wood with ashlar used sparingly, if at all. Walling in cob, or *torchis*, was probably once widespread, particularly in the east where its incidence, although now concentrated in the Rennes basin, still has a remarkably wide distribution. Roof covering was once almost entirely of thatch everywhere north of the Loire, rye thatch being preferred except in low-lying areas where reed was used, but for the poorer dwellings broom was common, and remained widely in use for farm buildings until the mid-twentieth century. Some oak-shingle roofing is known along the Marches, and south of the Loire the 'Roman' tile roof is ubiquitous. Red tiles of French manufacture are occasionally found and Bridgwater tiles were imported into the northern coastlands in the nineteenth century. Slate began to replace thatch in the coastal areas from the late-eighteenth century onwards. It may long have been used where locally available, but with the coming of the railways and the import of cheaper, lighter slates from Anjou, it rapidly gained ground, almost entirely replacing thatch in many areas. By the 1970s thatched buildings, in any number, were confined to the southern littoral with only local occurrence elsewhere. Floor covering was almost everywhere of earth, or *terre battue*, until the mid-twentieth century and stone paving was only rarely found. These materials and their use are not unique to Brittany, for they occur also in the British Isles and other parts of western Europe.

A variety of construction techniques is found. Tunnel- and slab-vaulted roofs are known in a few specialist buildings, corbelling is encountered in a small number of circular buildings including two pigsties, and the ordinary stone vault is universally used in the construction of bake-ovens. Timber roof structure varies considerably. Two examples of the aisled-hall truss exist in Saint-M'Hervé, and a few aisled market halls survive, though they were once more common in the towns. As aisled houses are known in south-west France and the Alps and aisled barns and market halls are common over much of France, it seems probable, in the absence of further evidence, that the form was introduced into Brittany from the east in early modern times. Other roof-types include rafter roofs, which may be a late feature, king-post and upper king-post trusses. The distribution of the full cruck is meagre, but sufficient to be able to say that it was probably once widely known. With the introduction of chimney stacks and insertion of loft floors, the cruck truss seems to have given way to the upper cruck. The collar and tie-beam truss, believed to be related to the cruck, is widespread in the west.

Distribution maps show that roofs without either king-posts or upper king-posts predominate west of the language divide and that roofs incorporating the king-post predominate in Haute-Bretagne. Whilst king-posts occur in the east at all levels of society, in the west they are confined to the *manoirs* and other high-quality houses. The king-post and the more common upper king-post appear to have been introduced from metropolitan France at an unknown date and to have become established in the east by modern times. Only at the upper levels of rural society were they absorbed into Basse-Bretagne, where the conservative peasantry continued to use collar and tie-beam roofs either with upper crucks or with straight principal rafters.

At what date the open hearth began to be replaced by the hearth with chimney, at the upper levels of rural society, is not known. Certainly by the sixteenth century, hearths with chimney stacks incorporated in the gable wall were being constructed at the middling level of society. Archaeological evidence shows that the centrally placed open hearth was probably universal in peasant houses of the Middle Ages, and a few examples of the hall with open hearth survived until the 1940s. Other examples demonstrate an intermediate evolutionary stage with the hearth against, but not built into, the gable wall, and with a wattle-and-clay chimney hood. Open-hearth houses are associated with fully-hipped roofs, but the migration of the hearth to one end gradually led to the construction of full gables which are now almost universal. Only in the areas of orthostat walling have hipped roofs survived for special reasons, with the hip confined to the lower end of the building. The gable-end chimney-stack is general. Rarely is a stack axially placed in a peasant house, although some *manoirs* are provided with heated upper rooms requiring axial stacks. Except for bake-ovens in outshots, the lateral stack is a rare feature. The chimney-stack, which probably appeared in the sixteenth century in peasant houses, came gradually to oust the open hearth, but the new fashion must have been slow to make progress in many areas and large numbers of poor people continued to live in primitive houses with open hearths throughout the nineteenth century. The transition seems to have lasted for a period of at least four to five hundred years. Chimney stacks are now almost always of stone or brick, but a few wattle-and-clay structures survive.

Doorway and window dressings may be wholly of ashlar, or of a mixture of ashlar and rubble, sometimes with a wood lintel. Schist rubble jambs and wood lintels are common in many areas. Gothic, round-headed, three-centred, ogee, cambered, square-headed, and shouldered doorheads are known. The round-headed type, popularly but wrongly regarded as typical, is a Renaissance feature introduced from France in the sixteenth century, gradually replacing the Gothic arch, but the square-headed doorway is the most 'typical'. Tentative date-sequences have been established. Windows were unglazed until the nineteenth century and openings were traditionally fitted with wood frames having shutters opening inwards. Superior construction is shown by transomed, or mullioned and transomed, windows, with two or four shutters.

Evidence from sample quadrats shows not only a great variety of building material, but regional variations in detail: breadth of chimney-stacks, raised gables, type of ridge finish, size of window openings, variations in roof pitch and the use of a cove. There is considerable regional variation in walling and roofing material, in architectural detail, in colour, texture and form.

Circular buildings survive in large numbers: well-covers, bake-ovens, dove-cots, windmills, pigsties and a number of specialist buildings. Both in form and construction, they parallel similar examples from Wales, Ireland and other parts of western and Mediterranean Europe. There is firm evidence of circular construction in the prehistoric and Early Christian periods and the survivors are the last in a long tradition.

Sub-rectilinear buildings provide the link between the

typologically earlier circular forms and the later rectilinear ones, for there is evidence both of the rounded corners of permanent stone buildings in a few regions, and of the oval forms of *lokennou*. The date at which the simple oval and circular houses, known from the Middle Ages, that could have lasted only a generation or so, were replaced by permanent houses of the traditional styles now common, is unknown. Probably it was not the same everywhere. Primitive sub-rectilinear buildings of twentieth-century date provide evidence of the 'open' long-house in its simplest form. Often with walls of low banks of earth or stone, these structures suggest ways in which excavated medieval oval plans may have been roofed. They parallel dwellings excavated in western Britain, some of which illustrate a three-cell form, but there is as yet no evidence of a second living room, beyond the hall, in medieval Breton peasant houses.

The single-cell dwelling with a hall on the ground floor and storage loft above, and of one, one-and-a-half, or two storeys, appears to be the standard form of dwelling throughout Brittany for the landless rural classes, or those without livestock. These are chiefly the homes of poor people and include the *penty* of the *journalier*. Other groups of higher social status such as the clergy, not directly engaged in agriculture, might have occupied a one-cell dwelling. Some buildings are of high quality and examples are known with bed-outshots, lateral chimney-stacks and gable-entry, features known in the British Isles but as yet only in small numbers in Brittany. The existence of the bed-outshot, in what may yet prove to be considerable numbers, greatly extends its known distribution, but, in contrast, the table-outshot is almost unknown in the British Isles, and its distribution in Brittany is confined to Léon. The presence of such large numbers of one-cell houses in Brittany may be an indication that they were once common over much of western Europe and that their relative scarcity in England and Wales may be the result of their having given way to more elaborate forms.

The earliest known long-houses are those of Pen-er-Malo and Kerlano. In this elementary form, the type survived well into the twentieth century, with no partition to separate the hall at the upper end from the byre at the lower end. Entry was by a common lateral doorway and an evolutionary sequence is discernible in which a low half-partition is first placed to delimit the byre end. Cattle could be tethered to this and conveniently fed from troughs placed in the cross-passage which took on the characteristics of a feeding walk. Later, and probably not before the nineteenth century, full partitions came to be built on the 'hall' side of the cross-passage, rather than the 'byre' side. Only rarely is a stone partition

encountered and the hearth and chimney are always at the upper end of the hall. The chimney-stack never backs on to the cross-passage as in Wales. Subsequently there developed in Haute-Bretagne a long-house sub-type with separate entry to the byre but maintaining internal communication. The last stage of development is represented by a further sub-type in which internal communication no longer exists. The Breton long-house is remarkable for having maintained the 'elementary' form until the twentieth century, although in this it is not unique, for similar examples are known from the Cantal and there are Irish parallels. Indeed, the long-house, and its derivatives, is known across the whole of northern France, in the Massif Central, and in the south-west as far as the Pyrenees. Nevertheless, in Brittany, a second cell, or parlour, at the upper end of the hall, known in England during the medieval period, failed to develop and the Breton long-house represents a survival in the twentieth century, in numbers unparalleled elsewhere, of the primitive man-beast relationship.

The first-floor hall is widely distributed, both as an independent unit as well as a constituent element in a row of buildings. It is associated with the upper levels of rural society, and the quality of construction usually indicates a degree of economic prosperity and importance with such dwellings intended for the minor nobility, gentry and clergy. Some of the earliest known medieval houses appear to be of the first-floor hall type and may provide a link with the first-floor halls of medieval castles.

The two-cell house is a relatively recent development, and some may result from the conversion of the byre of a long-house. There is evidence that the function of the lower end of long-houses may have changed frequently from byre to *chambre* as needs demanded. From the later eighteenth century, two-cell houses developed in coastal areas and spread inland to become known in the interior a hundred years later. Only after World War I was the type to become widespread. This two-cell peasant house is not to be confused with the two-cell Renaissance *manoir* known from the end of the sixteenth century onwards.

Multi-cell houses are more complex, and it is probable that types and sub-types remain to be discovered. Archaeological evidence in existing buildings suggests that some *manoirs* may have developed from a single hall, although examples of a type of three-unit plan are known with hall, cross-passage and service rooms and a third cell, beyond the hall, seeming to have been used as a stable or byre rather than as a parlour as in English three-unit houses. The cross-passage is known only in embryo form and seems never to have been bounded, in its original state, on both sides by wood or stone partitions. The Renaissance house, even when near-symmetrical on the ground floor, had a cross-passage open to the hall on one side. Complex multi-cell forms survive and evidence in probate inventories points to others. A lack of specialization is apparent, for whilst the hall continued as the common living room, other rooms served multiple purposes. It was common for beds to be found in all rooms, but only in the gentry houses of the eighteenth century have rooms been identified as true bedrooms, and they probably also had a 'withdrawing' function as well. Many multi-cell houses came to be occupied by peasant families — perhaps some always were — who lived entirely in the hall, using the other rooms for a multitude of storage purposes.

Field and documentary evidence illustrates a wide range of farm buildings, some in line with the house, others forming partially, or wholly, enclosed courtyards of varying degrees of regularity. The minute courtyards of the western peninsulas contrast sharply with those *manoirs* that have a full range of specialist buildings including a dove-cot. It is evident that, in general, courtyards are the result of evolution over a period of time rather than of one period of build. Farm buildings first developed at the upper levels of rural society, and large numbers of farms before World War I consisted only of a long-house and a few *lokennou*. Only the larger and better-built farms in the nineteenth century had specialist outbuildings.

Hearth is synonymous with 'house', and the number of families in a hamlet was the same as the number of *feux*. Many superstitious practices surrounded it. Fuel was of local provenance: wood, gorse, heath, peat or even turf and cow-dung. Before the twentieth century, diet was largely cereal-based and almost wholly so for the poorest people. Prosperous farmers ate meat two or three times a week, others only once a week and the poorest people only on a few occasions in a year if they were fortunate. Cider was the common drink except in Léon where milk and water were drunk during the week and wine on Sundays. Although food gradually improved in quality and quantity from the mid-nineteenth century onwards, yet it remained relatively simple and was prepared on the open fire with a range of utensils shown by the probate inventories to be relatively restricted. A man's wealth lay in the number and quality of his implements and livestock rather than in the material possessions of the household. The size of his dung-heap was a better index to prosperity than the number, range and variety of his furniture and utensils. The lesser gentry lived much as their tenants did, except that meat appeared more frequently on their tables, and their possessions, though not necessarily greater in number, may have been better in quality.

Simplicity of living and its confinement to the common hall goes far to assist an understanding of the architectural and archaeological evidence of the house. Layout of interiors is the subject of regional variation. Furniture styles show local variations and the distinctive coloured furniture of the *pays de Guérande* and the Île d'Ouessant stands apart. The positioning of the conjugal bed on the side of the hearth opposite the window is invariable, but the position of the table, whether it is centrally located in the midst of the hall, or placed perpendicularly to the wall next to the window, sharply divides Haute-Bretagne from Basse-Bretagne. Hygiene was rudimentary before the end of World War II, and lavatories were virtually unknown, although *garderobes* existed in some medieval and Renaissance houses. Given these regional variations, the interior of the Breton house is characterized by a remarkable uniformity.

There are proportionately few surviving medieval buildings, and it seems likely that the 'permanent' building styles now regarded as traditional came to take the place of earlier temporary structures only after the unsettled medieval period was over. The overwhelming proportion of surviving 'traditional' building is post-medieval in date. It is probable that replacement of the medieval dwellings of the greater part of the population varied in both time and place, and this may help to explain why the earliest surviving buildings in one area may be of sixteenth-century date, whilst in others they are of seventeenth- or eighteenth-century date. Late colonization of the *landes* was a further factor: such settlements may have no buildings of earlier date than the eighteenth or nineteenth century.

Although buildings were replaced at all periods, evidence suggests periods of greater building activity, some of which may be those in which the flimsy structures of the Middle Ages first came to be replaced by 'permanent' houses. In Finistère, this seems to have occurred in the late-eighteenth and nineteenth centuries, but elsewhere it was earlier. Much rural building dates from the late-sixteenth and seventeenth centuries following union with France, for although trade had played an important part in medieval Brittany, the peaceful conditions that followed the Union in 1532 led to increased mercantile activity both by land and by sea. Trade and commerce prospered and the profits were used to rebuild both publicly and privately. The sixteenth and seventeenth centuries were also great periods for the building of churches, *châteaux* and *manoirs*. A peasant art flourished on a scale unknown either before or since, adapting the new Renaissance ideas of decoration to local materials, so that dressed stone and sculpture appeared, often on a luxurious scale. It is to the sixteenth and seventeenth centuries that most of the earliest surviving *manoirs* belong, as do the great ecclesiastical achievements of Léon and Cornouaille with their *enclos paroissiaux*. The biggest single item in the creation of this wealth was the trade in linen and hemp. Most farms grew flax, and as the probate inventories show, many had spinning wheels and tools for the processing of the fibre. Linen for clothing and ships' sails was widely produced. Whilst some was undoubtedly intended for domestic use, much was sold. Certain areas, notably Léon, owe their relative prosperity to the trade, and it undoubtedly furnished the necessary surplus wealth for the reconstruction of houses both in town and country. The agricultural revolution of the nineteenth century led to the introduction of the two-cell house in the interior, but there is no trace of the further development of house-types familiar to British scholars. Brittany appears poor and conservative even in comparison with Ireland. Whilst the tendency to conserve may be an inherent characteristic of the people, other factors must also be sought. The nineteenth-century improvements in agriculture were not accompanied, as elsewhere, by a massive rural depopulation. As population increased, pressure became intense, much marginal land was enclosed and many squatter settlements were built. Tenancy may also have been a factor. Vallaux was of the opinion that the *domaine congéable* was a principal factor in the failure to improve housing and farm buildings,[784] as it gave no incentive to the tenant to improve the land as it was not his, and as he could be dismissed at will. Likewise the landowner was discouraged from improvement as it would increase his liability for compensation should he choose to evict a tenant. Both owner and occuper were thus discouraged from initiative. If a wall fell, it had to be rebuilt exactly as it was. If an entire house collapsed, it had to be replaced identically. Thus it may not be accidental that the areas where old buildings and traditions have been well preserved are sometimes those in which the *domaine congéable* was strongest, notably in the *pays vannetais*.

An outstanding characteristic of Breton farms is the tendency for them to be grouped in *rangées* of two to a dozen or more houses. These may be found over the whole country, but are strikingly conspicuous in north Morbihan and in parts of Ille-et-Vilaine where they reach their greatest development, and they appear to be related to former openfield. No example has yet been observed wholly contemporary in date for, in every case, vertical joints suggest that the *rangées* have grown with the passage of time. Whilst the earliest surviving building on a site is almost certainly several centuries later than the first dwelling erected in connection with the working of the

adjacent fields, the multi-cell row may betray a gradual and successive re-building of earlier structures. Alternatively, it may witness an initial settlement of a single farm, perhaps on an enclosed *lande*, or a hamlet of two or three farms. As population grew, aided by the practice of partible inheritance, the openfield was subdivided to provide land for heirs, and extra dwellings were built to accommodate their families. Several *rangées* illustrate a range of buildings dating from the seventeenth to the twentieth century, consistent with what is known of population increase. In a recent contribution to the subject, some useful information relating to the family occupation of the *rangée* in Morbihan has been outlined.[785] However, the *rangée* appears to be significantly related to associated former openfield, and most *rangées* are not wholly contemporary, but display organic growth often over several centuries. Two more recent studies outline the type of *rangée* of the Presqu'île de Rhuys and the traditional buildings of Belle-île respectively.[786] Whilst emphasizing the art-historical aspects of this subject, these add most usefully to our knowledge of the *rangée*.

It is unclear whether the practice of converting houses into byres is a recent phenomenon, or whether it has long been practised. If, as farms prospered and new houses were built, the old house was turned over to livestock, then many of the *rangées* of ten or twelve houses may never have accommodated that number of families. Alternatively, there may have been periods when houses, having been used as byres, were reconverted to dwellings as population increase demanded. The occurrence of a farmyard shared by more than one farm is a feature known in the British Isles and associated with a kin-group, working the land in common. Oral evidence suggests that this may once have been so in Brittany: there is no other convincing explanation for this grouping of farms. The hypothesis is made more convincing by the survival, in some cases, of internal communication throughout the *rangées*.

There are distinctive regional variations in the vernacular architecture of the Province, but too facile a correlation with other cultural distributions is probably best avoided, given the present stage of knowledge. The survival of the Gallic tongue, the extent to which the Armorican population survived the Breton settlement, and the relative proportions of the two populations are the subject of renewed controversy.[787] Immigration routes and the areas first colonized are also unknown. The most striking spatial aspect of the vernacular architecture is the dichotomy between the distribution of features whose existence is known over the whole province, and those which show some localization. Basic house-plans are to be found everywhere, indicating a response to economic and other factors and suggesting some antiquity. The long-house probably appeared not later than the Gallo-Roman period, and the single-cell house is as old as the concept of the house itself, for a family could hardly have lived in less than one room, although in earliest times that was as likely to have been circular or oval as rectilinear. Later regional variations are the localized distributions of the bed- and table-outshots of the north-west and pigsty-outshot of the Grande Brière and *pays de Guérande*. The first-floor hall is also widespread and there is no reason to believe that the multi-cell plans are in any way related to minor cultural divisions, except for two types noted in western Finistère. Basic plan-forms are thus universal. A notable exception is the category of circular farm buildings now almost exclusively confined to Bretagne *bretonnante*. Distribution maps of carpentry forms indicate some regional tendencies, the most striking variations associated with the ethnic divide. This is not to explain the distributions in ethnic terms. The forms now concentrated in the west, or Breton-speaking areas, were once probably common over the whole of the Province. East of the language divide they have been largely displaced by newer forms, derived from metropolitan France, which have as yet made progress in the west only at the higher levels of society. Certain distributions display a link with areas known to be culturally conservative, like the Grande Brière. Cultural differences between Haute-Bretagne and Basse-Bretagne are evident in prehistory, as distribution maps of the *allées couvertes* and certain Bronze Age distributions show.[788] It may be that the carpentry distributions reflect cultural divisions whose origins lie deep in prehistory. It is, however, too soon to develop an argument along these lines, for more data on carpentry forms is required. Greater knowledge of the Breton settlement, languages and dialects is needed for the Early Christian period. For the moment, it is sufficient to note the simple correlation with the ethnic divide. This basic cultural division is reflected in the interior arrangement of the houses, notably table position, and in roof form. The 'old' hipped roof of thatch survives only in the west, whereas the 'new' Renaissance hipped roof is most strongly represented in the east, occurring in the west only at the highest levels of society.

Building material, detail and finish show much stronger regional variations. The southern littoral stands out, as does the Rennes Basin, Cornouaille, Léon, and Trégorrois, whilst the western peninsulas form different and highly distinctive micro-regions. Traditional historic regions like the Goëllo, Penthièvre, Rohan and the

Vendelais are reflected in the superficial features of the houses.

The vernacular architecture of Brittany is characterized by the general uniformity of certain *traits* and by strong regional variation of others. Uniformity, notably of house-plan, appears largely to be a response to economic stimuli at the lower levels of society, being influenced in recent centuries by new fashions at higher social levels. Regional variations may reflect cultural divisions whose origins lie deep in prehistory and which have found expression in different ways throughout historical time. Strong kinship ties are reflected in the Breton house to a degree long since forgotten in many parts of western Europe. This is most noticeable in the development of the *rangée*, but may also explain the former occupation of certain multi-cell dwellings. The overall impression is of a province whose vernacular architecture is at the same time both extremely conservative and yet extraordinarily virile in the execution of detail and the working of stone. Primitive conditions survived until the mid-twentieth century, notably along the southern littoral. The extreme west, from the late-eighteenth century onwards, illustrates sharp contrasts between conservatism and innovation, whilst the survival until recently of *loges*, the open hearth and the widespread practice of living in one room is remarkable. Some families in the *pays de Baud* and on the Île d'Ouessant lived in the most primitive conditions. Whilst this may be explained in part by the nineteenth-century increase in population and the extreme poverty which resulted, it can hardly be doubted that the life-styles reflect a retarded stage of cultural development. In certain respects and in limited areas, Breton domestic buildings represent a form of life that can fairly be described as protohistoric, not achieving the cultural development to be expected of the medieval period. Most of the population, in so far as they lived entirely in one room, preserved a medieval pattern of living, that of the common hall, well into the twentieth century, differing from the true medieval hall only in that the hearth had migrated to a gable wall, by the provision of a chimney to evacuate smoke, and by the presence of a greater quantity of furniture and utensils.

Breton vernacular architecture is thus characterized by conservatism, the persistence of the common hall, failure to develop specialist rooms and by the close juxtaposition of humans and livestock. There are close parallels with other parts of Atlantic Europe, notably western Ireland and western Scotland. In comparison with most of Atlantic Europe, Brittany seems poor, often terribly poor, and extremely conservative, with an almost total failure to develop specialist rooms. In its use of materials, notably dressed stone, the simplicity of economic conditions and household organization is countered by richness of colour, texture, form and detail which display a skill and confidence whose vitality and sometimes exuberance are on a scale, and to an extent, scarcely matched in western Europe.

SEVENTEEN

REFERENCES

E.A.R.   Enquête d'Architecture Rurale, Chantier 1425, Musée des Arts et Traditions populaires, Paris
A.D.C.N.   Archives départementales des Côtes-du-Nord
A.D.F.   Archives départementales du Finistère
A.D.I.V.   Archives départementales d'Ille-et-Vilaine
A.D.L.A.   Archives départementales de la Loire-Atlantique
A.D.M.   Archives départementales du Morbihan

Preface
1. Meirion-Jones, 1977b.
2. Charpy, 1973.

Chapter 1. Introduction
3. Mercer, 1975, 1.
4. Brunskill, 1975, 107.
5. Campbell, 1937; 1938.
6. Erixon, 1937; 1938.
7. Peate, 1946; 1956; 1957; 1957-58; 1963; 1964.
8. Evans, 1939; 1940; 1942; 1951; 1957.
9. Addy, 1898; 1933.
10. Innocent, 1916.
11. Peate, 1946.
12. Fox and Raglan, 1951; 1953; 1954.
13. Brunskill, 1952; 1963; Marsden, 1958; Wood-Jones, 1963.
14. Mercer, 1975.
15. Smith P., 1975.
16. Brunskill, 1952; 1963; Marsden, 1958; Wood-Jones, 1963.
17. Fox and Raglan, op. cit.
18. Barley, 1961.
19. Hoskins, 1953.
20. Brunskill, 1965-66.
21. A.D.L.A.
22. Meirion-Jones, 1977a; 1980c. See also Lassure and Lassure (eds.), 1976; 1977; 1978; 1979; 1980.
23. Meirion-Jones, 1978a.
24. Vallaux, 1904; 1905a; 1905b.
25. Fournier, 1934.
26. Gautier, M., 1947a.
27. Guilcher, 1948; 1949; 1950.
28. Le Lannou, 1950.
29. Bernard, 1950a; 1951; 1952.
30. Colin, 1943; 1947a.
31. Keravel, 1954.
32. Buffet, 1947; 1954; 1960; 1969.
33. Choleau, 1905; 1907; De Cambry, 1799; Elegoet, 1978; Géniaux, 1902; Hélias, 1970; 1975; Lalaisse and Ropartz, 1866; Le Guennec, 1936 (reprinted 1975); 1937 (reprinted 1976); 1968; 1979; Le Maître, 1976; Le Scouëzec, 1979; Maguereze, 1840 (reprinted 1972); Picard, 1904; Puig de Ritalongi, 1894; Vaillat, 1913; De Vieillechèze, 1902.
34. Giese, 1931.
35. Aubry, Dupuis and Fenard, 1971; J.-C. Bans, 1979; P.G. Bans, 1975; 1976; 1978; 1979a; 1979b; J.-C. and P.G. Bans, 1979a; 1979b; Bouchy and Dufour, 1971; Cogné and Cogné, 1971; Gohel, 1976; Hamon, 1976; 1977-78; Laloy and Vivier, 1976; Le Floc'h, 1965; Meirion-Jones, 1973a; 1973b; 1973c; 1976a; 1976b; 1977a; 1977b; 1978a; 1978b; 1978c; 1978-79; 1979a; 1979b; 1979c; 1979d; 1980a; 1980b; 1980c; 1980d; 1981a; 1981b; Meuret, 1979; Miroudel, 1967; Mussat, 1971; 1976; 1979a; 1979b; Ministère des Affaires Culturelles, n.d.; 1969; 1972; 1973; 1974; Secrétariat d'État à la Culture, 1975; Agence d'urbanisme de la communauté urbaine de Brest et de son environnement, 1977a; 1977b; 1978a; 1978b; 1979; Ministère de la Culture et de la Communication, 1978; 1979; Ministère de la Culture et de l'Environnement, 1977; 1978.
36. André, 1974; 1978-79; 1979; Bertrand, 1970; 1971; 1972-73; Bertrand and Lucas, 1975; Lucas, 1972-73; Meirion-Jones, 1976a; 1976b; 1977b; 1978c; 1978-79; 1979c; 1979d; 1980b; Aumasson, 1977; Bardel, 1977; 1978-79; 1979; Batt, 1978-79; 1979; Giot, 1979.

Chapter 2. The Physical Landscape of Brittany.
37. Young, 1792, 82, 321.
38. Le Lannou, II, 1952, 373-374.
39. id., I, 1950, 62.
40. ibid., 94-108.
41. De la Borderie, I, 1896, 48; Chadwick, 1969, 293.
42. Le Lannou, I, 1950, 111.
43. Couffon, 1946, 19-34.
44. Le Lannou, I, 1950, 112.
45. Young, 1792, 82, 321.

Chapter 3.   The Cultural Landscape
46. Daniel, 1958, 100.
47. Chadwick, 1965, 236.
48. Meynier, 1944a.
49. Bowen, 1972, 26.
50. Grenier, 1943, 15-37.
51. Giot, L'Helgouac'h and Monnier, 1979; Giot, Briard and Pape, 1979.
52. Chadwick, 1965, 241.
53. ibid., 255.
54. ibid., 257.
55. ibid., 258.
56. ibid., 270-273; Fleuriot and Giot, 1977.
57. Loth, 1883, 176.
58. Chadwick, op. cit., 276.
59. Bowen, 1969, 160-190.
60. ibid., 182.
61. Fleuriot and Giot, 1977.
62. Colin, 1949; Giot, 1949; 1951a; 1951b; Fleuriot and Giot, 1977, 141.
63. Le Lannou, I, 1950, 179.
64. Gautier, M., 1947b, 135-137.
65. Gourvil, 1968, 45.
66. ibid., 41; Falc'hun, 1970, 158.
67. Gourvil, 1972, 952.
68. Largillière, 1925, 21.
69. Le Lannou, I, 1950, 185.
70. Meynier, 1945a, 167.
71. Thébaut, 1950.
72. Gourvil, 1968, 56; Falc'hun, 1970, 158.
73. Le Lannou, I, 1950, 193.
74. ibid., 196.
75. ibid., 197-199.
76. Souillet, 1943.
77. ibid., 97.
78. ibid., 94, 95.
79. Le Lannou, I, 1950, 203.
80. Guilcher, 1946c, 46.
81. Gourvil, 1972, 950.
82. Le Lannou, I, 1950, 206.
83. Meynier, 1955, 28.
84. Flatrès, 1944, 166.
85. ibid., 172, 173.
86. Flatrès, 1957, 356, 357.
87. ibid., 360; Déniel, 1943, 114-115.
88. Le Cam, 1951; Hamon, 1976; 1977-78.
89. Fichou-Perquis, 1952.
90. Flatrès, 1957, 355; 1978.
91. Meynier, 1949a.
92. Chaumeil, 1949.
93. Colin, 1947b; Flatrès, 1944; 1957; 1958a; 1958b; 1959; 1971a; 1971b; 1977; 1979; Meynier, 1943b; 1943c; 1944b; 1945b; 1949b; 1955; 1966.
94. Meynier, 1955.
95. Dobet, 1947; Meynier, 1945b; 1966.
96. Meynier, 1966, 608.
97. id., 1944a.
98. Guilcher, 1946b.
99. id., 1946a.
100. Meynier, 1966.
101. Flatrès, 1944; 1957.
102. Souillet, 1943.
103. Chaumeil, 1953.
104. Lefeuvre, 1907.
105. Flatrès, 1971; Meynier, 1949b.
106. Flatrès, 1971, 92.
107. Guilcher, 1946a.
108. Flatrès, 1971, 92.
109. Falc'hun, 1963.
110. Meynier, 1962, 1966.
111. Dobet, 1943; Gautier, 1945; 1946; Guilcher, 1943; 1946b; Juillard *et al.*, 1957; Meynier, 1949b.
112. Meynier, 1962, 130, 135.
113. id., 1949b.
114. id., 1955, 30.
115. Bernard, 1950b; Flatrès, 1944; Huon, 1943; Le Coz, 1948.
116. Fichou-Perquis, 1952; Juillard *et al.*, 1957.
117. Meynier, 1949b, 266; 1955, 30.
118. Flatrès, 1944.
119. id., 1957, 447, 451.
120. Charaud, 1943; Guilcher and Meynier, 1944.
121. Charaud, 1948; De Châteaubriant, 1923.
122. Charaud, 1953; Fichou-Perquis, 1952; Flatrès, 1944; Gautier, 1945; Juillard *et al.*, 1957, 83; Le Cam, 1951.
123. Le Cam, 1951.
124. Meynier, 1955.
125. Gautier, M., 1946.
126. Fichou-Perquis, 1952.
127. Gautier, M., 1945
128. Guilcher, 1946b.
129. Flatrès, 1944.
130. Flatrès, 1944; Limon, 1852.
131. Juillard *et al.*, 1957, 89. See also *Le lycée amoricain*, vols. 7 and 8, 1823-30.
132. Fournier, 1934, 76.
133. Le Lannou, I, 1950, 241.
134. Ministère de la Santé et de la Population, 1939.
135. Gautier, M., 1947, 260; Vallaux, 1905a, 106.
136. Vallaux, 1905a 108-109
137. Le Lannou, I, 1950, 236.
138. ibid., 237.
139. Vallaux, 1905a, 116.
140. Le Lannou, I, 1950, 243, 244.
141. Vallaux, 1905a, 114.
142. Ministère de la Santé et de la Population, 1939.
143. Fournier, 1934, 69, 75.

Chapter 4.   Building Materials
144. Aubry, 1971; Cogné and Cogné, 1971; Meuret, 1979; Mussat, 1971; 1979.

Chapter 5. Construction — I

145. Sebillot, I, 1968, 269; Le Braz, I, 1928, 157.
146. Baudoin, 1939.
147. Le Braz, I, 1928, 157.
148. Sebillot, I, 1968, 270.
149. Buffet, 1954, 65-67.
150. E.A.R., Finistère. Little research has been done on the building trades and craft organizations. See, however, Couffon, 1940; 1946.
151. Buffet, 1954, 66.
152. Bachelot de la Pylaie, 1850, 479.
153. Pelras, 1966, 351.
154. Baudouin, 1908.
155. Géniaux, 1912, 8.
156. E.A.R., Morbihan.
157. ibid. These houses at Talforest and Kerspec are illustrated in Meirion-Jones, 1978-79.
158. André, Bertrand and Clément, 1976.
159. Vigarié, 1971, 139.
160. E.A.R., Loire-Atlantique.
161. Buffet, 1954, 57.
162. ibid., 58.
163. Gohel, 1976, 30.
164. E.A.R., Morbihan.
165. Buffet, 1954, 58.
166. ibid., 59.
167. E.A.R., Côtes-du-Nord.
168. Stothard, 1820, 197, 255.
169. Blackburn, 1880, 59.
170. Daniel, 1960; L'Helgouach, 1976.
171. De Cambry, 1799, 382.
172. E.A.R., Côtes-du-Nord.
173. E.A.R., Finistère.
174. E.A.R., Morbihan.
175. E.A.R., Côtes-du-Nord.
176. E.A.R., Ille-et-Vilaine.
177. Commission d'Inventaire de Bretagne, Rennes. Dossiers: 35 Betton; 35 Bain-de-Bretagne; 35 La Chapelle-des-Fougeretz; 35 Cesson-Sevigné; 56 Ploërmel; 56 Pontivy; 22 Saint-Aaron; 22 Saint-Maden; 29 Landéda.
178. Ministère de la Santé publique, 1939.
179. De Cambry, 1799, 34.
180. Fleury, 1899, 321.
181. Stothard, 1820, 200.
182. Blackburn, 1880, 31.
183. P. Sebillot, 1885, 150.
184. Bouët and Perrin, 1844, 239; Hélias, 1975, 437.
185. Hélias, 1975, 65-67.
186. E. Gautier, 1950, 51.
187. Buffet, 1954, 67.
188. Souvestre, 1836, 217.
189. De Cambry, 1799, 117; Bachelot de la Pylaie, 1850, 405; Souvestre, 1838, 103-4.
190. Fleury, 1899, 321.
191. Fenton, 1970.
192. Meirion-Jones, 1976b.

193. A.D.F., 4E 141/25; 141/20; 141/22; 141/33.
194. A.D.F., 4E 141/22.
195. A.D.F., 42G4.
196. A.D.F., 4E 110/3.
197. A.D.F., 4E 110/3; 148/14.
198. A.D.F., 4E 37/63.
199. A.D.F., 4E 110/5.
200. A.D.F., 4E 264/131.
201. A.D.C.N., Série 3E, Cojan, 1768.
202. Du Fail, 1549, 45.
203. Buffet, 1954, 63.
204. Le Lannou, I, 1950, 253.
205. A.D.F., 4E 110/9; 110/4.
206. Ministère de la Guerre, 1919, 169; Le Bail, 1925, 37.
207. Buffet, 1954, 64.
208. Le Bail, 1925, 37.
209. Bachelot de la Pylaie, 1850, 254.
210. Vaillat, 1913, 282.
211. Roger, 1911, 22.
212. Lestang, 1894, 299.
213. Fleury, 1899, 321.
214. M. Gautier, 1947a, 289.
215. Buffet, 1954, 65.
216. M. Gautier, 1947a, 289.
217. Vallaux, 1905a, 136.
218. Gauthier, 1936, 22; 1950, 51; 1956, 6.

Chapter 6. Construction — II

219. Meirion-Jones, 1978b; 1979a.
220. Bardel, 1976, 56.
221. Cleac'h and Letissier, 1976, 37.
222. Daniel, 1960, 84 *et seq.*
223. Badel, 1976, 56.
224. Commission d'Inventaire de Bretagne, Rennes. Dossiers: 35 Billé; 35 Châtillon-sur-Seiche.
225. Banéat, II, 1973, 175.
226. Horn, 1963.
227. Secrétariat d'État à la Culture, 1975, 36.
228. Bachelot de la Pylaie, 1850, 256.
229. Le Scouëzec, 1979, 16.
230. Meirion-Jones, 1977a, 355.
231. E.A.R., Finistère.
232. Meirion-Jones, 1977a, 358.
233. ibid., 357.
234. Gauthier, 1936.
235. Commission d'Inventaire de Bretagne, Rennes. Dossier: 29 Kergloff.
236. E.A.R., Morbihan.
237. Groupe Habitat Populaire, 1974.
238. Laloy and Vivier, 1976.
239. Commission d'Inventaire de Bretagne, Rennes. Dossiers: 35 Plechâtel; 35 Poligné.
240. Meirion-Jones, 1981b.
241. J.T. Smith, 1964, 126.
242. E.A.R., Morbihan.
243. J.T. Smith, 1955; 1958; Meirion-Jones, 1977a, 355.
244. Mercer, 1975, 109.

245. Deneux, 1927; Hewett, 1969.
246. Alcock, 1973; J.T. Smith, 1975; J.-C. Bans, 1979; J.-C. Bans and P.G. Bans, 1979a; 1979b.
247. Meirion-Jones, 1977a, 357.
248. Alcock, 1973; Alcock and Barley, 1972; Peate, 1946; 1956; 1957; 1957-58; Raglan, 1956; J.T. Smith, 1964; Walton, 1954; 1957.
249. Childe, 1933, 121.
250. Bertrand, 1970; 1971; 1972-73; Bertrand and Lucas, 1975; Branigan, 1968; Lucas, 1972-73; Meirion-Jones, 1979a, 18; 1981a (forthcoming); Van Es, 1967.
251. J.-C. Bans, 1979; P.G. Bans, 1979b; J.-C. Bans and P.G. Bans, 1979a; 1979b; Hekker, 1961; Hinton, 1967; McCourt, 1960-62; 1964-65; Meirion-Jones, 1977a; 1979a; 1981a (forthcoming); J.T. Smith, 1964; Trefois, 1937; Walton, 1960-62.
252. Meirion-Jones, 1976a.
253. Guilcher, 1949, 29.
254. Le Braz, 1905, 183.
255. Souvestre, 1860, 276.
256. Périer de Lahitolle, 1867, 168.
257. Vallaux, 1905a, 271, 273.
258. E.A.R., Morbihan.
259. Meirion-Jones, 1978-79.
260. Guilcher, 1949, 30.
261. Aumasson, 1977.
262. Meirion-Jones, 1978-79.
263. Following English usage, the term 'hall' is used to denote the common living room in this work (see Chapter 8).
264. E.A.R., Morbihan.
265. E.A.R., Côtes-du-Nord.
266. E.A.R., Loire-Atlantique.
267. De Cambry, 1799, 33.
268. Bachelot de la Pylaie, 1850, 172-3.
269. ibid., 405.
270. Souvestre, 1838, 103-4.
271. Le Bail, 1925, 38.
272. Sée, 1908-9, 633
273. Dupuy, n.d., 17.
274. E.A.R., Morbihan.
275. E.A.R., Loire-Atlantique.
276. A.D.C.N., Série 5M.2; A.D.I.V., Série 20M.e. 1-3.
277. Mussat, 1979a.
278. Secrétariat d'État à la Culture, 1975, 170.
279. Le Lannou, I, 1950, 250.
280. Fournier, 1934, 52.
281. Gautier, M., 1947a, 290.
282. ibid., 286.
283. Gauthier, 1965.
284. Vallaux, 1905a, 133-4.
285. ibid., 134-5.
286. Ministère de la Santé publique, 1939, 104, 113; E.A.R., Finistère.

Chapter 7. Circular Buildings
287. Erixon, 1937, 124.
288. ibid., 132.
289. Peate, 1946, 32.
290. ibid., 45.
291. Evans, 1942, 81.
292. Buchanan, 1956, 105.
293. Henry, 1949, 299; 1957, 153.
294. Cayla, 1954; Delamarre, 1934; Desaulle, 1965; Formigé, 1914a; 1914b; Fournier, 1933; Galy, 1964; Lachastre, 1963; Lassure, 1976; Lassure (ed.), 1977a; 1977b; 1978; 1979; Sartiges, 1921a; 1921b.
295. Allen, 1969.
296. Walton, 1969.
297. Giot, Briard and L'Helgouach, 1971, 22.
298. Giot, Briard and L'Helgouach, 1969, 18.
299. ibid., 1969, 27.
300. Rollando, 1971, 66.
301. De la Grancière, 1901, 276.
302. ibid., 276; id., 1902a, 121, 141; id., 1902b, 120, 389.
303. Le Rouzic, 1903, 256.
304. Professor P.-R. Giot, personal communication, 20 May 1977; Giot, Briard and Pape, 1979, 278.
305. Lecornec, 1973.
306. Giot, 1970.
307. id., 1960b.
308. Giot and Colbert de Beaulieu, 1969, 75.
309. Addy, 1933, 24.
310. Barbier, 1952, 15; 1960, 249; De la Borderie, 1896, vol. 1; Gaultier du Mottay, 1883, 288; Grand, 1958, 325.
311. Strabo, IV, 4, 3.
312. Grand, 1958, 325.
313. Barbier, 1952, 17.
314. ibid., 27, 35.
315. De la Borderie, 1896, vol. 1, 296; Giot, 1979, 9-12.
316. Grand, 1958, 326.
317. Couffon, 1943, 27; De la Borderie, 1896, vol. 1; Grand, 1958, 325.
318. Barbier, 1952, 17.
319. Devailly and Riché, 1969, 125.
320. Grand, 1958, 93.
321. Couffon, 1943, 28, 35.
322. Fournier, 1934, 53.
323. A.D.F., 42.G.4.
324. ibid.
325. Grand, 1958, 93.
326. Banéat, I, 1973, 271.
327. Couffon and Le Bars, 1959, 357.
328. ibid., 341.
329. Grand, 1958, 92.
330. Chadwick, 1969, 297.
331. Gauthier, 1965, 35.
332. Fournier, 1934, 53.
333. ibid., 53.
334. Du Halgouet, 1925; Sée, 1905-6, 499.
335. Salmon, 1971, 36.
336. Ministère des Affaires Culturelles, 1972, t. II, xvi, 14.
337. Gauthier, 1963.

338. Barbier, 1960, 521.
339. ibid., 522.
340. ibid., 523-26.
341. Frotier de la Messelière, 1940.
342. Ministère des Affaires Culturelles, 1969, t. I, 97.
343. Gauthier, 1963.
344. Ogès, 1949, 88.
345. M. Gautier, 1969.
346. ibid.
347. ibid., 85.
348. Le Braz, 1925, 44; Périer de Lahitolle, 1867, 168; Souvestre, 1860, 276; Vallaux, 1905a, 271, 273.

Chapter 8. Sub-rectilinear, Early and Primitive Rectilinear Buildings and Related Structures.

349. Meirion-Jones, 1976a; 1977b.
350. id., 1973b.
351. Piggott, 1948.
352. Meirion-Jones, 1976a.
353. Guilcher, 1949, 69.
354. Beresford, 1975, 18.
355. Meirion-Jones, 1976a.
356. ibid.
357. J.T. Smith, 1974, 241.
358. Hewett, 1969, 111.
359. Roberts, 1974; 1975.
360. Beresford, 1975, 41.
361. Giot *et al.*, 1971, 22.
362. Meirion-Jones, 1976a; 1977b.
363. Professor P.-R. Giot, personal communication, 20 May 1977; Giot, Briard and Pape, 1979, 278.
364. Rollando, 1971, 76.
365. Giot, n.d., 104.
366. Giot *et al.*, 1969, 74.
367. A.D.F., 42.G.4.
368. Evans, 1942.
369. Buchanan, 1957.
370. Fenton, 1970.
371. Meirion-Jones, 1976b.
372. Giot *et al.*, 1971, 38.
373. De la Grancière, 1901, 276.
374. Chadwick, 1969, 49; De la Grancière, 1901, 276; 1902a, 121, 141; 1902b, 120, 389.
375. Giot, 1960a, 193.
376. Meirion-Jones, 1976a; 1977b.
377. Bertrand, 1970; 1971; 1972-73; Bertrand and Lucas, 1975.
378. Lucas, 1972-73.
379. ibid.
380. André, 1974.
381. Bardel, 1976; 1977.
382. Briard and Peuziat, 1976.
383. Lecornec, 1973.
384. Sanquer, 1967, 35.
385. ibid., 37.
386. Aumasson, 1977.

387. André, 1978-79; 1979; Aumasson, 1977; Bardel, 1976; 1977; 1977-78; 1979; Batt, 1978-79; 1979.
388. Meirion-Jones, 1973b; 1973c.
389. id., 1978-79; 1977b.
390. id., 1978-79.
391. Vallaux, 1905a, 273.
392. Maho, 1975.
393. Meirion-Jones, 1978-79.
394. Gauthier, 1956, 46.
395. De Cambry, 1799, 33.
396. Guilcher, 1949, 73.
397. ibid., 29.
398. Vallaux, 1905a, 271.
399. Fournier, 1934, 53.
400. Vallaux, 1905a, 136.
401. Le Braz, 1905, 84.
402. ibid., 183.
403. Le Grand, 1957, 95.
404. Souvestre, 1845, 144.
405. id., 1860, 208.
406. ibid., 276.
407. Du Châtellier, III, 1837, 53.
408. Périer de Lahitolle, 1857, 168.
409. André, Bertrand and Clément, 1975, 35.
410. Choleau, 1905; 1907.
411. Le Bourhis, 1908.
412. Picard, 1904.
413. Du Châtellier, 1897, 55-56.
414. Meirion-Jones, 1979d.
415. A.D.C.N., Série 5M.2., Comités d'Hygiène et de la Salubrité, 1848-69.
416. E.A.R., Côtes-du-Nord.
417. E.A.R., Morbihan.
418. Meirion-Jones, 1973c.
419. Guilcher, 1949, 29.
420. Fox, 1951.
421. Meirion-Jones, 1978c.
422. Hurst, 1971.
423. Addyman, 1972.
424. Laver, 1909.
425. Ó Danachair, 1954-56; 1966-67.
426. Hurst, 1971.

Chapter 9. The Single-cell House

427. E. Gautier, 1950, 37.
428. Colin, 1947a, 62.
429. Bernard, 1950a, 72.
430. Fournier, 1934, 50.
431. Vallaux, 1905a, 135-37.
432. Flatrès, 1957, 359; 1977, 320.
433. P. Smith, 1975, 159, 163.
434. Briard and Peuziat, 1976, 29.
435. E.A.R., Côtes-du-Nord; Finistère.
436. E.A.R., Morbihan; Loire-Atlantique; Ille-et-Vilaine.
437. E.A.R., Finistère.
438. These and other examples are fully illustrated in Meirion-Jones, 1979b.

439. ibid.
440. E.A.R., Côtes-du-Nord, Ploulec'h.
441. Meirion-Jones, 1979b; Brooksby, 1976; Ó Danachair, 1956; Walton, 1961.
442. Meirion-Jones, 1979b.
443. The author is grateful to Eric Mercer for this suggestion. Personal communication, 19 October 1979.
444. Rosot, 1970; *La vie à la Campagne*, 1922.
445. Giese, 1931.
446. Gohel, 1976; Hamon, 1976; 1977-78; Le Cam, 1951.

Chapter 10.   The Long-house and its Derivatives
447. Peate, 1946, 51; 1963, 440.
448. J.T. Smith, 1963; Fox and Raglan, 1951; 1953; 1954.
449. Jones and Smith, 1963; J.T. Smith, 1963.
450. Mercer, 1975, 34.
451. Worth, 1953; Alcock, 1969; Jones, 1971.
452. Chesher and Chesher, 1968.
453. Brunskill, 1954.
454. Roussell, 1934; Walton, 1957b; Fenton, 1978.
455. Aalen, 1966; Evans, 1939; 1957; Ó Danachair, 1955; 1964.
456. Peate, 1963; 1964.
457. Hurst, 1971.
458. J.T. Smith, 1963.
459. Meirion-Jones, 1973b; 1977a; 1977b; 1979c; P.G. Bans, 1979b.
460. J.T. Smith, 1963.
461. Peate, 1946.
462. Hurst, 1971, 113.
463. Peate, 1946, 59.
464. Vallaux, 1905a, 141.
465. Meirion-Jones, 1973a; 1973b, 135.
466. Flatrès, 1949, 147; Pesez, 1971, 318.
467. P.G. Bans, 1976.
468. Peate, 1946.
469. Fox and Raglan, 1953.
470. Meirion-Jones, 1978-79.
471. E.A.R., Morbihan.
472. E.A.R., Morbihan.
473. E.A.R., Loire-Atlantique.
474. E.A.R., Finistère.
475. E.A.R., Côtes-du-Nord.
476. E.A.R., Ille-et-Vilaine.
477. De Cambry, 1799, 32.
478. ibid., 33.
479. Peate, 1946, 59.
480. Bachelot de la Pylaie, 1850, 249.
481. ibid., 405.
482. d'Aiguillon, 1756.
483. Souvestre, 1838, 16.
484. ibid., 103.
485. Stothard, 1820, 195, 225.
486. Blackburn, 1880, 67.
487. Bouët and Perrin, 1844, 43.
488. Hélias, 1975, 34.
489. Roger, 1919, 23.

490. Le Lannou, I, 1950, 257.
491. Guilcher, 1949, 35.
492. Fournier, 1934, 50-53.
493. Vallaux, 1905a, 123.
494. Sée, 1908-9, 634.
495. Dupuy, n.d., 17.
496. Keravel, 1954, 70.
497. Goubert, 1974, 191.
498. Lestrang, 1894, 299.
499. MM. les Inspecteurs de l'Agriculture, 1884, 101, 114.
500. Buffet, 1947, 41.
501. id., 1954, 74.
502. Gauthier, 1956, 46.
503. Hélias, 1975, 33, 367.
504. Giese, 1931, 346.
505. E. Gautier, 1950, 39.
506. Vallaux, 1905a, 135, 141.
507. Géniaux, 1912, 7, 8.
508. Bardel, 1976; 1977; Briard and Peuziat, 1976.
509. Gauthier, 1956, 46.
510. E.A.R., Loire-Atlantique.
511. De Cambry, 1799, 33.
512. Meirion-Jones, 1973b.
513. Guilcher, 1949, 36.
514. Hughes, 1960.
515. Peate, 1946.
516. Evans, 1939.
517. J.T. Smith, 1963; personal communication, 2 February 1972.
518. Meirion-Jones, 1977a.
519. Hawkes, 1947.
520. Peate, 1944; J.T. Smith, 1963.
521. Evans, 1939.
522. P.G. Bans, 1976.
523. Hemp and Gresham, 1942; Jones and Smith, 1966-67.
524. J.T. Smith, 1970.

Chapter 11.   The First-floor Hall
525. Secrétariat d'État à la Culture, 1975; Ministère des Affaires culturelles, 1969.
526. Barley, 1961, 5-7.
527. Wood, 1965, 16.
528. P. Smith, 1975, 338; Ó Danachair, 1977-79.
529. Ramm, McDowall and Mercer, 1970.
530. P. Smith, 1975, 21, 135.
531. Derruau, 1949, 410-415.
532. Le Lannou, I, 1950, 258.
533. M. Gautier, 1947a, 285; Le Lannou, I, 1950, 258.
534. Fournier, 1934, 50.
535. Guilcher, 1949, 38.
536. Souvestre, 1845, 22.
537. Gauthier, 1965, 23, 25.
538. Le Lannou, I, 1950, 258.
539. E.A.R., Côtes-du-Nord.
540. E.A.R., Morbihan.
541. E.A.R., Loire-Atlantique.

542. E.A.R., Ille-et-Vilaine.
543. Secrétariat d'État à la Culture, 1975, 491.

Chapter 12.   The Two-cell House
544. Vallaux, 1905a, 141.
545. Le Lannou, I, 1950, 265.
546. M. Gautier, 1947a, 286.
547. Fournier, 1934, 53.
548. Vallaux, 1905a, 137.
549. Gauthier, 1965.
550. Guilcher, 1949, 26.
551. MM. les Inspecteurs de l'Agriculture, 1844, 101.
552. Keravel, 1954, 68.
553. Bernard, 1950a, 72.
554. id., 1951, 71.
555. Pelras, 1966, 347. A good recent summary of the houses of this region and their contents and farm buildings is given in an exhibition catalogue: Ministère de la Culture et de la Communication, 1979.
556. Colin, 1947a, 62.
557. Le Grand, 1957, 96.
558. id., 1958, 162.
559. Du Châtellier, III, 1837, 16, 35.
560. Ministère de la Santé, 1939, 98, 103, 111, 116.
561. Pelras, 1966, 347.
562. Bernard, 1950a, 72; 1951, 71.
563. E.A.R., Finistère.
564. E.A.R., Morbihan.
565. E.A.R., Loire-Atlantique.
566. A.D.C.N., Série 3E, Cojan, 1782.
567. A.D.C.N., Série 3E, Fairier, La Chèze, 1838.
568. A.D.C.N., Série 3E, Chevallier, Pommerit-le-Vicomte, 1835.
569. A.D.I.V., 4E. Étude Hanout-Levindré, Yvon 80, 1845.
570. A.D.I.V., 4E.I.162, Étude Piton, Vitré, 1806.
571. A.D.L.A., E V/27.
572. A.D.L.A., E XI/11.
573. A.D.L.A., E XI/11.
574. A.D.L.A., E XI/56.
575. A.D.F., 4E 110/124.
576. A.D.F., 4E 248/24.
577. A.D.F., 4E 194/161.

Chapter 13.   Multi-cell Houses
578. Souvestre, 1845, 23.
579. E.A.R., Côtes-du-Nord.
580. Ministère des Affaires Culturelles, 1969, 35, 63, 68, 88, 89, 102, 158.
581. Secrétariat d'État à la Culture, 1975, 491, 504, 550, 619.
582. Frotier de la Messelière, 1938; 1940; 1947; 1948; 1949a; 1949b; 1951; 1952.
583. Frotier de la Messelière, 1940, 247.
584. Le Guennec, 1968; 1975; 1976.
585. Ministère des Affaires Culturelles, n.d.; 1973; 1974; Ministère de la Culture et de l'Environnement, 1977; Ministère de la Culture et de la Communication, 1979.

586. Desvaux-Marteville, 1973-74.
587. Salmon, 1971.
588. A.D.F., 4E 110/122.
589. A.D.F., 4E 110/122.
590. A.D.F., 4E 110/185.
591. A.D.F., 4E 110/185.
592. A.D.F., 4E 248/26.
593. A.D.F., 4E 141/12.
594. Série 3E, Sabot/Guerin, Plenée-Jugon, 1781.
595. A.D.I.V., E^N 4518.
596. A.D.L.A., E XI/56.
597. A.D.L.A., E XIII/747.
598. Frotier de la Messelière, 1940, 249.
599. Fournier, 1934, 79.
600. Souvestre, 1845, 22.

Chapter 14.   Farm Buildings
601. Le Lannou, I, 1950, 260, 262; M. Gautier, 1947a, 284-5, 287.
602. Vallaux, 1905a, 135.
603. De Cambry, 1799, 32.
604. Fournier, 1934, 50, 53, 60.
605. Guilcher, 1948, 62.
606. id., 1949, 65.
607. Bernard, 1950a, 72.
608. Pelras, 1966, 266.
609. Ministère de la Culture et de la Communication, 1979.
610. E.A.R., especially Finistère.
611. E.A.R., Finistère.
612. E.A.R., Côtes-du-Nord.
613. E.A.R., Morbihan.
614. E.A.R., Ille-et-Vilaine.
615. E.A.R., Loire-Atlantique.
616. A.D.F., 4E 148/30.
617. A.D.F., 4E 110/124.
618. A.D.F., 4E 110/123.
619. A.D.F., 4E 110/189.
620. A.D.F., 4E 110/188.
621. A.D.F., 4E 110/186, 187.
622. A.D.C.N., Série 3E, Sabot/Guerin, Plenée-Jugon.
623. A.D.C.N., Série 3E, Chevallier/Mazé, Pommerit-le-Vicomte.
624. A.D.I.V., 4E.1.187, Étude Piton, Vitré.
625. A.D.M., E^N 3297.
626. A.D.C.N., Série 3E, Goudelin, Mazé, 1776.
627. A.D.F., 4E 110/124.
628. A.D.F., 4E 110/10.
629. A.D.F., 4E 110/4.
630. A.D.F., 4E 110/9.

Chapter 15.   Hearth and Home
631. Sebillot, I, 1968, 72.
632. Souvestre, 1836, 11; Sebillot, II, 1968, 73-79; Souvestre, 1838, 75; Pelras, 1966, 435-436.
633. Sebillot, II, 1968; Souvestre, 1836, 13.
634. Bachelot de la Pylaie, 1850, 174.

635. Du Châtellier, 1863, 189; Pelras, 1966, 435-36; Le Braz, II, 1928, 22, 73.
636. Le Braz, II, 1928, 76-80, 121, 232.
637. Sebillot, II, 1968, 46.
638. Le Braz, II, 1928, 53-54.
639. De Cambry, 1799, 30, 67, 119, 159, 196, 199, 275, 282.
640. Hélias, 1975, 126.
641. Bachelot de la Pylaie, 1850, 172.
642. Souvestre, 1845, 145.
643. Du Châtellier, III, 1837, 17, 36, 55, 71, 81.
644. Le Braz, 1905, 22.
645. Ministère de la Guerre, Comité d'Action économique de la Xe région, 1919, 175.
646. Hurst, 1961, 211; P. Smith, 1967, 774; 1975, 231; Mercer, 1975, 59.
647. De Cambry, 1799, 58, 67, 275, 281.
648. ibid., 35, 162, 199.
649. ibid., 35, 53, 120, 126, 159.
650. Bouët and Perrin, 1844, 172.
651. De Cambry, 1799, 187, 393.
652. ibid., 130, 197.
653. Bernard, 1951, 76; 1952, 167.
654. Goubert, 1974, 207, 208, 209, 212.
655. Bouët and Perrin, 1844, 47, 50; Souvestre, 1838, 103-4.
656. Souvestre, 1845, 214.
657. Colin, 1943, 77; 1947a, 75.
658. Stothard, 1820, 255.
659. Goubert, 1974, 206.
660. Hélias, 1975, 24.
661. Blackburn, 1880, 59-60.
662. Du Châtellier, III, 1837, 17, 36, 53, 71, 81.
663. A.D.I.V., Série 20M.e.1-3.
664. A.D.C.N. Série 5M.2, 1848-69. MM. les Inspecteurs de l'Agriculture, 1844, 98.
665. Ministère de la Santé publique et de la Population, 1939.
666. E. Gautier, 1950, 87.
667. Pelras, 1966, 378.
668. Vaillat, 1913, 282.
669. Goubert, 1974, 222.
670. J.-S. Gauthier, n.d.; Maumené, 1922; Rosot, 1970; Hélias, 1969; 1970; Janneau, 1973; Buffet, 1947; 1954; Jambon, 1977.
671. Du Fail, 1549, 159.
672. Sée, 1908-9, 633, 634. See also Sée, 1896; 1906.
673. De Cambry, 1799, 33.
674. ibid.
675. ibid., 34.
676. De Fréminville, c, 1850, 34.
677. Stothard, 1820, 196.
678. ibid., 200.
679. Géniaux, 1912, 8.
680. Bachelot de la Pylaie, 1850, 115.
681. ibid., 173.
682. ibid., 175-77.
683. ibid., 275, 277.
684. ibid., 479.
685. Souvestre, 1838, 16, 103-4.
686. id., 1836, 217.
687. id., 1860, 134.
688. ibid., 276; Meirion-Jones, 1979d.
689. Blackburn, 1880, 31, 67.
690. Du Bois Saint-Sevrin, 1888, 283.
691. Géniaux, 1902a, 321; 1902b, 657; 1912, 7.
692. Vaillat, 1913, 282.
693. Roger, 1919, 22-24, 51.
694. Bouillé, 1926, 2; Du Halgouet, 1944, 147; Goardou, 1948, 302; Hélias, 1970, 25; Le Doaré, 1948, 301; Quentel, 1948, 302; Sperenze, 1948, 302.
695. Hélias, 1975, 52; Perrin, 1806, plates 5,6,7,8,13; Bouët and Perrin, 1970, 39, 43, 45, 52, 65.
696. Musée de Bretagne, Rennes, 58.9.18.
697. id., 49.205.
698. id., 58.9.60.
699. id., D.67.3.
700. Le Lannou, I, 1950, 265.
701. Gautier, 1947a, 286.
702. Vallaux, 1905a, 137.
703. Gauthier, 1932, 32.
704. Rosot, 1970, 5.
705. Marchal, 1920, 52.
706. ibid., 56.
707. Buffet, 1954, 73-85.
708. Sebillot, 1885, 148.
709. Lalaisse and Ropartz, 1866; Choleau, 1905; 1907; Puig de Ritalongi, 1894; Sée, 1896; 1906; Maguereze, 1840; 1972; Le Maître, 1976; Elegoat, 1978; Le Scouëzec, 1979; Goardon, 1974; 1975; Le Floc'h, 1965; Le Bourhis, 1908; Picard, 1904.
710. Dupuy, n.d., 20, 21, 28; Keravel, 1954, 77.
711. Le Floc'h, 1965, 227.
712. Goubert, 1974, 190.
713. ibid., 191.
714. Colin, 1943, 79.
715. id., 1947a, 73.
716. Pelras, 1966, 355; Bernard, 1950a, 72; 1951, 164. A good recent summary of the houses of this region and their contents is given in an exhibition catalogue: Ministère de la Culture et de la Communication, 1979.
717. Bresson, 1934, 95.
718. Du Châtellier, 1835-37, 16, 36.
719. Giese, 1931, 343.
720. Luzel, 1888, 241.
721. Ogès, 1949, 22.
722. Le Bail, 1925, 39.
723. Ogès, 1949, 28.
724. A.D.C.N., Série 2E: famille de Liscoët.
725. Vallaux, 1905a, 137, 140.
726. Le Braz, 1905, 22.
727. Guilcher, 1949, 30-31.
728. Hélias, 1975, 16.
729. Ardouin-Dumazet, 1903.

730. Bohéas, 1883.

731. Fournier, 1934, 52.

732. Ministère de la Guerre . . ., 1919, 217.

733. MM. les Inspecteurs de l'Agriculture, 1844, 101.

734. ibid., 100-3.

735. A.D.C.N., Série 5M.2, 1848-69.

736. E. Gautier, 1950, 37-39.

737. ibid., 48.

738. ibid., 50.

739. A.D.I.V., Série 20.M.e.1-3.

740. Lestang, 1894, 298.

741. Fleury, 1899, 317.

742. Buffet, 1947, 34-69; 1969, 167-173.

743. Gauthier, 1956, 45.

744. Bernard, 1951; 1952.

745. Keravel, 1954.

746. Colin, 1943; 1947a.

747. Lick, 1970.

748. A.D.C.N., Série 3E, Rouvrais, Merdrignac, 1841; 1835; 1833; 1834; Sabot, Plénée-Jugon, 1781; 1784; 1785; Fairier, La Chèze, 1767; 1778; *an* 4; Chevallier, Pommerit-le-Vicomte, 1837; 1838; 1835; 1771; 1772; 1767; Bouché, Saint-Nicholas-du-Pélem, 1790; Cojon, Plougonver, 1789; 1788; 1787; 1783; 1782; 1775; 1769; 1763; A.D.I.V., 4E.I.187; 162; 163; 4E/Étude Hanout-Levindré, Pleine-Fougères, 1766; 1768; 1773; 1774; 1791; 1809; 1810; *an* 10; *an* 11; 1845. A.D.L.A., E XII 747, E II 2049, E XII 746, E V 27, E XI 20, E XI 33, E XI 11, E XI 10, E XI 40, E XI 41, E 1499, E 1515, E 1507, E 1536, E 1557, E XI 56, E II 687. A.D.F. 4E 148/31; 141/31, 12, 13, 15, 8; 110/124, 123, 122, 189, 188, 187, 186. 185, 5; 248/26, 24, 22, 93, 92, 91, 90, 89; 37/171, 170, 169, 167; 194/30, 28, 101, 98, 161, 160. A.D.M., E^N 2587-2617; E^N 4482, 4483, 4487, 4506, 4517, 4518; E^N 3297.

749. E.A.R., Finistère, Côtes-du-Nord, Morbihan, Ille-et-Vilaine, Loire-Atlantique.

750. A.D.I.V., 4E.I. 162/Étude Piton, Vitré.

751. A.D.I.V., 4E. Étude Hanout-Levindré, Pleine-Fougères, Notaire Yvon/80.

752. A.D.L.A., E V/27.

753. A.D.L.A., E V/27.

754. A.D.L.A., E XI/11.

755. A.D.L.A., E XI/56.

756. A.D.C.N., Série 3E, Sabot/Guerin, Plénée-Jugon.

757. A.D.F., 4E 110/122.

758. A.D.F., 4E 110/123.

759. A.D.F., 4E 37/167.

760. A.D.F., 4E 194/161.

761. A.D.I.V., 4E.I.187, Étude Piton, Vitré.

762. A.D.C.N., Série 3E, Étude Bouché, Saint-Nicholas-du-Pélem.

763. Bachelot de la Pylaie, 1850, 176; Ogès, 1949, 28.

764. E.A.R., Morbihan. These plans are illustrated in Meirion-Jones, 1978-79.

765. De Cambry, 1799, 34.

766. Bachelot de la Pylaie, 1850, 173.

767. E.A.R., Côtes-du-Nord.

768. E.A.R., Loire-Atlantique.

769. E.A.R., Morbihan.

770. E.A.R., Finistère, Ille-et-Vilaine, Loire-Atlantique.

771. Ministère de la Santé, 1939.

772. Dupuy, n.d., 7, 10.

773. Colin, 1943, 80.

774. A.D.F., 4E 141/12.

775. Roger, 1919, 24.

776. Goubert, 1974, 191-4.

777. Dupuy, n.d., 15.

778. Hélias, 1975, 159.

779. A.D.I.V., Série 20.M.e.1-3; A.D.C.N., Série 5M.2.

780. Dupuy, n.d., 26, 27, 29.

781. Hélias, 1975, 14.

782. E. Gautier, 1950, 42, 44.

783. M. Gautier, 1947a; Le Lannou, I, 1950.

Chapter 16. *The Vernacular Architecture of Brittany: Conclusions*

784. Vallaux, 1905a, 136.

785. P.G. Bans, 1976.

786. Hamon, 1976; 1977-78.

787. Fleuriot and Giot, 1977.

788. Giot *et al.*, 1971, 18, 26.

EIGHTEEN

BIBLIOGRAPHY

Aalen, 1966   Aalen, F.H.A., 'The Evolution of the traditional house in western Ireland', *J. Roy. Soc. Antiq. Ireland*, 96 (1966), 47-58.

Addy, 1933   Addy, S.O., *The evolution of the English house*, London (1898), 2nd ed., rev. Summerson, J., London (1933).

Addyman, P.V.   Addyman, P.V.'The Anglo-Saxon house: a review', *Anglo-Saxon England*, 1 (1972), 273-307.

Agence d'urbanisme 1977a   Agence d'urbanisme de la communauté urbaine de Brest et de son environnement, *Le patrimoine architectural et les sites: Commune de Guilers*, Brest (1977).

1977b   Agence d'urbanisme de la communauté urbaine de Brest et de son environnement, *Le patrimoine architectural et les sites: Commune de Plouzané*, Brest (1977).

1978a   Agence de l'urbanisme de la communauté urbaine de Brest et de son environnement, *Le patrimoine architectural et les sites: Commune de Bohars*, Brest (1978).

1978b   Agence de l'urbanisme de la communauté urbaine de Brest et de son environnement, *Le patrimoine architectural et les sites: Commune de Gouesnou*, Brest (1978).

1979   Agence d'urbanisme de la communauté urbaine de Brest et de son environnement, *Le patrimoine architectural et les sites: Commune de Guipavas*, Brest (1979).

Alcock, 1969   Alcock, N.W., 'Devonshire farmhouses, Part II', *Trans. Devonshire Association*, 101 (1969), 83-106.

1973   Alcock, N.W., *A Catalogue of cruck buildings*, London and Chichester (1973).

Alcock and Barley, 1972   Alcock, N.W., and Barley, M.W., 'Medieval roofs with base-crucks and short principals', *Antiquaries J.*, 52 (1972), 132-168.

Allen, 1969   Allen, E., *Stone shelters*, Cambridge, Mass. and London (1969).

André, 1974   André, P., 'Le site médiéval de Kerlano en Plumelec (Morbihan)', *Archéologie en Bretagne*, no. 2 (avril 1974), 27-34.

1978-79   André, P., 'Lann-Gouh: le village abandonné', *Archéologie en Bretagne*, 20-21 (1978-79), 71-73.

1979   André, P., 'Melrand: le village abandonné de Lann-Gouh. Troisième campagne de fouilles', *Archéologie en Bretagne*, 24 (1979), 35-36.

André et al, 1976   André, P., Bertrand, R., and Clément, M., 'En Morbihan permanance d'un type d'habitat: la maison à pignons en abside', *Archéologia*, 97 (août, 1976), 28-36.

L'architecture rurale, 1977a   *L'architecture rurale en pierre sèche: revue de l'architecture populaire et anonyme*, C.E.R.A.P.S: Paris, 1 (1977).

1977b   *L'architecture rurale en pierre sèche: revue de l'architecture populaire et anonyme, essai d'analyse architecturale*, C.E.R.A.P.S: Paris, Supplément no. 1 (1977).

1978   *L'architecture rurale en pierre sèche: revue de l'architecture populaire et anonyme*, C.E.R.A.P.S: Paris, vol. 2 (1978).

1979   *L'architecture rurale*, C.E.R.A.R: Paris, 3 (1979).

1980a   *L'architecture vernaculaire rurale*, C.E.R.A.R: Paris, Supplément no. 2 (1980).

1980b   *L'architecture vernaculaire rurale*, C.E.R.A.R: Paris, Supplément no. 3 (1980).

L'architecture rurale, 1980c — L'architecture vernaculaire, C.E.R.A.R: Paris, 4 (1980).

Ardouin-Dumazet, 1903 — Ardouin-Dumazet, -., Les îles de l'Atlantique, d'Hoëdic à Ouessant, 2ème ed., Paris and Nancy (1903).

Aubry et al, (1971) — Aubry, M.-L., Dupuis, R. and Fenard, S., 'Maisons paysanne de la Bretagne rennaise', 'Maisons paysannes de France, (1971, no.3), 10-14.

Aumasson, 1977 — Aumasson, P., '35 — Bain-de-Bretagne: fortifications médiévales au Coudray — La Haute Ville. Fouilles d'Août 1977', Archéologie en Bretagne, no.15 (1977), 22-25.

Bachelot de la Pylaie, 1850 — Bachelot de la Plylaie, J.-M., Études archéologiques et géographiques, Bruxelles (1850). Reprinted, Quimper (1970).

Banéat, 1973 — Banéat, P., Le département d'Ille-et-Vilaine: histoire, archéologie, monuments, 3rd ed., 4 vols, Paris (1973).

J.-C. Bans, 1979 — Bans, J.-C., 'Les granges à "courbes" de l'Ancien Régime en Limousin', La Revue félibréenne et régionaliste Limouzi, no.72 (Oct. 1979), 3-20.

P.G. Bans, 1975 — Bans, P.G., Les maisons rurales traditionnelles en Basse-Bretagne, MS, Centre d'Ethnologie française (1975).

1976 — Bans, P.G., 'Maison longue et famille étendue en Bretagne', Études rurales, 62 (1976), 73-87.

1978 — Bans, P.G., 'Pour une "ethnohistoire" de la maison rurale: l'exemple de la Basse-Bretagne', Bull. Soc. archéol. Finistère, 106 (1978), 339-373.

1979a — Bans, P.G., Notes sur les maisons rurales en Basse-Bretagne, MS (revised version) (1979).

1979b — Bans, P.G., Aspects de l'architecture rurale en Europe occidentale, Établissements humains et socio-culturel environnement; no.5, UNESCO, Paris (1979).

Bans and Bans, 1979a — Bans, J.-C. and Bans, P.G., 'Notes sur les charpentes "cruck" en France et sur les problèmes d'interprétation qu'elles posent dans le cadre d'une théorie générale des constructions rurales européennes', L'architecture rurale, 3 (1979), 9-32.

1979b — Bans, J.-C, and Bans, P.G., 'Notes on the cruck truss in Limousin', Vernacular Architecture, 10 (1979), 22-29.

Barbier, 1951 — Barbier, P., Les vestiges monastiques des îles de l'embouchure du Trieux: l'Île Saint-Maudez et l'Île Verte, Saint-Brieuc (1952) Also Mémoires, Société d'Emulation des Côtes-du-Nord, 80 (1951), 1-35.

Barbier, 1960 — Barbier, P., Le Trégor historique et monumental, Saint-Brieuc (1960).

Bardel, 1976 — Bardel, J.-P., 'Vieux habitats en forêt de Pont-Calleck en Berné (Morbihan)', Archéologie en Bretagne, 11, no.3 (1976), 33-39.

1977 — Bardel, J.-P., '56 Berné-Coupe 12A de la Forêt domaniale de Pont-Calleck ensemble médiéval', Archéologie en Bretagne, 15 (1977), 28.

1978-79 — Bardel, J.-P., 'Berné, Pont-Calleck, le village déserté (Campagne 1978)', Archéologie en Bretagne, 20-21 (1978-79), 69-69.

1979 — Bardel, J.-P., 'Berné, Pont-Calleck: le village déserté', Archéologie en Bretagne, 24 (1979), 37-38.

Bardel and Bardel, 1976 — Bardel, J.-P., and Bardel, A., 'Les souterrains médiévaux en Bretagne'. Archéologia, no.97 (août, 1976), 50-57.

Barley, 1961 — Barley, M.W., The English farmhouse and cottage, London (1961).

Batt, 1978-79 — Batt, M. 'Karhaes-Vihan: un village médiéval déserté', Archéologie en Bretagne, 20-21 (1978-79), 37-42.

1979 — Batt, M., 'Brennilis: Karhaes-Vihan, un village médiéval déserté. Fouilles de 1979', Archéologie en Bretagne, 24 (1979), 18-22.

Baudoin, 1939 — Baudoin, -., 'Les oeufs dans la construction des maisons paysannes', Folklore paysan, 2, no. 3 (mai, juin, juillet, 1939), 78-79.

Baudouin, 1908 — Baudouin, M., 'La croix blanche des fermes du bocage vendéen', Bull. et. Mém de la Soc. d'Anthropologie de Paris (1908), 1-36.

Beresford, 1975 — Beresford, G., The medieval clay-land village; excavations at Goltho and Barton Blount. The Society for Medieval Archaeology, Monograph Series, No. 6 (1975).

Bernard, 1950a — Bernard, D., 'Cléden-Cap-Sizun', Bull. Soc. archéol. Finistère, 76 (1950), 58-181.

1950b — Bernard, D., 'Quelques observations sur la forme des champs auprès de la Pointe du Raz', Nouvelle Revue de Bretagne, 4 (1950), 372-373.

Bernard, 1951 — Bernard, D., 'Cléden-Cap-Sizun', *Bull. Soc. archéol. Finistère*, 77 (1951), 35-108.

1952 — Bernard, D., 'Cléden-Cap-Sizun', *Bull. Soc. archéol. Finistère*, 78 (1952), 13-139.

Bertrand, 1970 — Bertrand, R., 'La poterie onctueuse du village médiéval de Pen-er-Malo en Guidel (Morbihan)', *Travaux, Société lorientaise d'Archéologie* (1970). Unpaginated.

1971 — Bertrand, R., 'Un habitat rustique du XIIᵉ siècle à Pen-er-Malo en Guidel', *Travaux, Société lorientaise d'Archéologie* (1971). Unpaginated.

1972-73 — Bertrand, R., 'Le site médiéval de Pen-er-Malo en Guidel. Le bâtiment A: étude de matériel', *Travaux, Société lorientaise d'Archéologie*, (1972-73), 15-17.

Bertrand and Lucas, 1975 — Bertrand, R., and Lucas, M., 'Un village côtier du XIIᵉ siècle en Bretagne: Pen-er-Malo en Guidel (Morbihan)', *Archéologie médiévale*, 5 (1975), 73-101.

Blackburn, 1880 — Blackburn, H., *Breton folk*, London (1880).

Bohéas, 1883 — Bohéas, P., *Topographie médicale de l'Île d'Ouessant* (Finistère), Thèse de médicine, Paris (1883).

Bouët and Perrin, 1970 — Bouët, A., and Perrin, O., *Breiz-Izel ou Vie des Bretons de l'Armorique*, Paris (1844). Reprinted (1970).

Bouillé, 1926 — Bouillé, J., *L'habitation bretonne*, Coll. de l'art régionale en France, Paris (1926).

Bouchy and Dufour, 1971 — Bouchy, A.-M., and Dufour, H., Plougastel-Daoulas: la vie de la famille et du village: le cycle de la vie individuelle dans la société paysanne de 1890-1940. D.E.S., Faculté des lettres et sciences humaines, Université de Bretagne Occidentale, Centre d'études Celtiques (1971), 305 pp.

Bowen, 1969 — Bowen, E.G., *Saints, seaways and settlements*, Cardiff (1969).

1972 — Bowen, E.G., *Britain and the western seaways*, London (1972).

Branigan, 1968 — Branigan, K., 'The origins of cruck construction — a new clue', *Medieval Archaeology*, 12 (1968), 1-11.

Bresson, 1934 — Bresson, M.-M., 'L'habitat rural dans la région du Cap Sizun (Bretagne)', *Comptes-rendus du Congrès international de Géographie, Paris, 1931*, tome III, Paris (1934), 91-96.

Briard and Peuziat, 1976 — Briard, J., and Peuziat, J., 'L'habitat ancien de Kervini en Poullan (Finistère)', *Archéologie en Bretagne*, 12, no. 4 (1976), 29-36.

Brooksby, 1976 — Brooksby, H., 'Bed-outshuts in the Gower, west Glamorgan', *Vernacular Architecture*, 7 (1976), 21-23.

Brunhes, 1920 — Brunhes, J., 'Les types régionaux de maisons et carte générale des toits', Chapter 14 in *Histoire de la nation française, tome I, Introduction générale: Géographie humaine de la France*, Paris (1920), 411-444.

Brunskill, 1952 — Brunskill, R.W., 'Traditional domestic architecture in the Eden valley', unpublished M.A. thesis, University of Manchester (1952).

1954 — Brunskill, R.W., 'The development of the small house in the Eden valley from 1650 to 1840', *Trans. Cumberland and Westmorland antiq. archaeol. Soc.*, 53 (1954), 160-189.

1963 — Brunskill, R.W., 'Traditional domestic architecture of the Solway plain'. unpublished Ph.D. thesis, University of Manchester (1963).

1965-66 — Brunskill, R.W., 'A systematic procedure for recording English vernacular architecture', *Transactions, Ancient Monuments Society*, 13 (1965-66), 43-126.

1975 — Brunskill, R.W., 'Vernacular architecture of the norther Pennines: a preliminary view', *Northern History*, 11 (1975), 107-142.

Buchanan, 1956 — Buchanan, R.H., 'Corbelled structures in Lecale, County Down', *Ulster J. Archaeol.*, 19 (1956), 92-112.

1957 — Buchanan, R.H., 'Stapple thatch', *Ulster Folklife*, 3 (1957), 19-28.

Buffet, 1947 — Buffet, H.-F., 'La maison, le mobilier et le costume', Chapter 2 in *En Bretagne morbihannaise: coutumes et traditions du vannetais bretonnant au XIXᵉ siècle*, Grenoble and Paris (1947), 34-69.

1954 — Buffet, H.-F., 'La maison', Chapter 3, 'Le mobilier', Chapter 4, in *En Haute-Bretagne*, Paris (1954), 56-72; 73-85.

1960 — Buffet, H.-F., *Ille-et-Vilaine: aspects géographiques, historiques, touristiques et économiques du département* (1960) pp. 184.

1969 — Buffet, H.-F., 'Les maison rurales au pays de Port-Louis', *Les cahiers de l'Iroise*, 16, no. 3, Nouvelle Série (Juillet-Septembre, 1969), 167-173.

Campbell, 1937   Campbell, Å., 'Notes on the Irish house — I', *Folk-liv*, 1 (1937), 207-234.

1938   Campbell, Å., 'Notes on the Irish house — II', *Folk-liv*, 2 (1938), 173-196.

Cayla, 1954   Cayla, A., 'L'art de la pierre sèche dans les pigeonniers du Haut-Quercy', *Bull. de la Soc. des Études littéraires, scientifiques et artistiques du Lot*, Cahors, 75 (1954), 181-185.

Chadwick, 1965   Chadwick, N., 'The colonization of Brittany from Celtic Britain', *Proceedings of the British Academy*, 51 (1965), 235-299.

1969   Chadwick, N., *Early Brittany*, Cardiff (1969).

Charaud, 1943   Charaud, A.-M., 'Quelques questions de structure agraire dans les pays de la Loire-Inférieure', *Bull. Assoc. Géogr. français*, (1943), 107-113.

1948   Charaud, A.-M., 'L'habitat et la structure agraire de la Grand Brière et des Marais de Donges', Annales de Géographie, 57 (1948), 119-130.

Charpy, 1973   Charpy, J., *Guide des archives du Finistère*, Quimper (1973).

Châtelard, 1930   Châtelard, M., 'L'habitation dans les Pyrénées ariègeoises', *Revue géogr. des Pyrénées et du Sud-Ouest*, 1 (1930), 306-330.

Chaumeil, 1949   Chaumeil, L., 'Les chemins creux de Bretagne', *Annales de Bretagne*, 58 (1949), 55-58.

1953   Chaumeil, L., 'L'origine du bocage en Bretagne', *Eventail de l'histoire vivante* (Hommage à Lucien Febvre), Paris (1953), 163-185.

Chesher and Chesher, 1968   Chesher, V.M., and Chesher, F.J., *The Cornishman's House*, Truro (1968).

Childe, 1933   Childe, V.G., 'Scottish Megalithic tombs and their affinities', *Trans. Glasgow archaeol. Soc.*, N.S., 8 (1933). 120-137.

Choleau, 1905   Choleau, J., *Le journalier agricole du pays de Vitré*, Vannes (1905).

1907   Choleau, J., *Conditions des serviteurs ruraux bretons, domestiques à gages et journaliers agricoles*, Paris (1907).

Cleac'h and Letissier, 1976   Cleac'h, G., and Letissier, M., 'Un ermitage de style irlandais: l'ermitage de Saint-Hervé en Lanrivoaré', *Archéologia*, no. 97 (août, 1976), 37-41.

Colin, 1943   Colin, E., 'Quelques aspects de la vie rurale du pays de Porzay (fin du XVIIIe siècle — début du XIXe siècle), d'après les archives notariales', *Bull. Soc. archéol. Finistère*, 70 (1943), 73-83.

1947a   Colin, E., 'L'evolution de l'économie rurale du pays de Porzay de 1815 à 1930 d'après les archives notariales', *Bull. Soc. Archéol. Finistère*, 73 (1947), 60-80.

1947b   Colin, E., 'Un problème de géographie agraire: structure et finage des champs bretons', *Nouvelle Revue de Bretagne*, 1 (1947), 351-353.

Colin, 1949   Colin, E., 'A propos de l'anthroplogie des Bigoudens', *Nouvelle Revue de Bretagne*, 3 (1949), 227.

Cogné and Cogné, 1971   Cogné, J., and Cogné, A., 'Le problème du choix des pierres dans la restauration et dans la construction en Bretagne', *Maisons paysannes de France* (1971, no. 3), 7-9.

Coque, 1956   Coque, R., 'L'évolution de la maison rurale en Amiénois', *Annales de Géographie*, 65 (1956), 401-417.

Couffon, 1940a   Couffon, R., 'État sommaire des architectes, maîtres-maçons et maîtres d'oeuvres des Côtes-du-Nord', *Bull. de la Soc. d'Emulation des Côtes-du-Nord*, 72 (1940), 161-186.

1940b   Couffon, R., 'Table sommaire des artisans et artistes originaires des Côtes-du-Nord ayant travaillé antérieurement au XIXème siècle', *Bull. Soc. d'Emulation des Côtes-du-Nord*, 72 (1940), 187-245.

1943   Couffon, R., 'Essai sur l'architecture religieuse en Bretagne du Ve siècle', *Mém. Soc. d'Hist. et d'Archéol. de Bretagne*, 23 (1943), 1-40.

1946a   Couffon, R., 'État sommaire des architectes, maîtres-maçons et maîtres d'oeuvres des Côtes-du-Nord', *Bull. de la Soc. d'Emulation des Côtes-du-Nord*, 76 (1946), 200 *et seq.*

1946b   Couffon, R., 'Table sommaire des artisans et artistes originaires des Côtes-du-Nord ayant travaillé antérieurement au XIXème, *Bull. Soc. d'Emulation des Côtes-du-Nord*, 76 (1946), 198-204.

1946c   Couffon, R., 'Toponymie bretonne: La fôret centrale, les plous', *Mém. Soc. d'Hist. et d'Archéol. de Bretagne*, 26 (1946), 19-34.

Couffon and Le Bars, 1959   Couffon, R., and Le Bars, A., *Répertoire des églises et chapelles du diocèse de Quimper et de Léon,* Saint-Brieuc (1959).

D'Aiguillon, 1756   D'Aiguillon, le Duc, Rapport sur la visite de l'Île d'Ouessant, Saint-Mathieu, 29.5.1756. Archives de l'Inspection du Génie, Paris, no. 6.

Daniel, 1958   Daniel, G.E., *The megalith builders of western Europe,* London (1958).

1960   Daniel, G.E., 'Brittany', Chapter 4 in *The Prehistoric chamber tombs of France,* London (1960), 71–111.

De Cambry, 1799   De Cambry, J., *Voyage dans le Finistère ou état de ce département en 1794 et 1795,* Paris (1799), 32–35.

De Châteaubriant, 1923   De Chateaubriant, A., *La Brière,* Paris (1923).

De Fréminville, 1850   De Fréminville, -. (ed.), J. De Cambry, *Voyage dans le Finistère,* Paris (c. 1850). Reprinted, Brionne, Eure (1970).

De la Borderie, 1896   De la Borderie, L.-A.-Le Moyne, *Histoire de Bretagne,* 7 vols., Rennes (1896 ff.).

De la Grancière, 1901   De la Grancière, A., 'La préhistoire et les époques Gauloise, Gallo-Romaine et Mérovingienne dans le centre de la Bretagne armorique', *Bull. Soc. polymathique du Morbihan,* 29 (1901), 276.

1902a   De la Grancière, A., 'Époque du Fer au Gauloise: enceinte fortifiée de Castel-Finans', *Bull. Soc. polymathique du Morbihan,* 30 (1902), 121.

1902b   De la Grancière, A., 'Dernières explorations dans la région montagneuse de Quénécan entre le Blavet et le Sar (1899-1900)', *Bull. Soc. polymathique du Morbihan,* 30 (1902), 120, 389.

Delamarre, 1934   Delamarre, M.-J.-B., 'Contribution de l'habitat rudimentaire — les cabanes en pierre sèche des environs de Gordes, Vaucluse', *Comptes-rendus du Congrès international de Géographie de Paris, 1931,* tome III, Paris (1934), 293–298.

Delaruelle, 1933   Delaruelle, -., 'La maison élémentaire de la région Toulousaine', *Revue géogr. des Pyrénées et du Sud-Ouest,* 4 (1933), 373–383.

Demangeon, 1920   Demangeon, A., 'L'habitation rurale en France. Essai de classification des principaux types', *Annales de Géographie,* 29 (1920), 352–375.

Demangeon, 1926   Demangeon, A., 'De l'influence des régimes agraires sur les modes d'habitat dans l'Europe occidentale', *Comptes rendus du Congrès international de Géographie, Cairo, 1925,* tome IV, Cairo (1926), 92–97.

1927   Demangeon, A., 'La géographie de l'habitat rural', *Annales de Géographie,* 36 (1927), 1–23; 97–114.

1936   Demangeon, A., *Enquête sur l'habitation rurale en France,* Tours (1936).

1937a   Demangeon, A., *Les maisons des hommes, de la hutte au gratte-ciel,* Paris (1937).

1937b   Demangeon, A., *La définition et le classement des maisons rurales,* Paris (1937).

1939   Demangeon, A., 'Maison rurales de France et musées de plein air', *Folklore paysan,* 2, no. 2 (1939), 33–35.

1942   Demangeon, A., 'Esaai d'une classification des maisons rurales,' and 'L'habitation rurale en France: essai de classification des principaux types', *Problèmes de géographie humain,* Paris (1942), 230–235; 261–287.

Deneux, 1927   Deneux, H., 'L'évolution des charpentes du XIᵉ au XVIIIᵉ siècles', *L'architecte* (1927), 19–89.

Deniel, 1943   Deniel, J., 'La structure sociale agraire de Saint-Martin-des Champs (Finistère)', *Annales de Bretagne,* 50 (1943), 114–115.

De Planhol, 1968a   De Planhol, X., 'Les limites septentrionales de l'habitat rural de type lorrain', in Jäger, H., Krenzlin, A., and Uhlig, H. (eds) *Beiträge zur genese der siedlungs und agarlandschaft in Europa, Geographische Zeitschrift,* Beihefte 18, Wiesbaden (1968), 145–163.

1968b   De Planhol, X., *L'habitat et l'habitation rurale de type lorrain,* Rapport présénte par . . . S.I., OREAM-Lorraine (1968).

1969   De Planhol, X., 'L'ancienne maison rurale lorraine', *Norois,* 63 et 63 bis (1969), 315–336.

1971   De Planhol, X., 'Aux origines de l'habitat rural lorrain', *Les congrès et colloques de l'Université de Liège,* 58: *L'Habitat et les paysages ruraux d'Europe,* (1971), 69–91.

Derruau, 1949   Derruau, M., 'Le contraste de l'habitat', *La Grande Limagne, auvergnate et bourbonnaise,* Part IV, Clermont-Ferrand (1949), 405–442.

Desaulle, 1965 — Desaulle, P., *Les bories de Vaucluse. Région de Bonnieux. La technique, les origines, les usages (contribution à l'étude des constructions en pierre sèche de la France)*, Paris (1965).

Desvaux-Marteville, 1973-74 — Desvaux-Marteville, E., 'Les manoirs du Perche: d'une image littéraire à la réalité archéologique', *Archéol. médiévale*, 3-4, (1973-74), 365-392.

Devailly and Riché, 1969 — Devailly, G., and Riché, P., 'De l'Armorique à la Bretagne', Chapter 4 in Delumeau, J., (ed.), *Histoire de la Bretagne*, Toulouse (1969), 117-152.

De Vieillechèze, 1902 — De Vieillechèze, A., 'La Croisic, vieux logis, vieilles gens', *Bull. de la Soc. archéol. de la Loire-Inférieure*, no. 43A (1902).

Dobet, 1943 — Dobet. F., 'Quelques remarques sur les champs dans les communes de Ploumagoar et de Coëtmieux (Côtes-du-Nord)', *Annales de Bretagne*, 50 (1943), 110-111.

1947 — Dobet, F., 'Quelques exemples d'ensembles cadastraux circulaires', *Annales de Bretagne*, 54 (1947), 138-144.

Du Bois Saint-Sevrin, 1888 — Du Bois Saint-Sevrin, F., 'Mobilier d'une bourgeoise de Saint-Malo au XVIIe siècle', *Bull. Soc. archéol. Finistère*, 15 (1888), 283-304.

Du Châtellier, (1835-37) — Du Châtellier, A., *Recherches statistiques sur le département du Finistère*, 3 vols., Nantes (1835-37).

1863 — Du Châtellier, A., *L'agriculture et les classes agricoles de la Bretagne*, Paris (1863).

Du Fail, 1549 — Du Fail, N., *Les Baliverneries d'Eutrapel*, Lyon (1549).

Du Halgouet, 1925 — Du Halgouet, H., 'Du droit de colombier et de garenne', *Mém. Soc. d'Hist. et d'Archéol. de Bretagne*, 6 (1925), 57-82.

1944 — Du Halgouet, H., 'La Bretagne inconnue: demeures seigneuriales (Coëtcaudec, Le Plessis-Josso, Les Ferrières, Cadoudal)', *Mém. Soc. d'Hist. et d'Archéol. de Bretagne*, 24 (1944), 147-165.

Dupuy, n.d. — Dupuy, A., *La Bretagne au XVIIIe siècle*, Brest (n.d.).

Elegoet, 1978 — Elegoet, F., *Mémoires d'un paysan du Léon*, La Baule (1978).

Erixon, 1937 — Erixon, S., 'Some primitive constructions and types of lay-out with their relation to European rural building practice', *Folk-liv*, 1 (1937), 124-155.

Erixon, 1938 — Erixon, S., 'West European connections and cultural relations', *Folk-liv*, 2 (1938), 137-172.

Evans, 1939 — Evans, E.E., 'Donegal survivals', *Antiquity*, (1939), 207-222.

1940 — Evans, E.E., 'The Irish peasant house', *Ulster J. Archaeol.*, 3rd series, 3 (1940), 165-169.

1942 — Evans, E.E., *Irish heritage*, Dundalk (1942).

1951 — Evans, E.E., *Mourne country*, Dundalk (1951).

1957 — Evans, E.E., *Irish folk ways*, London (1957).

Falc'hun, 1963 — Falc'hun, F., *Histoire de la langue bretonne d'après la géographie linguistique*, 2nd ed., Paris (1963).

1966 — Falc'hun, F., *Les noms de lieux celtiques: 1ère série*, Rennes (1966).

1970 — Falc'hun, F., *Les noms de lieux celtiques: 2ème série*, Rennes (1970).

Fenton, 1970 — Fenton, A., 'Clay building and clay thatch in Scotland', *Ulster Folklife*, 15-16 (1970), 28-51.

1978 — Fenton, A., *The island blackhouse and a guide to 'The Blackhouse' No.42, Arnol*, Edinburgh: H.M.S.O. (1978).

Fichou-Perquis, 1952 — Fichou-Perquis, G., 'Un exemple de champs ouverts en Bretagne intérieure', *Cinquantième anniversaire du Laboratoire de Géographie de Rennes*, Rennes (1952), 287-292.

Flatrès, 1944 — Flatrès, P., 'Le pays Nord-Bigouden', *Annales de Bretagne*, 51 (1944), 158-205.

1949 — Flatrès, P., Review of I.C. Peate, *The Welsh house*, in *Annales de Bretagne*, 56 (1949), 147.

1957 — Flatrès, P., 'La structure rurale du Sud-Finistère d'après les anciens cadastres', *Norois*, 4 (1957), 353-367; 425-453.

1958a — Flatrès, P., 'L'étendue des finages villageois en Bretagne', *Norois*, 18 (1958), 181-189.

1958b — Flatrès, P., 'Note sur les champs ouverts de la Presqu'île de Crozon', *Penn-ar-Bed*, Brest, 14 (1958), 1-3.

1959 — Flatrès, P., 'Les structures rurales de la frange atlantique de l'Europe', *Annales de l'Est*, 21 (1959), 193-202.

1971a — Flatrès, P., 'Hamlet and village', in Buchanan, R.H., Jones, E., and McCourt D. (eds), *Man and his habitat*, London (1971), 165-185.

Flatrès, 1971b — Flatrès, P., 'Les anciennes structures rurales de Bretagne d'après le cartulaire de Redon. Le paysage rurale et son évolution. *Études rurales*, 41 (1971), 87-93.

1977 — Flatrès, P., 'Historical geography of western France', Chapter 9 in Clout, H.D. (ed.), *Themes in the historical geography of France,* London, New York and San Fransisco (1977), 301-342.

1978 — Flatrès, P., 'Les "placîtres" en Bretagne', in M. Kielczewska-Zaleska (ed), *L'évolution de l'habitat et des paysages ruraux d'Europe, Actes de la conférence tenue à Varsovie en septembre 1975,* Warsaw, *Geographia Polonica,* 38, (1978), 89-95.

1979 — Flatrès, P., 'L'évolution des bocages: la région de Bretagne'. *Norois,* 103 (1979), 303-320.

Flatrès-Mury, 1970a — Flatrès-Mury, H., 'Deux aspects de l'habitat rural: "cours" et "plants" sur les confins normands, bretons et manceaux', *Norois,* 17, no.65 (1970), 21-37.

Flatrès-Mury, 1970b — Flatrès-Mury, H., 'Matériaux et techniques de construction rurale dans l'Ouest de la France: l'example des confins normands, bretons et manceaux', *Norois,* 17, no. 68 (1970), 547-566.

Fleuriot and Giot, 1977 — Fleuriot, L., and Giot, P.-R., 'Early Brittany', *Antiquity,* 51 (1977), 106-116.

Fleury, 1899 — Fleury, J., 'Les maisons-types dans la région du Bas-Léon', Chap. 15 in Ministère de l'Instruction Publique . . ., *Enquête sur les conditions de l'habitation en France. Les maisons-types,* tome II, Paris (1899), 317-323.

Formigé, 1914a — Formigé, J., 'Notes sur les cabanes en pierres sèches de Vaucluse', *Bull. Soc. Nat. Antiq. Fr.* (1914), 126.

1914b — Formigé, J., 'Cabanes de pierres sèches dans le Vaucluse', *Bull. monumental,* 78 (1914), 47-57.

Fournier, 1934 — Fournier, L., 'La population et l'habitat', *Monographie géographique de la commune de Bulat-Pestivien (Côtes-du-Nord).* Thèse lettres, Caen (1934), Saint-Brieuc (1934), 39-55.

Fournier, 1933 — Fournier, P.-F., 'Les ouvrages en pierres sèches des cultivateurs d'Auvergne et la prétendue découverte d'une ville aux côtes de Clermont', *L'Auvergne littéraire, art. et hist.,* 10, no. 68, fasc. 3 (1933), 3-79.

Fox, 1951 — Fox, C.F., 'Three round-gabled houses in Carmarthenshire', *Archaeologia Cambrensis,* 101 (1951), 106-112.

Fox and Raglan, 1951-54 — Fox, C.F., and Raglan, Lord, *Monmouthshire houses,* Cardiff, I (1951), II (1953), III (1954).

Frotier de la Messelière, 1938 — Frotier de la Messelière, Le Vicomte, *Géographie historique du département des Côtes-du-Nord* (1938).

1940 — Frotier de la Messelière, Le Vicomte, 'Les manoirs bretons des Côtes-du-Nord', *Bull. et Mém. Soc. d'Emulation des Côtes-du-Nord,* 72 (1940), 247-270.

1947 — Frotier de la Messelière, Le Vicomte, *Le pays de Quintin, son passé, ce qu'il en reste,* Saint-Brieuc (1947).

1948 — Frotier de la Messelière, Le Vicomte, *Catalogue illustré des monuments ruraux des Côtes-du-Nord dans le Trégor et le Goëllo,* Saint-Brieuc (1948).

1949a — Frotier de la Messelière, *Le Vicomte, Le Poher, Finistère et Côtes-du-Nord,* Saint-Brieuc (1949).

Frotier de la Messelière, 1938 — Frotier de la Messelière, Le Vicomte, *Le Pouldouvre et le Canton de Dinan-Est,* Saint-Brieuc (1949).

1951 — Frotier de la Messelière, Le Vicomte, *Au coeur du Penthièvre,* Saint-Brieuc (1951).

1952 — Frotier de la Messellière, Le Vicomte, *Le Porhoët des Côtes-du-Nord,* Saint-Brieuc (1952).

Galy, 1964 — Galy, G.-R., 'L'habitat en pierres sèches. Essai de méthodologie', *Bull. Assoc. des Géographes français,* nos. 328-329 (novembre-décembre, 1964), 57-69.

Gaultier du Mottay, 1883 — Gaultier du Mottay, -., 'Répertoire archéologique', *Mém. Soc. archéol. et hist. des Côtes-du-Nord,* (1883), 288.

Gauthier, 1927 — Gauthier, J.-S., 'La maison bretonne', *La Bretagne touristique* (15 fév. 1927), 32-34.

1932 — Gauthier, J.-S., 'La maison bretonne', *L'art populaire en France,* Strasbourg, 4 (1932), 27-42.

1936 — Gauthier, J.-S., 'Vieilles maisons rurales de la Loire Inférieure', *Bull. Soc. archéol. hist. Nantes et de la Loire-Inférieure,* 76 (1936), 20-28.

Gauthier, 1950 — Gauthier, J.-S., 'Les maisons rurales de la Loire-Inférieure', *Bull. de l'Assoc. bretonne et Union régionaliste bretonne*, 4ᵉ série, 59 (1950), 49-61.

1956 — Gauthier, J.-S., 'Folklore de la Loire-Inférieure: 1ᵉʳᵉ partie: L'habitat', *Nantes-Tourisme*, 7 (1956), 1-64.

1963 — Gauthier, J.-S., 'Les colombiers, les fuies, les pigeonniers', *Nantes-Tourisme*, tome 14, 3ᵉ trimestre, no. 62 (1963), 5-9.

1965 — Gauthier, J.-S., *La maison bretonne*, Châteaulin (1965).

n.d. — Gauthier, J.-S., *Meubles et ensembles bretons*, Paris (n.d.).

E. Gautier, 1950 — Gautier, E., *La dure existence des paysans et des paysannes. Pourquoi les Bretons s'en vont*, Paris (1950).

M. Gautier, 1945 — Gautier, M., 'Pseudo-pratiques communautaires en Bretagne méridionale', *Annales de Bretagne*, 52 (1945), 92-96.

1946 — Gautier, M., 'Remarques sur la terminologie agraire en Bretagne', *Annales de Bretagne*, 53 (1946), 136-139.

1947a — Gautier, M., 'L'habitat', Chapter 1, Livre II, in *La Bretagne Centrale*, La Roche-sur-Yonne (1947), 282-290.

M. Gautier, 1947b — Gautier, M., 'Traces de l'invasion bretonne médiévale en pays gallo', *Annales de Bretagne*, 54 (1947), 135-137.

1969 — Gautier, M., 'Un type d'habitation rurale à fonction "industrielle". Les moulins de Bretagne et de Vendée', *Norois*, 63 et 63 bis (1969), 73-100.

Géniaux, 1902a — Géniaux, C., 'L'hiver dans les fermes', *La Revue Mame*, 386 (23 février, 1902), 321-326.

1902b — Géniaux, C., 'L'agouvrô', *La Revue Mame*, 407 (20 juillet, 1902), 657-662.

1912 — Géniaux, C., *La Bretagne vivante*, Paris (1912).

Giese, 1931 — Giese, W., 'Beiträge zur Volkstümlichen Siedlung und Wirtschaft in den Monts d'Arrée (Basse-Bretagne)', *Volkstum. u. Kultur der Romanen*, 4 (1931), 343-377.

Giot, 1949 — Giot, P.-R., 'Sur "l'origine étrangère de groupes ethniques bretons"', *Nouvelle Revue de Bretagne*, 3 (1949), 66-69.

1951a — Giot, P.-R., 'Armoricains et Bretons, étude anthropologique', *Travaux de l'Institut d'Anthropologie de la Faculté des Sciences de Rennes* (1951).

Giot, 1951b — Giot, P.-R., 'Qui sont les Bretons?', *Nouvelle Revue de Bretagne*, 5 (1951), 18-21.

1960a — Giot, P.-R., *Brittany*, London (1960).

1960b — Giot, P.-R., 'Les souterrains armoricains à l Âge du Fer', *Annales de Bretagne*, 62 (1960), 45.

1970 — Giot, P.-R., *Barnenez*, Rennes (1970).

n.d. — Giot, P.-R., *La Bretagne avant histoire*, Rennes (n.d.).

1979 — Giot, P.-R., 'Île de Bréhat: fouilles de l'Île Lavret', *Archéologie en Bretagne*, 24 (1979), 9-12.

Giot, et al., 1969 — Giot, P.-R., Briard, J., and L'Helgouach, J., 'La préhistoire', Chapter 1 in Delumeau, J. (ed)., *Histoire de la Bretagne*, Toulouse (1969), 11-58.

Giot, et al., 1971 — Giot, P.-R., Briard, J., and L'Helgouach, J., 'Préhistoire et protohistoire armoricaines', Chapter 1 in Delumeau, J. (ed.), *Documents de l'histoire de la Bretagne*, Toulouse (1971), 7-24.

Giot, et al., 1979a — Giot, P.-R., Briard, J., and Pape, L., *Protohistoire de la Bretagne*, Rennes (1979).

Giot, et al., 1979b — Giot, P.-R., L'Helgouach, J., and Monnier, J.-L., *Préhistoire de la Bretagne*, Rennes (1979).

Giot and Colbert de Beaulieu, 1969 — Giot, P.-R., and Colbert de Beaulieu, J.-B., 'Au seuil de l'histoire', Chapter 2 in Delumeau, J. (ed.), *Histoire de la Bretagne*, Toulouse (1969), 59-88.

Y. Goardou, 1948 — Goardou, Y., 'Plan des fermes bretonnes', *Nouvelle Revue de Bretagne*, 2 (1948), 302.

H. Goardon, 1974 — Goardon, H. 'Moeurs et coutumes du Cap Sizun au début du XXᵉ siècle', *Bull. Soc. archéol. du Finistère*, 102 (1974), 223-279.

1975 — Goardon, H., 'Moeurs et coutumes du Cap Sizun au début du XXᵉ siècle', *Bull. Soc. archéol. du Finistère*, 103 (1975), 225-275.

Gohel, 1976 — Gohel, L.-M., 'La construction de terre en Haute-Bretagne. Histoire et techniques', *Arts de l'Ouest: études et documents*, Rennes, 1 (1976), 23-48.

Goubert, 1974 — Goubert, J.-P., *Malades et médecins en Bretagne, 1770-1790*, Rennes (1974).

Gourvil, 1968 — Gourvil, F., *Langue et littérature bretonnes*, Paris (1968).

1972 — Gourvil, F., 'Les noms de lieu bretons: initiation toponymique', *Bull. Soc. archéol. Finistère*, 99 (1972), 937-960.

Grand, 1958 — Grand, R., *L'art Roman en Bretagne*, Paris (1958).

Grenier, 1943 — Grenier, A., 'Les civilisations primitives de l'Armorique', in *Conférences universitaires de Bretagne*, Paris (1943), 15-37.

Groupe Habitat Populaire, 1974 — Groupe Habitat Populaire (Unité pedagogique d'architecture de Nantes), *Architecture rurale du pays blanc: plaquette de conseils*, Nantes (1974).

Guilcher, 1943 — Guilcher, A., 'Quelques exemples de champs ouverts dans la Bretagne du sud', *Annales de Bretagne*, 50 (1943), 111-112.

1946a — Guilcher, A., 'Le finage des champs dans le cartulaire de Redon', *Annales de Bretagne*, 53 (1946), 140-144.

1946b — Guilcher, A., 'Points de vue nouveaux sur la structure agraire de la Bretagne', *L'Information géographique*, (jan.-fév. 1946), 9-15.

1946c — Guilcher, A., 'Le mot ker', *Mém. Soc. d'Hist. et d'Archéol. de Bretagne*, 26 (1946), 35-48.

1948 — Guilcher, A., 'L'habitat rural à Plouvien', *Bull. Soc. archéol. Finistère*, 74 (1948), 3-74.

1949 — Guilcher, A., 'L'habitat rural à Plouvien', *Bull. Soc. archéol. Finistère*, 75 (1949), 26-98.

Guilcher, 1950 — Guilcher, A., *L'habitat rural à Plouvien, Finistère*, Brest (1950).

Guilcher and Meynier, 1944 — Guilcher, A., and Meynier, A., 'À propos de la note de Mlle Charaud sur la structure agraire en Loire-Inférieure', *Bull. Assoc. Géogr. français* (1944), 77-78.

Hamon, 1976 — Hamon, F., 'L'habitat traditionnel dans la Presqu'île de Rhuys', *Penn ar Bed*, 10, no. 85 (juin, 1976), 380-390.

1977-78 — Hamon, F., 'Un exemple de standardisation de l'architecture rurale au XVIIe siècle: Belle-Île-en-Mer', *Transactions, Ancient Monuments Society*, N.S., 22 (1977-78), 104-111.

Hawkes, 1947 — Hawkes, C.F.C., 'The excavation at Iwerne, 1897', *Archaeol. J.*, 104 (1947), 48-62.

Hekker, 1961 — Hekker, R.C., 'Fachwerkbau in Südlimburg', *Arbeitskreis für deutsche Hausforschung: Bericht über die Tagung in Aachen, 1961* (1961), 49-74.

Hélias, 1969 — Hélias, P., *Savoir-vivre en Bretagne*, Châteaulin (1969).

Hélias, 1970 — Hélias, P., *Logis et ménages*, Châteaulin (1970).

1975 — Hélias, P., *Le cheval d'orgeuil: mémoires d'un Breton du pays bigouden*, Paris (1975).

Hemp and Gresham, 1942 — Hemp, W.J., and Gresham, C., 'Park, Llanfrothen, and the unit system', *Archaeologia Cambrensis*, 97 (1942), 98-112.

Henry, 1949 — Henry, F., 'Early Irish monasteries, boat-shaped oratories and beehive huts', *County Louth archaeol. J.*, 11 (1949), 296-304.

1957 — Henry, F., 'Early monasteries, beehive huts and dry-stone houses in the neighbourhood of Caherciveen and Waterville (Co. Kerry)', *Proc. Royal Irish Academy*, 58, sec. C. no. 3 (1957), 45-166.

Hewett, 1969a — Hewett, C.A., *The development of carpentry, 1200-1700: an Essex study*, Newton Abbot (1969).

1969b — Hewett, C.A., 'The dating of French timber roofs by Henri Deneux: an English summart', *Transactions, Ancient Monuments Society*, 16 (1969), 89-108.

Hinton, 1967 — Hinton, D., 'A cruck house at Lower Radley, Berks', *Oxoniensia*, 32 (1967), 13-33.

Horn, 1963 — Horn, W., 'Les halles de Questembert', *Bull. Soc. polymathique du Morbihan*, 90 (1963), 1-16.

Hoskins, 1953 — Hoskins, W.G., 'The re-building of rural England, 1570-1640', *Past and Present*, 4 (1953), 44-89.

Hughes, 1960 — Hughes, T.J., 'Aberdaron', in Davies, E., and Rees, A.D., (eds.) *Welsh rural communities*, Cardiff (1960), 119-181.

Huon, 1943 — Huon, R., 'Champs ouverts et allongés de Binic (Côtes-du-Nord)', *Annales de Bretagne*, 50 (1943), 112-114.

Hurst, 1961 — Hurst, J.G., 'The kitchen area of Northolt manor, Middlesex', *Medieval Archaeology*, 5 (1961), 211-299.

1971 — Hurst, J.G., 'A review of the archaeological evidence (to 1968)', Chapter 2 in Beresford, M.W. and Hurst, J.G. (eds.), *Deserted medieval villages* (1971), 117.

Innocent, 1916 — Innocent, C.F., *The development of English building construction*, London (1916).

Jambon, 1927 — Jambon, J., *Les beaux meubles rustiques du vieux pays de Rennes*, Rennes (1927); Marseilles (1977).

Janneau, 1973 — Janneau, G., *Meubles bretons*, Paris (1973).

Jones, 1971 — Jones, S.R., 'Devonshire farmhouses, Part III', *Trans. Devonshire Association*, 103 (1971), 35-75.

Jones and Smith, 1963 — Jones, S.R. and Smith, J.T., 'The houses of Breconshire, Part I', *Brycheiniog*, 9 (1963), 1-78.

1966-67 — Jones, S.R., and Smith, J.T., 'The houses of Breconshire, Part IV', *Brycheiniog*, 12 (1966-67), 1-91.

Juillard, *et al.*, 1957 — Juillard, E., Meynier, A., de Planhol, X., and Sautter, G., 'Structures agraires et paysages ruraux', *Annales de l'Est*, 17 (1957), 7-188.

Keravel, 1954 — Keravel, P., 'Fermes du pays de Quimper à la fin du XVIIe siècle et au début du XVIIIe siècle', *Bull. Soc. archéol. Finistère*, 80 (1954), 63-81.

Lachastre, 1963 — Lachastre, J., 'Constructions en pierres sèches de Daglan. Eléments caractéristiques, essai de classification', *Bull. de la Soc. hist. et archéol. du Périgord*, Périgueux, 90, 3e livraison (1963), 121-128.

Lalaisse and Ropartz, 1866 — Lalaisse, H., and Ropartz, -., *Scènes de la vie rurale*, Nantes (1866).

Laloy and Vivier, 1976 — Laloy, P., and Vivier, B., *Haute-Bretagne. Ille-et-Vilaine. Habitat rural en pays de Vilaine*, Comité départemental du tourisme d'Ille-et-Vilaine, Rennes (1976).

Largillière, 1925 — Largillière, R., *Les saints et l'organisation chrétienne primitive dans l'Armorique bretonne*, Rennes (1925).

Lassure, 1976 — Lassure, C., *Bibliographie de L'architecture rurale en pierre sèche du Quercy et du Périgord: revue analytique et critique*, Paris (1976).

Lassure, 1977-80 — Lassure, C., (ed.) (1977-80) See under 'L'architecture rurale'.

Lassure and Lassure, 1976 — Lassure, C. and Lassure, J.-M., *Les vestiges lithiques de l'ancien vignoble cadurcien*, Paris (1976).

Laver, 1909 — Laver, H., 'Ancient types of huts at Athelney', *Proc. Somerset archaeol. Soc.*, 55 (1909), 175-189.

Le Bail, 1925 — Le Bail, A., *L'agriculture dans un département français: le Finistère agricole (étude d'économie rurale)*, Angers (1925).

Le Bourhis, 1908 — Le Bourhis, F., *Étude sur la culture et les salaires agricoles en Haute-Cornouaille*, Rennes (1908).

Le Braz, 1905 — Le Braz, A., *La terre du passé*, 3rd ed., Paris (1905).

Le Braz, 1928 — Le Braz, A., *La légende de la mort chez les Bretons armoricains*, 2 vols., Paris (1928). Reprinted, Marseilles (1974).

Le Cam, 1951 — Le Cam, L., 'Le problème de l'openfield sur les rives du Golfe du Morbihan', *Annales de Bretagne*, 58 (1951) 164-170.

Lecornec, 1973 — Lecornec, J., 'Le site à enclos de Kerlande à Brandivy (Morbihan)', *Annales de Bretagne*, 80 (1973), 61-70.

Le Coz, 1948 — Le Coz, J., 'La structure agraire dans le Canton de Fouesnant', *Annales de Bretagne*, 55 (1948), 191-194.

Le Crann, 1948 — Le Crann, J., Une société rurale dans les Montagnes d'Arrée: Saint-Rivoal au début du XXe siècle, unpublished, Mémoire de maîtrise, Faculté des lettres et sciences humaines, Université de Bretagne Occidentale, Brest, Centre d'Études Celtiques (1972).

Le Doaré, 1948 — Le Doaré, J., 'Plan des fermes bretonnes', *Nouvelle Revue de Bretagne*, 2 (1948), 299-301.

Lefeuvre, 1907 — Lefeuvre, P., *Les communs en Bretagne à la fin de l'ancien régime*. Rennes (1907).

Le Floc'h, 1965 — Le Floc'h, V., *La vie rurale à Plouivel, paroisse de Cornouaille, 1675-1789*, Mémoire de D.E.S., Rennes (1965).

Le Grand, 1957 — Le Grand, A., 'Le Canton de Briec au début du XIXe siècle', *Bull. Soc. archéol. Finistère*, 83 (1957), 80-101.

1958 — Le Grand, A., 'Le Canton de Briec au début du XIXe siècle', *Bull. Soc. archéol. Finistère*, 84 (1958), 160-190.

Le Guennec, 1936 — Le Guennec, L., *Nos vieux manoirs à légendes: Cornouaille, Léon, Tréguier* (1936); reprinted Quimper (1975).

1937 — Le Guennec, L., *Choses et gens de Bretagne* (1937); reprinted Quimper (1976).

1968 — Le Guennec, L., *Nos vieux manoirs à légendes*, deuxième série: *Vieux manoirs fortifiés Tréguier, Léon, Cornouaille*, Quimper (1968).

1979 — Le Guennec, L., *Le Finistère monumental*, tome 1: *Morlaix et sa région*, Quimper (1979).

Le Lannou, 1950 — Le Lannou, M., *Géographie de la Bretagne*, Rennes, I (1950).

1952 — Le Lannou, M., *Géographie de la Bretagne*, Rennes, II (1952).

Le Maître, 1976 — Le Maître, L.-P., *Les sillons de Beuzec au pays de Concarneau*, 2nd ed. Quimper (1976).

Le Rouzic, 1976 — Le Rouzic, Z., 'Habitations gauloises de la station de Kerhillio (commune d'Erdeven)', *Bull. Soc. polymathique du Morbihan*, 31 (1903), 256.

Le Scouëzec, 1979 — Le Scouëzec, G., *Brasparts: une paroisse des Monts d'Arrée, Paris (1979)*.

Lestang, 1894 — Lestang, -., 'Les maisons-types dans la région de Vannes', Chapter 45 in Ministère de l'Instruction Publique . . ., *Enquête sur les conditions de l'habitation en France. Les maisons-types*, tome I. Paris (1894), 298–300.

L'Helgouach, 1975 — L'Helgouach, J., 'Fouilles récentes de mégalithes morbihannais', *Les dossiers de l'archéologie*, no. 11 (juillet-août, 1975). 32–41.

Lick, 1970 — Lick, R., 'Les intérieures domestiques dans la seconde moitié du 18ᵉ siècle d'après les inventaires après décès de Coutances', *Annales de Normandie*, 20 (1970), 293–316.

Limon, 1852 — Limon, J.-M., *Usages et règlements locaux en vigeur dans le Finistère*, Quimper (1852).

Loth, 1883 — Loth, J., *L'èmigration bretonne en Armorique*, Paris (1883).

Lucas, 1972–73 — Lucas, M., 'Le site médiéval de Pen-er-Malo en Guidel: les bâtiments B et C', *Travaux, Société lorientaise d'Archéologie* (1972–73), 18–20.

Luzel, 1888 — Luzel, F.-M., 'Inventaire du mobilier d'un cultivateur bas-breton au commencement du XVIᵉ siècle (1510)', *Bull. Soc. archéol. Finistère*, 15 (1888), 241–252.

Lycée Armoricain, 1823–30 — *Lycée Armoricain (le):* l'agriculture, constructions rurales, 16 vols. Nantes,(1823–30) especially vols. 7 and 8.

Maguereze, 1840 — Maguereze, J-J., *Ethnologie basse-bretonne*, Saumur (1840). Also *Les cahiers de Baud* (1972), 7–8.

Maho, 1975 — Maho, H., 'Guénin: vers le création d'un conservatoire des arts et traditions populaires au pays de Baud', *Morbihan: Cahiers de l'UMIVEM*, no. 14, (automne, 1975) 17–19.

Marchal, 1920 — Marchal, M., 'La maison rurale en Haute Bretagne', *L'Hermine de Bretagne*, 2 (1920), 52–61.

Marsden, 1958 — Marsden, T.L., Minor domestic architecture in the county of Rutland and vicinity, Unpublished Ph.D. thesis, University of Manchester (1958).

Maumené, 1922 — Maumené, A., (ed.), 'Maisons et meubles bretons', *Vie à la Campagne*, Numéro extraordinaire (15 Dec. 1922).

McCourt, 1960–62 — McCourt, D., 'Cruck trusses in north-west Ireland', *Gwerin*, 3 (1960–62), 165–185.

1964–65 — McCourt, D., 'The cruck-trss in Ireland and its west European connections', *Folk-liv*, 28–29 (1964–65), 64–78.

Meirion-Jones, 1973a — Meirion-Jones, G.I., 'Settlement and vernacular architecture in Brittany', *Vernacular Architecture*, 4 (1973), 3–6.

1973b — Meirion-Jones, G.I., 'The long-house in Brittany: a provisional assessment', *Post-Medieval Archaeology*, 7 (1973), 1–19.

1973c — Meirion-Jones, G.I., 'The long-house: a definition', *Medieval Archaeology*, 17 (1973), 135–137.

1976a — Meirion-Jones, G.I., 'Some early and primitive building forms in Brittany', *Folk Life*, 14 (1976), 46–64.

1976b — Meirion-Jones, G.I., 'An interpretation of the structure', in Finlaison, M.D. (ed.), 'A medieval house at 13 and 13A Old Street, St. Helier', *Annual Bulletin, Société Jersiaise*, 21 (1976), 482–486.

1977a — Meirion-Jones, G.I., 'Vernacular architecture and the peasant house', Chapter 10 in Clout, H.D. (ed.), *Themes in the historical geography of France*, London, New York and San Francisco (1977), 343–406.

1977b — Meirion-Jones, G.I., The lesser rural domestic buildings of Brittany: their construction, distribution and evolution. Unpublished Ph.D. thesis, 2 vols. University of London Library (1977).

1978a — Meirion-Jones, G.I., *La maison traditionnelle: Bibliographie d'architecture vernaculaire en France*, Centre National de la Recherche Scientifique: Centre de Documentation Sciences Humaines, Paris (1978).

1978b — Meirion-Jones, G.I., 'The roof-carpentry of Brittany. I — Construction excluding cruck forms', *Vernacular architecture*, 9 (1978), 17–25.

1978c — Meirion-Jones, G.I., 'The sunken-floored hut in Brittany', *Medieval Village Research Group, Twenty-sixth Annual Report* (1978), 32–34.

1978–79 — Meirion-Jones, G.I., 'Un problème d'évolution de la maison bretonne: le foyer ouvert', *Archéologie en Bretagne*, 20–21 (1978–79), 18–26.

Meirion-Jones. 1979a — Meirion-Jones, G.I., 'The roof-carpentry of Brittany. II — Cruck construction', *Vernacular architecture*, 10 (1979), 15-21.

1979b — Meirion-Jones, G.I., 'The bed-outshot in Brittany', *Ulster Folk Life*, 25 (1979), 29-53.

1979c — Meirion-Jones, G.I., 'The Breton lon-house', *Paysages ruraux européens, Travaux de la Conférence européenne permanente pour l'étude du paysage rural, Rennes-Quimper, 26-30 septembre 1977*, Rennes (1979), 25-49.

1979d — Meirion-Jones, G.I., 'Une maison aux meubles de pierre dans les Monts d'Arrée', *Archéologie en Bretagne*, 23 (1979), 41-48.

1980a — Meirion-Jones, G.I., 'L'architecture vernaculaire de la Bretagne: un résumé', *Mémoires de la Société d'Histoire et d'Archéologie de Bretagne*, 57 (1980).

1980b — Meirion-Jones, G.I., 'Les loges à sol surcreusé en Bretagne', *Archéologie en Bretagne*, 25 (1980), 47-52.

1980c — Meirion-Jones, G.I., 'La ricerca sull'architettura rurale in Francia', *Quaderni Storici*, Ancona-Roma, no. 43 (April 1980), 194-209.

1980d — Meirion-Jones, G.I., 'La maison-longue en Bretagne', *Archéologie en Bretagne*, Part I, 26(1980), 41-57; Part II, 27(1980), 31-44; Part III, 29 (1981), 49-67.

1981a — Meirion-Jones, G.I., 'Cruck construction: the European evidence' in Alcock, N.W. (ed)., *Cruck construction: Introduction and Catalogue*, Council for British Archaeology, Research Report No. 42, London (1981), forthcoming.

1981b — Meirion-Jones, G.I., 'The seventeenth-century *greniers-à-sel* at Honfleur, Calvados', *Archaeological Journal*, 138 (1981), 248-258.

Mercer, 1975 — Mercer, E., *English vernacular houses: a study of traditional farmhouses and cottages*, Royal Commission on Historical Monuments, England, London (1975).

Meuret, 1979 — Meuret, J.-C., 'Images d'une sortie aux marches de Bretagne: Brains, Les Marches, Chelun (Ille-et-Vilaine)', *Maisons paysannes de France* (1979, no. 3), 24-26.

Meynier, 1943a — Meynier, A., 'Champs et chemins de Bretagne', *Conférences universitaires de Bretagne* (1943).

1943b — Meynier, A., 'Un enquête sur le bocage breton', *Annales de Bretagne*, 50 (1943), 102-103.

1943c — Meynier, A., 'Vocabulaire des champs bretons', *Annales de Bretagne*, 50 (1943), 103-110.

1944a — Meynier, A., 'Sur de curieux alignements de chemins et de monuments en Bretagne', *Annales de Bretagne*, 51 (1944) 125-129.

1944b — Meynier. A., 'Notre enquête sur les champs bretons', *Annales de Bretagne*, 51 (1944), 136-139.

1945a — Meynier, A., 'La commune rurale française', *Annales de Géographie*, 53 (1945), 161-179.

1945b — Meynier, A., 'Les ensembles cadastraux circulaires en Bretagne', *Annales de Bretagne*, 52 (1945), 81-92.

1949a — Meynier, A., 'A propos de chemins creux de Bretagne', *Annales de Bretagne*, 58 (1949), 345-347.

1949b — Meynier, A., 'Quelques énigmes d'histoire rurale en Bretagne', *Annales, Economies, Sociétés, Civilisations*, 4. no. 3 (1949), 259-267.

1955 — Meynier, A., 'En Armorique et dans l'Ouest britannique: problèmes de structure agraire', *Annales, Economies, Sociétés, Civilisations*, 10, no. 1 (1955), 27-36.

1962 — Meynier, A., 'Les études de géographie agraire au laboratoire de géographie de Rennes', *Norois*, 9 (1962), 127-147.

1966 — Meynier, A., 'La genèse du parcellaire breton', *Norois*, 13 (1966), 595-610.

Ministère de la Guerre, 1919 — Ministère de la Guerre, Comité d'Action Economique de la Xᵉ Région, *Le développement économique des Côtes-du-Nord, agriculture, industries, commerce*, Saint-Brieuc (1919).

Ministère de la Reconstruction, 1947 — Ministère de la Reconstruction et de l'Urbanisme, *Résultats statistiques d'une propriété bâtie dans les communes rurales (Bretagne)*, Paris (1947).

Ministère de la Santé, 1939 — Ministère de la Santé Publique et de la Population: Commission d'Étude de l'Habitation Rurale, *Enquête sur l'habitation rurale en France*, 2 vols, Paris (1939).

Ministère de l'Instruction Publique, 1894, 1899 — Ministère de l'Instruction Publique, des Beaux Arts et des Cultes: Comitè des Travaux Historiques et Scientifiques, *Enquête sur les conditions de l'habitation en France*, tome I, Paris (1894); tome II, Paris (1899).

Ministère des Affaires Culturelles, n.d. — Ministère des Affaires Culturelles: Direction de l'Architecture, Centre de Recherches sur les Monuments Historiques, *Beffrois de charpentes, étude de structures*, Paris (n.d.).

1972 — Ministère des Affaires Culturelles: Direction de l'Architecture, Centre de Recherches sur les Monuments Historiques, *Charpentes*, 6 vols, Paris (1972).

n.d. — Ministère des Affaires Culturelles: Direction de l'Architecture, Centre de Recherches sur les Monuments Historiques, *Eglises à pans de bois, étude de structures*, tome I, *Champagne*, Paris (n.d.).

n.d. — Ministère des Affaires Culturelles: Direction de l'Architecture, Centre de Recherches sur les Monuments Historiques, *Maisons à pans de bois*, 8 vols, Paris (n.d.).

n.d. — Ministère des Affaires Culturelles: Commission d'Inventaire Bretagne, *L'habitat rural en pays de Fougères: Catalogue d'exposition*. Rennes (n.d.).

n.d. — Ministère des Affaires Culturelles: Direction de l'Architecture, Centre de Recherches sur les Monuments Historiques, *Maisons à pans de bois, Bresse*, Paris (n.d.).

1969 — Ministère des Affaires Culturelles, *Inventaire général des monuments et des richesses artistiques de la France. Commission régionale de Bretagne. Finistère: Canton Carhaix-Plouguer*, 2 vols, Paris (1969).

1973 — Ministère des Affaires Culturelles: Inventaire général des monuments et des richesses artistiques de la France, Commission régionale Bretagne, *Patrimoine architectural Cancalais: Catalogue d'Exposition, Mairie de Cancale 24 juillet au 15 septembre 1973*, Rennes (1973).

1974 — Ministère des Affaires Culturelles: Inventaire général des monuments et des richesses artistiques de la France, Commission régionale Bretagne, *Manoirs, fermes et chapelles autour de Tréguier: Catalogue de l'exposition, Canton de Tréguier, printemps-été, 1974*, Rennes (1974).

Ministère des Affaires Culturelles, n.d. — Ministère des Affaires Culturelles: Commission régionale d'Inventaire Bretagne, *Jubés de Bretagne: exposition organisée par le Ministère des Affaires culturelles avec le concours des conseils généraux de la Région Bretagne*, Rennes (n.d.).

Ministère de la Culture et de la Communication, n.d. [1978] — Ministère de la Culture et de la Communication, Inventaire général des monuments et des richesses artistiques de la France, Commission régionale de Bretagne, Département des Côtes-du-Nord, *Arrondissement de Guingamp: Indicateur du Patrimoine Architectural*, Paris (n.d.) [1978].

1979 — Ministère de la Culture et de la Communication, Inventaire général des monuments et des richesses artistiques de la France, Commission régionale Bretagne, *Architecture rurale et mobilier au Cap Sizun; Exposition réalisée avec le concours du Conseil Général du Finistère, Catalogue I.G.M.R.A.F. no. 87, juillet 1979, Audièrne*, Rennes (1979).

Ministère de la Culture et de l'Environnement, 1977 — Ministère de la Culture et de l'Environnement, Commission régionale d'inventaire Bretagne, *Châteaux et Manoirs de l'arrondissement de Guingamp: Exposition organiseé avec le concours du Conseil Général des Côtes-du-Nord, Château de la Roche-Jagu, juin-octobre, 1977*, Guingamp (1977).

1978 — Ministère de la Culture et de L'Environnement, *Inventaire général des monuments et des richesses artistiques de la France, Commission régionale de Bretagne: Morbihan, Canton, Belle-Île-en-Mer*, Sivom de Belle-Île-en-Mer (1978).

MM. les Inspecteurs de l'Agriculture 1844 — MM. Les Inspecteurs de l'Agriculture, *Agriculture des Côtes-du-Nord*, Paris (1844).

Miroudel, 1967 — Miroudel, -., La maison rurale en Ille-et-Vilaine, D.E.S. Faculté des lettres et sciences humaines, Université de Rennes (1967).

Mussat, 1971 — Mussat, A., 'Introduction à la connaissance des maisons rurales bretonnes', *Maisons paysannes de France*, (1971, no. 3), 4-6.

1976 — Mussat, A., 'Un thème d'étude: l'habitat rural traditionnel', *Arts de l'Ouest: études et documents*, Rennes, 1 (1976), 5-21.

Mussat, 1979a — Mussat, A., 'L'habitat rural traditionnel en Bretagne', *Maisons paysannes de France* (1979, no. 2), 10-13.

1979b — Mussat, A., *Arts et cultures de Bretagne: un millénaire*, Paris (1979).

National Museum of Wales, 1972 — National Museum of Wales, *Art treasures of Western Morbihan: La Cornouaille Morbihannaise, Exhibition organised by the Ministry of Cultural Affairs and the General Council of Morbihan, Cardiff, 20 October to 18 November 1972*, Rennes (1972).

Ó Danachair, 1954-56 — Ó Danachair, C., 'Semi-underground habitations', *J. Galway archaeol. hist. Soc.*, 26 (1954-56), 75-80.

1955 — Ó Danachair, C., 'Stand und Aufgaben der Hausforschung in Irland', *Bericht des Arbeitskreises für deutsche Hausforschung* (1955).

1956 — Ó Danachair, C., 'The bed outshut in Ireland', *Folk-liv*, 20 (1956), 26-31.

1964 — Ó Danachair, C., 'The combined byre and dwelling in Ireland', *Folk Life*, 2 (1964), 58-75.

1966-67 — Ó Danachair, C., 'Some notes on traditional house types in county Kildare', *J. Kildare archaeol. Soc.*, 14 (1966-67), 234-246.

1977-79 — Ó Danachair, C., 'Irish tower houses and their regional distribution', *Béaloideas*, 45-47 (1977-79), 158-163.

Ogès, 1949 — Ogès, L., *L'agriculture dans le Finistère au milieu du XIXᵉ siècle*, Brest (1949).

Peate, 1946 — Peate, I.C., *The Welsh house*, 3rd. ed., Liverpool (1946).

1956 — Peate, I.C., 'The cruck truss', *Man*, 56 (1956), 146-147.

1957 — Peate, I.C., 'The cruck truss', *Man*, 57 (1957), 48.

1957-58 — Peate, I.C., 'The cruck truss: a reassessment', *Folk-liv*, 21-22 (1957-58), 107-113.

1963 — Peate, I.C., 'The Welsh long-house: a brief re-appraisal', Chapter 18 in Foster, I.Ll., and Alcock, L. (eds.), *Culture and environment*, London (1963), 439-444.

1964 — Peate, I.C., 'The long-house again', *Folk Life*, 2 (1964), 76-79.

Pelras, 1966 — Pelras, C., 'Goulien, commune rurale du Cap Sizun (Finistère): étude d'ethnologie globale', Cahiers du Centre de Recherches Anthropologiques, no. 6, *Bull. et Mém. de la Soc. d'Anthropologie de Paris*, t. 10, XIᵉ série (1966), 141-587.

Périer de Lahitolle, 1867 — Périer de Lahitolle, E., 'Les domaines congéables: études d'histoire et d'économie agricoles', *Bull. Soc. polymathique du Morbihan* (1867), 167-168.

Perrin, 1808 — Perrin, O., *Galerie des moeurs, usages et costumes des Bretons de l'Armorique*, Paris (1808).

Pesez, 1971 — Pesez, J.-M., 'Le village médiéval', *Archéologie médiévale*, 1 (1971), 307-321.

Picard, 1904 — Picard, Y., *L'ouvrier agricole de Saint-Pol-de-Léon*, Brest (1904).

Piggott, 1948 — Piggott, S., 'Primitive house-types in Iberia', *Antiquity*, 22 (1948), 40-42.

Puig de Ritalongi, 1894 — Puig de Ritalongi, A.G., *Les bigoudens: origines, types, costumes, moeurs et coutumes*, Nantes (1894).

Quenedey, 1911 — Quenedey, R., 'Les combles des maisons du XVIᵉ siècle à Rouen', *Bulletin monumental*, 75 (1911), 247-264.

1919 — Quenedey, R., 'Les combles annéciens', *Revue savoisienne* (1929), 1-8.

Quentel, 1948 — Quentel, H., 'Plan des fermes bretonnes', *Nouvelle Revue de Bretagne*, 2 (1948), 302.

Raglan, 1956 — Raglan, Lord, 'The cruck truss', *Man*, 56 (1956), 101-103.

Ramm, et al., 1970 — Ramm, H.G., McDowall, R.W., and Mercer, E., *Shielings and bastles*, Royal Commission on Historical Monuments, England, London (1970).

Robert, 1936 — Robert, J., 'Un habitat de transition: Vallorcine', *Revue de Géographie alpine*, 24 (1936), 667-700.

1939a — Robert, J., *La maison rurale permanente dans les Alpes françaises du Nord. Étude de géographie humaine*, Thèse lettres, Tours (1939).

1939b — Robert, J., *L'habitat temporaire dans les montagnes pastorales des Alpes françaises du Nord. Étude de géographie humaine*, Thèse complémentaire, Grenoble (1939).

1942 — Robert, J., 'Habitat temporaire et nomadisme dans les Alpes françaises du Nord', *L'Information Géographique*, 6, no. 1 (1942), 1-8.

1946 — Robert, J., 'Un habitat temporaire: l'écurie-grange dans les Alpes françaises du Nord', *Annales de Géographie*, 55 (1946), 102-111.

1949 — Robert, J., 'La maison rurale et le bois dans les Alpes de Haute-Savoie', *Revue de Bois*, Paris, 4, no. 2 (1949), 9-12.

Robert, 1951   Robert, J., 'Types de maisons rurales dissociées dans le centre de la Gâtine tourangelle', *Congrès International de Géographie, Lisbonne, 1949*, tome III, Lisbonne (1951), 133-140.

1954   Robert, J., 'Un habitat temporaire: les montagnettes dans les Alpes françaises du Nord', *Mélanges géographiques offerts au doyen E. Bénévent*, Gap (1954), 167-182.

1972   Robert, J., 'La maison agricole: essai de classification et définitions', *Norois*, 19, no. 75 (1972), 541-548.

Roberts, 1974   Roberts, D.L., 'The persistence of archaic framing techniques in Kesteven, Lincolnshire — I', *Vernacular Architecture*, 5 (1974), 19-20.

1975   Roberts, D.L., 'The persistence of archaic framing techniques in Kesteven, Lincolnshire — II', *Vernacular Architecture*, 6 (1975), 33-38.

Roger, 1919   Roger, H., *Le Finistère, ses habitants, leurs moeurs, les richesses de ce pays*, Montpellier (1919).

Rollando, 1971   Rollando. Y., *La préhistoire du Morbihan*, 3rd ed., Vannes (1971).

Rosot, 1970   Rosot, Y., *Le meuble rustique en Bretagne*, Châteaulin (1970).

Roussell, 1934   Roussell, A.A., *Norse building customs in the Scottish isles*, Copenhagen and London (1934).

Salmon, 1971   Salmon, M.-J., *L'architecture des fermes du soissonnais: son évolution du XIIIᵉ au XIXᵉ siècle*, Sazeray, Indre (1971).

Sanquer, 1967   Sanquer, R., 'Plouédern: motte féodale de Leslouch' in 'Chronique d'archéologie antique et médiévale', *Bull. Soc. archéol. du Finistère*, 93 (1967), 35-37.

Sartiges, 1921a   Sartiges, Le Vicomte de, 'Les cabanes de pierres sèches du Sud de la France', *Bull. Soc. préhistorique française*, 18 (1921), 338-358.

1921b   Sartiges, Le Vicomte de, *Les cabanes en pierre sèche du Sud de la France*, Le Mans (1921).

P. Sebillot, 1885   Sebillot, P., 'Les maisons rustiques en Haute Bretagne', *Revue d'Ethnographie*, 4 (1885), 148-157.

P.-Y., Sebillot, 1968   Sebillot, P.-Y., *Le folklore de la Bretagne*, 2 vols., Paris (1968).

Sécretariat d'État à la Culture, 1975a   Sécretariat d'État à la Culture, *Inventaire général des monuments et des richesses artistiques de la France. Commission régionale de Bretagne. Morbihan: Cantons Le Faouët et Gourin*, Paris (1975).

1975b   Sécretariat d'État à la Culture, Commission d'Inventaire Bretagne, *Les Malouinières: exposition organisée avec le concours de la Société d'Histoire et d'Archéologie de Saint-Malo et de la Ville de Saint-Malo*, Rennes (1975).

Sée, 1896   Sée, H., *Étude sur les classes rurales en Bretagne au Moyen-Age*, Paris (1896).

1905-6   Sée, H., 'Les classes rurales en Bretagne du XVIᵉ siècle à la Révolution', *Annales de Bretagne*, 21 (1905-6), 474-520.

1906   Sée, H., *Les classes rurales en Bretagne du XVIᵉ siècle à la Révolution*, Paris (1906), Reprint, Brionne (1978).

1908-9   Sée, H., 'Les classes rurales en Bretagne du XVIᵉ siècle à la Révolution, Parts VI and VII', *Annales de Bretagne*, 24 (1908-9), 619-664.

J.T. Smith, 1955   Smith, J.T., 'Medieval aisled halls and their derivatives', *Archaeol. J.*, 112 (1955), 76-93.

1958   'Medieval roofs: a classification', *Archaeol. J.*, 115 (1958), 111-149.

1963   Smith, J.T., 'The long-house in Monmouthshire: a re-appraisal', Chapter 16 in Foster, I.Ll., and Alcock, L. (eds.), *Culture and environment*, London (1963), 389-414.

1964   Smith, J.T., 'Cruck construction: a survey of the problems', *Medieval Archaeology*, 8 (1964), 119-151.

1970   Smith, J.T., 'Lancashire and Cheshire houses: some problems of architectural and social history', *Archaeol. J.*, 127 (1970), 156-181.

1974   Smith, J.T., 'The early development of timber buildings: the passing-brace and reversed assembly', *Archaeol. J.*, 131 (1974), 238-267.

1975   Smith, J.T., 'Cruck distributions: an interpretation of some recent maps', *Vernacular Architecture*, 6 (1975), 3-18.

P. Smith, 1967 — Smith, P., 'Rural housing in Wales', Chapter 11 in Thirsk, J. (ed.), *The agrarian history of England and Wales*, IV, 1500-1640, London (1967), 767-813.

1975 — Smith, P., *Houses of the Welsh countryside: a study in historical geography*, Royal Commission on Ancient and Historical Monuments in Wales, London (1975).

Souillet, 1943 — Souillet, G., 'Chronologie et répartition des noms de lieux en *-ière* et en *-ais* dans la Haute-Bretagne', *Annales de Bretagne*, 50 (1943), 90-98.

Souvestre, 1836 — Souvestre, E., *Les derniers Bretons*, Paris (1836).

1838 — Souvestre, E., *Le Finistère en 1836*, Brest (1838).

1845 — Souvestre, E., *Le foyer breton*, Paris (1845).

1860 — Souvestre, E., *Les derniers paysans*, Paris (1860).

Speranze, 1948 — Speranze, N., 'Plan des fermes bretonnes', *Nouvelle Revue de Bretagne*, 2 (1948), 301-302.

Stothard, 1820 — Stothard, A.E., *Letters written during a tour through Normandy, Britanny, and other parts of France in 1818*, London (1820).

Strabo — Strabo, *Geography*, IV, 4,3.

Thébaut, 1950 — Thébaut, A.-M., 'Le territoire communal breton', *Annales de Bretagne*, 57 (1950), 229-236.

Trefois, 1937 — Trefois, C.F., 'La technique de la construction rurale en bois', *Folk* (1937), 55-72.

1950 — Trefois, C.V., *Ontwikkelings Geschiedenis van onze Landelijke Architectuur*, Antwerpen (1950).

Trépos, 1960 — Trépos, P., 'Enquêtes sur le vocabulaire breton de la ferme', *Annales de Bretagne*, 67 (1960), 325-376.

1961 — Trépos, P., 'Enquêtes sur le vocabulaire breton de la ferme', *Annales de Bretagne*, 68 (1961), 601-698.

Vaillat, 1913 — Vaillat, L., 'La maison en Bretagne', *L'art et les artistes*, 96 (mars 1913), 281-284.

Vallaux, 1904 — Vallaux, C., 'La vie et les saisons en Basse-Bretagne', *Bretagne Nouvelle* (mars 1904).

1905a — Vallaux, C., *La Basse-Bretagne: étude de géographie humaine*, Thèse lettres, Caen (1905); Paris (1906).

1905b — Vallaux, C., 'L'évolution de la vie rurale en Basse-Bretagne', *Annales de Géographie*, 14 (1905), 36-51.

Van Es, 1967 — Van Es, W.A., 'Wijster: a native village beyond the Imperial frontier, 150-425 A.D.', *Palaeohistoria*, 11 (1967), 386.

Vie à la Campagne, 1922 — *Vie à la Campagne*, see Maumené, A. (ed.).

Vigarié, 1969 — Vigarié, A., 'Recherche d'une explication de la maison cauchoise', *Norois*, 63 et 63 bis (1969), 177-187.

1971 — Vigarié, A., 'Les énigmes de la maison cauchoise', *Annales de Normandie*, 21 (1971), 137-151.

Walton, 1954 — Walton, J., 'Hogback tombstones and the Anglo-Danish house', *Antiquity*, 28 (1954), 68-77.

1957a — Walton, J., 'The cruck truss', *Man*, 57 (1957), 15-16.

1957b — Walton, J., 'The Skye house', *Antiquity*, 31 (1957), 155-162.

1960-62 — Walton, J., 'Cruck trusses in the Dordogne', *Gwerin*, 3 (1960-62), 3-6.

1962 — Walton, J., 'The built-in bed tradition in north Yorkshire', *Gwerin*, 3, no. 4 (1961), 114-125.

1969 — Walton, J., 'Megalithic building survivals', in Jenkins, J.G. (ed.), *Studies in Folk Life*, London (1969), 106-122.

Wood, 1965 — Wood, M., *The English mediaeval house*, London (1965).

Wood-Jones, 1963 — Wood-Jones, R.B., *Traditional domestic architecture in the Banbury region*, Manchester (1963).

Worth, 1953 — Worth, R.H., 'The Dartmoor house', in *Dartmoor*, Newton Abbot (1953), 403-418.

Young, 1792 — Young, A., *Travels, during the years 1787, 1788 and 1789 undertaken more particularly with a view of ascertaining the cultivation, wealth, resources and national prosperity of the Kingdom of France*, London (1792).

INDEX AND GLOSSARY